SHAPES to CUT
Plants & Shapes

Illustrated by Gary Mohrman

Teaching & Learning Company

1204 Buchanan St., P.O. Box 10
Carthage, IL 62321-0010

Table of Contents

Plants

Bean Stalk	5
Cactus	6
Dandelion	7
Day Lily	8
Ivy Leaf	9
Leaf–Beech	10
Leaf–Maple	11
Leaf–Oak	12
Palm Tree	13
Pansy	14
Poinsettia	15
Poppy	16
Tree	17
Tulip	18

Shapes

Circle	19
Diamond	20
Hexagon	21
Moon Crescent	22
Octagon	23
Oval	24
Polygon	25
Rectangle	26
Square	27
Star	28
Teardrop	29
Triangle (Equilateral)	30
Triangle (Isosceles)	31
Triangle (Right Angle)	32

Cover by Gary Mohrman

Copyright © 1998, Teaching & Learning Company

ISBN No. 1-57310-135-4

Printing No. 98765

Teaching & Learning Company
1204 Buchanan St., P.O. Box 10
Carthage, IL 62321-0010

The purchase of this book entitles teachers to make copies for use in their individual classrooms only. This book, or any part of it, may not be reproduced in any form for any other purposes without prior written permission from the Teaching & Learning Company. It is strictly prohibited to reproduce any part of this book for an entire school or school district, or for commercial resale.

All rights reserved. Printed in the United States of America.

How to Use This Book

The patterns in this book provide simple shapes with round corners, thick lines, gentle angles and useful images for your children's first cutting experiences. Use the shapes individually to enhance a learning center or unit or use them in combination to create lively learning experiences.

It is usually easier if the children color the picture first and then cut it out. Some interesting effects can be achieved by having the children color white paper with markers (crayons and watercolors not recommended) and then copying the image onto the colored paper. If you do not want the children to color the picture, then you might copy it onto colored paper.

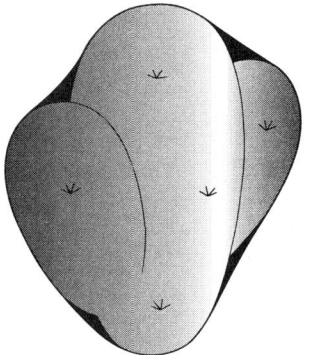
color shape

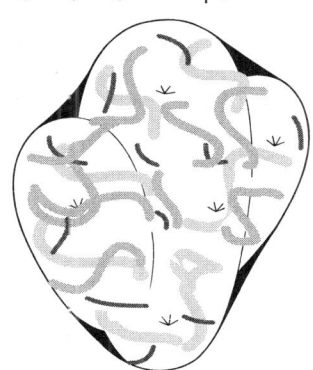
marker paper

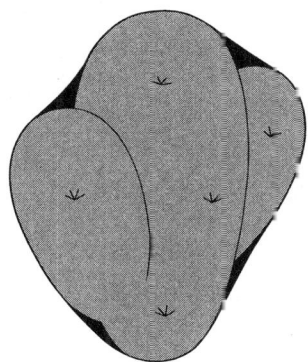
colored paper

Other ideas include:
- tracing the picture onto thin interfacing (found in fabric stores) and coloring with marker. These make wonderful flannel board items.
- cutting the pattern out of tagboard or plastic (large ice cream container lids work well, check your school cafeteria) and using as a stencil.
- cutting the pattern out of a sponge and using for sponge painting.

Some things you can make with these patterns:

Puffy Stuff
Make fronts and backs. Before gluing shut, fill with a small amount of cotton batting or paper towel.

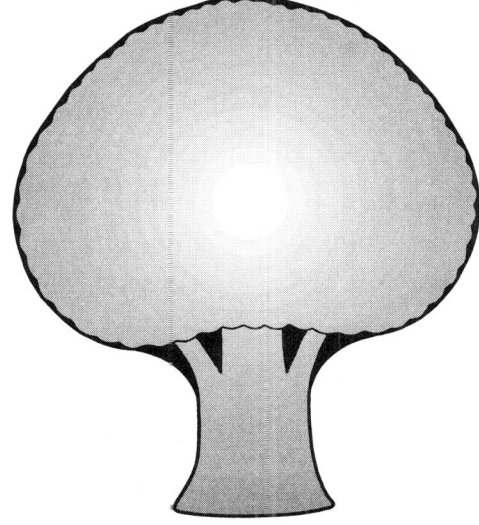

Flash Cards
Write beginning sounds or other facts on the shapes, use for review.

Mobiles

Make fronts and backs and hang from a coat hanger with string or yarn.

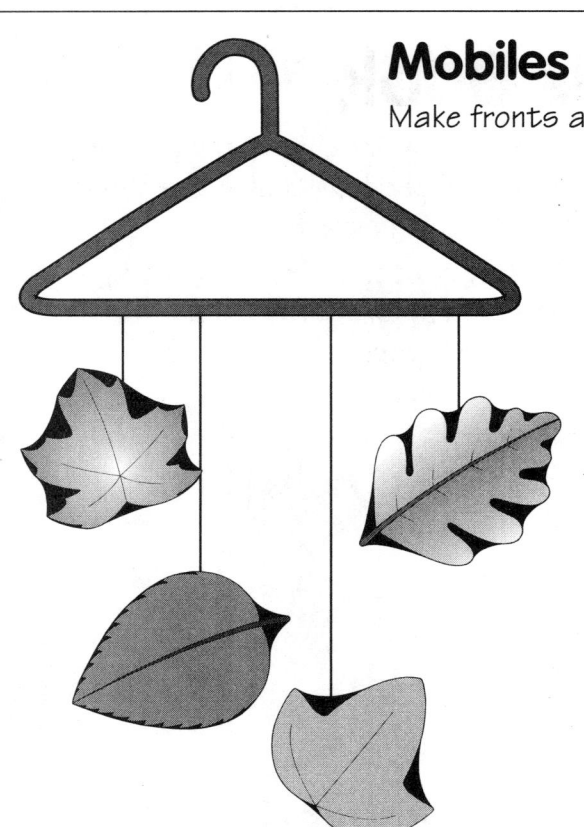

Stick Puppets

Attach a craft stick to the back and use to tell a story.

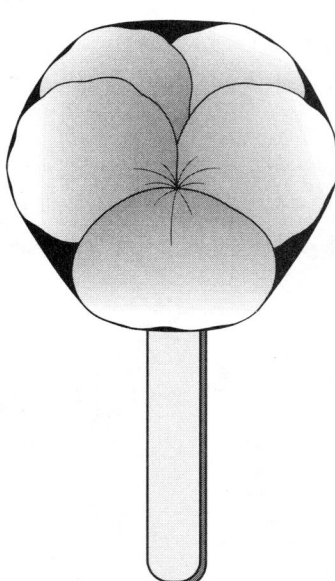

Shape Books

Some more things you can make with these patterns:

- bulletin board displays, door decorations, window decals
- name tags or place cards
- stationery
- portfolio covers or report covers
- flannel board pieces (cut from flannel or interfacing)
- gift wrap (cut from sponge and dip in tempera paint for sponge painting)
- stand-up figures (Make a front and back and glue together. Stand up with a small amount of clay.)
- sorting materials (Copy onto colored paper. Make sure you have at least two of the items in the same color. Cut out. Have children sort by color, shape, etc.)

You'll find many creative uses for the patterns in this book, and your young children will love having a collection of shapes to cut!

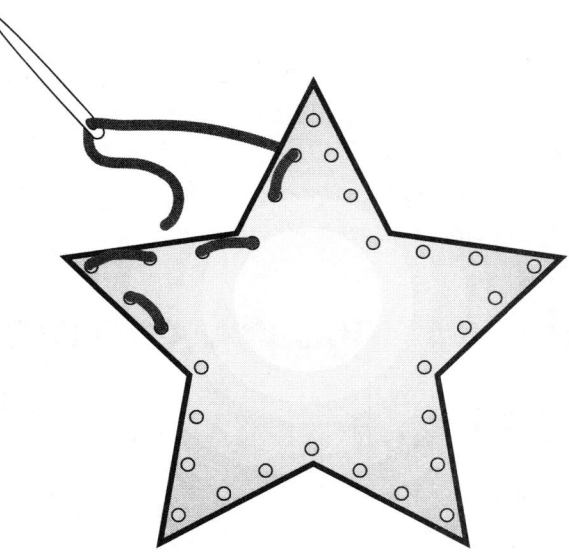

Lacing Items

Cut pattern from felt, glue two or three thicknesses together for strength. Use a hole punch to make holes around the edges about 1" (2.5 cm) apart. Supply blunt plastic needle and length of yarn.

Bean Stalk

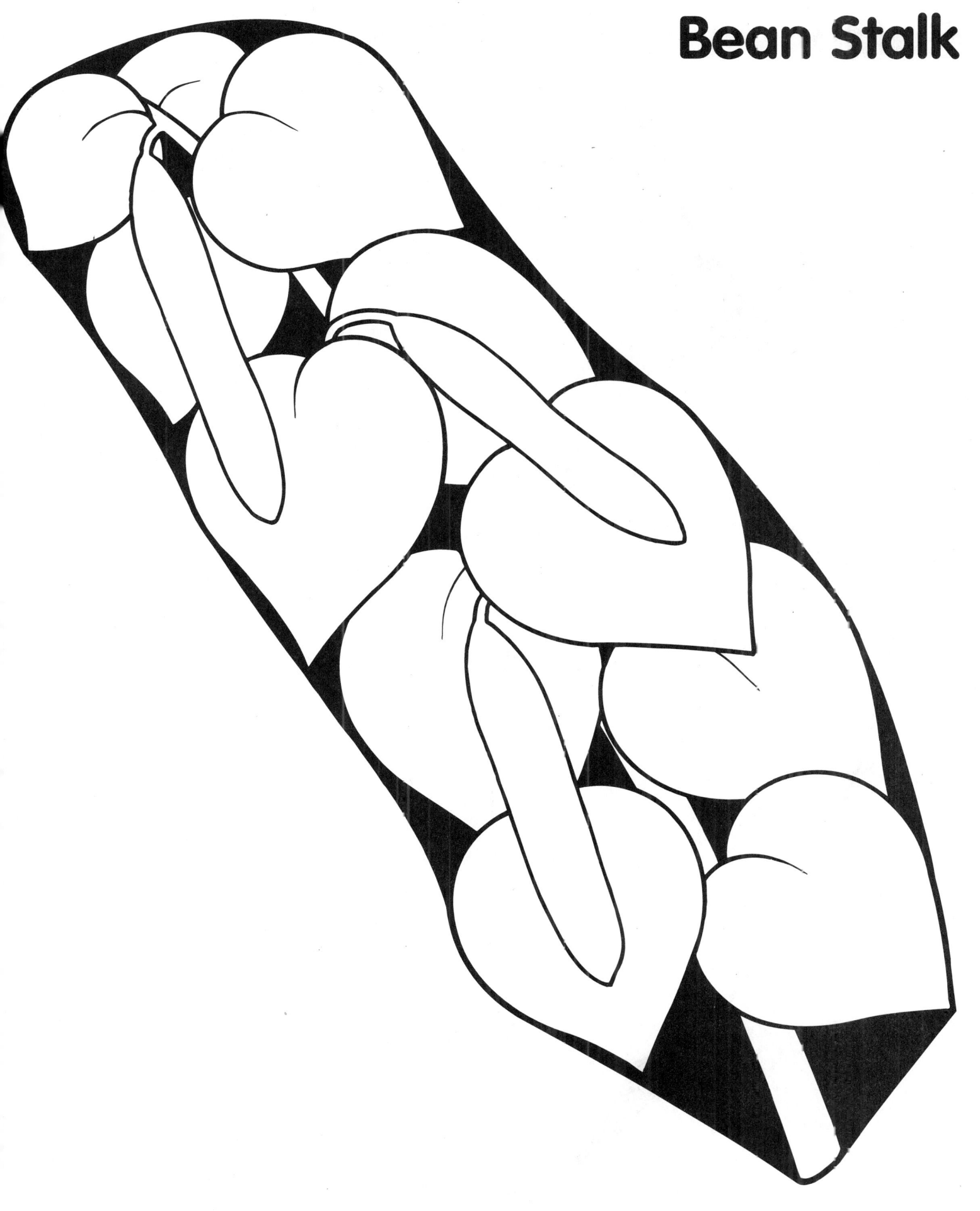

Cactus

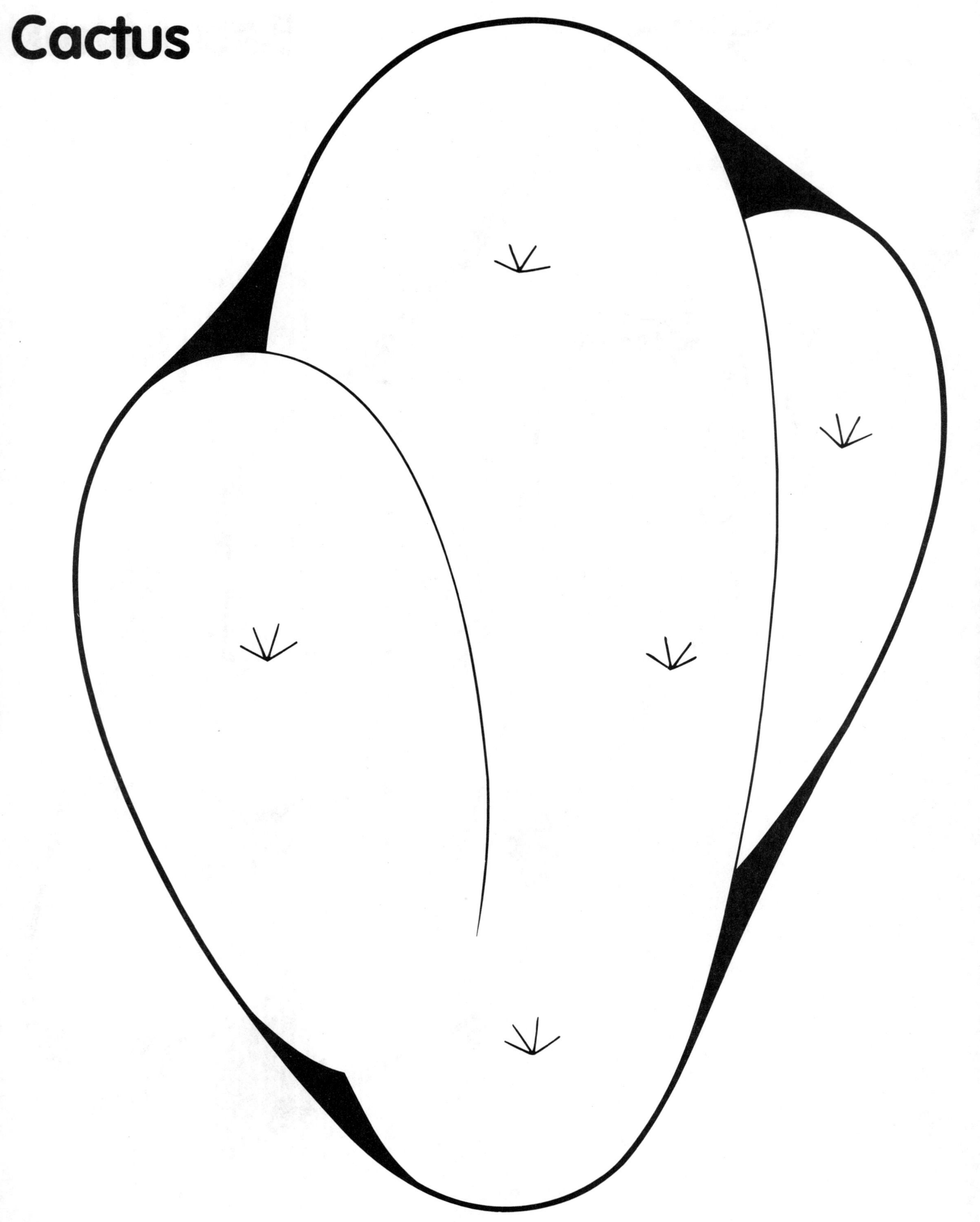

Dandelion

Day Lily

Ivy Leaf

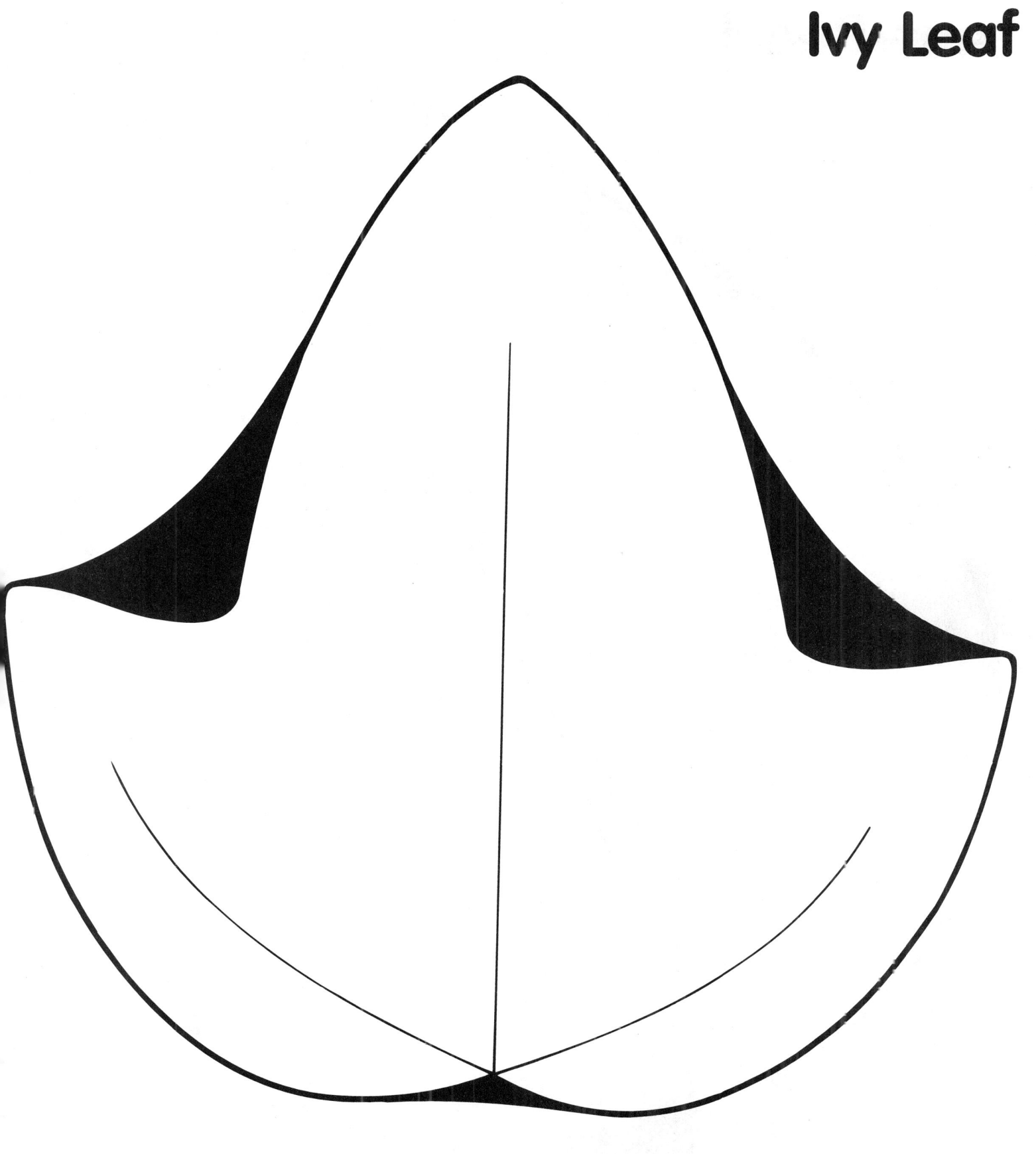

Leaf–Beech

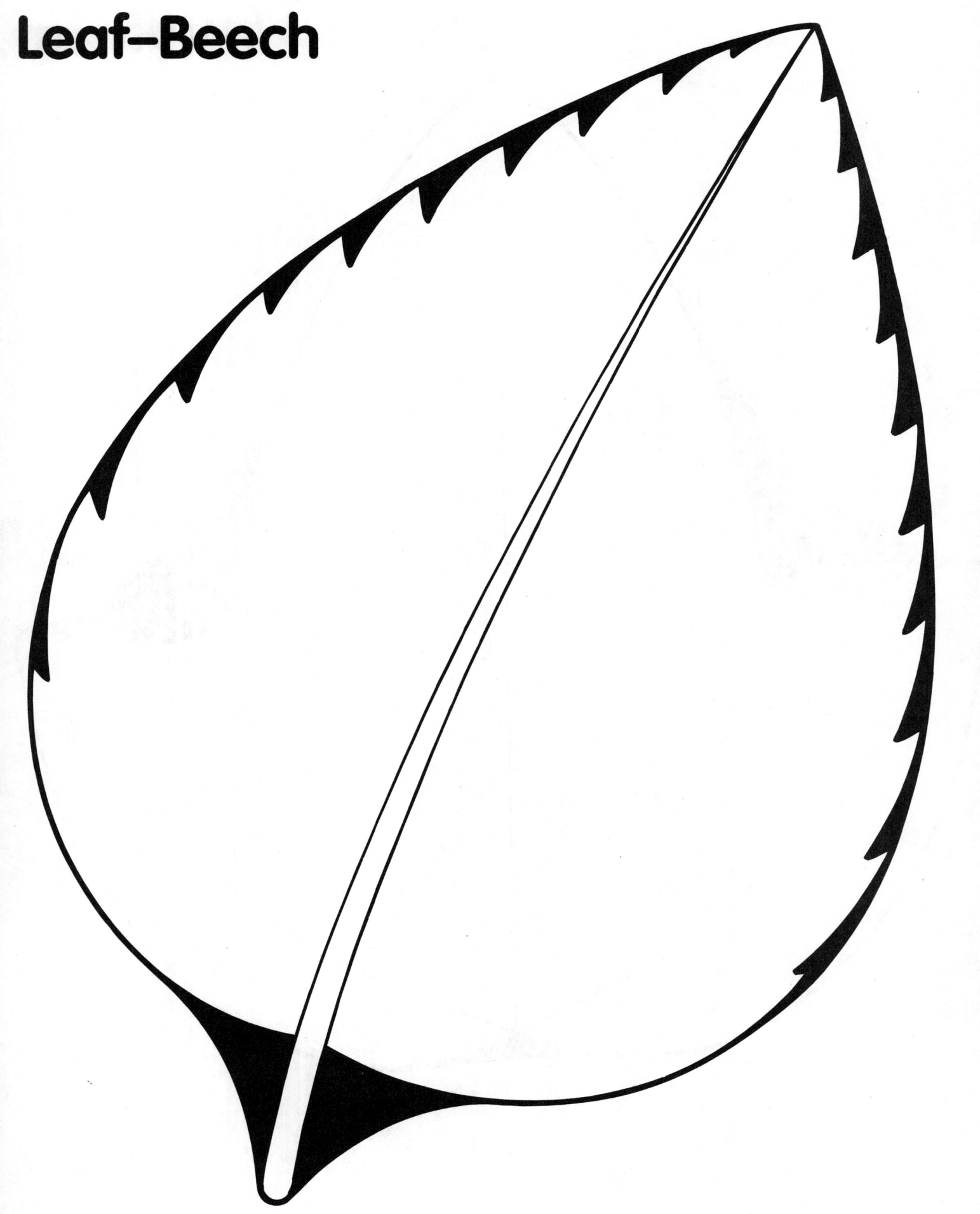

Leaf-Maple

Leaf-Oak

Palm Tree

Pansy

Poinsettia

Poppy

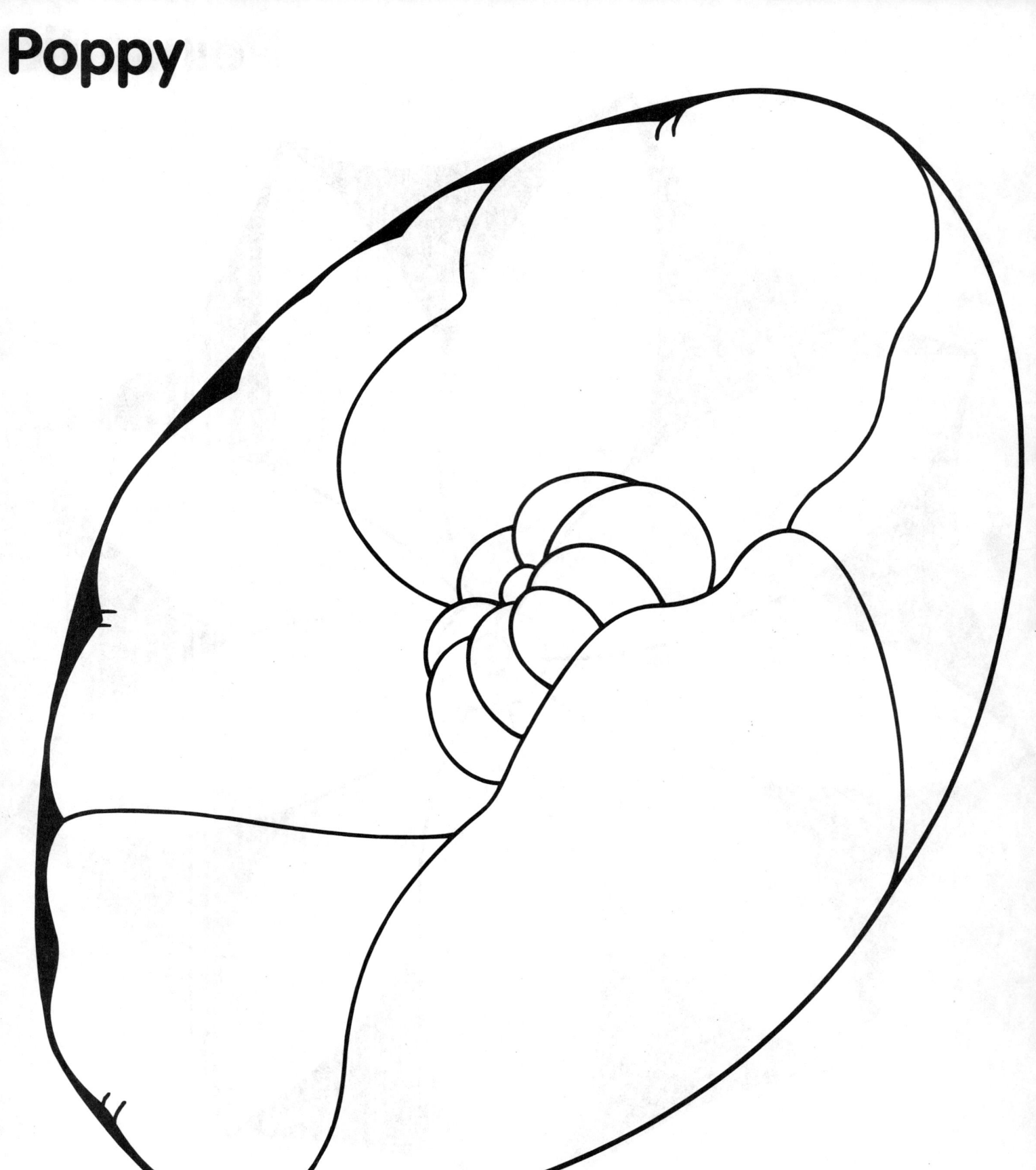

Tree

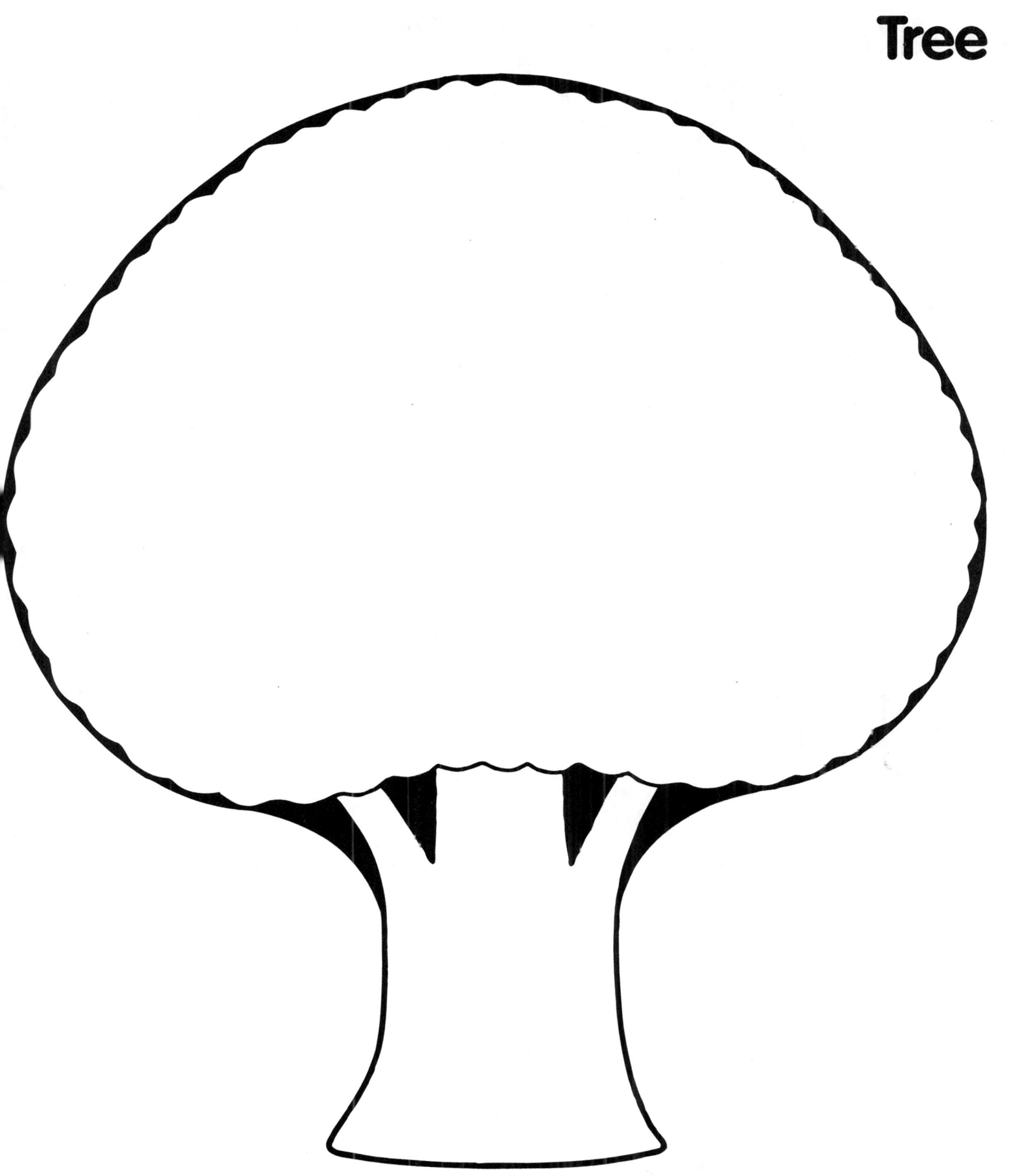

Tulip

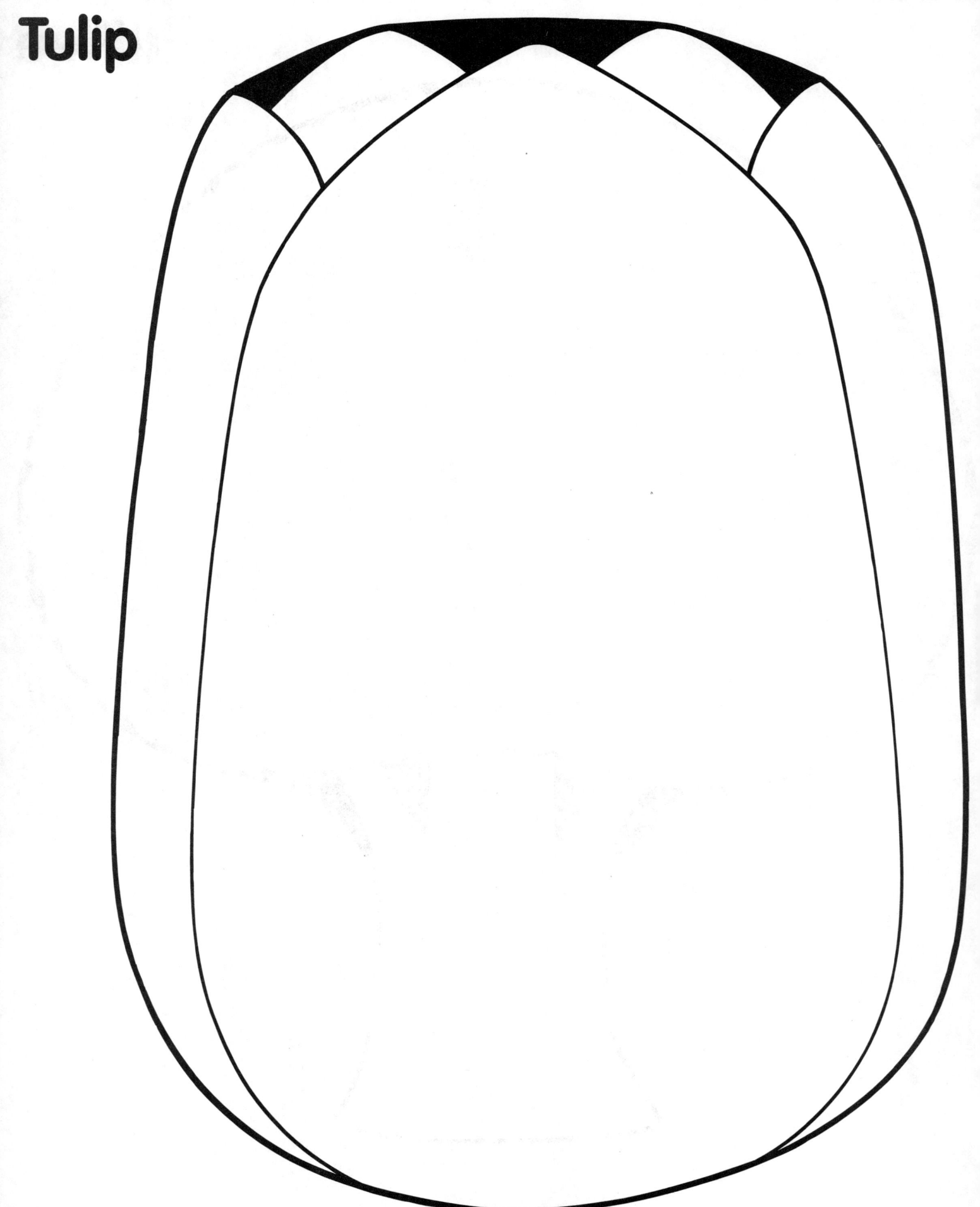

Circle

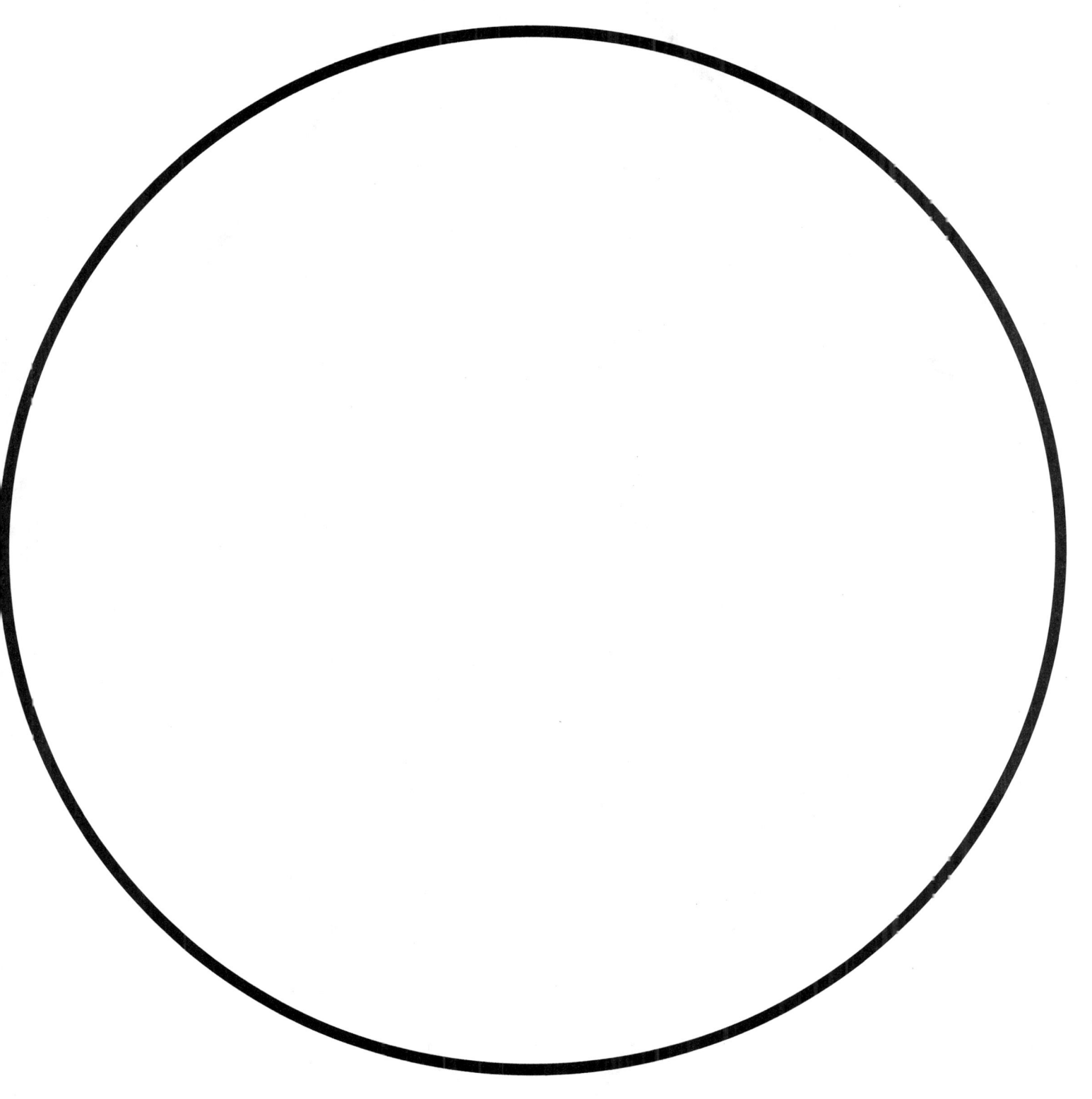

Diamond

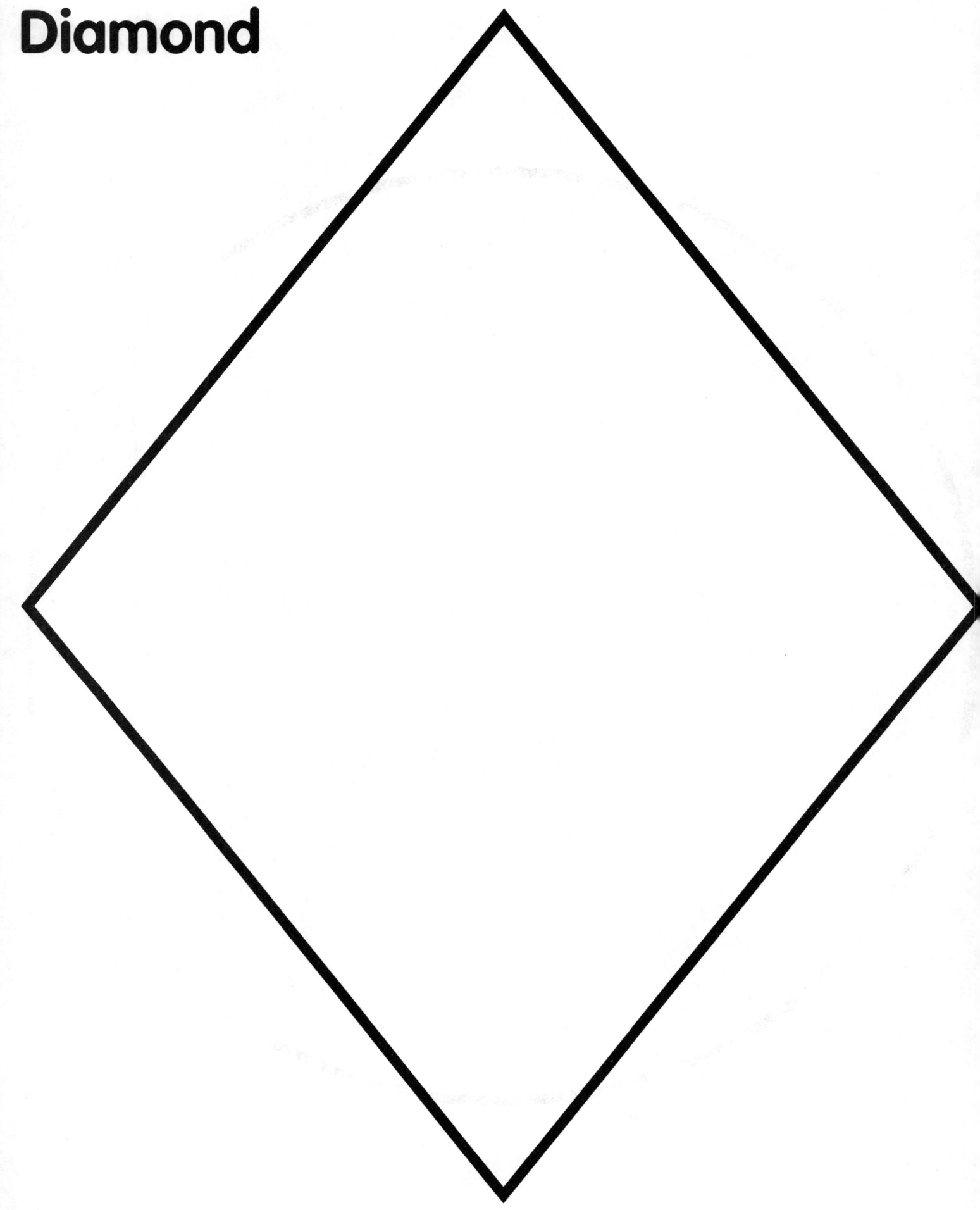

Hexagon

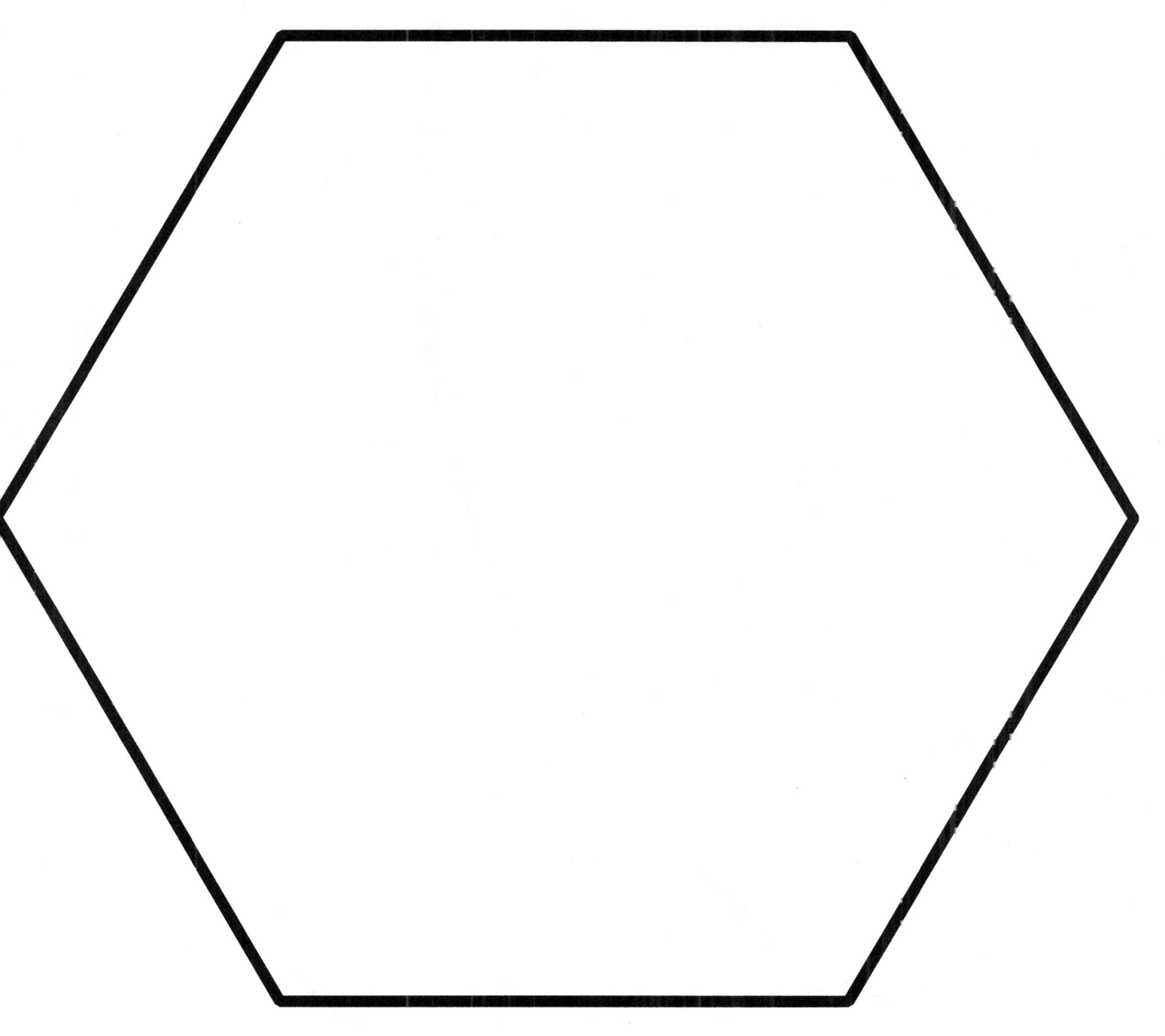

Moon Crescent

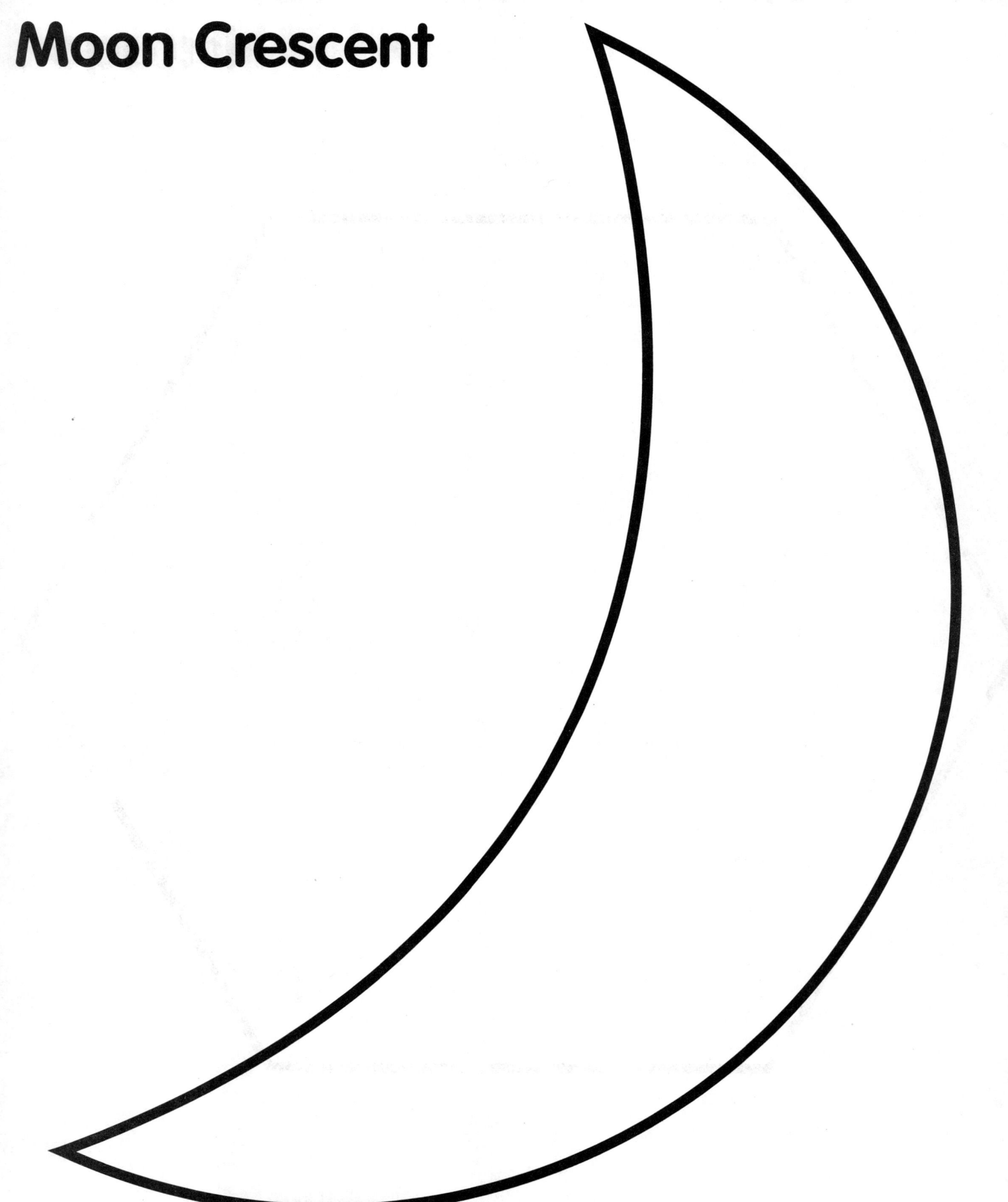

Octagon

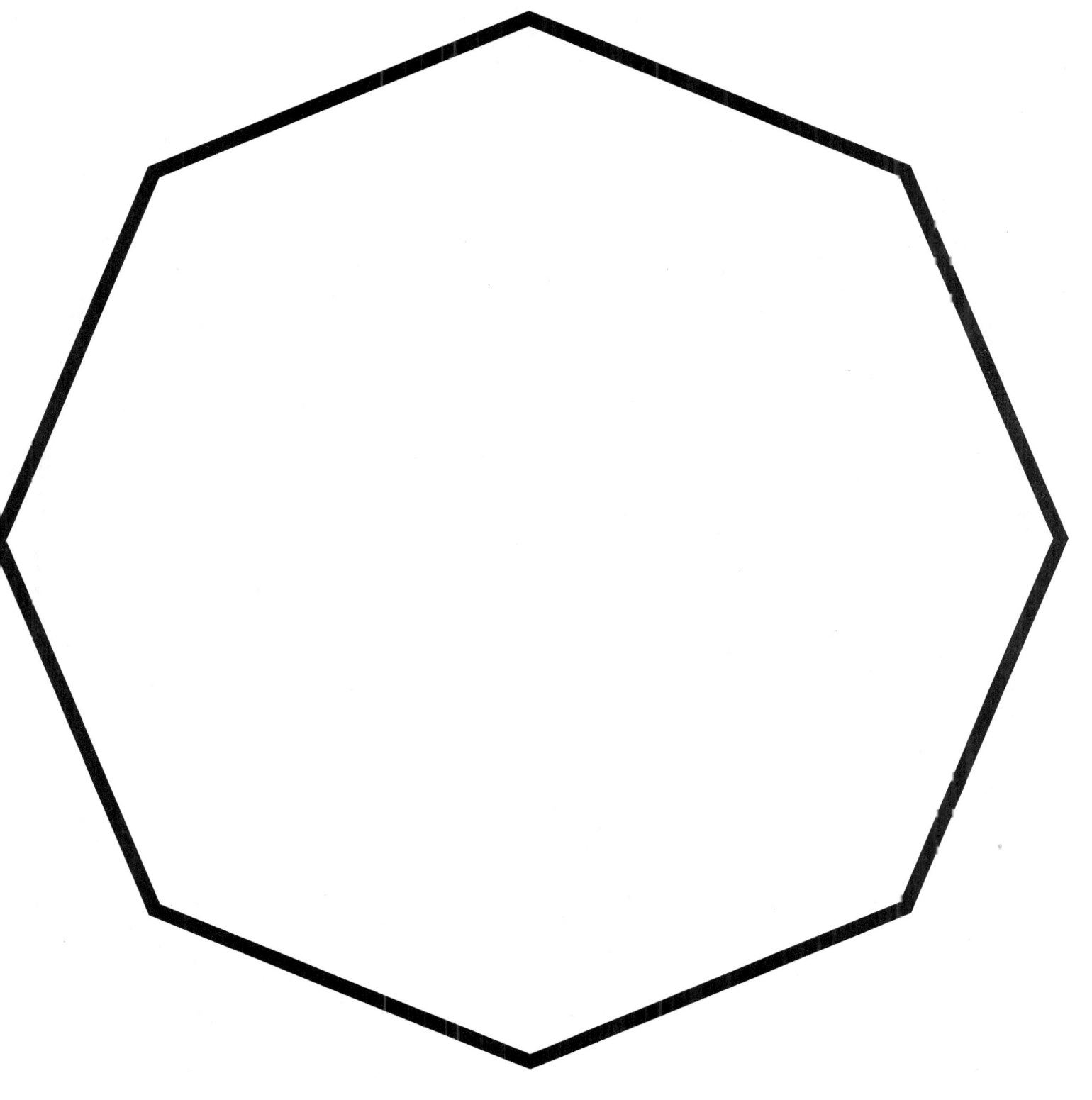

Oval

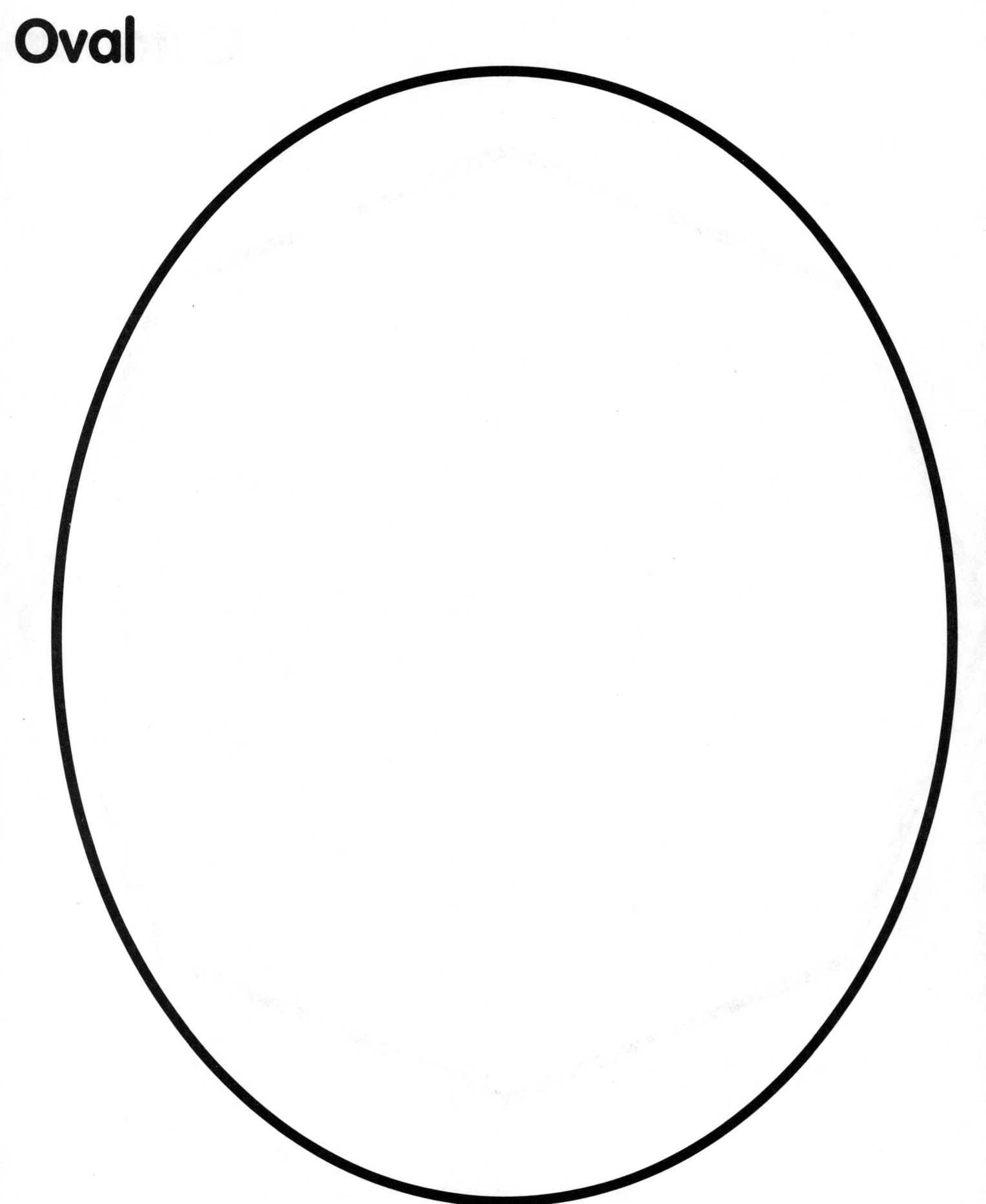

Polygon

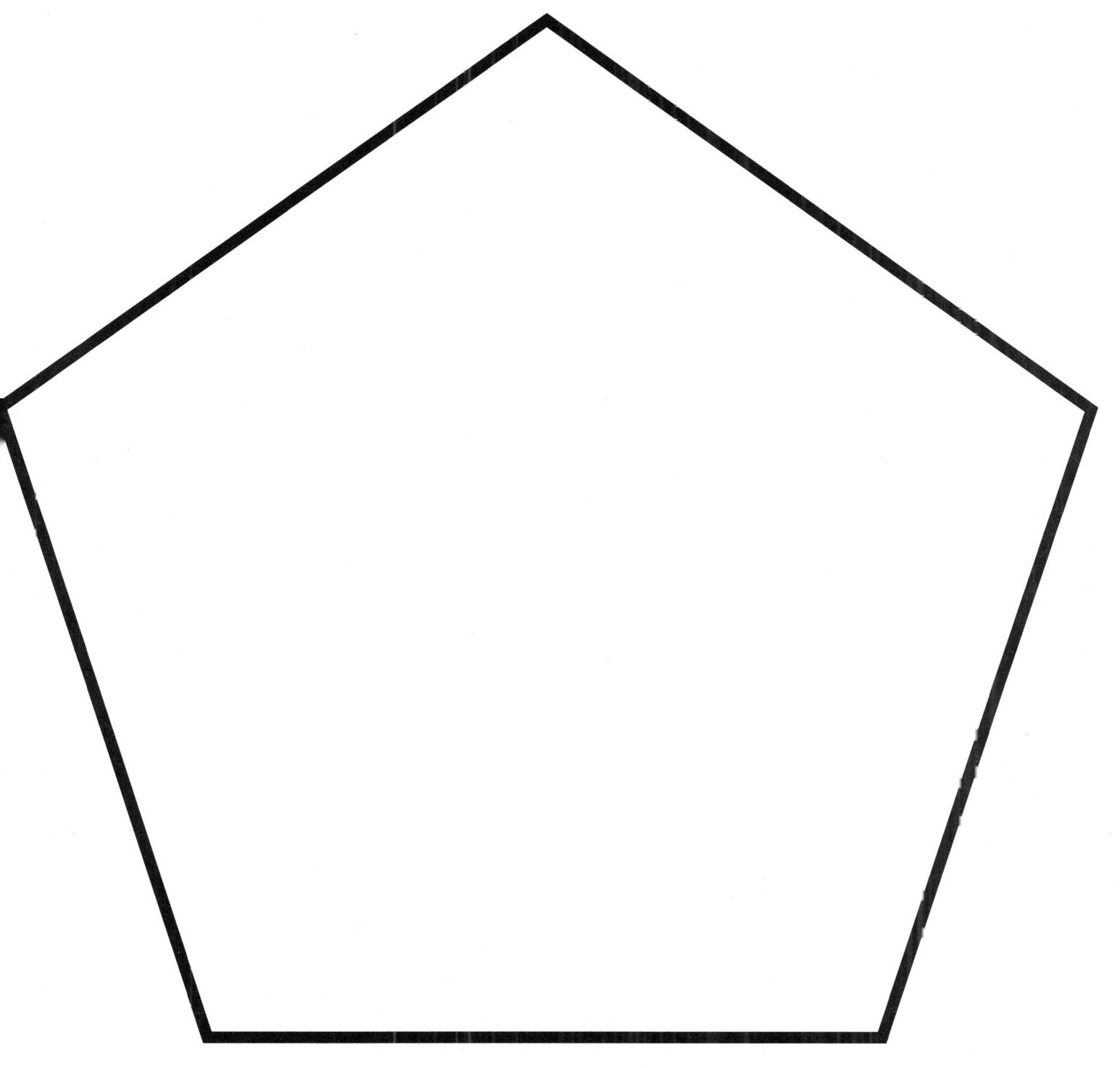

Rectangle

Square

Star

Teardrop

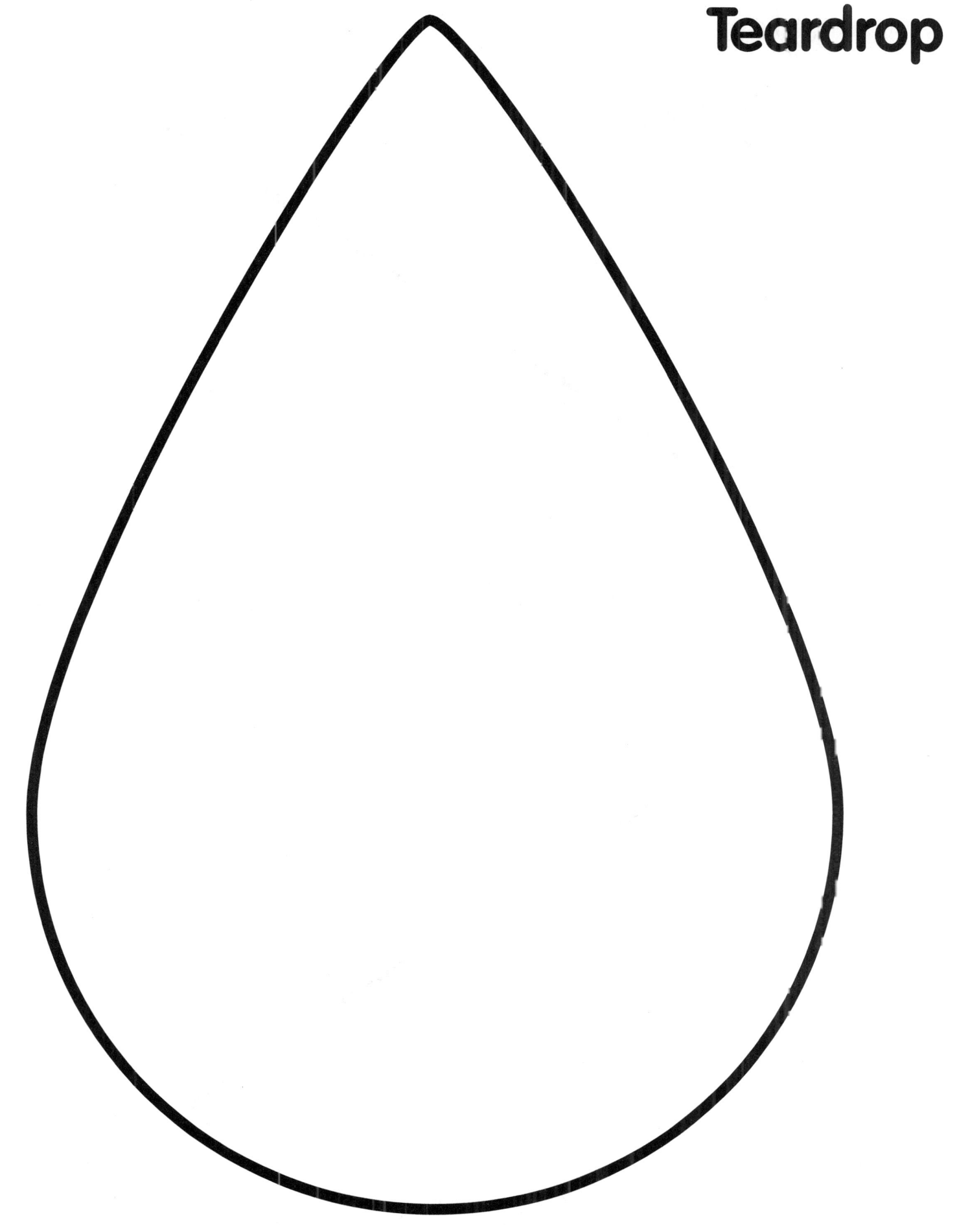

Triangle (Equilateral)

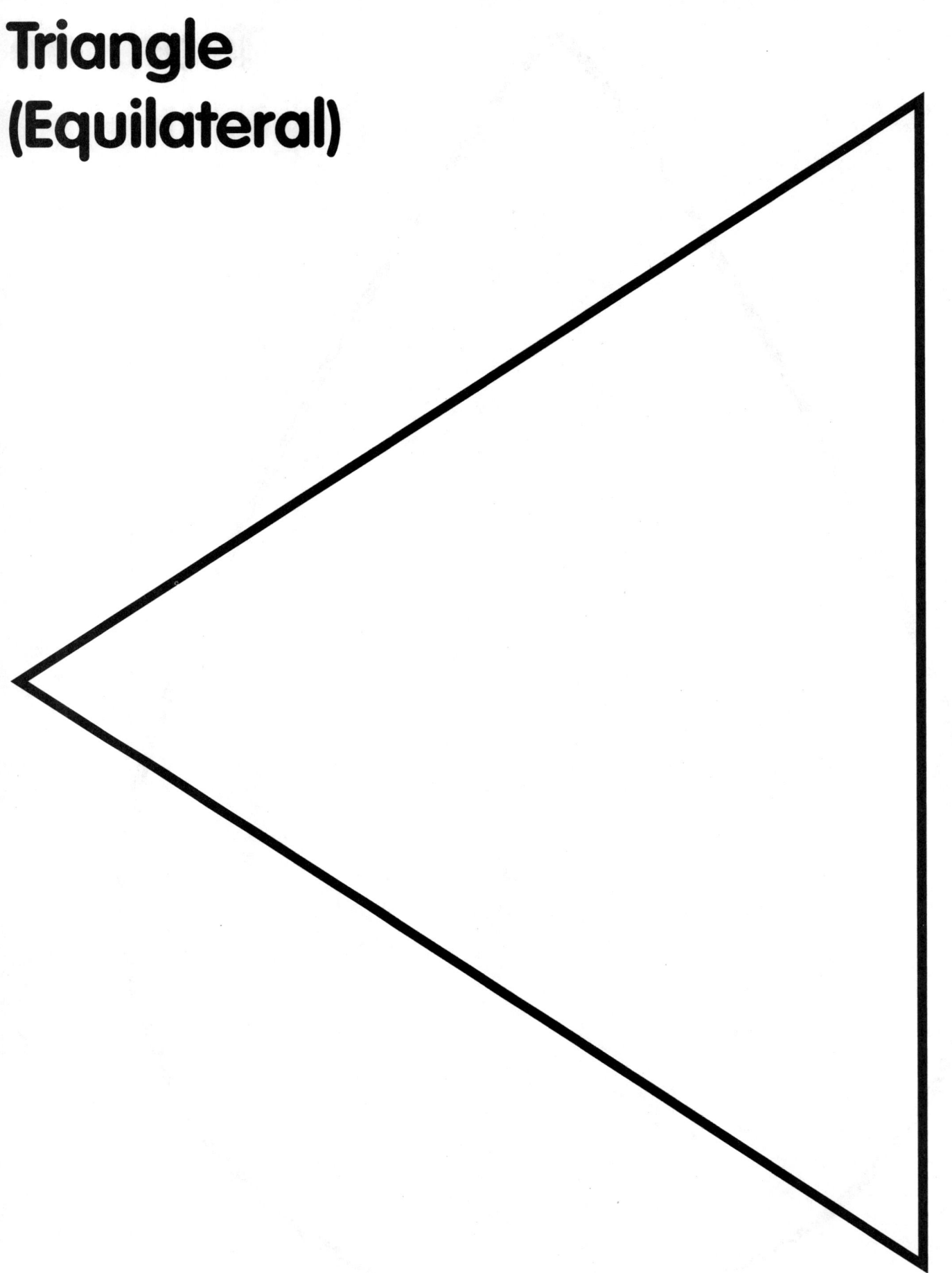

Triangle (Isosceles)

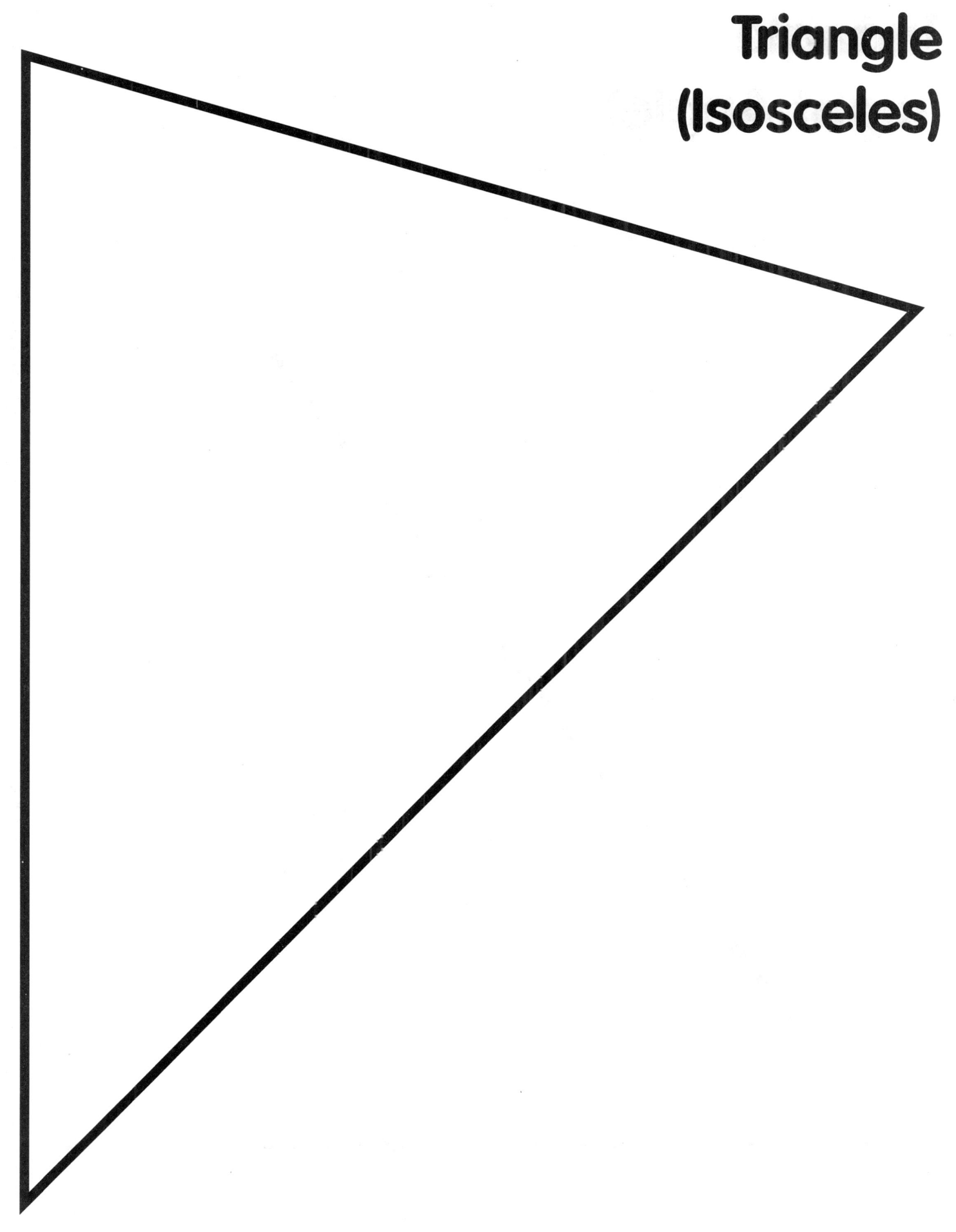

Triangle (Right Angle)

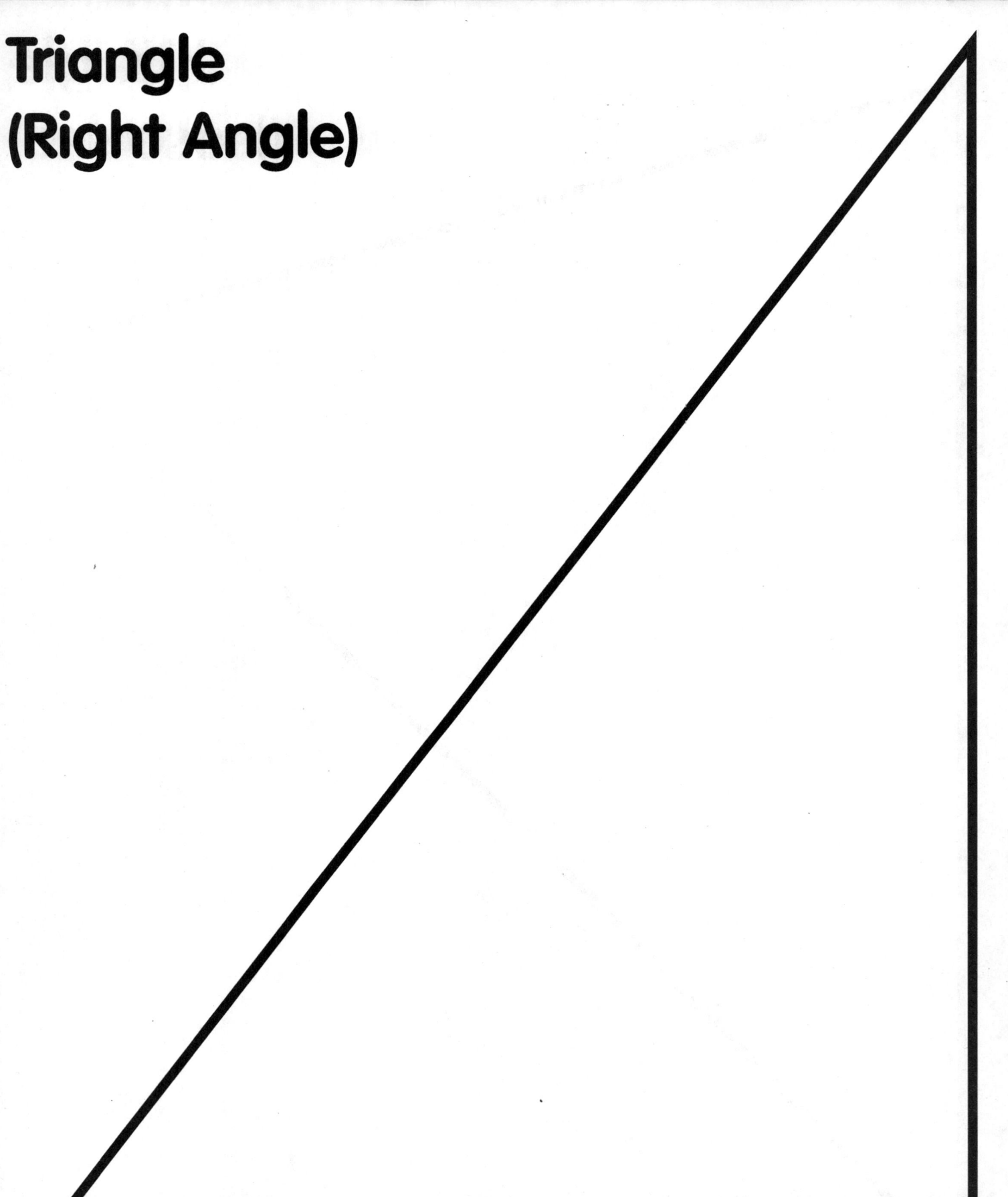

California real estate practice

California real estate practice

Hyman Maxwell Berston
Professor of Business and Real Estate Coordinator
City College of San Francisco

1981   Fourth edition

Homewood, Illinois   60430

© RICHARD D. IRWIN, INC., 1968, 1973, 1977, and 1981

All rights reserved. No part of this publication may be reproduced, stored in a retrieval system, or transmitted, in any form or by any means, electronic, mechanical, photocopying, recording, or otherwise, without the prior written permission of the publisher.

ISBN 0-256-02539-8
Library of Congress Catalog Card No. 80–84357
Printed in the United States of America

4 5 6 7 8 9 0 K 8 7 6

Preface

Since its publication in 1968, *California Real Estate Practice* has been adopted for use in 90 schools and colleges throughout the state. The text has been thoroughly revised and updated with respect to content, illustrations, tables used, and real estate forms presented. The result is this current edition.

The text has been designed basically for use in real estate practice classes and incorporates fundamental theory with actual practice. The everyday activities of the broker and salesperson are taken into account. Various tables and charts and 63 real estate forms are illustrated, and a detailed analysis of the purpose and content of the most important forms is given.

A number of problems and examples have been used in an attempt to explain and show the practical application of the material presented. Each chapter contains questions for discussion, and 250 multiple-choice questions with answers appear in Appendix B as an aid to students who may be preparing to take the state broker or salesperson license examinations. A *Teacher's Manual*, available for instructors, contains answers to the questions for discussion and suggestions for presenting the chapter material to the class. Extensive testing material is provided, including multiple-choice question tests of the type given by the California Department of Real Estate.

California presently leads the nation in real estate education and research. Approximately 97 community colleges offer courses in real estate, and most have established a Real Estate Certificate program in addition to offering the associate in arts degree with a specialization in real estate. Additionally, courses are offered by private schools and colleges, by the California Association of Realtors, by local boards of Realtors, and in adult classes sponsored by local school districts.

For a person to secure a real estate broker license, California real estate law now requires completion of college-level courses in Real Estate Practice, Real Estate Law, Real Estate Appraisal, Real Estate Finance, Real Estate Economics or Basic Accounting, and an additional course taken from an approved list of electives.

Twenty-nine years as a practicing Realtor and teacher of real estate subjects have convinced the author that the way to achieve professionalization of the real estate business is through continued and increased emphasis on education. The real estate business is becoming increasingly complex and technical, and proper education and training are absolutely necessary in order to achieve the greatest degree of success.

Acknowledgments

The author wishes to thank sincerely the numerous coordinators, real estate instructors, and licensees throughout California who have aided in the preparation of *California Real Estate Practice*. Preceding the actual work on the revision, questionnaires were sent to a number of individuals asking for comments and suggestions. The response was excellent, and any improvements are clearly attributable to this response. The author received valuable suggestions and tips from students and licensees who have used the text in the classroom, the California Department of Real Estate, Title Insurance and Trust Company, California Association of Realtors, and the California Association of Real Estate Teachers.

A very special thank-you to my wife, Bertie, and my children—Debbie, Marilyn, Susan, Emanuel, and Judith—for their love and support.

H. M. Berston

Contents

List of illustrations xiii

1. **The real estate industry and the real estate broker** 1

   Trade and professional associations, 1
      Local real estate boards, 1
      National Association of Realtors, 2
      The California Association of Realtors, 5
      Use of the term *Realtor®* and *Realtor®-Associate*, 5
      Realtists, 5
      Affiliation not mandatory, 5
   California Department of Real Estate, 5
      The California Real Estate Commissioner, 6
   State Real Estate Advisory Commission, 6
   Education and research, 6
   Real Estate Recovery Fund, 6
   Commissioner's plan for professionalism, 6
   The real estate broker, 7
      Real estate salesman, 7
      When license not required, 7
      Penalty for violation, 8
      Obtaining a real estate license, 8
      Real estate broker's license, 8
      Real estate salesman's license, 9
   License examination content, 10
   Continuing education requirement, 10
   Common real estate law violations, 10
   Additional laws affecting the licensee, 12
      Regulation 2903, structural defects, disclosure, 12
      Regulation 2785, code of ethics and professional conduct, 12
   The licensee as an agent, 14
      Creation of the agency relationship, 14
      Agent's authority, 15
      The fiduciary relationship, 15
      Statements made by brokers and salesmen, 15
      When principal supplies false information, 16

2. **The real estate office** 17

   Basic company forms, 17
      Individual proprietorship, 17
      The partnership, 17
      The corporate form, 18
   Real estate office personnel, 18
      Sales manager, 18
   The broker and salespersons, 19
   Training program, 19
      On-the-job training and forms, 20
      Staff meetings, 20
      Outside training, 20
      Employee and independent contractor, 21
      Broker-salesman contract, 26
      Review of agreements, 26
   Costs of operating a real estate office, 26
      Computing desk cost, 26
   Maintaining trust fund records, 28
   Physical features of the real estate office, 28
      Location, 28
      Physical appearance and office layout, 28
   Real estate franchising, 30
      Policy and procedure manual, 30

3. **Listing and prospecting** 41

   Listings, 41
   Types of listings, 41
      Oral listing, 41
      Open listing, 41
      Exclusive agency listing, 42

Exclusive right to sell listing, 42
Multiple listing, 42
Net listing, 42
Option listing, 43
Analysis of the listing form, 43
The broker's commission, 46
Prospecting, 46
  The broker, 46
  The beginning salesman, 46
  Additional sources of listings and prospects, 48
  Obtaining the listing, 49
Proper procedures, 49

4. **Selling and marketing techniques** 52

Areas of sales preference, 52
Reasons for sale or purchase, 53
  Occupancy, 53
  Investment and speculation, 53
  Special uses, 53
Presale preparation, 53
  Know the property, 54
  Know the prospective purchaser, 54
  Know the owner, 54
Qualifying the prospective buyer, 54
Showing the property, 55
  Personal safety, 58
Following the inspection, 58
Points to emphasize to the buyer, 58
The real estate sales kit, 59
  Discussion with clients, 60

5. **The offer and the deposit receipt** 61

Where to prepare the offer, 61
Deposit receipt as a contract, 61
Preparing the deposit receipt, 62
  Termite inspection, 66
  Personal property and fixtures, 67
  Closing costs, 71
The counteroffer, 73
Nonperformance, 76
Option to purchase real estate, 76

6. **Advertising** 78

The A-I-D-A Approach, 78
Areas of advertising, 78
General advertising, 78
  Trade association advertising, 79
  Specific forms of general office advertising, 79

Classified advertising, 81
  Writing the classified ad, 81
  The heading of the ad, 82
  The body of the ad, 83
  Special forms, 83
  Box or block ad, 83
  Closing the ad, 83
Answering ad calls, 83
  Switch sheet and call register, 85

7. **Financing real estate** 86

The promissory note, 86
  Holder in due course, 87
  Interest charge, usury, and proposition 2, 88
Trust deeds and mortgages, 88
  With respect to parties, 88
  With respect to title, 89
  With respect to statute of limitations, 89
  With respect to remedy, 89
  With respect to redemption, 89
  Mortgage with power of sale, 89
Effects and incidents of security arrangements, 92
  Purchase money trust deed or mortgage, 92
  Reconveyance, 92
  Hypothecation, 92
  Lien priorities, 92
  Assignment of debt, 92
  Deficiency judgment, 92
  "Subject to" versus "assumption of," 94
  Offset statement, 94
  Subordination clause, 94
  Partial release clause, 94
  Acceleration clause, 94
  Impound or Trust account, 95
  Prepayment penalties and lock-in provisions, 95
  Open-end-loan, 95
  Points, 96
Second trust deeds and mortgages, 96
  Request for notice and notice of default, 96
  Chattel mortgage, 99
  Agreement of sale (land contract), 99
All-inclusive trust deed, 100
Creative finance, 100
  FLIP or graduated payment loan, 100
  Variable interest rate loan, 100
  Rollover loan, 100
  Portable loan, 101
  Swing loan, 101
  Reverse loan, 101

Truth-in-Lending Law, 101
   Real estate transactions, 101
   Disclosure, 101
   Right to rescind, 105
   Enforcement and penalties, 108
   Effect upon the real estate licensee, 108
Real Estate Settlement Procedures Act, 109
Sources of funds, 109
Institutional lenders, 110
   Savings and loan associations, 110
   Commercial banks, 113
   Insurance companies, 114
Noninstitutional lenders, 114
   Private individuals, 114
   Mortgage companies and investment trusts, 115
Government guaranteed and insured loans, 115
   FHA (Federal Housing Administration), 115
   Veterans Administration (GI loan), 118
   California-Veterans loans (Cal-Vet), 119
   FNMA and GNMA, 120
Prohibition against redlining, 121
Broker acting as loan agent, 121
   Broker's loan disclosure statement, 121
   Commissions and charges, 121
Real property securities dealer, 124
   Real property securities permit, 124

8. Escrow procedure and title insurance ... 126

Escrow defined, 126
Essentials of a valid escrow, 126
Complete escrow, 127
The escrow agent, 127
   Duties and responsibilities of the escrow holder, 127
   Escrow holder as an agent, 128
Termination of escrow, 128
Differing escrow practices, 128
Division of escrow charges, 128
Checklist for real estate transactions, 129
Chronological steps in the escrow, 130
   Southern California escrow steps, 130
   Northern California escrow steps, 132
Escrow problem and statements, 132
   Transaction facts and agreements, 132
   Escrow statements, 133
   Explanation of procedures, 133
Title insurance, 136
Types of policies, 136
   Standard coverage policy, 136
   Extended coverage policy, 143
   Payment of title insurance fees, 143
   Various risks, 143
Additional title company protections, 144

9. General taxation and real estate 145

Proposition 13—Jarvis-Gann, 145
   Basic intention of Proposition 13, 146
Assessment of real property, 146
The tax rate, 146
Tax collection calendar, 146
Board of equalization, 147
Reporting ownership change, 147
Property reassessment, 148
Homeowners' property tax exemption, 148
Tax credit for renters, 148
Senior Citizens Property Tax Assistance, 148
Senior Citizens Property Tax Postponement, 149
Solar tax credits, 149
Veteran's exemption, 149
Special assessments, 149
Documentary transfer tax, 150
Property exempt from taxation, 150
Tax sale and redemption, 150
California estate and gift taxes, 151
   The Estate and Gift Tax Act of 1980, 151
   California gift tax, 151
   Joint tenancy property, 151
   Payment of the gift tax, 151
   Gift tax exemptions, 151
   Additional gift tax exemptions, 152
   California gift tax rates, 152
California estate tax, 153
   Inheritance tax and probate proceedings, 153
   Cost basis, 153
   Stepped-up tax basis, 153
   Cost basis and gift tax, 154
   California estate tax rates, 154
   Professional advice, 154
Federal gift and estate taxes, 154
   Unified credit and tax rates, 155
   The marital deduction, 155
   Transfers within three years of death, 156
   Joint interests, 156
   Property basis, 156
   Farm or business property valuation, 156

10. The income tax and real estate 157

Capital gains and losses, 157
   Capital assets, 157
   Classification of real property, 158

Dealer or investor? 158
Short- and long-term capital gains, 159
Cost basis and adjusted basis, 159
Sale of residence, 160
Principal residence, 160
How to determine gain or loss, 161
Special problems regarding residences, 161
Age 55 or older, 161
Depreciation, 162
Estimated useful life, 162
Land not depreciable, 163
Basis for determining depreciation, 163
Salvage value, 163
Methods of depreciation, 163
Change of method, 165
Comparison of methods of depreciation, 165
Recapture of depreciation, 166
The Tax Reform Act of 1976 and Revenue Act of 1978, 166
Recapture of depreciation, 166
Loan points and prepaid interest, 166
Deduction of investment interest, 166
Construction taxes and interest, 166
Business use of homes, 167
Rental of vacation homes, 167
Installment and deferred payment sales plans and Installment Sales Revision Act of 1980, 167
General requirements, 167
Calculation of gain, 168
Other deferred-payment sales, 169
Disposition of installment obligations, 169
Schedule E, 169

11. Property management and leasing. 173

Certified Property Manager (CPM), 173
Written examinations, 173
Certificate, 173
Types of properties managed, 173
Employment opportunities, 173
Goals of management, 174
Classification of managers, 174
General property manager, 174
Individual building manager, 174
The resident manager, 174
Functions and specific duties, 174
Earnings, 175
Management contract, 175
Leasing, 175
Origin of leases, 175
Types of leasehold estates, 178

Requirements for creation of a lease, 178
Rights and obligations of the parties, 178
Analysis of lease form, 179
Rent, 179
Security, 179
Maintenance, repairs, and injury, 182
Reentry by lessor, 182
Assign or sublet, 182
Additional clauses for the lease form, 183
Termination of the lease, 183
Remedies of the lessor, 184
Utility shut-offs, 184
Preventing access, 184
Retaliatory eviction, 184
Proper maintenance, 185
Rental determination, 185
Oil, gas, and mineral leases, 185
Ground lease, 185
Sale-and-leaseback, 185
Lease-option arrangement, 187
Residential rental, 187

12. Appraisal and valuation of real property . . 189

Factors influencing value, 189
Different types of value, 189
Market value, 190
Definition of appraisal, 190
Methods of appraising, 190
The market comparison approach, 190
The cost approach, 192
The capitalization of income approach, 193
Appraisal organizations, 196
Depreciation, 197
Determining depreciation, 197
Depreciation for tax purposes, 198
Summary of appraisal and valuation methods, 198
Form of the appraisal report, 198
Income property statement, 199
Scheduled income, 199
Operating expenses, 199
Assessed value, 199
Investment information, 199

13. Property insurance 203

The insurance concept of property, 203
The packaging trend, 203
Commercial coverages—the multiperil policy, 204
Coinsurance, 204
Risks and coverages, 205
California homeowners insurance policy, 205

Multiperil policy, 205
Liability policy, 205
Workmen's compensation insurance, 205
Insurance licenses and licensing procedure, 205
  Agent, 205
  Broker, 208
  Solicitor, 208
  Certificate of convenience, 209
  General rules governing licensees, 209
Home warranty insurance programs, 209

14. Real estate mathematics 211

Interest, 211
  Simple and compound interest, 211
  Computing time, 211
  Interest formulas, 212
  60-day 6 percent method, 213
  Interest tables, 213
  Finding number of days, 213
Prorations, 215
Percentage, 216
  Commissions, 217
  Profit and loss, 217
  Net listing, 217
  Capitalization, 217
  Loan ratio, 218
  Discount, 218
Property tax, 219
Depreciation, 219
Amortization, 219
  Amortization schedule, 220
  Present balance of a loan, 220
Area measurement, 221
  Finding the square footage of a building, 225

15. Business opportunities brokerage 227

Definition of business opportunity, 227
Goodwill as applied to business, 227
Selling a business opportunity, 227
  Attention to certain legal requirements, 228
Specific rules and regulations, 228
  Uniform Commercial Code (UCC), 228
  Bulk sales and the UCC, 229
  California sales and use tax provisions, 230
  Alcoholic Beverage Control Act, 230
Technical qualifications license, 231
General chronological sale procedure, 231

16. Public sales, condominiums, and mobilehomes 233

Public sales, 233
Trustee's sale, 233
  Statement of condition, 233
  The notice of default, 233
  Trustor's right of reinstatement, 234
  Payment in full, 234
  Notice of sale, 234
  The sale, 234
  Holder of a second loan, 235
  Effect of sale on liens, 235
  Additional comments on trustee's sales, 235
  Possession after sale, 235
  Type of property sold, 236
Probate sales, 236
  Sale of estate property, 236
  Notice of sale, 236
  Listing probate property, 237
  Sale and opening of bids, 240
  Form of the bid, 240
  Raising the bid in court, 240
  Issuance of deed, 240
  Real estate broker's commission, 240
  Additional comments on purchase of probate property, 241
Mortgage foreclosure, 241
  Foreclosure sale, 241
  Method of bidding, 241
  Redemption rights, 241
  Right of possession, 241
Tax sale of real property, 241
  First sale, 241
  Second sale, 242
  Actual sale to public, 242
  Tax deed, 242
  Title insurance, 242
Sheriff's sale, 242
  Writs of attachment, judgment, and execution, 242
  Sale on writ of execution, 243
  Certificate of sale, 243
  Right of redemption, 243
  Final issuance of deed, 243
Additional sales of real property, 243
  Role of the real estate broker, 243
Condominium sales, 244
  Condominium features, 244
  The licensee and condominium sales, 244
Mobilehome sales, 245
  Regulating laws, 245
  Taxing mobiles as real property, 246
  Mobilehome parks, 246

Financing methods, 246
Escrow procedures, 247
Listing and purchase contracts, 247
Modular construction, 247

17. Real estate exchanges and trade-in programs 252

Exchanges, 252
    Reasons for an exchange, 252
    The tax-free exchange, 252
    Like kind defined, 253
    Boot defined, 253
    Depreciation considered, 253
    Basis for newly acquired property, 254
    Three-way exchange, 254
    Time-delay exchange—Starker case, 255
Involuntary conversion, 255
    Exchange examples, 255
    Analysis of exchange agreement form, 256
    Terms and conditions of an exchange, 256
    Acceptance, 257
Trade-in programs, 261
    Trade-in versus the exchange, 261
    The basic problem, 262
    Common trade-in programs, 262
    FHA trade-in assistance, 263
    Beginning a trade-in program, 266
    Guarantee agreement form, 266

Appendix A: Definitions of real estate and building construction words and phrases 267

Appendix B: Multiple-choice questions and answers 279

Appendix C 289

Index 335

List of illustrations

Figures

Organization chart of the real estate business, 2
Code of ethics, 3–4
Broker-salesperson contract, 22–23
Broker-salesman contract (employee), 24–25
Office operating costs diagram, 27
Examples of CAR forms for Real Estate Trust Fund Records and Requirements, 29
Policy and procedure manual, 30–38
Exclusive authorization and right to sell form, 44
Daily work plan form, 47
Estimated seller's net form, 50
Home buyer's problem analysis form, 56
Estimated buyer's cost form, 57
Real estate purchase contract and receipt for deposit form, 64–65
Structural pest control certification agreement, 68
Standard inspection report form, 69–70
Counteroffer, 74
Release of real estate purchase contract and receipt for deposit, 75
Average of California single family home prices, 79
Examples of classified advertisements for real estate, 82
Switch sheet and incoming call register, 84
Deed of trust, 87
Short form deed of trust, 90–91
A full reconveyance form, 93
Request for notice, 97
Notice of default, 98
Disclosure statements, 103–4
Notice of right to cancel, 106–7
Loan application form, 111–12
Mortgage loan disclosure statement, 122–23
Basic escrow procedures, 131
Seller's escrow statement, 134
Buyer's escrow statement, 135
Title insurance policy, 137–42
Property tax statement, 147
California estate and gift tax exemptions, 152
Schedule E: Supplemental income schedule, 170–71
Professional management agreement, 176–77

A standard lease, 180–81
CAR residential rental agreement, 186
A completed CAR competitive market analysis form, 191
Details of standard construction, 194–95
Veterans administration residential appraisal sheet, 200
Income property statement, 201
Standard fire insurance policy (business risks), 206
Standard fire insurance policy (personal risks), 207
Notice of intended sale, 230
Standard notice of sale, 237
Listing contract, 238
Purchase contract, 239
Listing and purchase contracts (mobile homes), 248–50
Exchange agreement form, 258–60
Guaranteed sales plan agreement form, 264–65
Independent contractor application, 289–90
Exclusive employment of broker to exchange, sell, lease, or option, 291
Selling your home or buying a home, 292
Multiple dwelling units—apartments, 293
Commercial-industrial buildings, 294
Residential analysis, 295
Receipt for increased deposit, 296
Release of real estate purchase contract, 297
Interim occupancy agreement, 298
Special studies zone disclosure, 299
All-inclusive purchase money promissory note, 300–301
All-inclusive purchase money deed of trust, 302–4
VA and FHA amendments, 305
Joint tenancy grant deed, 306
Grant deed, 307
Condominium grant deed, 308
Statement of identity, 309
Individual tax analysis, 310
Exclusive authorization to lease or rent, 311
Residential lease agreement after sale, 312
Exclusive authorization to lease or rent a single family dwelling, 313
Statement of condition, 314–15

Notice to pay rent or quit, 316
Thirty day notice of termination of tenancy, 317
Industrial and commercial leases, 318
Property analysis, 319
Comparative investment analysis, 320
Standard residential appraisal data sheet, 321–22
Business opportunity, 323
UCC financing statement, 324
Condominium DRE public report, 325–30
Exchange escrow instructions, 331
Exchange escrow statement, 332
Exchange basis adjustment, 333

Tables
Real cost of interest on a home loan, 58
Home ownership savings, 59

Projected California housing needs 1979–1984, 80
Government loan information, 116
Typical FHA loans, 118
Federal gift and estate tax rates, 155
Comparison of methods of depreciation, 165
Interest figured on $1,000, 214
Number of days between dates, 214
Proration for rents, taxes, and insurance, 215
Capitalization, 218
Monthly payments necessary to amortize a 15 percent loan, 220
Loan progress chart, 221
Monthly payments necessary to amortize an 9¾ percent loan, 222
Table of payments to amortize a $1,000 loan, 223
Fraction, decimal, and percentage equivalents, 224

1

The real estate industry and the real estate broker

Approximately 10 to 15 percent of all employed persons in the United States are engaged in the real estate business and its related activities. The business consists of the activities of private individuals and corporations, and the public activities of federal, state, and local governmental agencies. The state of California contains approximately 380,000 real estate broker and salesperson licensees.

The private segment of the real estate business is that of agency and brokerage practice, which involves selling, leasing, management, loan, and business opportunity brokerage. In addition, a broker may be engaged in related activities, such as construction, modernization of existing structures, and the development of unimproved land—commonly called subdividing. Besides improving land by creating lots and bringing in utilities, the developer may also construct homes and commercial buildings, and on a larger scale may create an entire community.

In performing the necessary functions in the real estate business, the broker must work with such specialists as surveyors, engineers, financial institutions who furnish necessary funds, title companies, architects, contractors, pest control men, attorneys, accountants, and many others whose special skills are necessary.

Government at all levels influences the real estate business through the many agencies and departments whose functions and responsibilities affect real estate. In the area of taxation are the administration of real property tax laws, valuation of real estate for tax purposes, assessment practices, and collection of real estate taxes. The management area involves acquisition, sale, leasing, and management of government lands and properties and public housing. Laws regulating the use of real estate involve building, health, zoning, fire, electrical, and plumbing codes, while other areas of enforcement include licensing laws and real estate laws.

Finally, and most important to the home-buying public, is the governmental role in financing, which involves the Home Loan Bank System, Federal Savings and Loan Insurance Corporation, Federal Housing Authority, Veterans Administration, and state veterans programs. Figure 1–1 illustrates the relationship between government agencies and segments of private enterprise, as well as professional, trade, and public organizations active in real estate.

TRADE AND PROFESSIONAL ASSOCIATIONS

Local real estate boards

A local real estate board, or board of Realtors, is a voluntary organization of individuals engaged in the real estate business in a particular locality. Full membership is restricted to those individuals who hold a real estate broker license, while real estate salesman licensees may obtain associate membership. In addition, most boards maintain an affiliate classification of membership which is open to banks, trust companies, title companies, escrow companies, and others whose duties or interests are related to the real estate business.

Local boards provide many services to their members, such as a multiple listing service, area maps, sales records and listing information, legal and other publications pertaining to local property, a library, real estate forms, educational materials, business and educational meetings, insurance protection, and other such benefits.

Virtually all local boards in California are affiliated with the California Association of Realtors and the National Association of Realtors. There are,

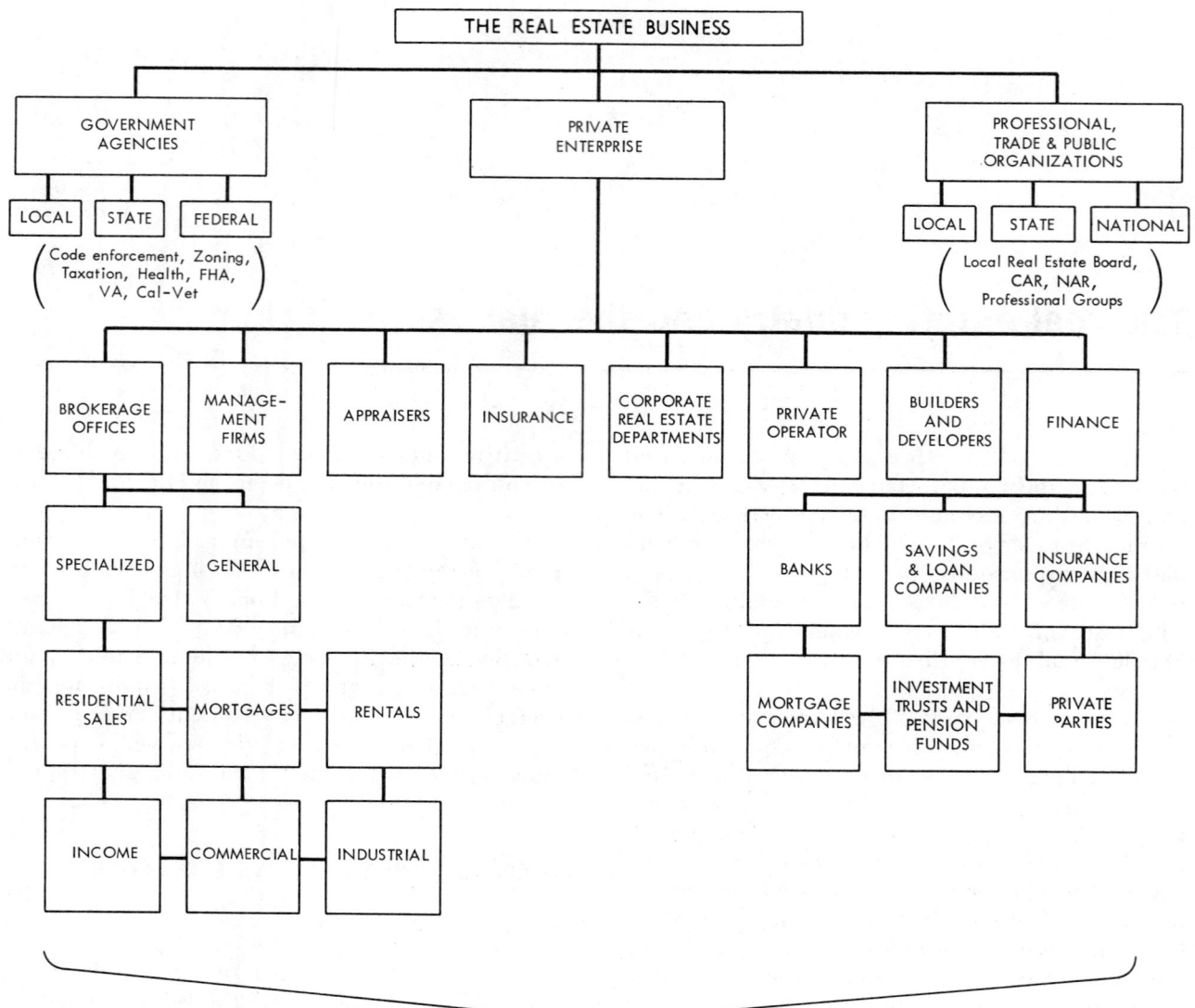

IN ADDITION, THERE MAY BE VARIOUS COMBINATIONS
OF THE ABOVE FOR SPECIAL PROJECTS OR PURPOSES.

FIGURE 1-1

however, a few independent boards in the state, some of which are strong in membership and influential in their communities. Many of the members of such boards are also members of boards affiliated with the state and national associations.

National Association of Realtors

The National Association of Realtors, 155 East Superior Street, Chicago, Illinois 60611, was organized in 1908 and currently has a membership of approximately 600,000 throughout the United States, and Puerto Rico. The national association unites the organized real estate interests through-out the United States and presents a common cause and program in behalf of national legislation affecting real property and the real estate industry. It is composed of local real estate boards throughout the nation, and the Code of Ethics of the NAR is subscribed to by the California Association of Realtors and local boards and is shown in Figure 1-2.

Because there are so many specialized areas of activity in the real estate business, there are many additional groups which have been founded within the framework of the NAR such as The American Institute of Real Estate Appraisers, The Institute of Farm Brokers, Society of Industrial Realtors, American Society of Real Estate Counselors, Wom-

CODE OF ETHICS

National Association of Realtors

California Association of Realtors

Preamble

Under all is the land. Upon its wise utilization and widely allocated ownership depend the survival and growth of free institutions and of our civilization. The interests of the nation and its citizens require the highest and best use of the land and the widest distribution of land ownership. They require the creation of adequate housing, the building of functioning cities, the development of productive industries and farms and the preservation of a healthful environment.

Such interests impose obligations beyond those of ordinary commerce. They impose grave social responsibility and a patriotic duty to which the REALTOR" should dedicate himself, and for which he should be diligent in preparing himself. The REALTOR", therefore, is zealous to maintain and improve the standards of his calling and shares with his fellow-REALTORS" a common responsibility for its integrity and honor. The term REALTOR" has come to connote competency, fairness and high integrity resulting from adherence to a lofty ideal of moral conduct in business relations. No inducement of profit and no instruction from clients ever can justify departure from this ideal.

In the interpretation of his obligation, a REALTOR" can take no safer guide than that which has been handed down through the centuries, embodied in the Golden Rule, "Whatsoever ye would that men should do to you, do we even so to them."

Accepting this standard as his own, every REALTOR" pledges himself to observe its spirit in all of his activities and to conduct his business in accordance with the tenets set forth below.

Where the word REALTOR" is used in this Code and Preamble, it shall be deemed to include REALTOR"-Associate. Pronouns shall be considered to include REALTORS" and REALTOR"-Associates of both genders.

ARTICLE 1

The REALTOR" should keep himself informed on matters affecting real estate in his community, the state, and nation so that he may be able to contribute responsibly to public thinking on such matters.

ARTICLE 2

In justice to those who place their interests in his care, the REALTOR" should endeavor always to be informed regarding laws, proposed legislation, governmental regulations, public policies, and current market conditions in order to be in a position to advise his clients properly.

ARTICLE 3

It is the duty of the REALTOR" to protect the public against fraud, misrepresentation, and unethical practices in real estate transactions. He should endeavor to eliminate in his community any practices which could be damaging to the public or bring discredit to the real estate profession. The REALTOR" should assist the governmental agency charged with regulating the practices of brokers and salesmen in his state.

ARTICLE 4

The REALTOR" should seek no unfair advantage over other REALTORS" and should conduct his business so as to avoid controversies with other REALTORS".

ARTICLE 5

In the best interests of society, of his associates, and his own business, the REALTOR" should willingly share with other REALTORS" the lessons of his experience and study for the benefit of the public, and should be loyal to the Board of REALTORS" of his community and active in its work.

ARTICLE 6

To prevent dissension and misunderstanding and to assure better service to the owner, the REALTOR" should urge the exclusive listing of property unless contrary to the best interest of the owner.

ARTICLE 7

In accepting employment as an agent, the REALTOR® pledges himself to protect and promote the interests of the client. This obligation of absolute fidelity to the client's interests is primary, but it does not relieve the REALTOR® of the obligation to treat fairly all parties to the transaction.

ARTICLE 8

The REALTOR® shall not accept compensation from more than one party, even if permitted by law, without the full knowledge of all parties to the transaction.

ARTICLE 9

The REALTOR® shall avoid exaggeration, misrepresentation, or concealment of pertinent facts. He has an affirmative obligation to discover adverse factors that a reasonably competent and diligent investigation would disclose.

ARTICLE 10

The REALTOR® shall provide equal professional services to all persons regardless of race, creed, sex, or country of national origin. The REALTOR® shall not be a party to any plan or agreement to discriminate against a person or persons on the basis of race, creed, sex, or country of national origin.

FIGURE 1-2

ARTICLE 11

A REALTOR® is expected to provide a level of competent service in keeping with the Standards of Practice in those fields in which the REALTOR® customarily engages.

The REALTOR® shall not undertake to provide specialized professional services concerning a type of property or service that is outside his field of competence unless he engages the assistance of one who is competent on such types of property or service, or unless the facts are fully disclosed to the client. Any person engaged to provide such assistance shall be so identified to the client and his contribution to the assignment should be set forth.

The REALTOR® shall refer to the Standards of Practice of the National Association as to the degree of competence that a client has a right to expect the REALTOR® to possess, taking into consideration the complexity of the problem, the availability of expert assistance, and the opportunities for experience available to the REALTOR®.

ARTICLE 12

The REALTOR® shall not undertake to provide professional services concerning a property or its value where he has a present or contemplated interest unless such interest is specifically disclosed to all affected parties.

ARTICLE 13

The REALTOR® shall not acquire an interest in or buy for himself, any member of his immediate family, his firm or any member thereof, or any entity in which he has a substantial ownership interest, property listed with him, without making the true position known to the listing owner. In selling property owned by himself, or in which he has any interest, the REALTOR® shall reveal the facts of his ownership or interest to the purchaser.

ARTICLE 14

In the event of a controversy between REALTORS® associated with different firms, arising out of their relationship as REALTORS® or as cooperating brokers, the REALTORS® shall submit the dispute to arbitration in accordance with the regulations of their board or boards rather than litigate the matter.

ARTICLE 15

If a REALTOR® is charged with unethical practice or is asked to present evidence in any disciplinary proceeding or investigation, he shall place all pertinent facts before the proper tribunal of the member board or affiliated institute, society, or council of which he is a member.

ARTICLE 16

When acting as agent, the REALTOR® shall not accept any commission, rebate or profit on expenditures made for his principal-owner, without the principal's knowledge and consent.

ARTICLE 17

The REALTOR® shall not engage in activities that constitute the unauthorized practice of law and shall recommend that legal counsel be obtained when the interest of any party to the transaction requires it.

ARTICLE 18

The REALTOR® shall keep in a special account in an appropriate financial institution, separated from his own funds, monies coming into his possession in trust for other persons, such as escrows, trust funds, clients' moneys and other like items.

ARTICLE 19

The REALTOR® shall be careful at all times to present a true picture in his advertising and representations to the public. He shall neither advertise without disclosing his name nor permit any person associated with him to use individual names or telephone numbers, unless such person's connection with the REALTOR® is obvious in the advertisement.

ARTICLE 20

The REALTOR®, for the protection of all parties, shall see that financial obligations and commitments regarding real estate transactions are in writing, expressing the exact agreement of the parties. A copy of each agreement shall be furnished to each party upon his signing such agreement.

ARTICLE 21

The REALTOR® shall not engage in any practice or take any action inconsistent with the agency of another REALTOR®.

ARTICLE 22

In the sale of property which is exclusively listed with a REALTOR®, the REALTOR® shall utilize the services of other brokers upon mutually agreed upon terms when it is in the best interests of the client.

Negotiations concerning property which is listed exclusively shall be carried on with the listing broker, not with the owner, except with the consent of the listing broker.

ARTICLE 23

The REALTOR® shall not publicly disparage the business practice of a competitor nor volunteer an opinion of a competitor's transaction. If his opinion is sought and if the REALTOR® deems it appropriate to respond, such opinion shall be rendered with strict professional integrity and courtesy.

ARTICLE 24

The REALTOR® shall not directly or indirectly solicit the services or affiliation of an employee or independent contractor in the organization of another REALTOR® without prior notice to said REALTOR®.

FIGURE 1-2 *(continued)*

ens Council, Institute of Real Estate Management, National Marketing Institute, Securities and Syndication Institute and others. In addition, there are independent organizations such as the Society of Real Estate Appraisers, American Society of Appraisers, National Association of Home Builders, American Bankers Association, U S. Savings and Loan League, and numerous trade and professional organizations which are closely related to the real estate business.

The California Association of Realtors

The California Association of Realtors, 505 Shatto Place, Los Angeles, California 90020, was formed at Los Angeles in 1905. It is the largest such organization in the United States and is composed of the members of approximately 180 local real estate boards in California and also individual members. At the present time, there are approximately 115,000 individuals on the CAR roster.

The following objectives and purposes of the California Association of Realtors are set forth in its constitution:

a. To unite its members and to promote high standards.
b. To safeguard the land-buying public.
c. To foster legislation for the benefit and protection of real estate and to cooperate in the economic growth and development of California.

A few of CAR's standing committees concern themselves with education, ethics and professional standards, exchanges, insurance, real property taxation, real estate teachers, legislation, political affairs, and finance. There are numerous divisions within CAR, such as the California Association of Real Estate Teachers and the Real Estate Certificate Institute. Others deal with such areas as property management, investment, syndication and industrial-commercial brokerage.

CAR now provides legal advice to members who may call a toll-free number, (213) 387–0392, and ask a CAR attorney questions ranging from landlord-tenant relations to real estate contract problems.

Use of the term *Realtor*® and *Realtor*®-*Associate*

In California, the term *Realtor*® may be used only by a licensed real estate broker who is either an individual member of the National Association of Realtors® or a full member of a local real estate board that is affiliated with the NAR. An individual who is licensed in California as a real estate salesman and is employed by a Realtor® or affiliated with a Realtor® as an independent contractor may apply for Realtor®-Associate membership in the NAR and use the Realtor-Associate designation.

In California, the unauthorized use of the term *Realtor*® is a violation of the California Real Estate Law. To every member authorized to use the term *Realtor*® the national association issues a certificate signed by the officers of the national association designating the member as a Realtor.®

Realtists

In 1947, a national organization of black real estate brokers known as the National Association of Real Estate Brokers was formed in Miami, Florida, and in turn adopted the name Realtist. The address of the National Association of Real Estate Brokers, Inc. is 1025 Vermont Avenue, N.W., Washington, D.C. 20005.

A Realtist must be a member of a local board as well as a member of the national organization. The California Association of Real Estate Brokers, affiliated with the National Association of Real Estate Brokers, was organized in 1955 and now has four board affiliates: Associated Real Property Brokers, Oakland; Consolidated Real Estate Brokers, Sacramento; Consolidated Realty Board, Los Angeles; and Logan Heights Realty Board, San Diego.

Affiliation not mandatory

One who is licensed by the California Division of Real Estate is not, of course, under any compulsion to join any of the trade or professional organizations. While a licensee may join his local board, which is affiliated with the CAR and the NAR (national association), he may remain entirely unaffiliated and merely use the designation, Licensed Real Estate Broker.

CALIFORNIA DEPARTMENT OF REAL ESTATE

The California Department of Real Estate was created by legislative act in 1917. It provided for the licensing and regulation of real estate agents and was the first legislation of its kind in the United States. Certain parts of the legislation were subsequently found unconstitutional. In 1919, legislation that deleted the unconstitutional provisions of the 1917 act was passed; and it, with subsequent amendments, has remained in effect since then. In 1943, the original law, the Real Estate Act, was codified and became part of the Business and Professions Code. It may be properly referred to as the Real Estate Law and comprises Division 4 of the Business and Professions Code beginning at Section 10000.

Among the strongest supporters of the real estate licensing law was the organized real estate industry itself. The law is designed primarily for the protection of the public in real estate transactions when the services of an agent are employed. By requiring qualifications for license and by the establishment and enforcement of definite standards and practices, the law has also played an important part in the professionalization of the industry and of those engaged in real estate and related activities.

The California Real Estate Commissioner

The California Real Estate Commissioner is appointed by the governor and is the chief executive of the division. The commissioner serves at the pleasure of the governor, and it is his duty to determine administrative policy and to enforce the provisions of the law.

Among the duties involved in administering the provisions of the law are the investigation of complaints against licensees, regulation of the sale of subdivisions, screening and qualifying of applicants for licenses, and the investigation of nonlicensees alleged to be performing acts for which a license is required by law.

The commissioner has all the powers granted by the Administrative Procedure Act to hold formal hearings for determination of issues involving a license, license applicant, or subdivider. After a hearing, the commissioner may suspend or revoke or deny the license, or issue an order halting sales in a subdivision.

The department also publishes the annual *Reference Book* and a long list of teacher's guides, student workbooks, research studies, and other educational aids and materials.

STATE REAL ESTATE ADVISORY COMMISSION

In 1937, a State Real Estate Board was established by legislative act; and in 1957, its name was changed to the State Real Estate Advisory Commission. Except for the commissioner himself, members serve without pay and are reimbursed only for actual and necessary travel expenses while on official business.

The Real Estate Law authorizes the advisory commission to:

1. Inquire into the needs of the real estate licensees of California, the department, and matters of business policy of the department.
2. Confer with the governor and other state officers on how the department may best serve the state and its licensees in the real estate business.
3. Make recommendations and suggestions to the commissioner as they see fit regarding licensees and the public.

EDUCATION AND RESEARCH

In 1956, the legislature created the Real Estate Education and Research Fund, separate from the Real Estate Fund, which supports the general operation of the Department of Real Estate. The new fund, sustained by a fixed portion of license fees, is used for the advancement of education and research not only at the University of California but at the California State Universities and California Community Colleges as well.

To assist the commissioner in allocating to the public institutions of higher learning monies appropriated by the legislature for this purpose, the commissioner in 1958 appointed the Commissioner's Real Estate Education and Research Committee, now known familiarly as the CREERAC. On the committee are representatives of the real estate industry, the real estate commissioner, the universities, the state colleges, and the community colleges of California. Areas of responsibility and emphasis are defined for each of the participants in the program.

REAL ESTATE RECOVERY FUND

In 1964, The legislature created a Real Estate Recovery Fund supported by real estate license fees. The fund provides for payment to innocent parties who obtain a judgment against a real estate licensee on the basis of fraud, misrepresentation, deceit, or conversion of trust funds in a real estate transaction in the event that the licensee does not have sufficient assets to pay the judgment. Of approximately 700 claims filed since the fund began, 78 percent have been paid in whole or part, totaling $1,900,000.

COMMISSIONER'S PLAN FOR PROFESSIONALISM

In 1966, the real estate commissioner's office drafted and distributed a "Blueprint for Professionalization of the Real Estate Business in California." In the text of the paper, it was explained that the intention was to provide a frame of reference and general plan of procedure for raising the standards of real estate practitioners in California.

For many years, both nationally and in the state of California, articulate real estate practitioners have been urging the cause of professionalism. Through the years, not only did the California Association of Realtors support legislation raising licensing standards, thus providing increased protection for the public dealing through licensees, but it steadily enlarged opportunities for its members to increase their knowledge and improve their skills.

Two of the principal ingredients for achievement of professional status are (a) specialized education in depth and (b) recognition by the public that a professional type of service is indeed involved. As to the former, educational attainment, California, because of its unique real estate education, research, and recovery fund, has reached the position where its public collegiate institutions, and some private collegiate institutions as well, offer widespread opportunities for real estate education in depth. Thus, this essential of professionalism is available to all who wish it.

In recent years, numerous recommendations and proposals have been made, such as requiring a college degree for the broker license, requiring two years full-time experience as a salesperson with no credit for prior experience or education in order to become a broker, increasing broker requirement courses from six to eight, and requiring a pre-license course for the salesperson license.

Even though legislation was introduced to accomplish some of the recommendations, it was not successful, and none as yet have been enacted into law.

THE REAL ESTATE BROKER

The general public thinks of a real estate broker as an agent whose duty it is to bring a seller and buyer together and thus negotiate the sale and/or purchase of real property.

The Real Estate Law gives a much more detailed definition of a real estate broker. It defines him as a person who actually does, or offers or attempts to do, certain acts. These acts are done for compensation or in expectation of a compensation. These acts are done for others and are with regard to, or in connection with, real property.

The acts are as follows:

1. Sells or offers to sell; buys or offers to buy.
2. Solicits prospective sellers or purchasers.
3. Solicits or obtains listings.
4. Negotiates the purchase, sale, or exchange of real property.
5. Leases or rents, collects rents, or negotiates the sale, purchase, or exchange of leases.
6. Negotiates real property loans and deals with borrowers, lenders, or note holders in connection with real estate loans.
7. Buys, sells, or exchanges real property contracts or promissory notes secured by liens on real property.
8. Claims or collects an advance fee in connection with an advance fee listing to sell, lease, exchange, or rent real property or to obtain a loan thereon.
9. Collects payments or performs other functions in connection with real property contracts or promissory notes secured by liens on real property.
10. Assists in filing an application for the purchase of lease of, or in locating or entering on, lands owned by the state or federal government.

Real estate salesman

A real estate salesman is a person who, for a compensation or in expectation of a compensation, is employed by a licensed real estate broker to do one or more of the acts set forth in the definition of a real estate broker, above. A salesman must be affiliated with a licensed broker and cannot operate independently under a salesman's license.

When license not required

The definition of a real estate broker and a real estate salesman does not include the following, and a broker's license or salesman's license does not have to be held by the following:

1. Anyone who directly performs any of the defined acts with reference to his own property or, in the case of a corporation which, through its regular officers receiving no special compensation therefore, performs any of the acts defined with regard to the corporation's own property.
2. Anyone holding a duly executed power of attorney from the owner.
3. Services rendered by an attorney at law in performing his duties as such attorney at law.

4. Any receiver, trustee in bankruptcy, or any person acting under the order of the court.
5. Any trustee selling under a deed of trust.

The above exemptions are the most common. For further details regarding exemptions from license requirements, the reader is referred to Section 10133.1, Real Estate Law, *Department of Real Estate Reference Book.*

While a person dealing with his own property does not have to be licensed, there is often a question about how many transactions within a year may be engaged in before the owner is deemed to be a broker and thus to fall under the licensing provisions. The following section from the Real Estate Law, Section 10131.1, should provide ample clarification as regard this point:

1. The acquisition for resale to the public, and not as an investment, of eight (8) or more real property sales contracts or promissory notes secured directly or collaterally by liens of real property, during a calendar year, or
2. The sale to, or exchange with, the public of eight (8) or more real property sales contracts or promissory notes secured directly or collaterally by liens on real property during a calendar year.

The law further provides that the transactions negotiated through a real estate licensee shall not be considered in determining whether a person is a broker and subject to the license requirement.

Penalty for violation

Without a license, one cannot legally collect a commission or fee for performance of any of the acts defined as within the authority of the licensed broker or salesman. One who purports to act as a real estate broker or real estate salesman without being duly licensed may, on conviction, be punished by fine or by imprisonment or both.

It is also a violation of the law for any individual to pay a compensation to a nonlicensee for performing any acts which require a license.

Obtaining a real estate license

Applications and forms for all examinations and licenses issued by the Real Estate Commissioner must be made on forms furnished by the Department of Real Estate. Forms, as well as a booklet entitled, "Instructions to License Applicants," can be obtained by calling at any of the department's offices throughout the state or writing to the principal officer in Sacramento.

Principal Office

Sacramento 95816
1719 24th Street
916-445-3995

Branch Offices

Fresno 93721
State Office Bldg., Rm. 3084
2550 Mariposa St.
209-488-5009

Los Angeles 90012
State Office Bldg., Rm. 8107
107 S. Broadway
213-620-5903

Sacramento 95823
4433 Florin Rd., Suite 300
916-445-6776

San Diego 92101
State Bldg., Rm. 5008
1350 Front Street
714-237-7345

San Francisco 94107
185 Berry Street
415-557-2136

Santa Ana 92701
Rm. 324
28 Civic Center Plaza
714-558-4491

Duplicate sets of fingerprints are also required of all applicants who have not filed prints with the department during the immediately preceding five-year period.

Real estate broker's license

The applicant for the real estate broker's license must:

1. Be at least 18 years of age.
2. Have had previous experience or education as required by law.
3. Be honest, truthful, and of good reputation.
4. Submit proof of having completed six statutory college courses as required by law.
5. Pass the examination.

Experience and education. The Real Estate Law requires two years active experience as a licensed real estate salesman within the past five years or equivalent experience. This experience must be in the general field of real estate or may be in the form of graduation from a college.

Most candidates for the broker's license base their claims for qualification upon two years of experience as a real estate salesman. However, the commissioner does not allow any person who has been merely licensed as a salesman for two years to qualify. The applicant must submit proof that he was actively employed as a full-time 40-hour-per-week salesman or part-time for the equivalent of two years full-time. A form is provided for the applicant so that he may obtain the signature of his employing broker or brokers, who must certify as to the required employment.

The requirement may be met by a combination of full-time experience as a licensed salesman and certain equivalent qualifying real estate experience. All claims of equivalent qualifying real estate experience must be supported by valid evidence in the form of letters or statements from responsible parties who have been in a position to note the applicant's duties or activities as they have related to the general field of real estate. Examples of such equivalent experience are:

1. Employment in the real estate department of a savings and loan association or bank.
2. Experience as a subdivider or contractor.
3. Experience and employment in the field of real estate appraisal.
4. Employment as a public employee in such departments as that of the tax assessor or city planning department.
5. Employment in a title insurance or escrow company.

Equivalent experience may also include formal collegiate education. Some examples are:

1. An individual who holds a baccalaureate degree from any accredited college or university may qualify without any experience as a real estate salesman licensee.
2. An applicant may qualify with one year full-time employment as a licensed salesman and graduation from a California Community College with a major in real estate.

Statutory courses. In addition to the salesman experience or equivalent requirement, all applicants for the California Real Estate Broker License must submit proof of having completed six college-level courses as follows:

I. Legal Aspects of Real Estate
Real Estate Practice
Real Estate Finance
Real Estate Appraisal
II. Real Estate Economics, *or* Accounting
III. A course selected from one of the following: real estate principles, business law, property management, real estate office administration, escrows, or an advanced course in legal aspects of real estate, real estate finance, or real estate appraisal.

The four courses listed in Group I must be completed by the broker applicant. The additional two courses required may be satisfied by completing both of the courses listed in Group II or by completing one of the courses from Group II and one of the courses listed in Group III.

The required courses must be college level courses with a value of three semester-units or four quarter-units each. Three semester- or four quarter-units means 45 hours of classroom work, so that the six courses will require a total of 270 hours.

An attorney who is a member of the California or other state bar association will generally qualify for the real estate broker examination on the basis of education and experience and is exempt from the statutory courses requirement.

Broker's license examination. The makeup and content of the license examination are discussed in the chapter. The examination fee, which must accompany the application for the broker license, is $85. If the applicant does not pass the examination, his fee is not refundable but will be held to his credit for a period of two years. If the applicant passes the examination, he is so notified and may then apply for the broker's license, which is valid for four years.

The examination is scheduled for one day, and the applicant is allowed a maximum of two and one-half hours in the morning session and two and one-half hours in the afternoon session to complete the test which consists of 200 multiple-choice questions. To pass, an applicant must answer a minimum of 150 questions correctly.

Real estate salesman's license

The applicant for the real estate salesman license must:

1. Be at least 18 years of age.
2. Be honest, truthful, and of good reputation.
3. Pass the examination.

Salesman's license examination. There is no specific experience, education, or course requirement that must be met prior to taking the salesman's examination. The initial step for the applicant for a real estate salesman license is to fill out, and forward with the $60 examination fee, an application that can be obtained at any Department of Real Estate office and at many local board of Realtors offices.

The applicant is scheduled for examination, and if he passes the test, he is entitled to file the application for license as well as the signature of the broker who intends to employ him. This application for a four-year license is filed with a required fee.

The examination for the salesman's license is similar in content to that of the broker's license but is not so thorough and searching in nature. It has been devised with emphasis on testing whether the candidate has sufficient practical and everyday working knowledge. It is, in form, a totally objective three and one-quarter hour test having a total of 150 multiple choice-questions. To pass, an applicant must answer at least 105 questions correctly.

LICENSE EXAMINATION CONTENT

In 1973, California real estate salesman's and broker's examinations were revised to separate questions that are universal and multi-state in their application from those that deal with subject matter peculiar to real estate law and practice in California.

The purpose was to institute a certain element of reciprocity between states that agree with California to administer the same multi-state portion as part of their own salesman's and broker's license examination.

However, effective July 1980, California no longer participates in any multi-state reciprocal testing program.

The ratio of questions with respect to specific areas in the California salesman's and broker's examinations is given in the *Department of Real Estate Reference Book* as follows:

1. *In law*—a reasonable understanding of general real estate law and the license law and its application to real estate transactions. This includes the analysis of listings and deposit receipts. Total weight: 50 percent.
2. *In matters of public control*—a general understanding of the impact of federal, state, and local authority in zoning, subdividing, in exercising the power of eminent domain and in general real estate transactions. Total weight: 10 percent.
3. *In valuation*—a sufficient knowledge of valuation methods to enable the licensee to serve his clients and the general public in a useful and dependable manner in carrying out his function in the real estate market. Total weight: 15 percent.
4. *In finance*—a general knowledge of available financial sources, procedures, practices and government participation sufficient to assist clients in obtaining and utilizing credit in real estate transactions. Total weight: 10 percent.
5. In special areas pertaining to real estate with which the licensee should be sufficiently familiar to perform his duties and live up to his responsibilities adequately including:
   a. *Income taxation*—applied to sale of residences, types of installment sales, capital gains, corporations, real estate investment trusts.
   b. *Land development*—water supply, sewage, drainage, streets, community facilities.
   c. *Canons of business ethics, including familiarity with the Code of Ethics promulgated by the National Association of Realtors.*
   d. *Rentals*—property management.
   e. *Escrows*—nature and purposes, requisites, obligations of parties.
   f. *Arithmetical calculations*—as required for computation in real estate transactions.
   g. *Title insurance.*
   h. *Residential building design, and construction.*

   Total weight: 15 percent.

CONTINUING EDUCATION REQUIREMENT

All real estate broker and salesman licensees, effective January 1981, as a condition for license renewal every four years, are required to evidence completion of 45 clock hours of instruction in educational courses, seminars, or conferences in current real estate related areas. License renewals must be accompanied by certificates of attendance, official transcripts, or certified copies of attendance showing a total of no less than 45 clock hours of approved continuing education during the immediately preceeding four years.

The new law is consistent with the availability of real estate courses, educational seminars, and programs presently offered throughout the State. Courses required for licensure, general training or education to obtain a license or examination preparation offerings will not be acceptable toward meeting the continuing education requirement. Acceptable offerings must qualify for continuing education credit purposes through application to and approval by the Real Estate Commissioner, and approved offering entities are required to issue a uniform certificate of attendance to each student successfully completing approved offerings.

COMMON REAL ESTATE LAW VIOLATIONS

Sections 10176 and 10177 of the Real Estate Law should be thoroughly understood by all real estate licensees. Violations with regard to these sections constitute the foundation for most license suspensions or revocations.

Section 10176 is concerned with the actions of a licensee while engaged in the practice and performing any of the acts within the scope of the Real Estate Law, while Section 10177 applies to situations in which the person involved was not necessarily acting as an agent or as a licensee.

In discussing violations, we should realize that the vast majority of those engaged in the real estate business are honest individuals who conduct business in an honorable and ethical way. Many mistakes and violations are made, not intentionally, but because the licensee was unaware that he was committing a violation. It is important that the licensee know what he may not do as well as what he may do.

Section 10176(a), misrepresentation. The licensee must disclose to his principal material facts that his principal should know. Failure to do this is cause for disciplinary action. A large percentage of the complaints the commissioner receives allege misrepresentation on the part of the salesman and/or broker. California courts have consistently said that real estate purchasers are relieved from any responsibility to independently investigate facts represented as true by an owner or broker unless the purchaser knows the statements are false.

Section 10176(b), false promise. Although it may seem that a false promise and a misrepresentation are the same thing, they are not. A misrepresentation is a false statement of fact, while a false promise is a false statement about what the promisor is going to do in the future. The false promise is usually proved by showing that the promise was impossible of performance and that the person making the promise knew it was impossible.

Section 10176(c), misrepresentation through agents. This section gives the commissioner the right to discipline a licensee who misrepresents or makes false promises through other real estate agents, and also for a continued and flagrant course of misrepresentation.

Section 10176(d), divided agency. A licensee must inform all his principals if he is acting as an agent for, or receiving a commission from, more than one party in a transaction.

Section 10176(e), commingling. Commingling is the mixing together of the funds of a licensee and those of his principals. To avoid this, the licensee is cautioned to maintain a trust account and to keep all moneys entrusted to him separate from his own personal funds. If we go a step beyond the mere mixing together of funds, we come to an even more serious offense—conversion. Conversion is the misappropriation and use of the funds of another. If a licensee takes a deposit and then spends it immediately, he has converted these funds.

Section 10176(f), definite termination date. This section requires that an exclusive listing have a definite termination date. Generally, if the termination date is specified, or if a definite period of time is indicated, the requirement is satisfied.

Section 10176(g), secret profit. A licensee is prohibited from making a secret profit in a real estate transaction. An example would be a broker who makes a low offer, usually through a dummy purchaser, when the broker already has a higher offer from a legitimate buyer. When the dummy buyer, who is really acting for the broker, acquires the property, it is then sold to the real buyer whom the broker has waiting. The profit to the broker is generally much more than a mere commission would have been.

Section 10176(h), listing-option. This section requires that when a licensee uses a form that is both an option and a listing, he must inform his principal of the amount of profit he will make and must obtain his principal's written consent to the profit.

Section 10176(i), dishonest dealing. This is a catchall type of section and covers all acts that require a real estate license.

Section 10176(j), signatures of prospective purchasers. This section makes it a violation for brokers engaged in the sale of business opportunities to use what is known as a "sendout list." Brokers who have no written or oral listings to sell the businesses give the list to a prospective purchaser. The purchaser signs the list of businesses for sale and, in doing so, promises that he will pay a commission to the broker who furnished him the list should he eventually buy one of the listed businesses, even though he may not deal with the broker who furnished the list.

We shall now briefly review Section 10177, which covers acts performed while the person involved may or may not have been acting as a real estate agent or as a licensee.

Section 10177(a), obtaining license by fraud. If it is found that a licensee obtained his license by fraud, misrepresentation, or deceit, the commissioner may revoke the license. This section is commonly used when it is found that the license failed to mention a previous criminal record on his license application.

Section 10177(b), convictions. This section permits the commissioner to proceed against a licensee who has been convicted of either a felony or a misdemeanor that involves moral turpitude.

Section 10177(c), false advertising. This section covers false advertising as it relates to subdivision and general property sales.

Section 10177(d), violations of other sections. This section gives the commissioner the authority to proceed against a licensee for violation of any of the other sections of the Real Estate Law, the rules and regulations of the commissioner, and the subdivision laws.

Section 10177(e), misuse of trade name. This section refers to the misuse of any terms or insignia of any real estate organization. It applies to those who use the term *Realtor* without the right to do so.

Section 10177(f), conduct warranting denial. This is a general section of the law and covers any act involving crime or dishonesty. This section applies to those requiring a license.

Section 10177(g), negligence or incompetence. This section allows the commissioner to proceed against the licensee when it is shown that he is so careless or unqualified that to allow him to handle a transaction would endanger the interests of his clients or customers.

Section 10177(h), supervision of salesman. A broker is subject to disciplinary action if he fails to exercise reasonable supervision over the activities of his salesmen.

Section 10177(i), violating government trust. This section prescribes disciplinary liability for using government employment to violate the confidential nature of records thereby made available.

Section 10177(j), other dishonest conduct. This section specifies that any other conduct, not necessarily connected with real estate, which constitutes dishonest dealing or fraud may subject the one so involved to license suspension or revocation.

Section 10177(k), restricted license violation. Violation of the terms, conditions, restrictions, and limitations contained in any order granting a restricted license is grounds for disciplinary action.

Section 10177(l), inducement of panic selling. A cause for disciplinary action is the soliciting or inducing of the sale, lease, or the listing for sale or lease of residential property on the ground, wholly or in part, of loss of value, increase in crime, or decline of the quality of the schools due to the present or prospective entry into the neighborhood of a person or persons of another race, color, religion, ancestry, or national origin.

Licensees must be familiar with the commissioner's regulations dealing with discrimination and panic selling and comply with the requirements of federal and state laws dealing with the prohibition of discrimination in performing sales, leasing, rental or financing, or other usual real estate activities.

Section 10177(m), Franchise Investment Law. Violation of any provisions of the Franchise Investment Law or commissioner's regulations pertaining to this law.

Section 10177(n), securities. Violation of corporations code sections and commissioners regulations pertaining to securities.

ADDITIONAL LAWS AFFECTING THE LICENSEE

Sections 10176 and 10177 of the Real Estate Law are but a small part of the laws, rules, and regulations covering the actions of licensees or other persons engaged in any way in the real estate business. The alert licensee must be familiar with the California Real Estate Law, the rules and regulations of the commissioner, Administrative Procedure Act, Business and Professions Code, and additional excerpts from the California Code as they may apply. Specialized areas such as property loan brokerage and subdivisions are thoroughly regulated.

The real estate commissioner is empowered to adopt rules and regulations for the administration and enforcement of the Real Estate Law. These regulations are many and varied; Regulations 2903 and 2785 are examples.

Regulation 2903, structural defects, disclosure

A licensee shall disclose to any and all purchasers, or prospective purchasers, and to any and all sellers, or prospective sellers, or parties to an exchange, any and all knowledge he may have, as soon as it is practical for him to do so, of any infestation of wood-destroying organisms in any improvement or premises, the sale, purchase, or exchange of which said licensee negotiates.

Regulation 2785, code of ethics and professional conduct

In order to enhance the professionalism of the California real estate industry and maximize protection for members of the public dealing with real estate licensees, the following standards of professional conduct and business practices are adopted:

a. Unlawful conduct. Licensees shall not engage in "fraud" or "dishonest dealing" or "conduct which would have warranted the denial of an application for a real estate license" within the meaning of Business and Professions Code Sections 10176 and 10177 including, but not limited to, the following acts and omissions:

1. Knowingly making a substantial misrepresentation of the likely market value of real property to its owner (1) for the purpose of securing a listing or (2) for the purpose of acquiring an interest in the property for the licensee's own account.

2. The statement or implication by a licensee to an owner of real property during listing negotiations that the licensee is precluded by law, regulation or by the rules of any organization, other than the broker firm seeking the listing, from charging less than the commission or fee quoted to the owner by the licensee.

3. The failure by a licensee acting in the capacity of an agent in a transaction for the sale, lease or exchange of real property to disclose to a prospective purchaser or lessee facts known to the licensee materially affecting the value or desirability of the property, when the licensee has reason to believe that such facts are not known to, nor readily observable by, a prospective purchaser or lessee.

4. When seeking a listing, representation to an owner of the real property that the soliciting licensee has obtained a bona fide written offer to purchase the property, unless at the time of the representation the licensee has possession of a bona fide written offer to purchase.

5. The willful failure by a listing broker to present or cause to be presented to the owner of the property any offer to purchase received prior to the closing of a sale, unless expressly instructed by the owner not to present such an offer, or unless the offer is patently frivolous.

6. Presenting competing offers to purchase real property to the owner by the listing broker in such a manner as to induce the owner to accept the offer which will provide the greater compensation to the listing broker, without regard to the benefits, advantages, and/or disadvantages to the owner.

7. Knowingly underestimating the probable closing costs in a transaction in a communication to the prospective buyer or seller of real property in order to induce that person to make or to accept an offer to purchase the property.

8. Failing to explain to the parties or prospective parties to a real estate transaction the meaning and probable significance of a contingency in an offer or contract that the licensee knows or reasonably believes may affect the closing date of the transaction, or the timing of the vacating of the property by the seller or its occupancy by the buyer.

9. Knowingly making a false or misleading representation to the seller of real property as to the form, amount and/or treatment of a deposit toward purchase of the property made by an offeror.

10. The refunding by a licensee, when acting as an agent or sub-agent for seller, of all or part of an offeror's purchase money deposit in a real estate sales transaction after the seller has accepted the offer to purchase, unless the licensee has the express permission of the seller to make the refund.

11. Failing to disclose to the seller of real property in a transaction in which the licensee is acting in the capacity of an agent, the nature and extent of any direct or indirect interest that the licensee expects to acquire as a result of the sale. The prospective purchase of the property by a person related to the licensee by blood or marriage purchase by an entity in which the licensee has an ownership interest, or purchase by any other person with whom the licensee occupies a special relationship where there is a reasonable probability that the licensee could be indirectly acquiring an interest in the property, shall be disclosed.

b. Unethical conduct. In order to maintain a high level of ethics in business practice, real estate licensees should avoid engaging in any of the following activities:

1. Representing, without a reasonable basis, the nature and/or condition of the interior or exterior features of a property when soliciting an offer.

2. Failing to respond to reasonable inquiries of a principal as to the status or extent of efforts to market property listed exclusively with the licensee.

3. Representing as an agent that any specific service is free when, in fact, it is covered by a fee to be charged as part of the transaction.

4. Failing to disclose to a person when first discussing the purchase of real property, the existence of any direct or indirect ownership interest of the licensee in the property.

5. Recommending by a salesperson to a party to a real estate transaction that a particular lender or escrow service be used when the salesperson believes his or her broker has a significant beneficial interest in such entity without disclosing this information at the time the recommendation is made.

6. Claiming to be an expert in an area of specialization in real estate brokerage, e.g., appraisal, property management, industrial siting, etc., if, in fact, the licensee has had no special training, preparation or experience in such area.

7. Using the term *appraisal* in any advertising of offering for promoting real estate brokerage business to describe a real property evaluation service to be provided by the licensee unless the evalu-

ation process will involve a written estimate of value based upon the assembling, analyzing and reconciling of facts and value indicators for the real property in question.

8. Failing to disclose to the appropriate regulatory agency any conduct on the part of a financial institution which reasonably could be construed as a violation of The Housing Financial Discrimination Act of 1977 (anti-redlining)—Part 6 (commencing with Section 35800) of Division 24 of the Health and Safety Code.

9. Representing to a customer or prospective customer that because the licensee of his or her broker is a member of, or affiliated with, a franchised real estate brokerage entity, that such entity shares substantial responsibility, with the licensee, or his or her broker, for the proper handling of transactions if such is not the case.

10. Participating in the organized disclosure to a representative, agent, or employee of a public or private school, firm, association, organization or corporation conducting a real estate preparatory course the language of any question used in a state real estate license examination, at the request of such person or entity.

11. Demanding a commission or discount by a licensee purchasing real property for one's own account after an agreement in principle has been reached with the owner as to the terms and conditions of purchase without any reference to price reduction because of the agent's licensed status.

c. Beneficial conduct. In the best interests of all licensees and the public they serve, brokers and salespersons are encouraged to pursue the following beneficial business practices:

1. Measuring success by the quality and benefits rendered to the buyers and sellers in real estate transactions rather than by the amount of compensation realized as a broker or salesperson.

2. Treating all parties to a transaction honestly.

3. Promptly reporting to the California Department of Real Estate any apparent violations of the Real Estate Law.

4. Using care in the preparation of any advertisement to present an accurate picture or message to the reader, viewer, or listener.

5. Submitting all written offers as a matter of top priority.

6. Maintaining adequate and complete records of all one's real estate dealings.

7. Keeping oneself current on factors affecting the real estate market in which the licensee operates as an agent.

8. Making a full, open, and sincere effort to cooperate with other licensees, unless the principal has instructed the licensee to the contrary.

9. Attempting to settle disputes with other licensees through mediation or arbitration.

10. Complying with these standards of professional conduct and the Code of Ethics of any organized real estate industry group of which the licensee is a member.

Nothing in this regulation is intended to limit, add to, or supersede any provision of law relating to the duties and obligations of real estate licensees or the consequences of violations of law. Subdivision *a* lists specific acts and omissions which do violate existing law and are grounds for disciplinary action against a real estate licensee. The conduct guidelines set forth in subdivisions *b* and *c* are not intended as statements of duties imposed by law nor as grounds for disciplinary action by the Department of Real Estate but as guidelines for elevating the professionalism of real estate licensees.

THE LICENSEE AS AN AGENT

In most of his real estate transactions, the real estate broker or salesman acts as an agent for someone else. The person for whom he acts is called the principal. This principal generally seeks to buy or sell property from a third party. Thus, the broker or salesman represents his principal in dealings with third parties.

Creation of the agency relationship

The agency relationship between a licensee and his principal in the real estate business is created through a written contract called a listing. When initiated in this way, the basic principles of contract law are applicable. Listings will be discussed in greater detail in Chapter 3.

An agreement authorizing or employing a broker to purchase or sell real estate for compensation or commission is invalid unless the agreement is in writing, contains a termination date, and is signed by the party to be charged or by his agent. Aside from the open listing form, which may or may not contain a definite termination date and is seldom used by most brokers, all other listing forms must contain a definite termination date. It is required that the agent have equal written authority to bind his principal on any agreement within the class of contracts covered by the Statute of Frauds or other sections that make writing necessary.

Different types of listing forms are used, but the important thing to remember is to correctly fill in the forms and obtain the needed signatures. Being a contract, it must have the essential elements of a contract, including competent parties, a lawful object, proper offer and acceptance, and consideration.

Consideration is provided from the fact that the broker either does find the purchaser ready, willing, and able to buy, or agrees to make an effort to do so. Although he is not paid a commission for merely agreeing to try, the fact that he does try may be a valuable part of the contract, particularly when the contract constitutes an exclusive listing for a limited but fixed time.

Agent's authority

An agent has the authority to (1) do everything necessary, or proper in the ordinary course of business, for effecting the purpose of his agency and (2) to make representations about the facts involved in the transaction he is engaged in. Unless specifically authorized, he has no authority to act in his own name unless it is in the usual course of business to do so.

While an agent may do what is necessary or proper in order to carry out his duties, he must always be very careful that his principal has full knowledge of what the agent is doing and approves of his actions. The agent must not keep any secrets from his principal and must not do anything that would be against the best interest of his principal. There should always be full disclosure of facts between an agent and those whom he represents.

One of the greatest causes of complaints to the Real Estate Department arises out of deposits and the demand for their return. Many of these complaints state that the broker or salesman urged a deposit merely as a matter of form from the prospective purchaser and said that the deposit would be returned if the prospective purchasers changed their minds about the transaction and wanted the deposit returned. Usually this is an oral promise on the part of the broker or salesman. The important point here is that the deposit never belongs to the broker or salesman. Although the licensee may be empowered under the listing agreement to accept a deposit, the deposit is not the property of the licensee but, rather, that of the principal. The commissioner spells out quite thoroughly the rules and regulations dealing with the handling of deposits, and all licensees should be familiar with them.

The fiduciary relationship

The broker and his salesmen owe a definite loyalty to their clients and are prohibited by law from personally profiting by virtue of their agency, except by the agreed compensation for their services. The fiduciary character of the relationship between the broker and his clients is held by the courts in the same strictness as is the relationship between a trustee and beneficiary. The Civil Code forbids an agent from doing any act that a trustee is forbidden to do.

Although the agent generally represents the seller of the property, he owes a like duty of fairness and good faith to the buyer. Not only does he owe it to the buyer direct, but also, any misrepresentation or unlawful concealment gives the buyer the right to rescind the contract or possibly to sue the agent, his employing broker, and the owner of the property.

An agent is obligated to use reasonable care and skill in his work. He cannot compete with his principal on matters connected with the agency and, of course, cannot act as an agent for a competitor.

An agent cannot act for two principals in negotiations with each other unless both have knowledge of, and consent to, the dual agency.

The courts have held that an agent cannot acquire any interests adverse to his principal; that is, the agent cannot make any secret profit out of the subject of his agency. If he conceals an interest in the property sold or if he makes any secret profit whatsoever, he will have to return these moneys to his principal.

A real estate agents license is subject to suspension or revocation if the licensee claims, demands, or receives a commission, a fee, or other consideration as compensation or inducement for referral of customers to any escrow agent, structural pest control firm, or title insurance companies.

Statements made by brokers and salesmen

Real estate agents are constantly making statements to prospects concerning the condition of the premises being offered for sale. Usually, one or more of the parties involved in the transaction may have erroneous impressions concerning the property.

Such statements and impressions can be generally classified as follows:

1. Statements intended and understood as merely expressions of opinion.

2. Statements intended and understood to be part of the contract itself.
3. Mistakes.
4. Statements intended and understood as representations of fact.
5. Nondisclosure of material facts by silence.

A statement by the agent that the building he is offering for sale is "the best on the block" or that it is "very well constructed and in the best neighborhood in town" are examples of statements that are merely expressions of opinion. The prospective purchaser should recognize them as such, and the opinions would not place the licensee under any liability under the law.

Statements incorporated into the deposit receipt become part of the contract itself. If these statements or promises were made in good faith, their falsity results only in breach of contract, and the licensee is not liable under the law. The statements, however, must have been made in good faith.

When the parties to a transaction merely form untrue conclusions with respect to the property, the case is usually one of mutual mistake. The contract may be rescinded, and the licensee would not ordinarily be liable under the law.

Thus, if there was good faith on the part of the licensee and honest intent, statements that fall under 1, 2, and 3, above, usually will not place the licensee in a position of liability under the law. Litigation usually occurs with regard to statements that fall under 4 and 5.

Statements intended and understood as representations of fact which later prove to be false will fall under three general classifications.

Innocent misrepresentations. Such statements later found to be false permit rescission of the contract, and ordinarily no liability attaches against the licensee.

Negligent misrepresentations. The broker's or salesman's liability for negligent statements is considered to be a form of deceit. The liability can be enforced either by the injured party in a civil action for damage or by the commissioner in a disciplinary action to suspend or revoke the broker or salesman license.

Fraudulent misrepresentations. This kind of statement is made when the person who states a fact knows it to be false. This is clearly fraud and not only subjects the licensee to both civil and disciplinary action but also may result in criminal action against him.

We come finally to nondisclosure of material facts by silence. Liability for silence will result when the licensee has knowledge of facts that affect the property in question and he knows that the prospective purchaser or seller is unaware of these facts.

When principal supplies false information

When the principal supplies the agent with false information concerning a property, and the agent reasonably relies on this information and repeats it to a prospective purchaser, the agent will not be held liable.

The agent who makes such misrepresentations must show that they were made with the belief that they were true and that the agent did, in fact, believe them to be true. Since the seller of a property may not always give the broker correct information, the broker or salesman must be very cautious and thoroughly examine any information he feels inadequate or suspicious in any way. If the information given the licensee is such that any responsible licensee would have cause to question it, then a licensee who does not do so may find himself open to liability when he passes this information on to others.

QUESTIONS FOR DISCUSSION

1. A broker is defined as a person who performs certain acts with relation to real property. As an individual, list as many of these acts as you can that fall within an area with which you may have had some contact.
2. What is the main difference between a broker's license and a salespersons license?
3. When do individuals dealing with their own property have to be licensed?
4. In what ways do the requirements for broker's license generally differ from those for salespersons license?
5. How is the formal agency relationship created between the real estate broker and his principal?
6. How do the elements of contract enter into the creation of the agency relationship?
7. What is meant by the agent's fiduciary relationship?
8. For what types of statements to clients might a licensee be held liable at law?
9. Can a licensee be held liable for something he does not say?
10. What is the general rule with respect to when the broker earns a commission?

2

The real estate office

Most real estate offices in California are single-office operations, as opposed to firms that have a main office plus branch-office locations. In addition, the most common form of operation is the individual proprietorship—that is, a single broker who heads and runs the firm.

The main factor common to most successful offices is that they operate under clearly outlined procedures for all activities, and all personnel are expected to adhere to them. A study of unsuccessful offices will show that they operate with a general lack of adequate internal organization and, further, that they have a large turnover in sales personnel.

BASIC COMPANY FORMS

Three basic forms of company formation are found in the real estate business. These are (1) individual proprietorship, (2) partnership, and (3) corporation.

Individual proprietorship

Single ownership is the predominant form of real estate organization in California. It is an office run and operated by a single broker-owner, who makes and is solely responsible for all business decisions.

Approximately 25 percent of licensees in the state are employed in offices staffed by no more than three salespeople and run by a single broker. Some brokers, of course, do not choose to employ any salesmen at all, and in other cases, we find a husband-wife combination operating an office.

Some of the advantages of an individual proprietorship form of operation may be:

1. Absolute control of the business.
2. Decisions quickly made.
3. Independence of action.
4. Ownership of all profits.
5. Psychological and intangible rewards.

Some of the disadvantages of this form may be:

1. Limited availability of capital.
2. Unlimited legal liability.
3. Difficulty of handling all specialized phases of a real estate brokerage operation.
4. Need for continuous personal attention is necessary.
5. Success completely dependent on the ability of a single individual.
6. Difficulty of budgeting one's time to adequately service all clients.

The partnership

A partnership is an agreement between two or more persons to carry on, as co-owners, a business for profit. In the real estate partnership, all partners must hold a real estate broker or salesman license. A salesman licensee may by contract with a broker be a copartner, but the Department of Real Estate holds the broker responsible for supervising the salesman licensee and for all acts of the partnership in transacting real estate business.

Partnerships fall into two broad categories: a general partnership, created to conduct a general continuing type of business; and a limited partnership, formed for a specific and limited purpose, such as building or subdivision project. The limited partnership, or joint venture, is dissolved when the project is completed. The continuing real estate partnership is a general partnership.

A mutual agency relationship exists among partners; each partner is empowered to bind the firm, himself, and his partners to third persons on transactions within the scope of the partnership business. Obviously, this type of business form is a very sensitive one as far as each of the partners is concerned. They are in a sense married one to the other for the common purpose of sharing responsibilities, liabilities, profits, and the everyday work load involved in running a real estate organization. One of the main factors in the failure of the partnership as a business form is the partners' inability to work well together and to agree on business policies and practices to be followed.

Most successful partnerships are made up of persons who are able to work well with each other, who have a good general background in real estate, and, in addition, possess knowledge and experience in a specialized area of real estate. One partner may be expert in income properties, another partner in residential real estate, while another partner may specialize in commercial and industrial offerings. Other areas in which individual partners may excell are taxation, exchanges, office management, listing, selling, or property management.

The general advantages of the partnership may be:

1. The capital and specialized talents of the partners are pooled.
2. Tax liabilities are created by the individual partners, and the partnership is not taxed as such.
3. Increased scale of operations is possible with greater stability.

Some of the disadvantages may be:

1. Each partner is liable for the acts of the other.
2. Partnerships are built on the ability of the partners to work together.
3. Personal assets of each partner are subject to interests of creditors.

The corporate form

Less than one sixth of all California real estate firms are incorporated. An individual broker, as well as two or more brokers, may form a corporation. One must have the services of an attorney in order to incorporate, since certain statutory legal requirements must be met.

The decision to incorporate usually results because a firm grows to a size so large that the corporation form offers distinct tax advantages. Generally, large-scale operations lend themselves best to use of the corporate form, and because such operations carry with them the risk of tremendous liability, the limited liability feature of the corporation is very important. Individuals are liable only to the extent of their investment in the corporation, and their personal assets are thus protected.

The opportunity for raising capital through the sale of stock is another reason for incorporation. Some real estate offices incorporate and offer shares of stock to certain key personnel as inducements to remain with the firm. A salesperson for a corporation may now be a majority shareholder or serve as an officer or director of the corporation provided the designated broker for the corporation is also an officer and director and is thus in a position to exercise supervision and control over performance of licensed activities by salespersons who are licensed to the corporation.

Among the possible disadvantages are: the complexity and cost involved in organizing and forming the corporation; the difficulty in obtaining credit or making loans, since the creditors know they can take action only against the assets of the corporation; the fact that decisions cannot be made rapidly in many instances; and the knowledge that while there are certain tax advantages, the corporation is a victim of double taxation in that the profits of the corporation are taxed when earned and then the stockholders are again taxed when these profits are distributed in the form of dividends.

The three forms of real estate organization discussed thus far—the individual broker-owner, the partnership, and the corporation—generally concern the permanent operation of a business of a continuing nature. In many instances, parties join forces for a single project or transaction. Where this is the intent of the parties involved, we often find a joint venture or syndicate form used. These forms lend themselves best to the single purpose, one-time-only real estate project or transaction.

REAL ESTATE OFFICE PERSONNEL

Personnel in the typical offices consists of the broker or brokers who own and run the operation, the licensees employed as salesmen, and persons employed as secretaries and bookkeepers and for other office activities that do not require a real estate license.

Sales manager

In the smaller office, the broker will assume the responsibility for management of the operation and supervision of the salesmen, if any. A sales manager is not generally required unless the sales force numbers eight to ten or more persons. At this point, the volume of activity justifies the appointment of sales manager who will devote his time to salesmen's problems with regard to typical transactions, training programs, advertising preparation, public relations, participation in local board and service club activities, and relations with such person as escrow officers, loan officers, pest control inspectors, and others with whom the office constantly deals.

The compensation of the sales manager is usually based upon the sales production of the office, with a fixed minimum generally provided. The income of the sales manager generally reflects the size of the firm, the number of salesmen employed and supervised by him, and whether or not he is permitted to list and sell in addition to acting as sales manager.

It is interesting to note that good salesmen generally do not make good sales managers. The position of sales manager requires a certain degree of administrative ability and is much more an inside desk-job than a salesman is used to. The sales manager must understand company policy and be able to interpret and enforce such policy among the licensees under his control. He must set up sales quotas, plan and participate in weekly sales meetings, help to arbitrate disputes, and be a person who can gain the respect and confidence of those with whom he works.

THE BROKER AND SALESPERSONS

The sales staff should consist of individuals interested in real estate as a career and willing to put in the time and effort necessary to be successful. When interviewing an applicant for a salesman's position, the experienced broker will certainly be interested in the applicant's previous work experience, manner and appearance, education and/or special training, present family status, and personality.

Hiring unqualified individuals leads to a large turnover of personnel and tends toward a poor public image of the real estate agent and the real estate business.

During the past few years, a movement has begun to make the real estate licensee truly a professional person. Standards for licensees have gradually risen as a result of pressures from the public and the real estate industry. The California Association of Realtors has done a particularly effective job of sponsoring legislation to raise licensing standards and of encouraging the development of educational offerings throughout the state.

A recent California Association of Realtors membership survey reported in 1980 shows that while there is no single set of characteristics which fits all licensees, there are certain factors applicable to a majority or greater proportion of those surveyed.

The distribution of salespersons as to men and women is just about 50-50, with women slightly ahead. With respect to brokers, men substantially outnumber women. The average rate for brokers is 50 and for salespersons, 43, although 25 percent of salespersons are in the 18 to 35 age bracket.

Experience levels are diverse, with about 50 percent of salespeople having less than five years in real estate while 60 percent of brokers have over nine years experience. The broker typically spends 50 hours a week engaged in real estate activities while salespeople spend 44. About 30 percent of all licensees reported working in excess of 60 hours per week. Ninety percent of brokers and 80 percent of salespeople reported that they are engaged in real estate as a full-time activity.

Average business income is most difficult to state, with the ranges between high and low amounts varying widely. However, for full-time licensees, the median income for a broker can be stated as approximately $38,000 and for a salesperson, $21,000. The typical brokerage office employs between 7 and 15 salespeople. Twenty-five percent have a staff of three or less, while 20 percent employ over 25 salespeople. Twenty-five percent of real estate offices have a franchise affiliation and are generally larger offices. Approximately 85 percent of salespersons are employed as independent contractors.

Most licensees specialize in residential sales. Residential income properties come next followed by commercial and industrial real estate and building development. Specialization seems related to experience, with more experienced licensees specializing in areas such as business opportunities, farms, appraising, property management, unimproved acerage, building developments, and condominium development and conversions.

Ninety percent of real estate licensees report owning their own residence, with 80 percent having additional real estate holdings.

TRAINING PROGRAM

Almost without exception one finds that the most successful real estate firms also have the best training programs for their personnel. One of the chief reasons for the failure of beginning salesmen is the lack of guidance and training given to them by their employing broker.

The well-rounded, complete training program should encompass three general areas: (1) individual on-the-job training and forms (2) staff meetings, and (3) outside academic instruction.

On-the-job training and forms

Before a newly employed salesman is put on the floor of the office, where he will be expected to meet clients, answer the telephone, and conduct the business of the office in general, he will need a certain amount of intensive individual training. To a lesser degree, this training will have to continue even after he begins to be assigned floor time in the office. The initial training must give the salesman a complete understanding of the company's policies and procedures, its commission schedule, and in general what is expected of him and what he may expect from the office. The individual responsible for this initial training may be the owner-broker, the sales manager, or a senior salesman who is assigned this function.

Special emphasis should be given to the study and understanding of all the various forms used in the office, such as listing forms, deposit receipts, rental and lease agreements, and other specialized forms and records. A complete set of all forms used should be made available to the licensee for referral and study.

A complete set of forms published by the California Association of Realtors is contained in their publication, *Real Estate Standard Forms Reference Book.* Another excellent set of commonly used forms can be obtained from Professional Publishing Company, 122 Paul Drive, San Rafael, California.

Staff meetings

Staff meetings, or sales meetings as they are sometimes called, provide an excellent opportunity for both formal and informal personnel training. Such meetings are generally held in the morning hours, and although once a week seems to be the most popular frequency, many firms hold such meetings two or three times each week. Many techniques may be used.

Specific topic discussion. A topic of general interest may be considered, such as current market conditions, present state of financing, new legislation affecting real estate, successful sales techniques, or methods of listing.

Successful transactions. A recently completed transaction may be considered, with the salesman involved explaining the steps as they took place. This type of presentation generally results in a spirited discussion of how the deal was put together, what was done correctly, and what may have been done better.

Special projects report. Often, one or two members of the firm may study a special problem and then report their findings to the assembled group.

Current listings. All the firm's current listings are reviewed, with up-to-date information relevant to any particular listing.

Audio-visual presentation. A new film relating to real estate or a taped talk by an expert provides for an interesting presentation. An overhead projector may be used to project a form on a screen during a discussion of the use of the form and proper method of entering the necessary information thereon.

Outside speakers. In addition to a presentation by a member of the firm, many persons from the outside may be invited to speak to the staff.

Outside training

In addition to training within the firm, the licensee can obtain numerous textbooks and other reading material prepared for those in real estate.

A licensee may also enroll in formalized study courses conducted by the CAR, the University of California Extension Division, and virtually all the community colleges throughout the state.

CAR programs. The California Association of Realtors offers a variety of opportunities for the licensee to further his education in real estate. In addition to a number of excellent books dealing with various areas in real estate, the CAR also holds numerous conventions and meetings and sponsors courses and seminars throughout the state.

University of California and state colleges. The University of California offers a number of real estate courses in its regular and extension division and also provides correspondence courses. These range from broad general coverage of a specific area to a very advanced and detailed course offering. Some of the areas covered are real estate law, practice, finance, appraisal, management, economics, investment, design and structure, taxation, exchanges, analysis, and marketing. The state colleges also offer a variety of courses.

Community colleges. Virtually all of the community colleges in the state offer courses in real estate in both the day and evening divisions. Many also offer a summer program open to all. California leads the nation in number and variety of real estate courses offered in the university, state colleges, community colleges, and adult evening programs of local school districts. Of the fees collected by the Department of Real Estate from licensees, a portion goes to finance in part the programs offered at these institutions throughout the state.

The community colleges generally offer a real estate certificate to persons who complete certain prescribed requirements.

Local boards and private schools. In addition to all the foregoing programs, many local real estate boards have an educational committee and usually sponsor regular meetings featuring guest speakers on timely topics of special interest to local real estate practitioners. A number of private schools provide specialized courses and training programs.

Employee and independent contractor

An ordinary employee is one who is employed to render personal service to his employer and who, in rendering such service, remains entirely under the control and direction of his employer. An independent contractor, however, is one who does his work in his own way and is merely responsible for attaining a final result. The person hiring the independent contractor cannot tell him how to do his job, as is the case with an employee. An agent is generally distinguished from an employee or independent contractor, but with regard to real estate agents, the classification of the individual agent may vary depending upon the particular circumstances.

The classification of a person as an agent, employee, or independent contractor is important with respect to two general areas. The first is with respect to social security coverage and unemployment insurance. An employee is generally covered, while one who works for himself as an independent contractor may be without certain of these benefits. The law does, however, require workman's compensation insurance to be provided for any worker regardless of whether they are classified as an independent contractor or employee.

The second area is with respect to liability, and while a real estate licensee is an agent, he may also be classified as either an independent contractor or an employee. While a principal is generally responsible for the acts of his agent, there are situations in which the principal may not be liable if the agent is an independent contractor. This liability finds its most notable illustrations in the cases involving automobile accidents of employees while driving on the employer's business. If the wrongdoer was an independent contractor, as a real estate broker is usually classified, the property owner whom the broker represents will not be responsible for injuries caused by negligence of the broker. Since a real estate salesman is often considered to be an employee of the broker, virtually all brokers carry substantial public liability insurance for their salesmen and other office employees.

The California Association of Realtors has recently issued a publication dealing with the independent contractor and employee relationship. It is very important to distinguish whether the salesman is an employee or an independent contractor. In tort and contract areas, the salesman is presumed to be the agent of the broker, regardless of whether the salesman is designated an employee or independent contractor, and all acts of the salesman within the course and scope of his usual duties impose liability on the broker.

With regard to state unemployment insurance, statutory authorization allows a broker to disclaim the employee relationship if the salesman is remunerated on a commission basis only. In the withholding tax and social security areas, the broker can only insist on the freedom associated with an independent contractor relationship if the broker can establish that he exercises control of his salesmen only as to the results desired and not as to the details and means of the salesman's performance.

The California Association of Realtors makes available for use two different forms of broker-salesman contract. Figure 2–1 illustrates the form in which the status of the salesman is to be that of an independent contractor and states that the parties to the agreement are and shall remain independent contractors, and that the salesman is controlled by the broker only as to the result of the salesman's work, and not as to the means by which such result is accomplished. The other form, illustrated in Figure 2–2, classifies the salesman as an employee and contains a clause stating that the salesman has no authority, either expressed or implied, to represent anything to a prospective purchaser unless it is in the listing agreement or unless he receives specific written instructions from the broker. The broker has complete direction and control of the salesman, which is an important point in the employee classification.

BROKER - SALESPERSON CONTRACT

(INDEPENDENT CONTRACTOR)

CALIFORNIA ASSOCIATION OF REALTORS® STANDARD FORM

THIS AGREEMENT, made this _____ day of _____, 19____, by and between _____ hereinafter referred to as Broker and _____

_____ hereinafter referred to as Salesperson,

WITNESSETH:

WHEREAS, Broker is duly licensed as a real estate broker by the State of California, and

WHEREAS, Broker maintains an office, properly equipped with furnishings and other equipment necessary and incidental to the proper operation of business, and staffed suitably to serving the public as a real estate broker, and

WHEREAS, Salesperson is now engaged in business as a real estate licensee, duly licensed by the State of California.

NOW, THEREFORE, in consideration of the premises and the mutual agreements herein contained, it is understood and agreed as follows:

1. Broker agrees, at Salesperson's request, to make available to Salesperson all current listings in the office, except such as Broker may choose to place in the exclusive possession of some other Salesperson. In addition, at Salesperson's discretion and at Salesperson's request Broker may, from time to time, supply Salesperson with prospective listings; Salesperson shall have absolute discretion in deciding upon whether to handle and the method of handling any such leads suggested by Broker. Nothing herein shall be construed to require that Salesperson accept or service any particular listing or prospective listing offered by Broker; nor shall Broker have any right or authority to direct that Salesperson see or service particular parties, or restrict Salesperson's activities to particular areas. Broker shall have no right, except to the extent required by law, to direct or limit Salesperson's activities as to hours, leads, open houses, opportunity or floor time, production, prospects, reports, sales, sales meeting, schedule, services, inventory, time off, training, vacation, or other similar activities.

At Salesperson's request and at Salesperson's sole discretion Broker agrees to furnish such advice, information and full cooperation as Salesperson shall desire. Broker agrees that thereby Broker obtains no authority or right to direct or control Salesperson's actions except as specifically required by law (including Business and Professions Code Section 10177 (h)) and that Salesperson assumes and retains discretion for methods, techniques and procedures in soliciting and obtaining listings and sales, rentals, or leases of listed property.

2. Broker agrees to provide Salesperson with use, equally with other Salespersons, of all of the facilities of the office now operated by Broker in connection with the subject matter of this contract, which office is now maintained at _____
_____.

3. Until termination hereof, Salesperson agrees to work diligently and with Salesperson's best efforts to sell, lease or rent any and all real estate listed with Broker, to solicit additional listings and customers, and otherwise promote the business of serving the public in real estate transactions to the end that each of the parties hereto may derive the greatest profit possible, provided that nothing herein shall be construed to require that Salesperson handle or solicit particular listings, or to authorize Broker to direct or require that Salesperson to do so. Salesperson assumes and agrees to perform no other activities in association with Broker, except to solicit and obtain listings and sales, rentals, or leases of property for the parties' mutual benefit, and to do so in accordance with law and with the ethical and professional standards as required in paragraph 4 below.

4. Salesperson agrees to commit no act of a type for which the Real Estate Commissioner of the State of California is authorized by Section 10176 of the California Business & Professions Code to suspend or to revoke license.

5. Broker's usual and customary commissions from time to time in effect, shall be charged to the parties for whom services are performed except that Broker may agree in writing to other rates with such parties.

Broker will advise all Salespersons associated with Broker of any special commission rates made with respect to listings as provided in this paragraph.

When Salesperson shall have performed any work hereunder whereby any commission shall be earned and when such commission shall have been collected, Salesperson shall be entitled to a share of such commission as determined by the current commission schedule set forth in Broker's written policy, except as may otherwise be agreed in writing by Broker and Salesperson before completion of any particular transaction.

6. In the event that two or more Salespeople participate in such work, Salesperson's share of the commission shall be divided between the participating Salespersons according to agreement between them or by arbitration.

7. In compliance with Section 10138 of the California Business and Professions Code, all commissions will be received by Broker; Salesperson's share of such commissions, however, shall be payable to Salesperson immediately upon collection or as soon thereafter as practicable.

8. In no event shall Broker be personally liable to Salesperson for Salesperson's share of commissions not collected, nor shall Salesperson be entitled to any advance or payment from Broker upon future commissions, Salesperson's only remuneration being Salesperson's share of the commission paid by the party or parties for whom the service was performed. Nor shall Salesperson be personally liable to Broker for any commission not collected.

9. Broker shall not be liable to Salesperson for any expenses incurred by Salesperson or for any of his acts except as specifically required by law, nor shall Salesperson be liable to Broker for office help or expense. Salesperson shall have no authority to bind Broker by any promise or representation unless specifically authorized in writing in a particular transaction. Expenses which must by reason of some necessity be paid from the commissions, or are incurred in the collection of, or in the attempt to collect the commission, shall be paid by the parties in the same proportion as provided for herein in the division of commissions.

FIGURE 2-1

Salesperson agrees to provide and pay for all necessary professional licenses and dues. Broker shall not be liable to reimburse Salesperson therefor.

In the event Broker elects to advance sums with which to pay for the account of Salesperson professional fees or other items, Salesperson will repay the same to Broker on demand and Broker may deduct such advances from commissions otherwise payable to Salesperson

10. This agreement does not constitute a hiring by either party. It is the parties' intention that so far as shall be in conformity with law the Salesperson be an independent contractor and not Broker's employee, and in conformity therewith that Salesperson retain sole and absolute discretion and judgment in the manner and means of carrying out Salesperson's selling and soliciting activities. Therefore, the parties hereto are and shall remain independent contractors bound by the provisions hereof. Salesperson is under the control of Broker as to the result of Salesperson's work only and not as to the means by which such result is accomplished. This agreement shall not be construed as a partnership and Broker shall not be liable for any obligation incurred by Salesperson.

11. In accordance with law, Salesperson agrees that any and all listings of property, and all employment in connection with the real estate business shall be taken in the name of Broker. Such listings shall be filed with Broker within twenty-four hours after receipt of same by Salesperson.

Salesperson shall receive a commission in accordance with the current commission schedule set forth in the Broker's written policy based upon commissions actually collected from each firm listing solicited and obtained by Salesperson. In consideration therefore Salesperson agrees to and does hereby contribute all right and title to such listings to the Broker for the benefit and use of Broker. Salesperson and all other Salespeople associated with Broker to whom Broker may give the listing. Salesperson shall have the rights provided in paragraph 13 hereof with respect to listings procured by Salesperson prior to termination.

12. On completion of work in process, this agreement may be terminated by Salesperson at any time. Except for cause, this agreement may not be terminated by Broker except on 30 days' prior written notice to Salesperson. On the occurrence of any of the following causes Broker may terminate this agreement:

(a) Election of Broker to sell its entire business, or to cease doing business at the office specified in paragraph 2;
(b) Any breach of this agreement by Salesperson;
(c) Cessation of Salesperson to be licensed;
(d) Failure of Salesperson to comply with any applicable law, or regulation of the Real Estate Commissioner;
(e) The filing by or against Salesperson of any petition under any law for the relief of debtors; and
(f) Conviction of Salesperson of any crime, other than minor traffic offenses.

13. When this agreement has been terminated, Salesperson's regular proportionate share of commission on any sales Salesperson has made that are not closed, shall, upon the closing of such sales, be paid to Salesperson, if collected by Broker, and except in cases of termination for cause Salesperson shall also be entitled to receive the portion of the commissions, received by Broker after termination, allocable to the listing (but not the sale) as set forth in Broker's current commissions schedule, on any listings procured by Salesperson during Salesperson's association with Broker, subject, however, to deductions as provided in paragraph 14.

14. In the event Salesperson leaves and has transactions pending that require further work normally rendered by Salesperson, Broker shall make arrangements with another Salesperson in the organization to perform the required work, and the Salesperson assigned shall be compensated for completing the details of pending transactions and such compensation shall be deducted from the terminated Salesperson's share of the commission.

15. Arbitration—In the event of disagreement or dispute between Salesperson in the office or between Broker and Salesperson arising out of or connected with this agreement which cannot be adjusted by and between the parties involved, the disputed disagreement shall be submitted to the Real Estate Board of which Broker is a member for arbitration pursuant to the provisions of its Bylaws, said provisions being hereby incorporated by reference, and if the Bylaws of such Board include no provision for arbitration, then arbitration shall be pursuant to the rules of the American Arbitration Association, which rules are by this reference incorporated herein.

16. Salesperson shall not after the termination of this contract use to Salesperson's own advantage, or the advantage of any other person or corporation, any information gained for or from the files or business of Broker.

17. Salesperson agrees to indemnify Broker and hold Broker harmless from all claims, demands and liabilities, including costs and attorney's fees, to which Broker is subjected by reason of any action by Salesperson taken or omitted pursuant to this agreement.

18. All notices hereunder shall be in writing. Notices may be delivered personally, or by mail, postage prepaid, to the respective addresses noted below. Either party may designate a new address for purposes of this agreement by notice to the other party. Notices mailed shall be deemed received as of 5:00 P.M. of the second business day following the date of mailing.

WITNESS the signatures of the parties hereto the day and year first above written. In duplicate.

WITNESS

BROKER

ADDRESS

WITNESS

SALESPERSON as INDEPENDENT CONTRACTOR

ADDRESS

FIGURE 2-1 *(continued)*

BROKER-SALESMAN CONTRACT
(EMPLOYEE)
CALIFORNIA ASSOCIATION OF REALTORS® STANDARD FORM

1. This agreement entered into this _____ day of _____ 19____ by and between _____ hereinafter called Broker and _____ _____ hereinafter called Salesman, hereby agree, subject to termination at will be either party, to the following conditions and details of their relationship:

BROKER

2. Broker is defined as the operator of a real estate firm or business, licensed as a broker under the laws of the State of California by the Real Estate Commissioner, to sell or otherwise deal in real estate, and who employs one or more salesmen.

SALESMAN

3. Salesman is defined as: (a) A person duly licensed under the laws of the State of California by the Real Estate Commissioner as a salesman and employed by Broker. (b) A person duly licensed under the laws of the State of California by the Real Estate Commissioner as a broker and employed by Broker as a real estate salesman.

GENERAL CONDITIONS

4. Salesman shall read and be governed by the Code of Ethics of the National Association of Realtors,® the real estate law of the State of California and the by-laws of the local real estate boards, and any future modifications or additions thereto. A copy of the code of ethics and of the local Board by-laws are attached hereto.

BROKER OBLIGATIONS

5. Broker maintains offices adequately and properly equipped with furnishings, equipment and facilities reasonable and adequate for the proper operation of a general real estate brokerage business, staffed with trained employees engaged in serving the public as a real estate broker.

6. As a part of these facilities, Broker procures and maintains listings for sale, lease and rental of real estate as well as purchasers, lessees and renters thereof, and has for some time and does now enjoy the good will and reputation for fair dealing with the public generally.

7. Broker is duly and regularly licensed as a real estate broker under license issued by the Real Estate Commissioner of the State of California and maintains memberships in the local real estate board, the California Association of Realtors® and the National Association of Realtors®

8. Broker agrees to make available to Salesman all current listings in the office except such as Broker may find expedient to place exclusively in the possession of some other salesman.

9. Salesman has not authority, either express or implied, to represent anything to a prospective purchaser unless it is in the listing agreement or unless he receives specific written instructions from Broker.

10. Broker shall provide, within limitations herein set forth, Salesman with advertising and with necessary office equipment, including space, desk, telephone, telegrams, signs, business cards, stationery, escrow assistance, legal advice and supervisory assistance and cooperation with salesman in connection with his work.

11. All advertising shall be approved and placed by Broker.

12. Broker must first approve the ordering of all title searches and the opening of all escrows.

13. In the event any transaction in which Salesman is involved results in a dispute, litigation or legal expense, Salesman shall cooperate fully with Broker and Broker and Salesman shall share all expense connected therewith, in the same proportion as they would normally share the commission resulting from such transaction if there were no dispute or litigation. In any event, the salesman shall not be financially responsible for any expenses that are in excess of the amount that he would have normally received as his share of the commission had there been no dispute or litigation. It is the policy to avoid litigation wherever possible and Broker reserves the right to determine whether or not any litigation or dispute shall be prosecuted, defended, compromised or settled, and the terms and conditions of any compromise or settlement or whether or not legal expense shall be incurred.

14. Salesman shall not make any long distance calls or send any telegrams without prior approval of Broker. All telephone calls and telegrams over $1.00, including tax, shall be paid one-half by Salesman for whose benefit the cost was incurred, and one-half by Broker.

15. All Salesmen shall receive an equal amount of floor time.

16. All Salesmen shall be allowed to purchase a home from among the firm's listings, providing the Broker is paid the normal share of commission due Broker as Broker's share of commission. Said purchase of a home shall be for the Salesman's own use and occupancy. If another Salesman is involved through having obtained the listing, said Salesman shall receive his normal listing fee in the same manner as if a sale had been made to someone not connected with the office.

17. No salesman shall be required to work an average of more than six days a week.

18. Broker shall close his office and his open houses on the following legal holidays: Fourth of July, Thanksgiving Day, Christmas Day and Easter Sunday.

COMMISSIONS

19. Broker agrees to pay Salesman as and for Salesman's compensation for services rendered on a commission basis for all work done by Salesman in accordance with fee schedule adopted by Broker's office, a copy of which is attached hereto and shall be considered a part of this agreement. No commission shall be considered earned or payable to Salesman until the transaction has been completed and the commission collected by the Broker. Commissions earned shall be payable twice each month, on the _____ and _____ day of each month.

FIGURE 2–2

20 The schedule of commissions and divisions thereof as attached hereto shall be used in every transaction, and any variation therefrom shall first be approved by Broker. Any arrangement for division of commission with other brokers shall be first approved by Broker. In the event two or more salesmen employed by Broker participate in a commission on the same transaction, it shall be divided between the participating salesmen according to prior agreement or by arbitration.

21 Any expense incurred in negotiating the sale, including travel expense, hotels, meals, maps, special services employed, listing fees, multiple listing commissions, etc., shall first be deducted from the gross commission received.

SALESMEN'S OBLIGATIONS

22 Salesman agrees to conduct his activities and regulate his habits so as to maintain and to increase, rather than diminish the good will and reputation of Broker.

23 Salesman shall furnish his own automobile and pay all expenses thereof and shall carry liability and property damage insurance satisfactory to the Broker, name Broker as co-insured and deliver copy of endorsement to Broker.

24 Salesman shall remain continuously licensed by the State of California to sell real estate and shall pay the required renewal fee.

25 Salesman shall not obligate Broker for materials or sevice or the purchase of real property or anything or in any other way, without first obtaining consent of Broker, verbally or in writing.

26 Salesman shall use only real estate forms approved by Broker.

27 Broker reserves the right to reject any exclusive listing deemed unsatisfactory, and to return said listing to the owner.

28 Salesman acknowledges that he is an employee of Broker and that he will abide by all written rules and regulations now in force or subsequently adopted by Broker. Broker agrees to carry compensation insurance for all employees.

29 All letters received, and a copy of all letters written by Salesmen pertaining to the business of Broker shall be the property of Broker, and be turned over to Broker for Broker's records. All letters written by Salesmen shall be approved by Broker before mailing or delivering.

30 All money, documents or property received by Salesman in connection with any transaction of Broker shall be delivered to Broker immediately. All checks or money orders shall be made payable to either Broker, to a title company or to another Broker-approved escrow holder. In the event that all or any portion of the deposit is forfeited, and the seller has received his share of the funds, a division of the remainder of such deposit shall be made between Broker and Salesman in the same proportion as though the amount received was a commission received in connection with the transaction.

31 In connection with any transaction, if it becomes necessary or desirable to receive all or part of the commission in property other than cash, then approval of Broker shall first be obtained. In such event, Broker and Salesman may agree as follows
   a. To divide such property between Broker and Salesman in kind, in the same proportion as their respective interests in the commission involved; or
   b. Broker may pay Salesman his full share of the commission in cash, in which event Broker shall have the full ownership of the property so received; or
   c. To retain such property in the names of Broker and Salesman and thereafter to dispose of the same at such time at such price and on such terms as Broker and Salesman shall agree. Any profit or loss or any carrying charges or other expenses with respect to such property, shall be shared between Broker and Salesman in the same proportion as their respective interests in the commission involved.

32 This agreement for division of commission shall not apply to subdivision sales or acreage for subdivisions or large or unusual transactions which require special time and services on the part of the Broker. Commissions received and paid on such transactions will be subject to special written agreement.

ARBITRATION

33 In the event of disagreement or dispute between Salesmen in the office or between Broker and Salesman arising out of or connected with this agreement, which cannot be adjusted by and between the parties involved, such questions shall be submitted to the local real estate Board committee governing such disputes or if this is not agreed upon, the problem must be submitted to a temporary Board of Arbitration for final adjustment. Such board shall be selected in the following manner: Each of the parties to the disagreement or dispute shall select one member who shall be a licensed broker or licensed salesman. Such selection shall be made within five days from the time notice is given in writing by either party to the other, that arbitration is desired. The two arbitrators thus selected, in case they cannot reach a decision after a single conference or adjustment thereof, shall name a third arbitrator who shall be a person not licensed by the Real Estate Commissioner, Such arbitration may follow the provisions of Sections 1280 through 1293 of the Code of Civil Procedure for the State of California.

TERMINATION OF CONTRACT

34 This contract and the association created hereby may be terminated by either party hereto, at any time, upon notice to the other, said notice to be in writing; but the rights of the parties to any commission which accrued prior to said notice shall not be divested by the termination of the contract.

35 When this agreement has been terminated for any reason, any deals Salesman has made that are not closed shall be considered his property and upon closing of said deals, full Salesman's share of commission shall be paid to him; and Salesman shall receive agreed listing commissions on his listings if sold within the life of such listings, and commission received by Broker. This shall not apply to any extension of the said listings beyond the original listing period.

36 In the event salesman leaves and has deals or listings pending that require further services normally rendered be Salesman, the Salesman and Broker, or Broker alone, shall make arrangements with another Salesman in the organization to perform the required services, and the Salesman assigned shall be compensated for takingcare of of pending deals or listings.

37 Broker and Salesman agree to all the foregoing terms and conditions and to use their skill, efforts and abilities in cooperating to carry out the terms of this agreement for the mutual benefit of Broker and Salesman.

38 In Witness Whereof, the parties hereto have set their hands this day and year first above written.

_____
BROKER

_____
SALESMAN

FIGURE 2–2 *(continued)*

Broker-salesman contract

Commissioners Regulation 2726 requires that every real estate broker must have a written agreement with each of his salesmen. This is required in connection with an individual working as a salesman for a broker, whether the individual holds a real estate salesman or a real estate broker license. The agreement must be dated and signed by the parties and include the amount and type of supervision to be exercised by the broker, the duties of the parties, and compensation arrangement. Signed copies of agreement shall be available for inspection by the commissioner or his designated representative on request and shall be retained by the parties for a period of three years from date of termination of the agreement.

Thus, there should be no doubt as to the status or position of the salesman or broker-salesman in the real estate organization. The commissioner prescribes no particular form for the agreement; and if the office policy and procedures manual includes the material required in Regulation 2726, then a signed statement by the parties that this policy and procedures manual constitutes their working arrangement will suffice.

Review of agreements

Commissioners regulation 2725 requires that all real estate agreements prepared or signed by a salesman which would materially affect the rights or duties of the parties to the transaction shall be reviewed, initialed and dated by his broker within five working days of execution thereof or before the close of escrow, whichever occurs first. However, while retaining overall responsibility for supervision, specific authority to review and initial such agreements may be delegated by the broker as follows:

1. To a licensed real estate broker who has entered into a written agreement relating thereto with the broker.
2. Where circumstances warrant, to a real estate salesman licensed to him, providing such salesman has entered into a written contract relative thereto with the broker and has accumulated at least two years full-time real estate salesman's experience during the preceding five-year period.

COSTS OF OPERATING A REAL ESTATE OFFICE

The California Association of Realtors recently conducted a survey of real estate firms throughout the state to determine a breakdown of the average expenses involved in running an office. Figure 2–3 shows the results of the survey.

The shaded portion represents all commissions paid. The unshaded portion is defined as the "Company Dollar" and is then projected as a 100 percent dollar. It includes the amount left to the broker-owner after payment of all commissions, including salesmen, multiple, and co-op commissions splits.

The percentages shown are, of course, only averages and will vary from office to office, depending on the size of the operation, high or low periods of business activity, type of specialization, and efficiency of operation.

Each real estate firm, regardless of the size or type of operation, has a fairly basic cost of operation which must be returned each month before a profit is earned. This basic cost varies, but the expenses that contribute to it are the same type for all offices. The common expenses are:

1. Fixed salaries (if any) of managements, salesmen, and other employees.
2. Rent, maintenance, and utilities.
3. Stationery, supplies, and office materials.
4. Equipment, office machines, and depreciation of these items.
5. Telephones and automatic answering services or systems.
6. Specific and promotional advertising.
7. Automobile and travel expenses.
8. Professional association, local board, and multiple listing organization expenses.
9. Insurance costs and possible health plan costs.
10. Legal, accounting, and other specialized service fees.

Computing desk cost

After a broker has been able to determine, with some safe degree of accuracy, the monthly cost of the above listed expenses, he will then be able to determine the average number of salesmen that his office can properly sustain. Since each salesman will take up one desk space, we refer to this cost as the desk cost to the office.

Let us assume that broker Smith estimates the monthly cost for operating his office to be $3,000, and the floor area of the office can properly accom-

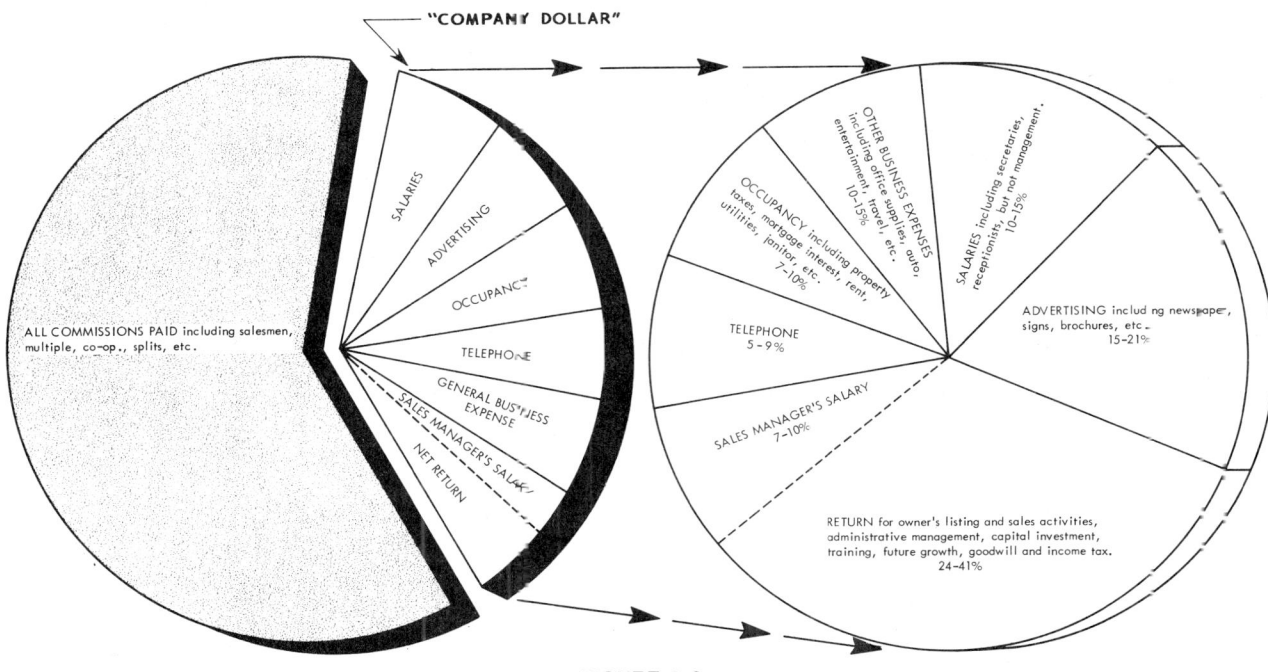

FIGURE 2–3

modate ten desk for salesmen. The desk cost then will be $3,000 divided by ten, or $300. Thus, each salesman in the office must return $300 to the office each month before there is any profit to the broker.

If the office operates on a 50-50 split with the salesman, each salesman will have to produce $600 in commissions each month before the office will break even. Naturally, since the broker wants to make a profit rather than merely break even, each salesman will have to produce much more than $600 a month in commissions. It is from this basic area of calculations that the broker will eventually be able to determine the sales quota in terms of dollar amount of sales that each licensee in his office will be expected to meet.

The broker has many problems to consider. A common one is that not all salesmen produce equally well. One salesman produces more and thus contributes more to the office in the way of commissions. Another consideration relates to the type of listing and sale. If a property is listed and sold by the office alone, the entire commission on the sale comes into the office, but if the sale involves cooperation with another real estate firm, then only one half the commission will come into the office. As an example, let us assume the sale of a $98,000 house at a commission rate of 6 percent.

A. Exclusive listing. Listed and sold by salesman Jones of ABC Realty.

Commission of 6 percent of a sale price of $98,000 equals $5,880. On a 50-50 split basis, Jones receives $2,940, and the office gets $2,940.

B. Exclusive listing. Listed by salesman Jones but sold by salesman Thomas of Metropolis Realty Company.

Commission of 6 percent on a sale price of $98,000 equals $5,880. ABC Realty receives $2,940 and Metropolis Realty $2,940. On a 50-50 split basis, salesman Jones will receive $1,470, and the office gets the other $1,470. The commission split would be identical if the property had been listed by Metropolis Realty and sold by salesman Jones of ABC Realty.

C. Listed by salesman Jones of ABC Realty and sold by salesman Brown of ABC Realty.

Commission of 6 percent on a sale price of $98,000 equals $5,880. Basis for commission split is 20 percent to listing salesman, 40 percent to selling salesman, and 40 percent to the office. Salesman Jones receives $1,176, salesman Brown receives $2,352, and the office receives $2,352.

Although the examples given above do not show all the various ways in which the commission might have been divided, they do point up that the dollar amount of sales will not always give an exact picture of the amount of commission money coming to the office.

MAINTAINING TRUST FUND RECORDS

The maintenance of adequate trust fund records is essential because of the nature of the real estate broker's fiduciary responsibility. The size of the office and the number of transactions involved will to some extent determine the type and complexity of the records kept, but regardless of size or volume of business, all brokers must keep an accurate and officially acceptable record of all trust funds passing through the office.

Section 10148 of the Business and Professions Code states that "all listings, deposits receipts, cancelled checks, trust records, and other documents" executed or obtained by a licensed real estate broker in connection with any transaction for which a real estate license is required shall be retained for a period of three years. Further sections of the code make it mandatory that certain types of records be kept available for inspection for a period of four years from date of the transaction.

Even though a broker does not maintain a trust account in a bank because he places trust funds directly into escrow, he is still responsible for keeping records of all trust funds received by him, including uncashed checks held pending receipt of instructions from his principal. Section 2831 of the California State Real Estate Commissioner's Regulations states that the record shall set forth in columnar form: *(a)* date funds received; *(b)* from whom received *(c)* amount received; *(d)* with respect to funds deposited to bank trust account, date of said deposit; *(e)* with respect to funds previously deposited to trust bank account, check number or date of related disbursement; *(f)* with respect to funds not deposited in bank trust account, nature of other depository and date funds were deposited; *(g)* daily balance of bank trust account if one is maintained.

Each broker who maintains a formal trust cash receipts journal and a formal cash disbursement journal, or other similar records, in accordance with standard recognized accounting procedures, will have complied with the above requirements. All records and funds shall be open to inspection by the commissioner or his deputies. The CAR provides each of the necessary forms and instructions for their use in their binder-form publication *Real Estate Trust Fund Records and Requirements*. Figure 2–4 illustrates portions of a few of these forms.

PHYSICAL FEATURES OF THE REAL ESTATE OFFICE

The two areas we shall now discuss—location and the physical appearance and layout of the office—are important factors in the operation of any successful real estate firm. Location will determine the geographic area to be served, and physical appearance will influence the opinion of many persons regarding the efficiency and businesslike attitude of the firm.

Location

The broker should locate his office in the area he intends to serve best. Most of the business transacted by the typical real estate office will be in the neighborhood where the office is located. The location will quite often depend on whether the broker wants to engage in general real estate sales or to specialize in a particular type of property.

An office dealing mainly in commercial and industrial properties would locate in the central business district, while an office dealing mostly in residential properties would locate in a suburban area or in the residential area it intends to serve best. There are, of course, exceptions to any general rule, and the broker who operates alone, without any sales staff, and transacts much of his business away from the office may find the precise location unimportant. Such a broker may have an office in a large downtown office building. Many large and long-established real estate firms are located in the central business district, and yet they handle many residential sales in addition to commercial, industrial, leasing, and the like. However, many of these large organizations have established one or more branch offices to better serve certain areas.

Physical appearance and office layout

The main requisite of the office exterior is that it be attractive and clean; this, of course, holds true for the interior as well. The office should be located on a street that is adequately served by public transportation, and it is most important that there be adequate parking facilities for clients.

A business sign sufficient to identify the firm is a must, and it should be big enough to enable persons driving by to spot it without difficulty. It should be of the type that can be illuminated at night, and its color and style of lettering may be the same as those the firm uses on the signs it will affix to properties it lists for sale. An emblem, slogan, or trademark may be incorporated into the design. The exterior appearance of the firm should blend together to give a professional, businesslike picture to the passerby. A real estate office should not look like a hot-dog stand or a drive-in.

COLUMNAR RECORD OF ALL TRUST FUNDS RECEIVED AND PAID OUT

CALIFORNIA ASSOCIATION OF REALTORS® STANDARD FORM

19 Date Received	From Whom Received Or To Whom Paid	Description	TRUST FUND BANK ACCOUNT									Daily Balance of Trust Bank Account
			RECEIVED				PAID OUT				
			Amount Received	Cross Ref.	Date of Deposit	xx	Amount Paid Out	Check No.	Date of Check	xx	

RECORD OF ALL TRUST FUNDS RECEIVED – NOT PLACED IN BROKERS TRUST ACCOUNT

CALIFORNIA REAL ESTATE ASSOCIATION STANDARD FORM

TRUST FUNDS INCLUDING UNCASHED CHECKS RECEIVED			Description Property or Identification	Disposition of Uncashed Checks or Other Funds Forwarded to Escrow or Principal	Date Forwarded
Date Received	Received From	Amount			

SEPARATE RECORD FOR EACH PROPERTY MANAGED

CALIFORNIA ASSOCIATION OF REALTORS® STANDARD FORM

Owner _____
Address _____
Property _____
Tenant's Name _____
Units _____
Remarks _____

Deposit _____
Monthly Rent _____
Commission:
   Leases _____
   Collection _____
   Management _____

Date	Received From or Paid To	Description	Receipt or Check No.	Amount Received	Date Deposited	Amount Disbursed	Balance

SEPARATE RECORD FOR EACH BENEFICIARY OR TRANSACTION

CALIFORNIA ASSOCIATION OF REALTORS® STANDARD FORM

Description	Discharge of Trust Accountability For Funds Paid Out			Trust Accountability For Funds Received		Balance of Account
	Date of Check	Check No.	Amount	Date of Deposit	Amount	

FIGURE 2-4

The office interior should be well planned to provide adequate space and working area. It should not resemble a vast wasteland, nor should it look like the inside of a clothes closet. The area immediately inside the front entrance is the reception area. It should contain a large counter, receptionist's desk, and adequate seating facilities for customers who may be waiting for a particular salesman.

Behind the counter is the salesman's work area. Each salesman should have a separate desk and telephone. Each desk should have a nameplate that clearly identifies the salesman. The broker's desk may be in this area also, but usually he has a private office or an enclosed area that offers a certain degree of privacy.

A conference or closing room is a necessity. It is difficult for a salesman to talk to customers in the main part of the office while others are moving about and talking on the telephone. No one is able to concentrate, and discussions in this type of atmosphere are generally wasted. In an office not large enough to have a separate conference or closing room, the broker's office may be used.

Finally, each office should have a separate workroom or area in which are located such items as typewriters, mimeograph machine, photocopy machines, files, forms, signs, dictating machine, and the like.

Clean and sanitary rest room facilities for the use of the staff, as well as for clients, should be provided.

REAL ESTATE FRANCHISING

Franchising seems to be an increasingly important element in the marketing structure of the real estate industry. As it is generally known in the real estate business today, franchising is a form of marketing in which a parent company grants an individual brokerage firm the right to do business in a prescribed manner over a certain period of time in a specified location. The parent company is the franchisor, the individual receiving the benefits is the franchisee, and the right or privilege itself is the franchise.

A recent study conducted among California Realtors and reported by the California Association of Realtors states the following as possible advantages and disadvantages of becoming a real estate franchisee.

Advantages:

1. Marketing identification by use of a readily identifiable tradename or trademark, development of a specific image with large scale advertising.
2. Sales personnel recruitment, training programs and classes to prepare for licensing.
3. Assistance with office management and providing sales tools.
4. Guidance with respect to special problems common to the real estate business.
5. Client referral systems.

Disadvantages:

1. Relinquishing the importance of the individual firm name to that of the franchisor.
2. Initial expenses.
3. Continuing costs and fees.
4. A certain degree of control must be turned over to the franchisor.
5. Difficulty of relinquishing the franchise and returning to independent status.

Policy and procedure manual

Each real estate office should have some form of policy and procedure manual. It should contain an outline and basic discussion of the policies and procedures of the office.

The sample manual in Figure 2–5 is certainly not intended to represent the ultimate in construction or content but is illustrated here in order to show the areas that may be covered and to provide a basis for thought and discussion.

An additional form, applicable to this chapter, is illustrated in Appendix C as Figure C2–1.

QUESTIONS FOR DISCUSSION

1. What is your definition of a professional person, and how do you think professional status is attained?
2. As a salesperson looking for an office to affiliate with, what thing should you look for?
3. When you decide to start your real estate company, what business form will you select and why?
4. Assume that you are a broker with openings in your firm for two additional salespeople. What should you look for in interviewing applicants?
5. Discuss the different opportunities offered to real estate licensees in your community for furthering their real estate education.
6. With respect to the Policy and Procedure Manual presented in the chapter, discuss what you feel are its strong points and what you feel may have been lacking in presentation.
7. How can you best determine the basic costs in-

volved prior to opening your own real estate office as an individual proprietor?

8. Why do you think so much special emphasis is placed on the subject of trust fund records?

9. Assume that you are going to open your own office and have rented an area approximately 30 feet wide and 150 feet deep. Discuss various ways of physically dividing the area with respect to traffic pattern and layout.

10. Discuss the advantages and disadvantages of working for an established real estate company as against opening and operating your own firm.

POLICY AND PROCEDURE MANUAL

This manual constitutes the policies, practices, and procedures of ABC Realty Company, 123 Tenth Avenue, Central City, California.

ABC Realty Company is an equal opportunity employer. Salesmen and saleswomen are employed without regard to race, color religion, or national origin,.

ABC Realty Company has as its objective, service to its clients, to the community, and to its staff. Each associate salesperson will have a copy of this manual. After he has read it he will sign his name on the last page of the office copy of this Policy and Procedure Manual. His signature creates a contractual relationship between ABC Realty Company and the associate salesperson.

The purpose of this manual is to outline the policies and working procedures clearly so that everyone will thoroughly understand his rights and responsibilities with respect to the organization and to his associates.

ABC Realty Company is a member of the Central City Board of Realtors and of the Central City Multiple Listing Service (M.L.S.). Every salesperson must become a member of both the board and M.L.S.

OFFICE HOURS

The office will be open from 9 a.m. until 5:30 p.m., Monday through Saturday. On Sundays the office will be open from 11 a.m. until 6 p.m. These hours do not limit the time or hours of individual endeavor. If office facilities are necessary for the convenience of a customer or to close a transaction, the salesman may use the office for such specific purpose any evening or on Sundays or holidays. Every member of the staff is expected to work an average of 40 hours a week.

VACATION AND LEAVE

Every staff member is entitled to 2 days off each week. Each staff member is allowed up to 21 days sick leave each year. During the first two years of employment, each staff member will be allowed two weeks vacation time each year. After two years, the allowance will be three weeks. When a salesman is absent for any of the above reasons, the broker will service his prospects.

FLOOR TIME

A schedule of floor time will be prepared at the end of each month for the coming month. Salesmen have daily floor time in four-hour shifts. If a salesman cannot keep his floor time, he must arrange for a substitute. All substitutions must be cleared with the office secretary. If a substitute is not available, the broker will take the floor time and assign all prospects acquired to various salesmen. Each salesman is responsible for

FIGURE 2-5

his floor time in the office. If he must leave to show a property, or for any other reason, he must see that the floor is covered. Promptness and dependability are basic principles insisted upon by the firm.

DUTIES OF FLOOR SALESMAN

The floor salesman will be entitled to all new prospects who come into the office during his time on the floor. All new prospects who telephone will be referred to the floor salesman provided that such prospects do not request a particular salesman by name.

Anyone entering the office is to be courteously greeted. If the client requests a specific member of the firm, every effort should be made to locate him. If this is impossible, the floor salesman or secretary should take the name, telephone number, and the message. If the client insists on immediate service, the broker will carry on for the absent salesman whenever possible. Should a sale be made, the absent salesman will receive his usual commission. If another salesman must assist the customer, he is to receive 10 percent of the office share of the commission in the case of a sale.

AGREEMENTS

Each salesman is free to make any commission arrangement he wishes with any other salesman in the office, with the object of encouraging salesmen to cooperate on prospective listing and buying customers. Such agreements must be accompanied by a memorandum signed by both salesmen.

OPEN HOUSE

A salesman is expected to hold an open house on Sundays and/or weekdays on properties he has listed, assuming of course, that such procedure is agreeable to the seller.

OFFICE LOG

A daily log book is maintained by the office secretary. This book is of vital importance to all members of the staff. All persons—drop-ins, prospects, and others who come in person or telephone—must be listed in the log book. Name, address, telephone number, the reason for calling, and disposition of the case are to be recorded. The floor salesman is responsible for entering, on the loose-leaf sheet affixed to the log book each morning by the secretary, the names of persons he interviews or who are referred by telephone to him. New listings, sales reported, cancellations, financial information, and other pertinent material is to be entered by members of the staff. The secretary will transfer the information into the permanent log book each day.

FIGURE 2-5 *(continued)*

3

PERSONAL APPEARANCE

Each salesman should give close attention to his personal appearance. He should be well groomed and neatly and conservatively dressed. Those licensees who wish to be regarded as professionals by the public must look the part.

PERSONAL COMMUNICATION

Every salesman should call in to the office at least twice during the day to pick up messages. On his days off, he should let the secretary know where he can be reached.

CAR AND ENTERTAINMENT

Every salesman must have a well running car, of good appearance, and clean both inside and out. Salesmen should keep careful account of car expenses incurred for business use. Entertainment expenses should be itemized, and receipts obtained for the Internal Revenue Service. Salesmen will not be reimbursed by the office for these expenses.

INSURANCE

Salesmen must have car insurance. The amount for public liability is to be not less than $100,000 - $300,000 with $50,000 property damage. There must be a clause affixed thereto insuring ABC Realty Company. It is mandatory that every member of the staff carry Health, Accident, and Disability insurance. Such insurance will be carried by this office on all salesmen who have been associated with this organization for three years or longer.

All members of the staff will make their own Social Security payments. The bookkeeper will supply forms and give necessary assistance.

EDUCATION

Each salesman is required to enroll in a real estate course or professional seminar each year. The office will pay one half the tuition fee if any. Attendance at local Board of Realtors estate board educational meetings, CAR educational conferences, and such related functions is emphasized by the office. Attendance at the weekly staff meeting is mandatory for all staff members.

CONDUCT IN GENERAL

Courtesy to staff and to prospects, to clients, and to members of other firms is essential to the proper function of this office.

FIGURE 2-5 *(continued)*

4

When properties are shown, the salesman shall have complete information on them. Appointments must be arranged in advance, and, if they cannot be kept, the seller or tenant must be notified promptly. If calls are made with the seller's permission when the seller is out, cards must be left and the time of the call should be entered on the back of the card. When keys are borrowed from another office, they must be promptly returned to the office in question. The use of a locked receptacle for keys (Lok-Box) is to be explained to sellers and should be used only with their permission. Signs may be placed on a property only with the permission of the seller.

TELEPHONE

When answering the telephone, the salesman should give the name of the firm and his own name. Exact addresses of properties listed should not be given over the telephone. Personal calls during business hours should be kept to a minimum since lines must be kept open for business use.

DAY BOOK

Every salesman must keep a day book. Items to be recorded are daily activities, telephone calls made and received, prospects contacted, properties shown or inspected, sales, listings taken, and any other pertinent information. This day book is the salesman's only record of his daily activities and is necessary during conferences with the broker or in the event that controversies arise.

SALES KIT

Each salesman should have a sales kit containing at least the following items:

1. Listing forms, office and multiple.
2. Purchase contract and receipt for deposits.
3. Blank checks.
4. Loan amortization booklet.
5. Title insurance cost schedule.
6. City map and zoning map.
7. City and parochial school locations map.
8. Carbon sheets and company stationery.
9. Envelopes and stamps.
10. Business cards.

PROSPECTS

OFFICE PROSPECTS

An office prospect is one who is secured through general office advertising or who comes into the office of his own accord. Such prospects are referred to the floor salesman. Referrals specifically to the broker, or prospects who write to the firm or who are secured by the broker personally, will be assigned by him to the salesman best suited to

FIGURE 2-5 *(continued)*

handle the prospect. Where possible, these assignments will be rotated. Prospects taken from a salesman for lack of contact will be also treated. All prospects not within the definition of Individual Prospects shall be classified as Office Prospects.

INDIVIDUAL PROSPECTS

An individual prospect is a person secured by the salesman personally. The contact may be social, personal, or through firm advertising bearing the name of the salesman.

CUSTOMER PROSPECT FILE

Every salesman shall fill out two cards on every prospect either assigned to him or personally acquired by him. One card will go into his own file and the other into the office file. Cards are provided by the office for this purpose and they should be filled in with such information as down payment available, family size, income bracket, and special wants or desires of the prospect. The salesman's name and the date must be entered and a statement telling how the prospect happened to come to this firm.

CANVASS

When this card is properly filed, it serves notice on all members of the firm that the salesman now has the exclusive right to canvass that prospect for 21 days. Should the broker consider that a prospect is being neglected or improperly handled, he may reassign him to another salesman or assist the original salesman with the prospect.

LISTINGS

A successful office is one which has a good supply of properly priced listings. When a salesman takes a listing, he should not give the seller an opinion on price unless he is absolutely sure of the fair market value or the price (within 10%) at which the property will sell. If he is in doubt he should consult the Sold File and the Multiple Listings records.

All necessary information should be obtained such as reason for selling, size of lot, existing financing, available financing, secondary financing, down payment required, and all of the other information necessary. Previous title searches, if any are available, should be inspected for restrictive covenants, easements, and tax information.

Care should be taken to have both husband and wife sign a listing, as well as any other person who may have an interest in the property. Salesmen must consistently contact seller at least once each week with respect to progress being made on the sale of the property.

Listings must be in writing, signed, and taken to the office secretary, who will submit them to the broker in conformance with Commissioners Regulation 2725, and then file them in the appropriate office file.

FIGURE 2–5 *(continued)*

6

THE REAL ESTATE PURCHASE CONTRACT AND RECEIPT FOR DEPOSIT

All salesmen will use office deposit receipt forms. All blank spaces must be carefully and legibly filled in with pen or typewriter. Checks for deposit should be in the amount of at least 5 percent, and if possible, 10 percent of the offer. A straight note to be paid on date of acceptance or when escrow is opened, or on some specific date, is also acceptable as a deposit. Salesmen should always avoid taking cash.

All such checks, notes, or cash should be given as soon as possible to the bookkeeper who will place them in the safe until an escrow is opened or they are deposited in the company's trustee account, depending on arrangements with the buyer.

All conditions must be clearly and concisely stated. Financing conditions such as present loan balance and terms and conditions, whether an assumption or whether the buyer is to take subject to loan and fees, should be explicitly stated. If a new loan is to be obtained, the approximate amount, interest, monthly payments, length of loan, points, and who is to pay them must be clearly stated. Secondary financing must be equally clearly outlined as well as any problems regarding termite work.

The title and/or escrow company desired should be indicated, as well as data respecting occupancy. Seller's privileges after closing of escrow should be precisely stated. When the purchase contract and receipt for deposit are completed, they shall be submitted to the broker in conformance with Commissioners Regulation 2725.

COMMISSIONS

Commissions are to be 6 percent of the selling price for the sale of improved properties up to $100,000 and 5 percent on the amount over this. The commission on unimproved properties shall be 10 percent, with a minimum fee of $500.

DIVISION OF COMMISSIONS

In general, all commissions will be split on a 50/50 basis, one half going to the broker and one half to the salesman or salesmen involved.

Transactions within the office:

Salesman A lists the property and also sells it. He will receive 50 percent and the office will receive 50 percent.

Salesman A lists and Salesman B sells. A receives 25 percent, B receives 25 percent, and the office receives 50 percent.

Broker lists and Salesman A sells. Each gets 50 percent of the commission.

Broker sells and Salesman A lists. Each gets 50 percent of the commission.

On a transaction involving additional staff members, the commission split will be by agreement between the salesmen and the broker.

FIGURE 2-5 *(continued)*

Transactions involving another office:

When ABC Realty lists a property and another office sells it, or when ABC Realty sells another office's listing, the entire commission involved will be split 50/50 between the two offices. The 50 percent received by ABC Realty will be divided one half to the office and one half to the salesman involved.

Commissions on Multiple Listings will be divided on the same basis as explained above.

After consultation, and with the consent of the broker, a salesman may buy and sell property on his own account, provided that buyer and seller are informed in writing of his status and that he pays full commissions.

COMMISSIONS ON EXCHANGES

Commissions on exchanges, unless otherwise stipulated, shall be at the regular 6 percent rate on all pieces of property involved in the transaction. The owner of each piece of property shall be liable for his commission, and he should be so informed. Commissions will be pooled in the event that other offices are involved in the transaction and will be divided equally between the participating offices unless there have been other arrangements made previously.

RENTAL COMMISSIONS

Only the rental agent in this office will handle rentals. Commissions for leases or other rental agreements may be charged tenants or owners by agreement. Usual commission will be according to the schedule established by this office. Salesmen bringing in a rental listing which is successfully rented will receive 5 percent of the rental commission obtained. The office will receive 15 percent and in the event that it is an office listing, the office will receive 20 percent as its share. All prospects obtained as the result of a rental listing will be considered the prospects of the salesman who obtained the listing.

PRESENTING THE OFFER

On receipt of an offer, the salesman must submit it to the broker for inspection. The salesman may then, alone or accompanied by the broker, present the offer to the seller. If there are two or more offers made before presentation of the first to the seller, all offers are to be presented simultaneously to the seller. However, where there is a counteroffer, the salesman who has the first offer in time will have the first opportunity to present a counteroffer to his prospect.

OBLIGATIONS OF THE BROKER

The broker agrees to furnish a pleasant, attractive, and commodious office. There will be a desk for each employee, a typewriter available for his use, a dictating machine, stationery, forms, maps, a reverse telephone directory, copies of local laws and zoning ordinances, files, telephones, and janitorial, secretarial, and bookkeeping services.

FIGURE 2–5 *(continued)*

8

The broker will assign office space and the use of the closing room and will assist each and every member of the staff. Each staff member is expected to confer at least once each week with the broker. There will be a general sales meeting every Monday morning at 9 a.m. which every member of the staff is expected to attend. The purpose of these meetings is to review and discuss current market data, credit and financing trends, and everyday matters of concern to the office.

The broker will assist the salesman with his sales and financial problems. He will also assist in making referrals to specialists when necessary, such as attorneys, appraisers, and builders.

CLERICAL OFFICE PERSONNEL

SECRETARY—RECEPTIONIST

The secretary-receptionist will assist the broker with correspondence and real estate and insurance forms. She will answer the telephone, sharing this task with floor salesmen; file listing and prospect cards; and keep the files up to date.

The secretary will assign to the bookkeeper-stenographer some of the salesmen's letters which must be transcribed from the dictating machine. She will handle all escrow forms for the salesmen and the broker.

BOOKKEEPER—STENOGRAPHER

The bookkeeper-stenographer will answer the telephone when the secretary is busy. She will assist the secretary with stenographic and filing matters. She will keep the books of the office for both real estate and insurance matters. The bookkeeper will handle all checks and funds coming into the company and will therefore be bonded by a licensed bonding company.

RENTAL AGENT—INSURANCE AGENT

The rental agent, a real estate licensee with an insurance license, will also handle insurance under the direction of the broker. He will be paid 50 percent of the commissions from insurance premiums as well as a percent of rental commissions.

ARBITRATION

All interoffice disputes of any kind are to be submitted to arbitration. Each party involved will name one staff member, and those thus selected will then appoint another member. The broker, unless involved in the dispute, will be an additional member or he may appoint the firm's attorney as his representative on the arbitration committee. All salesmen who sign the statement at the end of this policy manual automatically give their consent to abide by the committee's decision.

FIGURE 2-5 *(continued)*

9

The secretary will take notes during the meeting. The result of the decision will be entered into the records of the firm in the appropriate file. Disputes involving other offices will be turned over to the local real estate board for arbitration. It is the policy of the office to avoid lawsuits of any kind whenever possible.

TERMINATION OF EMPLOYMENT

A salesman contemplating leaving should give 30 days notice to the broker. When a salesman is to be discharged, unless for violation of a provision of the Real Estate Law, the broker must give him 30 days notice.

All listings, whether obtained by the salesman personally or assigned by the office, become the property of the office.

The salesman is to make every effort to close any pending transactions. Any which are completed will be considered his, and the commission will be paid to him when received from the escrow office of the title insurance company.

All transactions on which the departing salesman was working on the date he left will be considered office transactions in which he has no interest. They will be assigned by the broker to another salesman, or handled by the broker.

The broker is required to report any unethical conduct to the Real Estate Commissioner of the State of California. Therefore, before the broker can sign the authorized release of the salesman, he must be satisfied as to his conduct.

When a salesman leaves the office, he is to receive his salesman's license which has been displayed in the office, and his authorized release is to be properly signed by the broker.

STATEMENT OF AGREEMENT

I, _____, a licensed real estate salesman associated with the ABC Realty Company of Central City, having read all of the foregoing policy manual, do unqualifiedly agree to abide by all of the procedures, rules, and regulations set forth therein.

Signature:_____   Date:_____

FIGURE 2–5 *(concluded)*

3

Listing and prospecting

In Chapter 1, when dealing with the duties and responsibilities of the real estate broker, we discussed the subject of agency and the fact that the listing agreement creates the agency relationship between the broker and his client. In this chapter, we shall discuss the various types of listings and methods of correct preparation of listing forms; then we shall discuss the ways in which the broker and salesman obtain these listings.

LISTINGS

A listing is an employment contract that establishes the agency relationship between a broker (the agent) and a property owner (the principal) for the purpose of attempting to negotiate the sale or purchase of real property.

Generally speaking, a verbal agreement to pay a commission is not enforceable in court unless the broker has a written listing signed by the owner of the property. The listing must show the intention of the owner to pay a commission to the broker when he procures a buyer with whom the owner enters into an agreement for the purchase of the property.

There are a few exceptions to this general rule. Although no broker should make a practice of trying to sell a property without the protection of a properly executed listing form, the question arises as to whether or not a broker can collect a commission even though he was not working under a listing from the owner.

The courts have held that where the only agreement to pay a commission is contained in an agreement of sale between the buyer and seller, the broker is entitled to his commission on performance of the provisions contained in the sales agreement. The requirement that a contract with a broker to sell real property be in writing may also be satisfied by evidence that the buyers and sellers signed escrow instructions providing for payment of a commission out of moneys deposited in escrow and that the escrow was satisfactorily completed.

It is important to remember that the subject of commission payable to the broker arises three times during the normal real estate transaction:

1. At the time the listing agreement is completed.
2. At the time the sales agreement is completed.
3. In the instructions prepared by the escrow officer, attorney, or whoever else may be acting in this capacity.

TYPES OF LISTINGS

Oral listing

As the name implies, an oral listing contains nothing in writing and, although used occasionally by some brokers, should be avoided as unsound business practice. The broker must be extremely careful in working on a property when there has been only an oral discussion between the broker and the property owner regarding the price, terms, commission, and so on, since the broker is putting forth time and expense without the protection of a written contract.

The broker may talk to a buyer about a piece of property and even show him the property, and later find that the buyer had subsequently contacted the owner and purchased the property directly from him, thus eliminating the commission the broker would have earned.

Open listing

Open listings, and all listings to be discussed subsequently, are listings in writing. In an open listing, the seller may employ a number of brokers, each of whom will have an equal opportunity to sell the property and earn a commission. Under an open listing, the commission is payable only to the first broker who procures a buyer with whom the seller enters into an agreement. An open listing may or may not contain a specified term, whereas all subsequent listings that will be discussed must contain a definite termination date.

The seller may sell the property himself and pay no commission, and he may withdraw the property from the market at any time he wants, since the open listing contains no definite term of employment.

Open listings, which are sometimes referred to as nonexclusive listings, are used by builders and developers, attorneys, executors, administrators of estates, and others who do not want to be bound to any particular broker or set of specific requirements.

Exclusive agency listing

In an exclusive agency listing, one broker is designated as the exclusive agent by the property owner, and only this one broker has a listing for the sale of the property. The listing is for a specified term, but the owner still has the right to sell the property himself without having to pay a commission.

This type of listing is slightly better than the open listing in that it excludes other brokers. If another broker has a client who is interested in buying, he will have to contact the broker named in the listing and work with him. However, since the property owner reserves the right to sell the property himself, another broker may bypass the broker who has the listing and go directly to the owner.

Exclusive right to sell listing

The exclusive right to sell listing is the one most commonly used by brokers throughout the United States. This listing gives the broker named the exclusive authorization and right to sell the property and excludes the owner from doing so without paying the broker a commission. The broker thus becomes the sole agent, and if the property is sold by the owner or by anyone else during the term of the listing, the broker is entitled to his commission.

Most exclusive right to sell listings contain the further provision that in the event the owner, after expiration of the listing, sells the property to a person or persons with whom the broker negotiated during the term of the listing, then the broker shall be entitled to his commission.

This is the best type of listing for both the broker and the property owner. By entering into this form of listing, the owner shows that he has complete confidence in the broker and is content to let the broker handle the entire transaction. In turn, the broker will certainly give the property his full attention, advertise it properly, and try to effect a sale in the shortest time possible. The broker named in the listing may, if he wishes, cooperate with other brokers who may have an interested buyer. This type of cooperation between two brokers—one with the property for sale and the other with an interested buyer—is practiced quite often. The owner pays the commission agreed on in the listing, and the cooperating brokers divide the commission between themselves as they see fit.

Multiple listing

A multiple listing is an exclusive right to sell listing used by brokers who belong to a multiple listing service or exchange, usually in conjunction with their local real estate board. Under this arrangement, brokers pool their listings so that a listing by any one broker who belongs to the multiple listing service is made available to all of the other members of the organization. The initials MLS are commonly used to designate this type of listing and to indicate that a broker may be a member of a multiple listing service.

In some areas, an MLS broker must submit all his listings for distribution to fellow members, while in other areas a broker may use an MLS form for the listing if he wants, but may also list a property he does not want to be distributed to members and retain this as an exclusive listing within his office.

The broker who obtains the MLS listing has control over the negotiations, and other MLS members must work through him. If the listing broker sells the property himself, he, of course, earns the entire commission. If he must cooperate with another MLS broker, then the commission is divided by agreement between the brokers involved.

Net listing

A net listing allows the broker to receive as his commission any amount in excess of the selling price fixed by the seller. In the listings we have discussed previously, the commission has been stated as a fixed percent of the final selling price. In the net listing, the broker and seller agree on a specific price the seller will accept, and the broker receives whatever he is able to get over and above the amount the seller wants.

Net listings generally are not used to any great extent. They often give rise to a claim of unfairness by the seller, who will usually say that the net price agreed on was too low and that the broker should have known this and set a higher receiving price for the seller.

In California, a broker must disclose to the seller the amount of his commission in connection with a net listing before the seller signs a sales agreement.

Option listing

An option listing gives the broker an option to purchase the property himself. When exercising this option, the broker is in a fiduciary position and must make disclosure of all outstanding offers to purchase and any other material information in his possession. The reasoning behind this is quite obviously to be certain that the broker does not take unfair advantage of the seller. An example is a broker who waits until he finds a third party to whom he can make a profitable resale of the property and then exercises his option to purchase it. The seller here is not aware that the broker has a buyer waiting. Since the option under an option listing is usually exercised only after a period of time during which the broker is supposedly trying to sell the property in the usual way, it follows that the broker may not try too hard once he finds a buyer who is willing to pay a price well above the option price. The temptation is strong for the broker to wait until he can exercise his option, buy the property, and then sell to the waiting buyer, thus making a good deal more than the usual commission.

A variation of the option procedure is commonly used in trade-in situations. The subject of property exchanges and trades is discussed in Chapter 17.

ANALYSIS OF THE LISTING FORM

Although the exact wording and form of listings may vary somewhat throughout the state, they are basically the same as far as their major provisions are concerned. The example in Figure 3–1 is an Exclusive Authorization and Right to Sell listing form prepared by the California Association of Realtors. The numbered parts of the form in the illustration correspond to those of the explanations that follow.

1. The name of the real estate broker or of the real estate firm is shown here. Often, the listing form will be prepared by a licensed salesman rather than by the broker himself, and the salesman should be careful not to write in his own name at this point. It is the broker who is being appointed agent, and the name of the broker or company must be shown. If the salesman is filling in the form, he will sign his own name at the bottom. The words "exclusively and irrevocably" are very important, since it is these words preceding the term which identify this as an exclusive-right-to-sell listing.

The term of the listing is entered—usually a term of 30, 60, or 90 days. Although 90 days is the most common, there is no set term. If the broker feels that a particular piece of property may take a longer than average time to sell, he may ask the owner for a longer period. The city and county in which the property is located are entered, and then a space is provided for entering the location of the property. This may be done in a variety of ways. Some brokers merely enter the street and number of the property, while others enter not only the mailing address but also the lot and block number of the property which may be obtained from the owner's tax bill or from the county recorder's office. If the property is large in area, such as country or ranch property, the broker may enter the legal metes and bounds description.

2. The purchase price at which the property is being offered for sale is stated.

A space is provided for the specific terms under which the seller is offering the property to a prospective purchaser. These terms must be discussed in detail by the broker and the seller and must be completely understood by both since it is on these terms that the broker will offer the property to the public. Included here are items relating to the financial arrangements and possible second loan to be carried back by the seller. Instead of noting specific terms, many brokers prefer to state, "All cash or other terms acceptable to seller." This does not bind the seller to accept any offer other than all cash and allows the seller to consider any other offer which may be made by the buyer.

Items of personal property, such as stove and refrigerator, which will be included in the purchase price are shown.

The agent is authorized to accept a deposit from a prospective purchaser. Most forms contain this

EXCLUSIVE AUTHORIZATION AND RIGHT TO SELL

THIS IS INTENDED TO BE A LEGALLY BINDING AGREEMENT—READ IT CAREFULLY.
CALIFORNIA ASSOCIATION OF REALTORS® STANDARD FORM

1. **Right to Sell.** I hereby employ and grant Prestige Properties hereinafter called "Agent," the exclusive and irrevocable right commencing on May 3, 19-- , and expiring at midnight on August 2, 19-- , to sell or exchange the real property situated in City and , County of San Bernardino , California described as follows:

Lot and improvements commonly known as 1790 Western Avenue, San Bernardino, California, 92403

2. **Terms of Sale.** The purchase price shall be $ 159,500. , to be paid in the following terms:

All cash, or other terms acceptable to seller.

(a) The following items of personal property are to be included in the above-stated price:

Stove, refrigerator and all wall-to-wall carpeting.

(b) Agent is hereby authorized to accept and hold on my behalf a deposit upon the purchase price.

(c) Evidence of title to the property shall be in the form of a California Land Title Association Standard Coverage Policy of Title Insurance in the amount of the selling price to be paid for by Seller 1/2 Each

(d) I warrant that I am the owner of the property or have the authority to execute this agreement. I hereby authorize a FOR SALE sign to be placed on my property by Agent. I authorize the Agent named herein to cooperate with sub-agents.

3. **Notice: The amount or rate of real estate commissions is not fixed by law. They are set by each broker individually and may be negotiable between the seller and broker.** Bold Type - Civil Code

Compensation to Agent. I hereby agree to compensate Agent as follows:

(a) Six percent (6) % of the selling price if the property is sold during the term hereof, or any extension thereof, by Agent, on the terms herein set forth or any other price and terms I may accept, or through any other person, or by me, or Six percent (6) % of the price shown in 2, if said property is withdrawn from sale, transferred, conveyed, leased without the consent of Agent, or made unmarketable by my voluntary act during the term hereof or any extension thereof.

(b) the compensation provided for in subparagraph (a) above if property is sold, conveyed or otherwise transferred within 120 days after the termination of this authority or any extension thereof to anyone with whom Agent has had negotiations prior to final termination, provided I have received notice in writing, including the names of the prospective purchasers, before or upon termination of this agreement or any extension thereof. However, I shall not be obligated to pay the compensation provided for in subparagraph (a) if a valid listing agreement is entered into during the term of said protection period with another licensed real estate broker and a sale, lease or exchange of the property is made during the term of said valid listing agreement.

4. If action be instituted to enforce this agreement, the prevailing party shall receive reasonable attorney's fees and costs as fixed by the Court.

5. In the event of an exchange, permission is hereby given Agent to represent all parties and collect compensation or commissions from them, provided there is full disclosure to all principals of such agency. Agent is authorized to divide with other agents such compensation or commissions in any manner acceptable to them.

6. I agree to save and hold Agent harmless from all claims, disputes, litigation, and/or judgments arising from any incorrect information supplied by me, or from any material fact known by me concerning the property which I fail to disclose.

7. This property is offered in compliance with state and federal anti-discrimination laws.

8. Other provisions: None

9. I acknowledge that I have read and understand this Agreement, and that I have received a copy hereof.

Dated May 3, 19-- San Bernardino , California

(s) Arthur Smith   (s) Ada Smith
OWNER   OWNER
1790 Western Avenue,   San Bernardino, California 921-8832
ADDRESS   CITY—STATE—PHONE

10. In consideration of the above, Agent agrees to use diligence in procuring a purchaser.

Prestige Properties   110 Main Street, San Bernardino, California 92408
AGENT   ADDRESS—CITY
By (s) J. M. Carter, Realtor   921-8000   May 3, 19--
                                PHONE   DATE

For these forms address California Association of Realtors®
505 Shatto Place, Los Angeles 90020. All rights reserved
Copyright 1978 by California Association of Realtors.® Revised 1980   **FORM A-11**

NO REPRESENTATION IS MADE AS TO THE LEGAL VALIDITY OF ANY PROVISION OR THE ADEQUACY OF ANY PROVISION IN ANY SPECIFIC TRANSACTION. IF YOU DESIRE LEGAL ADVICE, CONSULT YOUR ATTORNEY.

FIGURE 3–1

provision to make it quite clear that any deposit money accepted by the broker is held for the benefit of the seller and does not belong to the agent.

A statement dealing with the issuance of a policy of title insurance and who shall pay for the policy is shown. In California, it is customary for proof of title to be in the form of a title insurance policy prepared and issued by a title insurance company. The main purpose is to be certain the buyer receives a good marketable title, free of all liens and encumbrances except those he agrees to assume. Whether buyer or seller pays for the title insurance policy varies throughout the state and is discussed in detail in Chapter 8.

Seller warrants ownership of the property and agrees to permit the brokers sign to be affixed to the property. State law specifically allows placement of a sign on real property with respect to sale, rental, or exchange. The sign must be of a reasonable size as determined by the city or county having jurisdiction and must be permitted to show the name, address, and phone number of the owner or his agent. The broker is allowed to cooperate with other real estate licensees.

3. The amount of the commission is set down as a percentage of the selling price and is also usually written out in the space provided. A percentage figure should be given, since the selling price of the property usually will not be the asking price of the seller; thus a stated percentage can later be applied to the amount the property finally brings. The amount of the broker's commission is not fixed by law but is strictly a matter of agreement between the seller-principal and the broker-agent. Assembly Bill 802, effective July 1980 and added to the Business and Professions Code as Section 10147.5, requires that any printed or form agreement which fixes the compensation to be paid to a real estate licensee for the sale of residential real property containing not more than four residential units shall contain the following statement in not less than ten-point boldface type immediately preceding any provisions of such agreement relating to compensation of the licensee: Notice: The amount or rate of real estate commissions is not fixed by law. They are set by each broker individually and may be negotiable between the seller and broker.

Since this is an exclusive-right-to-sell form, valid for a stated period of time, the seller agrees that should he sell the property himself during this time, withdraw it from the market, or lease or rent it, he will be responsible for the payment of a commission to the broker. The amount of the commission is based on the stated percentage as applied to the stated asking price on the listing.

A safety clause is provided which protects the broker's commission with respect to a common situation. A buyer has been shown the property by the broker, or has talked to the broker about a particular piece of property, and then goes to the owner and attempts to purchase directly from him. The owner and buyer may wait until the broker's listing has terminated and then deal with each other. In any event, the seller expects to avoid the need to pay the broker a commission and thus save the buyer some money by accepting a reduced amount for the property.

It is very important, therefore, that a broker or salesman keep complete and accurate records of the names of all persons with whom he comes into contact regarding the sale of a particular piece of property. Many licensees make it a practice to supply the seller with a list of such names in writing to be able to later show that they had negotiated with those persons named during the term of the listing.

4. This provision is common in most contracts and reminds the parties that in a lawsuit, attorneys fees and court costs are generally added to any amounts the court may award.

5. The listing also gives the broker the exclusive and irrevocable right to act as agent in the exchange of the property, and this section deals with exchanges and cooperation with other real estate agents.

6. Although the owner agrees to hold the agent harmless from any liability or damages with respect to incorrect or missing information, the broker must be sure to obtain all relevant information about the property when securing the listing and not always rely completely upon facts supplied by the owner. In order to avoid an accusation of negligence, the broker must be very careful with respect to statements made to clients and must conduct his own investigation with respect to the property.

7. This "civil rights" provision complies with requirements of federal and state law. The seller is made aware that racial discrimination is against the law.

8. Space is provided for insertion of additional provisions which may relate to any number of subjects, such as certain repairs to be made by the seller or the way in which the seller will give possession of the property at close of escrow.

9. The listing agreement must be dated and signed by the property owner. Since California is a community property state, it is important that

both the husband and wife sign all documents pertaining to any real estate transaction. This may not be necessary where separate property is involved, but since most property held by husband and wife is community, the broker should be on the safe side and obtain both signatures.

The law requires that a copy of any document pertaining to the sale or purchase of real property must be given to those persons signing such a document.

10. The broker signs the agreement, or the name of the broker or the firm is entered and is followed by the signature of the licensed salesman. It is important to note that the broker agrees to use "diligence" in procuring a purchaser. Some forms contain a more detailed list of the acts that will be expected of the broker, such as advertising and showing the property, cooperating with fellow brokers, and furnishing information to the seller regarding progress being made during the listing term.

THE BROKER'S COMMISSION

A broker is usually entitled to a commission when he produces a buyer, "ready, willing, and able" to purchase the property on terms and conditions acceptable to both buyer and seller.

If an agreement is entered into and the buyer refuses to perform, the broker may receive one half the forfeited deposit. If the seller refuses to perform, the broker usually is still entitled to his full commission. Some contracts may expressly provide that no commission is payable except on a completed sale.

A broker is generally not entitled to reimbursement for expenses incurred by him in attempting to sell a property. If he fails to sell the property during the term of the listing, he not only loses a commission but also must bear the loss for advertising and other expenses.

The amount of commission to be received is a matter of agreement between principal and agent.

PROSPECTING

We shall conclude this chapter with a brief discussion of some of the methods commonly employed to obtain listings and prospective clients.

The broker

A successful broker, or experienced salesman, has both a continuous supply of prospects who want to purchase property and an adequate supply of marketable listings to sell.

A licensee may obtain a listing in three general ways:

1. A person who wants to sell property knows the licensee personally or is referred to the licensee by a mutual friend.
2. The licensee is able to convince a prospective seller that he should sell and that the licensee should be the one to represent him.
3. A subsequent listing which arises as the result of a sale.

A person in the real estate business must be known by the people in his community. We usually find that the successful broker belongs to many groups, clubs, church and civic organizations, and professional societies where he is able to meet and work with many people. He has an outgoing personality and is able to communicate with individuals at all levels. He knows his business and leaves a good impression on those with whom he comes into contact.

Real estate is in great measure a business of referrals. A broker deals with persons who are sent to him by others. One satisfied client sends the broker many more and will himself deal with the broker again and again through the years. Many successful licensees have built up such a successful following that they no longer spend much time looking for new prospects but instead are kept quite busy taking care of old customers and referrals sent by them. Success in the real estate business does not come quickly but instead is the result of hard work, honest dealing, and time.

In connection with proper time utilization, some type of Daily Work Plan, such as that shown in Figure 3–2, is a necessity.

The beginning salesman

Although he may obtain some prospects in the ways previously mentioned, the salesman just starting in the business will also have to resort to (a) neighboring canvassing, (b) open house, and (c) dealing with persons who call or stop at the real estate office.

Neighborhood canvassing. Most salesmen start by ringing doorbells in the neighborhood where their office is located. In this way, the salesman becomes known to property owners and tenants in the area. This method is known as "farming," and the area being worked by the licensee is referred to as his farm.

"YA GOTTA WORK THE TERRITORY"

DAILY WORK PLAN

Name_____   Date_____

Today's Plan   Today's Accomplishments

8:00 .   Showing Property
8:30 .   .
9:00 .   .
9:30 .   New Properties Inspected
10:00 .   .
10:30 .   .
11:00 .   Soliciting Expired Listings
11:30 .   -
12:00 .   -
12:30 .   Phone Solicitation
                                                "Cold"
1:00 .   .
1:30 .   -
2:00 .   "By Owner"
2:30 .   .
3:00 .   Door-to-Door Canvassing
                                                "Cold"
3:30 .   .
4:00 .   -
4:30 .   "By Owner"
5:00 .   -
5:30 .   -
6:00 .   Previous Client Follow-up
6:30 .   .
7:00 .   _____
7:30 .   _____
8:00 .   .
8:30 .   .
9:00 .

The salesman will be surprised at the number of people he will get to know and the number of leads he will receive from them. Not only will he be able to obtain listings but also prospective purchasers, since a person who sells one property will often buy another.

Open house. Although not all persons who stop to look at an open house are interested in buying, the licensee will soon learn to identify those who are, and once he is able to determine what they want and what they can afford, he should be able to proceed and finally effect a sale.

Not all brokers agree that the open house method of merchandising real estate is a good one, and in many areas, properties are not kept open nor are signs affixed. The buyer must go to a real estate office directly in order to find out about and inspect available listings.

Office calls. All salesmen usually are required to be in the real estate office on a certain day during the week. This is usually called floor time. The salesman will answer any telephone calls in connection with advertisements placed by the firm in the newspaper. Those who call regarding these ads are often potential buyers, as evidenced by the fact that they have been reading the real estate section of the newspaper and are interested enough to call for further information with respect to a particular advertisement.

Other calls the salesman may receive could be from an owner interested in selling his property, from someone who wants an appraisal, from a family looking for a place to rent or lease, or from other licensees in the area. In addition to telephone calls, the salesman deals with persons who come into the office in person seeking information. Of course, any one of them could become the salesman's next client.

Additional sources of listings and prospects

Legal publications. Although not a source for obtaining many exclusive listings, legal notices and publications inform the broker about properties offered for sale. These are usually open listings, and the broker who finds a purchaser will earn his commission. Sales of this type are: *(a)* tax sales by city and county tax collectors, *(b)* sales by the state, *(c)* sales by the court, *(d)* estate sales, *(e)* sales by attorneys and banks, *(f)* involuntary auction sales, and *(g)* foreclosure sales. Public sales of real property are discussed in Chapter 16.

Multiple listing book. Being a member of a multiple listing association is very helpful for the salesman. In addition to providing him with numerous listings, the MLS books help him to keep up with prices and sales in various neighborhoods. These books should be kept on file because they are an excellent reference source, especially when comparisons are needed in trying to determine the correct price at which to list a property.

Telephone canvassing. Many licensees obtain from the telephone company a reverse directory, which contains listings by street address rather than by name. The salesman can telephone all the persons on a particular block or street. In this way, he can talk to persons who were not at home when he rang their doorbells. Some persons find talking over the telephone easier than standing in their doorways, and many salesmen prefer this method of canvassing.

Local newspaper. Most successful licensees make it a habit to regularly read the real estate section of their local newspapers. Keeping up with the advertisements allows one to know what is for sale in the area and who has the listing. Many properties are not in multiple listing, but virtually all property for sale is advertised in the newspapers. Since all brokers generally cooperate with one another, a call to the listing office will bring all the information needed regarding price, type of property, financing, and how and when the property may be shown.

One should never skip over property advertised "for sale by owner," for quite often the owner will cooperate with the licensee, and if he gets his price, he will usually be willing to pay a commission. Many persons try to sell their property themselvs, thinking it an easy thing to do. They soon find out how complicated it really is, and the salesman or broker who calls may be able to convince the owner that the property should be listed with the licensee.

Builders. Builders are always looking for a good buy on parcels of unimproved land. They are too busy to do much looking for themselves and often deal with brokers. In many urban areas, older buildings are purchased, torn down, and replaced with new structures, since this is the only way the builder can obtain a site at that particular location.

Investors. Many persons prefer to invest their money in real estate and hold it in anticipation of a fixed return. Benefits such as depreciation, tax shelter, and rising prices are important factors to be considered. Licensees who are able to successfully deal with investors will have repeated business with them year after year.

Speculators. All successful brokers have a group of clients who regularly speculate in real estate. Some speculators buy run-down properties, improve them, and then put them on the market, while other speculators seek to purchase property that is priced low and then immediately attempt to resell it. The broker who finds these properties for his speculative clients will make a commission when they buy and will usually be given the listing when the property is resold, thus making an additional commission.

Obtaining the listing

A great deal has been written concerning the various methods by which a broker may convince a property owner to list the property with him. The licensee who is a good lister will emphasize to the prospective seller some or all of the following principles.

Specialization. The real estate broker is a specialist who has the experience and technical knowledge necessary to move a property at a price and on conditions fair to both buyer and seller. The purchase and sale of real estate is extremely complex and requires that many forms be properly prepared and understood. Does the seller understand what is involved in an escrow, title search, deposit receipt, and termite inspection? The broker does, while the average person does not.

Financing. Proper financing is the decisive factor in the success of many real estate transactions. The broker works with all the lending institutions in the community and knows where to obtain the best financing at any given time. Can the seller explain to the buyer what is meant by a prepayment penalty, an acceleration clause, points, or a second loan? Can the seller explain the procedures involved in obtaining an FHA or a VA Loan? Most sellers can be shown that the broker is the person to do the job properly.

Negotiation with the buyer. The seller and buyer cannot usually communicate properly with each other. The buyer is generally too timid to tell the property owner what objections he may have regarding the property or the terms and conditions, but he will discuss these with the broker, who may be able to overcome them and thus effect the sale.

Saving the seller time. When a piece of property is advertised for sale, someone must be constantly available to answer the telephone and to show the property. Does the seller have sufficient time to do this? Can he afford to take time away from his normal occupation, and is his wife ready for persons who will knock on the door at all hours of the day without having first called to make an appointment? The seller should be advised that he may waste a great deal of time in talking to persons who seem interested only to find later that they are not qualified to purchase his property for a variety of reasons. The broker qualifies the prospect first, and only then does he arrange for an inspection of the property.

Advertising and showing. The seller should be made aware of the expense involved in continuous classified advertising. The broker knows how and when to advertise the property and, of course, bears the full expense of such advertising. The broker is able to show the property to its best advantage. Since the broker has talked to the prospective purchaser before he is shown the property, features the buyer is looking for can be emphasized and expanded on during the showing. Questions with regard to zoning, building codes, and costs of minor remodeling can readily be answered by the broker.

Professional standards. The broker operates within a prescribed set of laws, rules, and regulations and will forfeit his license to operate should he be proved dishonest in his dealings. The seller should have peace of mind in knowing that the sale of his property is being handled by a professional. He will not have to worry about a buyer's trying to take advantage of him because of a lack of knowledge on his part.

Saving the commission. An unwillingness on the part of the seller to pay the brokerage commission is a reason the property owner commonly gives for his refusal to correctly list the property with a broker. It should be explained to the seller that a mistake on his part, with respect to any of the numerous forms and conditions involved in the normal transaction, can cost him as much, and in many cases more, than the commission being earned by the broker.

PROPER PROCEDURES

With respect to listing, Realtors generally agree that certain procedures are necessary to insure success. The following outline represents a consensus of the views of successful Realtors regarding proper procedures in connection with the listing and sale of real property.

1. *Fully explain all terms of the listing contract.* Your clients must know what they are signing and it is the licensees' responsibility to fully explain any instrument requiring your clients' signatures.

ESTIMATED SELLER'S PROCEEDS
California Association of Realtors® Standard Form

SELLER: ARTHUR AND ADA SMITH

PROPERTY ADDRESS: 1790 WESTERN AVENUE, SAN BERNARDINO, CALIFORNIA

BROKER: PRESTIGE PROPERTIES

This estimate is based on costs associated with __conv.__ financing.

ESTIMATED CLOSING DATE: 6/20/--
PROJECTED SELLING PRICE: $ 146,500.

ENCUMBRANCES
First Trust Deed	$ 59,600.
Second Trust Deed	8,900.
Other Encumbrances	
TOTAL	$ 68,500.

PROJECTED GROSS EQUITY $ 78,000.00

ESTIMATED COSTS
Escrow	$ 129.
Sub Escrow	
Recording	6.
Drawing Deed	
Title Insurance	550.
Transfer Tax	161.
Notary	4.
Pre-Payment Penalty	
Forwarding or Transfer	50.
Reconveyance	75.
Interest	900.
Discount @ %	
Preparation of Documents	
Taxes	
Appraisal	
Structural Pest Control Inspection	
Structural Pest Control Repairs	825.
FHA-VA or Lender	
Home Warrantee	
Brokerage	8,790.
Buyer's Fees	
Miscellaneous Fees	
TOTAL	$ 11,490.

ESTIMATED CREDITS
Prorated Taxes	$ 110.00
Prorated Insurance	
Prorated Rents	
Impound Accounts	
Other	
Other	

TOTAL ESTIMATED COSTS $ 11,490.00
LESS ESTIMATED CREDITS $ 110.00

NET SELLER'S COSTS $ 11,380.00
PURCHASE MONEY NOTE (if any)
ESTIMATED SELLER'S CASH PROCEEDS $ 66,620.00

This estimate based upon the above projected selling price, type of financing, and estimated closing dates, has been prepared to assist the seller in computing his costs. Lenders and escrow companies will vary in their charges; therefore, these figures cannot be guaranteed by the broker or his representatives.

I have read the above figures and acknowledge receipt of a copy of this form.

Seller: (s) Arthur Smith Date: May 3, 19--
(s) Ada Smith Date: May 3, 19--

Presented by: (s) J. M. Carter
Address: 110 Main Street, San Bernardino
Phone No.: 921-8000

The estimated seller's proceeds calculated above will vary according to any difference in unpaid loan balances, bonds assessments, other liens, impound account, if any, and any expenses for required repairs. All estimates and information are from sources believed reliable but not guaranteed.

FIGURE 3-3

2. *Describe your firms marketing procedures.* Tell your clients how and what you plan to do in order to best facilitate and complete a sale of the property.
3. *Explain how multiple listing works.* Many individuals do not know the difference between multiple listing and other methods of listing. If you recommend multiple listing, tell the seller why you feel this is best and explain the procedures involved.
4. *Advise sellers how to treat showings by other licensees.* Prepare the sellers in the proper way to deal with other agents who will come to show the property. Any questions or inquiries of a technical nature should be referred to the listor. Individuals who are not real estate licensees may stop by to ask questions and should be referred to the listing office to arrange for inspection.
5. *Suggest any repairs or improvements you feel may be necessary.* The broker can often suggest minor repairs or improvements, such as painting, which can be done inexpensively and will greatly aid in the sale of the property.
6. *Explain closing costs and the approximate net amount the seller can expect to obtain.* Figure 3-3 illustrates a CAR form which can be used in arriving at these amounts.
7. *Discuss open house scheduling with the seller.* Determine in advance the dates on which you plan to hold the property open for inspection so that the sellers can have enough time to plan other activities away from the property during the showing.
8. *Fully explain all terms and conditions of offers you present.*
9. *Describe escrow and closing procedures.*
10. *Keep in regular contact with your clients.*

Regular progress reports should be made during the transaction. After close of escrow, the successful licensee will continue to keep in periodic touch because satisfied clients are the best source of future referrals and listings.

Additional forms, applicable to this chapter, are illustrated in Appendix C as Figures C3-1 thru C3-4.

QUESTIONS FOR DISCUSSION

1. Discuss the more important provisions that should be included in a listing agreement.
2. Describe a multiple listing service and what you think are its advantages and disadvantages.
3. In what conditions might you, as a broker, be willing to use an open listing?
4. Discuss the advantages and disadvantages of an option listing.
5. Do you agree with the present methods of arriving at the amount of the broker's commission, or do you believe that the commission should be set by law?
6. What are the general ways in which a broker obtains salable listings?
7. How should a new real estate licensee obtain prospective clients?
8. Discuss listings as they may protect the interests of the licensee.
9. What are some of the more important duties of the licensee required in a listing, and some of his responsibilities to the owner of the property?
10. Discuss the different times during a usual real estate transaction when the parties can discuss or negotiate the commission to be paid to the broker.

4

Selling and marketing techniques

The people who sell real estate and the product that they sell have one thing in common—each one is different from every other. The most accurate statement of the prerequisites for success in real estate sales is that the salesman must have a desire to work hard and succeed, the ability to learn, and a personality that will enable him to deal successfully with the general public.

The selling function in real estate is divided into four phases: (1) securing listings, (2) prospecting for and securing potential buyers by various means, (3) bringing a buyer and seller together through negotiations, and (4) successfully closing the transaction by effecting the sale.

In this chapter, we shall examine: some of the motivating factors that influence persons to engage in the purchase and/or sale of real estate, what the salesman should attempt to know about his clients, important considerations in showing properties to prospective buyers, points to emphasize, and the materials and information the salesman should have available.

Selling real estate differs from selling many other products.

1. The product being sold is quite complex and very individualized.
2. The sales period is longer and more time-consuming.
3. The transfer of property involves many legal requirements and restrictions which must be understood by the salesman.
4. The licensee quite often is acting as an intermediary between two parties and must sell each party in order to make the sale and earn his commission.
5. Each product to be sold has its own special features and problems, such as location, value, financing, and many others the salesman must be aware of.

Real estate licensees spend approximately 60 percent of their work time with prospective buyers and sellers helping them to arrive at a decision. Thirty percent of the licensees' time is spent obtaining leads, making appointments, getting facts and answers to certain questions, and gathering specific information. The remaining 10 percent is spent in self-improvement and continuing education activities, such as seminars, courses, and reading current publications and materials relating to the real estate business.

AREAS OF SALES PREFERENCE

Regardless of whether the real estate salesman specializes in residential, income, commercial, industrial, or recreational properties, he may want to spend most of his time, as far as representation and negotiations are concerned, in one of three general areas: (1) listing properties, (2) seeking specific properties for a prospective purchaser, and (3) creating sales possibilities.

Many salesmen find that they have a special talent for obtaining listings.

Equally in evidence are those licensees who prefer first to line up individuals who want to buy and then to concentrate on finding them a property they will purchase.

In addition to both of the above, there are those who create sales possibilities and put the deal together. A broker may show an individual the benefit to be derived from trading his present property for a newer or larger holding; he may bring a builder and an owner of unimproved land together and become the exclusive agent for the sale of a number of new buildings; or he may become expert in property management and leasing, exchanges, finance, and any of the other common areas of specialization that will allow him to seek out the investor and the property owner rather than waiting for them to come to him.

It is obvious that while a licensee may prefer to be a lister or a seller, the most successful salesman is the one who can be both with equal ability and, in addition, is able to eventually specialize to the degree that he can create many sales situations.

REASONS FOR SALE OR PURCHASE

If the real estate licensee understands the basic situations that motivate people to buy and/or sell real estate, he will be able to train himself in advance to cope successfully with the problems common to any particular situation and thus avoid the embarrassment of being taken by surprise or caught off guard when dealing with the client. He will also be able to recognize the best time to approach an individual and turn him into a satisfied client.

The three most common reasons for the purchase of real estate are (1) for occupancy, (2) for investment and speculation, and (3) for special uses.

Occupancy

Anyone engaged in general brokerage will agree that most sales of real estate are made to persons who wish to occupy the building they purchase. Homeownership is as American as apple pie and the Fourth of July. A house is security and protection, it is a feeling of belonging to the community, a safeguard against inflation, and a symbol of family stability. The following are but a few of the many prospective purchasers available to the broker:

1. Newly or recently married couples who want a house of their own.
2. Persons who have been renting and have decided to apply their monthly payments to the purchase of their own property.
3. A family that has outgrown its present house and needs a larger one.
4. Those who want to move up and buy a better or more expensive house.
5. Parents who, when their children have grown, find that their present house is too large and want something smaller.
6. Persons who must, for one reason or another, change their location.
7. Those who want to purchase a second home for climatic or recreational reasons.

Investment and speculation

All types of real estate—residential, income, commercial, and recreational properties—are purchased for investment purposes. The benefits of a tax shelter, appreciation, equity buildup, and spendable cash income are a few of the reasons for the purchase of property for investment.

It is not always easy to distinguish between an investor and a speculator, since those engaged in speculation are also, in a sense, investors. The speculator is generally thought of as one who invests for a short term as against one who keeps his investment for a longer period. The purchase of a building for quick resale, the repair and modernization of an older building recently purchased and now once again on the market, and the construction and sale of a new office building or shopping center complex—all these, while they are also investments, are correctly classified as speculations.

Special uses

Many individuals, groups, and organizations seek to purchase real estate for special uses. Among the more common are:

1. The purchase of real estate to be used in connection with retailing, manufacturing, entertainment or recreation, or for any type of profit-making business use.
2. Facilities to be used by social, fraternal, church, educational, and other such profit or nonprofit groups.
3. The acquisition of real estate by various governmental agencies at all levels.

PRESALE PREPARATION

Too many salesmen prefer to wait until they have found an interested purchaser and only then attempt to seek solutions to many of the common problems that arise during the preliminary negotiations. If too many obstacles present themselves, the buyer will begin to lose confidence in the broker, and the sale will be lost. The successful broker will not only be prepared with answers and solutions to those problems that do arise, but he will also be able to manage the sale so as to minimize and often eliminate those conditions that may prevent a sale. To the greatest degree possible and practical, a licensee should know (a) the property he is attempting to sell, (b) the prospective purchaser, and (c) the owner of the property.

Know the property

The successful salesman knows his product thoroughly. This is easy for most persons engaged in selling, since the product remains the same and only the customers change. The real estate salesman not only deals with different buyers but also his product is never the same, since no two properties are alike. The only exception may be the salesman employed to sell new tract houses, each almost identical to the other. Very few licensees restrict their activities to such sales, and each property they are attempting to sell will differ in many respects to any other. The broker will have to be ready with information regarding:

1. The location and the neighborhood with respect to schools, transportation, religious institutions, recreational areas, shopping centers, special features, and socioeconomic level of the people who live in the area.
2. A practical approximation of the price the property will bring, the existing financing and availability of new financing, down payment required, monthly payments necessary, property taxes, secondary financing, special assessments, and, if applicable, rental data, gross and net income, expenses, and matters such as depreciation for income tax purposes.
3. The physical condition of the property with respect to any termite and dry rot damage, plumbing, wiring, and roof. Degree of building and zoning code violation, if any, legal uses, construction, and layout.
4. When and how may the property be shown to prospective purchasers and certain items that may not be included in the purchase price, such as drapes, stove and refrigerator, carpeting, special fixtures, and plants.
5. Size of rooms, size of lot, and exchange or trade possibilities.

Know the prospective purchaser

With respect to the buyer, the broker will have to determine:

1. What are his basic physical needs? What is the size of his family and what special features is he seeking in the property he will ultimately purchase?
2. What can the buyer afford to pay, what is his income, and what does he have for a down payment?
3. Does the buyer understand the nature of closing costs and the approximate amount he will have to pay?
4. Does the buyer understand the problems of financing, and does he realize that his financial picture will determine to a great extent the location and type of property he will be able to purchase?
5. Is this client psychologically desirous of purchasing, or is he merely looking around and as yet undecided about what he really wants to do?
6. Does the buyer have another piece of property to sell before he can purchase something else?

Know the owner

With respect to the owner who has put his property on the market, the broker will have to determine:

1. Does the owner really want to sell?
2. Does he understand, so far as is practical, the market value of the property and the approximate price it may be expected to bring?
3. Will the seller be in the market for another piece of property when he sells this one?
4. Will the seller cooperate in showing the property, or will he place unreasonable restrictions on the broker?
5. Has the seller an adequate understanding of closing costs, possible termite inspection, secondary financing, and other related matters?

QUALIFYING THE PROSPECTIVE BUYER

When a broker meets a prospective seller, he tries to obtain a listing; when he meets a prospective buyer, he must be able to adequately qualify that buyer before he can begin to show him any properties.

The buyer must not only be shown properties he will want to buy, but he must also be in a financial position to actually make the purchase. Many beginning licensees waste a good deal of time showing clients properties they may like but cannot really afford to buy. Quite often, this client will be lost to another salesman who has the ability to adequately qualify the prospect. He will then show the buyer properties that can actually be sold to him.

Two areas of vital importance, then, are (1) determination of the needs and desires of the client with respect to the physical features of the property, and (2) financial ability of the buyer, with particular emphasis on the amount of down payment needed, amount of loan he can qualify for, and monthly payment he is able to make. Figure 4–1 illustrates the CAR Home Buyer's Problem Analysis which may be used to list the prospective purchasers needs and qualifications, and Figure 4–2 is used to estimate the buyer's cost.

SHOWING THE PROPERTY

If at all possible, the broker should never show the buyer a property that the broker has not inspected first. It is impossible to do the best job of showing without knowing what will be shown. Every piece of property is in some way different from every other. Even in an area of tract houses where the physical plan of each house is the same, the interior cleanliness, decoration, and general condition should not be the subject of guesswork prior to showing.

Don't confuse the buyer by showing him too many properties. It is difficult for the average prospect to inspect more than three properties at any one showing and still remember the particular points of interest about each one. Too often, the buyer will be confused, and the broker will be unable to obtain any kind of an offer. If the broker has correctly qualified the prospect, he should be able to obtain an offer to purchase before he has had to show any more than three to six individual properties, and it is not uncommon for many brokers to sell the first or second property shown to the buyer.

Let the owner know you are coming to inspect. Ideally, the owner or tenant should not be at home when the broker brings clients to look at the property. If someone is at home, he should be introduced briefly and then disappear during the inspection. If the owner follows the broker and purchaser about, the client will hurry through the property without really giving it a thorough inspection and will later lose interest in that particular building. Further, the client will not have time to ask questions about certain features which may pose a problem and which the broker might have been able to answer to the satisfaction of the buyer.

Try to have the property clean and neat. A dirty house gives the impression that the owner not only is dirty himself but also has probably been negligent regarding the general care and maintenance of the property over the years.

Brokers know that "$200 worth of paint may bring $2,000 more for the property," since, psychologically, buyers want clean property. A purchaser may say that he can redecorate and would like to save money by getting a dirty house or one that is in need of repair, but usually this is just not true, and it is the clean building that the buyer will purchase. Only a small minority of buyers will actually purchase a house in need of minor repair and redecorating and save money by doing the necessary work themselves. This is the reason that professional speculators are able to make a substantial profit on properties they purchase by often doing no more than repainting, refinishing floors, and adding new lighting fixtures where needed and then quickly reselling.

Don't argue with the client. This may seem to be too elementary to mention, but many real estate salesmen are guilty of just such actions. With regard to the appearance and general characteristics of a property, the broker must be careful never to interject his personal feelings to the extent that he finds himself in strong disagreement with his client. Personal tastes vary, and the broker must remember that it is the buyer who will have to live in the property. The inexperienced salesman will often act as though any adverse comments by the purchaser are to be taken as a personal affront against the licensee; but the successful salesman knows that while certain objections on the part of the buyer can be solved by tactful discussion, many will have to be taken without reply. No property will be 100 percent perfect to the buyer, and the decision to purchase will generally be made on the basis that the good points far outweigh a few minor poor ones.

Don't rush the client. The broker should allow enough time for the buyer to adequately inspect the property. He should make sure that the buyer sees all the rooms, the basement, the yard, and anything else of special importance. Since buyers are often timid about going through someone else's house, the broker should lead the way but remain in the background and should not subject the buyers to the constant drone of his voice throughout the tour. The more experience a salesman has, the better he will be able to judge the amount of supervision needed when showing a property to a particular client.

Choose a good route to the property. If the purchasers are not familiar with the neighborhood in which the property is located, the broker should plan his route of approach so that the buyers will pass the church, school, shopping center, playground, and whatever else may be of interest. Since first impressions are very important, a correctly planned approach will give the broker a chance to sell the area surrounding the property.

HOME BUYER'S PROBLEM ANALYSIS
CALIFORNIA ASSOCIATION OF REALTORS® STANDARD FORM
(a check list to aid in determining the Buyer's qualifications and needs)

PERSONNEL DATA:

Name: (husband)_____ Phone (Office)_____
    (wife)_____ (home)_____
Address: (home)_____
    (work) (husband)_____ (wife)_____
Other Family Data: Boys_____ Cars_____
    Girls_____ Boat_____
    Relatives_____ Schools_____
    Pets_____ Church_____

NEEDS:

Bedrooms_____ Separate Din. Rm._____
Baths_____ Din. Rm./Fam. Comb._____
Sq. Ft._____ Separate Fam. Rm._____
1 or 2 Story_____ Fam. Rm./Kitch. Comb._____
Style_____ Fireplace_____
Lot Size_____ Garage Capacity_____
Location_____ Unusual Needs_____
Possession_____

FINANCES:

Capabilities: Down Payment Max.:_____Now
    Or from Sale of Own Home_____
    Monthly Payment:_____
      (Including Taxes, Insurance)_____
      (Excluding Taxes, Insurance)_____
    Type Loan Needed_____
Other Equities: Amount, Details_____
Location_____
Trade-In Possibility Data:_____

EMPLOYMENT NOTES:

Husband: Company_____ Address_____
    Position_____ How Long_____ Salary_____
Wife: Company_____ Address_____
    Position_____ How Long_____ Salary_____

ADDITIONAL ITEMS:

How Came in Contact:_____
Other Data:_____

For these forms address California Association of Realtors®, 505 Shatto Place, Los Angeles 90020. All rights reserved. Copyright 1970.

FIGURE 4–1

ESTIMATED BUYER'S COST
California Association of Realtors® Standard Form

BUYER: HAROLD AND JANE GREEN

PROPERTY ADDRESS: 1790 WESTERN AVENUE, SAN BERNARDINO, CALIFORNIA

BROKER: PRESTIGE PROPERTIES

This estimate is based on costs associated with _____ Conv. financing.

Loan Amount $ 110,000.   Interest 13 %   Term 30 years.

ESTIMATED BUYER'S EXPENSES

Loan Origination Fee	$ 1,750.00
Appraisal Fee	
Credit Report	20.00
Tax Impounds	
Insurance Impounds	
Lenders Prepaid Interest	471.00
Other Lender Fees	
Tax Service	17.50
Title Insurance Policy	
ALTA Policy	101.50
Escrow Fee	129.00
Recording Fees	10.00
Notary Fees	4.00
Preparation of Documents	
Fire Insurance	475.00
Structural Pest Control Inspection	75.00
Structural Pest Control Repairs	
Home Warranty	
Prorate Taxes	110.00
Other	
TOTAL ESTIMATED EXPENSES	$ 3,163.00
Estimated Expenses	3,163.00
Less Buyer's Credits	
Net Estimated Expenses	3,163.00
Down Payment	36,500.00
TOTAL CASH REQUIRED	$ 39,663.00

Projected Closing Date: 6/20/--
Proposed Purchase Price: $ 146,500.

ESTIMATED CREDITS:

Prorated Taxes	
Rents	
Security Deposits	
Other	
Other	
TOTAL CREDITS	$ -0-

PROJECTED MONTHLY PAYMENTS:

Principal & Interest	1,216.82
Taxes	150.00
Insurance	39.58
Other	
Other	
TOTAL	$ 1,406.40

This estimate based upon the above proposed purchase price, type of financing, and projected closing date has been prepared to assist Buyer in computing his costs. Lenders and escrow companies will vary in their charges; therefore, these figures cannot be guaranteed by the broker or his representatives. All estimates and information are from sources believed reliable but not guaranteed.

I have read the above figures and acknowledge receipt of a copy of this form.

Buyer (s) Harold Green   Date May 7, 19--

(s) Jane Green   Date May 7, 19--

Presented by: (s) J. M. Carter
Address: 110 Main Street
Phone No. 921-8000

FIGURE 4–2

Personal safety

Quite often, the real estate licensee will initially be dealing with clients who are strangers. It is generally best to meet and get acquainted with a new client at the real estate office. It may not be wise to make a telephone appointment and meet a stranger at a vacant property.

It is best to let your office know where you are going and the name of the client and to make some type of arrangement to call in periodically. Drive your own car when showing properties and during business activities, and do not carry large sums of money or wear obviously expensive jewelry or accessories.

FOLLOWING THE INSPECTION

After the buyer has thoroughly inspected the property, the broker should reemphasize those features of the property he thinks most closely relate to the needs and desires of the purchaser.

Assuming that the broker believes the prospect is qualified and the prospect has expressed his interest and basic approval of the property just inspected, the time has come for the broker and buyer to discuss formulation of the offer to be presented to the seller. The following chapter will deal with the offer and preparation of the deposit receipt.

POINTS TO EMPHASIZE TO THE BUYER

In addition to a discussion relating to a specific piece of property, there are many general points to emphasize to a prospective purchaser regarding the advantages of real property ownership.

1. A tenant pays a certain amount of money each month, which is lost to him forever. All he has to show for this expenditure is a box full of rent receipts. The renter is buying a piece of property for someone else (the owner), when he might just as well be buying for himself.
2. In addition to equity buildup, the property owner gains through appreciation, which in many areas of California has been between 10 and up to 35 percent each year. Many persons who purchased property three years ago have seen the value of their property double; the appreciation is equal to the original purchase price.
3. Real estate taxes and the interest paid on a loan are deductable items on the buyer's income tax return. Table 4–1 shows the real cost of home loan interest to the purchaser.

TABLE 4–1
The real cost of interest on a home loan

Taxable income (adjusted gross income minus allowable deductions)			Net cost at				
Single taxpayer	Married taxpayers	Tax bracket	11%	12%	13%	14%	15%
8,500	11,900	21%	8.7	9.5	10.3	11.1	11.9
11,000	16,000	24	8.4	9.1	9.9	10.6	11.4
17,000	25,000	32	7.5	8.2	8.8	9.5	10.2
21,000	30,000	37	7.0	7.6	8.2	8.8	9.5
28,000	36,000	43	6.3	6.8	7.4	8.0	8.6
34,000	46,000	49	5.6	6.1	6.6	7.1	7.7
42,000	50,000	55	5.0	5.4	5.6	6.3	6.6

Interest payments are deductible for income tax purposes. Example: Mr. and Mrs. Smith have a taxable income of $36,000 and are in the 43 percent tax bracket. If they purchase real property and borrow money at 13 percent, the real cost of interest to them is 7.4 percent.

4. The purchaser of income property can deduct real estate taxes, interest on a loan, certain expenses in connection with the operation of the property, certain repairs, and depreciation. Table 4–2 illustrates the savings involved in home purchase and the actual monthly cost to the purchaser.
5. The actual amount of cash needed to purchase real estate is but a small percentage of the entire selling price. If one purchases a building with a 20 percent cash down payment and the building increases in value 10 percent each year, the amount of increase will equal the down payment in approximately two years, and the owner will have doubled his actual cash investment.
6. The purchase of property affords future potential income in that when it is fully paid for, the owner of the property has purchased himself an annuity. He can sell the property, and if he carries back the first loan himself, he will receive both the cash down payment at the time of the sale and a monthly payment for many years to come.
7. If a property is partially or fully paid off, the owner may refinance and purchase more property, or he may trade up to a bigger and more expensive property without the necessity of advancing any additional cash.
8. The population of California and per capita income are expected to continue to increase. The steady increase in population, as well as building material cost increases and wage increases in the building trades, will result in a

TABLE 4–2
Home ownership savings

720 Wonderful Way	Mr. and Mrs. U. R. Smart	
Down payment: $28,000	Loan: $87,000 at 12.5% interest	Purchase price: $115,000

Monthly payments (principal and interest)	(1)	$ 928.52
Monthly real property tax	(2)	+95.83
Monthly insurance	(3)	+35.12
Total monthly payments	(4)	$1,059.47
Deductible items for income tax purposes		
Monthly interest	(5)	906.25
Monthly real property tax	(6)	+95.83
Total deduction	(7)	$1,002.08
Monthly income tax savings		
43% tax bracket (assuming $38,000 taxable income) times $1,002.08 equals	(8)	430.89
Total monthly payments (4)	(9)	1,059.47
Income tax savings (8)	(10)	−430.89
Monthly cost	(11)	$ 628.58
Equity buildup and inflation factor		
Monthly cost (11)	(12)	628.58
Monthly equity buildup on loan	(13)	−22.27
Monthly cost	(14)	$ 606.31
Monthly cost (14)	(15)	606.31
Inflation factor, increase in value ½% per month	(16)	−575.00
Monthly cost	(17)	$ 31.31
Monthly savings account interest lost on down payment of $28,000 at approximately 9½% per annum	(18)	+221.67
Monthly cost of home ownership to Mr. and Mrs. Smart	(19)	252.98

Assuming inflation factor of 1 percent per month, the monthly cost of $252.98 becomes instead a profit of $322.02 per month.

---

constant upward pressure on real estate prices.
9. The purchase of real estate allows privacy, freedom of action, and peace of mind for the owner and his family.

THE REAL ESTATE SALES KIT

Every licensee should equip himself with a sales kit and always keep it close by whenever he is on the job. The kit consists of a briefcase containing the following materials and items.

To aid in listing:
- a. Listing forms (local, CAR, MLS).
- b. Competitive market analysis forms and others the salesman may prefer to use as an aid in appraisal and valuation.
- c. A printed booklet or brochure advertising the firm and enumerating the services it offers.
- d. Business cards and stationery.
- e. MLS cards of properties recently sold.
- f. 100-foot measuring tape.
- g. Example of classified advertisements currently being run by the firm.

To aid in selling:
- a. Deposit receipt forms (local, CAR, MLS).
- b. Loan application forms.
- c. Blank notes and checks.
- d. Amortization payments booklet.
- e. Schedule of escrow fees, title insurance costs.
- f. Exchange or trade-in forms.
- g. Statement of identity forms.
- h. Complete information re: FHA, VA, Cal-Vet loans.

Miscellaneous material to aid in both of the above:
- a. Daily appointment book.
- b. Math tables booklet to aid calculating and proration.
- c. Street maps.
- d. Latest copy of the *Department of Real Estate Reference Book* and/or *Realty Bluebook*.
- e. Special forms and materials required locally.

- f. Extra pen, pencil, eraser, scratchpad, carbon paper.
- g. Stamps, envelopes.
- h. Directory of local board and MLS members.
- i. Map showing location of schools and colleges in the area.
- j. A calculator specifically programmed to do financial and business mathematics.

In addition, the licensee should carry the following in the trunk of his car:
- a. For Sale, For Rent, Sold, and other commonly used signs.
- b. A spare lockbox.
- c. Hammer and nails (for putting up all those signs).

Discussion with clients

While the sales kit is intended to provide the licensee with whatever he may need in the course of negotiations with clients, it certainly is not intended as a means for turning the salesman's automobile into a real estate office. The client, be he potential seller or purchaser, should discuss matters of importance with the broker in a businesslike atmosphere free from any unnecessary interruptions. The broker's office or the client's house are the two most common locations used. When listing, the broker will usually find himself at the client's house, since this is the property generally being listed. It is often difficult to retain the full attention of the husband and wife while the children are playing, the telephone may suddenly ring, or the television set is on in the next room. When the broker is dealing with a prospective buyer, it may be easier to get him to the real estate office. If the buyer evidences sufficient interest following the property inspection, the broker should bring him back to the office for a review of pertinent facts. The average person, seller or buyer, becomes extremely nervous when the time comes to sign on the dotted line, and the experienced broker knows that the slightest distraction to the client can nullify an otherwise successful transaction. In order of preference then, the best place to transact business with clients are in (*a*) the broker's office, (*b*) the client's house, (*c*) the client's place of business. Definitely not recommended as a general rule are such places as the salesman's automobile or the local tavern, while having a drink.

An additional form, applicable to this chapter, is illustrated in Appendix C as Figure C4–1.

QUESTIONS FOR DISCUSSION

1. How does the sale of real estate differ from the sale of other products?
2. What are some of the areas of specialization and sales preference open to a licensee in the real estate business?
3. Discuss the three most common reasons people purchase real estate, and give examples of such purchases.
4. What do you think are some of the more important facts a broker should know about a piece of property he has listed?
5. With respect to the buyer, what are some of the important factors the licensee will have to determine when attempting to sell a property?
6. What is meant by qualifying the buyer?
7. What are some important rules to be followed when showing a property?
8. What selling point might the licensee use with the buyer?
9. What might the licensee wish to determine with respect to the owner of a listed property?
10. What do you think about the possible advantages or disadvantages of the open house method of marketing residential property?

5

The offer and the deposit receipt

In Chapter 4, we discussed the many factors involved in correctly laying the groundwork that will result in the broker's having a prospective purchaser who is seriously interested in a specific piece of property. The broker must now prepare the formal offer to be presented to the seller. Much has been written about asking the buyer to make the offer, asking for a deposit check, and other methods of motivating action. Each sale is truly an individual case, and each client is different in many respects from any other. The more experience the licensee has, the easier it will be for him to determine the correct approach for the particular client.

Very simply, actually writing up the offer is something the broker should be leading up to from the first time he begins to show the prospective purchaser different properties. All this time, the broker should have bene educating his client toward the time when an offer will have to be made. If he has been successful during the preliminary stages, the buyer should be able to proceed with preparation of the offer as easily and comfortably as possible. The buyer should understand what he is doing and what is involved.

Rarely does the buyer offer the full asking price for the property and also agree without exception to the terms and conditions set forth by the seller. One of the most difficult tasks facing the salesman is to obtain an offer that represents a fair market price. Assuming that the property has been listed correctly, that is, the asking price is within approximately 5 percent of the price the property should actually sell for, the broker should be able to obtain an offer that will have an excellent chance of being accepted by the seller. If the listed price is too high, or if the offer is below fair market value, there will be no initial acceptance but, instead, a counter-offer by the seller. A specific condition, not acceptable to either party, may result in continued negotiation.

When two licensees are involved in the transaction, the lister has an obligation to try to obtain the best price and terms possible for the seller, while the licensee who represents the buyer may prepare an offer that reflects his desire to obtain the property at the lowest price possible. Whether two brokers are involved or only one is representing both parties, it is important to remember not to prepare what is quite obviously a very poorly composed or low offer. To give the buyer false hope and to upset the seller will only result in a difficult situation for the licensee.

WHERE TO PREPARE THE OFFER

A quiet, businesslike atmosphere, free from any distractions or interruptions, will bring the best results. Various mathematical computations and the usual technical explanations will require that all parties be able to give full attention.

DEPOSIT RECEIPT AS A CONTRACT

The deposit receipt is one of the most important forms used by the real estate licensee. It not only constitutes a receipt for a deposit to bind an offer by prospective purchasers, but when properly signed by the purchasers and accepted by the sellers and signed by them, it becomes a contract for the purchase and sale of real property.

In addition to its contract purpose the acceptance section at the bottom of the deposit receipt form also restates the obligation of the sellers to pay the real estate broker a specified sum as his commission. Although the sellers may have previously agreed to payment of a commission in the listing contract, the exact amount of the commission based on the actual agreed-on selling price is stated on the deposit receipt. Since the broker may be selling property for which he has no listing, he is protected by the properly completed deposit receipt, which will enable him to his commission on completion of the transaction.

As a contract, the deposit receipt is essentially like any other, and because it deals with real property, it must be in writing and signed by the parties involved in order to be valid under the Stature of Frauds. There must be: *(a)* parties capable of contracting; *(b)* their consent, that is, genuine offer and acceptance; *(c)* a lawful object; and *(d)* sufficient consideration.

In a real estate sales transaction, the seller usually states the price, terms, and conditions under which he is willing to sell the property when he completes the listing agreement with his broker, or even if he attempts to sell the property himself. These terms and conditions are known as his offer. When a prospective purchaser accepts these terms and conditions set forth by the seller, the result is a binding contract. Usually, however, the buyer does not completely accept the terms and conditions asked for by the seller and, instead, makes his own offer to the seller.

It makes no difference whether the offer comes from the property seller or from the buyer; if negotiation finally leads to a definite offer on the one side and unconditional acceptance of the other side, a contract has been effected. All that is legally required to complete the contract for the sale of the real property is to reduce the terms and conditions to writing and have the parties sign the contract. This is done on the deposit receipt form.

All forms such as deposit receipts, listing agreements, exchange agreements, and any other agreement for the sale or exchange of real property should have and contain the following provisions:

1. Date of the agreement.
2. Names and addresses of the parties to the contract.
3. Description of the property.
4. Consideration.
5. Reference to creation of new mortgages or trust deeds, if any.
6. Reference to existing mortgages or trust deeds, if any.
7. Any other provisions that may be required or requested by either party.
8. Date and place of closing.

PREPARING THE DEPOSIT RECEIPT

Different forms of Deposit Receipts are in use throughout the state. While they are basically the same, the phraseology of various sections of the form have been changed in certain parts of the state to conform more closely to the general practice in that particular area.

Although we will use the CAR Real Estate Purchase Contract and Receipt for Deposit as an illustration, it makes no difference which of the rather standardized deposit receipt forms is used, since they will all show the same general procedure.

1. The seller will provide the buyer with a deed.
2. A policy of title insurance will be issued.
3. The buyer will sign a note secured by a deed of trust for any money he may have to borrow in order to effect the purchase of the property.

All this will have occurred between the time the deposit receipt has been signed and accepted by the parties to the transaction and the successful completion of the transaction at close of escrow.

Throughout our discussion of deposit receipt preparation, we shall assume the most basic of all real estate transactions—the sale of a single-family residence. The parts of the deposit receipt form in Figure 5–1 correspond to those of the explanations which follow.

A. Location. Enter the name of the city or town in which the agreement is being filled out and the current date in the upper right corner of the deposit receipt.

B. Received from. Enter the name(s) of the person(s) making the purchase offer. The name of the purchaser and legal status should be shown.

Examples:

Llewelyn Snyder and Marie Snyder (his wife).
John Shaffer (a single man).
Paul Fisher (a married man).
George Martin (a licensed real estate broker) and Elizabeth Martin (his wife).
William McCarthy (a licensed real estate salesman) and Mabelline McCarthy (his wife).

[*Not True*] The law does not require a real estate licensee to disclose, to individuals with whom he may deal, possession of a real estate license, as long as the licensee is acting as a principal and not as an agent in connection with the transaction.

Commissioners Regulation 2727 states that a real estate salesman or a real estate broker acting in the capacity of a real estate salesman, who enters into an agreement as a principal involving the purchase or sale of real property while licensed to, or in the case of a broker/salesman, while subject to the supervision of a broker, shall make a written disclosure of the fact of purchase or sale to the supervising broker within five days from execution of the agreement and before close of escrow.

In other words, disclosure doesn't have to be to individuals with whom the licensee deals, but it must be to a supervising or employing broker.

The above are only a few examples of the many possible. If the persons making the offer are related, always make clear the relationship. If one person is married and the other is not, this also should be made clear.

> A single man or woman is one who has never been married.
> An unmarried man or woman is one who has been married but is now legally divorced, and the final divorce decree has been issued by the court.
> A married man or woman is a legally married person.
> A widow or widower is one who has lost a spouse and has not remarried.

C. The amount and form of the deposit. Enter the amount and form of the deposit the purchasers give the broker at the time the offer is made. The amount must be spelled out and also written numerically. Example:

Two thousand dollars .... ($2,000.00)

If a mistake is made and the two amounts differ, the amount written out will be deemed correct and will prevail. The deposit should be substantial enough to protect the seller in the event the buyer changes his mind without a valid reason after the seller has accepted the offer. The problem of getting a substantial deposit from the purchaser at the time the offer is made is common. A buyer usually does not want to give the licensee a large deposit prior to sellers acceptance of the offer. To facilitate a later increase of deposit, paragraph 2 provides a means of increasing the deposit when the offer is accepted.

The form of the deposit may be cash, a personal check, a cashier's check, or anything of value acceptable to the seller. The deposit may also take the form of a promissory note when a check or cash is not immediately available. The broker should use a straight note form payable on demand to the broker with no interest. On the back of the note the broker should state that the note is being taken in conjunction with the deposit receipt in question and should describe the property involved.

D. The offered price. Enter the amount being offered by the purchaser, both numerically and written out. Example:

Fifty thousand dollars .... ($50,000.00).

E. Property description. There are various ways of identifying and stating the description of the property. The main thing to remember is that the description should be accurate and thorough enough to absolutely identify the specific property in question. Examples:

> Lot and improvements commonly known as 25 Gary Drive, San Francisco, California.
> Assessors Block 1833, Lot 3, commonly known as 25 Gary Drive, San Francisco, California.
> Assessors Block 1833, commonly known as 25 Gary Drive, San Francisco, California. Legally described as . . . (full legal description given if known).

Quite often, the legal description will have to be the one used, since the property may be an unimproved lot or country land without a street address or block and lot number.

Paragraph 1. *Buyer will deposit in escrow with.* Enter the name of the firm to act as escrow. It may be an escrow company, a bank, or a title insurance company; and it should be remembered that the determination of who will act as escrow is by agreement of the parties involved in the sale.

In northern California, the escrow function is usually handled by the title insurance company. In Southern California, some brokers use the title company to perform the escrow function, while others use a separate escrow company and the title insurance company merely issues the policy of title insurance. A period of 30 to 60 days from date of acceptance is usually allowed to complete the escrow and close the transaction.

Terms and conditions of the sale. In this area of the deposit receipt, the broker enters the terms and conditions of the sale. The broker writes in the word "terms," and under it he includes in detail the means by which buyer will compile the amount being offered as the purchase price. It will generally include some cash, a first loan, and perhaps a second loan. "Conditions" will include all matters, other than financing, that the parties want to be included on the deposit receipt. We will first discuss some examples of terms and then look at some of the common conditions included in the ordinary deposit receipt.

CALIFORNIA ASSOCIATION OF REALTORS® STANDARD FORM

REAL ESTATE PURCHASE CONTRACT AND RECEIPT FOR DEPOSIT

THIS IS MORE THAN A RECEIPT FOR MONEY. IT IS INTENDED TO BE A LEGALLY BINDING CONTRACT. READ IT CAREFULLY.

(A) _____ San Francisco _____, California. _____ July 8 _____, 19 --

(B) Received from __James A. Byar and Mary Byar, husband and wife_____

(C) herein called Buyer, the sum of __One Thousand Dollars ---------------__ Dollars $ __1,000.__
evidenced by cash ☐, cashier's check ☐, or _____, personal check ☒ payable to __San Francisco Title Insurance Company__, to be held uncashed until acceptance of this offer, as deposit on account of purchase price of

(D) __One Hundred Fifty-two Thousand Dollars ---------------__ Dollars $ __152,000.__

(E) for the purchase of property, situated in __City of San Francisco__, County of __San Francisco__, California, described as follows: __Assessors Block 1833, Lot 3, known as 25 Gary Drive, San Francisco__

1. Buyer will deposit in escrow with __San Francisco Title Ins. Company__ the balance of purchase price as follows:

TERMS: $ 38,000. cash down payment, including deposit.

$ 114,000. 1st loan to be obtained by James and Mary Byar from ABC Savings and Loan Association. Interest not to exceed 11½ percent per annum, term of 30 years, with monthly payments including principal and interest to be approximately $ 1,129.

$ 152,000. purchase price

CONDITIONS:
1. Subject to a structural pest control inspection report. Buyer to pay for cost of report and seller for cost of any indicated corrective work to a limit of $ 2,500.

2. Wall-to-wall carpeting, window treatments, stove and refrigerator presently in premises to remain and be included in purchase price.

3. Parties to pay normal and usual closing costs.

Set forth above any terms and conditions of a factual nature applicable to this sale, such as financing, prior sale of other property, the matter of structural pest control inspection, repairs and personal property to be included in the sale.

2. Deposit will ☒ will not ☐ be increased by $ __14,200.__ to $ __15,200__ within __10__ days of acceptance of this offer.
3. Buyer does ☒ does not ☐ intend to occupy subject property as his residence.
4. The supplements initialed below are incorporated as part of this agreement.

Other
__X__ Structural Pest Control Certification Agreement ____ Occupancy Agreement _____
____ Special Studies Zone Disclosure ____ VA Amendment _____
____ Flood Insurance Disclosure ____ FHA Amendment _____

5. Buyer and Seller acknowledge receipt of a copy of this page, which constitutes Page 1 of____ Pages.

X __(s) James A. Byar__ X __(s) Sam Seller__
BUYER   SELLER

X __(s) Mary Byar__ X __(s) Virginia Seller__
BUYER   SELLER

A REAL ESTATE BROKER IS THE PERSON QUALIFIED TO ADVISE ON REAL ESTATE. IF YOU DESIRE LEGAL ADVICE CONSULT YOUR ATTORNEY.

THIS STANDARIZED DOCUMENT FOR USE IN SIMPLE TRANSACTIONS HAS BEEN APPROVED BY THE CALIFORNIA ASSOCIATION OF REALTORS® AND THE STATE BAR OF CALIFORNIA IN FORM ONLY. NO REPRESENTATION IS MADE AS TO THE APPROVAL OF THE FORM OF SUPPLEMENTS. THE LEGAL VALIDITY OF ANY PROVISION, OR THE ADEQUACY OF ANY PROVISION IN ANY SPECIFIC TRANSACTION. IT SHOULD NOT BE USED IN COMPLEX TRANSACTIONS OR WITH EXTENSIVE RIDERS OR ADDITIONS.

FIGURE 5–1

REAL ESTATE PURCHASE CONTRACT AND RECEIPT FOR DEPOSIT

The following terms and conditions are hereby incorporated in and made a part of Purchaser's Offer

6. Buyer and Seller shall deliver signed instructions to the escrow holder within ____10____ days from Seller's acceptance which shall provide for closing within ____60____ days from Seller's acceptance. Escrow fees to be paid as follows: _____Buyer pays escrow fees._____

7. Title is to be free of liens, encumbrances, easements, restrictions, rights and conditions of record or known to Seller, other than the following: (1) Current property taxes, (2) covenants, conditions, restrictions, and public utility easements of record, if any, provided the same do not adversely affect the continued use of the property for the purposes for which it is presently being used, unless reasonably disapproved by Buyer in writing within ____5____ days of receipt of a current preliminary title report furnished at ____Buyers____ expense, and (3) _____
Seller shall furnish Buyer at ____Buyers____ expense a standard California Land Title Association policy issued by ____San Francisco Title____ Company, showing title vested in Buyer subject only to the above. If Seller (1) is unwilling or unable to eliminate any title matter disapproved by Buyer as above, Seller may terminate this agreement, or (2) fails to deliver title as above Buyer may terminate this agreement; in either case, the deposit shall be returned to Buyer.

8. Property taxes, premiums on insurance acceptable to Buyer, rents, interest, and _____ shall be pro-rated as of (a) the date of recordation of deed; or (b) _____
Any bond or assessment which is a lien shall be ____paid____ by ____Seller____ ____Seller____ shall pay cost of transfer taxes, if any.

9. Possession shall be delivered to Buyer (a) on close of escrow, or (b) not later than ____3____ days after close of escrow or (c) _____

10. Unless otherwise designated in the escrow instructions of Buyer, title shall vest as follows: _____
_____James A. Byar and Mary Byar, husband and wife, as Joint Tenants_____
(The manner of taking title may have significant legal and tax consequences. Therefore, give this matter serious consideration.)

11. If Broker is a participant of a Board multiple listing service ("MLS"), the Broker is authorized to report the sale, its price, terms, and financing for the information, publication, dissemination, and use of the authorized Board members.

12. If Buyer fails to complete said purchase as herein provided by reason of any default of Buyer, Seller shall be released from his obligation to sell the property to Buyer and may proceed against Buyer upon any claim or remedy which he may have in law or equity; provided, however, that by placing their initials here Buyer: ( ) Seller: ( ) agree that Seller shall retain the deposit as his liquidated damages. If the described property is a dwelling with no more than four units, one of which the Buyer intends to occupy as his residence, Seller shall retain as liquidated damages the deposit actually paid, or an amount therefrom, not more than 3% of the purchase price and promptly return any excess to Buyer.

13. If the only controversy or claim between the parties arises out of or relates to the disposition of the Buyer's deposit such controversy or claim shall at the election of the parties be decided by arbitration. Such arbitration shall be determined in accordance with the Rules of the American Arbitration Association, and judgment upon the award rendered by the Arbitrator(s) may be entered in any court having jurisdiction thereof. The provisions of Code of Civil Procedure Section 1283.05 shall be applicable to such arbitration.

14. In any action or proceeding arising out of this agreement, the prevailing party shall be entitled to reasonable attorney's fees and costs.

15. Time is of the essence. All modifications or extensions shall be in writing signed by the parties.

16. This constitutes an offer to purchase the described property. Unless acceptance is signed by Seller and the signed copy delivered to Buyer, in person or by mail to the address below, within ____2____ days, this offer shall be deemed revoked and the deposit shall be returned. Buyer acknowledges receipt of a copy hereof.

Real Estate Broker ____ABC REALTORS____   Buyer ____(s) James A. Byar____
(F) By ____(s) H. M. Maxwell____   ____(s) Mary Byar____
Address ____135 Tenth Avenue, S.F., 94118____ Address ____912 - 32nd Avenue, San Francisco____
Telephone ____564-1919____   Telephone ____758-1238____   ____94121____

ACCEPTANCE

The undersigned Seller accepts and agrees to sell the property on the above terms and conditions. Seller has employed ____ABC REALTORS____ as Broker(s) and agrees to pay for services the sum of
(G) ____Eight Thousand, Six Hundred____ Dollars ($ ____8,600.____), payable as follows:
(a) On recordation of the deed or other evidence of title, or (b) if completion of sale is prevented by default of Seller, upon Seller's default or (c) if completion of sale is prevented by default of Buyer, only if and when Seller collects damages from Buyer, by suit or otherwise and then in an amount not less than one-half of the damages recovered, but not to exceed the above fee, after first deducting title and escrow expenses and the expenses of collection, if any. In any action between Broker and Seller arising out of this agreement, the prevailing party shall be entitled to reasonable attorney's fees and costs. The undersigned acknowledges receipt of a copy and authorizes Broker(s) to deliver a signed copy to Buyer.

Dated: ____July 9, 19--____ Telephone ____752-8899____   Seller ____(s) Sam Seller____
Address ____25 Gary Drive, San Francisco, 94112____   Seller ____(s) Virginia Seller____

Broker(s) agree to the foregoing. Broker ____ABC REALTORS____   Broker _____
Dated: ____July 9, 19--____ By ____(s) H. M. Maxwell____   Dated: _____ By _____

Page __2__ of __2__ Pages

FIGURE 5-1 *(continued)*

The various ways in which a purchase may be financed will be treated in Chapter 7, dealing with real estate finance. Now let us look at the sale of the house at 25 Gary Drive, San Francisco, and note a few of the ways in which the terms might be set forth on the deposit receipt.

Example 1—cash over conventional loan:
All cash to seller as follows:

Down payment of $32,000 cash, including deposit.

Subject to purchaser obtaining a first loan secured by this property in the amount of $120,000 from American Savings and Loan Association, with interest at 12 percent annum, for a term of 30 years, payable at approximately $1,235 per month.

Example 2—cash down payment plus first and second loans:

Down payment of $25,000 cash, including deposit.

Subject to purchaser obtaining a first loan secured by this property in the amount of $115,000 from Bayview Federal Savings and Loan Company, with interest not to exceed 11½ percent, for a term of 30 years, payable at approximately $1,139 per month.

Purchaser to execute a note secured by a second deed of trust on this property, in favor of the seller, in the amount of $12,000, payable at $120 per month or more, including interest at 12 percent per annum, with the entire balance due five years from date of this note, or immediately on the sale or transfer of this property if prior to the due date of the note.

It is obvious then that there are numerous ways to state the terms of financing, depending on the method used, such as:

a. A down payment plus a conventional loan.
b. A down payment, a conventional first loan, and a second loan.
c. A down payment and assumption of an existing first loan.
d. A down payment and assumption of an existing first and second loan.
e. All cash to the seller.
f. A new, or assumption of an existing, FHA loan.
g. A new, or assumption of an existing, Veterans Administration (GI) loan.
h. A California Veterans Loan.
i. Exchange of property the buyer presently owns for the one he is purchasing, or a down payment and a note secured by a deed of trust on a property the buyer owns.

The broker must remember that at this point in the deposit receipt he must clearly and adequately state exactly how the purchaser plans to finance the purchase and obtain the necessary funds, which when totaled will equal the amount being offered to the seller.

Conditions. Having completed the description of "terms," the broker now enters the word "conditions" on the deposit receipt. The first item usually discussed here is the "termite report" and corrective work that may be indicated by the report.

Termite inspection

A termite inspection is not required by law. A building may be sold without any termite inspection as long as the purchaser and seller agree to this condition. However, government guaranteed or insured loans require a termite clearance, and some savings and loan associations and banks require a termite report before they will complete the loan, while others do not. Many times, the purchaser himself will insist on an inspection of the building. What must be made clear on the deposit receipt is *(a)* who will pay for the termite inspection and *(b)* who will pay for the corrective work that may be recommended in the report if it is decided that such work is to be done.

Effective October 1979, every time a pest control company makes an inspection of real property, the inspector must post a tag at the entrance of the attic, subarea, or garage giving the company name and date of inspection. If any corrective work is subsequently completed on the property, the company must post an additional tag in the same location.

The law requires that whenever a licensee is an agent in a transaction in which the delivery of a structural pest control inspection report, notice of work completed, or certification prescribed by Section 8519 of the Business and Professions Code is a condition of a contract effecting the transfer, the licensee shall (1) cause delivery of the appropriate documents to the transferee, (2) determine that the transferor has caused such delivery, or (3) advise the transferee that Section 1099 of the Civil Code requires that the appropriate documents be delivered to the transferee.

The licensee must maintain a record of the action taken by him to effect compliance with this regulation in accordance with Section 10148 of the Business and Professions Code.

The California Association of Realtors, provides a structural pest control agreement, illustrated in Figure 5-2, which may be used in the event that the seller agrees to an inspection and to pay for any indicated corrections. Figure 5-3 illustrates a standard pest control inspection report.

Licensees who do not choose to use the CAR termite form may enter the following on the deposit receipt.

> Property to be examined by a licensed pest control operator at the expense of the buyer; any work, to repair damage from infestations of wood-destroying organisms or to correct conditions that caused infestation, to be done at the expense of the seller; funds for such work to be held in escrow and disbursed on the clearance by the inspection and delivery of a certificate of completion and termite clearance.

Sometimes the above wording is shortened and the following written in:

> Seller to provide buyer with standard termite clearance. Buyer to pay for cost of inspection and seller for costs of correction.

We have so far been discussing a case in which the seller is willing to have an inspection of the property and pay for corrections needed. Now let us look at the other extreme, when (a) the seller does not want to pay for any work, and (b) the seller does not want to pay for any work and does not want to allow any inspection of his property.

a. Property is to be purchased in its present as-is condition, with seller not to be responsible for any corrective work whatsoever. Subject to buyer's approval of existing pest control inspection report issued by (name of pest control firm) and dated (date of report).

b. Property is to be purchased in its present as-is condition, with seller not to be responsible for any corrective work whatsoever, no pest control inspection report having been issued.

If the buyer is purchasing the property as is and without benefit of a report, the seller and the broker must exercise extreme caution not to make any representations one way or another concerning the condition of the property, and the broker would probably be wise, in connection with the use of b above, to state also that the buyers have physically entered upon the property and observed its apparent condition. A seller or real estate licensee who is aware of any existing damage and fails to tell the purchaser will be liable at law for full cost of any corrective work necessary.

Another situation that may frequently occur is one in which the buyer wants to make his offer conditional on his acceptance of a subsequent termite report, or the seller wants his acceptance of an offer to be subject to his approval of a subsequent report. In these cases the licensee may write the following:

> This offer is subject to a structural pest control inspection report acceptable to both the buyer and seller.

This is an extremely unwise condition to include in the deposit receipt, since in so doing, the licensee has given the buyer or the seller a way of backing out of the transaction after receipt of the report. Although the termite report may not be the actual reason at all, either party may be able to use it as an excuse not to go through with the transaction.

Some licensees feel that when a piece of property is placed on the market, it may be advantageous to have the property inspected and have a report issued before the receipt of an offer from a prospective buyer. If the property is newer, or appears to be in good condition, many brokers advise their principals to order a report as soon as possible. Knowing exactly what corrective measures may be needed, if any, and the cost involved will make it much easier for the broker to negotiate with the prospective buyer.

Often, the seller does not want to obligate himself to pay for all the necessary work a report may show is needed but, at the same time, does not insist that he be relieved of all responsibility in this regard. The seller is willing to obligate himself for an amount that seems reasonable to him. In such a case, the broker will work his entry on the deposit receipt so that it limits the seller's liability. The following is an example.

> This offer is subject to a structural pest control inspection report. Buyer to pay for cost of the report (not to exceed $100), and seller to pay for indicated corrective work up to, but not in excess of, two thousand, five hundred dollars ($2,500).

Personal property and fixtures

Anything the buyer assumes will be included in the purchase price but might in any way be in doubt should be put in writing on the deposit receipt. The most common entry refers to carpeting and drapes, and so we often see the following:

STRUCTURAL PEST CONTROL CERTIFICATION AGREEMENT

California Association of Realtors Standard Form

This agreement is part of and is hereby incorporated in that "Real Estate Purchase Contract and Receipt for Deposit" between the parties hereof dated _____ 19_____, pertaining to the property described as follows:

_____

1. _____ agrees at his expense to furnish
                      Seller/Buyer

_____ within _____ days from date
                 Buyer/Seller

of SELLER's approval of this agreement with a current written report of an inspection by a licensed Structural Pest Control Operator of the main building and all attached structures.

_____
(specify any additions or exceptions)

2. If no infestation or infection of wood destroying pests or organisms is found, the report shall include either in the form of an endorsement or as a separate written statement by the inspecting licensed Structural Pest Control Operator a CERTIFICATION to provide in accordance with B & P Code 8519(a): "This is to certify that the above property was inspected on _____ (date) in accordance with the Structural Pest Control Act and rules and regulations adopted pursuant thereto, and that no evidence of active infestation or infection was found".

3. All work recommended in said report to repair damage caused by infestation or infection of wood-destroying pests or organisms found and all work to correct conditions that caused such infestation or infection shall be done at the expense of SELLER.

_____
(specify any additions or exceptions)

Funds for work to be performed shall be held in escrow and disbursed upon receipt of a CERTIFICATION on the "Notice of Work Completed" to provide, in accordance with B & P Code 8519(b): "This is to certify that the property described herein is now free of evidence of active infestation or infection".

4. With the additions or exceptions, if any, noted below, BUYER agrees that any work to correct conditions usually deemed likely to lead to infestation or infection of wood-destroying pests or organisms, but where no evidence of existing infestation or infection is found with respect to such conditions, is NOT the responsibility of the SELLER, and that such work shall be done only if requested by BUYER and then at the expense of BUYER.

_____
(specify any additions or exceptions)

5. If inspection of inaccessible areas is recommended in the report, BUYER has the option of accepting and approving the report or requesting further inspection be made at the BUYER's expense. If further inspection is made and infestation, infection, or damage is found, repair of such damage and all work to correct conditions that caused such infestation or infection shall be at the expense of SELLER. If no infestation, infection or damage is found, any repairs to entry of the inaccessible areas shall be at the expense of BUYER.

6. _____ hereby selects the following licensed
                    Seller/Buyer

Structural Pest Control Operator to inspect the property: _____
SELLER consents to such inspection.

COPY OF REPORT TO BUYER

SELLER acknowledges his responsibility under Civil Code Section 1099 to deliver to BUYER as soon as practical before transfer of title or the execution of a real property sales contract as defined in Civil Code Section 2985 a copy of the inspection report, a "NOTICE OF WORK COMPLETED" OR A "CERTIFICATION pursuant to B & P Code 8519" as may be required.

SELLER directs _____
                 name of Broker

to deliver such copies of the above documents as may be required.

BUYER AND SELLER ACKNOWLEDGES RECEIPT OF A COPY OF THIS AGREEMENT WHICH INCORPORATES THE EXCERPTS FROM THE BUSINESS AND PROFESSIONS CODE AND THE CIVIL CODE printed on the reverse hereof.

Date Approved and Accepted	Date Approved and Accepted
BUYER	SELLER

REQUEST FOR STRUCTURAL PEST CONTROL CERTIFICATION REPORT

To _____
    Name of Operator   Address of Operator

You are instructed to make a Structural Pest Control Inspection of the main building and all attached structures.

_____
(specify any additions or exceptions)

Located at _____

For purposes of clarification you are requested to identify and separate in your report as clearly as possible, your findings and recommendations as follows:

SECTION 1)   Work recommended to repair damage caused by existing infestation or infection of wood-destroying pests or organisms and all work recommended to correct conditions that caused such infestation or infections.

SECTION 2)   Work recommended to correct conditions usually deemed likely to lead to infestation or infection of wood-destroying pests or organisms, but where no evidence of active infestation or infection is found with respect to such conditions.

Your quotations for cost of any recommended work should be segregated as above and be as itemized as possible.
Inspection of inaccessible areas, if any, shall not be made without specific authorization.
If your report discloses no infestation or infection, you shall issue a CERTIFICATION to that effect in accordance with B & P Code 8519(a).
If your report discloses infestation and infection and you subsequently are requested to perform recommended work in whole or in part your NOTICE OF WORK COMPLETED shall contain a CERTIFICATION to that effect in accordance with B & P Code 8519(b) or (c), whichever is applicable.

The undersigned agrees to pay $ _____ for your inspection and report in the above form, providing you deliver said report as indicated below on or before _____ 19_____.

Dated _____
    Person ordering the report   Address   City   State   Zip   Phone

Copies to:

Name of listing Broker	Address	Other	Address
Name of selling Broker	Address	Other	Address

FIGURE 5–2

STANDARD INSPECTION REPORT FORM

This form is prescribed by the Structural Pest Control Board with whom a copy must be filed, by licensee.
THIS IS AN INSPECTION REPORT ONLY, NOT A NOTICE OF COMPLETION.

Structural Pest Control Board
1020 N Street
Sacramento 14, Calif.

FIRM NAME AND ADDRESS
H. J. DAVIES CO.
3934 Geary Blvd.
San Francisco, Calif. 94118

FIRM LICENSE NUMBER	STAMP NUMBER	DATE OF INSPECTION
3091	807A	January 6, 19--

INDICATE INFESTATIONS AND CONDITIONS SHOWN IN BOX BELOW BY AN X IN THE PROPER SQUARE

S	K	F	B	FG	EC	Z
X		X		X	X	

CONSTRUCTION (X TYPE): 1. STUCCO [X] 3. BRICK [ ] 5. FRAME [X] 7. OTHER [ ]

CODE FROM DIRECTORY	CITY CODE	ADDRESS OF PROPERTY INSPECTED — BLDG. NO.	STREET	CITY
		850	Funston Avenue	San Francisco

Inspection Ordered By .... ABC Realty Company, 123 Tenth Avenue, Central City
Report Sent To and Date ... "   "   "   January 7, 19--

Owner's Name and Address ..
Buyer's Name and Address ...

INSPECTED BY P. Kesecker   LICENSE NO. 3418   SIGNED BY

Is this a complete inspection report Yes [ ] No [ ]. If no explain below in accordance with Sec. 1994. Number of pages of this report [ ]
Will this report comply with Regulation 1991 if all recommended work is completed? Yes [ ] No [ ] If no, explain below.
See reverse side for applicable sections of Structural Pest Control Act and Regulations.

EVIDENCE OF: (ALSO SEE DIAGRAM AND EXPLANATION BELOW)

LOCATIONS OF INFESTATIONS, INFECTIONS AND CONDUCIVE CONDITIONS ON DIAGRAM

LEGEND	1	2	3	4	5	6	7	8	9	10	11	12	13	14	15	16	17	18
S—Subterranean Termites	*	*	*		*	*												
K—Dry-wood Termites																		
Z—Dampwood Termites																		
F—Fungus or Dry Rot	*						*											
B—Beetles—Other Wood Destroying Insects																		
FG—Faulty Grade Levels	*		*				*											
EC—Earth-wood Contacts				*			*											
CD—Cellulose Debris																		
EM—Excessive Moisture Conditions																		
IV—Insufficient Ventilation																		
SL—Shower Leaks																		
IA—Inaccessible Areas					*													
D—Structural Damage																		
A—Attic																		
FI—Further Inspection Recommended																		

DIAGRAM AND EXPLANATION OF FINDINGS AND METHODS OF RECOMMENDED CORRECTIONS

General Description: This is a two story, single family frame dwelling. Stucco and wood exterior. Flat roof. No Attic. Garage in basement. No excessive moisture conditions found. Ventilation apparently normal. Faulty grade levels, See Item 1, 3, and 7. Concrete foundations coated with cement coating. Improved basement areas. Eight foot average joist clearance. Masonry front stairs. Wood service stairs. No structurally attached planters, patios or abutments.

FIGURE 5–3

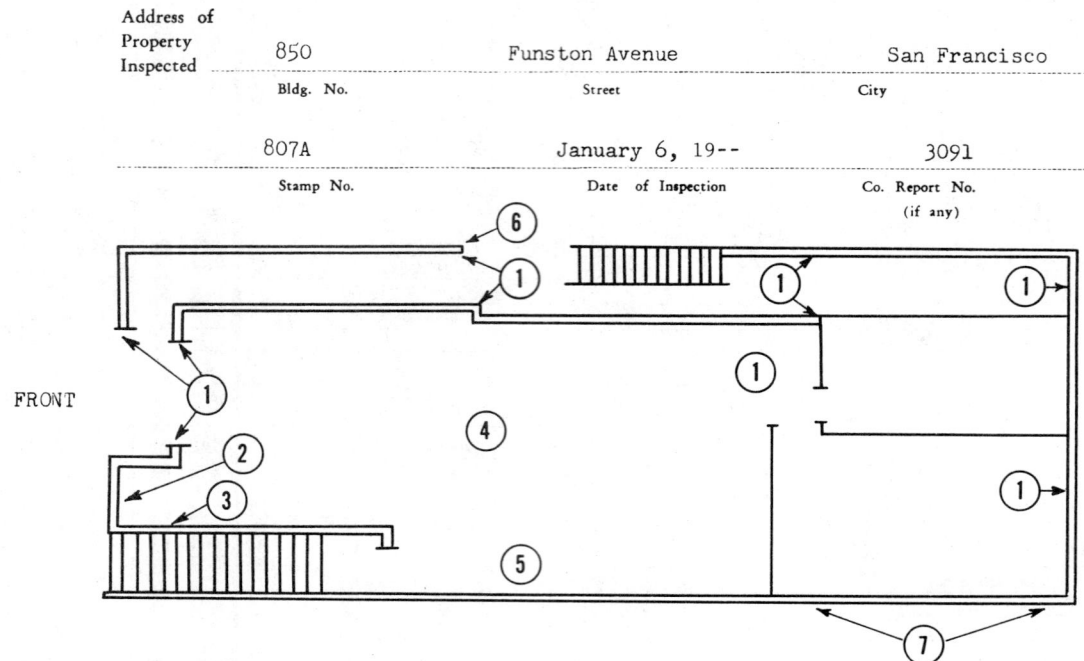

SECOND PAGE OF STANDARD INSPECTION REPORT ON THE PROPERTY LOCATED AT:

Address of Property Inspected: 850 Funston Avenue San Francisco
Bldg. No. / Street / City

807A   January 6, 19--   3091
Stamp No. / Date of Inspection / Co. Report No. (if any)

Findings and Recommendations:

1. Basement Areas - The indicated door framing extends well into concrete. Wood-rot and termite damage. Cut off and repair framing. Install concrete bases. Apply toxic chemicals.

2. Front Wall - Termite infestation in front wall. Scrape down termite tubes. Apply toxic chemicals.

3. Front Stairs - Bottom of framing extends through concrete. Termite infestation. Cut off and repair bottom of framing. Install concrete footings. Apply toxic chemicals.

4. Basement Areas - Covered walls and ceilings, wood framing not exposed.

5. Basement Areas - Termite infestation over foundation behind furnace. Scrape down termite tubes. Drill and apply toxic chemicals. Re-fill holes.

6. Service Alley - Termite infestation in corner. Scrape down termite tubes. Apply chemicals.

7. Perimeter Wall - Portions of foundation below exterior grade. Soil contact to base of wall, minor wood-rot. Cut off and repair bottom of wall. Increase foundation height. Apply toxic chemicals.

FIGURE 5-3 *(continued)*

All wall-to-wall carpeting and all drapes presently in the building shall remain and be included in the purchase price.

In addition to the foregoing, we commonly find such entries as:

The purchase price shall also include the stove and refrigerator presently in the building.

or

All furnishings presently in the building are to be included in the purchase price. These items are to be identified and listed separately on a Bill of Sale form, which shall be made a part of the escrow.

Anything affixed to a building with the intent that it be made a permanent part of the building is generally considered to be real property and automatically goes with the building for the purchase price stated in the deposit receipt.

Many times, however, there is a question about whether carpeting, drapes, a crystal chandelier in the entry hall or dining room, or other such items are to be automatically included in the purchase price. The buyer may think he is getting these items, while the seller may intend to remove some or all of them. It is obvious, then, that many kinds of items and fixtures may have to be mentioned in the deposit receipt in order to avoid future complications, which may delay closing of the transaction. Fixtures are items of personal property attached or incorporated into the land or building in such a manner that they become real property and are then considered part of the land or building.

The courts in California have utilized several general tests to determine whether or not an item of personal property has become a fixture. The two most important are (a) the intention of the person attaching or incorporating the personal property into the land or building, and (b) the particular method by which the property is actually incorporated or attached and the degree of damage that might result to the property were the item to be removed.

Closing costs

An item that will often appear under "conditions" on the deposit receipt relates to the closing costs to be paid by the buyer and/or seller in connection with the sale and purchase of the property. The buyer should never be allowed to assume that the deposit he puts down on the property will automatically take care of the closing costs. The responsible broker will explain to the prospective purchaser, even before the offer is made that a certain amount of money will be needed to pay for closing costs in connection with the purchase and that this money will have to be deposited in escrow prior to closing of the transaction. The purchaser should know that these costs are in addition to the purchase price. Closing costs, which will be discussed in greater detail in Chapter 8, dealing with escrows, generally include such items as the policy of title insurance, loans fees, and expenses as the result of insurance and tax prorations.

The broker may enter either of the following:

In addition to the down payment specified above, the purchaser is to pay normal closing costs incident to this transaction.

or

Buyer to be responsible for the payment in escrow, or approximately $3,000 for closing costs in connection with this sale and purchase.

Having completed our discussion of terms and conditions, let us now turn to the remaining printed portion of the deposit receipt (Figure 5-1).

Paragraph 2. If the purchaser gives the broker a small deposit at the time he makes the offer, it is general practice to have the deposit increased upon acceptance of the offer, usually to 10 percent of the purchase price. Thus, if a purchaser makes an offer of $135,000 on a property when conventional financing is planned and gives the licensee $2,000 as a deposit at the time the offer is made, the purchaser will have to deposit an additional $11,500 at the time that the seller accepts the offer and signs the deposit receipt.

Paragraph 3. The statement by the purchaser with respect to intention to occupy is important to the bank or savings and loan association. A copy of the purchase contract is generally submitted along with the loan application, and with respect to the purchase of single-family residences, a number of lenders are wary of speculators. Although intention not to occupy may merely signify an investment purchase, it can also mean a speculative purchase. A real estate licensee who falsifies such a disclosure is subject to disciplinary action by law.

Paragraph 4. Supplements incorporated as part of the purchase agreement are shown.

Paragraph 5. The law requires parties signing any document to be given a copy.

Paragraph 6. This clause provides spaces to state the number of days given to deliver escrow instructions and to close escrow. The payment of escrow fees is by local custom and is discussed in Chapter 8.

Paragraph 7. "Title is to be free of . . ." restricts the condition of the title to items of public record. In the blank line provided, some brokers enter: "Title subject to liens, encumbrances, conditions, and restrictions of public record only."

At this point, unless the broker has already had a preliminary title search made, it is difficult to know just what a search will disclose concerning the overall condition of the title. Certain restrictions may be disclosed which the purchaser does not wish to accept. Some brokers add a clause stating that the offer is subject to the buyers approval within a specified time of easements or other property restrictions disclosed by the preliminary title search.

Here we have a situation similar to that with regard to termite inspection. If the broker has a preliminary title search before writing up the offer, he will know the condition of the title and can discuss it with the prospective purchaser when the offer is made. In most cases, however, it is only after an offer has been received and accepted by the seller that escrow is opened and a title search ordered to disclose the condition of the title the seller has to convey.

If the preliminary title search reveals any defects in the title, it is the responsibility of the seller to remove them and to pay for any expenses incurred in so doing. If a seller is unable to convey a marketable title, or if the property is destroyed or substantially damaged prior to the actual transfer of title, the buyer is released from his contractual obligation and any deposits are returned.

Paragraph 7 further provides a space in which to enter the name of the title insurance company that will issue the title insurance policy, and to state who will pay for the title policy. Who pays for the title insurance policy is a matter of local custom and is discussed in Chapter 8.

Paragraph 8. "Property taxes, premiums on insurance . . ." is fairly self-explanatory and merely indicates that, where necessary, there shall be a proration of items as of the date of transfer of title. The necessary prorations are done by the escrow officer, and the results are shown on the buyer's and seller's statements. The items most commonly involved are taxes, rents, interest, insurance premiums, and expenses for which the buyer and/or seller may now be responsible. The amount of any bond or assessment that is a lien against the property is generally paid by the seller, as are any existing delinquencies. The seller customarily pays for any transfer taxes.

Paragraph 9. Normally, possession of the property passes from the seller to the buyer as of the close of escrow, since at this time, recordation of the deed and other necessary documents takes place, and title passes to the buyer.

It is very important for the broker to be certain that the seller understands this, since many times the seller thinks he has a reasonable amount of time after close of escrow in which to move out.

The broker must remember that while it may be normal for the seller to be a bit hesitant and want some time in which to move, the buyer becomes the legal owner of the property as of close of escrow and recordation and is responsible for his loan payments and taxes. In complete fairness to both the buyer and seller, if occupancy is not given on close of escrow, the deposit receipt shoud contain a condition stating *(a)* the exact number of days the seller has to remain on the property and *(b)* an amount of rent (per day) the seller is to pay to the buyer for these additional days beyond the close of escrow. The amount is the cost per day to the new owner for loan payment, insurance, and taxes.

If the buyer and seller agree, the escrow officer may be instructed to withhold from the seller's funds an amount equal to the entire rental for the agreed-to period of occupancy. When the escrow officer is later notified that the former owner has vacated the property, he will forward the amount of rental to the buyer. If the seller vacates before the full amount of time agreed on, the escrow officer will forward to the buyer what is due him and refund the difference to the seller.

Paragraph 10. This paragraph specifies the way in which the buyers wish to take title.

When the buyers ask the broker his opinion about how they should take title, the broker must remember that such advice may be regarded as practicing law, and the buyers should be advised to consult their attorney. This part of the deposit receipt form may then be left blank or the statement may be made that instructions are to follow and the information may later be given to the escrow officer.

Paragraph 11. If the broker is a member of multiple listing, the broker is given permission to disclose certain information about the transaction as required of members. However, the broker need not disclose any information in connection with the sale if the buyers and sellers wish such facts to be kept confidential.

Paragraph 12. California courts have generally held that clauses which provide for automatic retention or forfeiture of deposits are not valid.

To conform with the California Liquidated Damage Law, effective July 1978, this new liquidation damage clause is provided should buyer and seller wish to use it. If the buyer and seller initial the appropriate places in the clause, the law provides that if the buyer fails to perform and there is a breach of contract, the seller may retain as liquidated damages, from the deposit actually paid an amount not to exceed three percent of the purchase price of the property.

If the buyer and seller do not initial the appropriate places in the clause, it will not apply, and any disputes the parties may have with respect to the contract or deposit will hve to be settled by instituting legal action.

Paragraph 13. If acceptable to the parties and retained in the purchase contract, this clause provides that if a dispute is strictly with respect to disposition of buyer's deposit in event of a default, the matter shall be settled by arbitration in accordance with rules of the American Arbitration Association.

Paragraph 14. Standard clause contained in most contracts should legal action be necessary.

Paragraph 15. Time is of the essence of this contract. Most contracts contain a statement to the effect that time is of the essence. This phrase has its origin in the law and simply means that the time requirements of the contract must be strictly adhered to.

Paragraph 16. The usual amount of time given the seller to consider and accept the offer is one to two days, although the time is flexible and depends upon the particular situation. Most responsible brokers agree that an offer should be presented to the seller as soon as possible. It must be remembered that the prospective purchaser may withdraw his offer at any time prior to acceptance by the seller.

F. Space is provided for entering the name and address of the real estate firm and the signature of the licensee preparing the offer. A space is provided for the purchaser's signatures. If the purchasers are husband and wife, the licensee must obtain the signatures of both parties. A copy must be given to parties signing the contract.

G. The acceptance portion contains space for entering the name of the broker or brokers involved, the total sum of commission to be paid, and conditions upon which payment of the commission is due. Condition *(c)* takes into account that the parties may not have initialed the liquidated damages clause and that a suit in court or other negotiations may be necessary.

In the event that the listing and selling brokers are different, space is provided for inserting the names of the cooperating brokers. If the sellers are husband and wife, the broker must obtain the signatures of both parties. As with the buyer, the seller must also be given a copy of this deposit receipt; it is the broker's responsibility to be sure that all parties who have signed the deposit receipt receive a copy. It is sufficient that husband and wife receive a single copy.

The form concludes with a brief reminder of the respective functions of the real estate broker and attorney, and a brief statement with respect to the use limitations of this new form.

THE COUNTEROFFER

If the same broker represents both the buyer and the seller, he may have a better chance of writing up an offer that is completely acceptable to the seller and requires no counteroffer. The broker who obtains the listing is often (but not always) in a position to know just what the sellers are willing to accept and can base his discussion with the prospective purchasers on these facts. The broker who represents only the buyers is, of course, trying to get the best deal possible for them, and the terms and conditions of the offer he prepares may often weigh heavily in favor of his clients.

It is most advantageous if the selling broker and the listing broker are able to satisfactorily communicate with each other prior to the writing-up of the offer so that there will be a closer understanding of what is required to make the sale.

When all attempts to secure an acceptance of an offer have failed, the broker should certainly try to obtain a counteroffer from the seller. If the changes are minor, the counteroffer may be written on the reverse side of the original offer and begins with the following statement:

> All conditions of the deposit receipt as stipulated on the reverse side are acceptable to the seller with the following exceptions:

The broker then lists the exceptions, which may include such items as the purchase price, financing, possession, or termite provisions. The counteroffer is then signed and dated by the seller. If the changes in the original offer are major ones or are extremely long, then the broker should prepare a separate counteroffer. A CAR Counteroffer commonly used in such cases is illustrated in Figure 5–4.

Another alternative is for the broker to prepare a new deposit receipt containing changes the seller

COUNTER OFFER

THIS IS INTENDED TO BE A LEGALLY BINDING AGREEMENT — READ IT CAREFULLY

CALIFORNIA ASSOCIATION OF REALTORS ® STANDARD FORM

This is a counter offer to the Real Estate Purchase Contract and Receipt for Deposit dated _____, 19_____,
in which _____
is referred to as buyer and _____
is referred to as seller.

Seller accepts all of the terms and conditions set forth in the above designated agreement with the following changes or amendments:

_____
_____
_____
_____
_____
_____
_____
_____
_____
_____
_____
_____

The seller reserves the right to continue to offer the herein described property for sale and accept any offer acceptable to him at anytime prior to personal delivery to seller or _____, seller's authorized agent, of a copy of this counter-offer, duly accepted and signed by buyer. Unless this counter offer is accepted in this manner on or before _____, 19____ at _____ it shall be deemed revoked and the deposit shall be returned to the buyer.

Receipt of a copy hereof is hereby acknowledged.

DATED: _____, 19____   _____
                                                                              SELLER
TIME: _____   _____
                                                                              SELLER

The undersigned buyer nereby accepts the above counter offer.

_____
_____
_____
_____
_____

Receipt of a copy hereof is hereby acknowledged.

DATED: _____, 19____   _____
                                                                              BUYER
TIME: _____   _____
                                                                              BUYER

Receipt of buyer's acceptance is hereby acknowledged and seller agrees to sell on the terms and conditions set forth above.

DATE: _____, 19____   _____
                                                                              SELLER
TIME: _____   _____
                                                                              SELLER

NO REPRESENTATION IS MADE AS TO THE LEGAL VALIDITY OF ANY PROVISION OR THE ADEQUACY OF ANY PROVISION IN ANY SPECIFIC TRANSACTION. A REAL ESTATE BROKER IS THE PERSON QUALIFIED TO ADVISE ON REAL ESTATE. IF YOU DESIRE LEGAL ADVICE CONSULT YOUR ATTORNEY.

FIGURE 5-4

RELEASE OF REAL ESTATE PURCHASE CONTRACT AND RECEIPT FOR DEPOSIT

CALIFORNIA ASSOCIATION OF REALTORS® STANDARD FORM
THIS IS INTENDED TO BE A LEGALLY BINDING CONTRACT. READ IT CAREFULLY.

The undersigned Buyer and Seller who were parties to that certain Real Estate Purchase Contract and Receipt for Deposit dated, _____, 19____, covering the following described property:

_____
_____
_____
_____
_____
_____
_____
_____

hereby mutually release each other from any and all claims, actions or demands which each may have up to the date of this Agreement against the other by reason of said Real Estate Purchase Contract and Receipt for Deposit.

It is the intent of this Agreement that all rights and obligations arising out of said Real Estate Purchase Contract and Receipt for Deposit are declared null and void.

_____ holding
(Name of Broker or Escrow Holder)

the deposit under the terms of said Real Estate Purchase Contract and Receipt for Deposit is hereby directed and instructed to disburse said deposit in the following manner:

$_____ TO _____
$_____ TO _____
$_____ TO _____
$_____ TO _____

Dated _____   Dated _____

Buyer _____   Seller _____

             _____   _____

Dated _____   Dated _____

Broker _____   Broker _____

By _____   By _____

FIGURE 5–5

wants. The seller signs and dates the acceptance portion of the deposit receipt, and it is presented to the buyer. If it is acceptable, the buyer signs it, thus creating a completed deposit receipt and binding contract.

Negotiations may continue back and forth for some time until there is a meeting of the minds, but the effective broker keeps trying as long as there is a chance for agreement between buyer and seller.

If another broker brings in an offer during these negotiations, or if the listing broker receives an offer from a prospective purchaser, these offers must be presented to the seller for his consideration and possible acceptance.

Thus, speed is of the essence in a real estate transaction, for while you may be discussing some minor point of contention with your client, another broker will bring in just the offer the seller wants and successfully sell the property.

NONPERFORMANCE

What happens if the deposit receipt is properly signed by all parties to the transaction and then one of them decides that he does not want to go through with the transaction as agreed?

If the buyer fails to perform, the seller may do any of the following:

1. The seller may declare the contract void and return the buyer's deposit.
2. The seller may declare the contract void and refuse to return the buyer's deposit. The buyer, of course, may agree to a forfeit of his deposit, or he may bring suit against the seller for a return of the deposit.
3. The seller may sue the buyer for specific performance or damages.

If the seller fails to perform, the buyer may do any of the following.

1. He may agree to termination of the contract and the return of his deposit.
2. He may agree to termination of the contract and allow the seller to keep the deposit (although this rarely occurs).
3. He may sue the seller for specific performance.

For all practical purposes, it may be correctly said that suits for specific performance rarely occur in everyday transactions. The time and expense involved make this remedy impractical. Only in a very large and complex transaction will court action for specific performance occur.

Figure 5–5 illustrates a form which releases both parties from a deposit receipt.

OPTION TO PURCHASE REAL ESTATE

An option agreement was discussed in Chapter 3 in connection with a broker taking an option agreement and listing combined. An option agreement is a separate form of contract, however, and it is used in a variety of cases independent of any listing agreement.

The option agreement is defined as a contract to make a contract or as an agreement to hold an offer open for a specific period of time usually in consideration for a monetary payment.

An option to purchase property is usually obtained from an owner (optionor) by a prospective purchaser (optionee) in order to give the purchaser the exclusive right to buy it during the term of the option. If the prospective purchaser decides to exercise the option and purchase the property, the monetary consideration for the option is usually credited toward the purchase price. If the optionee does not decide to purchase, the consideration is retained by the optionor.

The terms and conditions of sale may be fully contained in an option agreement, but in certain transactions where the terms and conditions are very complex and detailed, an option agreement is attached to a purchase contract which is later signed and completed by the optionor and optionee.

Options are used in different ways. Builders may request an option on a number of lots, a corporate purchaser may use options to acquire adjacent parcels of land, or a lessee may request a lease-option agreement from an owner in order to later purchase the property.

Additional forms, applicable to this chapter, are illustrated in Appendix C as Figures C5–1 thru C5–4.

QUESTIONS FOR DISCUSSION

1. Discuss the essentials of a valid estate contract.
2. How may the problem of termite inspection be minimized by the broker?
3. Discuss the problem of fixtures with regard to the sale of a residence, and explain how it may be minimized by the broker.
4. What are the important provisions that should be included in any agreement for the sale of real property?
5. How does the deposit receipt form used by brokers

in your community differ, if at all, from the CREA form discussed in the text?

6. Discuss any particularly unique conditions that may be included in a deposit receipt in your particular locality.

7. Assuming you are the listing broker, what courses of action might you suggest to your seller with respect to the deposit of a buyer who wants to back out of the agreement through no fault of the seller?

8. What do you think the seller of a vacant property should do if the buyer wants occupancy prior to close of escrow?

9. With respect to purchase of a single-family residence, what are the advantages and disadvantages of a specific performance suit?

10. As a real estate licensee, when and where do you prefer to meet with your clients to prepare the purchase contract?

6
Advertising

Students of advertising are informed that the first advertisement in the American newspaper to offer a commodity for sale was placed by William Bradford in the *Boston News-Letter,* May 8, 1704, as follows.

> At Oysterbay, on Long Island in the Province of N. York. There is a very good Fulling-Mill to be Let or Sold, as also a Plantation, having on it a large new Brick house, and another good house by it for a Kitchin and warehouse, with a Barn, Stable &c. a young Orchard and 20 acres clear Land. The Mill is to be Let with or without the Plantation; Enquire of Mr. William Bradford Printer in N. York, and know further.

Well over 250 years later, the broker who places a classified advertisement in the real estate section of his local newspaper wants the same result Mr. Bradford wanted—that the reader of the ad shall "Enquire . . . and know further."

The quantity and types of advertising the individual broker will undertake will, of course, depend on the size and the type of organization involved. The small office will continue to depend on classified advertising, For Sale signs on listed properties, and small ads in local neighborhood merchant's publications, while a large real estate firm will spend a substantial part of its budget on large-scale advertising of all types and forms.

THE A-I-D-A APPROACH

Regardless of the specific form or type of advertising used, the ultimate goal is the same and is generally referred to as the A-I-D-A Approach. The advertising media must begin by attracting *Attention;* once attention has been obtained, the next step is to create *Interest* in the specific product or service offered; then a *Desire* for the product or service must be stimulated; and, finally, the individual must be compelled to take *Action* to satisfy the desire. Thus, any successful form of advertising successfully stimulates Attention, Interest, Desire, and Action in the individual to whom such advertising is directed.

AREAS OF ADVERTISING

Real estate advertising falls into two general areas. The first area is general advertising, also commonly called institutional advertising. The second area is specific advertising, also commonly called Operational Advertising.

General advertising takes in all media and forms that the real estate office, allied organizations, and the industry as a whole employ in order to present a certain picture or image to the public. Specific advertising deals mainly with the ways in which a firm presents to the potential purchaser individual properties it has listed. The form mainly used is the classified advertisement in the real estate section of a newspaper.

GENERAL ADVERTISING

For the individual office, general advertising is concerned with the images of the firm, the broker, the salesmen, and other employees in the community in which they operate.

The firm should project the proper professional image in the community and should build a sound reputation for honesty, integrity, and adherence to a high standard of ethical behavior. Each person associated with a real estate office is, each and every day, the firm's walking advertisement to people with whom he or she may come into contact. Participation in the activities of the local board, the local multiple listing service, and the state and national associations will help to build the correct image and reputation desired.

Service activity is another area to be considered. Involvement in groups such as Rotary and Lions, in church and religious organizations, and in scouting, will bring the licensee into contact with many persons and broaden the base from which clients will be attracted. Another area is the civic one composed of local neighborhood merchants' associations, neighborhood homeowner groups, chambers of commerce, and private and public charitable groups. A broker should take part in as many of these activities as he can, and if possible, he should be active in planning and zoning work in his community. All this not only results in worthwhile work but also will increase the broker's area of influence and constantly add to the number of his personal contacts. The more friends and acquaintances the licensee can gather, the more referrals of real estate business he will obtain.

Trade association advertising

Local real estate boards, the California Real Estate Association, and the National Association of Realtors are constantly engaged in presenting to the public information and materials relating to the real estate industry. The advantages of homeownership, investment in real property, and the services rendered by the Realtor are constantly being stressed.

A continuing program of advertising is carried on by banks and title insurance companies, and much of it relates to the sale or purchase of real estate.

Since newspapers receive more real estate advertising dollars than does any other media, newspaper editors insert many items that tend to increase their readers' interest and desire about real estate in general. Figure 6–1 and Table 6–1 are examples of such materials.

Specific forms of general office advertising

The many specific forms of general advertising are limited solely by the imagination and ingenuity of the broker. The most common forms, however, are as follows.

Signs. Prerequisites for the success of a sign are that it be attractive, quickly informative, and unique, if possible. Whether the firm decides to use special colors, type of print, a slogan, or special arrangement, it should be carried through on all

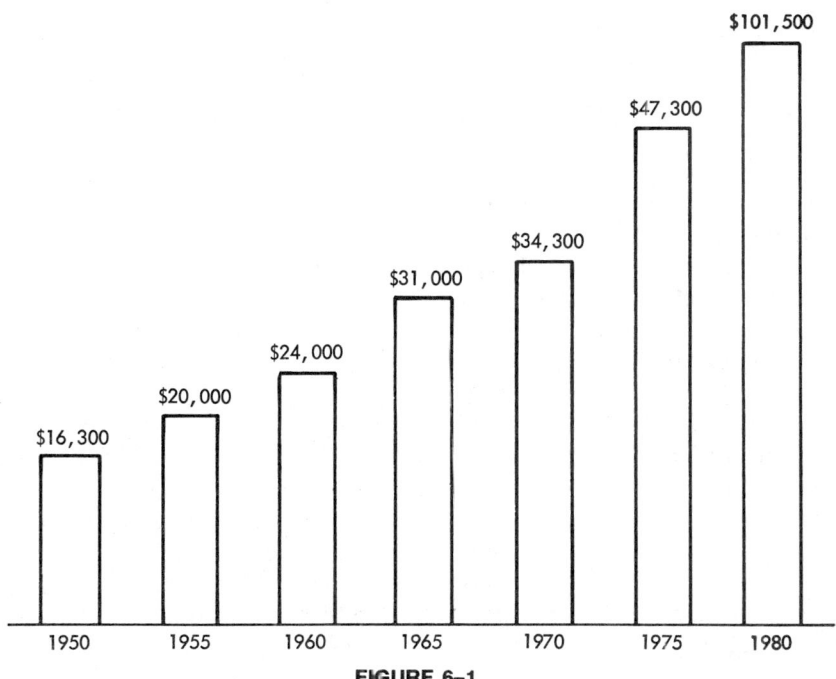

CALIFORNIA SINGLE FAMILY HOME PRICES
(in thousands of dollars)

FIGURE 6–1

TABLE 6–1
Projected California housing needs 1979–1984 (in thousands)

	1976	1977	1978	1979	1980	1981	1982	1983	1984
Natural increase*	—	174	178	181	184	187	190	194	197
Net migration†	—	204	233	210	210	210	210	210	210
Net change from preceding year*	—	375	411	391	394	397	400	404	407
Civilian Population‡	21,239	21,614	22,025	22,416	22,810	23,207	23,607	24,011	24,418
Household size§	2.73	2.71	2.67	2.64	2.61	2.58	2.56	2.54	2.52
Number of households	7,780	7,976	8,249	8,491	8,739	8,995	9,221	9,453	9,690
Number of new households	—	196	273	249	248	256	226	232	237
Vacancies	—	6	8	7	7	8	7	7	7
Demolitions	—	60	60	60	60	60	60	60	60
Housing need	—	262	341	309	315	314	293	299	304

* The figure for 1977 is from the California Statistical Abstract, 1978
† The figures for 1977, 1978: Population Research Unit of the Department of Finance as cited in L.A. Times, Dec. 20, 1978
‡ The figures for 1977: California Statistical Abstract, 1978
§ The figures for 1976–1978: Population Research Unit

printed materials used by the office where possible.

Cards and stationery. The same rules mentioned in relation to signs apply here. The makeup of the stationery letterhead and the business card should be in good taste and informative, and the quality of the paper and printing shold be such that the result is not a cheap, mass-produced appearance.

Giveaways. This type of advertising may be of limited value, but many firms still include in their advertising budget a sum for the purchase of giveaway items such as pencils, ball-point pens, calendars, and the like. The idea behind this type of advertising is to keep the name of the firm constantly before the user of the item. Akin to this type of advertising is a gift to a satisfied client, such as a subscription to *Sunset* magazine or a nameplate for the front entrance of a home.

Special publication ads. Many types of publications are produced on special occasions or reach a particular group of persons in the community. The local high school yearbook, the annual lodge yearbook, charity programs, and special Christmas or Easter publications are all areas for insertion of real estate firm advertisements. The type of advertisement is a general one and not related to any specific property but is intended merely to place the name of the firm before as many people as possible.

Direct mail. Such advertising consists of letters, pamphlets, brochures, postal cards, booklets, and other similar items, which may be mailed to a limited number of selected persons or to residents of a large geographic area. The material a large developer sends out may include informative and descriptive literature, a map of the tract or area of land offered, pictures and plans, and statements from experts or satisfied clients as to the attractiveness and value of the particular offering.

A real estate office might issue a monthly bulletin or booklet listing the various offerings available through the office and showing pictures of some of these properties. Often, a brochure with information and pictures will be prepared for a single offering, such as a motel, an office building, or an expensive house.

Another quite popular form of direct mailing is letters or postal cards sent to persons who live in the immediate vicinity of a property the office has listed for sale. Many times a neighbor will have a relative or a business acquaintance who may want to settle in the area, and the postal card will notify him that a house close to his is available. Even if the person does not have someone to refer, he may himself want to look at the property, and his coming into contact with a member of the firm may lead to his becoming a client in the future. After a sale has been made, many offices send a card.

TV and radio advertising. This area of advertising has not been generally used to any great extent by real estate offices. Television reaches a limited audience and is quite expensive as far as its use for an average listing is concerned. Among the few users of television may be a large developer who wants to advertise a big tract development, and the TV aspect is merely a part of a wide-scale plan of advertising that involves all forms and costs a considerable amount of money. The same is generally true of radio, with the exception of a small number of real estate firms who sponsor alone, or cosponsor with other local business firms, a regular news or sports type of program.

News releases. Many items in the news section of a newspaper, large city daily or small town weekly, are concerned with the sale, purchase, exchange, modernization, or construction of real property. The more often an individual broker can get his name or the name of his firm incorporated in a favorable news story, the better known he will become in his community. Many persons seek out a particular real estate firm, not because they have transacted business with them in the past or have been referred by someone, but simply because the firm has a favorable reputation and its name is known to all who reside in the area.

The broker should become acquainted with the person at his local newspaper who is responsible for accepting news releases. If the item submitted by the broker has genuine news value and is correctly prepared, it stands a chance of appearing in print. The information submitted should be typewritten and double-spaced on standard-size typing paper, and should tell and answer who, what, when, where, why, and how. The type of situation that lends itself to use as a news release may be: (*a*) announcement of the sale of a particularly large or well-known property, (*b*) a new monthly sales record, (*c*) announcement of construction of a new tract of homes or an apartment complex, (*d*) moving of the firm to larger and more modern quarters, (*e*) opening of a branch office to better serve a particular locale, and (*f*) announcement of a recreational or retirement development. The broker alert to the value of this type of publicity will attempt to use the news release whenever possible, since it not only is an excellent means of attracting potential clients but also is free of charge to the broker.

Outdoor advertising. This type of advertising usually takes the form of a billboard, either free-standing along a roadway or affixed to a building, or of a message painted directly on a building. Billboard ads are generally used only by large developers and are usually found along a highway leading to the particular tract of houses for sale.

Individual offices seldom regularly use billboards. The only exception is the broker in a smaller community who may maintain a sign adjacent to the main highway into town in order to present the name and location of the office to persons entering. In many resort and vacation areas, a broker will maintain next to his office a large bulletin board type of sign with a blackboard surface that enables him to write in with chalk various rentals available as well as properties for sale.

Window displays. A commonly used method of presenting information to the public is through the use of an attractive display in the windows of the real estate office and elsewhere. Interesting messages attractively presented, along with pictures of properties either recently sold or now for sale, will cause passersby to stop and take note.

CLASSIFIED ADVERTISING

The most common form of specific advertising is the classified advertisement. This is by far the most used method of real estate advertising, consuming the bulk of the advertising budget. A recent survey by the National Institute of Real Estate Brokers reported that almost 50 percent of all sales made by brokerage firms can be directly traced to classified advertising.

A new broker's most difficult job is to begin his program of classified advertising. Once he has mastered the techniques of writing a good ad and has experienced the results obtained, the process becomes less difficult, and the broker merely continues to use the type and form of ad he believes gains the best results for him. Samples of classified ads are shown in Figure 6–2.

In a survey conducted by the University of California, recent home buyers in the San Francisco-Oakland Bay Area were asked, "What attracted you to a particular real estate office and led to the purchase of this home?" The answers were:

32 percent, newspaper advertisement.
27 percent, For Sale sign on the property.
30 percent, individual referral and personal contact.
7 percent, open house.
4 percent, other.

Writing the classified ad

Classified advertising is expensive, and a continuing program requires that the broker write an ad that is direct and to the point. If it is too wordy, it will cost more than it should. If too small and abbreviated, it will fail to attract the attention of the reader, and the broker will not get his money's worth from the ad.

The parts of the ad may be thought of as the (*a*) heading, (*b*) body of the ad, and (*c*) closing.

• 3200 sq. ft. of charm

This gracious home is located on over ½ acre high in Friendly Hills. Custom built and thoughtfully planned in every detail by present owner. 4 Bdrms. and Rumpus Rm. or could be 5th bedroom, plus delightful 29 ft. family room w/frplc. and inside BBQUE. 4 baths, sep. formal dining room. 20 ft. master bdrm. with view and private bath. Lovely grounds provide beautiful setting for the SPARKLING 40' POOL. Large covered patio and tropical landscaping give complete seclusion. Many special features include 2 forced-air furnaces, 2 water heaters, extra closed and storage space, carpeting, draperies, shutters, sprinklers. A most outstanding value at $289,000

COUNTRY CLUB

Here is a neighborhood which reflects pride of ownership. It is refined and exclusive. The home has over 2100 sq. ft. of living space including 3 large bedrooms, family room.

18-HOLE GOLF COURSE
$179,000 and $183,500
Immediate Occupancy
san juan hills
This is your last chance

to buy the popular "Islander" model designed for the growing family. Four king-sized bedrooms (including the favorite master bedroom suite complete with separate dressing room and yards of closets), three baths, large family room. Balanced Power kitchen with all the extras.

Speculator

OR DECORATOR—A chance to use your imagination. This FABULOUS VIEW is structurally sound, but it needs glamourizing. 3 bedrms., 2½ baths. UNUSUALLY SPACIOUS. A possible 100% return on a SMALL INVESTMENT.

ORANGES—LEMONS & ROSES
A profusion of fruit bearing trees midst horticultural splendor & a huge shade tree adorns this large fenced yard. 2 bedrooms and dining room or den, 1½ ba. Blk. from school, church & shopping. Wide street w/sidewalks. PRICED for IMMED. SALE. $89,950.

---

1 BR., DEN-2 BATH
AND
2 BR., DEN-3 BATH

Luxury homes surrounded by the Capistrano Country Club's soon-to-be completed

---

✓ $5,000 DOWN!

30' POOL + 2 Bedroom, 2 bath-Ranch! NEAR Valley Plaza! EVAPORATIVE AIR. 17' Living Room wall-to-wall carpeting. Tile family

---

"A LOVE AFFAIR"

Is inevitable when you see this handsome 4-bedroom, 2½ bath home + a tremendous 15x30 family room, approx. 2500 sq. ft., wall-to-wall carpets, drapes. F.A. heat, beautifully landscaped, within walking distance

FIGURE 6-2

The heading of the ad is most important, since this is what attracts reader attention. Remember that your ad will be competing with many others on the same page, and you want the reader, as he scans across the page, to be attracted to your particular ad. If the heading attracts the reader's attention, he will then go on to read the body of the ad, which should contain whatever the broker feels is most important about the particular piece of property, such as number of rooms, baths, special features, price, grounds, and location. Finally, each ad should contain as a closing the name, address, and telephone number of the firm.

The classified ad allows the broker to use a small space for a tightly worded teaser message. It should lay the foundation of desire in the mind of the reader. This is the secret—create curiosity, desire, and action with pertinent description and imaginative phrases that make properties come alive for your prospective clients. Basic facts will always work to your advantage if you search out the words that make them excitingly desirable.

The heading of the ad

Each property has at least one and usually several outstanding selling points. The broker should pick out the selling point he wants to stress the most and feature it in his heading. The following are a few of the many types of features that may be stressed in the heading.

Location. Many persons look for property in a particular geographic area or section of a city. They will quickly spot an ad that immediately indicates the area of their choice.

Physical feature. Emphasis may often be placed on a particular physical feature of the property offered for sale. The broker may want to point up the number of bedrooms and baths, the square footage, a pool, many rooms, a family room, a modern kitchen, or a den.

Price and terms. A low down payment, a reduced price, or an exceptional buy are items of interest to prospective purchasers. Many persons may be able to make substantial monthly payments but do not have a big down payment, so a small initial payment is an important factor for them in looking for a house. The availability of an FHA loan is important as is any means that will allow purchase with a minimum amount of cash necessary. Regulation Z of the Truth-in-Lending Law affects the use of credit terms in advertising the sale of residential property. It is permissible to advertise in general terms, but if the specific amount of down payment or interest charge is stated, the broker must include other required information in the advertisement. The Truth-in-Lending Law is discussed in detail in Chapter 7, Finance.

Special features. In addition to the physical features within a building, many special features will attract a buyer, such as a view, gracious grounds, an adjacent recreational facility, or a particular type of architecture and style.

Speculation or work needed. Often, a broker will have a piece of property that is dirty and in need of repair. If repaired, it would sell for much more, so the appeal is to either a speculator who may want to buy the property, fix it up, and then sell it, or to a person who is a handyman and feels that he can save money by moving in and taking care of the necessary repairs over a period of time.

Attention getters. Many types of headlines are used merely for the purpose of attracting attention so that the reader will continue to the body of the ad. Because the heading is meaningless by itself, the reader usually is curious enough to finish the message.

Any imaginative licensee can think up many additional headings, and in many cases, a heading may incorporate more than one of the features already discussed.

The body of the ad

Having been attracted to the advertisement by the heading, the body of the ad should present whatever information the broker feels necessary in order to compel the reader to inquire further. Where newspaper advertising rates are high, the broker may arrange his ads in various ways, depending on the amount of his advertising budget and the number of ads he runs in the newspaper each week. The broker may:

1. Use a large-size heading and condense the body of the ad in order to save space.
2. Use a small heading and put more of the message into the body of the ad.
3. If his budget allows, use a large heading and also a good size and descriptive body to present the necessary information.
4. Use a block ad instead of individual ads. The block ad places all the offerings of the firm in one large advertisement, and individual headings are usually kept down to a single line preceding each individual offering.

Special forms

Builders, developers, and some large firms often run advertisements that are unique in form and take a large amount of space. The size is usually such that anyone reading the classified section cannot help but notice this particular ad. The advertising department of most larger newspapers usually employs a person who is expert in this field and will help the advertiser to set up and arrange the design of his particular advertisement. This service is available to the small broker as well and can be very helpful to one inexperienced in arrangement and construction of material.

Box or block ad

Many brokers prefer to lump together in a single ad all the properties they want to advertise, while other brokers prefer to run a separate ad for each offering. When the different offerings are run together, they are referred to as box, block, or column ads, while individual ads are called either individual or single ads. The choice is one of individual taste on the part of the broker. Since most brokers want the reader to feel that their particular firm has a good variety of listings, the broker with a few ads to run may place them individually throughout the classified page, thinking that the reader who spots the name of the firm a number of times will be favorably impressed. On the other hand, the broker who has several offerings to present may feel that one large block ad with the name of the firm clearly evident, usually in large type at the top, will also be quite impressive to the reader. Many newspapers give a slightly reduced rate to the broker who regularly advertises and uses a minimum number of column inches of space each week, as against the broker who places a number of single ads at will.

Closing the ad

The most common method of closing the ad is to give the name, address, and telephone number of the firm. This is usually in a type size somewhat larger than the body of the ad. In single ads, the closing is usually at the bottom only, while in other forms, the information may be at both top and bottom.

ANSWERING AD CALLS

Successful advertisements and signs on property result in calls from prospective purchasers, and the real estate licensee must be ready to properly handle and take care of such calls. The goal of the licensee is to make an appointment with the caller

CALIFORNIA ASSOCIATION OF REALTORS
505 Shatto Place   Los Angeles, California 90020

SWITCH SHEET

1. Ad Heading _____   3. Ad Heading _____

   Other Properties   Price, etc.   Other Properties   Price, etc.

   1. _____   _____   1. _____   _____
   2. _____   _____   2. _____   _____
   3. _____   _____   3. _____   _____

2. Ad Heading _____   4. Ad Heading _____

   Other Properties   Price, etc.   Other Properties   Price, etc.

   1. _____   _____   1. _____   _____
   2. _____   _____   2. _____   _____
   3. _____   _____   3. _____   _____

For these forms address California Association of Realtors, 505 Shatto Place, Los Angeles 90020. All rights reserved. Copyright 1973 by California Association of Realtors.

FORM SW-1

FILE REF. _____

Incoming Call Register

GOALS
1. Create Favorable Image
2. Make appointment soon as possible

REMINDER QUESTIONS

Name?   Address?   Phone No.?   What area preferred?   What type home?
What price range?   How many in family?   Ages?   What area work in?   Will you sell present home?   Any special requirements?   Would you like list of available homes in preferred area?   What is convenient time for appointment?

Ad Reference _____ Date _____   Family Information _____

Address of Home In Ad _____   Now Owns or Rents _____

Name of Caller _____   ➤ Date and Time of Appointment _____

Address _____ Phone _____   Comments _____

Area Desired _____   _____

Special Requirements _____   Follow Up _____

Type of Home _____ Price Range _____

Type or Place of Employment _____

FORM ICR-1   For these forms address California Real Estate Association
505 Shatto Place, Los Angeles 90020. All rights reserved.

FIGURE 6-3

to show property. In order to do this, the licensee must be familiar with all of the company listings including those being advertised and those which display a company sign.

To prepare for ad calls, the licensee should paste on a sheet of paper copies of all company ads currently appearing in local newspapers and have them on his desk. He must also have quick access to information on all other company listings. When a prospective purchaser calls about a specific property, the licensee must know the property and be able to discuss its main features, price, and terms. In addition, he must be familiar with similar properties or acceptable alternatives.

Switch sheet and call register

Figure 6–3 illustrates a switch sheet and incoming call register. The switch sheet is used to show properties similar to those being advertised. The incoming call register follows the principle that whoever asks the questions controls the conversation. The caller will refer to a particular ad or piece of property and ask a few questions. The licensee must answer the caller's inquiries and then take control of the conversation by use of the questions on the call register.

After a few minutes of conversation, the caller should begin to feel at ease with the licensee, and the licensee can arrange for an appointment to meet the caller, show specific properties, and successfully effect a sale.

Being prepared is a necessary ingredient to success in making appointments and subsequent sales.

QUESTIONS FOR DISCUSSION

1. What are the essential elements of any successful form of advertising?
2. What are some of the ways in which the individual licensee may become involved in the general advertising of the firm?
3. How do you feel about the practice of putting For Sale signs on property?
4. How does trade association advertising help the individual broker?
5. What type of real estate firm do you think could best benefit by direct mail advertising?
6. What do you feel are the advantages or disadvantages of a box or block ad?
7. Who do you think should pay for the cost of advertising in a small- or medium-size real estate firm?
8. In what way might an ad for a single-family residence differ from an ad for an apartment building?
9. How may a news release be helpful to a real estate broker?
10. What is meant by a word-of-mouth advertising?

7

Financing real estate

Very few persons who purchase real estate are capable of paying, or would want to pay, all cash for the property. In virtually all real estate transactions, some form of financing is necessary to enable the buyer to borrow the money he needs to effect the purchase. Usually, a purchaser has a certain amount of money for a down payment and borrows the remainder needed to meet the purchase price. The purchaser will execute a note for the money borrowed and secure this note by executing a deed of trust in favor of the lender.

Persons entering into a discussion of real estate finance will use the term "mortgage" many times. Actually, a true mortgage contract is very seldom used in California. The device used instead is the deed of trust. Thus, when an individual in California refers to a mortgage on his property, he is really referring to a loan, which is actually in the form of a note secured by a deed of trust. Title Insurance and Trust Company, one of California's largest, reported that in 1976, the deed of trust was used in 98.8 percent of all property transactions recorded by them. A discussion of the reasons behind the widespread use of the deed of trust as against the mortgage will follow discussion of the promissory note.

THE PROMISSORY NOTE

The promissory note is the principal instrument used to evidence the obligation or debt and is a negotiable instrument. California Civil Code contains the Uniform Commercial Code, which defines the rules governing promissory notes.

There are basically three kinds of promissory notes.

The *straight note* calls for payment of interest only during the term of the note and the full amount of the principal when the note falls due.

The *installment note* calls for periodic payments on the principal, such payments being separate from the interest payments.

The *fully amortized installment note* is most commonly used in California. This note requires certain periodic payments (usually monthly) of fixed amounts. The amount includes payment on both the principal and interest and is calculated so as to render the note fully paid at the end of the term. The periodic payments are usually referred to as installments, and thus, many persons refer to this type of note as an installment note. However, the correct definition is a fully amortized installment note.

The promissory note is a negotiable instrument freely transferrable in commerce. In order to be negotiable, the Uniform Commercial Code requires that the following be incorporated into the note: (a) The note must contain an unconditional promise, (b) in writing, (c) made by one person to another, (d) signed by the maker, (e) promising to pay on demand or at a fixed or determinable future time, (f) a certain sum of money, (g) payable to order or to the bearer.

The negotiability of a note is not affected by inclusion of a clause adding court costs and reasonable attorney's fees if litigation becomes necessary in order to collect; neither does inclusion of an acceleration clause, which provides that default in one or more of the payments makes the entire principal amount immediately due. In fact, these and similar provisions actually make the note more attractive to lenders and thus may be said to enhance negotiability.

It should be remembered with regard to real estate loans that the lender usually reserves the right to approve any person or persons to whom the loan may be subsequently transferred by the original borrower.

7 / FINANCING REAL ESTATE

Do Not Destroy This Original Note: When paid, said Original Note, together with the Deed of Trust securing same, must be surrendered to Trustee for Cancellation and retention before reconveyance will be made.

NOTE SECURED BY DEED OF TRUST
(INSTALLMENT—INTEREST INCLUDED)

$ 93,000.00   Sacramento, California, October 1, 19--

In installments as herein stated, for value received, I promise to pay to ABC Savings and Loan Association, 100 Kennedy Drive, Sacramento, California _____, or order,
at 100 Kennedy Drive, Sacramento, California
the sum of Ninety-three Thousand .... (93,000.00) DOLLARS,
with interest from October 1, 19-- on unpaid principal at the rate of 11½ per cent per annum; principal and interest payable in installments of Nine hundred twenty dollars and 98/100 Dollars
or more on the 1st day of each month, beginning on the 1st day of November, 19--

_____ and continuing until said principal and interest have been paid.

Each payment shall be credited first on interest then due and the remainder on principal; and interest shall thereupon cease upon the principal so credited. Should default be made in payment of any installment when due the whole sum of principal and interest shall become immediately due at the option of the holder of this note. Principal and interest payable in lawful money of the United States. If action be instituted on this note I promise to pay such sum as the Court may fix as attorney's fees. This note is secured by a DEED OF TRUST to TITLE INSURANCE AND TRUST COMPANY, a California corporation, as trustee.

(s) John Purchaser

(s) Mary Purchaser

TO 417.1 CA (11-68)   THIS FORM FURNISHED BY TITLE INSURANCE AND TRUST COMPANY
DO NOT DESTROY THIS NOTE

FIGURE 7-1

Figure 7-1 is an illustration of a fully amortized installment note. Reference to an amortization table will disclose that $93,000 at 11½ percent, with payments of $920.98 monthly, will mean a term of 30 years. The date of the last payment due is not shown on the note, since the note states that the borrowers are to pay $920.98 "or more" on the first day of each month. This allows the borrowers, should they so desire, to increase their monthly payment and pay the loan off in a shorter time. The provision under which such prepayment may take place is only one of a number of subjects that will be covered in a separate agreement between the borrower and lender. All lending institutions have a rather lengthy set of conditions and regulations under which the loan is being made, and the borrowers must accept these prior to obtaining the loan.

Holder in due course

If any of the previously listed essential requirements for negotiability is missing in the document, it is still valuable and transferrable in much the same manner as an ordinary contract. As such, the transferee or assignee will receive no more than the transferor had, and defenses that were good against the assigner are good against the assignee. However, it is possible with regard to a valid negotiable instrument that the transferee may receive more than the transferor had. If the holder of the instrument transfers it to a third party, who takes the notes as a holder in due course, then the one who takes the note may enjoy a favored position.

A holder in due course is one who has taken a negotiable instrument with the following conditions present:

1. The instrument, when taken, was complete and regular in appearance and form.
2. The instrument, when negotiated, was not overdue and was without notice of previous dishonor.
3. The instrument was taken in good faith and for a valuable consideration.
4. At the time it was negotiated to him, the person receiving the note had no knowledge of any infirmity in the instrument or any defect in the title of the negotiator.

If one who takes a note and qualifies as a holder in due course brings an action to collect on the note, the maker of the note cannot use any of the following defenses to refuse payment.

1. A lack or failure of consideration. The maker of the note cannot refuse payment by claiming that he has not received what the payee promised to give him for the note.
2. A claim of prior payment or cancellation. If the maker of the note actually pays the amount due to the payee but fails to receive proof that he has paid, and the payee meanwhile transfers the note to a holder in due course, the original maker may be still held responsible. This is one of the reasons why one who pays off a note should be sure he receives proof of payment. Such proof will usually be the note itself marked paid.
3. A claim of fraud in the inducement.
4. A setoff. A claim that the note was a setoff might be made when, for instance, the maker owes the payee $20,000 on the note, but the payee owes the maker $30,000 on another obligation.

The previous defenses, then, are good against the original payee but are not good against a subsequent holder in due course. However, certain real defenses are good against any person, a payee or holder in due course included. These defenses are:

1. Forgery, where the alleged maker did not really sign the note.
2. Material alteration, when an important change is made in the obligation without the knowledge of the parties involved.
3. Incapacity, where the maker is a minor or an incompetent.
4. Illegality of the instrument. If the instrument is executed in connection with an illegal act or if the rate of interest is usurious, then illegality of the instrument results.

Interest charge, usury, and Proposition 2

Section 1915 of the California Civil Code defines interests as "the compensation allowed by law or fixed by the parties for the use, forbearance, or detention of money." Any charge connected with a loan, whether it be called interest, service charge, placement charge, or points, may be considered by the courts as interest in determining if a usurious charge is being made. Thus, it may well be that when these additional charges are considered, along with the stated rate of interest on the note, the actual payment for the use of money may exceed the allowed maximum. No illegal interest can be collected in California on a note that is found to exceed the legal maximum, and in certain cirsumstances, the borrower can collect damages from the lender. A note that provides for a prepayment penalty is not considered usurious, nor does acceleration of maturity result in usury. It is interesting to note that California law exempts the following from restrictions of the usury law: banks, savings and loan associations, credit unions, industrial loan companies, and nonprofit cooperation associations.

Proposition 2, enacted in 1979, now defines the usury rate of interest as 10%, or the prevailing San Francisco Federal Reserve Bank discount rate plus 5%, whichever is higher.

Exempt from the usury law is any loan made or arranged by a California licensed real estate broker and secured wholly or in part by a lien on real property; or, a purchase money trust deed carried back by an owner who sells his real property.

TRUST DEEDS AND MORTGAGES

Mortgages and deeds of trust differ in many respects, and a comparison of these differences will make clear to the reader the reasons why the deed of trust is preferred by lenders and is the instrument generally used in California today. The mortgage and deed of trust differ with respect to *(a)* parties, *(b)* title, *(c)* statute of limitations, *(d)* remedy, and *(e)* redemption.

With respect to parties

In a mortgage, there are two parties—the mortgagor and the mortgagee. The mortgagor borrows the money to purchase the property, and the mortgagee is the lender.

In a deed of trust, there are three parties—the trustor, the trustee, and the beneficiary. The trustor borrows the money to purchase, and the beneficiary is the lender. The trustee is the third party to whom the borrower conveys the title to the property as security for the obligation owed to the lender. A deed of trust is shown in Figure 7–2.

Mortgage		*Deed of trust*	
Mortgagor	Borrower	Trustor	Borrower
Mortgagee	Lender	Beneficiary	Lender
		Trustee	Holds title for the benefit of the lender

With respect to title

A mortgage does not convey any degree of title; it merely creates a lien. The mortgagor executes a note and a mortgage in favor of the mortgagee, who then has a lien on the property, which he may enforce if the mortgagor defaults on his obligation.

The deed of trust also may be considered a lien against property, but it has the additional important element of the passage of title to a third party for the benefit of the lender. It may seem that with a deed of trust, the borrower does not have title in the property any longer because he has given it to the trustee; this is not entirely correct. California law provides that the trustee has legal title only to the extent that it may become necessary for him to effect a sale of the property for the benefit of the beneficiary should the trustor default in his obligation. Otherwise, the trustor holds true title to the property, referred to as *equitable title,* and may sell, lease, or further encumber it so long as he does nothing adverse or inconsistent with the right of the beneficiary.

When the beneficiary notifies the trustee that the note has been paid in full, the rights and interests given the trustee in the deed of trust are reconveyed to the trustor. A request for full reconveyance is part of the trust deed, as shown in Figure 7–2 (continued).

With respect to statute of limitations

In a mortgage, an action to foreclose is barred when the statute of limitations has run out on the principal obligation. Thus, the rights of the mortgagee must be enforced during the term of the note.

With a deed of trust, the rights of the beneficiary are not ended when the statute of limitations has run on the note, for the trustee has title with power of sale for the benefit of the beneficiary and can sell the property to pay off the debt.

With respect to remedy

In a mortgage agreement, the only remedy of the mortgagee is foreclosure by court action. The deed of trust, however, allows the beneficiary the option of either foreclosing by court action or proceeding with a trustee's sale of the property. Obviously, the trustee's sale procedure is the method used with the deed of trust. This is one of the main reasons for the existence and lenders' use of the deed of trust. Some lenders employ a form mortgage document that includes a power of sale, which will be discussed later in this chapter. The actual procedures and steps used in foreclosing under a mortgage and in exercising the power of sale under a deed of trust (trustee's sale) are discussed in Chapter 16, dealing with public sales of real property.

With respect to redemption

Under a mortgage that has been foreclosed by court action, the right of the mortgagor to redeem exists for one year after the sale. It is not uncommon for legal proceedings to run for as long as two years after a sale before the rights of the mortgagor are finally eliminated.

Under a deed of trust, sale of the property by the trustee is an irrevocable, final, and absolute sale, and the trustor has no right of redemption. Approximately four months elapses from the time the trustor defaults on his obligation and a notice of default is filed to the actual sale of the property by the trustee. During this time, the trustor may save the property from being sold, but once the trustee's sale takes place, it is final.

Our preceding comparison of the mortgage and the deed of trust should help the reader to understand the main reasons for the almost total use of the deed of trust by lenders in California. The two most important reasons are: (1) the ease and facility, without having to resort to court action, with which the property may be sold to satisfy the debt if the borrower defaults; and (2) the short period of redemption prior to the sale and the fact that the sale, once made, is absolute.

Mortgage with power of sale

Some lenders occasionally use a conventional mortgage form that has written into it a power-

RECORDING REQUESTED BY

AND WHEN RECORDED MAIL TO

Name: John Purchaser
Street Address: 200 Monterey Street
City & State: Sacramento, California 95822

SPACE ABOVE THIS LINE FOR RECORDER'S USE

SHORT FORM DEED OF TRUST AND ASSIGNMENT OF RENTS (INDIVIDUAL)   A.P.N. _____

This Deed of Trust, made this   1st   day of   October, 19--   , between

whose address is   John Purchaser and Mary Purchaser, husband and wife , herein called TRUSTOR,
200 Monterey Street (number and street)   Sacramento (city)   California (state)   95822 (zip) ,

Title Insurance and Trust Company, a California corporation, herein called TRUSTEE, and

ABC Savings and Loan Association, Sacramento, California , herein called BENEFICIARY,

Witnesseth: That Trustor IRREVOCABLY GRANTS, TRANSFERS AND ASSIGNS to TRUSTEE IN TRUST, WITH POWER OF SALE, that property in   City of Sacramento,   Sacramento   County, California, described as:

Lot 29, Block B, Parklake Addition (as recorded July 12, 1919, Book 3, Page 59 of maps), City of Sacramento, County of Sacramento, State of California. Commonly known as: 200 Monterey Street, Sacramento, California.

TOGETHER WITH the rents, issues and profits thereof, SUBJECT, HOWEVER, to the right, power and authority given to and conferred upon Beneficiary by paragraph (10) of the provisions incorporated herein by reference to collect and apply such rents, issues and profits.

For the Purpose of Securing: 1. Performance of each agreement of Trustor incorporated by reference or contained herein. 2. Payment of the indebtedness evidenced by one promissory note of even date herewith, and any extension or renewal thereof, in the principal sum of $ 93,000.00 executed by Trustor in favor of Beneficiary or order. 3. Payment of such further sums as the then record owner of said property hereafter may borrow from Beneficiary, when evidenced by another note (or notes) reciting it is so secured.

To Protect the Security of This Deed of Trust, Trustor Agrees: By the execution and delivery of this Deed of Trust and the note secured hereby, that provisions (1) to (14), inclusive, of the fictitious deed of trust recorded in Santa Barbara County and Sonoma County October 18, 1961, and in all other counties October 23, 1961, in the book and at the page of Official Records in the office of the county recorder of the county where said property is located, noted below opposite the name of such county, viz.:

COUNTY	BOOK	PAGE	COUNTY	BOOK	PAGE	COUNTY	BOOK	PAGE	COUNTY	BOOK	PAGE
Alameda	435	684	Kings	792	833	Placer	895	301	Sierra	29	335
Alpine	1	250	Lake	362	39	Plumas	151	5	Siskiyou	468	181
Amador	104	348	Lassen	171	471	Riverside	3005	523	Solano	1105	182
Butte	1145	1	Los Angeles	T2055	899	Sacramento	4331	62	Sonoma	1851	689
Calaveras	145	152	Madera	810	170	San Benito	271	383	Stanislaus	1715	456
Colusa	296	617	Marin	1508	339	San Bernardino	5567	61	Sutter	572	297
Contra Costa	3978	47	Mariposa	77	292	San Francisco	A332	905	Tehama	401	289
Del Norte	78	414	Mendocino	579	530	San Joaquin	2470	311	Trinity	93	366
El Dorado	568	456	Merced	1547	538	San Luis Obispo	1151	12	Tulare	2294	275
Fresno	4626	572	Modoc	184	851	San Mateo	4078	420	Tuolumne	135	47
Glenn	422	184	Mono	52	429	Santa Barbara	1878	860	Ventura	2062	386
Humboldt	657	527	Monterey	2194	538	Santa Clara	5336	341	Yolo	653	245
Imperial	1091	501	Napa	639	86	Santa Cruz	1431	494	Yuba	334	486
Inyo	147	598	Nevada	305	320	Shasta	684	528			
Kern	3427	60	Orange	5889	611	San Diego	Series 2 Book 1961, Page 183887				

(which provisions, identical in all counties, are printed on the reverse hereof) hereby are adopted and incorporated herein and made a part hereof as fully as though set forth herein at length; that he will observe and perform said provisions; and that the references to property, obligations, and parties in said provisions shall be construed to refer to the property, obligations, and parties set forth in this Deed of Trust.

The undersigned Trustor requests that a copy of any Notice of Default and of any Notice of Sale hereunder be mailed to him at his address hereinbefore set forth.

STATE OF CALIFORNIA,   City and
COUNTY OF   Sacramento   } ss.

On   October 1, 19--   before me, the undersigned, a Notary Public in and for said State, personally appeared   John Purchaser and Mary Purchaser

_____ , known to me to be the person S whose name S are subscribed to the within instrument and acknowledged that   they   executed the same. WITNESS my hand and official seal.

Signature   (s) Arthur Notary

Signature of Trustor

(s) John Purchaser

(s) Mary Purchaser

Title Order No. _____

Escrow or Loan No. _____

TO 1939 CA (8-74) (OPEN END)

(This area for official notarial seal)

FIGURE 7–2

―――――――――――――― DO NOT RECORD ――――――――――――――

The following is a copy of provisions (1) to (14), inclusive, of the fictitious deed of trust, recorded in each county in California, as stated in the foregoing Deed of Trust and incorporated by reference in said Deed of Trust as being a part thereof as if set forth at length therein.

To Protect the Security of This Deed of Trust, Trustor Agrees:

(1) To keep said property in good condition and repair; not to remove or demolish any building thereon; to complete or restore promptly and in good and workmanlike manner any building which may be constructed, damaged or destroyed thereon and to pay when due all claims for labor performed and materials furnished therefor; to comply with all laws affecting said property or requiring any alterations or improvements to be made thereon; not to commit or permit waste thereof; not to commit, suffer or permit any act upon said property in violation of law; to cultivate, irrigate, fertilize, fumigate, prune and do all other acts which from the character or use of said property may be reasonably necessary, the specific enumerations herein not excluding the general.

(2) To provide, maintain and deliver to Beneficiary fire insurance satisfactory to and with loss payable to Beneficiary. The amount collected under any fire or other insurance policy may be applied by Beneficiary upon indebtedness secured hereby and in such order as Beneficiary may determine, or at option of Beneficiary the entire amount so collected or any part thereof may be released to Trustor. Such application or release shall not cure or waive any default or notice of default hereunder or invalidate any act done pursuant to such notice.

(3) To appear in and defend any action or proceeding purporting to affect the security hereof or the rights or powers of Beneficiary or Trustee; and to pay all costs and expenses, including cost of evidence of title and attorney's fees in a reasonable sum, in any such action or proceeding in which Beneficiary or Trustee may appear, and in any suit brought by Beneficiary to foreclose this Deed.

(4) To pay: at least ten days before delinquency all taxes and assessments affecting said property, including assessments on appurtenant water stock; when due, all incumbrances, charges and liens, with interest, on said property or any part thereof, which appear to be prior or superior hereto; all costs, fees and expenses of this Trust.

Should Trustor fail to make any payment or to do any act as herein provided, then Beneficiary or Trustee, but without obligation so to do and without notice to or demand upon Trustor and without releasing Trustor from any obligation hereof, may: make or do the same in such manner and to such extent as either may deem necessary to protect the security hereof, Beneficiary or Trustee being authorized to enter upon said property for such purposes; appear in and defend any action or proceeding purporting to affect the security hereof or the rights or powers of Beneficiary or Trustee; pay, purchase, contest or compromise any incumbrance, charge or lien which in the judgment of either appears to be prior or superior hereto; and, in exercising any such powers, pay necessary expenses, employ counsel and pay his reasonable fees.

(5) To pay immediately and without demand all sums so expended by Beneficiary or Trustee, with interest from date of expenditure at the amount allowed by law in effect at the date hereof, and to pay fee any statement provided for by law in effect at the date hereof regarding the obligation secured hereby any amount so demanded by the Beneficiary not to exceed the maximum allowed by law at the time when said statement is demanded.

(6) That any award of damages in connection with any condemnation for public use of or injury to said property or any part thereof is hereby assigned and shall be paid to Beneficiary who may apply or release such moneys received by him in the same manner and with the same effect as above provided for disposition of proceeds of fire or other insurance.

(7) That by accepting payment of any sum secured hereby after its due date, Beneficiary does not waive his right either to require prompt payment when due of all other sums so secured or to declare default for failure so to pay.

(8) That at any time or from time to time, without liability therefor and without notice, upon written request of Beneficiary and presentation of this Deed and said note for endorsement, and without affecting the personal liability of any person for payment of the indebtedness secured hereby, Trustee may: reconvey any part of said property; consent to the making of any map or plat thereof; join in granting any easement thereon; or join in any extension agreement or any agreement subordinating the lien or charge hereof.

(9) That upon written request of Beneficiary stating that all sums secured hereby have been paid, and upon surrender of this Deed and said note to Trustee for cancellation and retention and upon payment of its fees, Trustee shall reconvey, without warranty, the property then held hereunder. The recitals in such reconveyance of any matters or facts shall be conclusive proof of the truthfulness thereof. The grantee in such reconveyance may be described as "the person or persons legally entitled thereto." Five years after issuance of such full reconveyance, Trustee may destroy said note and this Deed (unless directed in such request to retain them).

(10) That as additional security, Trustor hereby gives to and confers upon Beneficiary the right, power and authority, during the continuance of these Trusts, to collect the rents, issues and profits of said property, reserving unto Trustor the right, prior to any default by Trustor in payment of any indebtedness secured hereby or in performance of any agreement hereunder, to collect and retain such rents, issues and profits as they become due and payable. Upon any such default, Beneficiary may at any time without notice, either in person, by agent, or by a receiver to be appointed by a court, and without regard to the adequacy of any security for the indebtedness hereby secured, enter upon and take possession of said property or any part thereof, in his own name sue for or otherwise collect such rents, issues and profits, including those past due and unpaid, and apply the same, less costs and expenses of operation and collection, including reasonable attorney's fees, upon any indebtedness secured hereby, and in such order as Beneficiary may determine. The entering upon and taking possession of said property, the collection of such rents, issues and profits and the application thereof as aforesaid, shall not cure or waive any default or notice of default hereunder or invalidate any act done pursuant to such notice.

(11) That upon default by Trustor in payment of any indebtedness secured hereby or in performance of any agreement hereunder, Beneficiary may declare all sums secured hereby immediately due and payable by delivery to Trustee of written declaration of default and demand for sale and of written notice of default and of election to cause to be sold said property, which notice Trustee shall cause to be filed for record. Beneficiary also shall deposit with Trustee this Deed, said note and all documents evidencing expenditures secured hereby.

After the lapse of such time as may then be required by law following the recordation of said notice of default, and notice of sale having been given as then required by law, Trustee, without demand on Trustor, shall sell said property at the time and place fixed by it in said notice of sale, either as a whole or in separate parcels, and in such order as it may determine, at public auction to the highest bidder for cash in lawful money of the United States, payable at time of sale. Trustee may postpone sale of all or any portion of said property by public announcement at such time and place of sale, and from time to time thereafter may postpone such sale by public announcement at the time fixed by the preceding postponement. Trustee shall deliver to such purchaser its deed conveying the property so sold, but without any covenant or warranty, express or implied. The recitals in such deed of any matters or facts shall be conclusive proof of the truthfulness thereof. Any person, including Trustor, Trustee, or Beneficiary as hereinafter defined, may purchase at such sale.

After deducting all costs, fees and expenses of Trustee and of this Trust, including cost of evidence of title in connection with sale, Trustee shall apply the proceeds of sale to payment of: all sums expended under the terms hereof, not then repaid, with accrued interest at the amount allowed by law in effect at the date hereof; all other sums then secured hereby; and the remainder, if any, to the person or persons legally entitled thereto.

(12) Beneficiary, or any successor in ownership of any indebtedness secured hereby, may from time to time, by instrument in writing, substitute a successor or successors to any Trustee named herein or acting hereunder, which instrument, executed by the Beneficiary and duly acknowledged and recorded in the office of the recorder of the county or counties where said property is situated, shall be conclusive proof of proper substitution of such successor Trustee or Trustees, who shall, without conveyance from the Trustee predecessor, succeed to all its title, estate, rights, powers and duties. Said instrument must contain the name of the original Trustor, Trustee and Beneficiary hereunder, the book and page where this Deed is recorded and the name and address of the new Trustee.

(13) That this Deed applies to, inures to the benefit of, and binds all parties hereto, their heirs, legatees, devisees, administrators, executors, successors and assigns. The term Beneficiary shall mean the owner and holder, including pledgees, of the note secured hereby, whether or not named as Beneficiary herein. In this Deed, whenever the context so requires, the masculine gender includes the feminine and/or neuter, and the singular number includes the plural.

(14) That Trustee accepts this Trust when this Deed, duly executed and acknowledged, is made a public record as provided by law. Trustee is not obligated to notify any party hereto of pending sale under any other Deed of Trust or of any action or proceeding in which Trustor, Beneficiary or Trustee shall be a party unless brought by Trustee.

―――――――――――――― DO NOT RECORD ――――――――――――――

REQUEST FOR FULL RECONVEYANCE
To be used only when note has been paid.

To TITLE INSURANCE AND TRUST COMPANY, TRUSTEE: Dated_____

The undersigned is the legal owner and holder of all indebtedness secured by the within Deed of Trust. All sums secured by said Deed of Trust have been fully paid and satisfied; and you are hereby requested and directed, on payment to you of any sums owing to you under the terms of said Deed of Trust, to cancel all evidences of indebtedness, secured by said Deed of Trust, delivered to you herewith together with said Deed of Trust, and to reconvey, without warranty, to the parties designated by the terms of said Deed of Trust, the estate now held by you under the same.

MAIL RECONVEYANCE TO:

_____
_____
_____

By _____

By _____

Do not lose or destroy this Deed of Trust OR THE NOTE which it secures. Both must be delivered to the Trustee for cancellation before reconveyance will be made.

Short Form Deed of Trust
WITH POWER OF SALE
(INDIVIDUAL)

Title Insurance and Trust Company
AS TRUSTEE

TITLE INSURANCE AND TRUST
A TICOR COMPANY

COMPLETE STATEWIDE TITLE SERVICE WITH ONE LOCAL CALL

FIGURE 7-2 *(continued)*

of-sale clause. This allows the mortgagee, on default by the mortgagor, to sell the property without the necessity of court proceedings. The mortgagor is usually bound to execute a deed to the purchaser after the mortgagee sells the property.

The main difference between the mortgage with the power of sale and the deed of trust is with regard to the statute of limitations. The mortgage with power of sale is in the same position as the conventional mortgage; a sale is barred when the statute of limitations has run on the principal obligation (the note). The opposite is true under the deed of trust, and even though judicial enforcement of the debt may not be possible, the trustee can still sell the property under his power of sale in order to satisfy the debt.

EFFECTS AND INCIDENTS OF SECURITY ARRANGEMENTS

Some of the more common incidents of security arrangements will be defined and discussed, as well as certain special rules of law with which the licensee should be familiar.

Purchase money trust deed or mortgage

When a borrower gives a mortgage or deed of trust to a lender for money used to purchase property, the mortgage or deed of trust is called a "purchase money" mortgage or "purchase money" deed of trust. Also, if a seller carries back all or a portion of the purchase price and receives a note secured by a mortgage or deed of trust, these become a purchase money mortgage or purchase money deed of trust. Whether money borrowed is or is not purchase money is so clearly defined because under California law, a lender cannot obtain a deficiency judgment if the sale of the property does not bring enough to pay off the note. There is an exception to this rule, however: a third-party lender may secure a deficiency judgment when the purchase money loan was made on a building of four or more units or designed for housing more than four families.

Reconveyance

When a purchaser borrows money to buy property and signs a note secured by a deed of trust, the note is for the money borrowed, and the deed of trust puts the property up as security for the note. When the note has been paid, the lender-beneficiary requests the trustee to record a full reconveyance.

The deed of trust illustrated in Figure 7–2 contains the form of such a request. Figure 7–3 shows a full reconveyance which is prepared by the trustee and recorded. This gives evidence that the note has been paid, and the lien against the property is removed. Whatever interest the lender had in the property is thus reconveyed to the borrower-trustor.

Hypothecation

To hypothecate a piece of property means to give it as security without the necessity of giving up possession of it. Thus, when a purchaser executes a note and deed of trust for the money to purchase the property, he is said to have hypothecated his property under the terms of the deed of trust.

Lien priorities

Section 2897 of the Civil Code states that different liens on the same piece of property generally have priority according to their time of creation and subject to the operation of the recording laws. Certain liens, such as tax liens and mechanic's liens, are given preferential treatment. Notice is an important element in the determination of priority; it may be actual or constructive through recordation. The lien created by a purchase money mortgage or purchase money trust deed has priority over all other liens created by or against the purchaser, subject to the operation of the recording laws.

Assignment of debt

When a note secured by a mortgage or deed of trust is assigned by the creditor to another, it carries with it the security. An assignment of the mortgage or deed of trust without the note transfers nothing to the assignee. When a note is transferred, the transferee is entitled to the security.

An assignment of a mortgage or deed of trust may be recorded, and this recordation gives constructive notice to all persons. When the assignment of the mortgage has been recorded and the note transferred, the debtor is not protected if he pays the original creditor.

Deficiency judgment

Aaron defaults on a $75,000 note and deed of trust held by Baker. At a subsequent sale, the prop-

RECORDING REQUESTED BY	
AND WHEN RECORDED MAIL TO	
Name	
Street Address	
City & State	

————— SPACE ABOVE THIS LINE FOR RECORDER'S USE —————

TITLE ORDER NO.   TITLE OFFICER

TO 430—1 C

FULL RECONVEYANCE

TITLE INSURANCE AND TRUST COMPANY, a California corporation, as duly appointed Trustee under Deed of Trust hereinafter referred to, having received from holder of the obligations thereunder a written request to reconvey, reciting that all sums secured by said Deed of Trust have been fully paid, and said Deed of Trust and the note or notes secured thereby having been surrendered to said Trustee for cancellation, does hereby RECONVEY, without warranty, to the person or persons legally entitled thereto, the estate now held by it thereunder. Said Deed of Trust was executed by

Trustor,

and recorded in the official records of   County, California, as follows:

REC.   AS INSTR. NO.   IN BOOK   PAGE

DESC.

In Witness Whereof, Title Insurance and Trust Company, as such Trustee, has caused its corporate name and seal to be hereto affixed by its Assistant Secretary, thereunto duly authorized on the date shown in the acknowledgement certificate shown below.

TITLE INSURANCE AND TRUST COMPANY, as such Trustee

By_____
Assistant Secretary

STATE OF CALIFORNIA,
COUNTY OF_____ } ss.

On_____, before me, the undersigned, a Notary Public in and for said State, personally appeared_____, known to me to be an Assistant Secretary of TITLE INSURANCE AND TRUST COMPANY, the corporation that executed the foregoing instrument as such Trustee, and known to me to be the person who executed said instrument on behalf of the corporation therein named, and acknowledged to me that such corporation executed the same as such Trustee. WITNESS my hand and official seal.

Signature_____

(This area for official notarial seal)   Name (Typed or Printed)

FIGURE 7-3

erty is sold for $72,000, leaving Baker with a deficiency of $3,000. Baker may wish to go into court seeking to obtain a deficiency judgment against Aaron for $3,000. If the property in question is a house, and the money was borrowed by Aaron for the purchase of this house, Baker will not be able to obtain a deficiency judgment. No deficiency judgment is allowed if (a) the security is a purchase money mortgage or trust deed, and (b) the remedy of foreclosure is accomplished by a trustee's sale.

"Subject to" versus "assumption of"

When a property is sold or exchanged and the existing mortgage or trust deed is to be transferred to the purchaser, he may either "assume" the existing obligation or take the property "subject to" the existing obligation.

When a purchaser assumes an existing loan, he accepts full responsibility for repayment with the consent of the existing lender who must approve the assumption.

If the buyer takes subject to the existing obligation, he is responsible for making the necessary payments if he wants to eventually receive clear title to the property, but the seller remains legally liable for the promissory note. If the buyer fails to make the necessary payments, then the seller (former owner) will be held responsible for the obligation. Further, if one assumes an obligation, he may be liable for a deficiency judgment if conditions will allow one; but if he purchases subject to the obligation, he cannot be held liable for a deficiency judgment.

Offset statement

When a purchaser buys a property and assumes or takes subject to existing obligation, he should receive an offset statement from the property owner or owner of the lien against the property (the lender). This statement should set forth the current status, terms, and conditions of the existing liens against the property.

Subordination clause

A subordination clause is an agreement written into a mortgage or deed of trust, providing that said obligation may be subordinated in priority to an anticipated future lien.

A subordination may be specific, giving priority to one or more specified encumbrances, or it may be an automatic future subordination, which automatically provides priority—without further action of the holder of the encumbrance to be subordinated—for one or more encumbrances, the terms and conditions of which are specified in the subordination agreement, to be created in the future. An automatic subordination agreement, if any, is ordinarily contained in the trust deed that is to be subordinated.

The use of a subordination agreement is usually associated with the development of unimproved land as follows:

Builder Brown wants to purchase from farmer Franklin a ten-acre unimproved parcel of land on which to build a number of houses for sale to the public. Brown does not want to tie up a large amount of capital in purchase of the land, so he arranges with Franklin to give him a modest down payment and then execute a note and deed of trust in favor of Franklin for the balance of the purchase price. Having obtained title to the land, Brown now proceeds to banker Baldwin for a construction loan. Baldwin will refuse to make the loan, since most lending institutions are prohibited by law from making any real estate loans not secured by first liens. In this case, the first lien is held by farmer Franklin. Thus, when he originally negotiated with Franklin for the purchase of the land, builder Brown would have had incorporated into the agreement a subordination clause that would allow him to later obtain the construction loan and have it take priority as a first lien. Most sellers will agree to this condition, since the purchase price they will receive will depend in large measure on the future development and improvement contemplated by the purchaser and developer of the property.

Partial release clause

Generally speaking, an obligation must be paid in full before the mortgagee or trustee can be compelled to release any part of his security. It is possible, however, for a provision to be made in the mortgage or deed of trust for the release of certain portions of the security when a certain amount of the obligation has been paid.

This device is often used by subdividers who are developing residential property and want to release certain lots when the purchaser's total payments have reached a predetermined amount.

Acceleration clause

A deed of trust or mortgage clause that on the happening of a certain event gives the lender the right to immediately demand payment of all sums owing to him is called an acceleration or alienation clause. Examples of an acceleration clause are *(a)* a statement in a mortgage or deed of trust that should the borrower default on payments for a certain period of time the entire obligation shall become immediately due and payable, or *(b)* a statement in a second trust deed, called a "due on sale clause," which makes the note immediately due and payable if the borrower should sell the property prior to the end of the note term.

A 1978 California Supreme Court decision *(Wellenkamp* v. *Bank of America)* now prohibits California chartered lending institutions from accelerating an existing loan upon sale of a property without showing impairment of their security. If the buyer is qualified to make the payments, such loans can now be assumed. The United States District Court has ruled that federally chartered lending institutions are exempt from the Wellenkamp ruling and can, if they wish, call any loan containing a due on sale clause when the property is sold.

Impound or trust account

Impounds are moneys accumulated in a special account called an impound or trust account. These moneys are used to pay certain expenses on the property when they become due, usually taxes and insurance. Many conventional lenders require the establishment of such a special account in connection with the making of a loan for the purchase of real property, and a portion of the payment made each month by the borrower is set aside in the impound account. FHA and VA loans require such an account. The rationale given by lenders for the establishment of such impounds is that the monthly accumulation of these funds will allow for payment of taxes and insurance without the necessity of the borrower's having to come up suddenly with the required amounts at one particular time.

The California Civil Code states that with respect to single-family, owner-occupied dwellings, lenders cannot require impound accounts as a condition of the loan unless such impounds are required by state or federal regulations, such as a loan guaranteed by the VA or insured by the FHA; a loan exceeding 90 percent of the appraised value of the property; or where the borrower fails to pay two consecutive tax installments on the property prior to their delinquency dates.

Lender and borrower can mutually agree to an impound account if, prior to execution of the loan, the lender has furnished the borrower a statement in writing that the account is not required as a condition of the loan and that interest will not be paid on impounded funds.

Prepayment penalties and lock-in provisions

A prepayment penalty is a charge made by a lender for paying all or part of the outstanding principal amount of a loan before the due date. This situation generally arises in connection with the sale of property on which the seller still owes a sum of money to a lender. Prepayment penalty charges differ among various lenders. Many savings and loan associations, for instance, charge a penalty of three to six months' interest on 80 percent of the outstanding balance of the loan.

With respect to residential property of four units or less and a single family, owner-occupied residence, the law allows prepayment of 20 percent of the loan in any year without penalty. If the loan is fully paid within five years of inception, a penalty not to exceed six months' interest on 80 percent of the loan balance is allowed, but no prepayment penalty is allowed after five years.

A lock-in period is a period from inception of a loan during which the lender will not allow prepayment. Customarily, savings and loan associations and banks have not imposed a lock-in period in connection with loans made by them, while such lock-in periods have been imposed by life insurance companies, pension funds, and certain savings banks. Since procedures among lenders vary, the borrower should investigate and make himself aware of any such provision which may be present in connection with a contemplated loan.

Section 2954.9 of the Civil Code states that any loan secured by residential property of four units or less can be prepaid at any time and the beneficiary can charge a prepayment penalty. With respect to an installment sale, a seller may restrict prepayment within the calendar year of the sale.

Open-end-loan

An open-end mortgage or trust deed is one that allows for future advances on the original loan using the same instruments as security. An example is that of a buyer who purchases a home in need of renovation and modernization and enters into an agreement with the lender that, upon completion of certain pre-agreed-upon work, the lender will increase the amount of the original loan. If a loan is not an open-end loan, then in order to borrow additional funds at a later date, an owner would either have to seek secondary financing or substitute for the old loan a new one that would require new fees and documents and probably a higher rate of interest.

Points

Discounts, or points, as they are usually called, are paid to lenders and are, in effect, prepaid interest. This method is used by many lenders in order to adjust the effective rate of interest so that it is equal to or nearly equal to the prevailing rate charged on conventional loans. The discounts (points) are absorbed mostly by the sellers, since under FHA-insured or VA-guaranteed loans, buyers may only be charged 1 percent. This 1 percent is called a loan origination fee and is used to cover the expense of obtaining FHA or VA approval.

In a tight money market, when conventional loan interest rates are high, the seller will usually have to pay a number of points to the lender in order to obtain the necessary loan for the buyer. A point is equivalent to 1 percent; thus, if the lender were to require that the seller pay three points for advancing a $75,000 loan to a prospective buyer under an FHA-insured loan, the seller will have to pay $2,250. Each point charged adds approximately $\frac{1}{8}$ percent to the yield on the loan, and thus, a lender who makes a loan at an annual interest rate of $11\frac{3}{4}$ percent and charges the borrower a 2 point loan fee is, in effect, increasing the yield of the loan to 12 percent.

With regard to conventional financing, there is no restriction on the number of points that may be charged the borrower. This charge for making a loan at most institutions is called a *loan fee, service charge, commitment fee,* or merely *points to the buyer.* This loan fee will be a part of the buyer's closing costs and will vary depending on the type of property involved and the particular lending institution. Although the buyer and seller may agree that each will pay a portion of the loan fee, the general practice is for the borrower (buyer) to pay all of the fee for the loan.

SECOND TRUST DEEDS AND MORTGAGES

Quite often in the purchase of property, the down payment and proceeds of a first loan are not sufficient to equal the purchase price, and thus, secondary financing in the form of a second trust deed or second mortgage is necessary.

This second loan is generally for a short term and usually carries a higher rate of interest of the related promissory note because of the higher risk factor involved and the junior lien status of the loan. Most second loans are usually written for from three to seven years but can be for any length of time the parties desire.

A second loan is in appearance much the same as the first, but the basic difference is that the second loan is a junior lien and is thus subordinate to the first loan in all respects. A second loan is wiped out by foreclosure of the first if the sale of the property brings only enough to pay off the first loan. Thus, the law gives the holder of the second loan the right of reinstatement. Should the borrower default on his payments, the holder of the second may reinstate the first loan (by assuming the payments) and may bring an action to foreclose or elect to use the power of sale, depending on whether the second loan is in the form of a mortgage or a deed of trust.

Request for notice and notice of default

Anyone interested in a particular deed of trust or mortgage with power of sale can make sure of being informed if a notice of default or a notice of sale is recorded. The holder of the second loan should record a request for notice with the county recorder. Some forms of mortgages and deeds of trust have such a request incorporated into the form, so that after recordation, a separate request for notice is not necessary.

The request for notice shown in Figure 7–4 must contain the recording data applying to the deed of trust or mortgage and the name and address of the person who wants the information. The recorder will enter this on the record of the deed of trust or mortgage, and if subsequently any notice of default or sale is recorded, the person named in the request will have to be notified.

For purposes of illustration, let us assume that Byer buys a house from Selar for $80,000. Byer receives a loan of $64,000 from ABC Savings and Loan Company. This first loan is secured by a note and deed of trust executed by Byer in favor of ABC Savings and Loan Company. Byer puts up $8,000 as the cash down payment, and Selar takes back a second loan secured by note and deed of trust in the amount of $8,000.

Subsequently, Byer defaults on the first loan payments, and ABC Savings and Loan Company records a notice of default (Figure 7–5) to start the period of reinstatement. If Byer does not reinstate,

7 / FINANCING REAL ESTATE

RECORDING REQUESTED BY

AND WHEN RECORDED MAIL TO

Name
Street Address
City & State

——— SPACE ABOVE THIS LINE FOR RECORDER'S USE ———

Request for Notice
UNDER SECTION 2924b CIVIL CODE

TO 422 C (9-67)

In accordance with Section 2924b, Civil Code, request is hereby made that a copy of any Notice of Default and a copy of any Notice of Sale under the Deed of Trust recorded as Instrument No._____ on_____, in book_____, page_____, Official Records of_____ County, California, and describing land therein as

Executed by_____, as Trustor,
in which_____is named as Beneficiary, and_____, as Trustee,
be mailed to_____
at_____
    Number and Street
_____
    City and State
Dated_____

STATE OF CALIFORNIA, }ss.
COUNTY OF_____
On_____before me, the undersigned, a Notary Public in and for said State personally appeared _____, known to me to be the person__ whose name_____subscribed to the within instrument and acknowledged that_____executed the same.
WITNESS my hand and official seal.

Signature_____
    Name (Typed or Printed)
If executed by a Corporation the Corporation Form of Acknowledgment must be used.

(This area for official notarial seal)

Title Order No._____ Escrow or Loan No._____

FIGURE 7–4

RECORDING REQUESTED BY

AND WHEN RECORDED MAIL TO

Name
Street Address
City & State

———— SPACE ABOVE THIS LINE FOR RECORDER'S USE ————

NOTICE OF DEFAULT

TO 613 C

as ①   under that certain deed of or transfer in trust executed

by

, as trustor to

, as trustee and

as beneficiary, dated   19   , and recorded   19   ,

in Book   , page   of Official Records, in the office of the County Recorder of

the   County of   State of California,

hereby gives notice that a breach of the obligations for which such transfer in trust is security has occurred, the nature of such breach being the failure to ②

and that the beneficiary has declared and does declare that all sums secured by said deed of trust are immediately due and payable and elects to cause the trust property to be sold to satisfy said obligations. In this instrument, whenever the context so requires, the singular number includes the plural.

Dated: _____

① "Trustee" or "Beneficiary."
② State each item of default such as failure to pay principal, or installments thereof, interest, taxes, insurance premiums, etc.

(CORPORATION)

STATE OF CALIFORNIA
COUNTY OF _____ } SS.
On _____ before me, the undersigned, a Notary Public in and for said County and State, personally appeared _____
known to me to be the _____ President, and _____
_____ known to me to be
_____ Secretary of the corporation that executed the within Instrument, known to me to be the persons who executed the within Instrument on behalf of the corporation therein named, and acknowledged to me that such corporation executed the within instrument pursuant to its by-laws or a resolution of its board of directors.
WITNESS my hand and official seal.

(Seal)
Signature _____
_____
Name (Typed or Printed)
Notary Public in and for said County and State

(INDIVIDUAL)

STATE OF CALIFORNIA
COUNTY OF _____ } SS.
On _____ before me, the undersigned, a Notary Public in and for said County and State, personally appeared _____
_____
_____, known to me to be the person__ whose name_____ subscribed to the within instrument and acknowledged that_____ executed the same.
WITNESS my hand and official seal.

(Seal)
Signature _____
Name (Typed or Printed)
Notary Public in and for said County and State

Application No._____

FIGURE 7–5

Selar will be in the position of having to do so. If Selar does not reinstate, ABC Savings and Loan Company will eventually order the trustee to sell the property, and Selar's security may be wiped out. A sale of real property under a senior lien (the first loan) cuts off junior liens (the second loan), except to the extent that the sales produces more than enough to pay the senior. Often, this does not occur, and the holder of the second lien will lose most, if not all, of his investment.

If Selar reinstates the first loan, he must continue to make the payments on it. At the same time, Selar will foreclose on the second loan, subject to the first. In foreclosing, Selar will go through the same steps and procedures as would the holder of the first. There is very little likelihood of Byer's being able to reinstate at this point; he would have to pay Selar the delinquencies due, together with the amount Selar has had to pay to reinstate and maintain the first.

At the time of the sale, Selar will bid in the amount owed him and will usually become the purchaser subject to the first. He will have regained the property he once sold, but he will now have to make the payments on the first loan held by ABC Savings and Loan Company. Selar may now rent the property if he can obtain a rental that will take care of the necessary payments and expenses, or he may once again put the property up for sale.

The use of a notice of default in connection with a trustee's sale is discussed in Chapter 16.

Chattel mortgage

A chattel mortgage is a contract whereby certain personal property is made security for a debt. It must be in writing, executed and acknowledged, and must be recorded in the office of the county recorder. It is but one of a number of personal property security devices.

In 1965, the Uniform Commercial Code (UCC) became law in California. The UCC regulates personal property security devices and recommends the use of an instrument called a security agreement. Since enactment of the UCC, the security agreement rather than a chattel mortgage has generally been used in connection with the sale of business opportunities when a lien is to be given on the personal property of a business. In addition, the UCC requires that a financing statement be filed in connection with a personal property security transaction.

Although the security agreement device seems to be replacing the chattel mortgage with regard to business opportunities, the broker should still be aware of the different classifications of personal property and the fact that, in certain cases, the chattel mortgage is still occasionally used, as well as a conditional sales agreement or a bill of sale accompanied by a note. A further discussion of the UCC and an illustration of a security agreement, will be found in Chapter 15.

Agreement of sale (land contract)

The agreement-of-sale form is more commonly known as a land contract and may also be referred to as an installment and contract, contract of sale, or installment sale contract. This form is basically a type of contract wherein the buyer makes payments to the seller over a certain period of time. The deed is given by the seller either on the final payment of the purchase price or when a specified amount has been paid, at which time the seller agrees to execute and deliver a deed to the property. Further, the buyer does not receive a policy of title insurance until he receives the deed.

Often, this agreement-of-sale form is used when the seller is, in effect, financing the transaction himself and the buyer is not providing the financing by borrowing from a lending institution. Builders may use this form, or it may be used by sellers for buyers who have little or no down payment. The buyer frequently is actually paying off the down payment, since he receives no deed for some time.

While this type of agreement, essentially an installment contract for the purchase of real estate, may have certain advantages to the seller, it has many distinct disadvantages to the buyer. In the usual real estate transaction, the buyer receives a deed from the seller and a policy of title insurance when he buys the property, but here he does not.

During the past few years, there have been numerous California court decisions concerning this form and the equitable interest in the property obtained by the buyer. These decisions frequently have so modified the intent of the form that the seller has lost many of the advantages he apparently had over the buyer, and he would have been better off to use the ordinary trust deed arrangement. Of particular importance is the recent decision of the California Supreme Court in the *Tucker* v. *Lassen Savings and Loan Association* case. The court held that an acceleration clause or "due on sale" clause with respect to an existing loan cannot automatically be exercised when the borrower sells the property using a contract of sale payable in installments.

In distinguishing between an "outright sale" with transfer of title and a land sale contract, the Supreme Court observed that in the normal case, the seller having received a small down payment and retaining legal title, has a considerable interest in maintaining the property until having been paid in full, thus preserving the first lender's security without impairment.

The court held that in the land contract situation, a "due on sale" clause can only validly be enforced when the lender can demonstrate a threat to one of his legitimate interests: the preserving of the security from waste or depreciation or the guarding against having to resort to the security upon default.

The Supreme Court thus has created restrictions upon enforcement of a "due on sale" clause in land sales contract situations, but one should not assume that a "sale" which would otherwise trigger the right to accelerate can be avoided by the device of a land sale contract. Each transaction must stand the test of the buyer's qualifications, the absence of impairment of the lender's security, and the seller's retention of legal title pending payment in full.

Proper use of the land contract, however, will permit transactions which, prior to the decision of the court, may have been precluded. A real estate licensee may negotiate such transactions but should refrain from preparing a land sale contract and refer this function to the attorneys of the parties.

ALL-INCLUSIVE TRUST DEED

An all-inclusive trust deed, commonly referred to as an overlapping or wraparound deed of trust, is an instrument that includes and yet is subordinate to existing trust deeds. It is in some respects similar to a contract of sale except that the title to the property is transferred and may be insured by a title insurance company.

When a note secured by an all-inclusive deed of trust is used, the buyer is the trustor and the seller is the beneficiary. Since the seller is the trustor on prior existing liens, the all-inclusive deed of trust cannot be used if such liens have a due-on-sale clause and provision in an existing note and deed of trust.

Because of the complexities involved, competent legal counsel should be consulted in connection with the use and preparation of the all-inclusive deed of trust.

CREATIVE FINANCE

The recent high interest, tight money market of 1980, has brought into renewed use the term, *creative financing*. It refers to other than traditional methods and forms of finance, some of which are still in a discussion stage, while others are being used in various parts of the state. A few of the more common are as follows:

FLIP or graduated payment loan

The Flexible Loan Insurance Program (FLIP) or graduated payment loan, already introduced in parts of California, allows smaller than usual loan payments to initially be made, with small increases in later years. After approximately five years, a payment level is reached which remains fixed for the loan term. It allows a buyer to have smaller payments at the beginning of the purchase and larger payments in later years when he can better afford to make such payments. With such an arrangement, more new buyers can qualify for financing and attain the ability to purchase a property.

Variable interest rate loan

A variable interest rate loan (VIR) is a loan in which the interest rate is not fixed and can increase or decrease according to a standard index. California banks and savings and loan associations offering a variable rate loan adjust the rate of interest based on the average cost of money to the lenders from the Federal Home Loan Bank (FHLB). The cost index is issued twice a year by the FHLB in San Francisco.

The law limits rate changes to once during any six-month period with a quarter percent increase limit and an overall limit during the loan term of 2½ percent of the original loan rate. On notification of an increase, a borrower may prepay all or part of the loan with no prepayment penalty allowed. If the cost index falls, the lender must reduce the rate of interest. Such loans are considered by lenders to be a more equitable method of financing home purchases because the borrower does not have to pay a higher rate of interest to subsidize others who purchased years ago at lower interest rates.

Rollover loan

A rollover loan permits a lender to renegotiate the rate of interest with the borrower every three to five years. For practical purposes, it results in a five-year loan with monthly payments figured on a 25- or 30-year basis. The Federal Home Loan Bank has approved such a loan limiting the rate of interest increase or decrease and specifying certain regulations with respect to late payment and prohibition of renewal fees. On a rollover loan with a 30-year term, the rate of interest increase or decrease is limited to five percent during the term of the loan, and the rate cannot fluctuate any more than ½ percent a year.

Portable loan

As the name implies, such a loan is written to be portable and can be transferred from an old to a new property without any additional charges or increase of interest rate. Existing loans can often be assumed by a purchaser, but with a portable loan, a seller gains the same type of advantage by being able to take the loan with him and transfer it to a newly acquired property.

Swing loan

A swing loan is a short-term loan on a borrowers principal residence to enable him to have a down payment and closing costs to buy another residence. After the purchase, the homeowner can sell the old residence and pay off the loan. Savings and loan associations can make such an unamortized interim loan to enable a borrower to make the down payment on a home purchase which they are financing. The loan can be in any amount which, together with the amount of any existing loan, does not exceed 80 percent of the fair market value of the property. In addition, the term of the swing loan is limited to 12 months with no prepayment penalty allowed. The borrower must use the loan proceeds to purchase a residence to be occupied as his principal residence, and the swing loan must be secured by a trust deed on a borrowers principal residence at the time the loan is made.

Reverse loan

A reverse loan enables older homeowners to borrow against their home equity and receive monthly payments needed to meet living costs and expenses. It can provide a monthly income for the homeowner without the necessity of having to sell the property. The amount advanced to the borrower plus interest charged is cumulativly totaled, and the lender is eventually repaid at such time as the property is sold or the borrower expires.

TRUTH-IN-LENDING LAW

On July 1, 1969, the Truth-in-Lending Law went into effect. The act is intended to enable consumers to know, through standardized language, exactly what they are paying in credit charges. Federal Reserve Regulation Z was issued under this law for the purpose of its implementation. The law does not set limits on interest or regulate trade practices. These are governed by individual state laws and may differ among the various states. Regulation Z merely requires that the consumer be fully advised of all of the details of his credit purchase. This requirement also applies to any advertising, in whatever form, that the seller engages in.

While the Truth-in-Lending Law regulates consumer credit of every form, we will, in our discussion, be concerned only with its effect upon real estate transactions. An extensive treatment of the law and Regulation Z, including sample forms, charts, and illustrations, may be obtained free by writing to the Federal Trade Commission, P.O.B. 36005, San Francisco 94102, and asking for the publication "What You Ought to Know about Truth-in-Lending." Supplementary material in connection with Regulation Z may also be obtained by writing to the Federal Reserve Bank, San Francisco, California.

Real estate transactions

All real estate credit in any amount is covered under Regulation Z when it is to an individual consumer. Any credit transaction that involves any type of security interest in real estate of a consumer is covered. Credit extended to corporations, partnerships, trusts, and governmental agencies is not covered by this act, nor does it apply to credit extended for business or commercial purposes, that is, nonconsumer purposes.

The act does require that any persons who, in the ordinary course of business regularly extend, or offer to extend, or arrange, or offer to arrange, for the extension of consumer credit, must make certain disclosures to the consumer.

Disclosure

The "finance charge" and the "annual percentage rate" are the two most important disclosures required. They tell the borrower how much he is paying for his credit and its cost in percentage terms. An exception is made in the sale of dwellings; the total finance charge in terms of dollars paid by both buyer and seller need not be stated. The annual percentage rate, however, must be stated clearly.

The finance charge. In general, the finance charge is the total of all costs imposed by a creditor and paid either directly or indirectly by the borrower or another party, such as points the seller may be required to pay in an FHA transaction as an incident to the extension of credit. It includes, in addition to interest, such costs as points or discounts, loan fees, finder's fees, inspection fees, timepiece differential, FHA mortgage insurance premiums, or even premiums on life insurance that a lender might require. The finance charge, however, does not include for purposes of real property transactions such charges as premiums or charges for title reports or title insurance, registration fees imposed by law, surveys, appraisal or inspection fees, transfer taxes, credit reports, legal fees for preparation of documents pursuant to a settlement, escrow, notary fees, utility costs, or payments to cover taxes not yet due and payable, but if any of these charges are included in the amount to be financed and are paid out of loan proceeds, they must be itemized and set forth separately in the disclosure statement.

The annual percentage rate. The annual percentage rate not only includes "interest" but also represents the relationship of the total finance charge to the total amount to be financed. Where points and other fees are involved, the rate shown will be higher than merely interest. A buyer who is told that the interest rate on his loan is to be 9 percent may wonder why it is shown as 9¼ percent on the disclosure statement. His broker will have to explain that the loan will carry an interest rate of 9 percent but that the annual percentage rate shown on the disclosure statement includes the total cost imposed by the lender for making the loan, which includes not only the interest on the sum borrowed but also the capitalized value of charges which must be paid by the borrower or anyone else at the inception of the loan.

The disclosure statement. A disclosure statement used by many savings and loan associations is shown in Figure 7–6, and a CAR form for brokers use is shown in Figure 7–7, and the law says that such disclosure shall be made before the credit transaction is consummated. Consummation may be generally defined here as the offer of credit to the borrower and his acceptance of the terms. In the normal real estate transaction, the disclosure of credit information would accompany the loan commitment. It would thus be after the purchase contract had been entered into but before close of escrow and consummation of the transaction. Certain problems arise in connection with second loans where, under the law, the lender may or may not be required to comply with the law. This will be discussed later in connection with the real estate licensee's role under Regulation Z of the Truth-in-Lending Law.

The following disclosures must be made:

1. The date on which the finance charges begin to accrue if it is different from the date of transaction.
2. Annual percentage rate of the finance charge.
3. Number, amount, and due dates or periods of payments scheduled to repay the indebtedness and, "except in the case of a loan secured by a first lien (or equivalent) on a dwelling to finance the purchase of that dwelling, or, in the case of credit sale of a dwelling," the sum of all these payments, using the term *total of payments*.
4. The method of computing the amount of any default or delinquency charge.
5. A description of any penalty charge that may be imposed by the creditor for prepayment of the principal sum.
6. Total amount of the finance charge, individually itemized, except in the case of a first mortgage lien given to finance the purchase of a dwelling.
7. Total amount of credit, including all charges, individually itemized, which are included in the amount of credit extended but which are not part of the finance charge, using the term *amount financed*.
8. Any finance charges, such as points and the like, including those paid out of loan proceeds, such as a discount, and any deposit balance or investment which the creditor required the borrower to make and which must either be paid by the borrower or another at settlement or before proceeds are disbursed, using the terms *prepaid finance charge* and *required deposit balance* as applicable.
9. The total finance charge, "except in the case of a loan secured by a first lien, or equivalent security interest, on a dwelling made to finance the purchase of that dwelling."
10. A description of any security interest retained by the creditor.

ABC SAVINGS AND LOAN ASSOCIATION
ADDRESS
NOTICE TO CUSTOMER REQUIRED BY FEDERAL LAW AND
FEDERAL RESERVE REGULATION Z
(To Be Executed in Duplicate)

CS&LL FORM Z-1
PURCHASE LOAN ON DWELLING

NAME OF BORROWER(S) _____ LOAN NO. _____

MAILING ADDRESS _____ LOAN AMOUNT $_____

A. Payments for principal and interest @ _____ % per annum on this transaction shall be in _____ monthly installments of $ _____ each, beginning on the _____ day of _____, 19___, and due on the _____ day of each month thereafter.

B. The FINANCE CHARGE on this transaction will begin to accrue on _____

C. CHARGES NOT PART OF FINANCE COSTS

	Pd. by Cash	Pd. from Loan
1. Title ins. premium	$_____	$_____
2. Recording fees	_____	_____
3. Appraisal fees	_____	_____
4. Credit report	_____	_____
5. Notary	_____	_____
6. To impounds	_____	_____
7. Prepare documents	_____	_____
8. _____	_____	_____
9. _____	_____	_____
Total Charges	$_____	$_____
Net proceeds to borrower		$_____
E. AMOUNT FINANCED		$_____

D. PREPAID FINANCE CHARGE
(Paid from any source)

1. Origination fee $_____
2. Loan fee pd. by buyer _____
3. Int. prepaid ( ) days _____
4. Mtge. ins. ( ) _____
5. _____ _____
6. _____ _____
7. _____ _____
8. _____ _____
9. _____ _____

PREPAID FINANCE CHARGE $_____

NOTE: Any figures in Sections C & D above with asterisks are estimated

F. **ANNUAL PERCENTAGE RATE** _____ %

G. LATE CHARGE — In the event a monthly payment is not paid by due date, the association will make the following charge: _____

H. PREPAYMENT PRIVILEGE — Borrower may prepay the loan in whole or in part in the following manner and under the following conditions: _____

I. SECURITY INTEREST — The association's security interest in this transaction is a trust deed covering real property and improvements located _____ and certain other rights and property relating thereto, all as described in the trust deed, a copy of which will be provided. The trust deed secures approved future advances and other indebtedness, the terms of which are described therein. The trust deed also covers after-acquired property located on or attached to the described real property. A security agreement _____ be taken on furniture, fixtures, and equipment situated therein.

J. INSURANCE — Fire and other hazard insurance protecting the property, if written in connection with this loan, may be obtained by borrower through any person of his choice, provided, however, the association may, for reasonable cause, refuse to accept an insurer on any such insurance which is required. If borrower desires property insurance to be obtained through the association's designated agency, the cost will be set forth in a separate insurance statement furnished by the association.

I(We) hereby acknowledge receiving and reading a completed copy of this disclosure along with copies of the documents provided. Notwithstanding any existing agreement with the association to the contrary, the association and each borrower understand that this is not an offer or commitment of the association to lend.

_____ _____
Association Borrower

By _____ _____
Title Borrower

Date _____ Date _____

FIGURE 7-6

REAL ESTATE LOAN DISCLOSURE STATEMENT
CALIFORNIA ASSOCIATION OF REALTORS® STANDARD FORM

BROKER/ARRANGER OF CREDIT: CREDITOR:

_____   _____
(NAME)   (NAME)

_____   _____
(ADDRESS)   (ADDRESS)

Purpose of Loan: _____

I.   Loan in the amount of $ _____ is to be secured by a note and Deed of Trust in favor of Creditor on property located at _____, which is ☐ is not ☐ expected to be the location of the Borrower's principal residence. (NOTE: If it is, a Notice of Right to Cancel must be provided unless this transaction involves a first lien for the purchase or initial construction of a dwelling.)

      The Deed of Trust may secure additional advances and may cover after-acquired property. The loan may also be secured by an assignment of proceeds from any required insurance protecting the property.

II. Charges included which are not part of the Finance Charge:
         1. Appraisal .... $ _____
         2. Credit report .... $ _____
         3. Notary .... $ _____
         4. Recording .... $ _____
         5. Title insurance .... $ _____
         6. Document preparation ...... $ _____
         7. Property insurance .... $ _____
         8. Termite inspection .... $ _____
         9. Other _____ $ _____
                         (DESCRIBE)
                 Total Charges ..... $ _____

      Property insurance may be obtained by Borrower through any person of his choice. If it is to be purchased through Broker or Creditor, the cost appears at Item II. 7 above.

      Credit life and disability insurance are not required to obtain this loan.

III. FINANCE CHARGE:
     A. Prepaid **FINANCE CHARGE**
                Loan Broker's commission .... $ _____
                Loan escrow fee .... $ _____
                Other _____ $ _____
                _____ $ _____
                        (DESCRIBE)   (Total of A) $ _____
     B. Interest for period of loan .... $ _____
                           FINANCE CHARGE   (A + B) $ _____
Finance Charge accrues from _____, 19_____.

IV. AMOUNT FINANCED:
      Amount of loan from Item I (includes all charges in Item II which are not paid in cash) ... $ _____
      Less Prepaid **Finance Charge** (Item III. A) .... $ _____
                                                          AMOUNT FINANCED $ _____

V. **ANNUAL PERCENTAGE RATE:** _____ %

VI. PAYMENT TERMS:
      Payable in _____ payments of principal and interest as follows: _____
monthly installments of $ _____ each, beginning _____, 19____, and a
final/balloon payment of $ _____ due on _____, 19____.
                                      TOTAL OF PAYMENTS (Item I + Item III. B) $ _____
      There are no arrangements for refinancing balloon payments.
      If any payment is not made within _____ days after it is due, a late charge must be paid by Borrower, as follows: _____.
In addition, Creditor has the option to accelerate the indebtedness and to declare all payments immediately due and payable.
      In the event of acceleration or other prepayment in full, unaccrued interest is cancelled and a default or prepayment charge will be computed as follows: _____
_____

                                                        I HAVE READ AND RECEIVED A COMPLETED COPY OF THIS STATEMENT.

Date _____, 19_____.   _____
*****IMPORTANT NOTE:**   (Borrower)
Asterisk denotes an estimate.   _____
                                                      (Borrower)
                                                      FORM LD-11

FIGURE 7–7

11. For a credit sale, land contract, or any others in which the credit is extended or arranged by the seller, the cash price, total down payment itemized to show cash and trade-in, and the unpaid balance of the cash price must be disclosed.

It should be noted that an important exception exists under the law. If circumstances require the issuance of a disclosure statement, the total amount of all monthly payments and the total finance charge need not be disclosed in connection with a purchase money first mortgage, or equivalent, to finance the construction or acquisition of a dwelling. Disclosure is required with regard to loans, secured or otherwise; to finance acquisition of raw acreage or building lots; refinancings; assumptions where the lender approves the new purchaser in writing; and certain second loans even though the first loan in the same transaction may be exempt from the requirement.

Right to rescind

The law gives the buyer the right to call off and cancel a credit transaction involving a security interest in any real property used or expected to be used as his principle residence. He has three business days after the credit contract is consummated or the disclosure statement is given, whichever is later, to rescind.

Excepted from this provision are purchase money first mortgages used to finance the acquisition or construction of a dwelling or the assumption of such an obligation. Thus, the purchaser has a right to cancel any credit transaction in which the lender takes back some security interest unless it is a first mortgage or assumption of a first mortgage given to finance the purchase or construction of a dwelling in which the buyer lives or expects to live. A contract of sale (also called a land contract or agreement of sale) is considered the equivalent of a first lien and is therefore not rescindable.

The right of recision requirement will not have any effect on second mortgages taken back by sellers who do not, in the regular course of business, extend credit. A person who does not regularly extend consumer credit in the course of his business is not considered a "creditor" and is exempt from compliance with the Truth-in-Lending Law, and therefore does not have to provide a disclosure statement or right to rescind.

If a second loan is taken by one who is deemed to be a "creditor" under the law, such as a builder, real estate licensee, institutional investor, or a private investor who invests in such loans primarily for income, the Truth-in-Lending Law will fully apply to the transaction and the right to rescind will exist.

Recision form. Whenever a borrower has the right to rescind a transaction, the creditor must give notice of the fact to the customer by furnishing him with two copies of a formal notice such as that shown in Figure 7–8. A customer may rescind a transaction by signing and dating the notice to cancel which he receives from the creditor and either (a) mailing the notice to the creditor at the address shown on the notice or (b) delivering the notice to the creditor at the address shown on the notice either personally, by messenger, or by other agents. A customer may also rescind by sending a telegram to the creditor at the address shown on the notice and stating that he has decided to cancel and also identifying in brief the transaction involved.

A customer who cancels a transaction will not be held liable for any finance charge or other type of charge, and any security interest acquired becomes void. The creditor, within ten days after receiving notice that the purchaser has decided to rescind, must return any deposit money received and terminate any security interest created.

A creditor should allow a sufficient time after the required three-day period for receipt of a letter or telegram which the customer may have sent. During the three-day period, the creditor must not take any action to perform under the contract since such action may be wasteful of time and effort should the customer decide to cancel. The law provides that the use of printed forms for the purpose of allowing a waiver of right of recision is prohibited. Waiver of right of recision is allowed in certain cases, but this can only be accomplished by the customer's submitting to the creditor a dated and signed personal statement modifying or waiving his right of recision.

Joint owners. Where joint ownership is involved and the right of recision exists, the right may be exercised by any one of the joint owners and applies to all of them. Where a modification or waiver of the right of recision exists, all joint owners must sign the statement required.

Where there are joint owners, the right to receive disclosures and notice of the right of recision, the right to rescind, and the need to sign a modification or waiver of such right, apply only to those joint owners who are parties to the transaction.

Advertising. Regulation Z of Truth-in-Lending affects the use of credit terms in advertising the

---
(Creditor)

(Office)

(City)

NOTICE OF RIGHT TO CANCEL

Name(s) of Customer(s) _____

Type of Loan _____

Amount of Loan _____ $ _____

Notice to Customer Required By Federal Law:

You have entered into a transaction on _____, 19____ which may result in a lien, mortgage, or other security interest on your home. You have a legal right under federal law to cancel this transaction, if you desire to do so, without any penalty or obligation within three business days from the above date or any later date on which all material disclosures required under the Truth in Lending Act have been given to you. If you so cancel the transaction, any lien, mortgage, or other security interest on your home arising from this transaction is automatically void. You are also entitled to receive a refund of any downpayment or other consideration if you cancel.

If you decide to cancel this transaction you may do so by notifying:

_____
(Name of Creditor)

at _____
(Address of Creditor's Place of Business)

by mail or telegram sent not later than midnight of _____, 19____.
(Date 3 business days after date of receipt of this notice.)

You may also use any other form of written notice identifying the transaction if it is delivered to the above address not later than that time. This notice may be used for that purpose by dating and signing below.

I hereby cancel this transaction.

_____, 19____   _____
(Date)   (Customer's Signature)

ACKNOWLEDGEMENT OF RECEIPT

I hereby acknowledge receipt of TWO copies of the foregoing Notice of Right to Cancel.

_____, 19____   _____
(Date)   (Customer's Signature)

_____
(All joint owners must sign)

See reverse side for important information about your right of rescission.

FIGURE 7–8

EFFECT OF RESCISSION

When a customer exercises his right to rescind, he is not liable for any finance or other charge, and any security interest becomes void upon such a rescission. Within 10 days after receipt of a notice of rescission, the creditor shall return to the customer any money or property given as earnest money, downpayment, or otherwise, and shall take any action necessary or appropriate to reflect the termination of any security interest created under the transaction. If the creditor has delivered any property to the customer, the customer may retain possession of it. Upon the performance of the creditor's obligations under this section, the customer shall tender the property to the creditor, except that if return of the property in kind would be impracticable or inequitable, the customer shall tender its reasonable value. Tender shall be made at the location of the property or at the residence of the customer, at the option of the customer. If the creditor does not take possession of the property within 10 days after tender by the customer, ownership of the property vests in the customer without obligation on his part to pay for it.

NOTICE OF INTENT TO PROCEED

I hereby certify that I have elected not to cancel or rescind the transaction referred to on the reverse side and that I have not delivered, mailed or filed for transmission by telegram to the Creditor any notice of cancellation or rescission of that transaction.

_____, 19_____
(Date and mail or deliver no sooner than
3 business days after date of receipt)

_____
(Customer's Signature)

_____
(All joint owners must sign)

FIGURE 7–8 *(continued)*

sale of residential real property. It is permissible to advertise in general terms, such as "low downpayment," "liberal terms available," or "FHA–VA financing available." Any finance charge, if mentioned, must be stated as "annual percentage rate," using that term.

The advertisement may state the annual percentage rate alone, but if the advertiser mentions any other credit terms, such as down payment, lack of down payment, monthly payment, amount of any finance charge, or the term of the loan, he must also mention the cash price, the required down payment, the annual percentage rate, and also the number, amount, and due dates of all payments.

Advertising includes newspapers, radio, TV, direct mail, giveaway literature, billboards, and posters.

Enforcement and penalties

A number of governmental agencies are involved in enforcement of the law. Penalties for violating the act can be both criminal and civil. For willful and knowing failure to comply, criminal punishment may result in a fine or imprisonment. A creditor who fails to disclose any required information may be civilly liable to the borrower for twice the finance charge but in no case less than $100 or more than $1,000. A creditor will have 15 days after discovering an error, before a civil action is begun or written notice of the error received from the customer, to correct the situation. Further, the creditor could avoid liability by showing through a preponderance of evidence that the violation was not intentional and resulted from a bona fide error. Civil liability could also extend to the assignee of the original creditor provided the assignee was in a continuing business relationship with the original creditor at the time the credit was extended or at the time of the assignment.

Effect upon the real estate licensee

The Truth-in-Lending Law defines a creditor as one who regularly extends or arranges for the extension of credit or offers to arrange for the extension of credit. According to the law, to arrange for the extension of credit means to provide or offer to provide consumer credit which is or will be extended by another person and where the person arranging such credit receives or will receive a fee or some other consideration for such service or has knowledge of the credit terms and participates in the preparation of the contract documents required in connection with the extension of credit.

The real estate licensee in general is not an arranger of credit under the Truth-in-Lending Law and is therefore not personally responsible for any of its requirements. Licensees do not ordinarily receive fees either from the mortgage broker or the mortgage lender for referring housing purchasers to them. The commission is paid by the seller of the property out of the proceeds of the sale, and while the licensee may direct the purchaser to a savings and loan company, bank, or other source of credit, the licensee is not paid separately for doing so. The regulations of the Truth-in-Lending Law, Regulation Z, in no way suggest that the licensee should refrain from making direct contacts with lenders in behalf of real property purchasers or that they should cease supplying preliminary credit information. The important point is that the lender or lender's agent should be the one to make the judgment on the acceptability of the purchaser as a credit risk.

The licensee should be careful not to prepare or assist in the preparation of any of the credit instruments, such as the loan application, note, deed of trust, mortgage, or installment sales contract. Thus, the real estate licensee is not a creditor or an arranger of credit if he does not receive any independent fee for helping to place the loan or assist in any way in the preparation of the credit instruments.

The licensee who lends his own money or who operates an independent separate mortgage banking or lending facility will be personally responsible for complying with the Truth-in-Lending Law. Land contracts, also referred to as an agreement of sale, conditional sale contract, or an installment sale contract, are discussed elsewhere in this chapter, and the same principles discussed above apply to the land contract. If the licensee does not receive a separate fee for selling the land contract independent of the sale of the real property itself and does not prepare or assist in the preparation of the land contract, he is not an arranger under the law and is not responsible for any disclosures.

Secondary financing. A seller who takes back a second loan as an accommodation to the purchaser and for the purpose of effecting the sale of his property is not a creditor under the law and does not have to comply with the disclosure provisions. Thus, the typical seller who is not in the business of selling or dealing in real estate is exempt from the law if he takes back a second trust deed. However, an individual who with some regularity extends funds for second loans may well be considered as being in the business of regularly extending credit and will have to comply with the law.

Even though an individual homeowner who takes back a second loan is usually exempt from compliance with the Truth-in-Lending Law, he must be the real lender to maintain his exemption. This may not be the case when he prearranges with a real estate licensee or second mortgage investor to discount and sell the instrument immediately. Thus, in cases where credit instruments are discounted by prearrangement, the real estate licensee should not rely on the seller's exemption and should comply fully with the disclosure provisions of the law. The licensee should make full disclosure of the terms of the second trust deed or contract of sale, and notification of the right to rescind must also be furnished to the purchaser. The seller's exemption from compliance with the law will not be lost because he may decide subsequently to sell his interest in the second loan or contract of sale. The exemption would be lost only in cases where it was clear from the outset that the seller had no intention of holding the instrument for any time at all but intended to sell it immediately.

REAL ESTATE SETTLEMENT PROCEDURES ACT

The Real Estate Settlement Procedures Act (RESPA) was enacted in 1974 and amended in 1976. The regulations of the act have been adopted by the Department of Housing and Urban Development (HUD) with respect to the sale or transfer of one- to four-family homes, co-ops, and condominiums financed through FHA, VA, or financial institutions with federally insured deposits. Current regulations require the following:

A uniform settlement statement must be made available to the borrower not later than the date of closing, unless waived by the borrower. HUD exempts such areas where settlement statements are usually provided as in the typical transaction using an escrow agent. If the borrower requests it, the borrower must be given the opportunity prior to close of escrow to inspect and review the settlements costs in connection with the transaction.

The lender is required to provide HUD's special information booklet to the borrower at the time the written loan application is received or within three days and also to furnish an estimate of the likely closing costs in connection with the transaction to be made by the lender. If the lender requires use of a particular attorney, title examiner, title insurer, or individual to conduct the settlement, the lender must state if any business relationship exists and give an estimate of that individual's charges.

Kickbacks or payment of unearned fees cannot be made in connection with the transaction. The sharing of commissions and referral fees between cooperating real estate brokers and agreements between real estate brokers and agents are not in violation of the law. RESPA regulations further state that a seller may not condition the sale of property on the buyer's purchase of title insurance from a particular title insurance company.

The purpose of the RESPA regulations is to provide full disclosure with respect to costs and charges in connection with real estate transactions and further benefits both the public and the real estate industry.

SOURCES OF FUNDS

There are many sources for obtaining funds necessary in real estate transactions. The entire real estate loan picture today is quite different from conditions that existed at the beginning of this century. Rates of interest have been appreciably reduced from those that used to be charged by mortgage lenders, and instead of paying off the total amount of the principal at maturity of the loan, today's methods call for amortizing loans by monthly payments that include principal, interest, taxes, and insurance. The term of the loan has also been extended from the former periods of under ten years to present terms of 15, 20, 25, and 30 years. Although the total interest payment will be higher, the monthly payment necessary will be lower, so that more persons are able to borrow money for the purchase of real estate.

The emergence of FHA insured and VA guaranteed home loans has had a great influence on the pattern of home purchases and on prescribed standards for lending practices as well as for building construction. Generally, they have offered the borrower the lowest rate of interest, a fairly high loan ratio to appraised value, and a long term. The same is true of programs initiated by various states, such as the Cal-Vet program in California. With the exception of new tract sales, however, considerable time and red tape are involved in obtaining and processing these types of loans. In periods of tight money, they may be difficult to obtain, and the seller may have to pay a considerable amount of points in order for the borrower to be able to obtain the loan.

In the sale of other than new or newer properties and when the buyer has a substantial down payment, conventional loans assume tremendous importance. These loans offer faster processing, have more flexible terms, and may offer the borrower a higher loan ratio. A substantial amount of conventional financing is also used in connection with newer properties in the higher price categories.

We shall discuss various lenders in the following order: (1) institutional lenders, which are (a) savings and loan associations, (b) commercial banks, (c) insurance companies; (2) noninstitutional lenders, which are (a) private individuals, (b) mortgage companies and investment trusts; (3) government guranteed loans, which are (a) FHA, (b) VA, (c) Cal-Vet.

Real estate licensees must be extremely cautious in discussing with clients the various factors with respect to real estate finance, such as loan ratios, interest rates, fees, term and prepayment penalties, since there is often as much change in these areas as among the various lenders. The discussion which follows with respect to lenders is general in nature; and in order for a licensee to be able to give current up-to-date information, he must constantly check upon conditions in his own particular locality.

INSTITUTIONAL LENDERS

Savings and loan associations

Among institutional lenders, savings and loan associations account for the greatest share of the home loan market. Loans made by institutional lenders without government gurantees are generally referred to as conventional loans.

The main function of the savings and loan association is to gather the savings of as many people as possible and to lend these savings safely to other people for the purposes of buying, building, making improvements, and refinancing. Loans are restricted to amortized first loans secured by a mortgage or deed of trust. Savings and loan associations do not advance funds for secondary financing. Figure 7–9 illustrates a typical savings and loan association loan application form.

In California, associations are either federally chartered or state chartered. All federally chartered associations and most state chartered associations are members of the Federal Home Loan Bank System and are subject to its supervision. In addition, most savings and loan associations have joined the Federal Savings and Loan Insurance Corporation.

Individual accounts are currently insured up to $40,000, and under certain conditions, a family of three can have as much as $200,000 insured by using multiple ownership accounts.

Each year, conventional loans account for an ever greater proportion of the real estate loan portfolio of California's savings and loan associations. Of the loans currently on their books, 95 percent are conventional, 3 percent VA, and 2 percent FHA. Factors to be considered separately with regard to savings and loan associations are (a) interest rate, (b) term, (c) loan fee, (d) prepayment penalty, and (e) loan ratio.

Interest rate. California savings and loan companies during 1980 paid savings account holders from 6 to slightly over 9 percent depending upon the term for which the money was deposited, and they paid up to 16 percent on 26-week money market certificates.

The rate of interest charged for loans has recently varied from 10 to 17 percent per annum. The newer and more select the property and the stronger the buyer, the lower the interest rate will be. The interest rate charged will be most important to the buyer who plans to keep his property for a long period of time. Although the difference in the monthly payment will vary only a few dollars between a loan at 11 percent and the same loan at 11½ percent, the amount of interest dollars the borrower will have to pay over a long period will vary considerably between the two loans.

In addition to the usual fixed rate of interest, some savings and loan associations use a variable interest rate which may periodically increase or decrease depending upon the average cost of money as determined by the Federal Home Loan Bank. These are termed Variable Rate Mortgages (VRMs).

Term. The term means the number of years given to repay the loan. A loan for a period of 30 years will require a lower monthly payment than the same loan for a 20-year term, since the sooner the borrower must repay the amount borrowed, the larger his monthly payment must be.

The term allowed on older properties will generally be between 15 and 20 years, while post-World War II buildings will get 20- to 30-year repayment terms. However, purchasers of select properties in large urban areas are often given 30-year repayment terms.

Many borrowers want a shorter term since they do not want to take forever to repay the loan, while other borrowers want a term as long as possible so that the monthly payment will be lower.

RESIDENTIAL LOAN APPLICATION

MORTGAGE APPLIED FOR	☐ Conventional ☐ FHA ☐ VA ☐ ______	Amount $	Interest Rate %	No. of Months	Monthly Payment Principal & Interest $	Escrow/Impounds (to be collected monthly) ☐ Taxes ☐ Hazard Ins. ☐ Mtg. Ins. ☐ ______

Prepayment Option

SUBJECT PROPERTY

Property Street Address	City	County	State	Zip	No. Units

Legal Description (Attach description if necessary) — Year Built

Purpose of Loan: ☐ Purchase ☐ Construction-Permanent ☐ Construction ☐ Refinance ☐ Other (Explain)

Complete this line if Construction-Permanent or Construction Loan	Lot Value Data / Year Acquired	Original Cost	Present Value (a)	Cost of Imps. (b)	Total (a + b)	ENTER TOTAL AS PURCHASE PRICE IN DETAILS OF PURCHASE.
	______	$	$	$	$	

Complete this line if a Refinance Loan

Year Acquired	Original Cost	Amt. Existing Liens	Purpose of Refinance	Describe Improvements [ ] made [ ] to be made
	$	$		Cost: $ ______

Title Will Be Held In What Name(s) — Manner In Which Title Will Be Held

Source of Down Payment and Settlement Charges

This application is designed to be completed by the borrower(s) with the lender's assistance. The Co-Borrower Section and all other Co-Borrower questions must be completed and the appropriate box(es) checked if ☐ another person will be jointly obligated with the Borrower on the loan, or ☐ the Borrower is relying on income from alimony, child support or separate maintenance or on the income or assets of another person as a basis for repayment of the loan, or ☐ the Borrower is married and resides, or the property is located, in a community property state.

BORROWER	CO-BORROWER
Name / Age / School Yrs ____	Name / Age / School Yrs ____
Present Address No. Years ____ ☐ Own ☐ Rent	Present Address No. Years ____ ☐ Own ☐ Rent
Street ______	Street ______
City/State/Zip ______	City/State/Zip ______
Former address if less than 2 years at present address	Former address if less than 2 years at present address
Street ______	Street ______
City/State/Zip ______	City/State/Zip ______
Years at former address ☐ Own ☐ Rent	Years at former address ☐ Own ☐ Rent
Marital Status ☐ Married ☐ Separated ☐ Unmarried (incl. single, divorced, widowed) — DEPENDENTS OTHER THAN LISTED BY CO-BORROWER: NO / AGES	Marital Status ☐ Married ☐ Separated ☐ Unmarried (incl. single, divorced, widowed) — DEPENDENTS OTHER THAN LISTED BY BORROWER: NO / AGES
Name and Address of Employer — Years employed in this line of work or profession? ____ years; Years on this job ____; ☐ Self Employed*	Name and Address of Employer — Years employed in this line of work or profession? ____ years; Years on this job ____; ☐ Self Employed
Position/Title — Type of Business	Position/Title — Type of Business
Social Security Number*** — Home Phone — Business Phone	Social Security Number*** — Home Phone — Business Phone

GROSS MONTHLY INCOME

Item	Borrower	Co-Borrower	Total
Base Empl. Income	$	$	$
Overtime			
Bonuses			
Commissions			
Dividends/Interest			
Net Rental Income			
Other† (Before completing, see notice under Describe Other Income below.)			
Total	$	$	$

MONTHLY HOUSING EXPENSE**

	PRESENT	PROPOSED
Rent	$	
First Mortgage (P&I)		$
Other Financing (P&I)		
Hazard Insurance		
Real Estate Taxes		
Mortgage Insurance		
Homeowner Assn. Dues		
Other		
Total Monthly Pmt.	$	$
Utilities		
Total	$	$

DETAILS OF PURCHASE

a. Purchase Price	$
b. Total Closing Costs (Est.)	
c. Prepaid Escrows (Est.)	
d. Total (a + b + c)	$
e. Amount This Mortgage	( )
f. Other Financing	( )
g. Present Equity in Lot	( )
h. Amount of Cash Deposit	( )
i. Closing Costs Paid by Seller	( )
j. Cash Reqd. For Closing (Est.)	$

DESCRIBE OTHER INCOME

B—Borrower C—Co-Borrower

NOTICE: † Alimony, child support, or separate maintenance income need not be revealed if the Borrower or Co-Borrower does not choose to have it considered as a basis for repaying this loan.

		Monthly Amount
		$

IF EMPLOYED IN CURRENT POSITION FOR LESS THAN TWO YEARS COMPLETE THE FOLLOWING

B/C	Previous Employer/School	City/State	Type of Business	Position/Title	Dates From/To	Monthly Income
						$

THESE QUESTIONS APPLY TO BOTH BORROWER AND CO-BORROWER

If a "yes" answer is given to a question in this column, explain on an attached sheet.	Borrower Yes or No	Co-Borrower Yes or No
Have you any outstanding judgments? In the last 14 years, have you been declared bankrupt?		
Have you had property foreclosed upon or given title or deed in lieu thereof?		
Are you a co-maker or endorser on a note?		
Are you a party in a law suit?		
Are you obligated to pay alimony, child support, or separate maintenance?		
Is any part of the down payment borrowed?		

	Borrower Yes or No	Co-Borrower Yes or No
Do you have health and accident insurance?		
Do you have major medical coverage?		
Do you intend to occupy this property?		
Will this property be your primary residence?		
Have you previously owned a home?		
Sales Price of previously owned home?	$	$

*FHLMC requires self employed to furnish signed copies of one or more most recent Federal Tax Returns or audited Profit and Loss Statements. FNMA requires business credit report, signed Federal Income Tax returns for last two years, and, if available, audited P/L plus balance sheet for same period.

**All Present Monthly Housing Expenses of Borrower and Co-Borrower should be listed on a combined basis.

***Neither FHLMC nor FNMA requires this information.

FHLMC 65 Rev. 3/77 FNMA 1003 Rev. 3/77

FIGURE 7–9

FIGURE 7-9 *(continued)*

Loan fee. Savings and loan associations usually charge a loan fee of from 1 to 3 percent of the amount of the loan. The loan fee is one of these items that make up the closing costs paid by the buyer-borrower. For instance, a buyer who borrows $80,000 and is charged a loan fee of 1½ percent will have to pay 1,200. This will be one of the closing cost items charged against him in escrow.

Prepayment penalty. Savings and loan associations generally charge a penalty of some sort if a loan is paid off before maturity. Since very few borrowers stay in the same location long enough to actually pay off a 20- to 30-year loan, the associations receive a considerable amount of revenue in this way.

Generally, the prepayment penalty charged will be three to six months of interest on the remaining balance of the loan. The charge is paid by the original borrower.

Many associations waive this penalty if the new purchaser finances through them. For this reason, the broker often will tell a purchaser to seek financing from the same savings and loan association that holds the seller's note, which may save the seller from paying a prepayment penalty. The price the seller will accept should then reflect such saving.

Loan ratio. Maximum loan ratios and terms allowed are set by law for savings and loan associations. Different regulations apply to different property classifications, such as single-family dwellings, two- to four-family buildings, five or more units, business property, and commercial property. Federally chartered savings and loan associations are allowed maximums slightly higher than those for state chartered associations.

The law prescribes the maximum limits and allows up to 95 percent of appraised value, but as a practical matter, all the savings and loan associations have set for themselves limits that are well below the maximum allowed. Since policies vary among the separate associations, the licensee must keep constantly abreast of the current practices of associations in his own locality.

In addition to their own loan, some associations will allow a second loan to be recorded against the property, while others will slightly lower the amount they will loan if they know that a second loan is to be recorded.

Most savings and loan associations will appraise the property at the same amount as the selling price if they believe the selling price reflects the current market value. This practice differs from that of banks, which often appraise a property at slightly below what it may bring on the open market. For this reason, in actual dollars loaned, a conventional loan from a savings and loan company usually will be more than one that may be obtained from a bank.

Commercial banks

Banks in California are either nationally chartered or state chartered. Federal laws regulate the national banks, while state laws regulate the state chartered institutions. In regard to activity in the real estate market, banks are traditionally known for their conversative appraisal and lending practices. Banks tend to favor short-term lending, so real estate loans, especially conventional ones, have never been a significant part of their lending program. They tend to favor business and short-term credit loans and automobile financing and recently have devoted much of their effort to the credit card field.

The distribution of all real estate loans held by California banks is approximately 60 percent conventional loans, 35 percent FHA insured loans, and 5 percent VA guaranteed loans. A large proportion of the conventional real estate loans were devoted to nonresidential properties in the business, commercial, and industrial areas. In making mortgage investments, liquidity and marketability are of prime importance. For banks, government underwritten loans have the important advantage of not having to be counted as part of their mortgage total, which is restricted by law to approximately 65 percent of their time deposits or the bank's combined capital and surplus, whichever is greater.

Policies and practices of various banks differ according to the particular banking firm and local area. The licensee must remain constantly informed about prevailing conditions in his own locale. Factors that will be considered separately are (*a*) loan ratio, (*b*) interest rate, (*c*) term, (*d*) loan fee, and (*e*) prepayment penalty.

Loan ratio. Fully amortized conventional real estate loans made by all national and state chartered banks are generally limited to 80 percent of the bank's appraised value of the property or the selling price, whichever is lower.

A most important fact to remember, however, is that the exception of new construction, the traditionally conservative banking approach to value results in the bank appraisal being 5 to 15 percent below the actual selling price of the property. The licensee must remember not to apply the bank's loan ratio to the selling price of the property as in savings and loan associations but rather to the bank's appraised value of the property.

Loans on prime residential properties will be made at between 70 and 80 percent of appraised value. Middle-aged and older properties regarded as acceptable will receive a loan of 60 to 70 percent of appraised value. Loans on economically sound farm properties will be made at approximately 66.66 percent of appraised value, and commercial and industrial properties will receive a 60 to 66.66 percent loan ratio.

Interest rate. Interest rates fluctuate, depending on conditions in the money market at any given time. Rates charged by banks have traditionally been slightly below those in effect at savings and loan associations; however, while some banks still follow this pattern, others charge the same interest rate as their local savings and loan associations.

Term. Bank terms vary from a high of 25 to 30 years for prime property, to 20 years for good property, and approximately 15 years for acceptable property.

Loan fee. One of the advantages of a bank loan has traditionally been the low loan fee charged to the borrower. During the past few years, however, most banks have begun to charge a percentage fee based on the amount borrowed. Those banks doing so are charging 1 to 3 percent of the loan amount.

Prepayment penalty. Some banks do not charge the borrower any prepayment penalty, and the borrower may, at any time, pay off the entire obligation without having a prepayment penalty assessed against him. Others charge a penalty of from 1 to 3 percent of the outstanding balance of the loan.

Insurance companies

Life insurance companies generally make conventional loans on all types of properties, but they favor loans on properties that require large amounts, such as shopping centers, developments, large commercial properties, industrial properties, and hotels. They invest heavily in mortgages insured by the FHA and in those guaranteed by the VA. Many loans are purchased from mortgage companies, who make loans in their respective communities and deliver them when completed to the insurance company. For a fee, the mortgage company usually serves as the agent for the insurance company in making such loans.

Of the loans held by insurance companies, approximately 50 percent are FHA and VA loans, 30 percent commerical income development properties, and 20 percent are on higher priced, new or rather recently built individual houses. The licensee who deals in resales of existing houses, duplexes, and smaller income units will seldom seek financing from an insurance company.

Life insurance companies incorporated in California or doing business in California are restricted to conventional mortgage loans of 75 percent of market value for single-family residences and 66.66 percent of market value for other types of property. There is no state restriction on term, but most insurance companies use 20 to 25 years. Interest rates are generally the same as those charged by commercial banks.

Since their investment objectives are long-term in nature, insurance companies generally do not have due-on-sale clauses in their loans. They generally have a lock-in provision during the initial portion of the term and charge a high prepayment penalty. Assumption of a loan is usually allowed if borrowers meet requirements.

Insurance companies at times have tended to favor those who are policyholders of the company or, when granting the loan, will require that the borrower take out an insurance policy with the company.

NONINSTITUTIONAL LENDERS

Private individuals

Private individual leaders make more loans from month to month than do any other class of leaders. Although at the present time they account for a little less than a quarter of the total mortgage debt, they rank number one as the source of junior mortgage (second) loans. Most of such loans are made on one- to four-family dwelling unit properties.

Aside from being sellers who carry back either first or second loans, individuals obtain loans through title companies, mortgage companies, and real estate brokers, by advertising, or through others who deal in real estate transactions. Many individuals have money to lend where real estate is to be the security. Many loan brokers deal with such private individuals, who are more than willing to pay the broker a fee for bringing them into transactions where they may make loans secured by real estate.

Individuals follow no uniform leading practices, and in general, they are not subject to national or state licensing laws or the requirements of other regulatory bodies. Thus, they can take greater risks in their investments, such as acceptance of high loan-to-value ratios. They usually do not use the technical credit analysis procedures that have been developed by institutional lenders, and many of the loans made by individuals would not be acceptable to institutional lenders.

Most loans made by private individuals are second loans. This is especially true in house resales. The term on these loans is usually from three to seven years; the average is five years. The interest rate charged will depend on the security risk involved.

Most second loans are carried back by the seller of a property. Such second loans generally contain a due-on-sale clause, which means that the entire amount is due the lender should the property be sold during the loan term. The monthly payment is usually 1 percent of the amount of the loan. This, of course, does not fully amortize the loan, and the borrower will have to make a substantial payment at the end of the term; such payment is generally called a balloon payment. Other aspects of second loans have been discussed previously in this chapter.

Mortgage companies and investment trusts

Mortgage companies operate primarily as mortgage loan correspondents of life insurance companies, mutual savings banks, pension funds, and other financial institutions. They may furnish mortgage loans to these institutions from only one metropolitan area, or one state, or sometimes several states. The mortgage companies, with their loan brokerage functions, are one of the many sources for mortgage loans. They make loans on houses, on income property, and also under FHA and VA.

Many mortgage companies have sizable funds of their own and are consistent lending sources in the mortgage market. Many also engage in additional business operations, such as property rentals, leases, management of properties, and insurance. A few even operate as real estate brokerage firms.

The companies are usually free of many of the lending limitations placed on other institutional leaders, and except for inspections by an examiner in conformity with state laws, they assume entire responsibility and make all decisions about their mortgage lending operations and their loan servicing. Some companies serve only as intermediaries and resell the loans as soon as they are made.

Mortgage companies are also active in construction lending. Such loans are made with their own funds or with the funds of the companies they represent. On the sale of the house, these funds are converted to long-term mortgage loans.

Probably the most dominant policy of these mortgage companies is to deal in mortgages that are most readily salable in the secondary market. As a result, these lenders prefer government insured or government guaranteed mortgages as well as conventional or uninsured mortgages for which they have advance purchase commitments. Generally, mortgage companies restrict their conventional loans to selected residential and business risks and to loans in price ranges suitable to the needs of investment firms that comprise the secondary mortgage market.

Investment trust formation was authorized under the tax laws enacted in 1960. The trust is taxed only on retained earnings, and if it distributes all its earnings to stockholders, it goes completely untaxed. With respect to taxation, the investors are treated the same as direct investors in real estate mortgages or in real estate.

The real estate investment trust differs from the stock investment company in that it invests primarily in real estate and real estate mortgages, while the stock company concerns itself with investment in stock and securities. A real estate investment trust, therefore, is an unincorporated trust or association of investors which is managed by one or more trustees and, because of the tax exemption provided by the law, is not taxed as a corporation.

Further information on investment trusts may be obtained from the nearest office of the State Division of Corporations.

GOVERNMENT GUARANTEED AND INSURED LOANS

Features of FHA, VA, and Cal-Vet loans are summarized in Table 7–1. Each is discussed separately in the text that follows.

FHA (Federal Housing Administration)

The FHA program has been in operation since its establishment in 1934. Since that time, the FHA has written mortgage and loan insurance in the aggregate amount of approximately $135 billion and has helped more than 39 million families improve their housing standards and conditions.

The FHA does not build houses or lend money. It acts only as an insurer of privately made loans from approved lenders. In California, the FHA will insure a loan secured by either a mortgage or a deed of trust. The soundness of the FHA concept has been shown by the fact that millions of mort-

TABLE 7-1
Government loan information

	FHA Title II (203b)	VA (GI Loan)	Cal-Vet
Loan eligibility	Anyone	W. W. II, Korean War, or post Korean	California Veteran, W. W. II, Korean War, or Vietnam
Source of funds	Approved lending institutions	Approved lending institutions	State bond issues
Loan security	Deed of trust or mortgage	Deed of trust or mortgage	Conditional sales contract
Interest rate	As set by government, plus 0.5% mortgage insurance	As set by VA	As set by state of California
Term	Maximum allowed 35 years Average 20 to 30 years	30-years, real estate 20 years, mobile homes	25-year maximum
Maximum purchase price allowed	No maximum	No limit, but loan cannot exceed VA appraisal (CRV, or certified reasonable value)	No limit
Maximum amount of loan	1 unit, 67,500; 2–3 units, 76,000–92,000; 4 units, 107,000	No maximum, but guarantee only 60% of loan to maximum of 25,000	$55,000 house $120,000 farm
Down payment	3% of 1st $25,000 of appraisal 5% of balance of appraisal 100% of excess of selling price over the appraisal	None required by VA, lender may require a down payment	5% of sales price, house 5%, farms
Prepayment penalty	None	None	2% during 1st 2 years
Assignable to	Anyone	Anyone	Cal-Vet at same interest Other Vets higher interest
Secondary financing	Not allowed concurrently with first (can add later)	Not allowed concurrently with first (can add later)	Not allowed
Monthly cost in addition to principal and interest	1/12 annual taxes 1/36 of 3-year fire insurance policy 1/12 of 0.5% mortgage insurance	1/12 annual taxes 1/36 of 3-year fire insurance policy	1/12 annual taxes, plus fee for life insurance
Government agency	Federal Housing Administration	Veterans Administration	State of California
Monthly salary required after federal taxes	3½ to 4 times monthly payment, including principal, interest, taxes, and insurance	3½ to 4 times monthly payment including principal, interest, taxes, and insurance	4 times monthly payment, plus 1/12 of taxes
Purpose of loan	Residence, to 4 units	Residence, to 4 units, condominiums or mobilehomes.	Residence, farm, mobilehome, condominium

gage and property improvement loans insured by the FHA have been made by banks, savings and loan associations, mortgage companies, and other FHA approved lending institutions. By protecting these lenders against loss, FHA insurance has enabled them to advance loans to moderate-income families who would otherwise have found it impossible to acquire the necessary funds for purchasing real estate. The FHA has helped to make the low down payment, long-term, fully amortized loan the standard throughout the nation.

In addition to its original programs of insuring loans made for the purposes of home purchase, home improvement, and multifamily rental housing, the FHA now insures loans for land development, low-income family housing, urban renewal housing, housing for the elderly, nursing homes, cooperative housing, condominiums, housing at military installations, housing for servicemen and their families when on active duty, and long-term loans for major home improvements.

Since this program is detailed and quite complex, all real estate licensees must keep their knowledge of FHA operations up-to-date. The licensee should obtain a copy of *The Digest of Insurable Loans*, published by the Federal Housing Administration, Washington 25, D.C., and usually available through all FHA regional offices.

When the Federal Housing Administration Act was originally passed by Congress, it contained two sections—Title I and Title II. Title I contains the provisions for modernization of existing houses and also provides for the conversion, repair, and alteration of existing structures. All these are generally referred to a home improvement loans. Title II provides for the purchase of new or existing properties. Title III was later established as a means of providing a secondary market for FHA insured mortgages. The most important and most used section of the FHA Act over the years has been Title II, which governs loans for the purchase of real estate.

Title I, home improvement and mobile home loans. Title I allows the FHA to insure lending institutions against loss on loans made to finance alterations, repairs, and improvements to existing structures. FHA limits its liability to 90 percent of the loss on individual loans and to 10 percent of all such loans made by the individual institution.

The individual lending institutions require the borrower to meet certain satisfactory income and credit requirements, and in addition, the borrower must own the property or have a lease that expires not less than six months beyond the maturity of the loan, or he must be purchasing the property on contract.

Title I, Section 2 also allows insurance of the purchase of a mobile home and lot which is to be the principal residence of the buyer. FHA standards of construction must be met, and the maximum term and insured loan amount is 12 years and $10,000 for single module mobile homes and $15,000 and 15 years for double module mobile homes.

Title II, home purchase loans. Title II of the FHA Act contains a number of sections. Selected sections are briefly outlined below and will be followed by a more detailed discussion of Section 203b, which deals with loans for construction or purchase of one- to four-family dwellings.

Section 203. To finance the construction or purchase of one- to four-family dwellings, single family dwellings for disaster-area residents, and low-cost single family homes in suburban and outlying areas.

Section 207. To finance the construction of large-scale rental housing projects, seasonal homes, loans to certain veterans, and for trailer or mobile-home parks.

Section 213. To finance the construction of nonprofit cooperatives of the management or sales type and the purchase of individual mortgages released from a sales-type project mortgage.

Section 220. To finance the rehabilitation of existing dwellings and the construction of new dwellings in designated urban renewal areas.

Section 221. To finance low-cost new or rehabilitated housing for the relocation of families displaced by slum clearance projects or other governmental action.

Section 222. To finance the purchase or construction of dwellings by servicemen on active duty with the Armed Forces, including the Coast Guard.

Section 223. To finance purchase or refinancing of existing multifamily dwellings.

Section 225. To finance additional advances under an open-end mortgage for repairs or improvements to one- to four-family dwellings.

Section 231. To finance the construction or rehabilitation of rental housing projects designed specifically for elderly persons.

Section 232. To finance the construction of facilities for skilled nursing care, convalescents, and others who do not need hospital treatment

Section 233. To finance single and multifamily units where the design and/or material used is of a nature to be considered experimental.

Section 234. To finance the purchase or construction of multifamily structures where the individual purchases the unit and is given deed to same along with undivided interest in common areas and facilities. This section is commonly known as the Condominium Housing Program.

Section 235. To provide home ownership assistance in the form of periodic payments by the FHA to mortgagees, which would reduce interest costs to the purchaser on market rate home mortgages and on the share of a cooperative association mortgage.

Section 236. To provide assistance to tenants and cooperators in the form of periodic interest reduction payments by FHA to the mortgagee for rental and cooperative housing projects serving low-income families.

Section 237. To finance home ownership for certain lower-income families who cannot qualify under normal standards because of their poor credit records but who can meet mortgage payments with appropriate budget and financial counseling.

There are, in addition to the above, many other programs for land development, group facilities, nonprofit hospitals, armed services housing and rentals, and programs in connection with the Department of Housing and Urban Development (HUD).

Whenever the terms *mortgage* and *mortgagee* are used in our discussion, the reader should remember that in California they include the terms *deed of trust* and *beneficiary*.

Title II, Section 203b. Title II has several subsections, but the one we shall be concerned with is Section 203b, which covers insured loans for the purchase of one- to four-family dwellings.

Secondary financing (second loans) to provide

the purchaser with additional funds over and above the FHA-insured loan is prohibited. No second loans are allowed if the purchaser receives FHA-insured financing.

Owner-occupied dwellings and condominiums are insurable as follows:

a. Up to 67,500 for a one-family dwelling.
b. Up to 76,000 and 92,000 for a two- or three-family dwelling.
c. Up to 107,000 for a four-family dwelling.

These figures represent the maximum permissible amount of loan that will be insured by FHA. Such loans are calculated as follows:

1. On proposed construction approved for FHA insurance prior to the beginning of construction or for existing dwellings over one year old, the limit is: 97 percent of the first $25,000 of FHA appraised value plus 95 percent of remainder of appraised value.

2. For construction completed less than one year and not approved for FHA insurance prior to its beginning, the limit is: 90 percent of appraised value.

3. A nonoccupant owner is limited to 85 percent of the amount an occupant owner could obtain. The maximum amounts are: $51,000 for a single family dwelling, $55,250 for a two- or three-family dwelling, $63,750 for a four-family dwelling.

4. Special terms are offered to a veteran who has not already received any direct, guaranteed, or insured loan from the Veterans Administration home loan program, known as the "GI bill": 100 percent of the first $25,000 of appraised value, plus 95 percent of the remainder of appraisal.

Most FHA-insured loans are made on property in classification 1, which is FHA-approved prior to construction or over one year old.

Term allowed. The term of repayment cannot be more than 35 years, but in practice, lending institutions limit FHA loans to a maximum of 30 years. The FHA itself recommends the 30-year maximum, and although this is generally used, loans are made for 25- and 20-year terms also.

Interest rate. To the prevailing rate of interest at any given time, an additional ½ percent must be added for mortgage insurance required by FHA. This charge is included in the borrower's monthly payment.

Table 7-2 illustrates the maximum loan and monthly payment necessary for regular FHA house purchases with an interest rate of 11 percent plus ½ percent for a total of 11½ percent.

FHA forms required. A variety of forms must be

TABLE 7-2
Typical FHA loans

FHA appraisal	Maximum FHA loan	Down payment	Monthly Payment		
			20-year term	25-year term	30-year term
45,000 ...	43,250	1,750	461.24	439.63	428.31
55,000 ...	52,750	2,250	562.56	536.20	522.39
65,000 ...	62,250	2,750	663.87	632.76	616.47
75,000 ...	71,750	3,250	765.19	729.34	710.55
$85,000 ...	$81,250	$3,750	$866.50	$825.90	$804.63

completed and processed when the sale of a property involves an FHA insured loan. Most commercial banks, savings and loan associations, and other lenders who accept applications for FHA-insured loans will have available all the necessary forms.

A considerable amount of time can be saved if the property seller applies for a conditional commitment before placing the property on the market or at the time the property is listed by the broker. Where tract homes are offered with FHA insured loans available, much of this preliminary work has already been done by the developer. When an individual owner lists his property for sale, it will be quite helpful if at the time the broker shows the property to a prospective purchaser, he already knows the FHA appraisal on the property and the amount of loan FHA will insure. Such action by the owner is optimal, however, and many times an FHA-insured loan will not be sought unless a prospective purchaser makes this a condition of the purchase contract.

Veterans Administration (GI loan)

The Veterans' Readjustment Benefits Act of 1966 and subsequent Veterans' Housing Act provide a program of loans for veterans of the U.S. Armed Forces. Eligible veterans and servicemen may obtain GI loans from private lenders for houses, mobile homes, condominiums, and buildings of up to four residential units.

Eligibility for loans. Veterans who served on active duty for 181 days or more, any part of it after January 31, 1955, and who were not dishonorably discharged, are eligible as post-Korean veterans. However, persons whose military service after January 31, 1955, consisted of "active duty for training" are not eligible. Members of the U.S. Armed Forces who have served at least two years in active duty status, even though not discharged, are eligible while they continue serving.

The Veterans Benefit Act of 1978 now provides eligibility for Vietnam-conflict veterans who served on active duty for 90 days or more, any part of it between August 5, 1964 and May 7, 1975.

Loan provisions. The VA will guarantee a home loan made by a private lender up to $25,000 or 60 percent of the loan, whichever is less. A lending institution will receive the government's guaranty, which is intended to be in lieu of a down payment or to reduce the down payment the lender normally requires.

The difference between a guaranteed and an insured loan is in the amount that will be paid to the lender in the event of a default. If there is a default on a guaranteed loan, the government pays the lender a specified maximum amount. This amount is reduced proportionately as the loan is paid off by the borrower. In the case of an insured loan, the VA will pay the net loss of the lender up to the amount of the lender's insurance account. The maximum amount of the loan the VA will guarantee is $25,000.

VA direct home loans are available for the purchase of residences in areas where such loans have been authorized, usually where private lenders are scarce and funds difficult to obtain. California is not such an area and is not eligible for any direct loans from the VA.

There is no maximum on the amount of a guaranteed loan itself, and most California lenders will make a guaranteed loan to a qualified veteran of up to $100,000.

Interest rate and term. The VA sets and periodically adjusts its interest rate, and the maximum term of a VA loan is 30 years.

Additional VA provisions. The loan amount is determined by a CRV, certificate of reasonable value. The CRV is ordered from the VA, and they assign an independent fee appraiser to determine the value of the property being purchased. Veterans must be informed of the reasonable value established by the VA before signing an offer or contract to pay a price greater than the CRV, although the veteran may pay more if he has the cash resources necessary.

No down payment is required by the VA. However, individual lenders may require a down payment. The VA loan is generally amortized on the standard plan of equal monthly payments, but the lender has flexibility in determining this procedure.

A lender is allowed to charge reasonable costs in connection with the loan. These costs usually include the VA appraisal, tax service, credit report, title policy, and recording fees. However, the purchaser is not allowed to pay any escrow charges.

In those parts of the state where termites may present a problem, the VA will generally require a termite inspection on the property.

Mobilehome loans. Loans made to veterans for the purchase of mobilehomes are guaranteed by the VA. The mobilehome must conform to certain VA specifications, and the maximum loan for the purchase of a double module mobilehome is $20,000 for a term of 20 years. If the purchase includes an undeveloped lot and site preparation or a developed lot, the VA will guarantee a mobilehome site loan up to $27,500 with a term of 20 years.

California-Veterans loans (Cal-Vet)

The California Veterans Farm and Home Purchase Program, created by the legislature in 1921, permits the state Department of Veterans Affairs to assist qualified veterans in acquiring farm or home properties. The state of California actually lends the funds, which are obtained through state bond issues.

Eligibility requirements. A veteran's eligibility is established by filing a loan application and discharge papers with the Department of Veterans Affairs, P.O. Box 1599, Sacramento, California.

A veteran must be a native Californian or have been a bona fide resident of the state at the time he entered the service. He must have served in time of war or participated in a military campaign or expedition for which a medal is authorized by the U.S. government. He must have served 90 days on active duty, a portion of which must have been in one of the following:

World War I: April 6, 1917 to November 11, 1918 (90-day requirement waived for World War I veterans only).
World War II: December 7, 1941 to December 1, 1946.
Korea: June 27, 1950 to January 31, 1955.
Vietnam: July 1, 1958 to end of U.S. military involvement.
Lebanon: July 1, 1958 to November 1, 1958.
Quemoy and Matsu: August 23, 1958 to June 1, 1963.
Taiwan Straits: August 23, 1958 to January 1, 1959.
Congo: July 14, 1960 to September 1, 1962.
Laos: April 19, 1961 to October 7, 1962.
Berlin: August 14, 1961 to June 1, 1963.
Cuba: October 24, 1962 to June 1, 1963.
Dominican Republic: April 27, 1965 to September 20, 1966.
Korea: October 1, 1966 to present.
Vietnam Medal: July 4, 1965 to present.

California veterans discharged with less than 90 days of service because of a war service-connected disability are eligible. To be eligible, all veterans must have been honorably discharged or still be in service.

Terms and conditions of loan (home purchase). The current amounts that may be loaned are up to $55,000 for the purchase of a house or condominium and up to $120,000 for the purchase of a farm. The rate of interest is subject to periodic redetermination and is set by the California legislature.

The house to be purchased must be a single-family dwelling and must meet certain standards set by the veterans department. The amount to be loaned may not exceed 95 percent of the department's appraisal of the house itself; the value of the land is not included in this appraisal. The veteran must pay in cash the difference between the department's loan and the sales price of the property, and no secondary financing is permitted in connection with the purchase of a house.

The current term of the loan is 25 years. However, the department may extend this term in special cases, but this is an exception rather than the rule. The veteran must agree to reside on the property, or agree that a member of his family will do so, within 60 days from date of purchase. He may not transfer, encumber, assign, or rent the property without the written consent of the veterans department.

Title to the property is held by the state of California and is transferred to the veteran on completion of his purchase contract. The Department of Veterans Affairs offers low-cost insurance coverage to a veteran making a loan. The premiums are added to the veteran's monthly payment and include life insurance, mortgage protection insurance, fire insurance, and other protective coverages.

The department will advance funds in a series of payments to a licensed and bondable contractor to pay for construction of a house when:

1. The veteran owns the lot.
2. The lot is inspected by the department and found acceptable.
3. The veteran furnishes plans and specifications approved by the department.
4. The veteran deposits in escrow any cash difference between loan and building cost.
5. The veteran pays a processing fee.
6. A formal building agreement is entered into by the veteran and the department.

On lot approval, the department will issue a conditional commitment. This may allow the veteran to obtain necessary temporary financing needed for construction.

The same general terms and conditions discussed previously apply to a veteran's purchase of a farm. The department will loan up to $120,000 for a term of 25 years. Loan payment with regard to a farm may be annual or monthly, whereas for the purchase of a house the payments must be monthly. The farm loan may be used to: (1) purchase a farm, (2) refinance a farm loan, (3) add new land to a farm, and (4) improve a farm.

The farm must be appraised by the Department of Veterans Affairs and found able to produce a reasonable net income for the operator. The veteran must plan to live on the farm.

California-Veterans Loans can be made for the purchase of a mobile home which is designed for single-family accupancy. The loan may include purchase of an approved site.

Secondary financing may be permitted if certain conditions are met, and improvement loans are also available.

FNMA and GNMA

The Federal National Mortgage Association (FNMA), popularly known as Fannie May, was originally established in connection with Title III of the National Housing Act and is engaged in the business of expanding the amount of capital available to finance home building and home buying. Its primary function is to buy FHA-insured and VA-guaranteed mortgages made by private lenders. These are purchased at a discount and then sold to other private lenders or investors.

The Housing and Urban Development Act of 1968 partitioned FNMA into two separate corporations resulting in the formation of the Government National Mortgage Association, called Ginnie May. The FNMA is authorized to issue and sell securities backed by a portion of its mortgage portfolio, with GNMA guaranteeing payment on such securities. GNMA also guarantees similar securities issued by other private issuers where they are backed by FHA, VA, and some Farm Home Administration mortgages or loans.

In February 1971, the FNMA established a procedure allowing all conventional lenders to grant insured mortgage loans through the Mutual Guarantee Insurance Corporation, which is commonly known as MAGIC. Participating lenders bid for available funds at auctions held by the FNMA, and the amount of the bid is governed by the current money market and the amount of discount the lender is prepared to allow FNMA to take when purchasing the loan from the lender. FNMA is obligated to purchase the mortgage loan from the lender at the price stated in the commitment for MAGIC loan funds and may in turn place the mortgages for sale on the secondary market to other investors.

The FNMA insures 75 percent of the loan amount against foreclosure losses, and MAGIC insures against foreclosure loss the amount between 75 percent and 90 percent of the balance of the loan.

PROHIBITION AGAINST REDLINING

New legislation prohibiting financial institutions from engaging in the practice known as redlining became effective January 1, 1978. Known as the Housing Financial Discrimination Act of 1977, the law provides a unique opportunity for real estate licensees to aid in stamping out redlining, a practice which is discriminatory and which, by restricting the free flow of mortgage capital, makes it more difficult for real estate licensees to put bona fide transactions together.

The Act prohibits financial institutions such as federal or state licensed savings and loans, state or national banks or credit unions, and thrift companies from engaging in discriminatory loan practices due, in whole or in part, to the consideration of conditions, characteristics, or trends in the neighborhood or geographic area surrounding the housing accommodations. Certain exceptions may be allowed if the financial institution can demonstrate that such consideration in the particular case is required to avoid an unsafe and unsound business practice. Consideration of race, color, religion, sex, marital status, national origin, or ancestry is also prohibited in regard to the composition of the neighborhood, the geographic area surrounding a housing accommodation, trends in the area, or in appraising a housing accommodation.

The Real Estate Commissioner will take disciplinary action against any real estate licensees found to be engaged in or connected with such activities.

BROKER ACTING AS LOAN AGENT

In the normal course of business, not only may a broker aid a prospective purchaser in making application for a loan from a financial institution, but quite often, the broker may himself become a representative or agent for a mortgage lending institution. The broker may also represent private interests who have funds to lend on notes secured by real property. Many real estate firms have set up a special loan division within the office or have established a subsidiary mortgage company.

It is required by law that anyone acting for compensation in negotiating a new loan or selling an existing loan secured by real estate must be a real estate licensee. Because of a number of complaints the Commissioner received over the years concerning exorbitant charges of some licensees in connection with the above activities, the Real Property Loan Brokerage Law was passed by the legislature. In 1961, the legislature revised and added to the existing law and passed Assembly Bill 1344, which is regarded as the most comprehensive mortgage loan legislation ever enacted up to that time. Further provisions have been added to the law by the legislature, including the Mortgage Loan Brokers Reform Act of 1973. The complete provisions of the law are contained in Article 7, Sections 10240 to 10249.2, Division Four, Real Estate Law, Business and Professions Code.

Broker's loan disclosure statement

The provisions of the law do not apply when the real estate licensee negotiates a loan in connection with a property sale or exchange or when he sells or exchanges a note in connection with such a transaction. The provisions of the law do apply when the licensee solicits or advertises for borrowers or lenders, or performs services for them in connection with loans secured by real property, or when the licensee either offers to or actually does sell, buy, or exchange a real property sales contract or a promissory note secured by real property.

When a licensee negotiates a loan to be secured directly or collaterally by a lien or real property, he must deliver to the borrower a statement containing certain information before the borrower becomes obligated to complete the loan. The California Real Estate Association form, Mortgage Loan Disclosure Statement, illustrated in Figure 7–10, is approved by the real estate commissioner for meeting the provisions of the law.

Commissions and charges

Besides being required to provide the borrower with a statement, the licensee is also restricted in the amount of commissions and other charges he

MORTGAGE LOAN DISCLOSURE STATEMENT
CALIFORNIA ASSOCIATION OF REALTORS® STANDARD FORM
(APPROVED BY STATE DEPARTMENT OF REAL ESTATE)

_____
(Name of Broker/Arranger of Credit)

_____
(Business Address of Broker)

I. SUMMARY OF LOAN TERMS
   A. PRINCIPAL AMOUNT OF LOAN . . . . $ _____
   B. ESTIMATED DEDUCTIONS FROM PRINCIPAL AMOUNT
      1. Costs and Expenses (See Paragraph III-A) . . . . $ _____
      2. Brokerage Commission (See Paragraph III-B) . . . . $ _____
      3. Liens and Other Amounts to be Paid on Authorization of Borrower
        (See Paragraph III-C) . . . . $ _____
   C. ESTIMATED CASH PAYABLE TO BORROWER (A Less B) . . . . $ _____

II. GENERAL INFORMATION CONCERNING LOAN
   A. If this loan is made, you will be required to pay the principal and interest at _____ % per year, payable as follows: _____ _____ payments of $ _____
      (number of payments) (monthly/quarterly/annual)
   and a FINAL/BALLOON payment of *$ _____ to pay off the loan in full.

> *CAUTION TO BORROWER: If you do not have the funds to pay the balloon payment when due, it may be necessary for you to obtain a new loan against your property for this purpose, in which case, you may be required to again pay commission and expenses for arranging the loan. Keep this in mind in deciding upon the amount and terms of the loan that you obtain at this time.

   B. This loan will be evidenced by a promissory note and secured by a deed of trust in favor of lender/creditor on property located at (street address or legal description): _____

   C. Liens against this property and the approximate amounts are:

Nature of Lien	Amount Owing
_____	_____
_____	_____
_____	_____

   D. If you wish to pay more than the scheduled payment at any time before it is due, you may have to pay a PREPAYMENT PENALTY computed as follows:

   E. The purchase of credit life or credit disability insurance is not required of the borrower as a condition of making this loan.

   F. The real property which will secure the requested loan is an "owner-occupied dwelling"*   YES _____ NO _____
      (Borrower initial opposite YES or NO)
   *An "owner-occupied dwelling" means a single dwelling unit in a condominium or cooperative or a residential building of less than three separate dwelling units, one of which will be owned and occupied by a signatory to the mortgage or deed of trust for this loan within 90 days of the signing of the mortgage or deed of trust.

FIGURE 7–10

III. **DEDUCTIONS FROM LOAN PROCEEDS**

   A. ESTIMATED COSTS AND EXPENSES to be paid by borrower out of the principal amount of the loan are:

	PAYABLE TO	
	Broker	Others
1. Appraisal fee	_____	_____
2. Escrow fee	_____	_____
3. Fees for policy of title insurance	_____	_____
4. Notary fees	_____	_____
5. Recording fees	_____	_____
6. Credit investigation fees	_____	_____
7. Other Costs and Expenses:	_____	_____
	_____	_____
	_____	_____

TOTAL COSTS AND EXPENSES . . . . $ _____

   B. LOAN BROKERAGE COMMISSION . . . . $ _____

   C. LIENS AND OTHER AMOUNTS to be paid out of the principal amount of the loan on authorization of the borrower are estimated to be as follows:

	PAYABLE TO	
	Broker	Others
1. Fire or other property insurance premiums	_____	_____
2. Credit life or disability insurance premiums (see paragraph II-E)	_____	_____
3. Beneficiary statement fees	_____	_____
4. Reconveyance and similar fees	_____	_____
5. Liens against property securing loan:	_____	_____
	_____	_____
	_____	_____
6. Other:	_____	_____

TOTAL TO BE PAID ON AUTHORIZATION OF BORROWER $ _____

The undersigned certifies that the lender for this loan will not be the broker or designated representative, either directly or indirectly, and that the loan will be made in compliance with the provisions of the California Real Estate Law.

_____ OR _____
(Broker)   (Designated Representative)

_____   _____
(License Number)   (License Number)

NOTICE TO BORROWER

DO NOT SIGN this statement until you have read and understand all of the information in it. All parts of the form must be completed before you sign.

The broker will rely on the INFORMATION ON LIENS in Paragraph II-C which was supplied by you. Be sure that you have stated all liens accurately. If you contract with the broker to arrange this loan and if the loan cannot be made because you did not state these liens correctly, you may be liable for payment of commission, fees and expenses.

The commission to be paid by you to the broker as shown in Paragraph III-B is customarily a percentage of the principal amount of the loan. The percentage that may be charged as a commission increases with the length of the loan. Keep this in mind in deciding upon the term for repayment of the loan.

Borrower hereby acknowledges the receipt of a copy of this statement.

DATED: _____   _____
                                          (Borrower)

                                          _____
                                          (Borrower)

FIGURE 7–10 (continued)

may make. Commission maximums set forth below are not intended to apply to any bona fide loans secured directly or collaterally by a first trust deed whose principal is $16,000 or more or to any bona fide loans secured directly or collaterally by any junior lien whose principal is $8,000 or more.

Commission maximums on first trust deeds are: (1) 5 percent for a loan of less than three years, (2) 10 percent for a loan of three years or more. Commission maximums for second or other junior trust deeds are: (1) 5 percent for a loan of less than two years; (2) 10 percent for a loan of two years but less than three years; (3) 15 percent for a loan of three years or more.

Section 10242 of the Real Estate Law details all of the charges which may be made for a loan in addition to the commission. Each of these charges must be supported by adequate records and cannot exceed the actual costs and expenses incurred by the licensee. If a loan is negotiated in violation of any provision of the mortgage loan broker law, the licensee is obliged to return any bonus, brokerage, or commission on demand to the borrower. Costs and expenses of making the loan, such as appraisal fees, escrow fees, title charges and notary, recording, and credit investigation fees charged to the borrower cannot exceed 5 percent of the principal of the loan provided, however, that if 5 percent of the loan is less than $195, the broker may charge up to that amount. Regardless of the size of the loan, the borrower cannot be charged more than $325 for costs and expenses, provided that in no event shall said maximum amount exceed actual costs and expenses paid, incurred, or reasonably earned.

For mortgage loan brokers making 400 or more loans per year or whose advertising costs connected with mortgage loan brokerage activities amount to more than 5 percent of gross revenue and at least $10,000 per year, the law requires submission of advertising by such brokers to the Department of Real Estate and requires an annual report to be submitted to the Commissioner.

REAL PROPERTY SECURITIES DEALER

Sections 10237 through 10239.35 of the Business and Professions Code relate to real property securities and real property securities dealers, spell out registration and regulatory requirements for such dealers, and are intended to control bulk transactions in trust deeds and real property sales contracts and investment plans dealing with them.

To secure endorsement as a real property securities dealer, an individual must have a real estate broker's license. An application for endorsement is sent to the commissioner together with a required fee and a corporate surety bond in the amount of $5,000. In lieu of the bond, the applicant may submit evidence of having filed with the state treasurer a cash bond in the amount of $5,000 or United States or state securities in the amount of $6,000.

A real property securities dealer is defined as any person acting as principal or agent who engages in the business of:

1. Selling real property securities, that is, promissory notes or sales contracts, as defined by subdivision (a) Section 10237.1 to the public.

2. Offering to accept or accepting funds for continual reinvestment in real property securities or for placement in an account, plan, or program whereby the dealer implies that a return will be derived from a specific real property sales contract or promissory note secured directly or collaterally by a lien on real property which is not specifically stated to be based upon the contractual payments thereon.

Sale to the public, however, is interpreted as excluding sales to corporations; pension, retirement, or similar trust funds; institutional lending agencies; or real estate brokers, attorneys, or licensed general building contractors.

A generalized definition of real property securities as set forth in Section 10237.1 holds them to be deeds of trust sold under an investment contract where the dealer guarantees the deed of trust in any one of several ways or makes advances to or on behalf of the investor. Also included in the definition is the sale of one of a series of promotional notes or sales contracts. Promotional refers to a note secured by a trust deed on unimproved real property; or a note executed after construction of an improvement on the property, but before the first sale; or executed as a means of financing the first purchase of property as so improved, and subordinated to another trust deed. An example of this latter type of promotional note would be a purchase money second trust deed on a house in a new subdivision.

Real property securities permit

Before selling real property securities to the public, a permit must be obtained from the real estate commissioner. This permit may be obtained to sell existing securities or may authorize the applicant to acquire and sell securities under a proposed plan or program. In the latter case, the permit would be obtained prior to acquisition of the securities. Before issuing a permit, the commissioner will inquire into the subject matter of the application to determine whether the proposed plan and proposed sale would be fair, just, and equitable. The fee for the application for a permit is the same as that required for a permit to issue stock in a California corporation, and fee schedules are available at any office of the Department of Real Estate.

An annual audit report listing total number of sales, dollar volume, and other pertinent data must be filed with the real estate commissioner by every real property securities dealer. All advertising material must be filed with the commissioner ten days prior to its use, and no dealer shall use any such material in any way after receiving notice in writing that such material contains any statement that is false or misleading or omits to state material information necessary to make the statement therein complete and accurate.

Securities dealer's statement. A disclosure statement called a real property security statement must be furnished to the purchaser of the real property security. The form of the statement is shown in Section 2977 of the commissioner's rules and regulations.

Additional forms, applicable to this chapter, are illustrated in Appendix C as Figures C7–1 thru C7–3.

QUESTIONS FOR DISCUSSION

1. With respect to the three basic types of promissory notes, discuss their differences.
2. What is an offset statement, and when is it generally used?
3. With respect to the statute of limitations, what is the main difference between a mortgage and a deed of trust?
4. What two remedies are available to a beneficiary in a deed of trust?
5. What is the main difference in redemption privileges between a mortgage and a deed of trust?
6. Can a deficiency judgment be obtained when there is a purchase money mortgage or purchase money deed of trust and a trustee's sale is used?
7. What is the main difference in the sale of a property between a buyer's taking subject to an existing obligation or assuming the existing obligation?
8. Give two examples of an acceleration clause.
9. How may the holder of a second loan protect his investment if the borrower defaults on the first loan?
10. What is the particular function of a chattel mortgage or security agreement?
11. When a purchase is made using a land contract or agreement of sale, what is particularly significant with respect to passage of title to the purchaser?
12. Discuss how points are used by various lenders.
13. What is a conventional loan, and what are the main sources of conventional loan funds?
14. Discuss the requirements for obtaining an FHA, VA, and Cal-Vet loan.
15. What are the conditions which require a broker to comply with the Real Property Loan Brokerage Law?

8

Escrow procedure and title insurance

When a broker has obtained a signed offer from a prospective buyer and an acceptance of the offer from the seller, he is then ready to go into escrow and close the transaction. A slight division of opinion is found in real estate textbooks regarding the difference between closing the deal and the escrow procedure. Some authors state that closing pertains to getting an offer in writing from the buyer and then obtaining the seller's acceptance and signature on the Purchase Contract and Receipt for Deposit. Other authorities believe that closing involves all the work and procedures necessary after the offer and acceptance have been obtained by the broker.

This textbook follows the position that closing the transaction includes not only obtaining the offer and acceptance but all of the work which follows. This means obtainment of a title insurance policy and initiation of the escrow procedure, which is successfully concluded when certain documents are officially recorded and funds involved are disbursed to those persons entitled to them.

ESCROW DEFINED

The California Financial Code, Section 17003, defines escrow as follows:

> Escrow means any transaction wherein one person for the purpose of affecting the sale, transfer, encumbering, or leasing of real or personal property to another person, delivers any written instrument, money, evidence of title to real or personal property or any other thing of value to a third person to be held by such third person until the happening of a specified event or the performance of a prescribed condition, when it is then to be delivered by such third person to a grantee, grantor, promisee, promissor, obligee, obligor, bailee, bailor, or any agent or employee of any of the latter.

The California Civil Code defines escrow as follows:

> A grant may be deposited by the grantor with a third person to be delivered on the performance of the condition, and, on delivery by the depository, will take effect. While in the possession of the third person, and subject to the condition, it is called an escrow.

ESSENTIALS OF A VALID ESCROW

To have a valid escrow, there must be a binding contract between buyer and seller, and the conditional delivery of transfer instruments to a third party. The binding contract may appear in any legal form; the most common are a deposit receipt, agreement of sale, exchange agreement, option, or mutual instructions of buyer and seller.

Escrow instructions supplement the original binding contract, above, and both the escrow instructions and the contract are interpreted together, if possible. If the supplemental escrow instructions should contain any terms in conflict with the original contract, the instructions, constituting the later contract, usually control. It is thus important that all conditions, whether in the original contract or in subsequent instructions, be clear and concise and that they be fully understood by all parties to the agreement.

In addition to a binding contract, there must be a conditional delivery of transfer instruments to a third party (usually called the escrow agent or escrow officer), together with instructions to deliver the instruments on fulfillment or performance of certain conditions.

The actual procedures followed by an escrow officer may vary, depending on the particular locale within the state. The licensee should understand that the procedures we shall discuss are general in nature, and he should, in addition, familiarize himself with certain special practices that may exist in his particular area.

COMPLETE ESCROW

A complete escrow contains all the necessary instructions that reflect an understanding by the parties in all the essential requirements of the transaction. If properly drawn and executed, it becomes an enforceable contract binding on all the parties. An escrow is termed "complete" when all the terms of the instructions have been met.

Generally, to have a correct escrow, a valid and binding contract must be entered into between the grantor and the grantee, and an irrevocable deposit must be made with the escrow holder. If a contract did not exist, the grantor could recover his deed from the escrow holder at any time before the conditions were performed. Where the contract does exist, the escrow officer exceeds his authority if he attempts to deliver any instruments to the grantee before the performance of any conditions specified, and in actual practice, the escrow officer will refuse such delivery prior to satisfactory performance of conditions.

THE ESCROW AGENT

All escrow agencies must be licensed by the California Corporation Commissioner. The regulations under which these escrow agents must operate will be found in Sections 17000 to 17614 of the California Financial Code.

Section 17004 of the Financial Code defines an escrow agent as "Any person engaged in the business of receiving escrows for deposit or delivery, for a compensation." Any corporation, partnership, firm, or individual who wants to engage in business as an escrow agent in California must be licensed.

Certain exceptions are made with regard to banks, savings and loan companies, insurance companies, title insurance companies, real estate brokers, and attorneys. An attorney may escrow a transaction only if it is incidental to the duty he is performing for his client or a client's estate as an attorney at law. A real estate broker may escrow only a transaction in which he acts as the broker.

Duties and responsibilities of the escrow holder

For a detailed description of the duties and responsibilities of the escrow holder, the licensee is referred to the sections mentioned above in the Financial Code. A few of the more important are as follows.

1. An escrow is confidential, and no information concerning the escrow may be given to any persons not a party to the escrow.
2. If disputes arise between the parties in an escrow, it is not the duty of the escrow agent to act as mediator. The escrow agent accepts and follows instructions from the parties and must be very careful not to give either party any advice that is not within the generally accepted scope of his duties as the escrow holder. For instance, one of the parties to the escrow may ask the escrow agent for some legal advice about alternative methods of taking title to real property. The escrow officer must give the party the same answer the real estate broker is so often cautioned to give; he must suggest that the party consult with his attorney.
3. An escrow holder may not deliver documents or funds unless there has been a strict compliance with the conditions of the escrow. If an instrument is delivered by the escrow holder before all the conditions of the escrow have been met, the delivery is not valid and title does not pass.
4. An escrow agent is prohibited by law from paying referral fees to anyone except a regular employee of the escrow company. Usually, this also prohibits payment of commissions to real estate licensees and to outsiders for sending business to a particular escrow company. Such fees include gifts of merchandise or other items of value.
5. An escrow agent may not permit any person to make an addition to, deletion from, or alteration of an escrow instruction or amended or supplemental escrow instruction unless it is signed or initialed by all persons who had signed or initialed the instructions or amendments thereto. An escrow holder must at the time of execution deliver any escrow instruction or amended or supplemental instruction to all persons executing it.

Termite reports. The question of ordering a termite report should never be raised by the escrow holder. This is strictly a matter for the parties to the escrow to decide on, and unless the subject of a termite report is made a condition to the escrow by one of the parties involved, the escrow holder should refrain from making any statement regarding the subject. Actually, the practice in California is for the parties to the contract to reach some agreement about a termite report before going into escrow. The agreement is usually stated on the deposit receipt. In Chapter 5, where deposit receipts are discussed, the subject of the termite report in connection with a sale of real property is dealt with more fully.

Escrow holder as an agent

The escrow holder in a sale of property through an escrow is at first the agent of both parties. When the conditions are performed, the escrow holder becomes the agent of each party—that is, of the grantor to deliver the deed and of the grantee to pay over the purchase money. This agency relationship is considered a limited one, and the only obligations to be fulfilled by the escrow holder are those set forth in the instructions and those that impart no general duties but are composed of facts connected with the transaction only.

TERMINATION OF ESCROW

An escrow is usually terminated when any one of the following occurs:

1. Full performance of the conditions of the escrow by the parties involved is the most common method by which an escrow is completed.
2. Cancellation by mutual consent of the parties involved usually occurs when the buyer and seller mutually agree to end negotiations and so instruct the escrow holder.
3. Revocation by one of the parties to the escrow occurs when one of the parties to the escrow decides not to meet conditions previously agreed on. The result may be the termination of the escrow; however, such action by some of the parties will usually result in legal litigation, and the escrow holder will do nothing pending a decision by the court.
4. An intervening condition or event may make it impossible for one of the parties to perform, a result if one of the escrow parties expires or becomes incapacitated prior to close of escrow.

DIFFERING ESCROW PRACTICES

Every real estate transaction involving the transfer of an equitable or legal title will involve a final closing statement or settlement sheet. Both the buyer and seller must be shown, in writing, the cash requirement, the proceeds, the expense or charge allotments, and the prorations in the transaction.

Customs in closing vary in different parts of California, particularly between the northern and southern parts of the state. In southern California, most transactions are closed in escrows performed by the escrow departments of banks, specialized escrow companies, or title insurance companies. The escrow function is an independent transaction, as is the issuance of a policy of title insurance. A separate fee is charged for each separate function. Although the title insurance company always issues the policy of title insurance, it may or may not perform the escrow function. Escrow instructions are generally more formalized, especially when a bank or specialized escrow company performs the escrow function.

In northern California, the prevailing practice is for the title insurance company to issue the policy of title insurance and also perform the escrow function. The title company charges one fee—for the policy of title insurance—and this takes care of the escrow function also; one fee covers both.

Practices also vary among firms. Many large real estate firms throughout the state perform the escrow function within their own offices and use the title company only to obtain the title insurance policy and see that the necessary instruments are publicly recorded.

In northern California, the form showing the financial aspects of the transaction is called the Buyer's Statement and the Seller's Statement. In southern California, this same type of form is referred to as the Settlement Sheet.

DIVISION OF ESCROW CHARGES

Division of the various charges in escrow also differs, depending on the particular locale involved. The customary divisions of charges is shown below, but the licensee should remember that this is customary and not mandatory. Occasionally, the parties to the escrow may decide to divide certain charges in other than the customary way, and there is nothing to prevent them from doing so.

The seller is generally responsible for:

1. Drawing instruments in favor of the purchaser.
2. Real estate transfer tax.
3. Any notarial fee on instruments in favor of purchaser.
4. Broker's commission.

The purchaser is generally responsible for:

1. Drawing instruments in favor of the seller or lender.
2. Recording fee for deed.
3. Recording fee for trust deed in favor of the lender.
4. Notarial fee on instruments in favor of seller or lender.

The title insurance policy fee is an important part of the closing costs. In the majority of counties, the buyer pays for the title insurance policy, while in some, the seller pays; in still others, the cost is divided equally between the buyer and seller.

Such items as taxes, insurance, and rents are prorated between the buyer and seller as of the date of close of escrow. In southern California where the escrow fee may be separate from the title insurance fee, the escrow fee is generally split 50–50 between the buyer and seller, or two thirds to the seller and one third to the buyer.

Any variation from what is customary in the division of fees should be agreed on by the parties in advance of close of escrow. Often, through sheer bargaining power, one party can be relieved of all or some of the customary charges that might otherwise be assigned against him.

CHECKLIST FOR REAL ESTATE TRANSACTIONS

The *Reference Book*, published by the California Division of Real Estate, contains an extensive checklist of items that may be part of a real estate transaction. Often, only certain of these items will apply in any one particular transaction. After looking over the list, the reader will appreciate the reason most brokers prefer to let an expert handle the escrow function in a transaction. For instance, when a title company performs the escrow function in connection with the issuance of a title insurance policy, many of the items shown on the checklist below become the responsibility of the title company rather than of the broker. An example is the preparation and examination of most of the documents and forms necessary to the transaction.

Factors to be considered and preparations to be made prior to and during the preparation of the purchase contract are:

1. The date of the contract.
2. The name and address of the seller.
3. Is the seller a citizen of full age and competence?
4. The legal status of the seller.
5. The full name of the seller's wife.
6. The name and legal status of the purchaser.
7. The full name of the purchaser's wife.
8. The address and telephone number of the purchasers.
9. The purchase price and the terms of the contract.
10. The kind of deed to be delivered.
11. What special agreement will have to be made regarding any personal property?
12. Is the mortgage to be assumed, or is the buyer purchasing subject to the mortgage?
13. What type of note will be involved?
14. Will a deed of trust be involved, and will there be any special conditions or provisions?
15. Do mortgages or trust deeds contain acceleration or restrictive conditions?
16. Are there to be any special reservations or exceptions in the deed?
17. Special conditions or provisions to be inserted into the contract.
18. Rights of tenants or lessees.
19. Items to be adjusted at close of escrow.
20. Division of charges in escrow.
21. Any special arrangements concerning liens, easements, assessments, taxes, covenants, or restrictions?
22. Place and date on which escrow is to be closed.
23. How will the buyer take title to the property?
24. Name and address of escrow holder and of broker making the sale.
25. How will the problems of termite inspection and possession be taken care of?

After acceptance of an offer and during escrow, the seller may need to furnish the following:

1. Copy of contract.
2. Latest tax, water, and receipted assessment bills.
3. Latest water meter readings.
4. Latest gas meter readings.
5. Information regarding last payment of interest on mortgages or trust deeds.
6. Insurance policies on the property.
7. Certificate or offset statement from any holder of a mortgage or deed of trust.
8. Any subordination agreements that may be called for in the contract.
9. Certificate showing satisfaction of mechanic's liens, chattel mortgages, judgments, or mortgages to be paid at or prior to close of escrow.
10. A rental statement listing tenants, amount of rents paid or due, and moneys being held as advance rents or deposits.
11. Assignment of leases affecting the property.

12. Notification to tenants regarding subsequent rent payments.
13. Bill of sale for any personal property involved in the sale.
14. Seller's last deed and deed he is to prepare for buyer.
15. Any instruments the seller is to prepare or deliver at close of escrow.
16. Any unrecorded instruments that may affect the title.

The purchaser should have and/or check on the following:

1. Purchaser's copy of the contract and certificate of title or policy of insurance showing title vested in the grantor.
2. Examination of the deed to see that it conforms to the contract.
3. Examination of property description on deed to see that it is correct.
4. Examination of the deed to see that it is properly executed.
5. Disposition of all liens that must be removed.
6. Sufficient cash to make necessary payment required at close of escrow.
7. Names and information concerning tenants, leases, and rent.
8. Bill of sale if any personal property involved.
9. Examination of preliminary title search or survey.
10. Any matters that may affect title or use of the property.
11. Bills for any unpaid taxes, water, or assessments.
12. Any unrecorded instruments that may affect title.
13. Copies of any loan papers signed in connection with the sale.
14. Examination of purchase money mortgages.
15. Examination of note and deed of trust.
16. Adjustments completed if called for in the contract.

CHRONOLOGICAL STEPS IN THE ESCROW

Although the sequence of steps in any type of escrow may vary slightly, there is a general order in which they occur. Figure 8–1 illustrates basic escrow procedures. We shall briefly look at the steps in a southern California escrow where the escrow function and issuance of a title insurance policy are performed separately. Then, we shall examine a northern California escrow where the title insurance company performs the escrow function and issues the policy of title insurance.

Southern California escrow steps

1. After obtaining a completed deposit receipt signed by all parties to the transaction, the broker will open an escrow and prepare escrow instructions. He will generally use a standard printed form prepared by the escrow holder for drafting instructions.
2. The escrow instructions are signed by all parties to the contract, and the escrow holder orders a title search from a title company. A report is subsequently made to the escrow officer by the title company.
3. The escrow officer requests a Beneficiary's Statement from the beneficiary shown on the recorded deed of trust. The statement will show the condition of the indebtedness and the unpaid balance of the loan.
4. Matters disclosed by the preliminary title report that are not approved by the escrow instructions are reported to the seller for clearance or to the buyer for approval.
5. When the escrow officer receives all the documents and funds necessary to close the escrow, he makes the necessary adjustments and prorations between the parties on what is called a settlement sheet.
6. The necessary instruments are then forwarded to the title insurance company with instructions to record them.
7. The title search is run to date as of the close of business on the date set for close of escrow, and if no change of title is found, the deed and other instruments are recorded on the following morning at 8 A.M. By filing the moment the recorder's office opens at 8 A.M., the title company can issue a title policy with the assurance that there are no intervening matters of record against the property.
8. On the day that recordation has taken place, the escrow officer will disburse funds to the parties entitled to them, cause any fire insurance policies to be transferred or amended, and present closing statements to the parties entitled to them. The title insurance company generally tries to issue the policy of title insurance to the purchaser on the same day or as soon after recordation as possible. Within a few weeks, the recorder's office will return the recorded deed to the escrow officer, who will forward it to the purchaser.

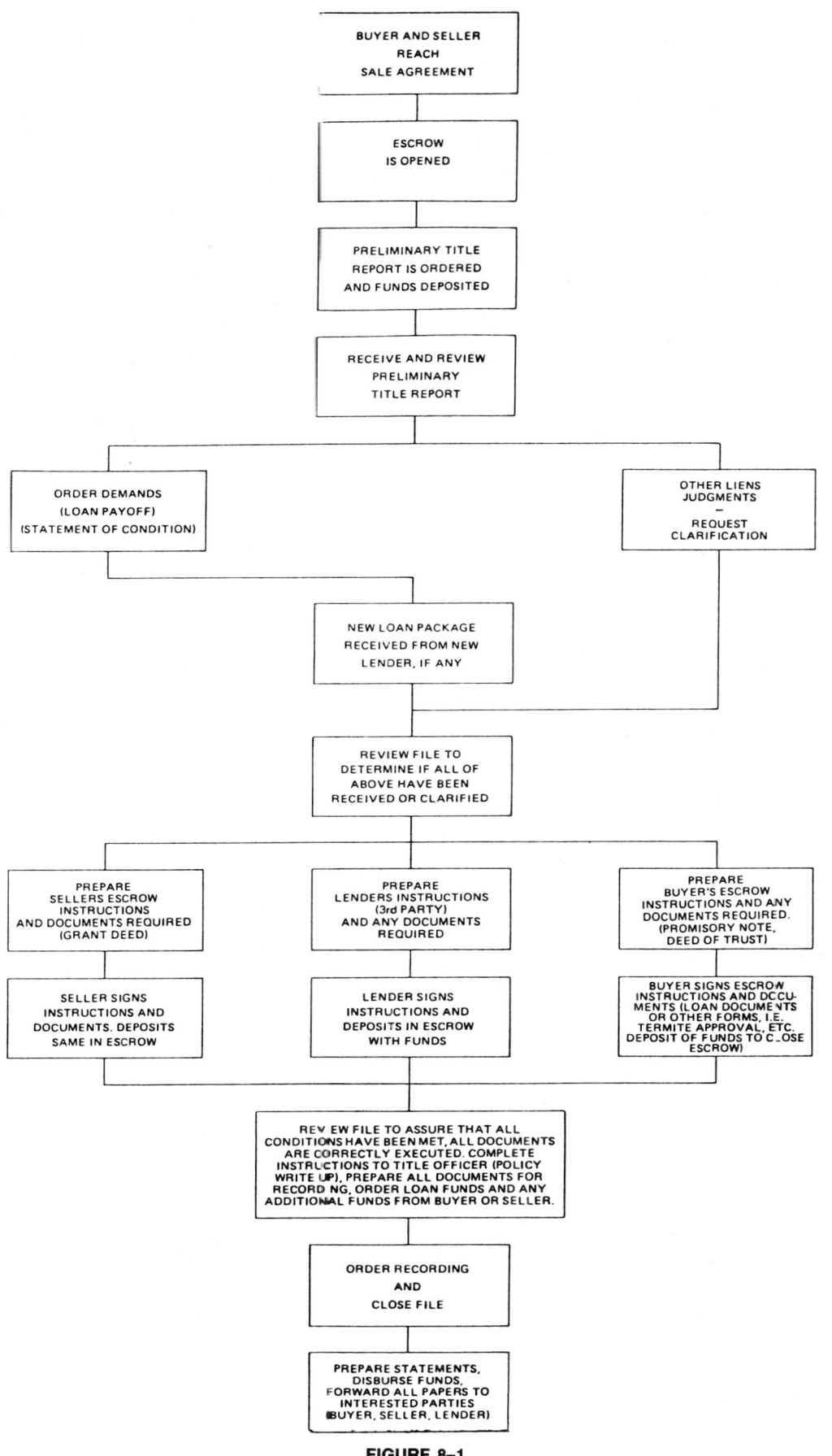

FIGURE 8-1

Northern California escrow steps

In many respects, the outline of steps below resembles the one for southern California. The main difference here is that the title company does both jobs; that is, it issues the policy of title insurance and takes care of recordation, and also performs the escrow function. The general sequence of steps is as follows:

1. After obtaining a completed deposit receipt signed by all parties to the transaction, the broker will open an escrow at the title company. If the broker does not maintain a trust account at a bank, he will at this point deposit with the title officer (who is also the escrow officer) any money received from the purchaser as deposit.
2. A preliminary title search is prepared, and sufficient copies are sent to the broker so that he may give one to the purchaser and one to the seller.
3. Matters disclosed by the preliminary title search are considered and are taken care of with the approval, if necessary, of buyer and/or seller. The title officer will receive any instructions that may be necessary in addition to those agreed on in the deposit receipt.
4. The title officer requests, from any beneficiary under an existing deed of trust, a statement of the condition of indebtedness and balance of the loan.
5. When the title officer receives all the documents necessary in order to close the escrow, he will make the necessary prorations in financial adjustments and prepare a seller's statement and a buyer's statement. These forms are also called buyer's and seller's instructions.
6. The instructions are presented to the respective parties to the transaction, and the parties sign their respective instructions and any other documents, such as a grant deed, note, and deed of trust, that may be necessary.
7. The title officer requests and obtains all funds necessary to close. The title search is run to date as of the close of business on the date set for close of escrow; and if no change of title is found, the deed and other pertinent instruments are recorded on the following morning at 8 A.M.
8. Following recordation, the title policy is issued and funds are disbursed to the parties entitled to them. Necessary insurance endorsements are obtained or may have been obtained just before recordation, and the policy and copies are sent to those entitled to them. When the title officer receives the recorded documents from the recorder's office, he will forward them to the necessary parties.

ESCROW PROBLEM AND STATEMENTS

An understanding of some common escrow procedures and the preparation of escrow statements for the seller and buyer are best explained by the use of an example involving a real estate transaction.

The basic facts concerning the transaction are given, followed by an explanation and the computations necessary in preparing the escrow statements for the parties involved. Prorations in connection with escrow are also discussed in the chapter dealing with real estate mathematics. Following the explanation, Figures 8–2 and 8–3 illustrate the actual escrow statement to be prepared for the sellers and buyers. These statements are also often referred to as settlement sheets.

Transaction facts and agreements

Taylor-Brown sale. The sale is of a residence at 390 Royal Court Road, San Tomas, California, belonging to John A. Taylor and Mary L. Taylor, husband and wife. Buyers are Thomas P. Brown and Carol V. Brown, husband and wife. The Realtor® is Ann Craig of ABC Realty Company.

1. Purchase price is $146,500.00 with buyers to obtain a loan of $110,000 with interest at 13 percent per annum, term of 30 years, and payments of $1,216.82 per month.
2. Closing date is May 25, 19—.
3. Buyers deposit 10 percent of purchase price with escrow and balance due at close of escrow.
4. Buyers' loan charges to XYZ Savings and Loan include loan fee of 1½ points plus $100.00; credit report, $20.00; tax service, $17.50; and interest at $39.18 per day from May 25 to June 1.
5. Buyers to pay $101.50 ALTA title policy premium for $110,000 loan amount.
6. Sellers' existing note and trust deed payable to XYZ Savings and Loan with principal balance of $59,594.00 and interest from April 1 at $15.10 per day; plus reconveyance fee $40.00; statement fee, $15.00; and late charge, $47.50.

7. Sellers' second note and trust deed payable to J. Smith with principal balance $8,887.50 and interest from April 1 at $2.47 per day and $30.00 reconveyance fee.
8. Both installments of property tax have been paid by seller at $523.75 per installment.
9. Buyers to pay $75.00 for termite inspection, sellers to pay $825.00 for termite work.
10. Buyers to pay insurance premium of $447.00 to L. Brown Insurance Company.
11. Buyers to pay $4.00 notary and $10.00 recording fees.
12. Sellers to pay 6 percent commission to ABC Realty Company.
13. Sellers to pay $550.00 premium for $146,500.00 title insurance policy.
14. Sellers to pay $4.00 notary and $6.00 recording fees.
15. Sellers to pay transfer tax of $161.15.
16. Escrow fee is $258.00. Sellers pay $129.00 and buyers pay $129.00.

Escrow statements

Forms of escrow statements vary from place to place, but it makes no difference what form is used—the principles remain the same. There are two general types:

1. The *ledger account* form, which represents a reproduction of the ledger accounts of the purchaser and seller. This is also called the debit and credit approach.
2. The *report* or accumulated deduction form, which is like an income statement if one is familiar with accounting. However, it requires no knowledge of accounting, and many claim it is more easily understood by the layman.

The *ledger account* form applying the facts presented in the Taylor-Brown sale is presented in Figures 8–2 and 8–3. The two statements to seller and buyer may be combined on a single sheet, or separate sheets may be made for each party.

Explanation of procedures

Following is an explanation of the procedures used in arriving at the figures shown on the escrow statements to the sellers and the buyers. The numbers in the escrow statements' right margins correspond to explanation numbers.

Sellers statement. The credit column shows amounts credited to the seller.

1. $146,500 purchase price.
2. Tax proration, $104.75. The seller has paid the second installment of property tax, $523.75, which is for January 1 to June 30. For this escrow calculation, every month is presumed to be 30 days. Mr. and Mrs. Brown become the owners on May 25 and must pay Mr. and Mrs. Taylor for 6 days in May and 30 days in June. The calculation is: $523.75 ÷ 180 × 36 = $104.75.

The debit column shows amounts to be paid by seller.

3. The premium for a standard CLTA owners title insurance policy for $146,500 is $550. Although the payment for title insurance is by agreement between the parties, the general custom in southern California is for the seller to pay, while the buyer pays in northern California.
4. Total escrow fee is $258, and by custom in southern California, the seller pays half, $129, and the buyer pays half, $129. In northern California, the buyer pays the full escrow fee.
5. Reconveyance fee, $30 in connection with second loan to J. Smith.
6. Notary fee, $4.
7. Transfer tax, $161.15. Based on $1.10 per $1,000 of sales price. Calculation is: $1.10 × 146.5 = $128.70.
8. Recording fee, $6.
9. Termite work, $825. This amount will be held by the escrow pending completion of work and issuance of certificate of completion by termite company.
10. Real estate commission, $8,790. Calculation is $146,500 × .06 = $8,790.
11. Amount necessary to pay off second loan, $9,023.35.
12. Amount necessary to pay off existing seller's loan to XYZ Savings. $60,527 for principal, interest, reconveyance fee, statement fee, and late charge. Because sellers did not make a May 1 loan payment, interest is charged for 30 days in April and 25 days in May. Calculation is: 55 × $15.10 = $830.50.
13. The total amount of expenses (debits) against the seller, 3 through 12, is $80,045.50. The amount credited to the seller, 1 and 2, is $146,604.75. The amount of money the sellers will receive at close of escrow is $66,559.25. Calculation is: $146,604.75 − $80,045.50 = $66,559.25.

ES 293 (12-73)

 **TITLE INSURANCE AND TRUST**

John A. and Mary L. Taylor

ESCROW STATEMENT
SELLER

ORDER NO.

SELLER ☒   BUYER ☐   BORROWER ☐

DESCRIPTION	DEBIT	CREDIT	
SALE/PURCHASE PRICE		146,500.00	1
DEPOSITS			
DEPOSIT RETAINED			
EXISTING LOAN ASSUMED			
NEW LOAN(S)			
PRO RATA TAXES 5/25/-- to 7/1/--		104.75	2
PRO RATA INSURANCE			
PRO RATA RENTS			
PRO RATA			
TITLE INSURANCE ☐ LOAN ☐ JOINT PREMIUM FOR $ 146,500.00 ☒ OWNERS POLICY ☐ ALTA POLICY	550.00		3
ESCROW FEE 1/2	129.00		4
RECONVEYANCE FEE	30.00		5
PREPARING DOCUMENTS			
NOTARY FEES	4.00		6
TRANSFER TAX	161.15		7
RECORDING	6.00		8
TAXES			
Termite Work	825.00		9
COMMISSION ABC Realty Company	8,790.00		10
INSURANCE PREMIUM			
LOAN PAYOFFS: J. Smith	9,023.35		11
Principal $ 8,887.50			
Interest at $ 2.47 per day from 4/1 to 5/25 135.85			
LOAN PAY OFFS XYZ Savings	60,527.00		12
Principal $ 59,594.00			
Interest at $ 15.10 per day from 4/1 to 5/25 830.50			
Reconveyance and Statement Fees 55.00			
Late Charge 47.50			
BALANCE/BALANCE DUE TO SELLER	66,559.25		13
TOTALS	146,604.75	146,604.75	14

APPROVED:

(s) John A. Taylor

(s) Mary L. Taylor

DATE:
May 25, 19--

ADDRESS:
390 Royal Court Road, San Tomas

564-1919
TELEPHONE:

FIGURE 8–2

ES 293 (12-73)

TITLE INSURANCE AND TRUST

Thomas P. and Carol V. Brown

ESCROW STATEMENT
BUYER

ORDER NO.

SELLER ☐ BUYER ☒ BORROWER ☐

DESCRIPTION	DEBIT	CREDIT	
SALE/PURCHASE PRICE	146,500.00		1
DEPOSITS		14,650.00	2
DEPOSIT RETAINED			
EXISTING LOAN ASSUMED			
NEW LOAN(S) XYZ Savings		110,000.00	3
PRO RATA TAXES 5/25/-- to 7/1/--	104.75		4
PRO RATA INSURANCE			
PRO RATA RENTS			
PRO RATA			
TITLE INSURANCE ☐ LOAN ☐ JOINT PREMIUM FOR $ ☐ OWNERS POLICY $ 110,000.00 ☒ ALTA POLICY	101.50		5
ESCROW FEE 1/2	129.00		6
RECONVEYANCE FEE			
PREPARING DOCUMENTS			
NOTARY FEES	4.00		7
TRANSFER TAX			
RECORDING	10.00		8
TAXES			
Termite Report	75.00		9
COMMISSION			
INSURANCE PREMIUM L. Brown Insurance Company	447.00		10
LOAN CHARGES XYZ Savings	2,061.76		11
Loan fee $ 1,750.00 Interest at $ 39.18 per Credit report 20.00 day from 5/25 to 6/1 Tax Service 17.50 $ 274.26			
LOAN PAY OFFS			
BALANCE/BALANCE DUE		24,783.01	12
TOTALS	149,433.01	149,433.01	13

APPROVED:
(s) Thomas P. Brown
(s) Carol V. Brown

DATE:
May 25, 19--

ADDRESS:
299 Lincoln Way, San Tomas

564-8090
TELEPHONE:

FIGURE 8–3

Buyer's statement. The debit column shows amounts to be paid by buyers.

1. $146,500 purchase price is shown.
4. Prorata property taxes. Buyer owes seller $104.75 as explained in seller's statement, 2.
5. Buyer pays $101.50 premium for $110,000 ALTA title policy insuring lender's interest.
6. Buyer's half of $258 escrow fee is $129.
7. Notary fee, $4.
8. Recording fee, $10.
9. Buyer pays for termite report, $75.
10. Property insurance policy, $447.
11. Buyer's loan charges to XYZ Savings, $1,750.00. Loan fee is 1½ points plus $100. ($1,650 + $100 = $1,750). Additional charges required by lender are for credit report, tax service, tax reserve, insurance reserve, and interest at $39.18 per day from close of escrow on 5/25 to 6/1, a total of seven days. Since regular loan payments represent interest charged for a preceding month, the regular loan payment of $1,216.82 will begin July 1.
13. The purchase price of $146,500 and closing costs of $2,933.01 equal $149,433.01.

The buyer is credited with the following amounts.

2. $14,650 representing 10 percent of purchase price deposited in escrow.
3. $110,000 loan from XYZ Savings.
12. Purchase price, $146,500, and closing costs, $2,933.01, equal $149,433.01. The buyer has been credited with a 10 percent deposit of $14,650 and loan proceeds of $110,000, which equals $124,650. To close escrow, the buyer must deposit the additional down payment, of $21,850 and $2,933.01 closing costs, totaling $24,783.01. Calculation is: $149,433.01 − $124,650.00 = $24,783.01.

TITLE INSURANCE

A transfer of the ownership of real property involves not only the preparation of necessary documents but also an examination and interpretation of public records for matters affecting that property in order to ascertain rights, interest, and liens of others. A policy of title insurance is an insured statement of the condition of the title of a particular piece of property. The policy shows who owns the land according to the public records and also what is recorded against the property in the way of taxes, mortgages, and deeds of trust, and any other liens and encumbrances of record.

It is thus very difficult to find a buyer who does not make use of a title report when buying a piece of property or a lender who will advance funds for the purchase of property without receipt of a title insurance policy. The title policy is a policy of indemnity since the title insurance company is insuring against loss in the event that its interpretation of the condition of title is incorrect. The beneficiary of the insurance is either the buyer of the property or the lender who has loaned money with the property as security for the loan.

A title insurance company, before issuing a policy, will perform an extensive search of the relevant public records to determine if any individual, other than the seller and including a government entity, has any right, lien, claim, or encumbrance which must be taken into account. This search can be very complex because in certain cases records may be located in various federal, state, county and municipal facilities.

Claims against title, even when they are without merit, frequently involve lengthy and expensive litigation, and part of the protection offered by a title insurance company is payment for any defense necessary against such claims.

TYPES OF POLICIES

Standard coverage policy

The basic form of coverage used in California, and illustrated in Figure 8–4, is known as the "California Land Title Association Standard Coverage Policy Form." This form has been established and standardized by the California Land Title Association (CLTA), the trade organization for the title companies in California, to comply with the form and coverage approved and recommended by the American Title Association for use throughout the United States. It may be issued to insure an owner only, or a lender only, or it may insure both the owner and lender and thus be a joint-protection standard coverage policy. A leasehold policy can be issued to insure a lessee or sublessee, and an easement policy is available to insure the owner of an easement.

The standard policy insures the ownership of the estate or interest in the described land and the priority and lien, upon said estate or interest, of the insured mortgage or deed of trust. Its coverage is not limited to matters revealed by public records and includes protection against such defects as forged instruments in the chain of title; acts of minors and incompetents whose disability is undisclosed; instruments which may be void; and

Policy of Title Insurance

SUBJECT TO SCHEDULE B AND THE CONDITIONS AND STIPULATIONS HEREOF, TITLE INSURANCE AND TRUST COMPANY, a California corporation herein called the Company, insures the insured, as of Date of Policy shown in Schedule A, against loss or damage, not exceeding the amount of insurance stated in Schedule A, and costs, attorneys' fees and expenses which the Company may become obligated to pay hereunder, sustained or incurred by said insured by reason of:

1. Title to the estate or interest described in Schedule A being vested other than as stated therein;

2. Any defect in or lien or encumbrance on such title;

3. Unmarketability of such title; or

4. Any lack of the ordinary right of an abutting owner for access to at least one physically open street or highway if the land, in fact, abuts upon one or more such streets or highways;

and in addition, as to an insured lender only;

5. Invalidity of the lien of the insured mortgage upon said estate or interest except to the extent that such invalidity, or claim thereof, arises out of the transaction evidenced by the insured mortgage and is based upon

    a. usury, or
    b. any consumer credit protection or truth in lending law;

6. Priority of any lien or encumbrance over the lien of the insured mortgage, said mortgage being shown in Schedule B in the order of its priority; or

7. Invalidity of any assignment of the insured mortgage, provided such assignment is shown in Schedule B.

Title Insurance and Trust Company

by *John E. Flood, Jr.*
President

Attest
Secretary

TO 1012 TI (5-77) California Land Title Association Standard Coverage Policy-1973   Cat. No. NN00240

FIGURE 8–4

Conditions and Stipulations

1. Definition of Terms

The following terms when used in this policy mean:

(a.) "insured": the insured named in Schedule A, and, subject to any rights or defenses the Company may have had against the named insured, those who succeed to the interest of such insured by operation of law as distinguished from purchase including, but not limited to, heirs, distributees, devisees, survivors, personal representatives, next of kin, or corporate or fiduciary successors. The term "insured" also includes (i) the owner of the indebtedness secured by the insured mortgage and each successor in ownership of such indebtedness (reserving, however, all rights and defenses as to any such successor who acquires the indebtedness by operation of law as described in the first sentence of this subparagraph (a) that the Company would have had against the successor's transferor), and further includes (ii) any governmental agency or instrumentality which is an insurer or guarantor under an insurance contract or guaranty insuring or guaranteeing said indebtedness, or any part thereof, whether named as an insured herein or not, and (iii) the parties designated in paragraph 2(a) of these Conditions and Stipulations.

(b.) "insured claimant": an insured claiming loss or damage hereunder.

(c.) "insured lender": the owner of an insured mortgage.

(d.) "insured mortgage": a mortgage shown in Schedule B, the owner of which is named as an insured in Schedule A.

(e.) "knowledge": actual knowledge, not constructive knowledge or notice which may be imputed to an insured by reason of any public records.

(f.) "land": the land described specifically or by reference in Schedule C, and improvements affixed thereto which by law constitute real property; provided, however, the term "land" does not include any area excluded by Paragraph No. 6 of Part I of Schedule B of this Policy.

(g.) "mortgage": mortgage, deed of trust, trust deed, or other security instrument.

(h.) "public records": those records which by law impart constructive notice of matters relating to the land.

2. (a.) Continuation of Insurance after Acquisition of Title by Insured Lender

If this policy insures the owner of the indebtedness secured by the insured mortgage, this policy shall continue in force as of Date of Policy in favor of such insured who acquires all or any part of said estate or interest in the land described in Schedule C by foreclosure, trustee's sale, conveyance in lieu of foreclosure, or other legal manner which discharges the lien of the insured mortgage, and if such insured is a corporation, its transferee of the estate or interest so acquired, provided the transferee is the parent or wholly owned subsidiary of such insured; and in favor of any governmental agency or instrumentality which acquires all or any part of the estate or interest pursuant to a contract of insurance or guaranty insuring or guaranteeing the indebtedness secured by the insured mortgage. After any such acquisition the amount of insurance hereunder, exclusive of costs, attorneys' fees and expenses which the Company may be obligated to pay, shall not exceed the least of:

(i) the amount of insurance stated in Schedule A;

(ii) the amount of the unpaid principal of the indebtedness plus interest thereon, as determined under paragraph 6(a) (iii) hereof, expenses of foreclosure and amounts advanced to protect the lien of the insured mortgage and secured by said insured mortgage at the time of acquisition of such estate or interest in the land; or

(iii) the amount paid by any governmental agency or instrumentality, if such agency or instrumentality is the insured claimant, in acquisition of such estate or interest in satisfaction of its insurance contract or guaranty.

(b.) Continuation of Insurance After Conveyance of Title

The coverage of this policy shall continue in force as of Date of Policy, in favor of an insured so long as such insured retains an estate or interest in the land, or owns an indebtedness secured by a purchase money mortgage given by a purchaser from such insured, or so long as such insured shall have liability by reason of covenants of warranty made by such insured in any transfer or conveyance of such estate or interest; provided, however, this policy shall not continue in force in favor of any purchaser from such insured of either said estate or interest or the indebtedness secured by a purchase money mortgage given to such insured.

3. Defense and Prosecution of Actions — Notice of Claim to be Given by an Insured Claimant

(a.) The Company, at its own cost and without undue delay, shall provide for the defense of an insured in litigation to the extent that such litigation involves an alleged defect, lien, encumbrance or other matter insured against by this policy.

(b.) The insured shall notify the Company promptly in writing (i) in case of any litigation as set forth in (a) above, (ii) in case knowledge shall come to an insured hereunder of any claim of title or interest which is adverse to the title to the estate or interest or the lien of the insured mortgage, as insured, and which might cause loss or damage for which the Company may be liable by virtue of this policy, or (iii) if title to the estate or interest or the lien of the insured mortgage, as insured, is rejected as unmarketable. If such prompt notice shall not be given to the Company, then as to such insured all liability of the Company shall cease and terminate in regard to the matter or matters for which such prompt notice is required; provided, however, that failure to notify shall in no case prejudice the rights of any such insured under this policy unless the Company shall be prejudiced by such failure and then only to the extent of such prejudice.

(c.) The Company shall have the right at its own cost to institute and without undue delay prosecute any action or proceeding or to do any other act which in its opinion may be necessary or desirable to establish the title to the estate or interest or the lien of the insured mortgage, as insured; and the Company may take any appropriate action, whether or not it shall be liable under the terms of this policy, and shall not thereby concede liability or waive any provision of this policy.

(d.) Whenever the Company shall have brought any action or interposed a defense as required or permitted by the provisions of this policy, the Company may pursue any such litigation to final determination by a court of competent jurisdiction and expressly reserves the right, in its sole discretion, to appeal from any adverse judgment or order.

(e.) In all cases where this policy permits or requires the Company to prosecute or provide for the defense of any action or proceeding, the insured hereunder shall secure to the Company the right to so prosecute or provide defense in such action or proceeding, and all appeals therein, and permit the Company to use, at its option, the name of such insured for such purpose. Whenever requested by the Company, such insured shall give the Company, at the Company's expense, all reasonable aid (1) in any such action or proceeding in effecting settlement, securing evidence, obtaining witnesses, or prosecuting or defending such action or proceeding, and (2) in any other act which in the opinion of the Company may be necessary or desirable to establish the title to the estate or interest or the lien of the insured mortgage, as insured, including but not limited to executing corrective or other documents.

4. Proof of Loss or Damage — Limitation of Action

In addition to the notices required under Paragraph 3(b) of these Conditions and Stipulations, a proof of loss or damage, signed and sworn to by the insured claimant shall be furnished to the Company within 90 days after the insured claimant shall ascertain or determine the facts giving rise to such loss or damage. Such proof of loss or damage shall describe the defect in, or lien or encumbrance on the title, or other matter insured against by this policy which constitutes the basis of loss or damage, and, when appropriate, state the basis of calculating the amount of such loss or damage.

Should such proof of loss or damage fail to state facts sufficient to enable the Company to determine its liability hereunder, insured claimant, at the written request of the Company, shall furnish such additional information as may reasonably be necessary to make such determination.

No right of action shall accrue to insured claimant until 30 days after such proof of loss or damage shall have been furnished.

Failure to furnish such proof of loss or damage shall terminate any liability of the Company under this policy as to such loss or damage.

5. Options to Pay or Otherwise Settle Claims and Options to Purchase Indebtedness

The Company shall have the option to pay or otherwise settle for or in the name of an insured claimant any claim insured against, or to terminate all liability and obligations of the Company hereunder by paying or tendering payment of the amount of insurance under this policy together with any costs, attorneys' fees and expenses incurred up to the time of such payment or tender of payment by the insured claimant and authorized by the Company. In case loss or damage is claimed under this policy by the owner of the indebtedness secured by the insured mortgage, the Company shall have the further option to purchase such indebtedness for the amount owing thereon together with all costs, attorneys' fees and expenses which the Company is obligated hereunder to pay. If the Company offers to purchase said indebtedness as herein provided, the owner of such indebtedness shall transfer and assign said indebtedness and the mortgage and any collateral securing the same to the Company upon payment therefor as herein provided. Upon such offer being made by the Company, all liability and obligations of the Company hereunder to the owner of the indebtedness secured by said insured mortgage, other than the obligation to purchase said indebtedness pursuant to this paragraph, are terminated.

6. Determination and Payment of Loss

(a.) The liability of the Company under this policy shall in no case exceed the least of:

(i) the actual loss of the insured claimant; or

(ii) the amount of insurance stated in Schedule A, or, if applicable, the amount of insurance as defined in paragraph 2(a) hereof; or

(iii) if this policy insures the owner of the indebtedness secured by the insured mortgage, and provided said owner is the insured claimant, the amount of the unpaid principal of said indebtedness, plus interest thereon, provided such amount shall not include any additional principal indebtedness created subsequent to Date of Policy, except as to amounts advanced to protect the lien of the insured mortgage and secured thereby.

(b.) The Company will pay, in addition to any loss insured against by this policy, all costs imposed upon an insured in litigation carried on by the Company for such insured, and all costs, attorneys' fees and expenses in litigation carried on by such insured with the written authorization of the Company.

(c.) When the amount of loss or damage has been definitely fixed in accordance with the conditions of this policy, the loss or damage shall be payable within 30 days thereafter.

7. Limitation of Liability

No claim shall arise or be maintainable under this policy (a) if the Company, after having received notice of an alleged defect, lien or encumbrance insured against hereunder, by litigation or otherwise, removes such defect, lien or encumbrance or establishes the title, or the lien of the insured mortgage, as insured, within a reasonable time after receipt of such notice; (b) in the event of litigation until there has been a final determination by a court of competent jurisdiction, and disposition of all appeals therefrom, adverse to the title or to the lien of the insured mortgage, as insured, as provided in paragraph 3 hereof; or (c) for liability voluntarily admitted or assumed by an insured without prior written consent of the Company.

FIGURE 8–4 ***(continued)***

8. Reduction of Insurance; Termination of Liability

All payments under this policy, except payment made for costs, attorneys' fees and expenses, shall reduce the amount of the insurance pro tanto; provided, however, if the owner of the indebtedness secured by the insured mortgage is an insured hereunder, then such payments, prior to the acquisition of title to said estate or interest as provided in paragraph 2(a) of these Conditions and Stipulations, shall not reduce pro tanto the amount of the insurance afforded hereunder as to any such insured, except to the extent that such payments reduce the amount of the indebtedness secured by such mortgage.

Payment in full by any person or voluntary satisfaction or release of the insured mortgage shall terminate all liability of the Company to an insured owner of the indebtedness secured by the insured mortgage, except as provided in paragraph 2(a) hereof.

9. Liability Noncumulative

It is expressly understood that the amount of insurance under this policy as to the insured owner of the estate or interest covered by this policy, shall be reduced by any amount the Company may pay under any policy insuring (a) a mortgage shown or referred to in Schedule B hereof which is a lien on the estate or interest covered by this policy, or (b) a mortgage hereafter executed by an insured which is a charge or lien on the estate or interest described or referred to in Schedule A, and the amount so paid shall be deemed a payment under this policy. The Company shall have the option to apply to the payment of any such mortgage any amount that otherwise would be payable hereunder to the insured owner of the estate or interest covered by this policy and the amount so paid shall be deemed a payment under this policy to said insured owner.

The provisions of this paragraph 9 shall not apply to an owner of the indebtedness secured by the insured mortgage, unless such insured acquires title to said estate or interest in satisfaction of said indebtedness or any part thereof.

10. Subrogation Upon Payment or Settlement

Whenever the Company shall have paid or settled a claim under this policy, all right of subrogation shall vest in the Company unaffected by any act of the insured claimant, except that the owner of the indebtedness secured by the insured mortgage may release or substitute the personal liability of any debtor or guarantor, or extend or otherwise modify the terms of payment, or release a portion of the estate or interest from the lien of the insured mortgage, or release any collateral security for the indebtedness, provided such act occurs prior to receipt by such insured of notice of any claim of title or interest adverse to the title to the estate or interest or the priority of the lien of the insured mortgage and does not result in any loss of priority of the lien of the insured mortgage. The Company shall be subrogated to and be entitled to all rights and remedies which such insured claimant would have had against any person or property in respect to such claim had this policy not been issued, and the Company is hereby authorized and empowered to sue, compromise or settle in its name or in the name of the insured to the full extent of the loss sustained by the Company. If requested by the Company, the insured shall execute any and all documents to evidence the within subrogation. If the payment does not cover the loss of such insured claimant, the Company shall be subrogated to such rights and remedies in the proportion which said payment bears to the amount of said loss, but such subrogation shall be in subordination to an insured mortgage. If loss should result from any act of such insured claimant, such act shall not void this policy, but the Company, in that event, shall as to such insured claimant be required to pay only that part of any losses insured against hereunder which shall exceed the amount, if any, lost to the Company by reason of the impairment of the right of subrogation.

11. Liability Limited to this Policy

This instrument together with all endorsements and other instruments, if any, attached hereto by the Company is the entire policy and contract between the insured and the Company. Any claim of loss or damage, whether or not based on negligence, and which arises out of the status of the lien of the insured mortgage or of the title to the estate or interest covered hereby, or any action asserting such claim, shall be restricted to the provisions and Conditions and Stipulations of this policy.

No amendment of or endorsement to this policy can be made except by writing endorsed hereon or attached hereto signed by either the President, a Vice President, the Secretary, an Assistant Secretary, or validating officer or authorized signatory of the Company.

No payment shall be made without producing this policy for endorsement of such payment unless the policy be lost or destroyed, in which case proof of such loss or destruction shall be furnished to the satisfaction of the Company.

12. Notices, Where Sent

All notices required to be given the Company and any statement in writing required to be furnished the Company shall be addressed to it at the office which issued this policy or to its Home Office, 6300 Wilshire Boulevard, P.O. Box 92792, Los Angeles, California 90009.

13. THE PREMIUM SPECIFIED IN SCHEDULE A IS THE ENTIRE CHARGE FOR TITLE SEARCH, TITLE EXAMINATION AND TITLE INSURANCE.

FIGURE 8–4 *(continued)*

SCHEDULE A

Amount $146,500.00 Premium $550.00

Effective Date   May 25, 19-- Policy Number   C-228

1. Name of Insured: XYZ SAVINGS AND LOAN ASSOCIATION, a corporation,
and
THOMAS P. BROWN and CAROL V. BROWN, husband and wife

2. The estate or interest referred to herein is at Date of Policy vested in:
THOMAS P. BROWN and CAROL V. BROWN, husband and wife, as joint tenants

3. The estate or interest in the land described in Schedule C is a fee.

SCHEDULE B

Part I

This policy does not insure against loss or damage by reason of the following:

1. Taxes or assessments which are not shown as existing liens by the records of any taxing authority that levies taxes or assessments on real property or by the public records.
Proceedings by a public agency which may result in taxes or assessments, or notices of such proceedings, whether or not shown by the records of such agency or by the public records.

2. Any facts, rights, interests or claims which are not shown by the public records but which could be ascertained by an inspection of the land or by making inquiry of persons in possession thereof.

3. Easements, liens or encumbrances, or claims thereof, which are not shown by the public records.

4. Discrepancies, conflicts in boundary lines, shortage in areas, encroachments, or any other facts which a correct survey would disclose, and which are not shown by the public records.

5. (a) Unpatented mining claims; (b) reservations or exceptions in patents or in Acts authorizing the issuance thereof; (c) water rights, claims or title to water.

6. Any right, title interest, estate or easement in land beyond the lines of the area specifically described or referred to in Schedule C, or in abutting streets, roads, avenues, alleys, lanes, ways or waterways, but nothing in this paragraph shall modify or limit the extent to which the ordinary right of an abutting owner for access to a physically open street or highway is insured by this policy.

7. Any law, ordinance or governmental regulation (including but not limited to building and zoning ordinances) restricting or regulating or prohibiting the occupancy, use or enjoyment of the land, or regulating the character, dimensions or location of any improvement now or hereafter erected on the land, or prohibiting a separation in ownership or a reduction in the dimensions or area of the land, or the effect of any violation of any such law, ordinance or governmental regulation.

8. Rights of eminent domain or governmental rights of police power unless notice of the exercise of such rights appears in the public records.

9. Defects, liens, encumbrances, adverse claims, or other matters (a) created, suffered, assumed or agreed to by the insured claimant; (b) not shown by the public records and not otherwise excluded from coverage but known to the insured claimant either at Date of Policy or at the date such claimant to the Company prior to the date such insured claimant became an insured hereunder; (c) resulting in no loss or damage to the insured claimant; (d) attaching or created subsequent to Date of Policy; or (e) resulting in loss or damage which would not have been sustained if the insured claimant had been a purchaser or encumbrancer for value without knowledge.

10. Any facts, rights, interests or claims which are not shown by the public records but which could be ascertained by making inquiry of the lessors in the lease or leases described or referred to in Schedule A.

11. The effect of any failure to comply with the terms, covenants and conditions of the lease or leases described or referred to in Schedule A.

FIGURE 8-4 *(continued)*

Part II

1. City and County Taxes for 19---19--, a lien, not yet payable. Assessor's lot 56, Block 619.
2. Public service easements appearing on map and granted to the Pacific Telephone and Telegraph Company and Pacific Gas and Electric Company in 222 O.R. 896. (Affects rear five feet.)
3. Declaration of restrictions by South Coast Insurance Company, a corporation, dated March 20, 1933, recorded April 10, 1933 in 8337 O.R. 821. No express words of forfeiture.
4. Trust Deed to secure the payment of $110,000.00 as follows:
   Trustor   : Thomas P. Brown and Carol V. Brown, husband and wife
   Trustee   : Columbia Reconveyance Company, a California corporation
   Beneficiary : XYZ Savings and Loan Association, a corporation
   Dated   : May 23, 19--
   Recorded   : May 23, 19-- Series Number A-89011.

SCHEDULE C

The specific land referred to in this policy is described as follows:

Being all that certain real property situated in the City of San Tomas, County of Los Angeles, State of California, described as follows, to wit:

Portion of Lot 56, Block 619, according to the map of Adams Terrace, filed July 18, 1931, in Book "P" of Maps, pages 21 and 22, in office of the Recorder of the City of San Tomas, County of Los Angeles, State of California, described as follows:

BEGINNING at a point on the northwest corner of the intersection of Royal Court Road and 20th Avenue; thence 200 feet northerly along the westerly line of Royal Court Road to point of beginning. Thence at a right angle 200 feet west; thence at a right angle 150 feet north; thence at a right angle 200 feet east; thence at a right angle 150 feet south to the point of beginning.

FIGURE 8-4 *(continued)*

ADDITIONAL PROTECTION INDORSEMENT
FOR HOME OWNERS

ATTACHED TO POLICY NO. C-228

ISSUED BY

Title Insurance and Trust Company

1. This Indorsement shall be effective only if at Date of Policy there is located on the land described in said Policy a one-to-four family residential structure, in which the Insured Owner resides or intends to reside. For the purpose of this Indorsement the term "residential structure" is defined as including the principal dwelling structure located on said land and all improvements thereon related to residential use of the property, except plantings of any nature and except perimeter fences and perimeter walls.

2. The Company hereby insures the Insured Owner of the estate or interest described in Schedule A against loss or damage which the Insured Owner shall sustain by reason of:

    a. the existence at Date of Policy of any of the following matters:

    (1) lack of a right of access from said land to a public street;

    (2) any taxes or assessments levied by a public authority against the estate or interest insured which constitute liens thereon and are not shown as exceptions in Schedule B of said Policy;

    (3) any unrecorded statutory liens for labor or material attaching to said estate or interest arising out of any work of improvement on said land in progress or completed at Date of Policy, except a work of improvement for which said Insured Owner has agreed to be responsible;

    b. the enforced removal of said residential structure or interference with the use thereof for ordinary residential purposes based upon the existence at Date of Policy of:

    (1) any encroachment of said residential structure or any part thereof onto adjoining lands, or onto any easement shown as an exception in Part II of Schedule B of said Policy, or onto any unrecorded subsurface easement;

    (2) any violation of any enforceable covenants, conditions or restrictions affecting said land and shown in Part II of Schedule B;

    (3) any violation of applicable zoning ordinances, but this Indorsement does not insure compliance with, nor is it in any way concerned with, building codes or other exercise of governmental police power;

    c. damage to said residential structure resulting from the exercise of any right to use the surface of said land for the extraction or development of minerals, if minerals are excepted from the description of said land or shown as an exception or reservation in Schedule B.

    The total liability of the Company under said Policy and all indorsements attached thereto shall not exceed, in the aggregate, the amount of said Policy and costs which the Company is obligated under the conditions and stipulations thereof to pay; and nothing contained herein shall be construed as extending or changing the effective date of said Policy.

    This indorsement is made a part of said Policy and is subject to the schedules, conditions and stipulations therein, except as modified by the provisions hereof.

Title Insurance and Trust Company

By *John J Eagan* Secretary

FIGURE 8–4 *(concluded)*

undisclosed rights of husband and wife when recorded instruments contain false recitals that an individual in question is unmarried.

The standard policy generally excludes claims not shown by the public record, mining claims, reservations in patents, and water rights. These exemptions result from the fact that the title insurance company does not ordinarily make a physical inspection or survey of the land or premises involved in a standard coverage policy. Where the buyer or lender is familiar with or has inspected the property in question, this type of coverage is sufficient.

Extended coverage policy

Extended coverage policies are available to both owners and lenders and, of course, cost more than the standard policy. The general exceptions contained in the standard policy are eliminated in the extended coverage policy.

The most commonly used extended coverage form policy is called the "American Land Title Association Policy—Additional Coverage," commonly known as an ALTA policy. In this policy, insurance is given that the lender has a valid and enforceable lien, subject only to the exclusions from coverage, if any, and such defects, liens, and encumbrances on the title as are shown on the policy. The policy expressly includes priority insurance to cover mechanic's liens and assessments for street improvements.

This type of extended coverage can also be issued for an owner, lender, or both together. The insurance is generally written by using the standard coverage form and deleting therefrom the printed general exceptions shown on the policy.

There are, in addition to the two policies and coverages already discussed, many other types of special coverages for specific situations.

Payment of title insurance fees

The title insurance policy fee forms a part of the "closing costs" in the purchase of real estate. In the following counties it is customary for the buyer to pay for the title insurance: Alameda, Calaveras, Colusa, Contra Costa, Lake, Marin, Mendocino, Napa, San Francisco, San Mateo, Solano, and Sonoma.

In the following cities, it is customary for the seller to pay: Del Norte, El Dorado, Fresno, Glenn, Humboldt, Imperial, Inyo, Kern, Kings, Lassen, Los Angeles, Madera, Modoc, Monterey, Mono, Nevada, Orange, Placer, Riverside, Sacramento, San Benito, San Bernardino, San Diego, San Luis Obispo, Santa Barbara, Santa Clara, Santa Cruz, Shasta, Siskiyou, Stanislaus, Sutter, Tehama, Tulare, Ventura, Yolo, and Yuba.

The buyer and seller generally split the title fee equally in Amador, Merced, Plumas, San Joaquin, and Tuolumne, while in Butte County, the fee is generally split on the basis of 75 percent to the seller and 25 percent to the buyer. There is no legal requirement, however, that the cost of title insurance be assigned or split in any particular way; and if the buyer and seller agree, either party may pay the entire cost regardless of the county in which the transaction takes place.

Various risks

Proper protection for a property owner is necessary because of the numerous risks and hazards which can be found in connection with title to real property. The following are examples of such risks:

1. Any instruments which have been forged or improperly executed.
2. Instruments executed by individuals with a legal disability, such as a minor or an incompetent.
3. Illegal acts of trustees or attorneys-in-fact.
4. Taxes which are now liens against a property.
5. Assessments or bonds which are liens against a property.
6. Fraud, duress, or coercion in securing essential signatures.
7. Unfiled mechanics liens or undisclosed restrictions.
8. False representation with respect to appointment of guardians or administrators.
9. Claims of undiscovered or unknown individuals who may be heirs or a decedent whose property has been distributed.
10. Joint tenancy deed or other instruments which are held to be invalid.
11. Defective court actions resulting from failure to include all necessary parties or failure to give proper notice.
12. Mistakes with respect to recording or indexing documents.
13. Mistakes due to individuals with similar or indentical names.
14. Instruments executed by individuals supposedly single but actually married.
15. Liens in favor of the United States or California and not disclosed in the records.

ADDITIONAL TITLE COMPANY PROTECTIONS

Various specific reports, guarantees, and protections are available to serve particular needs. A few of these are as follows:

Leasehold policy. Insurance for an owner of a leasehold or subleasehold.

Vendee policy. Insurance of the title to the interest of a vendee (purchaser) or successor or assignee of a vendee where a contract of sale or purchase has been recorded. The insured is the vendee, and title is shown vested in the vendee as to the equitable title created by the specific contract of sale and purchase, and in the vendor (seller) as to the legal title.

Open-end advances. Insurance is available to lenders making advances where an open-end loan is used. The protection is to insure the lender against loss as the result of ownership changes, impairment of the security device, or mechanics liens.

Mechanics liens. Protects against mechanics liens in connection with completed or in-progress structures which might gain priority over an insured mortgage or deed of trust.

Construction protection. Insures a lender that the foundations of a building being constructed are within specific boundaries and do not violate existing covenants, conditions, and restrictions and do not encroach on specific easements.

Litigation guarantee. This type of report is generally issued for the benefit of attorneys to furnish them with information pertinent to the commencement of a judicial proceeding. It discloses condition of record title, names and addresses of property owners, encumbrances, present deed on record, and any legal incapacities of the present owners.

Trustee's sale guarantee. Provides specific information to a trustee who must proceed with a trustee's sale. Gives information about title, ownership, and liens together with possible bankruptcy data about the owner and any information regarding federal tax liens.

Chain of title guarantee. Lists all recorded instruments in the chain of title of a specific real property parcel together with data concerning parties, dates, and recordings.

Property search guarantee. A property search is made for the purpose of determining what specific property is recorded in the name of a specific individual or corporation.

Restriction and easement guarantee. Provides copies of building and tract restrictions together with copies of easements which affect a particular property.

Additional forms, applicable to this chapter, are illustrated in Appendix C as Figures C8–1 thru C8–4.

QUESTIONS FOR DISCUSSION

1. Why may the escrow not act as mediator in disputes between the parties to the escrow?
2. What are the various methods by which an escrow can be terminated?
3. For which of the parties in an escrow is the escrow holder an agent?
4. How do escrow practices differ between northern and southern California?
5. How is the division of charges between buyer and seller made in your locality?
6. What escrow practices are used in your own locality?
7. What is the purpose of the seller's and buyer's statements?
8. What is the purpose of a proration?
9. Of what particular importance is the preliminary title search?
10. What particular circumstances allow a real estate broker to perform an escrow?

9

General taxation and real estate

The field of taxation and its relationship to dealings in real property have become quite complex. Tax laws have a great effect on most of the decisions made in real estate transactions, especially the larger ones. A knowledge of taxation and tax laws regarding property has become a necessity for the professional real estate broker, and many have taken college courses in this area.

It is important for those engaged in the real estate business to know the variety of taxes, their bases, and their effect on property transfers so that they may be able to counsel their clients correctly in this area. All persons, licensed or not, who take part in a real estate transaction will, to a certain degree, be made aware of the effect of taxation and tax laws upon real property. Brokers and their clients will often have to work along with accountants, attorneys, and others who specialize in the field of taxation. This chapter, as well as the following one, will deal with the more important aspects of taxation and its effect upon real property.

PROPOSITION 13—JARVIS-GANN

Officially passed by the voters June 6, 1978, and legally effective July 1, 1978, Proposition 13, commonly known as the Jarvis-Gann Amendment, is now law in California. This law, which adds Article XIII A to the State Constitution, is officially titled, "Tax Limitation—Initiative Constitutional Amendment" and its sections state as follows:

1. *(a)* The maximum amount of any ad valorem tax on real property shall not exceed one percent (1%) of the full cash value of such property. The one percent (1%) tax to be collected by the counties and apportioned according to law to the districts within the counties.

(b) The limitation provided for in subdivision (a) shall not apply to ad valorem taxes or special assessments to pay the interest and redemption charges on any indebtedness approved by the voters prior to the time this section becomes effective.

2. *(a)* The full cash value means the County Assessor's valuation of real property as shown on the 1975–76 tax bill under "full cash value," or thereafter, the appraised value of real property when purchased, newly constructed, or a change in ownership has occurred after the 1975 assessment. All real property not already assessed up to the 1975–76 tax levels may be reassessed to reflect that valuation.

(b) The fair market value base may reflect from year to year the inflationary rate not to exceed two percent (2%) for any given year or reduction as shown in the consumer price index or comparable data for the area under taxing jurisdiction.

3. From and after the effective date of this article, any changes in State taxes enacted for the purpose of increasing revenues collected pursuant thereto whether by increased rates or changes in methods of computation must be imposed by an Act passed by not less than two-thirds of all members elected to each of the two houses of the Legislature, except that no new ad valorem taxes on real property, or sales or transaction taxes on the sales of real property may be imposed.

4. Cities, Counties and special districts, by a two-thirds vote of the qualified electors of such district, may impose special taxes on such district, except ad valorem taxes on real property within such City, County, or special district.

5. This article shall take effect for the tax year beginning on July 1st following the passage of this Amendment, except Section 3 which shall become effective upon the passage of this article.

6. If any section, part, clause, or phrase hereof is held to be invalid or unconstitutional, the remaining sections shall not be affected but will remain in full force and effect.

Basic Intention of Proposition 13

The basic effect of this new law will be to place a limit on the amount of property taxes that can be collected by local governments, restrict the growth in the assessed value of property subject to taxation, require a two-thirds vote of the Legislature to increase state tax revenues, and authorize local governments to impose certain nonproperty taxes if two thirds of the voters give their approval in a local election.

In addition to implementation by the California Legislature and the California Board of Equalization, the California Supreme Court has found this new tax reduction amendment to the state constitution to be constitutional. Its intention is to reduce state income from property taxes necessitating a state reduction in expenditures.

ASSESSMENT OF REAL PROPERTY

The tax year is not based on the January 1 to December 31 calendar but rather on the fiscal year of July 1 to June 30. Every tax due on personal property is a lien on the real property of the owner. This is true of both city and county personal property taxes. Taxes due on real property are liens against the property assessed. Property taxes become a lien on property on the first day in March preceding the tax year.

As of this lien date, the assessment period begins. During this period, the office of the county assessor sets a valuation on the property for tax purposes. The Petris-Knox Bill, passed by the legislature in 1966, now makes it mandatory that all property on the tax rolls be assessed at 25 percent of actual cash value.

Assessors have a legal directive on how to determine values for tax purposes. The California constitution requires that all property shall be taxed in proportion to its value. "Value" is based on full cash value or market value, terms that the state supreme court holds are synonymous. The court further defines such value as the highest price that a property will bring if exposed for sale in the open market allowing a reasonable time to find a purchaser who buys with knowledge of all the uses to which it is adapted and for which it is capable of being used. Assessors divide the property value between land and improvements, and both amounts are shown in the tax bill and added together to arrive at full value.

When the valuation of property is completed, assessment rolls are prepared by the assessor and are then turned in to the county board of supervisors, who give them to the county auditor. The auditor lists the total number of acres of land, value of all real estate, personal property, improvements, and moneys. He thus arrives at the entire value of county property.

The same general procedure is followed by cities. Some make their own independent assessed valuations. The city board of supervisors performs the same function as the county board of supervisors. Some cities, such as Oakland in Alameda County, arrange with the county to handle all city tax assessments and collections. The city of San Francisco is unique in that it is a city and a county combined, and its supervisors are both city and county supervisors. The assessor is, likewise, city and county assessor.

THE TAX RATE

Previous to Proposition 13, at the same time that the assessor's office was preparing the assessment rolls, the various executive and administrative agencies of the county were preparing their yearly budgets to submit to the board of supervisors. Then, simply by knowing the amount of money necessary and by knowing the assessed value of county property, it was possible to arrive at the tax rate per $100 of assessed value to bring in the required amount of money.

Previously, tax rates varied among different localities, but now, with a 1 percent of market value tax limit, property owners will pay the same basic rate of approximately $4 per $100 assessed valuation. This is because assessments are 25 percent of market value.

Assessors divide the property value between the land and improvements, and so an owner's tax bill might show the full cash value of the land as $14,000 and improvements as $42,000, for a total full cash value of $56,000. The assessed value for tax purposes will be $3,500 for the land and $10,500 for the improvements for a total assessed value of $14,000, or 25 percent of the full cash or market value as required by law.

TAX COLLECTION CALENDAR

The tax rate, then, is approved by the board of supervisors by September 1, and the tax collector is required on or before November 1st of each year to mail a tax bill or copy of it to each fee owner of the property. See Figure 9–1.

The real property owner may pay his taxes in one payment, or he may pay in two installments. On the first day of November, the first installment

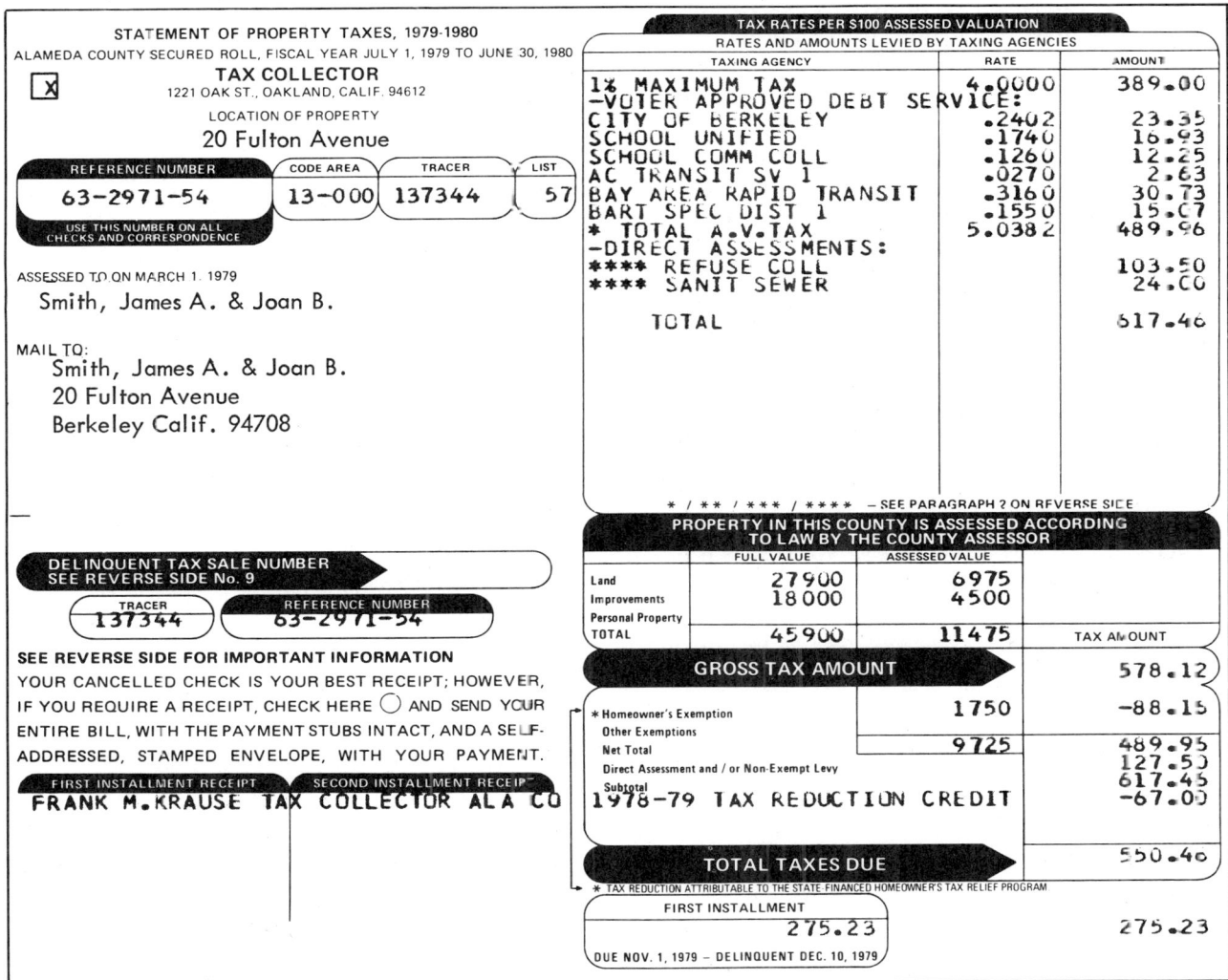

FIGURE 9–1

is due and covers the period of July through December. The first installment (first half) becomes delinquent if not paid by 5 P.M. December 10, at which time a penalty of 6 percent is added to the first installment. The second installment (second half) of the real property tax, which covers the period of January through June, is due on February 1 and becomes delinquent if not paid by 5 P.M. April 10.

To review:

1. Fiscal year basis—July 1 to June 30.
2. First Monday in March—taxes become a lien on real property.
3. First installment—due November 1 and delinquent on December 10 at 5 P.M.
4. Second installment—due February 1 and delinquent on April 10 at 5 P.M.

BOARD OF EQUALIZATION

The board of supervisors of each county is the county board of equalization, before whom an owner appears if he feels that his property has been overassessed. The state board is an elective body whose function is to check on the various county assessors and assure that the taxation process is properly conducted throughout the counties of the state. In some areas, the board of supervisors establishes a separate appeals board that hears appeals.

REPORTING OWNERSHIP CHANGE

Revenue and Taxation Code, Section 480, requires any individual acquiring an interest in real property to file a change of ownership statement with the county recorder or assessor of the county in which the property is located. The change of ownership statement must be filed within 45 days of the recording date or, if the ownership change is not recorded, within 45 days of the date of ownership change.

Local assessors and recorders will, on recordation of any ownership change, send a change of ownership form to the new owners of record, and such form must be completed and returned. It asks for specific information regarding the transfer, name of parties, how acquired, type of property, form of ownership, and details of financing.

PROPERTY REASSESSMENT

Real estate licensees must be aware of ownership changes which will result in a reassessment of property and tax increase as such information will be requested by prospective purchasers. The California state board of equalization has prepared a detailed and complex set of rules for county assessors with respect to which transfers will result in and which will not result in reassessment. A few of the more common reassessment transfers discussed in these rules are as follows:

The following will generally result in a reassessment of the property.

a. Traditional sale of real property from present to new owner.
b. Creation or transfer of a leasehold with a term of 35 years or more.
c. Transfer of lessors interest in real property subject to a lease with a remaining term of less than 35 years.

The following will generally not result in a reassessment of the property.

a. Creation of joint tenancy with original owner remaining on title.
b. Creation of a life estate.
c. Owners of tenancy in common create a joint tenancy.
d. Transfer of property between spouses.
e. Partnership owners add a partner.
f. Transfer of property to a revocable trust.
g. Transfer of separate property to a spouse.
h. Transfer to trustee for beneficial use of a spouse.
i. Property settlement or dissolution decree transfers.
j. Transfer due to expiration of a spouse.

HOMEOWNERS' PROPERTY TAX EXEMPTION

State Proposition 1-A, enacted in 1968, and subsequent additions provide that:

1. All household furnishings and personal effects of a householder are exempt from taxation.
2. A dwelling occupied by an owner as his principal place of residence will receive an exemption of $1,750 in assessed value.

A form upon which to make claim for the assessed value exemption is made available by the assessor and must be filed by the claimant prior to April 15. Only a person who both owns and occupies the property as his principal place of residence may file the claim for homeowner's property tax exemption. The form must be dated and signed by the claimant, under penalty of perjury, and contains statements that say in effect that:

a. The claimant holds title to the property or is buying under a contract of sale and is occupying the property as his principal place of residence.
b. The dwelling is a single living unit, either in a separate structure or a multiple-unit structure.
c. During the current fiscal year, neither the claimant nor anyone with whom the claimant shares ownership received or expects to receive from the state, county, or city any assistance (other than senior citizen's property tax assistance) containing an allowance for property tax on the described dwelling.
d. The claimant has not filed a claim for homeowner's exemption on any other property in California, and no other person whose principal residence is the dwelling identified in the claim has filed or will file a claim for the same dwelling.

The homeowner's property tax exemption excuses $1,750 of assessed value, which equals $7,000 of cash value. This results in tax savings to the homeowner of $70.

TAX CREDIT FOR RENTERS

California allows a renter's credit on the California income tax return to those individuals who meet certain requirements. The allowance varies depending on the adjusted gross income of the individual.

SENIOR CITIZENS PROPERTY TAX ASSISTANCE

Those who will be 62 years of age or over or totally disabled on January 1, have household income of not more than $12,000 for the calendar year, and are residents of California on January 1 may be entitled to some property tax relief. The Senior Citizens Property Tax Assistance Relief Law provides that any qualified owner may file each year for a refund of a portion of the property taxes levied on their principal residence.

The assistance is not automatic and will not be granted at the time the property taxes are paid. To claim assistance for property taxes paid for the fiscal year ending June 30, the taxpayer must file a claim with the Property Tax Assistance Division.

SENIOR CITIZENS PROPERTY TAX POSTPONEMENT

The Senior Citizens Property Tax Postponement Law gives qualified individuals who are 62 or older with household income of $23,100 or less the option of having the state pay all or part of the taxes on their homes. In return, a lien is placed on their property for the amount of taxes the state pays. The lien is payable when the homeowner sells the property, moves, or expires. A claim form must be filed for each year that a postponement of taxes is desired. Individuals who qualify for postponement may also qualify for property tax assistance. Claim forms or information regarding either the Property Tax Assistance or Postponement Programs may be obtained from the Franchise Tax Board Office in your area or by calling the Franchise Tax Board toll-free at 800–852–7050.

SOLAR TAX CREDITS   None

The state and federal governments allow a tax credit for solar installations. California provides a credit of 55 percent, not to exceed $3,000, for all installations (residential and nonresidential) which cost less than $12,000. If a solar system is installed in a building other than a single family residence and the cost is more than $12,000, the tax credit is 25 percent or $3,000, whichever is greater.

The solar tax credit is subtracted from the buyer's state income taxes. It is not just a deduction used to compute the total amount of income tax. If, for instance, the buyer's tax credit is greater than his total state tax bill, the unused credit is carried over to the next year or until the buyer has received the full credit due.

For example, if the buyer installs a solar water heating system that costs $3,000, he will be entitled to a tax credit of $1,650. If his state income tax is $900 for the year, he will get all of his withholding tax back and still have the remaining credit of $750 to apply the following year.

The federal government allows a 30 percent tax credit on the first $2,000 of the cost of installation and 20 percent of the next $8,000 for a total credit of $2,200 on the buyers' income tax.

The most common uses of solar systems are for swimming pool heating, household water heating, and space heating. Wind is generally considered a solar product and can be used to generate mechanical or electrical power.

There are two types of systems, active and passive. Active solar systems use air or water to store and circulate heat. In active systems, radiant solar energy becomes heat when it strikes a blackened surface. Active systems employ specialized hardware powered by mechanical or electrical energy to gather and carry heat; example—rooftop collectors made of glass and black-coated copper pipe. Liquids in the pipe absorb the sun's heat and then are circulated to a storage tank that feeds heat to household living areas and the water supply.

Passive solar systems collect heat without hardware; they make use of a structure itself to capture and store heat; example—large south-facing windows admit solar heat; if the walls of a building are made of brick, concrete, or adobe, they absorb heat and gradually release it. Temperature is modified throughout the day.

VETERAN'S EXEMPTION

A California veteran who has served in the military in time of war is entitled to an exemption of $1,000 on the assessed value of his property. The same advantage is given to the widow, widowed mother, or pensioned parent of a deceased veteran.

The property may not have an assessed valuation of over $5,000 or, if community property, $10,000. Claim for the exemption must be filed each year by the veteran or his spouse or other person entitled to do so with the assessor between the first Monday in March and the first Monday in May. This exemption applies only to real and personal property taxes and not to taxes levied by special assessment districts.

A veteran may not receive the $1,000 [4,000] veteran's exemption and the $1,750 [7,000] homeowner's exemption on the same property. If a veteran owns property other than his principal place of residence, the veteran may take the $1,750 homeowner's exemption on his residence and the $1,000 veteran's exemption on his other property if such other property qualifies.

SPECIAL ASSESSMENTS

While annual property taxes are levied for the support of general governmental functions, special assessments are levied for the cost of such specific local improvements as streets, sewers, irrigation, drainage, flood control, special lighting, and other public conveniences.

Special assessment districts are regulated by state law. Assessment districts issue bonds to finance the necessary improvements. Proposition 13 authorizes cities, counties, special districts, and school districts to impose such special taxes if two thirds of the voters approve. Such taxes cannot be based on the value or sale of real property.

Sometimes, if an improvement will be located completely within a particular city or county, the city or county merely establishes an improvement area and need not establish a separate assessment district for the particular improvement.

Often, a city issues improvement bonds that are sold to the general public to finance improvements.

Special assessments are usually of three general types:

a. Assessments at rates fixed annually and collected at the same time as the local taxes.
b. Separately collected assessments for the maintenance of special districts, such as irrigation districts.
c. Nonrecurring assessments levied for the cost of a particular local improvement.

The state of California has enacted various laws relating to special assessments and taxes and to the formation of assessment districts in the state.

DOCUMENTARY TRANSFER TAX

California law allows a county to adopt a documentary transfer tax to apply on all transfers of real property located in the county. Notice of payment is entered on the face of the deed or on a separate paper filed with the deed at time of recordation. A city within a county that has adopted the transfer tax may also adopt its own transfer tax ordinance with the tax fixed at half the rate charged by the county. In effect, this merely means that the county collects the total tax and turns half the amount over to the city.

In most counties, tax is computed at the rate of $1.10 per $1,000 or $0.55 per $500 or any lesser amount. If property is sold with a trust deed or mortgage against it and the existing encumbrance is assumed by the buyer, the tax is payable only on the seller's equity. If the trust deed or mortgage is newly executed in connection with the sale, the tax is payable on the entire purchase price of the property.

As part of closing costs in escrow, the documentary transfer tax is a charge against the seller. An example of the calculation of this charge appears in the chapter dealing with escrows.

PROPERTY EXEMPT FROM TAXATION

Properties owned by local, state, or federal governments are not subject to taxation. Obviously, this accounts for the large percentage of property excluded from the tax rolls. In California, almost three quarters of all the land is exempt from taxation. Properties owned by religious, charitable, and educational institutions are also exempt from taxation. It is said that these properties should be excluded because the institutions are nonprofit in nature and contribute to the religious, cultural, and charitable needs of the community.

There seems to be a never-ending discussion of the pros and cons of this arrangement in regard to the types and amounts of properties that should or should not be tax-exempt. The following are among the major examples of tax-exempt properties:

1. State, county, or city property.
2. Growing crops.
3. Nonprofit schools and colleges.
4. Churches.
5. Orphanages.
6. Notes, debentures, shares of capital stock, bonds, trust deeds, and mortgages.
7. Public schools.
8. Public libraries and museums.
9. Property used for welfare purposes.
10. Property owned by a veterans' organization.
11. Property exempt under a veteran's exemption.
12. Fruit and nut trees under three years of age.
13. Grapevines under three years of age.
14. Property exempt under U.S. laws.
15. California State Bonds.
16. Certain works of art displayed in a public gallery or museum.

TAX SALE AND REDEMPTION

On June 8 of each year, the tax collector publishes a delinquent list of properties on which taxes have not been paid during the previous fiscal year. After 21 to 28 days, the property is automatically "sold" to the state, and if the taxes due are not paid within the next five years, the state may sell the property at public sale. For a detailed discussion of this topic, see Chapter 16, Public Sales of Real Property.

CALIFORNIA ESTATE AND GIFT TAXES

The Estate and Gift Tax Act of 1980

Assembly Bill 2092, known as the Estate and Gift Tax Act of 1980, is now law. It is intended to conform the California laws with respect to taxable estates to the estate tax provisions of the Federal Internal Revenue Code of the United States and to eliminate a surviving spouse, and smaller estates generally, from payment of a California estate or gift tax.

In addition to elimination of spousal inheritance taxes, the new law greatly increases estate and gift tax exemptions with respect to other classes of beneficiaries. Taxpayers in certain instances may defer payment of estate taxes for up to ten years, and beneficiaries of farms or business partnerships may be able to defer payments for up to 15 years.

California gift tax

The California gift tax was enacted in 1939, has been amended several times, and is administered by the state controller and California Inheritance Tax Department. Copies of the law and regulations may be obtained from the California State Controller, Sacramento, California.

The tax is imposed on gifts of real and personal property and interests in such property. The tax is figured on the market value of the property as of the date the gift is made. Every donor who makes to an individual donee a gift or gifts exceeding $3,000 within a calendar year must file a return with the state controller by April 15 for gifts made during the preceding calendar year. The donor is the person making the gift, and the donee is the person receiving the gift.

Every donee who receives a gift for which a donor is required to file may also be required to file a donee's return by April 15 or to join with the donor in filing the donor's return. A trustee to whom property is transferred by gift must also file.

A transfer of community property between husband and wife is not subject to gift tax. However, a gift of community property to an individual other than a spouse is a taxable gift; each spouse is considered to have given half of the property.

A transfer of quasi-community property between spouses is treated as a nontaxable gift; but a gift of such property to an individual other than a spouse is a taxable gift. Quasi-community property is property belonging to a husband and wife which meets the California definition of community property but was acquired while both were living outside California. A conversion of quasi-community property of either spouse to community property, or into property held as joint tenants or as tenants in common, is not subject to a gift tax. If separate property of the husband or the wife is converted into community property, the conversion is treated as a nontaxable gift.

Joint tenancy property

It is quite common for husband and wife to hold property as joint tenants. Joint tenancy property is not subject to probate court proceedings, since it passes automatically to the surviving joint tenant. Creation of a joint tenancy in real property between a husband and wife is not considered a taxable gift.

Payment of the gift tax

After receiving the gift tax return, the controller has up to three years to determine the amount of tax due but usually takes approximately six months. When the controller decides on the amount of tax due, he notifies the donor. If the donor does not agree with the decision of the controller, he must pay the tax and then bring suit in the superior court to recover what he feels is due him. There is no provision for appeal before the tax is paid, but in actual practice, the controller usually consults the donor prior to determination of the amount of tax due so that there is no conflict once the controller makes his decision.

The tax becomes due immediately and is delinquent if it is not paid within 60 days. Proceedings for the collection of gift tax may be started at any time within ten years after the tax becomes delinquent.

Gift tax exemptions

The law allows certain exemptions from the payment of tax for those who give gifts. The exemptions are such that the average person may give away a considerable amount of money without having to pay any gift tax at all. Figure 9–2 shows California estate and gift tax exemptions. Exemptions for the gift tax are the same as those for the estate tax, which will be discussed later.

FIGURE 9-2
California estate and gift tax exemptions

Classification	Exemption
Class A	
Husband or wife	All
Minor child	$40,000
(includes adopted)	
Adult child, grandchild, parent, grandparent	$20,000
(relationship may be by blood or adoption)	
Mutually acknowledged child	
Descendant of mutually acknowledged child	
Class B	
Brother, sister	$10,000
(excludes, brothers- and sisters-in-law)	
Descendant of brother or sister	
(includes descendant by adoption)	
Wife or widow of son, husband or widower of daughter	
Class C	
Strangers in blood and individuals not class A or B	$3,000

Additional gift tax exemptions

In addition to the specific exemptions shown in Figure 9–2, the state of California allows an annual exemption of $3,000 to donees of all classes.

Example: John and Mary have three children and six grandchildren. They give to each of these persons the sum of $3,000 during the current year. They have given away the total sum of $27,000, and there is no gift tax for them to pay since they have not exceeded the sum of $3,000 to each donee.

Example: Martin and Janet have three children and six grandchildren. They give the sum of $6,000 to each of these individuals. The total amount given away is $54,000. Is there any tax to pay? The answer is no because each donor is allowed a $3,000 exemption against each donee each year, and thus together, a husband and wife are allowed to give $6,000 to each donee each year. Thus, if they want to, Martin and Janet can give away $54,000 total to the above individuals each and every year without any gift tax being required.

In both examples, the specific exemption of $20,000 each for adult children and grandchildren is not considered. The specific exemption is used if the gift exceeds the annual exemption of $3,000 per donee.

Example: Cynthia, age 23, receives a $25,000 gift from her mother.

Amount of gift	$25,000
Less $3,000 exemption	$22,000
Less specific exemption 20,000	$ 2,000 taxable gift

The taxable portion of the gift is $2,000, and the amount of tax is 2½ percent, or approximately $50.

The California gift tax, then, is computed separately on gifts made to each individual donee after applying the annual exemption and the specific exemption.

A gift of money, stocks, bonds, and the like is easier to compute, since one may give a specific amount as far as value is concerned. A gift of real property, however, is somewhat more complicated. In order to give property over the years and avoid as much gift tax as possible, on must give fractional interests each year rather than the whole property.

Use of gift tax exemptions and exclusions may mean tax savings and avoidance of estate and inheritance tax at a later date, assuming that an individual makes the decision to use the gift approach where applicable rather than dispose by will or another method, such as creation of a joint tenancy. In making a decision, there are many factors to be taken into consideration. The tax base awarded to property received by a donee is frequently mentioned as a factor to be considered with regard to gifts and will be discussed later.

California gift tax rates

The California gift tax rate schedule is as follows:

If the amount with respect to which the tentative tax to be computed is:	The tentative tax is:
Not over $25,000	2.5 percent of such amount
Over $25,000 but not over $75,000	$625, plus 5 percent of the excess of such amount over $25,000
Over $75,000 but not over $125,000	$3,125, plus 7.5 percent of the excess of such amount over $75,000
Over $125,000 but not over $175,625	$6,875, plus 10 percent of the excess of such amount over $125,000
Over $175,625 but not over $500,000	$11,875, plus 12.5 percent of the excess of such amount over $175,625
Over $500,000 but not over $1,000,000	$52,500, plus 15 percent of the excess of such amount over $500,000
Over $1,000,000 but not over $2,000,000	$127,500, plus 17.5 percent of the excess of such amount over $1,000,000

If the amount with respect to which the tentative tax to be computed is:	The tentative tax is:
Over $2,000,000 but not over $3,000,000	$302,500, plus 20 percent of the excess of such amount over $2,000,000
Over $3,000,000 but not over $5,000,000	$502,500, plus 22.5 percent of the excess of such amount over $3,000,000
Over $5,000,000	$952,500, plus 25 percent of the excess of such amount over $5,000,000

CALIFORNIA ESTATE TAX

The California estate tax procedure is administered by the California state controller and the California state Inheritance Tax Department. Copies of the law and regulations may be obtained from the California State Controller, Sacramento, California.

California estate tax is levied on the amount of inheritance received by beneficiaries after taking into account any allowable specific exemptions. The specific exemptions with respect to the California estate tax are the same as for the California Gift Tax illustrated in Figure 9–2. A surviving spouse acquires property free of estate taxes. Life insurance payable to a named beneficiary is exempt from such tax to a limit of $50,000. Such life insurance payments can be quite important to a surviving spouse with respect to payment of unexpected costs or fees.

Inheritance tax and probate proceedings

Property is usually held jointly by husband and wife in order to escape the time and expense of going through probate proceedings. Vesting title in the surviving spouse, if the property is held in joint tenancy, is a comparatively simple and inexpensive process compared with the commissions and fees payable to administrators, executors, and attorneys in a probate proceeding. In addition to the statutory fees, which are percentage amounts applied against the total value of the estate, there are additional fees allowed the executor, administrator, or attorney, as the case may be, in the event that they are required to perform any extraordinary service or incur other than regular expenses in connection with the probating of the estate. In order to avoid these fees and save the considerable time involved in the probate of an estate, most married couples hold title as joint tenants, thus eliminating probate proceedings.

State law provides that if a spouse expires without a will, or by will confers his or her interest in community property to the surviving spouse, such property after 40 days from date of expiration may be sold or otherwise dealt with by the surviving spouse without the necessity of probate with respect to the property. This law will eliminate the necessity for probate sale procedures in a great number of estates.

Cost basis

Married couples are often advised against holding property as joint tenants because of the problem of the tax basis, or cost basis, as it is often called. In addition to our discussion here, the method of determining the basis is covered in Chapter 10, Income Tax and Real Estate. The method of determining the basis for a residential property differs slightly from that of determining the basis for income or business properties where a depreciation deduction comes into the picture.

For our discussion, we will assume the property to be a single-family residential dwelling. The cost basis of this residence is the purchase price originally paid plus the costs at the time of purchase, such as title insurance, escrow fees, and loan fees. In addition, improvements added, such as a new bathroom, are included. Some years later, when the property is sold, the profit for tax purposes is the difference between the cost basis and the selling price, less costs of the sale, such as the broker's commission and other fees. This profit is known as the capital gain.

Example: Tom and Laura purchased a house some years ago at a cost of $44,000. They have added $12,000 worth of improvements and now sell the property for $152,000. The cost basis of $56,000 subtracted from a selling price of $152,000 equals a gain of $96,000. Assuming that Tom and Laura incurred $12,000 worth of expenses in connection with the sale, they will show a net gain of $84,000 and will be taxed on the basis of this $84,000 gain. As discussed in Chapter 10, the amount of tax will vary, depending on a number of factors.

Stepped-up tax basis

In California, a surviving spouse will inherit community property with what is called a stepped-up basis; that is, the value of the property at the time of inheritance becomes the new cost basis. Assuming Laura to be a surviving spouse, she will inherit the residence and receive a stepped-up basis. Instead of the old basis of $56,000, the residence will have a new basis of $152,000 (market value of property at time of inheritance), and if Laura now sells the property for $152,000, there is mathematically no gain and no tax to pay.

It is important to remember that only community property is treated in this way. If the property is held as joint tenancy property, Laura only gets a stepped-up basis on half of the property and half retains the old basis. If Tom and Laura held the property as joint tenants and Laura cannot prove that the property is community property, she will inherit the house with a new cost basis of $104,000. Half of the old base ($56,000 divided by 2) equals $28,000 plus $76,000, which equals $104,000. Now if Laura sells the property for $152,000, she will have a gain of $48,000. After deducting $12,000 of selling expenses, Laura has a taxable gain of $36,000.

If Tom and Laura had owned a large apartment building or income property that had greatly increased in value, we can see the importance to a surviving spouse with respect to a stepped-up basis on all or just half of a property. In California, if a surviving spouse can prove that a property held as joint tenants was, in fact, community property and had as its source community funds, the state will treat the property as community property for inheritance tax purposes and the surviving spouse will receive a stepped-up basis for the entire property. Additionally, joint tenancy property will avoid probate proceedings.

It is usually not difficult for a surviving spouse to show that real property, although held as joint tenants, was actually acquired during marriage with community funds. If a husband and wife wish to, they can prepare and sign a statement declaring specific property they own to be community property although they hold title as joint tenants in order to avoid probate proceedings.

Cost basis and gift tax

With respect to the sale of property acquired by gift, both California and federal laws hold that the cost basis to the donee now selling is the basis of the original donor. However, the value of property for purposes of determining the amount of gift tax that may be payable is the market value of the property at the time of the gift.

California estate tax rates

The California estate tax rate schedule is as follows:

If the amount with respect to which the tentative tax to be computed is:	*The tentative tax is:*
Not over $175,625	0 percent of such amount
Over $175,625 but not over $500,000	12.5 percent of such amount
Over $500,000 but not over $1,000,000	$40,625, plus 15 percent of the excess of such amount over $500,000
Over $1,000,000 but not over $2,000,000	$115,625, plus 17.5 percent of the excess of such amount over $1,000,000
Over $2,000,000 but not over $3,000,000	$290,625, plus 20 percent of the excess of such amount over $2,000,000
Over $3,000,000 but not over $5,000,000	$490,625 plus 22.5 percent of the excess of such amount over $3,000,000
Over $5,000,000	$940,625, plus 25 percent of the excess of such amount over $5,000,000

Professional advice

The subjects of taxation and methods of holding titles are quite complex, and most individuals and real estate licensees should seek the advice of either a certified public accountant, attorney, or bank officer with respect to taxation, title, or estate planning matters.

FEDERAL GIFT AND ESTATE TAXES

The Tax Reform Act of 1976 has brought about a major overhaul of estate and gift tax laws and is generally structured to favor small and medium sized estates.

The gross estate of a decedent includes all real and personal property owned by the decedent at time of death, such as stocks, bonds, checking and savings accounts, and real property. When the property that makes up the gross estate has been determined, it is given a value. The fair market value of the property is generally its value for estate tax purposes.

From the gross estate are deducted certain expenses, claims against the estate, expenses of administration, expenses of last illness and burial, transfers to exempt charitable and religious institu-

TABLE 9-1
Federal gift and estate tax rates

From	To	Tax is	Plus percent	Of excess over
—	$ 10,000	18% of such amount		
$ 10,000	20,000	$ 1,800	20%	$ 10,000
20,000	40,000	3,800	22	20,000
40,000	60,000	8,200	24	40,000
60,000	80,000	13,000	26	60,000
80,000	100,000	18,200	28	80,000
100,000	150,000	23,800	30	100,000
150,000	250,000	38,800	32	150,000
250,000	500,000	70,800	34	250,000
500,000	750,000	155,800	37	500,000
750,000	1,000,000	284,300	39	750,000
1,000,000	1,250,000	345,800	41	1,000,000
1,250,000	1,500,000	448,300	43	1,250,000
1,500,000	2,000,000	555,800	45	1,500,000
2,000,000	2,500,000	780,800	49	2,000,000
2,500,000	3,000,000	1,025,800	53	2,500,000
3,000,000	3,500,000	1,290,800	57	3,000,000
3,500,000	4,000,000	1,575,800	61	3,500,000
4,000,000	4,500,000	1,880,000	65	4,000,000
4,500,000	5,000,000	2,205,800	69	4,500,000
5,000,000	—	2,550,800	70	5,000,000

The tentative tax applies to the sum of *(a)* the amount of the taxable estate and *(b)* the amount of the adjusted taxable gifts.

tions, accrued taxes, unpaid mortgages, and executors' commissions and attorneys' fees.

What remains after deductions is called the net estate, and previously, this net estate in excess of $60,000 was taxed. Also a separate tax schedule was used for gifts which was approximately 75 percent of the estate tax rate schedule for corresponding brackets.

Unified credit and tax rates

With respect to the gift tax, previous law allowed a donor an annual exclusion of $3,000 per gift to each donee with no limitation as to the number of donees, plus a $30,000 lifetime exemption which was allowed only once but was cumulative until used up. A husband and wife had a $60,000 exemption, plus an annual exemption per donee of $6,000.

The Tax Reform Act of 1976 retains the annual exclusion of $3,000 per gift to each donee but replaces the $30,000 gift tax exemption and the $60,000 estate tax exemption with a unified credit of $47,000 (equivalent to an exemption of $175,625) for estate and gift taxes and provides a unified rate schedule for estate and gift taxes. The new federal gift and estate tax rates are illustrated in Table 9-1.

The unified credit of $47,000 is to be phased in over a five-year period as follows:

Year	Estate and gift tax credit	Estate or gift exemption equivalent
1977	$30,000	$120,700
1978	34,000	134,000
1979	38,000	147,300
1980	42,500	161,600
1981	47,000	175,600

In accordance with the new credit, a gross estate must be a certain amount before the filing of a tax return is necessary. For decedents expiring in 1977, an executor must file a return only if a gross estate exceeds $120,000. The amount increases to $134,000 in 1978, $147,000 in 1979, $161,000 in 1980, and $175,000 in 1981.

The marital deduction

The marital deduction is intended to equalize taxes between residents of states that are not community property states and residents of states that are community property states. It does this by accepting the concept of ownership prevailing between husband and wife in community property states, namely, that each owns half the property.

With respect to gifts, a married donor was previously allowed to deduct half the value of any interest in property given by the husband to the wife or by the wife to the husband. The Tax Reform Act of 1976 provides up to $100,000 of gifts to a spouse tax-free. The amount between $100,000 and $200,000 is fully taxable, and 50 percent of any amount over $200,000 is taxable.

With respect to estate taxes, the previous law allowed a deduction for property passing to a surviving spouse, but the deduction could not exceed half the value of the adjusted gross estate. The Tax Reform Act increases the estate tax marital deduction to the greater of $250,000 or half the decedents' adjusted gross estate.

Taking into account the previously discussed unified credit and value of the estate which the credit offsets, and adding to it the $250,000 marital deduction, the amount of estate as between married individuals that can be passed on tax-free is approximately:

Year	Amount tax-free	Estate value	Marital deduction
1977	$370,700	($120,700 +	$250,000)
1978	384,000	(134,000 +	250,000)
1979	397,300	(147,300 +	250,000)
1980	411,600	(161,600 +	250,000)
1981	425,600	(175,600 +	250,000)

Transfers within three years of death

Previously, a transfer of interest in property made by a decedent within three years of death was presumed to have been made in contemplation of death, and the full value of the property was included in the gross estate and taxed. However, the amount of gifts was not included in the estate if the executors were able to prove that the decedent was healthy and mentally competent and that the gifts were not made with the intent of avoiding estate taxes.

The areas in dispute were most often with respect to gifts of property in place of a testamentary disposition or the giving of a gift deed with instructions that it be recorded after expiration of the donor.

The Tax Reform Act of 1976 eliminates any conflict with respect to the donor's intent and requires that any gifts in excess of the annual exclusion of $3,000 per donee which are made within three years of expiration of the donor must be included in the donor's gross estate for tax purposes.

Joint interests

With respect to property owned in joint tenancy by husband and wife, the Tax Reform Act of 1976 now provides that if the joint tenancy was created by a transfer subject to gift tax at the time it was created, such property is now treated as belonging 50 percent to each spouse for estate tax purposes.

Property basis

Subject to certain adjustments, inherited property will not receive a stepped-up basis at time of inheritance but will carry decedents basis.

Farm or business property valuation

If certain conditions are met, the Tax Reform Act of 1976 allows property used in farming or some other trade or business to be valued on the basis of its present use, rather than the previous highest and best use method. This present use method, however, may not reduce a gross estate by more than $500,000.

Although this chapter may seem to be quite detailed in its presentation of the material covered, it actually presents only the basic essentials in an area that is extremely difficult and complex. The real estate licensee will have to work closely with accountants, attorneys, and other experts in order to achieve a high degree of professional success. The validity of the preceding statement will be all the more apparent as the reader proceeds to Chapter 10, which deals with the area of income taxes.

QUESTIONS FOR DISCUSSION

1. Discuss how the tax base in your community affects the taxes and burden of taxation on those who must pay.
2. What are your feelings regarding the taxing of the personal property of a homeowner, business, or industry?
3. How many different kinds and types of property in your community can you list that are tax-exempt?
4. What is the basic difference between the state and the federal gift tax?
5. What is the purpose of the martial deduction allowed in the federal estate tax?
6. Why may it be unwise for an elderly person to give a gift deed rather than make a testamentary disposition?
7. Why is it easier to avoid gift taxes when giving money than when giving real property?
8. What is the effect of a married couple's holding a piece of community property as joint tenants?
9. Do you feel it is proper for the state and federal government to collect gift or estate taxes?
10. What are special assessments, and how do they affect property in your community?

10

The income tax and real estate

All real estate transactions are influenced in varying degrees by our income tax laws. It is the effect of these laws on the individual that often defines the course of action he will take and the type of real estate transaction in which he will become involved.

An understanding of the basic principles in this area is essential for the real estate licensee. This chapter will consider capital gains and losses, sale of a residence, depreciation, installment and deferred payment sales, the Tax Reform Act of 1976, the Revenue Act of 1978, and Schedule E, which accompanies IRS Form 1040 of the U.S. Treasury Department.

The California taxpayer has two partners who share profits and losses, the U.S. government and the state of California. Tax laws affect real estate dealings either before acquisition, during ownership, or in connection with disposition. These laws can become quite complex, and both the licensee and his clients should realize that they will often need to seek the counsel of a CPA, a tax attorney, or other experts.

CAPITAL GAINS AND LOSSES

When an asset is sold or exchanged, the resultant gain or loss may be classified as either an ordinary gain or loss, or a capital gain or loss. While the tax on capital gains does not generally exceed a maximum of 28 percent, the tax on an ordinary gain may be as high as 70 percent. Obviously, it is extremely advantageous for an individual to be able to qualify for the capital gains treatment and the correspondingly lower tax rate, and much of the time spent in tax planning is directed toward achieving this benefit.

Capital assets

In order to be eligible for capital gains benefits, the asset sold or exchanged must be a capital asset or it must be an asset afforded the same treatment as a capital asset. The Treasury Department defines a capital asset by saying what it is not. Everything a person owns is a capital asset except:

1. Stock in trade.
2. Real or personal property includable in inventory.
3. Real or personal property held for sale to customers.
4. Accounts or notes receivable acquired in the ordinary course of a trade or business for services rendered, or from the sale of any of the properties described above, or for services rendered as an employee.
5. Depreciable property used in a trade or business.
6. Real property used in a trade or business.
7. A copyright, or a literary, musical, or artistic composition, or similar property created by one's personal efforts or acquired from the creator in a manner entitling the recipient to the creator's basis.
8. Certain federal, state, or municipal short-term obligations.

Since 1 through 8, above, are not capital assets, it appears that a substantial amount of real property is excluded from capital gains treatment. However, there always seem to be exceptions to the general rule, and although the definition of capital assets excludes business real property or any depreciable business property, the tax law contains a special provision for such property under Code Section 1231.

Section 1231 property. While the property defined under this section includes, in addition to certain real property, such items as livestock, timber, crops, domestic iron ore, and coal, we will be concerned only with the real property under this section, as follows:

1. Property used in a trade or business subject to depreciation and held for more than six months.
2. Real property used in a trade or business and held for more than six months.
3. Leases for an indefinite period, such as certain oil and gas leases, which are considered as real property.
4. Trade or business property involuntarily converted or other capital assets involuntarily converted and held for more than six months. Involuntary conversion occurs when money or other property is received for property that was destroyed, stolen, or condemned for public use.

Thus on all the above, 1 through 4, when there is a sale or exchange and the gains exceed the losses, each gain and loss is treated as though it were derived from the sale of a capital asset and is given capital gains treatment. If the losses exceed the gains, ordinary loss benefits will apply.

Were it not for the capital gains provisions in the tax law, the income derived from the sale or exchange of a large amount of real property would be classified as ordinary income and taxed in the same manner as are salaries, commissions, and the like. The income from the sale or exchange of real property is the difference between the amount realized on the sale or exchange and the seller's cost basis of the property. This point will be discussed later in the chapter.

Classification of real property

The preceding discussion of what constitutes a capital asset and how a capital gains treatment may be allowed brings us to the problem of how to classify real property in order to determine what treatment it will receive.

Real property held by the taxpayer for investment or production of income and not used in his trade or business or held primarily for sale to customers is a capital asset that will receive capital gains treatment. The real estate holdings of most individuals fall into this classification. Their primary means of livelihood have nothing to do with the purchase and sale of real estate. The property itself—income producing, a house, or unimproved land—is held basically as a long-term investment.

Real estate used by the taxpayer in a trade or business but not held for sale to customers is not a capital asset but is, instead, Section 1231 property, and if certain conditions are met, it will be given a capital gains treatment. Although a property may receive the capital gains treatment either because it is a capital asset or because it is Section 1231 property, determination of the type of property it is may be very important to the taxpayer. For instance, if a taxpayer sustains a loss from one sale and a gain from another, the tax consequences will be different if both sales involved capital assets or if one sale was of a capital asset and the other was of a Section 1231 property.

Finally, property held for sale to customers will not be given any capital gains benefits. Any gain or loss from the sale or exchange of such property will result in an ordinary gain or loss.

Dealer or investor?

One of the greatest areas of argument and litigation between individuals and the Internal Revenue Service is concerned with whether the taxpayer is classified as an investor or as a dealer. An investor receives the capital gains treatment, while a person deemed to be a dealer cannot. The real estate licensee often finds himself in a most difficult position in this regard and must plan his personal real estate transactions very carefully if he is to receive any capital gains benefits. The courts have held that it is possible for a person to be both a dealer and an investor at the same time. The dealer classification is not reserved for licensees alone; it will be applied to any person deemed to be in the real estate business to a certain degree, regardless of whether he deals openly on his own or through third persons in the acquisition and sale of real estate.

In attempting to determine whether an individual shall be classified as an investor or as a dealer with respect to a sale or exchange of real property, the Internal Revenue Service uses the following general guidelines.

Factors leading to classification as a dealer:

1. A real estate licensee who maintains an office or who is actively engaged in the real estate business.
2. The number of real estate transactions within a given period. A frequent number of purchases and sales or exchanges, continuously during any given year or years, by oneself or through third persons.
3. One who is primarily engaged in the business of subdividing, developing, or building.
4. The sale of property immediately after purchase or shortly thereafter; regular speculation and quick turnover.

Factors leading to classification as an investor:

1. Primary occupation or business is not in real estate.
2. Property being sold or exchanged has been held for an extensive period of time. Rental property held for investment.
3. Few purchases, sales, or exchanges over an extended period of time.
4. If the taxpayer can show that the sale or exchange is merely the liquidation of an investment, he will probably be allowed capital gains treatment.

Obviously, there may arise many instances in which it is difficult to decide whether the taxpayer is an investor or a dealer. Each case may have to be decided individually by the Internal Revenue Service. An individual may be deemed to be an investor in one transaction and a dealer in another.

Short- and long-term capital gains

After determining that the asset sold or exchanged is a capital asset, the taxpayer must determine whether the gain or loss is a short-term capital gain or loss or a long-term capital gain or loss. If the taxpayer holds the asset for less than 12 months, its sale or exchange results in a short-term capital gain or loss, but if the real estate is held for more than 12 months, its sale or exchange results in a long-term capital gain or loss. To determine the 12-month period, one should begin counting on the day following the day title was acquired. The same day of each succeeding month is the beginning of a new month, regardless of the number of days in the preceding month. The day the property is disposed of is included in the computation.

Short-term capital gains and losses are merged with each other by adding the gains and losses separately and subtracting one total from the other to obtain the net short-term capital gain or loss. Long-term gains and losses are merged in the same manner to determine the net long-term capital gain or loss, and the law limits the amount of ordinary income against which capital losses may be offset to $3,000.

The total net gain or loss is then determined by merging the net short-term capital gain or loss with the net long-term capital gain or loss. The taxpayer who is able to show a net long-term capital gain on the sale or exchange of his property, and who qualifies for the capital gains treatment, can deduct 60 percent of the capital gain from gross income and save a considerable amount of tax; such are the benefits of the capital gains treatment. While the federal tax law allows 60 percent of the capital gain to be exempt from taxation, the California tax law subjects capital gains to full taxation if property is held less than a year; 65 percent between one and five years; and 50 percent if held five years or longer.

Cost basis and adjusted basis

The basis of property is a key figure in computing the gain or loss when the property is sold or exchanged. The basis is also used in order to compute depreciation, which will be discussed later in this chapter. The original basis, also called the cost basis, is the original purchase price or cost to the taxpayer. In most cases, it is the original purchase price; however, the property may have been acquired by gift or inheritance, or in some other manner that requires use of a basis other than cost. There are many ways of acquiring property, and each will require a specific method of determining the cost basis. If the property was purchased, then the purchase price will be the basis, but the taxpayer will probably have to consult a tax expert if the property was:

1. Received for services rendered.
2. Received in a trade.
3. Converted to business or rental use.
4. Acquired in a nontaxable exchange.
5. Acquired by gift.
6. Acquired from a decedent.
7. Property to replace seized or destroyed property.

Adjusted basis of property is the original basis or cost increased or reduced as follows:

1. The original basis or cost of property should be increased by adding the cost of improvements that have a life of more than one year, purchase commissions, legal fees, title fees, certain capital expenditures the taxpayer is entitled to add to the original basis.
2. Settlement fee, the cost of purchase commissions, and legal and recording fees are also added to the original basis or cost of property.
3. Real estate taxes assessed on property at the time of purchase are added to the property if it was purchased prior to 1954.

The original basis or cost is decreased as follows:

1. Depreciation deductions taken are considered to be a return of capital and must be deducted from the original basis or cost.

2. Deductible losses that have been taken or are allowable are included.
3. If an easement was granted on the property, the amount of consideration received for the easement must be deducted.

When the adjusted basis amount is finally determined, it is the difference between the adjusted basis and the selling price of the property that the seller must report as gain. In addition, any selling costs, such as the broker's commission, may be deducted from the amount of the gain.

Example: Al and Millie Steinberg purchased a property for $120,000. Three years later, they sold the building for $190,000. Improvements made over the years totaled $16,200, and the cost of the sale, including the broker's commission, totaled $12,500. They have taken depreciation in the amount of $18,500. What is the amount of gain as the result of this sale?

Purchase price	$120,000	Original basis
Improvements	16,200	
	$136,200	
Depreciation deducted	18,500	
	$117,700	Adjusted basis
Sale price	190,000	
Less: Expenses of the sale	12,500	
	$177,500	Amount realized
Amount realized from sale	$177,500	
Less: Adjusted basis	117,700	
	$ 59,800	Gain

Al and Millie must report a capital gain of $59,800 on their income tax return and may be allowed to deduct 60 percent of this amount because of the capital gains treatment, leaving the sum of $23,920 to be taxed. The gain on this sale is, of course, a long-term capital gain, since Al and Millie held the property primarily for investment and for a period of longer than 12 months from the date of purchase.

SALE OF RESIDENCE

If a residence is sold or exchanged at a gain, the gain is taxable. Two special benefits are available to the taxpayer.

1. If within 18 months preceeding or after sale of the old residence, the seller buys and occupies another residence, the gain is not taxed at the time of the sale if the cost of the new residence equals or exceeds the adjusted sale price of the old residence. The seller is allowed additional time after selling the old residence if he is (a) constructing a new residence or (b) on active duty in the U.S. Armed Forces.
2. If the taxpayer is 55 years of age or older and can meet certain qualifications, special provisions, discussed later in the chapter, will apply to the sale.

If the seller purchases another residence within the time allowed, the tax may be postponed. Any gain not taxed in the year the old residence is sold is subtracted from the cost of the residence acquired to replace it, providing a lower basis to be used when the second residence is eventually sold. The tax may continue to be deferred as long as the taxpayer purchases another residence each time he sells his present one and meets certain qualifications.

Example: Jim Smith sells his residence and realizes a $25,000 gain on the sale. Immediately afterward, he purchases another residence for $98,000, which is more than the price he received for his old house. Smith will not be taxed on the gain; instead, the $25,000 will be deducted from the $98,000 purchase price of the new residence, giving it a basis of $73,000.

The above example indicates that the purchase price of the new residence is more than the adjusted sale price of the old residence, and this generally is the case. However, where the adjusted sale price of the old residence is more than the purchase price of a new residence, the gain taxed in the year of the sale is limited to the lesser of (a) the gain realized on the sale of the old residence or (b) the excess of the adjusted sale price of the old residence over the cost of the new one.

Where there is a loss on the sale or exchange of a residence, this loss may not be deducted and has no effect on the basis of a new residence.

Principal residence

The house that is sold and the house that is acquired to replace it must be principal residences of the taxpayer. Ordinarily, the house one lives in is his principal residence. Besides a single-family residence in the principal residence classification, the following also may be the principal residence of a taxpayer: a trailer, a houseboat, a cooperative apartment, or a condominium apartment. A taxpayer is limited to one principal residence.

Example: Ted Scourkes owns and lives in a house in Los Angeles during most of the year, but he occupies a house at Lake Tahoe during the summer. Internal Revenue Service will hold that the home in Los Angeles is his principal residence, while the Lake Tahoe house is not. Let us assume that Scourkes is transferred by his firm to San Francisco. He does not sell his Los Angeles or Lake Tahoe properties but merely moves to San Francisco where he rents a house. The Internal Revenue Service will now hold that Scourkes rented house in San Francisco is now his principal residence. It does not matter that Scourkes owns property elsewhere; it is the property one lives in that is considered the principal residence.

How to determine gain or loss

Although we have previously touched on this subject, it may be well to review the methods for determining gain or loss on the sale of property. Gain is the excess of the amount realized from a sale or exchange over the adjusted basis of the property sold or exchanged. Loss is the excess of the adjusted basis of the property over the amount realized from the sale or exchange.

The adjusted basis is the original cost or other basis adjusted for such things as casualty losses, improvements, and depreciation when appropriate. The amount realized from a sale or exchange of property is everything received for the property disposed of reduced by any cost incurred in effecting the transfer, such as commissions, advertising, and costs of legal fees.

Property, other than money, that may be received is included at fair market value. In the case of notes or other evidences of indebtedness received as a part of the sale price, the fair market value is usually the best amount that can be obtained from the sale to, or discount with, a bank or other purchaser of such notes or paper.

Indebtedness against the property. An indebtedness against the owner of the property or against the property, which is paid off as a part of the transaction or is assumed by the purchaser, must be included at its face value in the amount realized. If an indebtedness is attached to the property transferred, such indebtedness must be included at face value in the amount realized, even though neither the seller nor purchaser is personally liable for the debt.

Payment of boot. If a person trades a piece of property for another and in addition to giving the property must also pay some money, the amount of money paid is known as "boot." Thus, if an individual trades one property for another and pays cash to boot, the amount he realizes is the fair market value of the property received minus cash paid.

An example of computing gain or loss is the following. Bob Quigley sells a property with an existing $81,000 mortgage. He receives $60,000 in cash, and the buyer assumes the existing mortgage. The property has a cost basis to Quigley of $24,900, and his selling costs total $9,600. What is the amount of gain realized by Quigley?

Cash received	$ 60,000	
Mortgage assumed by buyer	81,000	
	$141,000	Selling price
Less: Quigley's cost basis	24,900	
	$116,100	
Less: Selling costs	9,600	
	$106,500	Gain

Special problems regarding residences

Many special problems arise with regard to the sale or exchange of a residence; some require quite complex calculations which should be attempted only by a tax expert. Examples of such situations are the following.

1. The property in question is only partially a residence as far as the owner is concerned. A person who owns a six-unit apartment house and lives in one of the apartments decides to sell the units and purchase a house. Only the portion of the selling price allocable to the residential unit of the former owner need be reinvested in the new residence in order to postpone the tax on that part of the gain. Quite often, the sale of a multiple-unit building in which the former owner was a resident must be treated as though it were a sale of two properties.

2. A building that was used as a residence and is subsequently converted to rental property takes on an entirely new dimension, for it now becomes business property or property held for the production of income.

3. A property owner may not sell but may trade in his house to a builder for a new one. In such a case, the transaction is generally treated as a sale and purchase.

Age 55 or older

Persons who sell or exchange their principal residence during the year may generally elect to exclude from their gross income part or all of the gain on the sale or exchange if (a) they were age 55 or older before the date of the sale or exchange and (b) they owned and used the property as their principal residence for a period of time, continuous or interrupted, totaling at least three years within the five-year period ending on the date of sale or exchange.

Taxpayers who meet these requirements can elect to exclude up to $100,000 of gain free of any taxes. The exclusion can only apply to a specific sale and no portion of the $100,000 can be carried over to a subsequent sale. If the taxpayer uses the exclusion and subsequently purchases and sells another residence, the exclusion cannot be used again, and tax will have to be paid if there is a gain.

Example: Arthur Wong sold his principal residence for $85,000 in 1979, when he was 57 years old. He is eligible to and does elect to exclude from his gross income for the current year the resulting gain. His selling price and selling expenses are shown below:

1.	Sale Price		$85,000
2.	Less:		
	Real estate commission	$ 5,100	
	Escrow costs or fees	500	
	Termite repairs	1,700	
		$ 7,300	7,300
3.	Amount Realized		$77,700
4.	Less Basis of Residence Sold:		
	Original purchase price	$22,500	
	Purchase escrow fees	300	
	Add copper pipes	900	
	Install 220 wiring	400	
	Terazzo front steps	300	
		$24,400	$24,400
5.	Gain Realized on Sale		$53,300

The exclusion of up to $100,000 of capital gain allows Arthur to receive a $53,300 tax-free gain.

Any individual who meets the ownership, use, and age requirements will be allowed to claim the special exclusion. Also, when the sale is being made by a husband and wife who otherwise meet the ownership and use requirements, if only one is over 55, they may elect the special exclusion.

DEPRECIATION

In Chapter 12, concerned with appraisal and valuation, we will discuss depreciation in terms of physical deterioration and functional, social, and economic obsolescence. Here, we discuss depreciation as brokers and investors generally do—as an offset against income in connection with properties held for investment or property used in a trade or business.

The Internal Revenue Code allows a deduction of depreciation as a reasonable allowance for the exhaustion, wear and tear, and normal obsolescence of property (1) used in a trade or business or (2) held for the production of income, and said depreciation may be deducted from gross income.

Depreciation taken on business or income property, then, will be subtracted from any rent or other income received from the property, thereby providing a partially tax-free income. At times, the depreciation allowance may exceed the income for a particular year, and the taxpayer may deduct this excess depreciation from any other income he may receive from other sources.

The Internal Revenue Service will not allow the taxpayer to take depreciation on his house, its furnishings, an automobile, or other items used only for personal or pleasure purposes. If, however, a personal item such as an automobile is used partially for business, the taxpayer will be allowed to depreciate that portion used for business.

Estimated useful life

One of the most important factors in the calculation of depreciation is to determine the useful life of the asset being depreciated. The useful life of an asset depends on how long one expects to use it, its age when acquired, policies concerning repairs, upkeep, and replacement, and other conditions. Useful lives prescribed by the Internal Revenue Service for depreciation purposes are applicable to all assets used in a particular industry or business rather than to individual assets. Longer or shorter useful lives than those given by the Internal Revenue Service may be used, but the taxpayer should consult his accountant to be sure that they are consistent with general practices in common use.

The Treasury Department publication, *Revenue Procedures 62–21*, commonly referred to as "depreciation guidelines," lists the number of years allowed on approximately 75 broad classes of assets. With regard to real property, the guideline lives are as follows:

Type of building	Years
Apartments	40
Banks	50
Dwellings	45
Factories	45
Farm buildings	25
Garages	45
Grain elevators	60
Hotels	40
Loft buildings	50
Machine shops	45
Office buildings	45
Stores	50
Theaters	40
Warehouses	60

One of the greatest areas of disagreement between taxpayers and the Internal Revenue Service centers around the useful life to be used in the depreciation of a particular asset. While 40 years may seem quite fair for a new apartment house, the taxpayer may feel that this same amount of time should not be used if the apartment house he has just purchased is 20 or 30 years old. However, the guideline lives given above make no mention of the age of the property to be depreciated and are not intended to refer only to new buildings. If this were the case, an investor could purchase a 30-year-old, eight-unit apartment house and attempt to write off his investment in ten years. It is also quite possible that the 30-year-old building in a certain location would sell for more than a ten-year-old building of the same size in a less desirable location. It is important, then, that whatever the guideline life used may be, the investor should not base his decision upon a haphazard guess or mere hearsay. He should decide only after careful consultation with his tax accountant, who is familiar with what the local Internal Revenue authorities will allow.

Land not depreciable

Current tax rules provide that land may not be depreciated; only the improvements thereon may be depreciated. Therefore, when an investor purchases a building, he must allocate the purchase price between the land and the building. It is difficult to state any exact mathematic formula to use in making this allocation, since values may vary widely depending on the particular property. In one case, the building may represent most of the value, while in another, the land itself is the main factor in arriving at the purchase price. Generally, the relative assessed valuations of the tax assessor are used in determining the allocation to be made.

Example: Eugene Brussell purchases a building for $300,000. The records of the tax assessor show that he has assessed the value of the land at $16,000 and the improvements at $14,000. The $42,000 value set on the improvements represents 70 percent of the total assessed value of $60,000. Brussell may now allocate 70 percent of the purchase price to the building and the remaining 30 percent to the land. The $300,000 purchase price is thus divided $210,000 to the depreciable building and $90,000 to the nondepreciable land.

Basis for determining depreciation

The basis for determining depreciation is the same as the basis used to determine gain if the property is sold. Usually, the cost of the property is its basis for depreciation after division is made in the amount to be allocated to building and the amount to land. In the previous example, Mr. Brussell's basis for depreciation is $210,000. If at any time during the term of ownership the owner improves the property, the additional cost is added to the basis and may be depreciated.

Salvage value

An asset may not be depreciated below its salvage value at the time it is disposed of or at the end of the guideline life assigned to it for depreciation purposes. The estimated salvage value must be deducted from the basis of the asset in determining the annual depreciation if either the straight-line or sum-of-the-years'-digits method is used. Not all assets will have depreciated in value over the years; for instance, a truck purchased new and used for five years will obviously be worth much less when it is replaced than when it was purchased, but a piece of real estate may be held for ten years and be worth much more when sold than when it was purchased.

The matter of salvage value in setting up a depreciation schedule for real property is something for the taxpayer and his accountant to decide. Interpretations vary, but since the value of a property at the end of its depreciable life is many times the salvage value of the building, most accountants merely use the allocated portion of the purchase price to the property when setting up the depreciation schedule and make no calculation whatsoever for salvage value, regardless of the depreciation method to be used. In line with this approach, in the following section, no arbitrary amount will be assigned as salvage value in any of the examples, since all the examples will deal with real property.

Methods of depreciation

The three methods most commonly used in the computation of depreciation are (1) straight-line, (2) declining balance, and (3) sum-of-the-years'-digits. The second and third are accounting methods for applying accelerated depreciation in the early years.

Straight-line method. This is the most used method of computing depreciation and may be used for any depreciable property. It gives the investor an equal amount of depreciation each year over the life assigned to the asset. The amount of yearly depreciation is determined by dividing the amount allocated to the building by the years of useful life.

Example: Dr. Louis Batmale purchases a piece of investment property consisting of rental units at a purchase price of $280,000. The purchase price is to be allocated 75 percent to the building and 25 percent to the land. A useful life of 30 years is to be assigned to the building for depreciation purposes. Seventy-five percent of the purchase price of $280,000 equals $210,000. The basis of $210,000 is divided by 30, equaling the sum of $7,000 which represents the yearly depreciation amount.

The straight-line method of depreciation causes a fixed percentage of depreciation to be taken each year during the assigned useful life of the depreciable asset. Shown below are the corresponding yearly depreciation percentage rates for selected terms of useful life using straight-line and declining balance methods of depreciation.

Years	Depreciation percent per year using straight-line	125 percent declining balance	150 percent declining balance	200 percent declining balance
5	20	25	30	40
10	10	12.5	15	20
15	6.6	8.3	10	13.3
20	5	6.25	7.5	10
25	4	5	6	8
30	3.3	4.17	5	6.67
35	2.86	3.58	4.29	5.72
40	2.5	3.125	3.75	5
45	2.22	2.78	3.33	4.44
50		2.5	3	4

Declining balance method. In this method, the amount of depreciation taken each year is subtracted from the cost or other basis of the property before computing the following year's depreciation, so that the same depreciation rate applies to a smaller or declining balance each year. Thus, the largest amount of depreciation is taken in the first year, with continually decreasing amounts of depreciation in successive years.

Within certain limits prescribed by the Internal Revenue Service, a depreciation rate may be used that is greater than the rate used in the straight-line method. In some circumstances, a rate twice the straight-line rate may be used; this is known as 200 percent depreciation. In other circumstances, the taxpayer is limited to a rate one and a quarter times the straight-line rate. This is known as 125 percent depreciation.

Rules governing the selection of the depreciation method will be discussed later in connection with the Tax Reform Act of 1976 and Revenue Act of 1978.

Example: Stanley Ritchie purchases for investment a building from the Ace Building Construction Company. The building is new, and Ritchie is the first user. The basis for depreciation is $160,000, and the depreciable life is 40 years. What is the depreciation deduction for the first three years using the straight-line method, and what is the amount of depreciation possible using the declining balance method for these years?

To determine the straight-line depreciation, we merely take the $160,000 basis and divide by 40, or we can multiply by the depreciation rate for 40 years, which is 2.5 percent.

$160,000 ÷ 40 equals $4,000

or

$160,000 × .025 equals $4,000.

The straight-line depreciation for the first year is $4,000, and the same amount for each succeeding year, since $4,000 each year over 40 years will return the $160,000 cost basis. Ritchie's depreciation for the first three years will amount to $12,000.

Since Ritchie is the first user of a new building, he may elect to use 200 percent depreciation—that is, twice the straight-line rate. Using this method, the depreciation for the first year will be $8,000. This is calculated by taking twice the straight-line rate of 2.5 percent, which is 5 percent.

.05 × $160,000 equals $8,000
for the first year's depreciation.

Since this is a declining balance method, the depreciation taken for the first year must be subtracted from the cost basis of $160,000 before calculating the depreciation for the second year.

$160,000 − $8,000 equals $152,000.
.05 × $152,000 equals $7,600
depreciation for the second year.

The second year's depreciation is now deducted from the cost basis in order to arrive at the third year's depreciation.

$152,000 − $7,600 equals $144,400.
.05 × $144,400 equals $7,220
depreciation for the third year.

Thus, at the end of three years, Ritchie will have taken $12,000 in depreciation using the straight-line method of $4,000 annually. The 200 percent declining balance method will have resulted at the end of the third year in a total depreciation of $22,820.

Let us now assume that Ritchie had purchased the building from its original owner when it was eight years old. We will use the same cost basis and depreciable life so that the straight-line rate will remain at $4,000 yearly. Since Ritchie has now purchased a used building and is considered a second or subsequent owner, he will be limited to 125 percent depreciation if he elects to use the declining balance method. The first three years of depreciation would be calculated as follows.

First year:
$160,000 × 0.3125 = $5,000
[1¼ times the straight-line rate of 2.5% is 3.125% which is expressed decimally as .03125].
Second year:
$160,000 − $5,000 = $155,000.
$155,000 × .03125 = $4,843.75.
Third year:
$155,000 − $4,843.75 = $150,156.25.
$150,156.25 × .03125 = $4,692.38.

Total depreciation taken after three years and using 125 percent depreciation is $14,536.13 as against $12,000 by the straight-line method.

Sum-of-the-years'-digits method. The sum-of-the-years'-digits method may be used only for property that qualifies for 200 percent depreciation—that is, first users of new residential property. In this method, the taxpayer applies a different fraction to the basis of the property. The denominator (bottom of the fraction) is the total of the numbers representing the depreciable life of the property. Thus, if the depreciable life is five years, the denominator is 15 (1 + 2 + 3 + 4 + 5 = 15). The number (top of the fraction) is the number of years of depreciable life remaining at the beginning of the year for which the computation is made. Thus, if the depreciable life is five years, the fraction to be applied to the basis of the property for the first year is ⁵⁄₁₅. The fraction for the second year is ⁴⁄₁₅, for the third year, ³⁄₁₅, and so on. In actual practice, this method is little used for real property; virtually all accountants prefer the 200 percent depreciation method.

Change of method

In certain circumstances, the Internal Revenue Service will allow the taxpayer to switch from a declining balance method to the straight-line method for the remaining depreciable life of the property. This has the effect of allowing accelerated depreciation in the early years with the balance of the allowable depreciation being taken in equal yearly amounts over the later years of depreciable life.

Comparison of methods of depreciation

Table 10–1 shows a comparison of the methods of depreciation that have been discussed. For purposes of illustration, we shall assume a basis of $10,000 and a depreciable life of ten years.

It is obvious that the accelerated methods of depreciation allow larger depreciation deductions in the earlier years than those allowed in the straight-line method. This depreciation is an offset against current income; however, the cost basis is reduced by this depreciation and will result in a greater gain when the property is later sold or exchanged. The advantage of each dollar of depreciation is that it offsets a dollar of income that would be taxed at ordinary income rates in the year received; the gain realized at the time of a later sale will usually be afforded capital gains treatment and, consequently, a much lower tax will be paid.

The length of time the investor plans to keep a property also has an important bearing on the method of depreciation selected. If he plans to retain the property for a long time, then the straight-line method will give him a more even offset against income. Since the income from a good piece of property increases over the years, an even depreciation offset is better than a method that continually decreases the offset.

The selection of a depreciation method should be made only after the investor has thoroughly examined the effect it will have on his overall business, investment, and tax picture.

TABLE 10–1
Comparison of methods of depreciation

Year	Straight-line	200 percent declining balance	125 percent declining balance	Sum-of-the-year's-digits
1	$ 1,000	$2,000	$1,250	$ 1,818
2	1,000	1,600	1,094	1,636
3	1,000	1,280	957	1,455
4	1,000	1,024	837	1,273
5	1,000	819	733	1,091
6	1,000	655	641	909
7	1,000	524	561	727
8	1,000	420	491	545
9	1,000	336	430	364
10	1,000	268	376	182
Total	$10,000	$8,926	$7,370	$10,000

Recapture of depreciation

Another important area of consideration for the investor is the recapture of depreciation rules and regulations. The recapture rules are designed to limit to a certain extent the capital gains treatment advantage.

There are many applications of these rules depending on the particular situation and type of property, and these are considered in our discussion of the Tax Reform Act of 1976 which follows.

THE TAX REFORM ACT OF 1976 AND REVENUE ACT OF 1978

The following discussion will consider some of the effects relating to real property as a result of the Tax Reform Act of 1976 and Revenue Act of 1978. Any newly enacted legislation, especially in the complex area of taxation, will be subject to changes. In addition, certain rules and procedures may differ between federal and state of California legislation. The real estate licensee must keep currently informed and work with tax experts such as a tax accountant or tax attorney when necessary.

Recapture of depreciation

Previously, special rules were provided for the recapture of depreciation allowed as a deduction with respect to real estate. In the case of nonresidential commercial real estate, any gain realized is treated or recaptured as ordinary income to the extent of post-1969 depreciation taken in excess of straight-line depreciation. In the case of residential property generally, this rule applied to property held during the first 100 months ($8\frac{1}{3}$ years) with a phaseout during the next 100 months; meaning that there was no recapture after $16\frac{2}{3}$ years. For certain government-subsidized housing acquired or constructed before January 1976, the phaseout began at 20 months ($1\frac{2}{3}$ years) and was completed at 120 months (10 years).

The law now modifies the rules relating to the recapture of depreciation on residential real estate. (The existing treatment of nonresidential real estate requiring the recapture of post-1969 depreciation in excess of straight-line depreciation is continued.) In the case of residential real estate, the law provides for the recapture of all post-1975 depreciation in excess of straight-line in the same manner as is presently the case for nonresidential real estate. In the case of government-subsidized housing, the law provides full recapture of post-1975 depreciation in excess of straight-line for the first 100 months ($8\frac{1}{3}$ years) and a phaseout of the amount recaptured during the second 100 months (up to $16\frac{2}{3}$ years).

Loan points and prepaid interest

Prepaid interest or points paid on a loan must be deducted over the period of the loan to the extent the interest represents the cost of using the borrowed funds during each taxable year in the period. An exception is made with respect to a loan in connection with the purchase or improvement of, and secured by, the taxpayer's principal residence. Points which are paid in connection with such a loan are considered prepaid interest, and the full amount of such points or any other prepaid interest may be deducted in full during the year in which paid.

A penalty charge for prepayment of a loan is deductible as interest in the year paid.

Deduction of investment interest

Prior law limited the deduction for interest on investment indebtedness to $25,000 per year plus the taxpayer's net investment income and long-term capital gain plus half of any interest in excess of these amounts. The law now limits deduction of investment interest to $10,000 per year plus the taxpayer's net investment income. No offset of investment interest is permitted against long-term capital gain.

Construction taxes and interest

The law now provides that with respect to real property held for purposes of business or investment, construction period interest and taxes are to be capitalized in the year in which they are paid or accrued and amortized over a ten-year period. A portion of the amount capitalized may be deducted for the taxable year in which paid or accrued. The balance must be amortized over the remaining years in the amortization period beginning with the year in which the property is ready to be placed in use or held for sale.

Construction period interest includes interest paid or accrued on indebtedness incurred on real property during its construction period. The construction period commences with the date on which the construction of a building or other improvement begins and ends on the date that the building or improvement is ready to be placed in use or held for sale.

Separate rules are provided in connection with commercial, residential, and government-subsidized housing, and the length of the amortization period is to be phased in over a seven-year period. In the case of a sale or exchange of property, the unamortized balance of the construction period interest and taxes is to be added to the basis of the property for purposes of determining gain or loss on the sale or exchange.

Business use of homes

The law now provides definitive rules relating to deductions for expenses attributable to the business use of homes. A taxpayer is not permitted to deduct any expenses attributable to the use of his home for business purposes except to the extent attributable to the portion of the home used exclusively on a regular basis: *(a)* as the taxpayer's principal place of business, *(b)* as a place of business which is used for patients, clients, or customers in meeting or dealing with the taxpayer in the normal course of business, or *(c)* in the case of a separate structure which is not attached to a dwelling, in connection with the taxpayer's trade or business.

Further, in the case of an employee, the business use of the home must be for the convenience of his employer. An exception to the exclusive use test is provided where the dwelling unit is the sole fixed location of a trade or business which consists of selling products at retail or wholesale and the taxpayer regularly uses a separate identifiable portion of the residence for inventory storage. An overall limitation is provided which limits the amount of the deductions to the gross income generated by the taxpayer's home business activity.

Rental of vacation homes

Previously, there was no definitive ruling relating to how much personal use of vacation property might result in the disallowance of deductions because the rental activities are not engaged in for profit. The law now provides a limitation on deductions for expenses attributable to the rental of a vacation home if the home is used by a taxpayer for personal purposes in excess of the greater of two weeks or 10 percent of the actual business use (rental time) during a year. In this case, the deductions allowed in connection with a vacation home cannot exceed the gross income from the business use of the vacation home, less expenses which are allowable in any event (such as interest and taxes).

In addition, if a vacation home is actually rented for less than 15 days during the year, no business deductions or income derived from the use of the vacation home are to be taken into account in the taxpayer's return for the taxable year.

INSTALLMENT AND DEFERRED PAYMENT SALES PLANS AND INSTALLMENT SALES REVISION ACT OF 1980

The sale of real property using a plan by which a part or all of the sale price is to be paid by the purchaser to the seller after the close of the tax year in which the sale is made is known as an installment or deferred payment sale. When this type of sale is made, the seller generally elects to use the installment sale method or, occasionally, the deferred payment method. If the seller meets certain requirements he will be able to report his taxable gain over a number of years and thus spread out his tax payments. Depending on the particular circumstances of the seller, it may be very advantageous to be able to spread out tax payments rather than having to pay all the tax in the year of the sale. The installment method of reporting income will relieve the seller of the burden of paying tax on income that has not been collected, and it permits him to include in his gross income only that portion of each collection which constitutes profit.

General requirements

The taxpayer must be the payee or mortgagee if a note or a first or second deed of trust or mortgage is given by the buyer for the unpaid balance of the selling price. If the buyer gives his note, mortgage, or deed of trust to another party in order to finance his purchase, and he pays the seller the proceeds he receives, the seller may not use the installment or deferred payment method of reporting taxable gain. With most ordinary purchases of real estate, the buyer borrows the necessary money from a bank or savings and loan company, so the outstanding debt is not owed to the seller. It is when the seller himself carries back the major portion of the financing that the installment method comes into use.

The former requirement that the sale is considered to be on the installment plan only if there is no payment to the seller in the year of the sale or that such payments do not exceed 30 percent of the selling price is eliminated and a seller can now accept any desired amount.

Payments received in the year of the sale include not only the down payment but also all other cash payments and property received in that year. Liabilities of the seller that are paid by the buyer in the year of the sale, such as liens and accrued interest and taxes, are included. Any deposit money or option payments that were received in any preceding year in accordance with the contract became part of the down payment and must be included.

Notes given to the seller or other evidences of indebtedness of the buyer are not included in payments in the year of the sale. Where property is sold subject to an existing loan and the buyer assumes the loan, the loan is not included in the collections received in the year of the sale unless such loan exceeds the seller's basis of the property.

Where the loan assumed by the buyer exceeds the seller's basis of the property, the excess of the loan over the adjusted basis of the property will be included in the payments received in the year of the sale. If the buyer pays off the seller's loan at the time of the sale instead of assuming it, he has, in effect, paid the seller an additional amount to the extent of the loan payment, and the seller must include this amount in the payments received in the year of the sale.

Calculation of gain

Deferred payment sales are now automatically reported as installment sales. The income from installment collections must be reported each year and is determined by the use of a gross profit percentage. The gross profit percentage for any sale is the percent that the gross profit to be realized is of the total contract price.

Example: Brown sells a property at a contract price of $200,000, and there is a gross profit of $50,000. The gross profit percentage is 25 percent ($50,000 divided by $200,000). Thus, 25 percent of each payment collected on the sale, including the down payment, is gain and must be included in gross income for the tax year in which collected. This percentage amount remains the same for all installment payments received on the sale.

Let us now consider an example of a sale that involves the assumption of an existing loan, a second loan, and a cash down payment, and let us determine what mathematical computations will be necessary if this is to be reported as an installment sale.

Assume that in 1974 Smith bought a lot for $16,000 and in 1975 he borrowed money to erect a house, which he occupied. The house cost $48,000, making Smith's total cost $64,000. In 1980, Smith sold the house to Jordan for a total of $110,000 and paid commission and other expenses amounting to $8,500 on the sale. Jordan paid $30,000 in cash and assumed Smith's existing loan in the amount of $38,000. Smith carried back a second loan of $32,000 for a term of five years at 12 percent annual interest with payments of $338. per month beginning January 1981.

The transaction qualifies as an installment sale, since the down payment of $30,000 received in the year of the sale does not exceed 30 percent of the selling price of $110,000. The existing first loan assumed by the buyer and the second loan both represent debts of the purchaser and are not considered in determining the amount of the payments received in the year of the sale. The percentage of each installment payment to be reported as profit is computed as follows:

Sale price of house	$110,000
Less: Commission and expenses	8,500
Net sale price	101,500
Cost basis of property to Smith	64,000
Gross profit to be realized on sale	$ 37,500
Contract price:	
Sale price	$110,000
Less: Loan assumed by Jordan	38,000
Contract price	$ 72,000

Gross profit percentage:

$$\frac{\text{Gross profit to be realized, } \$37,500}{\text{Contract price, } \$72,000} = 52\%$$

Accordingly, the profit realized on the 1980 receipts of $30,000 is 52 percent thereof, or $15,600. The monthly payments of $338. on the second loan will amount to $4,056 per year, and in 1981, the profit to be realized will be 52 percent of $4,056 or $2,109.12.

Since the property was a capital asset held by Smith for more than 12 months, the realized profit is a long-term capital gain. Thus, in determining his net long-term capital gains and losses on his income tax return, Smith will include for 1980 the $15,600 profit realized in that year, and on his 1981 return Smith will include the $2,109.12 realized in 1981. Since the annual amount received will be the same over the term of the second loan, Smith will have the same $2,109.12 of gain to enter on his annual tax return until the second loan is paid off in five years.

Other deferred-payment sales

A deferred-payment sale that does not meet the requirements set forth above for installment sales must be reported and any gain therefrom taxed in the year of the sale even though the sale is covered by obligations of the buyer which are payable to the seller over a term of years.

The gain or loss realized at time of sale is the difference between the sale price (including purchaser's obligations at their fair market value), reduced by the costs, if any, of making the sale, over the adjusted basis of property sold.

The sale price in this method takes into account any cash plus the fair market value of the buyer's obligations and other property received as consideration by the seller. Negotiable notes, mortgages, and land contracts the seller receives from the buyer are examples of obligations included at their fair market value in computing the amount realized from the sale of the property.

Fair market value generally represents the amount that an owner, who is not under a necessity of selling, is willing to take and that a buyer who is not under a necessity of buying, is willing to pay.

Example: a parcel of real estate was sold for $50,000, payable $40,000 down and the balance over a period of five years at $2,000 per year plus 11½ percent interest. The balance payable was represented by the purchaser's note, which had a fair market value of 75 percent of its face value. The assumption here is that the purchaser's note could be discounted by 25 percent and thus sold for 75 percent of its face value by the seller at the time of the sale. A commission of 6 percent, or $3,000, was paid to a broker for negotiating the sale. The real estate cost the seller $25,000, and was held by him for more than 12 months. Computation of gain is as follows.

Selling price	$50,000
Less: Commission	3,000
	$47,000
Less: Adjusted basis of property sold	25,000
Gain to be realized	$22,000
Gain recognized in year of sale:	
Cash	$40,000
Market value of note (75% of $10,000)	7,500
Total realized in year of sale	$47,500
Less: Commission of $3,000 and cost of property $25,000, total $28,000	28,000
Gain recognized in year of the sale	$19,500

The $19,500 may be reported as a long-term capital gain. Since only the market value of the note (75 percent of face value) was included to determine the profit recognized in the year of the sale, the seller must report as ordinary income 25 percent of each collection of principal he receives on the note. The interest on the note is also ordinary income.

Disposition of installment obligations

Gain or loss will usually result when an installment obligation, such as a note or mortgage, is disposed of by the seller. Such gains or losses are considered to result from the sale or exchange of the property for which the installment obligations were received. Thus, if the sale of the property resulted in a capital gain, the disposition of the obligation will result in a capital gain or loss; if the sale of the property produced income subject to ordinary tax, the disposition of the obligation will result in ordinary income or loss.

If the obligations are sold or exchanged, the gain or loss is measured by the difference between the basis of the obligations and the amount realized. If the obligations are disposed of by other than sale or exchange (for instance, by gift), the gain or loss is measured by the difference between the basis of the obligations and their fair market value at the time of such disposition.

SCHEDULE E

Schedule E (Form 1040) is called the Supplemental Income Schedule and includes income from pensions and annuities, rents and royalties, partnerships, and estates or trusts. Figure 10-1 shows a Schedule E prepared by Frank Conklin, 2000 Fine Street, Daly City. In it, the only supplemental income shown is received from a duplex that Mr. Conklin purchased for investment and has rented to tenants.

Mr. Conklin purchased this duplex from a friend who retired and moved to the country. The building is 35 years old and is in generally good condition. It is located in a good rental area, and Conklin believes that the $92,000 he paid is approximately $5,000 below market value. He put $25,000 cash down and received a loan from the seller in the amount of $67,000 with interest at 13½ percent and payments of $781.22 per month based on a 25-year term but with a due date of ten years.

Conklin took title to the building on January 9, with both units having been vacated prior to close of escrow. He had some painting and minor repair work done and at the beginning of February had rented the units for $435 each per month. He

SCHEDULE E (Form 1040) Department of the Treasury Internal Revenue Service	**Supplemental Income Schedule** (From pensions and annuities, rents and royalties, partnerships, estates and trusts, etc.) ▶ Attach to Form 1040. ▶ See Instructions for Schedule E (Form 1040).	19 --
Name(s) as shown on Form 1040 FRANK CONKLIN 2000 PINE STREET, DALY CITY, CALIFORNIA 94112		Your social security number 123 : 45 : 6789

Part I Pension and Annuity Income. If fully taxable, do not complete this part. Enter amount on Form 1040, line 17.
For one pension or annuity not fully taxable, complete this part. If you have more than one pension or annuity that is not fully taxable, attach a separate sheet listing each one with the appropriate data and enter combined total of taxable parts on line 4.

1a Did you and your employer contribute to the pension or annuity?. ☐ Yes ☐ No
 b If "Yes," do you expect to get back your contribution within 3 years from the date you receive the first payment? . . . . . ☐ Yes ☐ No
 c If "Yes," show: Your contribution ▶ $.................., d Contribution received in prior years . . . . ▶ | 1d | ....
2 Amount received this year . . . . | 2 | ....
3 Amount on line 2 that is not taxable. . . . . | 3 | ....
4 Taxable part (subtract line 3 from line 2). Enter here and include in line 18 below . . . . | 4 | ....

Part II Rent and Royalty Income or Loss. If you need more space, attach a separate sheet.
5a Have you claimed expenses connected with your vacation home (or other dwelling unit) rented to others (see Instructions)?. . . ☐ Yes ☑ No
 b If "Yes," did you or a member of your family occupy the vacation home (or other dwelling unit) for more than 14 days during the tax year? ☐ Yes ☐ No
6a Did you elect to claim amortization (under section 191) or depreciation (under section 167(o)) for a rehabilitated certified historic structure (see Instructions)?. . . . . ☐ Yes ☑ No
 b Amortizable basis (see Instructions) ▶

(a) Property code (describe in Part V)	(b) Total amount of rents	(c) Total amount of royalties	(d) Depreciation (explain in Part VI) or depletion (attach computation)	(e) Other expenses (explain in Part VII)	(f) Loss	(g) Income
Property A .	9,570.		3,220.	11,142.	4,792.	
Property B .						
Property C .						
Property D .						
Property E .						
7 Amounts from Form 4835 . .		/////				
8 Totals . .	9,570.		3,220.	11,142.	(4,792.)	

9 Total rent and royalty income or (loss). Combine amounts in columns (f) and (g), line 8. Enter here and include in line 18 below . . . . | 9 | (4,792.)

Part III Income or Losses from—

	(a) Name	(b) Employer identification number	(c) Loss	(d) Income
Partnerships				
	10 Add amounts in columns (c) and (d) and enter here	10	( )	
	11 Combine amounts in columns (c) and (d), line 10, and enter net income or (loss)		11	
	12 Additional first-year depreciation		12	( )
	13 Total partnership income or (loss). Combine lines 11 and 12. Enter here and include in line 18 below		13	
Estates or Trusts				
	14 Add amounts in columns (c) and (d) and enter here	14	( )	
	15 Total estate or trust income or (loss). Combine amounts in columns (c) and (d), line 14. Enter here and include in line 18 below		15	
Small Business Corporations				
	16 Add amounts in columns (c) and (d) and enter here	16	( )	
	17 Total small business corporation income or (loss). Combine amounts in columns (c) and (d), line 16. Enter here and include in line 18 below		17	

Part IV
18 TOTAL income or (loss). Combine lines 4, 9, 13, 15, and 17. Enter here and on Form 1040, line 18. ▶ | 18 | (4,792.)

19 Enter your share of gross farming and fishing income applicable to Parts II and III . . . . | 19 | E

283-064-2

FIGURE 10–1

Schedule E (Form 1040) 1979 Page **2**

Part V — Property reported in Part II

Property Codes	Kind and location of property
A	809 - 11 Fifth Avenue, Daly City, California - Duplex of 5 rooms each.
B	
C	
D	
E	

Part VI — Depreciation claimed in Part II. If you need more space, use Form 4562.

(a) Description of property	(b) Date acquired	(c) Cost or other basis	(d) Depreciation allowed or allowable in prior years	(e) Depreciation method	(f) Life or rate	(g) Depreciation for this year
Property A Total additional first-year depreciation (do not include in items below) ⟶						
809-11 Fifth Avenue	1/9/--	64,400.	-0-	S.L.	20 yrs.	3,220.
Totals (Property A)		64,400				3,220.
Property B Total additional first-year depreciation (do not include in items below) ⟶						
Totals (Property B)						
Property C Total additional first-year depreciation (do not include in items below) ⟶						
Totals (Property C)						
Property D Total additional first-year depreciation (do not include in items below) ⟶						
Totals (Property D)						
Property E Total additional first-year depreciation (do not include in items below) ⟶						
Totals (Property E)						

Part VII — Expenses claimed in Part II

Expenses (Description)	Properties A	B	C	D	E
Property Taxes	$ 950.	$	$	$	$
Loan Interest	9,022.				
Insurance	385.				
Water	180.				
Painting	250.				
Plumbing Repair	185.				
Roof Repair	170.				
Totals	11,142.				

283-064-1

FIGURE 10-1 *(continued)*

feels this is a good investment since the property in the area is appreciating at a rate of approximately 15 percent per year, and the rent he is receiving will approximately equal his monthly payments.

We will now look at Mr. Conklin's Schedule E form for the tax year.

The location and description of the property is entered in Part V. It is located at 809–811 Fifth Avenue, Daly City, California, and consists of two five-room units.

The total amount of rents, depreciation, expenses, and profit or loss is shown in Part II. Each of the units was rented for $435 per month effective February. Thus, Conklin received rent for 11 months for a total of $9,570.

The amount claimed for depreciation is $3,220. The purchase price was $92,000; and since Conklin's tax bill shows that his assessment is divided on the basis of just over 70 percent to the improvements and the remainder to the land, he will allocate the sum of $64,400 to the building as the basis for depreciation. Since the building is 35 years old, Conklin's accountant advises him that a depreciable life of 20 years is justified here. Thus, $64,400 divided by 20 years equals a yearly straight-line depreciation of $3,220.

Expenses of $11,142 are shown and are itemized in Part VII. Making up the total amount is $950 taxes, $385 insurance, $180 water, $9,022 loan interest, $250 painting, $185 plumbing repairs, and $170 for repair of the roof gutter.

The $3,220 depreciation and $11,142 expenses total $14,362 which exceeds the $9,570 rental income by $4,792 which Conklin may show as a loss. It is interesting to note that not only does Conklin receive $9,570 in rental income free from taxes, but also he will enter the $4,792 loss on another part of his Form 1040 and will offset $4,792 of his ordinary taxable income.

Information used in connection with the calculation of depreciation is shown in Part VI, and the amount of depreciation taken for the tax year is shown as straight-line depreciation of $3,220.

This example, involving a rather inexpensive and simple piece of income property, points up the advantages available to investors in real estate. In addition to the tax-free income feature, we must remember that the property in question is actually appreciating in value each year, and the monthly payments made by the tenants are used to pay off a loan, which results in an equity buildup for the owner.

An additional form, applicable to this chapter, is illustrated in Appendix C as Figure C10–1.

QUESTIONS FOR DISCUSSION

1. How can the taxpayer benefit by being able to classify a gain as capital rather than as ordinary?
2. Discuss the types of real property which qualify as Section 1231 property and the significance of this classification.
3. What are the factors leading to classification as a dealer rather than an investor?
4. What is the difference between a cost basis and an adjusted basis?
5. What is the difference between long-term and short-term capital gains?
6. Discuss the conditions which allow an owner to sell a principal residence and exclude payment of taxes on any gain.
7. What has the determination of estimated useful life to do with the subject of depreciation?
8. Discuss allowance of tax deductions with respect to business or vacation uses of residences.
9. What is meant by accelerated depreciation?
10. What are the three methods most commonly used in the calculation of depreciation?
11. What may be the advantage of selling property using an installment plan?
12. With respect to installment sales, what is meant by a 30 percent rule, and what is its present status?

11

Property management and leasing

In the real estate business, the specialized field of property management is a rapidly growing one. More and more licenses are devoting all of their time to the function of property management.

Since most brokerage offices must participate to a certain degree in the function of property management, all licensees should have at least an elementary knowledge of the general responsibilities and principles relating to management and leasing.

CERTIFIED PROPERTY MANAGER (CPM)

The Institute of Real Estate Management of the National Association of Realtors currently confers on those persons who meet their requirements the title of Certified Property Manager (CPM). To obtain this designation, a candidate must:

1. Be a member of a local real estate board or a member of the National Association of Realtors.
2. Have been actively engaged in the real estate management business in a responsible position for a minimum of three years.
3. Demonstrate his ability to manage real estate.
4. Pass certain minimum educational requirements.
5. Subscribe to the institute bylaws and pledge.
6. Give evidence of honesty and integrity.

Written examinations

In addition to the above requirements for the individual designation of Certified Property Manager, the candidate must:

1. Pass two written examinations prepared by the institute; or
2. Pass the examinations in the institute's Lecture Courses I and II, thereby eliminating part or all of the above examinations; or
3. Present proof of 15 years of active management experience in order to be allowed to take a special examination.

Certificate

A candidate who is accepted by the institute, having met all the requirements and passed all the necessary examinations, receives and may display an official certificate designating him a Certified Property Manager. The institute publishes *The Journal of Property Management*, issued quarterly.

TYPES OF PROPERTIES MANAGED

The most common types of properties managed for others are: office buildings, apartment buildings, commercial structures, residences, shopping centers, public buildings, recreational centers, hotels, motels, specialized factories, restaurants, and theaters. A few other types of special properties that have been gaining in importance in recent years are: parking lots, garages, harbors and their installations, and airports.

EMPLOYMENT OPPORTUNITIES

Individuals who are looking for a property management position should contact the property management departments of real estate firms and realize that property management departments are usually found in federal, state, and local governmental agencies and in commercial banks, savings and loan associations, real estate investment trusts, insurance companies, development and construction firms, and loan brokerage firms.

GOALS OF MANAGEMENT

Quite simply, the owner of a building wants to rent or lease space at a rate that will bring a sufficient return to enable him to pay the operating expenses, taxes, insurance, capital retirement, and other fixed charges and still show a certain return on the capital invested. The tenant wants to lease space at a rate that is within his income and will allow him to utilize the space at a profit to him.

To satisfy their requirements and those of their tenants, owners have found that the best method is to employ trained and experienced managers. The return far offsets the expense involved, and it is usually greater than the cost because a trained property manager is involved in the operation of the property.

CLASSIFICATION OF MANAGERS

The specific real estate management acts which require a real estate license are found in Section 10131 of the California Business and Professions Code. Basically, such acts include leasing or renting, offering to lease or rent, soliciting prospective tenants, and collecting rents. Individuals and companies who receive a compensation for performing such acts must generally be licensed. A license is not required for managers of auto and trailer parks, hotels, motels, or resident managers of apartment buildings.

There are generally three types of property managers—general property manager, individual building manager, and resident manager.

General property manager

This property manager is a licensee in a real estate office that manages a number of properties for various owners. He may devote his time exclusively to management, or he may be an active salesman and devote only a portion of his time to management.

Individual building manager

Certain properties are large enough in size to warrant full time attention by an individual property manager. A large urban office building or commercial complex are examples of such properties. Such a manager is usually paid a straight salary rather than being remunerated on a commission basis.

The resident manager (License Not Req'd)

The resident manager, or building superintendent as he is sometimes called, not only manages a property but also usually lives on the premises as well. He is generally employed by the real estate firm that manages the building or by the owner but is usually not a real estate licensee. The Institute of Real Estate Management of the National Association of Realtors offers special courses for resident managers, and those individuals who meet specific education and experience requirements receive the Accredited Resident Manager (ARM) recognition award.

In California, if an apartment building or complex has 16 or more residential units, a resident manager is required. If the owner resides on the premises, a resident manager is not required, and it is sufficient if there is a janitor or other resident of the building designated by the owner to respond to tenant complaints.

If the property consists of more than four but less than 16 dwelling units and the owner does not reside there, a written notice or sign must be affixed in plain view stating the name and address of the owner or his authorized agent.

FUNCTIONS AND SPECIFIC DUTIES

The professional property manager should:

1. *Be a specialist in merchandising.* He is selling a product, namely, the building he is managing. Whether he is showing an apartment or negotiating for the lease of commercial space, he must be able to sell the prospective tenant on the merits of his particular building.
2. *Be a leasing expert.* Leases can become quite complex and involved, and the property manager must be well versed in the different types and kinds of leases applicable or beneficial to particular types of clients.
3. *Have maintenance know-how.* One of the most important duties of the property manager is to take full charge of the maintenance problems inherent in the building under his direction.
4. *Understand accounting procedures.* Specialized records must be kept for any type of property. The manager must make reports to the owner and submit a detailed annual statement as well.
5. *Understand taxation aspects.* The effects of taxation are everywhere, and the property manager must understand property taxes and

their effect on the property under his control. He must understand the problems of depreciation that apply to the building owner and the relation of depreciation to the income and profit of the specific operation.

6. *Understand insurance.* Different forms of coverages must be carried on the property, and again there is a good deal of specialized knowledge that must be understood.
7. *Be a credit expert.* The credit rating of a prospective tenant is of vital importance to the manager, since he must be sure the tenant will be able to live up to the terms of his lease and is financially able to meet his obligations.
8. *Establish the rental schedule.* The manager must establish a proper rental schedule. He must make a thorough neighborhood analysis, which would include: (a) the character of the neighborhood, (b) economic level; (c) domestic status and family size; (d) availability of transportation, shopping, churches, schools, and recreational facilities; (e) physical aspects. The results of this survey must be related to the property under his control, and they will enable him to set up a realistic rent schedule to bring the maximum income to the owner.
9. *Supervise all purchasing.* The manager must know current prices for various items, and what is available on the market. He must keep up with technological advances in building materials and be able to get the best value for the money spent. In many cases, a worn-out item may be replaced with a new one of the same type, but quite often the manager has the opportunity to modernize and up-date the property by replacing an obsolete installation with a modern and more efficient one.
10. *Develop employee policies.* Many management operations succeed or fail in direct proportion to the ability of the manager to choose, train, and direct personnel. He must, therefore, know each job to be done so that he can properly direct those who do the job.
11. *Have a good general business background.* In addition to experience in the real estate business, a person who has the responsibility of managing properties worth thousands of dollars should have a solid background in general business and business administration

EARNINGS

The property management firm usually operates on a commission basis—that is, a percentage of the gross rent collected. The charge varies for different types of properties and in different areas and may be as low as 1 percent on a very large building and as high as 10 percent for a small residential building.

In addition to the commission, an additional fee is usually charged for the negotiation of new leases and for the supervision of major repairs or alterations to the building. Salaries for resident managers and office building managers depend largely on the local conditions and vary with the locale and size of the property involved.

MANAGEMENT CONTRACT

A management contract is a written contract that clearly sets forth the responsibilities of the broker and of the owner. It should indicate the terms and period of the contract, the policies pertaining to management of the building, management fees, and the authority and powers given by the owner to the broker who will manage the property.

Standard management agreement forms are available from local real estate boards. An excellent form, available from the California Association of Realtors, is reproduced in Fig. 11–1.

In his capacity as an agent, the manager is subject to all the legal restrictions imposed on an agent as well as to those specifically included in the contract.

LEASING

The negotiation of leases for clients is another part of the real estate licensee's everyday duties. Whatever his specialty may be, he must in varying degrees have a basic understanding of the landlord-tenant relationship and of the principles of leasing property.

We shall first discuss some of the basic principles of leases and leasehold estates and then continue with a detailed discussion of the leasing forms and conditions commonly in use. While the terms *landlord* and *tenant* apply to all rental situations, it is more correct to use the terms *lessor* and *lessee* when there is a written lease. Generally, however, the owner of the property is referred to as owner, lessor, or landlord. The person doing the renting is called the tenant or the lessee.

Origin of leases

Under the old English law, a distinction was made between freehold estates and less-than-free-

PROPERTY MANAGEMENT AGREEMENT

THIS IS INTENDED TO BE A LEGALLY BINDING AGREEMENT — READ IT CAREFULLY

CALIFORNIA ASSOCIATION OF REALTORS® STANDARD FORM

_____ (hereinafter "Owner"), and
_____ (hereinafter "Agent"),
agree as follows:

1. The owner hereby employs and grants Agent the exclusive right to rent, lease, operate and manage the property known as _____
_____
_____

upon the terms hereinafter set forth, for the period of _____ beginning on the date hereof and terminating the _____ day of _____, 19____; provided, however, that either party hereto may terminate this contract as of the _____ day of _____ during any year of the term hereof, by giving to the other party not less than 30 days prior written notice on an intention to so terminate.

2. Agent shall:
   (a) Use due diligence in the performance of this contract;
   (b) Render_____ statements of receipts, expenses and charges and to remit to Owner receipts less disbursements. In the
       monthly/other
       event the disbursements shall be in excess of the rents collected by the Agent, the Owner hereby agrees to pay such excess promptly upon demand of the Agent.
   (c) Accumulate as a reserve in the Owner's account each month approximately one-twelfth of the previous year's taxes, and bond payments or assessments, if any, and to pay same when due.
   (d) Deposit all receipts collected for Owner (less any sums properly deducted or otherwise provided herein) in a Trust account in a national or state institution qualified to engage in the banking or trust business, separate from Agent's personal account. However, Agent will not be held liable in event of bankruptcy or failure of a depository.
   (e) Bond by a fidelity bond in adequate amount any employee who handles or is responsible for Owner's monies.

3. The Owner grants Agent the following authority and powers and Owner shall pay the expenses in connection herewith:
   (a) To advertise the availability for rental of the herein described premises or any part thereof, and to display "for rent" signs thereof; to sign, renew or cancel leases for the premises or any part thereof; to collect rents or other charges and expenses due or to become due and give receipts therefor; to terminate tenancies and to sign and serve in the name of the Owner such notices as are appropriate; to institute and prosecute actions to evict tenants and to recover possession of said premises in the name of the Owner and recover rents and other sums due; and when expedient, to settle, compromise, and release such actions or suits or reinstate such tenancies. Any lease executed for the Owner by the Agent shall not exceed _____ years.
   (b) To make or cause to be made and supervise repairs and alterations, and to do decorating on said premises; to purchase supplies and pay all bills therefor. The Agent agrees to secure the prior approval of the Owner on all expenditures in excess of $ _____ for any one item, except monthly or recurring operating charges and emergency repairs in excess of the maximum, if in the opinion of the Agent such repairs are necessary to protect the property from damage or prevent damage to life or to the property of others or to avoid suspension of necessary services or to avoid penalties or fines or to maintain services to the tenants as called for in their leases.
   (c) To hire, discharge and supervise all labor and employees required for the operation and maintenance of the premises. Agent may perform any of its duties through Owner's attorneys, agents or employees and shall not be responsible for their acts, defaults or negligence if reasonable care has been exercised in their appointment and retention.
   (d) To make contracts for electricity, gas, fuel, water, telephone, window cleaning, ash or rubbish hauling and other services or such of them as the Agent shall deem advisable; the Owner to assume the obligation of any contract so entered into at the termination of this agreement.
   (e) To pay loan indebtedness, property and employees taxes, special assessments and insurance as designated by Owner.

4. The Owner shall:
   (a) Indemnify and save the Agent harmless from any and all costs, expenses, attorney's fees, suits, liabilities, damages or claim for damages, including but not limited to those arising out of any injury or death to any person or persons or damage to any property of any kind whatsoever and to whomsoever belonging, including Owner, in any way relating to the management of the premises by the Agent or the performance or exercise of any of the duties, obligations, powers or authorities herein or hereafter granted to the agent; to carry, at Owner's sole cost and expense, such public liability, property damage and worker's compensation insurance as shall be adequate to protect the interests of the Agent and Owner, the policies for which shall name the Agent as well as the Owner as the party insured.

FORM PMA-14

For these forms, address — California Association of Realtors®
505 Shatto Place, Los Angeles, California 90020
Copyright © 1977 California Association of Realtors® (Revised 1977)

FIGURE 11-1

(b) To pay the Agent:

    (1) For Management _____

    (2) For Leasing _____

    (3) In the event that the Owners shall request the Agent to undertake work exceeding that usual to normal management, then a fee shall be agreed upon for such services before the work begins. Normal management does not include modernization, refinancing, fire restoration, major rehabilitations, obtaining income tax advice, presenting petitions to planning or zoning committees, advising on proposed new construction or other counseling.

    (4) For assignment: The Owner hereby agrees that Agent may be compensated by the party or parties requesting an assignment of lease for services rendered in negotiating the consent of assignment.

    (5) Other _____
_____
_____

5. If it shall become necessary for Agent or Owner to give notice of any kind, the same shall be written, and served, by sending such notice by certified mail to the address shown under their signature.

6. This Agreement shall be binding upon the successors of the Agent, and the heirs, administrators, executors, successors and assigns of the Owner.

Parties acknowledge having read the foregoing prior to execution and receipt of a duplicate original dated this _____ day of _____ 19____.

WITNESS:

_____

_____

_____
OWNER

_____
ADDRESS

_____
AGENT

_____
ADDRESS

NO REPRESENTATION IS MADE AS TO THE LEGAL VALIDITY OF ANY PROVISION OR THE ADEQUACY OF ANY PROVISION IN ANY SPECIFIC TRANSACTION. A REAL ESTATE BROKER IS THE PERSON QUALIFIED TO ADVISE ON REAL ESTATE. IF YOU DESIRE LEGAL ADVICE CONSULT YOUR ATTORNEY.

FORM PMA-14

FIGURE 11-1 *(continued)*

hold estates. It is from the less-than-freehold estates classification that leases as we know them today are derived. The main feature of a leasehold estate is the degree of possession the lessee (tenant) has in the land and/or building of the lessor (owner).

During the term of the lease, the lessor has parted with his right of exclusive possession and has merely the basic title, called reversion, during the existence of the lease. A lease is usually referred to as a leasehold estate and is normally considered to be a form of personal property.

Types of leasehold estates

There are four basic types of leases, distinguished by the length of their duration: (1) tenancy for years, (2) periodic tenancy, (3) tenancy at will, (4) tenancy at sufferance.

Tenancy for years. This is the most common type of leasehold. The tenancy for years is for a fixed period of time, agreed on by the lessor and the lessee. The name is misleading, since the lease does not have to be for an even amount of years but rather for any agreed-on period of time. It may be for a number of years, months, or weeks. Under this type of lease, the lessee has the right to exclusive possession for a fixed period of time, agreed to by both parties, and usually shown on the face of the lease agreement.

Periodic tenancy. A periodic tenancy is created by the lessor and lessee to continue for successive periods of the same length, unless sooner terminated by notice. This type of tenancy does not terminate merely by the passing of time but, instead, is deemed to be renewed at the end of each of the periods by which the payment of rent is determined.

A periodic tenancy may be created when a lease runs out and the lessee remains and pays rent, which is accepted by the lessor. In this case, the tenancy is not renewed for the term of the original lease but rather for the amount of time equal to the time between rent payments.

The most common type of periodic tenancy is a tenancy from month to month. In the absence of any agreement respecting the length of time or the rent, the tenancy is presumed to be monthly. A periodic tenancy is usually terminated by giving a 30-day notice to the tenant if the rent is paid on a monthly basis or a notice equal to whatever number of days usually elapses between the payment of rent.

Tenancy at will. A tenancy at will is created by agreement between the parties involved but has no fixed term and is terminable at the will of either party. Originally, no notice had to be given to terminate this type of tenancy, but today most states require that some form of notice must be given.

Tenancy at sufferance. A tenant at sufferance is one who originally had lawful possession but whose right to remain on the premises has now passed. The owner may treat him as a trespasser, and he is not entitled to notice prior to ejection by owner. Some states require that notice be given even under this type of tenancy, but it is usually for a very few days. If, however, the owner of the property accepts the payment of rent from the tenant at sufferance, this type of tenancy usually ceases, and the person in possession becomes either a tenant at will or a periodic tenant.

Requirements for creation of a lease

A lease is a contract and is generally required to be in writing if its terms is one year or more. As a practical matter, it is wise business procedure to have all leases in writing, regardless of the term, to avoid any misunderstanding between the parties involved.

The lease should contain the names of the parties, a description of the property, amount of the rent, and length of time the lease will continue. In addition, there are usually many special conditions and clauses on the standard form.

The lessor must sign the lease and deliver it to the lessee. While it does not have to be signed by the lessee, it is common practice for the lessee to sign a copy and return it to the lessor. When the lessee enters into possession of the property and pays his rent, he automatically signifies his intent to agree to and abide by the provisions in the lease, even though he may not have signed and returned a copy of the lease.

As in any other contract, both parties to the lease are bound by the conditions in it, and any change in these terms and conditions must be agreed to by the parties involved. The lease may be recorded in the county where the property is located if the signature of the lessor is acknowledged, usually by a notary public, and such recordation will give constructive notice to all of the existence of the lease and the property involved.

Rights and obligations of the parties

The rights and obligations of the parties to a lease are varied and at times quite complex and should be adequately covered by the provisions of the lease agreement.

Some of the more important subjects to be covered, no matter how simple or complicated the form of the lease may be, are: (1) duration, (2) rent, (3) maintenance and improvements, (4) liability, (5) transfer by lessee, (6) termination, (7) special conditions and provisions.

Analysis of lease form

We shall use as an example of a standard lease—the form prepared and distributed by the California Association of Realtors and reproduced in Figure 11-2. Some of the provisions of the lease are self-explanatory, while others require some additional comments as follows:

1. The date on which the lease is made out is entered, together with the name of the lessor (landlord) and lessee (tenant), followed by the address, location, and description of the property leased, and including any special furnishings and fixtures.

2. Next, the term of the lease is stated. A space is provided for entering the exact data of beginning and ending of lease duration. Although there is generally no restriction to the amount of time property may be leased for, it is interesting to note that in some areas there are local laws and restrictions concerning the term. These often occur with respect to mineral, oil, and gas lands, and to property owned by a government or municipality.

Rent

3. Rent is the consideration paid by the tenant for use of the property. The lease should clearly state the amount of the rent in total and then set forth when, where, how, and in what amounts the rent is to be paid to the lessor by the lessee.

Sometimes, the lessor may ask the lessee for the first and last month's rent in advance at the time the lease is drawn up and signed by the parties. The Internal Revenue Service will consider this last month's rent as "prepaid rent," and the lessor must declare this as income in the year received. Many times, when the lessor collects an additional amount of rent in advance, the lessee may feel that should he decide to move from the premises, notice is unnecessary since the lessor will keep the additional amount.

In order to avoid declaring this prepaid rent as income in the year received, or risking the lessee's moving without notice, the lessor should call the extra money a security deposit. If he does this, the money need not be declared as income, and the lessee will still be obligated to pay the last month's rent when it is due. The security deposit then is returned when the lease terminates.

Security

4. The California legislature has resolved an area of confusion surrounding such terms in the landlord-tenant vocabulary as "cleaning deposit, rent guarantee and breakage fee" by including these terms in a single category to be called "Security."

Assembly Bill 94, effective January 1978, uses the single term *security* and defines it to mean any payment, fee, deposit or charge, including but not limited to an advance payment of rent, used or to be used for any purpose.

According to the new law, a security may not be greater than the equivalent of two months' rent for unfurnished residential property (three months' rent for furnished residential property) in addition to any rent paid *in advance* for the first month's rent. When the term of the lease is six months or longer, larger initial deposits are permitted.

The new law provides, among other things, that the landlord may use the security to:

Compensate for a tenant's failure to pay rent.

Repair damages (other than ordinary wear and tear) to the property caused by the tenant.

Clean the property upon termination of the tenancy.

The landlord holds the security *for the tenant*. After the tenancy is terminated and the tenant has moved out, the landlord has two weeks in which to return any unused security and to explain in writing how the remainder was used.

If a landlord unjustifiably claims any portion of a security, the landlord may be liable to pay the tenant $200 in punitive damages in addition to any actual damages. The landlord has the burden of proving the reasonableness of the amounts of the security not refunded to the former tenant.

The landlord may not attempt to avoid the provisions of this law by referring to the security furnished by the tenant as "nonrefundable." The law prohibits such characterization of a security, and such action might be construed as a bad faith claim, subjecting the landlord to payment of damages.

If a landlord conveys rental real property to another person, the landlord can do one of two things with the security being held for tenants (a real estate broker negotiating the sale or exchange should inform the seller of seller's obligation and, if so instructed by the seller, the broker may act on behalf of the seller in fulfilling these obligations):

RESIDENTIAL LEASE

THIS IS INTENDED TO BE A LEGALLY BINDING AGREEMENT — READ IT CAREFULLY

CALIFORNIA ASSOCIATION OF REALTORS® STANDARD FORM

_____, California _____ 19_____
_____, Landlord, and
_____, Tenant, agree as follows:

    1. Landlord leases to Tenant and Tenant hires from Landlord those premises described as: _____

together with the following furniture, and appliances, if any, and fixtures: _____

(Insert "as shown on Exhibit A attached hereto" and attach the exhibit if the list is extensive.)

    2. The term of this lease shall be for a period of _____ months; _____ years commencing _____ 19_____ and terminating _____ 19____.

    3. Tenant is to pay a total rent of $_____, payable as follows: _____

The rent shall be paid at_____
or at any address designated by the Landlord in writing.

    4. $_____ as security has been deposited. Landlord may use therefrom such amounts as are reasonably necessary to remedy Tenant's defaults in the payment of rent, to repair damages caused by Tenant, and to clean the premises upon termination of tenancy. If used toward rent or damages during the term of tenancy, Tenant agrees to reinstate said total security deposit upon five days written notice delivered to Tenant in person or by mailing. Balance of security deposit, if any, shall be mailed to Tenant at last known address within 14 days of surrender of premises.

    5. Tenant agrees to pay for all utilities and services based upon occupancy of the premises and the following charges: _____

except _____
which shall be paid for by Landlord.

    6. Tenant has examined the premises and all furniture, furnishings and appliances if any, and fixtures contained therein, and accepts the same as being clean, in good order, condition, and repair, with the following exceptions: _____

    7. The premises are leased for use as a residence by the following named persons: _____

No animal, bird, or pet except _____
shall be kept on or about the premises without Landlord's prior written consent.

    8. Any holding over at the expiration of this lease shall create a month to month tenancy at a monthly rent of $_____
payable in advance. All other terms and conditions herein shall remain in full force and effect.

    9. Tenant shall not disturb, annoy, endanger or interfere with other Tenants of the building or neighbors, nor use the premises for any unlawful purposes, nor violate any law or ordinance, nor commit waste or nuisance upon or about the premises.

    10. Tenant agrees to comply with all reasonable rules or regulations posted on the premises or delivered to Tenant by Landlord.

    11. Tenant shall keep the premises and furniture, furnishings and appliances, if any, and fixtures which are leased for his exclusive use in good order and condition and pay for any repairs to the property caused by Tenant's negligence or misuse or that of Tenant's invitees. Landlord shall otherwise maintain the property. Tenant's personal property is not insured by Landlord.

    12. Tenant shall not paint, wallpaper, nor make alterations to the property without Landlord's prior written consent.

    13. Upon not less than 24 hours advance notice, Tenant shall make the demised premises available during normal business hours to Landlord or his authorized agent or representative, for the purpose of entering (a) to make necessary agreed repairs, decorations, alterations or improvements or to supply necessary or agreed services, and (b) to show the premises to prospective or actual purchasers, mortgagees, tenants, workmen or contractors. In an emergency, Landlord, his agent or authorized representative may enter the premises at any time without securing prior permission from Tenant for the purpose of making corrections or repairs to alleviate such emergency.

    14. Tenant shall not let or sublet all or any part of the premises nor assign this lease or any interest in it without the prior written consent of Landlord.

    15. If Tenant abandons or vacates the premises, Landlord may at his option terminate this lease, and regain possession in the manner prescribed by law.

    16. If any legal action or proceeding be brought by either party to enforce any part of this lease, the prevailing party shall recover in addition to all other relief, reasonable attorney's fees and costs.

    17. Time is of the essence. The waiver by Landlord or Tenant of any breach shall not be construed to be a continuing waiver of any subsequent breach.

    18. Notice upon Tenant shall be served as provided by law. Notice upon Landlord may be served upon Manager of the demised premises at _____. Said Manager is authorized to accept service on behalf of Landlord.

    19. Within 10 days after written notice, Tenant agrees to execute and deliver a certificate as submitted by Landlord acknowledging that this agreement is unmodified and in full force and effect or in full force and effect as modified and stating the modifications. Failure to comply shall be deemed Tenant's acknowledgement that the certificate as submitted by Landlord is true and correct and may be relied upon by any lender or purchaser.

    20. The undersigned Tenant acknowledges having read the foregoing prior to execution and receipt of a copy hereof.

Landlord _____ _____ Tenant

Landlord _____ _____ Tenant

NO REPRESENTATION IS MADE AS TO THE LEGAL VALIDITY OF ANY PROVISION OR THE ADEQUACY OF ANY PROVISION IN ANY SPECIFIC TRANSACTION. A REAL ESTATE BROKER IS THE PERSON QUALIFIED TO ADVISE ON REAL ESTATE. IF YOU DESIRE LEGAL ADVICE CONSULT YOUR ATTORNEY.

For these forms, address — California Association of Realtors®
505 Shatto Place, Los Angeles, California 90020
Copyright ©1977 California Association of Realtors® (Revised 1977) LR-14

FIGURE 11-2

TENANT APPLICATION

Property Address: _____ Apt. No. _____

Name(s) of Applicant(s): _____

Other Name(s) used within last 3 years: _____

Names and Age of other Occupants: _____

_____

Pets (Number & Type): _____

Present Address: _____

    How long? _____ Reason for leaving: _____

    Name and Address of Owner or Owner's Agent: _____

Previous Address (Past 3 Years): _____

    How long? _____ Reason for leaving: _____

    Name and Address of Owner or Owner's Agent: _____

Previous Address (Past 3 Years): _____

    How long? _____ Reason for leaving: _____

    Name and Address of Owner or Owner's Agent: _____

Employment: Social Security Number _____ Drivers License Number _____

    Present Employer: _____ How long? _____

    Address: _____ Telephone: _____

    Employed as: _____ Salary: $ _____ per _____

Employment of any other Occupant: Social Security Number _____ Drivers License Number _____

    Present Employer _____ How long? _____

    Address: _____ Telephone: _____

    Employed as: _____ Salary: $ _____ per _____

Other Income: $ _____ Source: _____

Credit References (2): _____

Credit Cards: Issuer _____ Acct. No. _____ Issuer _____ Acct. No. _____

_____

Automobile License No. _____ State of Registry: _____

    Make & Model: _____ Year: _____ Color: _____

<u>IN CASE OF EMERGENCY</u>:

Name of Closest Relative: _____ Relationship: _____

    Address: _____ Telephone: _____

AUTHORIZATION TO VERIFY INFORMATION

I Authorize Landlord or his Authorized Agents to Verify the above information, including but not limited to obtaining a Credit Report and if this application is accepted I agree to execute the residential lease or rental agreement as set forth on the reverse side hereof.

Date _____ 19 _____ Applicant: _____

Telephone No. _____ Applicant: _____

    RECEIPT FOR DEPOSIT

        The undersigned acknowledges receipt of $ _____ in the form of ( ) Cash, ( ) Personal Check

        or ( ) _____ payable to _____ as deposit on the above described property.

Date _____ Agent _____

FIGURE 11–2 *(continued)*

Transfer the security to the new owner/landlord and notify the tenant by personal delivery or certified mail of such transfer, setting forth any claims made against the security. The notice must include the new security holder's name, address, and telephone number. If personal delivery is made, the tenant must acknowledge receipt on the landlord's copy by signing his name.

Alternatively, the landlord may return the security to the tenant after making any lawful deductions and furnishing a written itemized accounting to the tenant.

5. An apartment or flat may be let on a rental basis that includes all utilities or one that has the lessee pay all utilities. Whatever the arrangement, it should be clearly stated in the lease. Many times, the lessor will pay for certain utilities—the most common is water—and the lessee will pay for others.

6. This is an excellent provision which will prevent arguments at the termination of the lease with respect to what particular damage the tenants may have done to the premises.

7. This, again, is a common provision that will keep the lessee from allowing additional individuals to move into the premises. In a building containing many dwelling units, it is important that the lessor exercise control over the number of individuals living in any unit. The lessor also has the right to either restrict or allow pets.

Provisions 8, 9, and 10 are self-explanatory.

Maintenance, repairs, and injury

11. This provision states that the lessee shall keep the premises in good condition. This means that except for the normal expected wear and tear, the tenant in possession should not damage the premises.

With respect to injury, the general rule is that when all the premises are leased, the lessor is not liable for injuries to the tenant or others resulting from the defective condition of the premises. Such a condition results when the lessee leases an entire building from the lessor. Usually, however, a lessee is leasing only an apartment or a flat in a building containing other apartments or dwelling units. In such a situation, the lessor has a direct responsibility with regard to entrances, common hallways and stairs, and the elevator. If it can be shown that an injury was due to negligence on the part of the lessor and such negligence can be proven, the lessor probably will be held liable and have to pay damages. The lessee, however, is responsible for injuries occurring within his own dwelling unit.

Practically speaking, it is almost impossible to find an owner of rental property who does not carry some form of public liability insurance and other coverages to afford him protection in such cases. The tenant usually carries protective insurance also, and quite often, the lease is drawn to make this a requirement on the part of the lessee.

12. The lessee is told in this provision that the lessor must approve any painting or alterations which the lessee may desire to make. The owner of a building must be careful with respect to liability for any work done on the premises. If he has not ordered the work and does not want to be held responsible for payment, he must notify the individual performing the work of this fact. This is usually done on a form called a Notice of Nonresponsibility. Failure to do so may result in the owner's having to pay for work he did not order. The lessor should have a clear understanding with the lessee regarding this entire area of maintenance and repairs, and each should fully understand his responsibilities.

Reentry by lessor

13. This provision clarifies the lessor's right of entry. Some lease agreements state that if the lessee fails to pay rent or breaks any provision of the lease, that the lessor may enter the premises and remove occupants and possessions.

The lessor must be extremely careful with regard to his actions in this respect. Should he enter the premises and remove the personal effects of the lessee, he may be open to a suit for any injury or damage to the personal effects. Should the lessor enter the premises and forceably evict the lessee, he may be open to suit for any physical injury the lessee may claim.

Assign or sublet

14. This provision requires lessor's approval if the lessee wishes to sublet or assign the lease. If the lessor gives the lessee permission to assign his rights to another, the individual to whom the rights are assigned now assumes all the rights, duties, and responsibilities the original lessee had with respect to the lease.

If a lessee merely sublets the premises, he continues to be responsible to the lessor for payment of the rent. In this case, the sublessee must pay the original lessee who in turn pays the lessor.

15. The lessor must be sure that the lessee actually abandons or vacates the premises.

Provisions 16, 17, 18, 19, and 20 are self-explanatory.

The lease we have been using as an example is relatively simple with a minimum of provisions. It is not uncommon for a lease to contain anywhere from a dozen provisions up to as many as 50 separate provisions and conditions. The larger the property and the more complicated its use, the longer and more complex is the form of the lease.

ADDITIONAL CLAUSES FOR THE LEASE FORM

In addition to the provisions shown in our illustration lease, a few more which are commonly used are now presented for your information.

1. "The roof and exterior walls of the premises are not subject to this lease, and exclusive rights to the use thereof are reserved by the lessor." Such a provision may be necessary when large outdoor signs or other advertising matter are affixed to the walls or on the roof, for which the owner receives additional income.

2. "No signs, advertisements, or notices shall be inscribed, painted, or affixed to the outside or inside of the premises without the express consent of the lessor." This is a typical provision which allows the lessor to control an area that can often lead to problems. When a building is leased to a number of tenants for dwelling purposes, the lessor may not want tenants to erect signs of a commercial nature. Typical of these are such signs as "Alterations" or "Notary Public" or "Watch Repairing."

3. "Water beds are not allowed on the premises without the prior approval of the lessor." Some water beds hold over 200 gallons of water and weigh approximately 2,000 pounds, and excessive damage due to weight or water leakage may result.

Termination of the lease

There are many ways and differing reasons for which a lease agreement may be terminated by both or one of the parties involved. The more common are the following.

Expiration of the term. A lease is most commonly terminated when the end of the term agreed on in the lease has been reached. A lease should have some specific provision concerning what is to occur at the end of the term. The lessee may be given an option to renew on the same terms and conditions, he may be given the right only to negotiate a new lease, or he may be given notice by the lessor that he is to surrender the premises.

By tenant for failure of owner to provide quiet possession. A lessee is entitled to quiet possession of the premises he has leased. He is entitled to reasonable privacy and enjoyment, and failure of the lessor to provide such conditions is grounds for termination of the lease by the lessee. This is known as constructive eviction.

Although the lessee has the right to reasonable privacy, most leases give the lessor the right to enter and inspect the premises in order to make repairs and alterations that may be necessary or for the purpose of showing the property to prospective tenants during the closing weeks of the lease.

By tenant for owner's refusal to repair. Under most lease forms, the lessee is responsible for keeping the premises in good normal repair and for making minor repairs that may be necessary. The lessor is generally responsible for any major repairs that must be made. He is further responsible for any major structural repairs needed and cannot allow the building to become so dilapidated that it is no longer fit for occupancy. If the premises in question is a dwelling unit and if the owner refuses to make necessary repairs after being notified by the tenant, the tenant may either spend up to one month's rent for repairs or abandon the premises and not be responsible for further payment of rent or performance of other conditions in the lease.

As the result of eviction. Eviction is the dispossession of the lessee by the lessor. Actual eviction by law occurs after a lessor has brought action against the lessee, usually for failure to pay rent, and, on receiving an order from the court, has the lessee evicted. Constructive eviction occurs when a lessee is denied quiet enjoyment, or privacy, and therefore moves from the premises. When there is an eviction by law, the lessee may be liable for any monetary damages suffered by the lessor. When a constructive eviction occurs, the lessee is usually not required to pay the rent remaining in the lease.

By either party on destruction of the premises. Should the premises be destroyed, there is usually an automatic termination. If the damage is slight, however, the tenant may want to remain while the lessor makes the necessary repairs.

By either party on breach of a condition of the lease. Since violation of one of the conditions of the lease may result in termination, it is important that the lessor and lessee fully understand the provisions and terms of the lease they have signed.

By mutual agreement of the parties to the lease. Termination of the lease by mutual agreement is commonly called "surrender" and may be accomplished in two ways—by (1) mutual agreement and (2) operation of law.

Termination accomplished by mutual agreement is quite a simple matter. Parties to a lease frequently agree to its termination. The main point is that such termination must be by mutual agreement, and one party cannot force the other to terminate without a good and valid reason if the party does not want to do so.

Termination by operation of law is more complex and is usually the result of a court action. An example might be that of a lessee who moves out of an apartment without giving notice. The lessor subsequently reenters and takes possession. The lessor will then have a cause for court action and would probably bring suit to recover the remainder of the rent due under the terms of the lease. Generally, the lessor will attempt to re-lease the property and will be allowed to recover only the actual amount he loses plus any expenses incurred in repairing or cleaning the premises before leasing them again.

REMEDIES OF THE LESSOR

In our discussion thus far, we have touched on some of the remedies available to the lessor against the lessee. The same remedies are available as between a landlord and tenant when there is no lease and the tenancy is on a monthly basis. In such cases, the owner may recover possession of the premises by giving a 30-day notice to the tenant to vacate the premises.

The following is the legal process for eviction:
1. Three-day notice to pay rent or comply with a provision of the lease or rental agreement is given;
2. Complaint in unlawful detainer is filed with municipal clerk and summons is issued;
3. Summons and complaint served on tenant;
4. The tenant has the legal right to file a pleading in answer to the complaint, and in this event, a trial will be held.

If the tenant does not file a pleading and answer to the complaint, the following action will be taken:

5. Default of tenant is taken;
6. Default judgment is received;
7. Municipal court clerk issues writ of possession;
8. Writ of possession, instruction to sheriff, and approximately two hundred and fifty dollars ($250.00) is delivered to the sheriff;
9. Sheriff evicts tenant and stores furnishings.

Although the lessor has these specific remedies at law, in practice it is better if litigation can be avoided. Court proceedings are expensive when one considers the attorney's fee, and if the sheriff must evict the tenant, further expenses accrue to the owner of the property. Even though the lessor may be entitled to recover these expenses from the lessee, it usually follows that one who cannot pay his rent, if this is the reason for the eviction, will also be unable to pay any judgment.

Recent legislative enactments have substantially increased an owner's responsibility toward his tenants and require all rentals to be fit for human habitation. The basic items which must exist to meet the necessary standards are heating, plumbing, and effective weather protection. The premises must also be sanitary and in a reasonably safe condition.

Utility shut-offs

The law now provides increased financial liability for owners who willfully cause any interruption of utilities to tenants if the owner is acting with intent to evict a tenant. The owner can be liable for any expenses incurred by the tenant due to utility shut-offs.

Preventing access

An additional Civil Code section now makes it unlawful for an owner to prevent a tenant from gaining access to the property by locks being changed or any other such means. In addition, the owner cannot enter the premises and remove any of the tenants belongings if the intent is to evict the tenant.

Retaliatory eviction

If an owner attempts to evict a tenant for making repairs and deducting any costs from the rent or reporting the owner to some governmental agency, it is referred to as retaliatory eviction. The law provides for a 180-day period during which no such eviction can take place. The owner is prohibited from raising rent or taking any eviction action for a period of 180 days following the date the tenant has exercised any legal rights or reported any violations.

Proper maintenance

While the law requires an owner to maintain property in a clean and safe condition, the tenant must also maintain property and not cause any willful damage to the premises. The law excuses an owner from repairing damaged premises caused by any of the tenants.

Rental determination

Since there are various methods of determining the amount of rent to be charged under a lease, especially in commercial leases, several different types of leases have evolved. Among the more common are the gross lease, the net lease, and the percentage lease. All of these derive their names from the method used in the rental determination.

Gross lease. In this type of arrangement, the lessee pays to the lessor a fixed rate of rent at fixed periods of time. The lessor must pay the property taxes, the necessary insurance, the general upkeep, and the major repairs. The lessor, then, must regard the rent he receives as a gross rent. At the end of the year, he will determine the amount of his expenses over the year and deduct this from the gross rent to arrive at the actual net rental received.

Net lease. Under the net lease, the lessee pays all the taxes, insurance, and other general expenses involved in operation of the property, and the lessor receives a net rental figure. This arrangement is most commonly found in long-term business and commercial leases. The property owner wants a clear return to him and wants the tenant to take care of all maintenance and operating expenses. The lessor receives a steady profit on his investment, and on his income tax return, the lessee can deduct all amounts paid for rent, expenses, taxes, and maintenance in connection with the property.

Percentage lease. The amount of rent to be paid under a percentage lease is related to the gross amount of sales completed by the lessee. The percentage may be applied in various ways.

The rent may be stated as a fixed amount plus a percent applied to all gross sales in excess of a certain amount. Some leases state a fixed amount plus a percent of gross sales with a guaranteed minimum or a guaranteed minimum and maximum. Finally, the lease may state the rent only in terms of a certain percent of the gross or net sales of the lessee. The most common practice is to specify a fixed amount of rent plus a percentage agreement of some type.

The National Association of Realtors quotes the following as the most frequent percentages of gross sales used in percentage leases on certain types of businesses:

	%
Discount stores	
Appliances, radio, and TV	3
Bakery	6
Barber shop, beauty shop	8
Camera shop	6
Cleaner, laundry	10
Bar	7
Department store	2½
Drugstore	5
Florist	6
Furniture store	2½
Gift shop	6
Hardware store	4
Liquor store	5
Meat market	2
Men's wear, women's wear, and apparel	5
Paint store or variety	4
Shoe store	6
Supermarket-foods	1
Restaurant	5

Oil, gas, and mineral leases

In many parts of the country, real estate brokers specialize in leases that give rights to something contained under the surface of the land rather than on it. Large oil companies lease land they think contains gas or oil. The owner generally receives a flat fee or rental for allowing the company to drill on the land. Then, if the wells begin to actually produce, the owner will receive an additional amount, commonly called a royalty.

Ground lease

A ground lease, as the name implies, is a lease for unimproved property for a term of years. Such a lease is often made in connection with a large commercial or recreational development, and the land is quite often used for garage or parking purposes. Such leases often provide for the erection of improvements by the lessee, and these improvements ultimately become the property of the lessor.

Sale-and-leaseback

Sale-and-leaseback arrangements are often used by large business concerns. A simple illustration is a firm that cannot find the kind of building or facility in the particular location it wants. If sufficient capital is available, it can have a building constructed and then enter into a sale-and-leaseback arrangement with an investor. The firm now has the building it wants; it gets its investment back

RESIDENTIAL RENTAL AGREEMENT
(Month To Month Tenancy)

THIS IS INTENDED TO BE A LEGALLY BINDING AGREEMENT — READ IT CAREFULLY

CALIFORNIA ASSOCIATION OF REALTORS® STANDARD FORM

_____, California _____ 19____
_____, Landlord, and
_____, Tenant, agree as follows:

    1. Landlord rents to Tenant and Tenant hires from Landlord those premises described as: _____
_____
_____
together with the following furniture, and appliances, if any, and fixtures: _____
_____

(Insert "as shown on Exhibit A attached hereto" and attach the exhibit if the list is extensive.)

    2. The term shall commence on _____, 19 _____, and shall continue from month to month. This rental agreement may be terminated at any time by either party by giving written notice 30 days in advance.

    Tenant agrees to pay $ _____ rent per month payable in advance on the _____ day of each month and $ _____ representing prorated rent from date of possession.

    3. The rent shall be paid at _____
or at any address designated by the Landlord in writing.

    4. $ _____ as security has been deposited. Landlord may use therefrom such amounts as are reasonably necessary to remedy Tenant's defaults in the payment of rent, to repair damages caused by Tenant, and to clean the premises if necessary upon termination of tenancy. If used toward rent or damages during the term of tenancy, Tenant agrees to reinstate said total security deposit upon five days written notice delivered to Tenant in person or by mailing. Security deposit or balance thereof, if any, shall be mailed to Tenant at last known address within 14 days of surrender of premises.

    5. Tenant agrees to pay for all utilities and services based upon occupancy of the premises and the following charges: _____
except _____
which shall be paid for by Landlord.

    6. Tenant has examined the premises and all furniture, furnishings and appliances if any, and fixtures contained therein, and accepts the same as being clean, in good order, condition, and repair, with the following exceptions: _____
_____

    7. The premises are rented for use as a residence by the following named persons: _____
_____

No animal, bird, or pet except _____
shall be kept on or about the premises without Landlord's prior written consent.

    8. Tenant shall not disturb, annoy, endanger or interfere with other Tenants of the building or neighbors, nor use the premises for any unlawful purposes, nor violate any law or ordinance, nor commit waste or nuisance upon or about the premises.

    9. Tenant agrees to comply with all reasonable rules or regulations posted on the premises or delivered to Tenant by Landlord.

    10. Tenant shall keep the premises and furniture, furnishings and appliances, if any, and fixtures which are rented for his exclusive use in good order and condition and pay for any repairs to the property caused by Tenant's negligence or misuse or that of Tenant's invitees. Landlord shall otherwise maintain the property. Tenant's personal property is not insured by Landlord.

    11. Tenant shall not paint, wallpaper, nor make alterations to the property without Landlord's prior written consent.

    12. Upon not less than 24 hours advance notice, Tenant shall make the demised premises available during normal business hours to Landlord or his authorized agent or representative, for the purpose of entering (a) to make necessary agreed repairs, decorations, alterations or improvements or to supply necessary or agreed services, and (b) to show the premises to prospective or actual purchasers, mortgagees, tenants, workmen or contractors. In an emergency, Landlord, his agent or authorized representative may enter the premises at any time without securing prior permission from Tenant for the purpose of making corrections or repairs to alleviate such emergency.

    13. Tenant shall not let or sublet all or any part of the premises nor assign this agreement or any interest in it without the prior written consent of Landlord.

    14. If Tenant abandons or vacates the premises, Landlord may at his option terminate this agreement, and regain possession in the manner prescribed by law.

    15. If any legal action or proceeding be brought by either party to enforce any part of this agreement, the prevailing party shall recover in addition to all other relief, reasonable attorney's fees and costs.

    16. Time is of the essence. The waiver by Landlord or Tenant of any breach shall not be construed to be a continuing waiver of any subsequent breach.

    17. Notice upon Tenant shall be served as provided by law. Notice upon Landlord may be served upon Manager of the demised premises _____
at _____. Said Manager is authorized to accept service on behalf of Landlord.

    18. Within 10 days after written notice, Tenant agrees to execute and deliver a certificate as submitted by Landlord acknowledging that this agreement is unmodified and in full force and effect or in full force and effect as modified and stating the modifications. Failure to comply shall be deemed Tenant's acknowledgement that the certificate as submitted by Landlord is true and correct and may be relied upon by any lender or purchaser.

    19. The undersigned Tenant acknowledges having read the foregoing prior to execution and receipt of a copy hereof.

Landlord _____ _____ Tenant

Landlord _____ _____ Tenant

NO REPRESENTATION IS MADE AS TO THE LEGAL VALIDITY OF ANY PROVISION OR THE ADEQUACY OF ANY PROVISION IN ANY SPECIFIC TRANSACTION. A REAL ESTATE BROKER IS THE PERSON QUALIFIED TO ADVISE ON REAL ESTATE. IF YOU DESIRE LEGAL ADVICE CONSULT YOUR ATTORNEY.

For these forms, address — California Association of Realtors®
505 Shatto Place, Los Angeles, California 90020
Copyright © 1977 California Association of Realtors® (Revised 1977)

FIGURE 11-3

at the time of the sale; and it has a long-term lease for use of the building. Since the former owner is now in the position of being a lessee, all rent payments plus maintenance and repair costs are tax deductible. The same arrangement can be used for an existing building on which a substantial amount of the allowable depreciation has already been taken by the owner.

The benefits to the investor should be an excellent long-term tenant and the depreciation allowance available as an offset against the income. Sales-and-leaseback is also correctly classified as a form of financing device for the firm that utilizes this method. Sears, Roebuck and Company has extensively used the sale-and-leaseback method in establishing new retail outlets, and large insurance companies have been the purchasers.

A recapture provision may be incorporated into a sale-and-leaseback arrangement to allow the original owner to reacquire the property at the end of the lease term. Such an arrangement is quite complex, however, because of the effect of certain Internal Revenue Service tax rules and regulations.

Lease-option arrangement

During a time when loans are not easily available or when a purchaser does not have a sufficient down payment, a lease-option arrangement, or lease-purchase agreement as it is sometimes called, may be used. In this method, the prospective purchaser leases the property desired with an option to purchase at a later date for an agreed-on price. Usually, a certain amount of credit against the purchase price will be given for rent paid before exercise of the option to purchase.

RESIDENTIAL RENTAL AGREEMENT

Written agreements for a tenancy on a month-to-month basis are becoming increasingly popular throughout the country. Month-to-month agreements contain many of the provisions found in a standard residential lease and are used for apartments, flats, duplexes, and other common types of residential dwelling units. An example of such an agreement is the CAR Residential Rental Agreement, which appears in Figure 11–3. The reverse side of the Residential Rental Agreement contains the same tenant application form as the residential lease, Figure 11–2.

Basically, these agreements provide for a stated monthly rental, a cleaning charge, and often an initial deposit put up by the tenant at the time the agreement is signed. The cleaning charge is forfeited in part or whole by the tenant for property damage and/or cleaning required at the end of the agreement term. The deposit may also be forfeited if the tenant vacates the premises without giving proper notice as set forth in the agreement.

The amount of the deposit may be more than, less than, or equal to the rent for one month. This depends on the custom in a particular area or on the desire of the landlord. It is only natural that such a form should have come into wide usage. If the tenant vacates an apartment or other dwelling unit before the end of the lease term under a standard lease, the lessor may then go to court to try to recover damages, if any. However, the lessor can usually only collect the actual amount of rent lost. In most cases, the property owner will try to rerent the premises as soon as possible and will be able to do so within a month or two. Practically, then, it is usually unwise for the lessor to go to court over a tenant who skips out, since the fees the lessor will incur will more than offset the few months of rent he will be entitled to collect. In the month-to-month type of agreement, the deposit should be about enough to take care of any loss of this type incurred by the owner of the property from the time the tenant leaves to the time the dwelling unit is rented to another tenant.

A monthly tenancy agreement may be quite simple, or it may be lengthy and contain many conditions and provisions. Many of the conditions discussed in connection with leases may be incorporated into the monthly tenancy agreement.

The law now provides that the name and usual address of the person authorized to manage the premises *and* of an owner or person authorized to act on behalf of the owner for receipt of notices, demands, and process must be furnished in the lease or rental agreement; *or*, in the case of an oral rental agreement, be furnished in writing on demand of the tenant; or be posted in at least two conspicuous places on the premises, including every elevator.

Additional forms, applicable to this chapter, are illustrated in Appendix C as Figures C11–1 thru C11–7.

QUESTIONS FOR DISCUSSION

Property management

1. Discuss the different types of real estate managers, and their duties.

2. List some of the functions of the property manager with respect to the owner and to the tenant.
3. Comment on the nature of the management contract, and list some of the principal items that are included in it.
4. What general responsibilities do property managers have with respect to repairs and maintenance?
5. Discuss the general rules of agency that apply to property managers.
6. What are some of the records for which a property manager might be responsible?
7. What general responsibilities do property managers have with respect to funds received from rentals?
8. Discuss the factors that are generally taken into account in setting up rental schedules.
9. Discuss some of the types of insurance policies a manager might recommend for an apartment building with street-level commercial stores.
10. As a licensee who has decided to go into property management, discuss any preference you may have with respect to different types of properties.

Leasing

1. Discuss the fundamental types of leasehold estates.
2. Distinguish between a sublease and an assignment.
3. Discuss some of the more important subjects generally found in standard leases.
4. Why do most owners prefer to require a security deposit of lessees and tenants?
5. Discuss the duties of the lessor with regard to maintenance and repairs.
6. Identify and discuss the various ways a termination of lease may occur.
7. How many different types of leases can you identify and discuss?
8. What are the general duties and responsibilities of a lessee or tenant to the owner of the property?
9. What are the general duties and responsibilities of the property owner to the lessee or tenant?
10. What remedies are general available to a lessor?

12

Appraisal and valuation of real property

Since property valuation is the base of all real estate transactions, brokers and salesmen should be familiar with the theoretical aspects and concepts of value, the forces that influence values, and the methods by which such values may best be estimated. Every day, clients will question the broker about the worth, fair price, fair rental, fair basis for trade, or proper amount of insurance coverage for a particular property. The licensee must be able to answer such questions correctly and in detail. To be successful in the real estate business, the broker must determine whether he can profitably spend his time and effort in trying to sell a property at a listing price the owner is willing to set. In this regard, he must keep in mind that in accepting a listing, he obligates himself to put forth his best efforts to find a buyer for the property. He can do so only if he and the owner have set a fair price that will attract potential purchasers.

FACTORS INFLUENCING VALUE

Directional growth. In any estimate of value, attention should be paid to the directional growth of the area. This growth refers to the manner and direction in which the city or town tends to grow. Properties in the direction of growth tend to increase in value, especially if the growth is steady and rapid.

Location. The value of all types of properties is greatly affected by location; and quite often, all other factors being equal, the location is the greatest determinant of the market value of a particular property.

Utility. This factor involves judgment about the best use to which a property may be put and includes the capacity of the property to produce income. Local ordinances, such as building codes and restrictions, and zoning ordinances, affect the utility of a property.

Land composition. The type of soil, its size, shape, and slope all affect the value of the property. It is easier to build on a level lot than on a sloping one, and shipping centers must always be on level land. On the other hand, view lots, which tend to be quite valuable, usually have quite a bit of slope, as do hillside properties. Additional problems of slides and drainage play an important part in the determination of value.

Character of the neighborhood. The socioeconomic level of the neighborhood is a very important factor regulating value. The general age of the properties, the number and quality of the schools, transportation facilities, shopping centers, and recreational facilities are all quite important.

Economic trends. These include business trends, wage levels, available money and credit, interest rates, tax loads, and population growth.

Population and governmental regulations. Included here are such items as building codes, health codes and regulations, zoning laws, fire regulations, credit controls, and government guaranteed loans.

DIFFERENT TYPES OF VALUE

Although most of us think of value as monetary value, it is interesting to note that there are many types of value, such as:

1. Economic value
2. Appraised value
3. Potential value
4. Book value
5. Depreciated value
6. Face value
7. Cash value
8. Exchange value
9. Market value
10. Salvage value
11. Tax value
12. Assessed value
13. Replacement value
14. Rental value
15. Liquidation value
16. Mortgage loan value
17. Insurance value
18. Leasehold value
19. Nuisance value
20. Equity value

MARKET VALUE

When people refer to the value of property, they most generally mean the market value. The market value is the price for which a property will sell in the open market if the seller is not under any extreme pressure to sell and the buyer is not under any extreme pressure to buy, with a reasonable time allowed the broker to effect the sale. It is also assumed that both the seller and the prospective buyer are fully informed of all uses to which the property is adapted and for which it is capable of being used.

DEFINITION OF APPRAISAL

To appraise means to arrive at any estimate and opinion of the value of a property. An appraisal is usually a statement of the market value and/or value for loan purposes of a particular piece of property as of a specific date.

METHODS OF APPRAISING

It is generally accepted that there are three ways to approach a value estimate: (1) market comparison approach, (2) cost approach, and (3) income capitalization approach.

THE MARKET COMPARISON APPROACH

This is the most commonly used of all approaches to value. Quite simply, the broker finds comparables; that is, he finds properties very similar to the one he is appraising. These comparables must be properties that have sold recently. By comparing the selling prices of these properties, the broker can arrive at a valid estimate of value for the property he is appraising.

This approach is the one most generally used by real estate brokers and salesmen. It lends itself well to the appraisal of land, buildings, and other properties that exhibit a high degree of similarity and for which a ready market exists. This method is also particularly applicable as a check against the other two methods of appraising when the end result is to obtain a market value.

The mechanics of the process involve the use of market data of all kinds in order to closely compare the property being appraised with other similar properties. The sources used for determining a market value are:

1. The practical everyday experience the broker has obtained from dealing in properties in a given locale for a reasonable period of time.
2. The past listings in his own office, records of the local real estate board and multiple listing service.
3. Real estate advertisements in the local newspapers to learn asking prices for properties in the area.
4. Regular contact with other brokers, salesmen, loan officers, escrow officers, and others who are continually in touch with the local real estate market.
5. A knowledge of the influence of such factors as location, size of lot, condition, number, and size of units in a building, rental market, and operating expenses on the piece of property to be appraised.

Asking prices. One must remember that the asking price of a piece of property may not be its ultimate selling price. The price at which a property is listed may often indicate the probable top market value rather than the average actual selling price. Actual selling prices are what purchasers are willing to pay and are the truest indication of the market value of a property.

A property correctly listed is a property half sold. Too many brokers take a listings at any price no matter how ridiculous, but a broker does a disservice both to his client and to himself if he lists a property at an unrealistically high price.

Proper comparison. Proper comparison is most important. For nearly comparable properties, the value will decrease for such conditions as poor repair, poor design, and existing nuisances, while the price will increase for cleanliness, good design, special features, view, landscaping, and so on. Unless the sales being compared are of recent date, consideration must also be given to adjusting the values in keeping with the general economic conditions.

Some of the advantages of the market comparison approach are:

1. Easiest of the various methods to learn and to use.
2. Particularly applicable to single-family residences, which make up the bulk of real estate transactions.
3. Easiest method to explain to the layman.

It is important to remember that comparisons must be suitable, adequate in number, and reliable in source if they are to justify conclusions drawn from them. Note the example of a completed CAR Competitive Market Analysis Form, Figure 12–1.

COMPETITIVE MARKET ANALYSIS
CALIFORNIA REAL ESTATE ASSOCIATION STANDARD FORM

PROPERTY ADDRESS: 165 BALBOA AVENUE, SAN BERNARDINO, CALIFORNIA   DATE: July 25, 19--

FOR SALE NOW:	BED-RMS.	BATHS	DEN	SQ. FT.	1ST LOAN	LIST PRICE	DAYS ON MARKET	TERMS
127 Carter Avenue	3	2	No	1350	63,000	99,950	32	CTL or CTNL
801 Thomas Road	3	2	Yes	1450	52,600	104,500	7	20% Dn., 2nd to Seller
73 Anza Avenue	3	2	No	1250	61,200	95,950	61	CTNL
83 Center Street	3	2	No	1320	42,700	97,500	35	CTNL
980 Balboa Avenue	4	2	Yes	1430	70,100	104,950	12	CTL or CTNL

SOLD PAST 12 MOS.	BED-RMS.	BATHS	DEN	SQ. FT.	1ST LOAN	LIST PRICE	DAYS ON MARKET	DATE SOLD	SALE PRICE	TERMS
1153 Savannah Avenue	3	2½	Yes	1330	73,400	99,500	24	7/ 8/--	96,500	20% CTNL
23 Thomas Road	3	2	No	1300	48,600	93,950	17	6/21/--	91,000	20% CTNL
129 Connor Street	3	2	No	1270	64,800	92,500	22	5/18/--	90,950	CTL
1521 Moraga Avenue	4	2	Yes	1430	51,300	102,500	63	7/21/--	99,950	20% CTNL
173 Cervantes Street	3	2	Yes	1400	65,700	99,450	10	6/ 5/--	97,000	20%/ 11,900 2nd

EXPIRED PAST 12 MOS.	BED-RMS.	BATHS	DEN	SQ. FT.	1ST LOAN	LIST PRICE	DAYS ON MARKET	TERMS
328 Anza Avenue	3	2½	Yes	1425	47,200	106,950	90	CTNL
1920 Casper Street	3	2	No	1250	51,100	97,500	120	CTNL
1677 Balboa Avenue	4	2	Yes	1360	22,400	103,950	90	CTNL/ Submit Terms

F.H.A. ---- V.A. APPRAISALS

ADDRESS	APPRAISAL	ADDRESS	APPRAISAL
1204 Stern Circle	98,500		
1910 Balboa Avenue	95,000		

BUYER APPEAL
(GRADE EACH ITEM 0 TO 20% ON THE BASIS OF DESIRABILITY OR URGENCY)

1. FINE LOCATION: Close to schools/shopping 20 %
2. EXCITING EXTRAS: Beautiful garden and patio 20 %
3. EXTRA SPECIAL FINANCING: Possible seller 2nd 10 %
4. EXCEPTIONAL APPEAL: Well maintained 20 %
5. UNDER MARKET PRICE ___ YES ___ NO 0 %

RATING TOTAL 70 %

MARKETING POSITION

1. WHY ARE THEY SELLING: Business Transfer 20 %
2. HOW SOON MUST THEY SELL: 60 days 20 %
3. WILL THEY HELP FINANCE............YES 10 NO ___ %
4. WILL THEY LIST AT COMPETITIVE MARKET VALUE..YES 20 NO ___ %
5. WILL THEY PAY FOR APPRAISAL............YES 5 NO ___ %

RATING TOTAL 75 %

ASSETS: Centrally located. Nearby to public transportation and employment centers.
DRAWBACKS: Old-type gravity hot-air furnace located in basement.
AREA MARKET CONDITIONS: Steady demand for this neighborhood. Competitively priced properties sell in approximately 30 days.
RECOMMENDED TERMS: Conventional financing with 20% down. Seller may possibly carry 2nd loan.

TOP COMPETITIVE MARKET VALUE .... $ 97,000.

PROBABLE FINAL SALES PRICE .... $ 95,000.

SELLING COSTS

BROKERAGE	$	5,700
LOAN PAYOFF	$	43,612
PREPAYMENT PRIVILEGE	$	763
FHA --- VA POINTS	$	
TITLE AND ESCROW FEES: IRS STAMPS, RECONS, RECORDING	$	150
TERMITE CLEARANCE	$	65
MISC. PAYOFFS: 2ND T.D., POOL, PATIO, WTR. SFTNR., FENCE, IMPROVEMENT BOND.	$	
	$	
	$	
TOTAL	$	50,290

TOTAL .... $ 50,290.

NET PROCEEDS $ 44,710.   PLUS OR MINUS $ 300.

For these forms address California Real Estate Association, 520 So. Grand Ave., Los Angeles 90017. All rights reserved.

FORM CM 14
REV. 9/64

FIGURE 12-1

The cost approach

The cost approach to value (also called reproduction cost approach or replacement cost approach) is quite simple in principle. The cost approach is an estimate of the amount of money that would be necessary to duplicate the property under appraisal. Since people ordinarily will not pay more for a property than it would cost to replace the property or to obtain an equally satisfactory substitute property, the cost approach tends to set the upper limit of value.

The key to the correct use of the cost approach is the amount of depreciation the appraiser must allow for property that is not new. Before we discuss this further, let us consider the steps in the cost approach.

The first step is to make an independent estimate of the value of the land. This is always the current market value of the land, considered as vacant and available for improvement to its highest and best use.

The second step is to make an estimate of the replacement cost, new, of all improvements on the land. Accuracy requires the application of principles of building cost estimating.

Replacement cost to the appraiser means how much it would cost today to construct a building identical to the one being appraised. This implies taking an inventory of the materials and manufactured equipment that make up the property, and then applying to this inventory the current prices of similar materials, equipment, labor costs, and all overhead costs necessary to construct a suitable replacement of the property as of the appraisal date.

The methods in such estimates vary from the very technical and detailed procedures used by contractors and mortgage loan companies to the simpler shortcut methods, such as the square-foot and cubic-foot methods, used by most appraisers.

To use the simpler methods, an estimate of the total cost is made by comparison with other similar buildings whose costs are known and have been reduced to units per square foot of floor area of living space or per cubic foot of the building content. Applying these costs to the actual area of the property under appraisal will give an approximate valuation, provided the data about costs are accurate and the buildings and improvements are similar in quality and design. Corrections must be made for such differences as well as for changes in cost levels that may have taken place between the date of the basic costs and the date of the new estimate.

Cost figures may be obtained from local contractors or from numerous services that publish building costs. Actually, buildings costs will vary greatly, based on the efficiency of the builder and the amount of design and quality of construction, so that unless the appraiser is experienced in such matters, his estimates of value in this approach may be inaccurate. In appraising older buildings, it is also possible for an appraiser to use a depreciation rate that will cause his estimate under the cost approach to come out the way he wants it to and thus match the amounts he obtains by using the market comparison and capitalization of income approaches.

The third step in the cost approach method is to determine the existing depreciation of the property. This amount must be deducted from the replacement cost new to determine the value of the building. The difficulty of correctly estimating depreciation tends to increase with the age of the property and requires skill, experience, and good judgment on the part of the appraiser. A value determined by using the cost approach on any building more than a few years old is no more reliable than is the estimate of depreciation the appraiser used in his calculations.

There is no justification in always assuming that improvements depreciate at a rate corresponding to their age, although too often this is done by the inexperienced appraiser. It is common knowledge to the experienced broker that older property in a good location will sell for more than a newer property elsewhere. It is not uncommon for property to actually appreciate rather than depreciate in value as it gets older.

The fourth step in the cost approach method is to add the value of the land to the amount the appraiser has decided to apply to the value of the building, which he has determined by calculating the replacement cost new less depreciation.

The cost approach method is frequently used to get a ceiling on the value established by the other two approaches to value. It is particularly appropriate for appraising newly build properties where there is virtually no depreciation. It is also a good method for public service properties which have no active market and thus lack market data that can be used for a market comparison approach and which also produce no income on which to base an income capitalization approach. Examples of this type of property are (a) governmental buildings, (b) churches, (c) recreational structures, and (d) buildings that are very unique and specialized, so that few comparables exist in the community.

12 / APPRAISAL AND VALUATION OF REAL PROPERTY

The major details of building construction and explanation of building terms are illustrated in Figure 12–2.

The capitalization of income approach

The income approach is concerned with the present worth of future income of property. This method is particularly important in the valuation of income-producing property. It is measured by the net income one assumes the property will produce during its remaining economic life. The following is a simple example.

```
8-unit apartment house
Rental per unit—$350 per month.
  8 × $350 = $2,800 per month or $33,600 per year
Proven vacancy factor 5%:
  .05 × $33,600 = $1,680 per year
    $33,600
    −1,680
    $31,920 Gross income adjusted for vacancy factor
Annual expenses:
  Management................. $2,100
  Taxes......................  2,950
  Insurance .................    695
  Utilities..................  1,580
                              $8,525
    $33,600 Gross income
    −8,525 Expenses
    $25,075 Net income
Capitalization rate desired by purchaser, 8½%
```

$$\frac{25,075}{.085} = \$295,000 \text{ valuation}$$

Thus, if the purchaser pays $295,000 for the property, the $25,075 he receives each year represents an 8½ percent return on purchase price since 8½ percent of $295,000 is $25,075.

Three main steps are involved in the income capitalization approach.

First, a net annual income is derived by deducting total expenses from the gross income. Unless such figures have remained fairly constant, it is important that current trends in income and expenses be taken into account in figuring the net income.

Second, a selection is made of an appropriate capitalization rate or, as it is sometimes called, the present worth factor. This is the most important step in using the income approach to value. The rate selected depends on the return investors actually demand before they will be attracted by a particular investment. The greater the risk of recapturing the investment price, the higher is the accompanying rate as determined in the market for such properties.

By analyzing and knowing market prices on various types of income properties and checking against the net income produced, a broker can determine the going capitalization rate for various types of properties in his area of operation. The rate of return generally is higher on older properties and lower on newer buildings, although there may be exceptions to the rule.

It is important to note that a slight variation in the rate used makes a substantial difference in the capitalized value of the income. Using a net income of 21,000 capitalized at 6 percent, the property value is $350,000. Using a 7 percent capitalization rate, the property value is $300,000.

The third step after having determined the net income, then, is to apply the capitalization rate we have selected against the income and arrive at a figure that represents the appraised value of the property.

As important as the selection of a realistic rate is the proper determination of the net income of the property under appraisal. The net income figure is determined by deducting from the total gross income of the building, the following items:

Taxes	Vacancy factor
Utilities (gas, electric, water)	Repairs
	Janitorial
Refuse collection costs	Gardener
Insurance	Replacement reserve
License	Furniture depreciation
Management	

Not all buildings will have all the above expenses. A large office building or hotel would have a very complicated and detailed operating expense statement, whereas the typical smaller income property would have only the more common expenses, such as taxes, water, gas and electric, garbage, insurance, and miscellaneous expenses.

Once the net income has been established, the capitalization rate is applied and a valuation figure is determined. The net income, divided by the capitalization rate desired, equals the appraised value by the income capitalization method. The current net income is considered to be a perpetuity, and on this net income, appraisal is determined. Actually, a purchaser may improve a piece of income property after he buys it, and within a short time, he may have increased the net income and realized an even greater percentage return on his investment than he had anticipated at the time of purchase.

Determination of the capitalization rate. A look at some of the commonly recognized textbooks on appraisal discloses various methods, many of them mathematically complex and de-

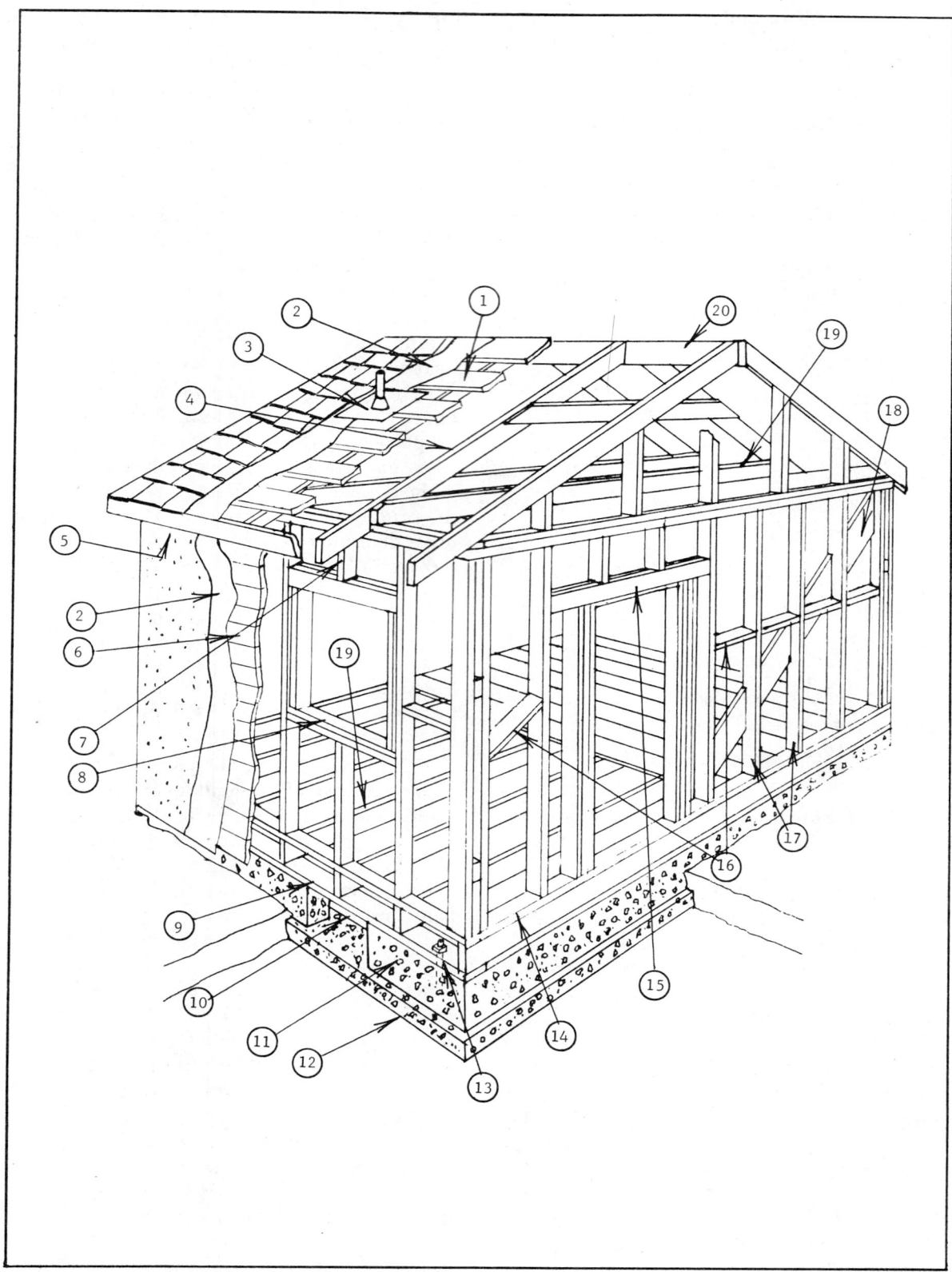

FIGURE 12-2

EXPLANATION OF DIAGRAM DETAILS

1. OPEN SHEATHING — Boards nailed to rafters as foundation for the roof covering. Open sheathing is used with wood shingles.

2. BUILDING PAPER — Heavy water proofed paper used between sheathing and roof covering or siding.

3. FLASHING — Sheet metal used to protect against water seepage.

4. RAFTERS — Sloping members of a roof used to support the roof boards and shingles. (Maximum 24" apart)

5. EAVE — Protruding underpart of roof overhanging exterior walls.

6. CLOSED SHEATHING — Boards nailed to studding as foundation for exterior siding. Closed means butted together.

7. CRIPPLE — Stud above or below a window opening or above a doorway.

8. SILL — Bottom portion lining doorway or window fits here.

9. MUD SILL — Treated member (or redwood) bolted to the foundation.

10. CRAWL SPACE — Unexcavated area under the house. Min. 18".

11. FOUNDATION — Concrete base of house.

12. FOOTING — Expanded portion of concrete foundation.

13. ANCHOR BOLT — Large bolt used for fastening mud sill to foundation. Bolt is anchored into concrete foundation.

14. SOLE PLATE — Support on which the studs rest.

15. HEADER (LINTEL) — The beam over a doorway or window.

16. FIRE STOP — Blocking used to restrict flames from spreading to attic. May be placed horizontally or diagonally.

17. STUDS — Vertical 2" x 4" framework of the walls spaced 16" on center.

18. BRACING — Board running diagonally across the wall framing to prevent sway.

19. JOISTS — Structural parts supporting floor or ceiling loads.

20. RIDGE BOARD — Highest point of construction in a frame building.

FIGURE 12-2 *(continued)*

tailed, for determining an appropriate capitalization rate to be used in the income capitalization method.

Those who are not expert appraisers must, of course, have some fairly simple and basic rules for determining the rate. The following rules will allow one to arrive at a capitalization rate that is just as valid and practical as one arrived at by the use of complicated mathematical formulas.

1. While one tries to make an investment that will bring the best rate of return possible, the lower limit should never be less than the current rate of interest for long-term loans on the particular type of property under appraisal.
2. Rates at any particular time tend to be uniform for comparable types of properties in any particular geographical area. The broker who deals with these properties day after day will certainly be aware of the general rates of return investors may expect to receive. One way that many licensees arrive at a quick estimate of the capitalization rate for a building being offered for sale is to divide the net income by the price being asked. Assuming a building offered for $320,000 showing a net income of $25,600, the capitalization rate would be found as follows:

$$\frac{\$25,600}{\$320,000} = .08 = 8\%$$

It is, of course, extremely important that the net income amount has been correctly determined. A further explanation of the mathematics of capitalization, including a Capitalization Table, can be found in Chapter 14.
3. Rates of return on investments other than real estate have an effect here. What the investor might realize on his investment in something other than real estate is an important consideration. If the rate of return will be little more than what might be received from good stocks or bonds, the investor may not want to purchase a piece of property (with all of the inherent problems of management, and so forth) and may, instead, decide to invest his money in stocks and bonds.
4. An important consideration is also the effect of the investment on the purchaser's tax setup. Income property may be depreciated for tax purposes and the depreciation used as an offset against income from the property. This may give the owner a considerable amount of tax-free income.
5. The rate the investor is willing to accept also is determined by such factors as: special features of the property which the purchaser wants and which cannot be measured purely in terms of income; the amount of appreciation the property will experience in the future; and plans for modernization and upgrading which will increase the net income. All these are important in the final decision the buyer makes about the rate of return he feels he should receive from a particular piece of property.
6. Many buildings may contain illegal dwelling units. Often, brokers look at properties where original large units have been divided into smaller ones. In some cases, additional units have been added. In any case, we often find that these units were not inspected and passed at the time of their construction and are thus in violation of local building and health codes. Many older properties are found in disrepair and contain numerous code violations. It is evident that on such properties, the investor will demand a different rate of return, since he faces a much higher risk factor as far as the stability of the property and its income are concerned. He also faces the possibility of a large expenditure for repairs and upkeep.

Since the capitalization rate measures the risk involved in the investment, it is generally true that the higher the risk, the higher the rate; the lower the risk, the lower the rate. Rates of return on income properties generally run anywhere from 5 to 12 percent, depending on the general age and condition of the property and the degree of risk involved.

Building and land residual methods. In some cases, the net income from real estate is divided between the land and improvements; different capitalization rates are applied to the net income from the land and to the net income from the improvements. The estimates of the value of the land and improvements are then added together to obtain the estimated value for the entire property.

Gross income multipliers. Licensees often use a quick method of arriving at an estimate of value by use of a "gross multiplier." For instance, a certain type of property may be said to generally sell for approximately 100 times the monthly gross income. This method is based upon the market relationship between rental value and the average sales prices of such properties.

APPRAISAL ORGANIZATIONS

Many organizations work to standardize and upgrade techniques of appraising. Among these are the American Institute of Real Estate Appraisers, the American Society of Appraisers, and the Society of Residential Appraisers.

To obtain the designation MAI (Member of the American Institute), the candidate must meet the age, experience, and study requirements, and must pass extensive examinations covering the entire field of appraising.

The Society of Residential Appraisers awards the SRA designation, and the American Society of Appraisers, ASA, and each of these organizations provide extensive educational programs and professional publications.

DEPRECIATION

Since depreciation is so important to the appraisal of real property, at this point we should define it in more detail.

Depreciation in its real sense means a loss in value from any cause. A simple illustration is an automobile. Each year it depreciates, it is worth less money. The reasons are (1) age and (2) wear. Depreciation in the real sense of the word is sometimes hard to relate to real estate. It is quite common to see aging buildings that are bringing prices higher than in years past. Instead of depreciation in value, property over the years has tended to appreciate in value.

In addition to depreciation in the sense of a loss in value, another common type of depreciation that affects property is depreciation for tax purposes. It is actually a method of returning to the investor in income or business property, over a certain number of years, an amount equal to the purchase price of the building.

Let us return to the traditional depreciation we first defined above—a loss in value from any source. This depreciation includes all the influences that reduce the value of property below its replacement cost new. The principal influences are physical deterioration, functional obsolescence, and economic and social obsolescence.

Physical deterioration is wear and tear from use and from the elements. It may also result from negligent care, damage by termites, and damage from dry-rot or from wood-destroying organisms.

By *functional obsolescence* is meant poor architectural design and style. The lack of modern facilities and out-of-date equipment and/or poorly planned interiors, and lack of adequate space.

By *economic and social obsolescence* is meant misplacement of the improvement. An area that 50 years ago was completely residential has changed over the years so that now it is a mixture of residential, commercial, and perhaps light manufacturing. What few residences remain are now economically and socially obsolete. They are wrong for the location as far as their use is concerned. Detrimental influence of supply and demand and zoning or legislative restrictions also cause this type of obsolescence.

While the first and second groups, above, are considered to be inherent in the property itself, the third group of influences consists of factors that are extraneous to the property itself. Physical and functional depreciation may be corrected by modernization and improvement of the existing structure. New wiring may be installed, plumbing modernized, kitchens and bathrooms brought up-to-date, and modern heating systems installed. Economic and social obsolescence is much more difficult to correct and usually necessitates an urban renewal and redevelopment project on a large scale.

Determining depreciation

In using the reproduction cost approach, the appraiser must determine the amount of depreciation that has occurred. Several methods are in current use.

Observed condition method. This is the most widely used in actual practice today. The appraiser must correctly determine the total cost of making all the necessary repairs in order to correct any curable physical deterioration and functional obsolescence, and in addition, he must estimate the actual loss in value as a result of all types of depreciation on the building.

Age-life method. This method is based on depreciation tables that have been developed to reflect age-life experience in the depreciation of structures of various types and uses assuming average care and maintenance. Such tables may be obtained from the Bureau of Internal Revenue under the titles *(a)* Income Tax Depreciation and Obsolescence, *(b)* Estimated Useful Lives, and *(c)* Depreciation Rates.

Additional methods. Appraisal textbooks generally explain methods other than those referred to above; and these methods are mainly mathematical ones that capitalize an income. One of the more popular is called the building residual method previously mentioned.

In this method, the land is valued independently of the building, and the fair annual net return of the land is deducted from the estimated net annual income of the property. The residual amount is said to be attributable to the depreciated building and is capitalized to indicate the building value. The depreciation figure is the difference between the residual value of the building, as shown above, and that of a new structure of a similar type.

Difficulties in determining depreciation. It is in the use of the replacement cost approach to appraisal that the determination of depreciation as discussed above is important. The replacement cost approach (or reproduction cost, as it is also called) is widely used today in the field of appraisal, and yet its validity rests mainly on a correct determination of depreciation. This determination is both difficult and confusing at times.

It is this weakness that causes the reproduction cost method to be really valid only if it is used to determine the value of new or nearly new properties for which reproduction costs can be accurately determined without having to determine a complicated depreciation figure.

Depreciation for tax purposes

The depreciation we have been discussing in this chapter on appraisal and valuation is generally referred to as traditional depreciation and is used in appraisal methods, particularly the reproduction cost approach.

However, what most brokers, accountants, and others in real estate dealing mean when they refer to depreciation is not traditional depreciation but depreciation as it relates to income tax and the Internal Revenue Service.

It is this depreciation for tax purposes that is of vital importance to real estate investors. The Internal Revenue Code states that depreciation (as used for tax purposes) is a reasonable allowance for the exhaustion, wear and tear, and normal obsolescence of property that is (1) used in a trade or business and (2) held for the production of income. This depreciation allowance may be deducted from the gross income received from such property in arriving at the net taxable income.

This type of depreciation was discussed in greater detail in Chapter 10, Income Tax and Real Estate.

SUMMARY OF APPRAISAL AND VALUATION METHODS

The *market comparison method* is by far the most logical and simple technique for establishing the value of property, and it is the method commonly used by brokers and salesmen in the field.

The value most sought by those dealing in real estate is the market value—that is, the price the property will sell for in the open market. Comparables exist for virtually all existent types and kinds of properties. The actual selling prices in the marketplace are much more valid for computation than are many of the complex mathematical processes that many appraisers use. Indeed, it is interesting to note that in many appraisal reports, the appraiser has purposefully used the mathematics in such a way that the figures obtained by the income capitalization and reproduction cost methods will agree with the amount obtained by the market comparison approach.

The *income capitalization method* has merit to a limited extent, since some of the assumptions the appraiser must make in using this approach are certainly matters of personal judgment alone and may or may not be entirely correct. It is very easy to misjudge in attempting either to arrive at a net income or to select the appropriate capitalization rate for use in the appraisal. Assuming that the net income is correct and the rate is proper for the particular location and market in which the property is located, this method is merely a check against the others.

The *replacement cost method* is correctly used only in appraising new or nearly new buildings. For other types of structures, this method merely sets an upper limit of value. The depreciation factor is the main problem in this approach. When replacement cost is employed in the appraisal of older properties, it is too easy for the appraiser to manipulate the depreciation allowance so that the result obtained will agree with the actual market price of the property.

Finally, for the broker who deals in properties in a given area, appraisal is not too difficult. He knows the prices being asked and the prices being paid. He knows the property, the rental market, typical expenses, and incomes. He knows other brokers, bankers, title men, loan officers, appraisers, and others engaged in the real estate business. He belongs to a local real estate board and multiple listing association, which gives him access to records of past sales in the area. Thus, he is able to adequately appraise the majority of buildings he comes in contact with. He relies on the most used method—a combination of market comparison and experience.

FORM OF THE APPRAISAL REPORT

The specific form, length, and contents of an appraisal report vary considerably depending on the client for whom the report is being prepared, the type of property being appraised, and the purpose for which the appraisal is being made. Some reports are only a single page or two, while others are quite formal and lengthy. A Veterans Administration Appraisal Report is illustrated in Figure 12–3. All reports, however, should contain basically the following information:

1. The date on which the value is estimated and the report prepared.
2. The estimate of value.
3. The purpose of the appraisal and its scope.
4. A description of the property.
5. A description of the general location and neighborhood.
6. The factual data necessary, together with its analysis and interpretation, by the use of one or more of the three common approaches.
7. Additional supporting material, such as maps, photographs, or plans.
8. The name and signature of the appraiser.

INCOME PROPERTY STATEMENT

The arrangement and presentation of information with respect to an income property in a clear and professional way can be of great help in the sale of such property. There are various forms in use, and an example is the Income Property Statement prepared by CAR and illustrated in Figure 12–4.

The statement begins by giving the name of the real estate firm and a description of the property being offered for sale. Sections for special features and general information are provided. The financing section discloses that a purchaser may assume an existing loan of $300,000 and the seller will carry back a second loan in the amount of $45,000.

Scheduled income

The building being offered consists of 16 furnished units with a total monthly income of $5,800. The number of bedrooms in each unit is shown, and the monthly rental is given for each.

Operating expenses

The proper presentation of operating expenses is extremely important, and these are given as yearly amounts. A recent survey of California Realtors showed that the order of presenting expenses shown is the most common method used.

Taxes is the largest item of expense and is shown first. Showing the various amounts for individual utilities is much preferred over merely showing a single sum. The cost of management spaces are arranged so that the broker may give the cost of professional management, resident manager expense, or both. If the manager receives a free apartment in addition to a salary, the broker should separate the amounts and make this clear in the presentation. The maintenance expense may either be an estimated percentage of the yearly scheduled income or the actual maintenance expense from the seller's records. Such actual figures are most valuable when based on the average of a number of preceding years.

Assessed value

This section shows the assessed valuation placed on the property by the local tax assessor. If the assessment is quite recent, the assessor's statement of fair cash value of the property as against the asking price will provide an interesting comparison. The various percentages used by the assessor will also provide the purchaser with a guideline for determining the basis for depreciation.

Investment information

The various terms used in the investment information section are an attempt at standardization of terms used by real estate brokers with reference to income properties.

Price, loan, and down payment. The asking price of the property is $400,000. The loans available are a first loan of $300,000 and a second loan of $45,000 totaling $345,000. Subtracting the loans from the purchase price gives a cash down payment of $55,000.

Scheduled income, vacancy factor, gross operating income. The scheduled income of $69,600 is the total annual income this property will produce for a year at the actual rents shown in the scheduled income area of this statement. The total monthly income of $5,800 × 12 = $69,600.

An estimated vacancy factor of 5 percent is used which equals $3,480. While 5 percent may be a fair representation, if actual performance or economic conditions indicate a higher or lower figure, then such a figure should be used. The vacancy factor estimate is subtracted from the scheduled income giving a gross operating income of $66,120.

Operating expenses and net operating income. The operating expenses of $19,415 are de-

VETERANS ADMINISTRATION
RESIDENTIAL APPRAISAL REPORT

CASE NUMBER: LH 37298

1. MAJOR STRUCTURES	A. TYPICAL COND.	B. BUILT-UP	C. AGE TYPE BLDG.	D. OWN OCCUP.	E. VACANCY	F. ZONING	G. LAND USE CHGS.	2. PROPERTY IS	3. BLDG. WARRANTY IN FORCE?
NEIGHBORHOOD	Good	100%	10	95	0	R-1	None	[X] OCCUPIED	[ ] YES [X] NO
BLOCK	Good	100%	10	95	0	R-1	None	[ ] VACANT	[ ] UNKNOWN

4. STATUS OF PROPERTY
- [ ] A. PROPOSED
- [ ] B. EXISTING, NOT PREVIOUSLY OCCUPIED
- [X] C. EXISTING, PREVIOUSLY OCCUPIED
- [ ] D. ALTERATIONS, IMPROVEM'TS. OR REPAIRS
- [ ] E. REFINANCING - VETERAN APPLICANT OWNS AND OCCUPIES RESIDENCE AS HOME

5. CONSTRUCTION COMPLETED BEFORE DATE HEREOF
- [ ] A. WITHIN 12 CALENDAR MOS.
- [X] B. MORE THAN 12 CALENDAR MOS.

6. NAME AND ADDRESS OF FIRM OR PERSON MAKING REQUEST (Complete mailing address. Include ZIP Code)

Aladdin Mortgage Company
123 Rainbow Parkway
Berkeley, California 94704

7. PROPERTY ADDRESS (Include ZIP Code)

456 Pioneer Way
Concord, California 94519

8. TYPE OF PROPERTY: [X] HOME [ ] MOBILE HOME LOT
9. MANDATORY HOME ASSOCIATION MEMBERSHIP? [ ] YES [X] NO
10A. NO. BLDGS. 1
10B. NO. LIVING UNITS 1

11. LOT DIMENSIONS: 60' X 120'

12. DESCRIPTION

	WOOD SIDING	CINDER BLOCK	SPLIT LEVEL	6 NO. ROOMS	1 DINING ROOM	2 CAR GARAGE	X GAS		CEN. AIR COND.	
X DETACHED	WOOD SHINGLE	STONE	% BASEMENT	3 BEDROOMS	1 KITCHEN	CAR CARPORT	UNDERGRD. WIRE		TYPE HEAT. & FUEL	
SEMI-DET.	ALUM. SIDING	BRICK & BLOCK	SLAB	2 BATHS	FAMILY RM.	X WATER (Public)	X SEWER (Public)		FA Gas	
ROW	ASB. SHINGLE	X STUCCO	X CRAWL SPACE	1/2 BATHS	UTILITY RM.	WATER (Comm.)	SEWER (Comm.)		ROOFING DESCRIP.	
CONDOMINIUM	X BRICK VENEER	1 STORIES	10 YRS. EST. AGE	1 LIVING RM.	1 FIREPLACE	WATER (Ind.)	SEPTIC TANK		Asph. Shgl.	

13. LEGAL DESCRIPTION

Lot 3, Block 24
Tract 1259
Contra Costa County,
California

14. TITLE LIMITATIONS, INCLUDING EASEMENTS, RESTRICTIONS, ENCROACHMENTS, HOMEOWNERS ASSOCIATION AND SPECIAL ASSESSMENTS, ETC.

PUE across rear 5 feet of lot.

15. OFFSITE IMPROVEMENTS

- **A. STREET SURFACE:** Asphalt
- **B. STREET ACCESS:** [ ] PRIV. [X] PUB.
- **C. STREET MAINT.:** [ ] PRIV. [X] PUB.
- **D. ADD'L. IMPROVEMENTS:** [X] STORM SEWER [X] SIDEWALK [X] CURB/GUTTER

16. REPAIRS NECESSARY TO MAKE PROPERTY CONFORM TO APPLIC. MPR'S

TOTAL ESTIMATED COST OF REPAIRS: $ -0-

17. REMARKS

- **A. DETRIMENTAL INFLUENCES:** None
- **B. REAL ESTATE MARKET IN COMMUNITY:** Moderate Demand
- **C. HIGHEST AND BEST USE:** Single-Family Residential
- **D. FEDERAL FLOOD HAZARD MAP ISSUED?** [X] YES [ ] NO
- **E. PROP. IN SPECIAL FLOOD HAZARD AREA?** [ ] YES [X] NO
- **F. EXPLAIN DEPRECIATION:** Normal physical deterioration

18. MARKET DATA

ITEM	SUBJECT PROPERTY	COMPARABLE NO. 1		COMPARABLE NO. 2		COMPARABLE NO. 3	
ADDRESS		20 Ranch Avenue		49 Miner Way		273 Golden Road	
SALE PRICE		$118,000		$108,000		$109,500	
TYPE OF FINANCING		Conv.		Conv.			
	DESCRIPTION	DESCRIPTION	ADJ.	DESCRIPTION	ADJ.	DESCRIPTION	ADJ.
DATE OF SALE	6/3/--	4/12/--	+$2,000	3/6/--	+$3,000	2/9/--	$
LOCATION	Good	Good		Good		Good	$4,000
SITE IMPROVEMENT	Average	Good	-500	Average		Average	
AGE/CONDITION	10/Good	12/Good		10/Average	+3,000	10/Good	
GARAGE/CARPORT	2/Garage	2/Garage		2/Garage		2/Garage	
CONSTRUCTION	Frame	Frame		Frame		Frame	
PORCHES, POOL, ETC.							
ROOM COUNT/SIZE ROOMS BDRMS BATH S.F. AREA	6 3 2 1,500	6 3 2 1,600 -2,500		6 3 2 1,500 -0-		6 3 2 1,400 +2,500	
NET ADJUSTMENT (Show + or - adjustment)		$ -1,000		$ +6,000		$ +6,500	
INDICATED VALUE OF SUBJECT PROPERTY		$ 117,000		$ 114,000		$ 116,000	

19. PROPERTY SHOWS EVIDENCE OF (Check)
[ ] TERMITE [ ] DRY ROT [ ] DAMPNESS [ ] SETTLEMENT [X] NO EVIDENCE

20. ESTATE (Check)
[X] A. FEE SIMPLE [ ] B. LEASEHOLD

21. REMAINING ECONOMIC LIFE (Years)
MAIN 50 OTHER 50

22. COST APPROACH
LA MAIN 1,500 [ ] CU. [X] SQ OTHER 500

23. DATA	DESCRIPTION	CONDITION	24. EQUIP.	DESCRIPTION	DEPR. VALUE	25. OTHER IMPROVEMENTS	DEPR. VALUE			
ROOF	Asp.Sh.	Good		GFWA Furnace	$ Bs.	Fireplace	$1,500	$ 55.00	RATE PER FT.	$15.00
FOUND.	Conc.	Good		Water Heater	100	Conc. Flatwork	800	$82,500	REPLMT. COST	$6,000
BSMT.	No			Built Ins:		Fence	800	$ 8,250	PHYSICAL DEP.	$ 600
FLOORS	Carpet	Good		Fan-Hood	150	W/W Carpeting	1,500	$	FUNCTIONAL	$
INT. WALLS	Gypsum	Good		Rng. Oven	300	Landscaping	1,000	$ 8,250	ECONOMIC	$
BATH FINISH	Gypsum	Good		Dshwash.	200			$74,250	TOTAL DEP.	$ 600
GUTTERS	Galv.	Good		Disposal	50				DEPR. COST	$5,400
									TOTAL DEPR. COST OF IMPR.	$79,650

26. ANNUAL TAXES

GENERAL	SPECIAL	OTHER					
$1,300	$	$	TOTAL	$800	TOTAL	$5,600	

- OTHER IMPR. AND EQUIP.: $ 5,680
- LAND VALUE: $30,000
- TOTAL DEPR. COST OF PROP.: $115,330

27. DOES PROPERTY CONFORM TO APPLICABLE MINIMUM PROPERTY REQUIREMENTS?
[X] YES [ ] NO (If "No" explain on reverse)

28. ESTIMATE FAIR MONTHLY RENT TIMES RENT MULTIPLIER (If applicable)
$600 × 190 = $114,000

29. RECONCILIATION
- **A. MARKET APPROACH:** $115,000
- **B. COST APPROACH:** $115,500
- **C. INCOME APPROACH** (If applicable): $114,000

NOTE: No determination of reasonable value may be made unless a completed appraisal report is received (38 U.S.C. 1810). I HEREBY CERTIFY that (a) I have carefully viewed the property described in this report, INSIDE AND OUTSIDE, so far as it has been completed; that (b) it is the same property that is identified by description in my appraisal assignment; that (c) I HAVE NOT RECEIVED, HAVE NO AGREEMENT TO RECEIVE, NOR WILL I ACCEPT FROM ANY PARTY ANY GRATUITY OR EMOLUMENT OTHER THAN MY APPRAISAL FEE FOR MAKING THIS APPRAISAL; that (d) I have no interest, present or prospective, in the applicant, seller, property, or mortgage; that (e) in arriving at the estimated reasonable value I have not been influenced in any manner whatsoever by the race, color, religion, national origin, or sex of any person residing in the property or in the neighborhood wherein it is located. I understand that violation of this certification can result in removal from the fee appraiser's roster.

30. I ESTIMATE "REASONABLE VALUE"
[X] "AS IS" [ ] "AS REPAIRED" [ ] "AS COMPLETED"

31. ESTIMATED REASONABLE VALUE: $115,000

32. SIGNATURE OF APPRAISER: (s) A. B. SMITH

33. DATE SIGNED: 7/1/--

FIGURE 12-3

INCOME PROPERTY STATEMENT
RESIDENTIAL
CALIFORNIA ASSOCIATION OF REALTORS® STANDARD FORM

PRESENTED BY **J. B. SMITH COMPANY**
1234 CENTER STREET, SANTA ANA
564-6892   541-5746

IMPROVEMENT **16 Furn. Apts. 12- 1 BR + 4- 2 BR**
ADDRESS **859 W. Cabria "Newlin Apts."**
CITY **Santa Ana, California**
(2) BLOCKS S OF **Quintara**
(½) BLOCKS E OF **Ulloa**
SALES REPRESENTATIVE **James Smith**
TELEPHONE **541-6892**   Res: **682-5431**   (Circle One)
SHOWING INSTRUCTIONS **Mrs. Hazard Apt.12**   OWNER - MANAGER - TENANT
TELEPHONE **642-5496 by appointment**   KEY

(Picture of property or business card may be placed in above space)

SPECIAL FEATURES
Excellent furnished rental units. Vacancy factor of 3.15% for previous 18 months. Located in good apartment area. Close to major shopping and public transportation. Utilities paid by tenants on 75% of units. Owner will sell or may trade for ranch property.

GENERAL INFORMATION:
LOT SIZE **66 x 290**   ZONE **C-1**   AGE **17**   CONST **WF + S**   ELEVATOR **No**   STYLE **Modern**
LEGAL **Lot 13 + 14 TR6968 AP-06216412**   PARKING **16**   STORIES **2**   SEWER **Yes**   HEAT **Gas**   AIR COND **No**

EXISTING INFORMATION:
FIRST LOAN **300,000.** PYMT **2,859.** INT **11%** ORIG **30** TO GO **20**   NO YEARS
LENDER **Park Savings + Loan**   LOCKED IN YES ___ NO **X**
SECOND LOAN ___ PYMT ___ INT ___ DUE ___ ACCEL ___
LENDER ___
OTHER LOANS ___ PYMT ___ INT ___ DUE ___ ACCEL ___

INVESTMENT INFORMATION BASED ON:
FIRST LOAN **300,000.** PAYMENT **2,859.** INTEREST **11%** NO YEARS **30**
LENDER **Park Savings + Loan**   COST $ **1 pt.**
SECOND LOAN ___ PAYMENT ___ INTEREST ___ DUE ___
LENDER ___
SELLER WILL CARRY **45,000.** PAYMENT **500.** INTEREST **12%** DUE **5 yrs.**

SCHEDULED INCOME:

#	DESC	RENT	#	DESC	RENT
1	1 BR	$350.	11	1 BR	$350.
2	1 BR	$350.	12	2 BR	$400.
3	1 BR	$350.	13	1 BR	$350.
4	2 BR	$400.	14	1 BR	$350.
5	1 BR	$350.	15	1 BR	$350.
6	1 BR	$350.	16	2 BR	$400.
7	1 BR	$350.			
8	2 BR	$400.			
9	1 BR	$350.			
10	1 BR	$350.			

TOTAL SCHEDULED MONTHLY INCOME $ **5,800.**

PROJECTED OPERATING EXPENSES:
Taxes	$ 5,250.
Insurance F&L	$ 800.
License & Fees	$ 85.
Utilities:	
Water	$ 2,420.
Electricity	$ 720.
Gas	$ 1,600.
Management	$ 3,600.
Trash	$ 720.
Gardener	$ 720.
Maintenance (Est.) __%	$ 3,500.
Other	
TOTAL	$ 19,415.

ASSESSED VALUE
	Amount	Percent
Land	$ 16,000.	16 %
Improvement	$ 80,000.	80 %
Pers. Prop	$ 4,000.	4 %
TOTAL	$100,000.	100%

PROJECTED INVESTMENT INFORMATION:
Price	$ 400,000.
Loan (2)	$ 345,000.
Down Payment	$ 55,000.
Scheduled Income	$ 69,600.
Vacancy Factor (Est.) **5** % $	3,480.
Gross Operating Income	$ 66,120.
Projected Operating Expenses	$ 19,415.
Net Operating Income (Est.)	$ 46,705.
Loan Payments	$ 40,308.
Gross Spendable (Est.)	$ 6,397.
Furniture Reserve (Est.)	$ 2,400.
Carpet Reserve (Est.)	$ 1,200.
Adj. Gross Spendable (Est.)	$ 2,797.
Paid on Principal	$ 3,858.
Projected Total Return	$ 6,665.
Earns **11.67** % on Sale Price	
Spendable of **5.08** % on Down Payment	
Earns **12.10** % on Down Payment	
Purchase Price is **5.7** Times Gross	

Above information is from sources believed reliable but not guaranteed.

For these forms, address California Association of Realtors®
505 Shatto Place, Los Angeles 90020
Copyright ©1969, 1978, California Association of Realtors® (Revised 1978)   FORM IPSR-11

FIGURE 12-4

termined by rounding off to the nearest dollar amount the total shown in the operating expenses column. This amount is subtracted from the gross operating income to give a net operating income of $46,705.

The net operating income of $46,705 is as accurate a figure as can be presently determined until the purchaser actually owns and operates the property himself. Rental income and expenses have been shown and an allowance for vacancy has been taken.

Loan payments and gross spendable. The monthly payments on the two available loans are shown as $2,859 and $500. The combined monthly payment of $3,359 is multiplied by 12 to arrive at a yearly loan payment of $40,308. Subtracting $40,308 from $46,705 gives a gross spendable of $6,397.

Furniture reserve and adjusted gross spendable. The gross spendable amount of $6,397 is the owner's to do with as he wants. In the property being presented, the units are furnished, and thus, the broker has wisely set aside a certain amount for eventual furniture and carpet replacement. The $3,600 is deducted here rather than from gross operating income since to do so will reduce net operating income and distort the picture when a capitalization rate is applied to it; $6,397 minus $2,400 furniture reserve and $1,200 carpet reserve gives an adjusted gross spendable of $2,797.

Paid on principal. $3,858 is the equity buildup to the owner on the first and second loans during the first year of ownership.

Total return. The total return is the sum of the adjusted gross spendable of $2,797 and the $3,858 paid on principal. If the units were not furnished or if the $3,600 had not been deducted for furniture and carpet reserve, the total return would be shown as the gross spendable of $6,397 plus $3,858 for a total return of $10,255. The broker has been more practical, however, in showing a prospective purchaser that he should set aside a certain amount to take care of replacements which will be necessary during his ownership, and the total return is thus shown as $6,655.

Earns on sale price. The statement shows 11.67 percent earned on sale price. This is calculated by dividing the net operating income by the sale price. We can say that this property will show approximately a 11.7 percent return based on the asking price of $400,000. To be exact, if we capitalize the net operating income of $46,705 by 11.7 percent ($46,705 ÷ .117) we arrive at a purchase price of $399,188.

Spendable on down payment and earns on down payment. Spendable of 5.08 percent on down payment is the adjusted gross spendable of $2,797 divided by the $55,000 down payment. Earns 12.10 percent on down payment is the total return of $6,655 divided by the down payment of $55,000.

Some brokers carry the percentage calculations out to hundredths of a percent as in this statement, while others merely calculate to tenth of a percent or round off to nearest whole percent. Rounding off to the nearest whole percent on this statement will give us 12 percent earns on sale price, spendable of 5 percent on down payment, and earns 12 percent on down payment.

Times gross. The purchase price is 5.7 times gross, and some brokers and purchasers like to use this as a means of comparing income properties in a particular location.

Additional forms, applicable to this chapter, are illustrated in Appendix C as Figures C12–1 thru C12–3.

QUESTIONS FOR DISCUSSION

1. What errors might an appraiser make with regard to the income approach to appraisal?
2. Which of the factors influencing value are most applicable to a single-family residence located in a housing tract?
3. What factors are most important in the use of the market comparison approach to valuation?
4. Discuss the types of properties in which the asking price and actual selling price are usually close and those properties in which a considerable difference may occur.
5. Which of the various appraisal methods could be used in determining the value of an apartment building?
6. What are some of the difficulties that might arise with respect to determining the net income of a large property?
7. At any given time, will the same capitalization rate be applied by investors to all income properties?
8. Discuss the types of depreciation generally considered inherent within the property itself.
9. Discuss the methods by which the appraiser seeks to determine the amount of depreciation that has occurred with respect to a given building.
10. What professional organizations and publications are available to the property appraiser?

13

Property insurance

In this chapter, we will confine our emphasis to those forms of insurance that cover the risks of ownership of real property. Although most insurance policies sold today are through insurance brokers and agents, a significant number of real estate brokers still sell insurance.

The insurance department of a real estate firm may be likened to that of a loan or property management department. It is a natural adjunct to the main business, and since all lenders generally require at least fire insurance coverage before they will release any funds to the escrow officer, the broker is in a good position to effect placement of the insurance on the properties he sells. Quite often, a purchaser prefers to deal with his own insurance broker, and the ethical real estate licensee will never attempt to place any undue influence on the client in order to obtain the insurance business.

The major areas in the insurance business are life insurance and property and casualty insurance. One who sells life insurance generally restricts himself to this area, as does the property and casualty agent. Basically, property insurance means fire insurance and extended coverages, while casualty insurance means liability coverages. In addition, there are coverages to protect against a consequential loss. Such a loss would result from the destruction of property leading to a business interruption or a loss of rental income.

THE INSURANCE CONCEPT OF PROPERTY

The insurance concept of property is divided into two groups—real and personal property. There are two broad subdivisions within the personal property concept: (1) property used in connection with a residence or a business, such as furniture, fixtures, machinery, and equipment; (2) property that is for sale or in the process of manufacturing, such as stocks of merchandise.

Insurance against loss to property is written primarily as fire and marine insurance. Ocean marine was the earliest form of insurance; from it developed inland marine coverages; and, eventually, fire insurance developed separately. Whereas the main emphasis of marine coverages was transportation, fire insurance concentrated on fixed locations—hence its application to real property. It can be said generally that fire insurance protects against loss to buildings and, with additional endorsements to the policy, covers against loss to furniture, fixtures, and stock. Other risks can be covered under a fire policy; these will be discussed later in this chapter. Inland marine insurance covers property in transit and property away from the insured premises.

THE PACKAGING TREND

The American system of insurance divides insurance into special lines, such as fire, casualty, and marine. This is not true of European insurance because there any kind of insurance may be written by any company any place in the world. The system of line specialization was based on the theory that expertise could be developed for each line, thus offering better solutions to complex problems.

Gradually, line specialization led to development of the package policy. A package policy combines several traditional lines into one policy.

For the policyholder, the advantages are in terms of cost, coverage, and convenience. One policy costs less than several. Duplicated coverages are eliminated, and at the same time, certain gaps in coverage are reduced or eliminated. Before package policies, the insured often neglected to purchase theft insurance when he bought fire insurance. A package takes care of such problems by including several automatic coverages. There is also only one agent, company, and renewal date.

In 1951, the Fireman's Fund Insurance Company issued the forerunner of the present and popular homeowners policy. Today, the homeowners policy is a single package that includes coverages formerly available only through separate contracts. Forms are available from basic coverages to what might be called the superdeluxe form, which covers just about everything the homeowner has in his possession and protects against virtually all possible perils.

Section I of the homeowners policy indemnifies the insured when either he or his property is injured or damaged. Section II covers liability imposed by law when others are injured or their property is damaged. Such damages can be the result of bodily injury or property damage while on the insured's premises or due to the activities of the insured. Generally, the law of negligence determines the fact and extent of liability. If a guest trips and accidentally falls while coming up the front stairs of the policyholder's house, the degree of liability depends on whether the steps were or were not in good repair, clean, and free from obstruction. Medical payments coverage provides medical expenses for any person, other than trespassers, injured on the insured's premises.

Section II also covers physical damage. If the insured damages the property of others, he is covered under his homeowners policy for damages he must pay to the injured party. In addition to the above, the policyholder may be covered for loss resulting from theft, larceny, burglary, and robbery. Farmers can purchase coverage similar to the homeowners policy. The general policy layout is the same, and there are special conditions for farmers and farm property; this type of policy is called a farmowners policy.

Homeowner policies are a package designed to provide those coverages most likely to be needed by property owners. They are flexible enough to suit the needs of the policyholders and offer reduced premiums when compared to separate policies.

COMMERCIAL COVERAGES—THE MULTIPERIL POLICY

The special multiperil policy has a purpose similar to the homeowners policy in that it combines line coverages for commercial enterprises. It starts with certain fundamental concepts: (1) a basic fire policy containing standard provisions; (2) special forms for special occupancies; (3) a uniform set of rules.

Special multiperil policies have been developed to cover special types and kinds of businesses and commercial enterprises, such as motel-hotel, apartment house, mercantile, institutional offices, processing-service, and manufacturing.

COINSURANCE

Most property owners do not carry fire insurance to cover the full value of their property, since very few fires result in a complete loss of the property insured. Most homeowners carry an amount of insurance equal to 70 or 80 percent of the full cash value of the property. Because of this partial coverage, the principle of coinsurance has been developed by insurance companies. The policyholder must generally carry insurance to cover a stated percent, usually 80 percent, of the value of his property. The company's liability for any loss is limited to the proportion of the loss that the amount of its policy bears to the amount obtained by applying the specified percentage to the value of the property at the time of the loss. Thus, if the policyholder fails to carry an amount of insurance equal to the specified percentage of the value of the property, he cannot recover his full loss. In effect, to the extent of the deficit, the policyholder takes the place of another insurance company and contributes proportionately to any loss—in other words, becomes a coinsurer. Remember: when we speak of property value here, we mean only the value of the buildings and improvements. Land is not considered nor insured because it cannot be lost.

An example of the operation of a requirement that the insured carry a policy of at least 80 percent of the value of his property follows:

Value of the improvements	$80,000
Amount of insurance policyholder should carry is 80 percent of the value	64,000
Amount of insurance policyholder actually carries	48,000
A fire occurs, and amount of actual loss is	12,000
Amount of company's liability is:	

$$\frac{48,000}{64,000} \times 12,000 = 9,000$$

Insurance company pays to policyholder	$ 9,000
Policyholder (insured) must stand the difference of	$ 3,000
Since the policyholder only carried 75 percent of the insurance coverage required ($48,000 instead of $64,000) the company will only be liable for 75 percent of the actual loss.	

For this reason, any person whose fire insurance policy contains an 80 percent clause should periodically check the amount of coverage he carries so that if the value of his property appreciates over the years, he will keep the amount of the insurance he should carry up to the proper level.

RISKS AND COVERAGES

Figures 13–1 and 13–2 outline the various risks and coverages generally available with regard to or in connection with real property.

California homeowners insurance policy

The standard form homeowners policy, to which may be added a borad form that covers contents, and a comprehensive personal liability form not only will cover all the perils listed in Figure 13–1 for the standard fire insurance policy but will also include coverage for bodily injury, property damage, defense, personal liability including medical payments, and voluntary property damage. A tenant may also be covered against the perils listed, excluding only those applicable to the building.

Multiperil policy

A special multiperil basic form policy is often used to cover a business. The basic policy, referred to as special multiperil, may be written with several endorsements to fit it to particular needs of any type of business.

The following may be insured: building, stock, merchandise, equipment, earnings, plate glass, neon signs, moneys and securities, and liability expenses for damages to others arising as the result of a business transaction or business in general.

The perils that may be covered collectively or individually are: fire and additional risks, bodily injury, property damage, defense, employee dishonesty, forgery, burglary, robbery, and breakage.

Liability policy

The standard forms used to cover liability are the standard liability policy, owners–landlords–tenants form, and the manufacturers and contractors form.

The following may be insured: any expenses when responsible for damage that may arise to others as the result of business activities, ownership or use of property, liability under a contract, professional services, expense for medical care of others, use of products, completed work, and activities of contractors.

The perils covered are: bodily injury, property damage, and defense.

Workmen's compensation insurance

Workmen's compensation insurance provides protection to the employer against the liability, imposed on him by law, to pay benefits to any workman because of injury sustained by him in the course of and arising out of his employment, without regard to fault or negligence on his part or that of any other person.

In California, all employers of one or more employees must secure liability for workmen's compensation. A standard workmen's compensation policy form in general use covers the employer for any injury that may result to an employee during the course of or in connection with his employment.

INSURANCE LICENSES AND LICENSING PROCEDURE

Under the insurance laws of the state of California, no person may transact insurance or act as an insurance agent, broker, or solicitor until he has obtained an appropriate license from the California State Insurance Commissioner. The three main licenses in the property and casualty field are agent, broker, and solicitor license.

Agent

An insurance agent is a person authorized by and acting on behalf of an insurer (company) to transact insurance. With an application for license as an insurance agent, at least one notice of company appointment of agent must be filed. This notice is a document wherein a company appoints the applicant as an agent when he obtains a license. An agent can transact insurance only with the companies that have appointed him as their agent. The company itself must qualify as an admitted insurer. An admitted insurer is one who has received a certificate of authority from the insurance commissioner to transact specified classes of insurance business in California.

Generally, there is no limit to the number of companies for which a licensee may act as an agent. Most agents represent a number of companies in order to be able to offer a wider variety of insurance services to their clients.

BUSINESS RISKS

OUTLINE OF STANDARD COVERAGES AVAILABLE AND POLICY FORMS USED

California Standard Form Fire Insurance Policy

Building, Equipment, Stock, Merchandise, Loss of Earnings, Extra Expense, Rental Income, and Leasehold may be insured together or individually.

I. Standard Form Fire Insurance Policy plus Building, Equipment, and Stock (Merchandise) Form will insure against:

    a) Fire   b) Lightning

II. To the above may be added an Extended Coverage Endorsement which will insure against:

    a) Windstorm   f) Riot

    b) Explosion   g) Vehicles

    c) Hail   h) Riot attending a strike

    d) Aircraft   i) Civil commotion

    e) Smoke

III. To the above may be added a Vandalism and Malicious Mischief Endorsement which will insure against:

    a) Vandalism   b) Malicious mischief

IV. To the above may be added the following endorsements which will cover the named perils or risks:

    a) Earthquake Endorsement   d) Leasehold Interest Endorsement

    b) Business Interruption Endorsement   e) Sprinkler Leakage Endorsement

    c) Rental Income Endorsement   f) Special Extended Coverages Endorsements

FIGURE 13-1

PERSONAL RISKS

OUTLINE OF STANDARD COVERAGES AVAILABLE AND POLICY FORMS USED

California Standard Form Fire Insurance Policy

Dwelling Building, Private Structures, Personal Property, Rental Value, and Additional Living Expense may be insured together or individually.

I. Standard Form Fire Insurance Policy plus Dwelling and Contents Form will insure against:

    a) Fire   b) Lightning

II. To the above may be added an Extended Coverage Endorsement which will insure against:

    a) Windstorm and hail   e) Civil commotion

    b) Explosion   f) Aircraft

    c) Riot   g) Vehicles

    d) Riot attending a strike   h) Smoke

III. To the above may be added a Vandalism and Malicious Mischief Endorsement which will insure against:

    a) Vandalism   b) Malicious mischief

IV. To the above may be added an Earthquake Damage Endorsement which will insure against:

    a) Earthquake

V. To the above may be added a Broad Form Endorsement which will insure against all of the above plus:

    a) Collapse

    b) Falling objects

    c) Weight of ice, snow, or sleet

    d) Breakage of glass

    e) Freezing of plumbing, heating, and air conditioning systems and domestic appliances

    f) Sudden and accidental tearing, cracking, burning, or bulging of appliance for heating water for domestic consumption (excluding any of the above as a result of wear and tear, deterioration or rust).

    g) Electrical injury to appliances

VI. For a Dwelling Building Only, the Dwelling Special Form will insure against all of the perils described in I, II, III, IV, and V above.

FIGURE 13-2

Specific requirements. There are no specific requirements with regard to degree of education or prior experience. The applicant for an agent's license has only to pass the examination given by the insurance commissioner, which consists of a number of questions. The applicant must obtain a score of 70 percent or better in order to pass. In addition to passing the examination, the applicant must be appointed by a company as its agent, as mentioned above. Although the commissioner imposes no special education or experience requirement, the applicant must realize that very few insurance companies will consent to appointing him as their agent unless they feel that he has the ability and potential for becoming a successful agent. It may thus be said that the industry itself sets certain standards for those who want to become insurance agents.

To obtain a license to act as a fire and casualty insurance agent, the applicant must:

1. Be a citizen or national of the United States or an applicant for citizenship.
2. Not be a minor.
3. Before being licensed, file at least one notice of company appointment.
4. Pass an examination given by the insurance commissioner.

Broker

An insurance broker is a person who acts for compensation on behalf of another person and transacts insurance with, but not on behalf of, an insurance company. A broker may be thought of as an individual who may place insurance and do business with whatever insurance company he wants, as opposed to an agent who may represent only those companies for whom he has been appointed an agent. One who has an insurance broker license may also obtain an agent's license, without examination, by filing an application form with the insurance commissioner, together with a notice of company appointment. Compensation for brokers and agents is generally a portion of the premium the client (insured) pays for the policy. The applicant for a broker's license must meet a more stringent set of requirements than the applicant for an agent's license.

Specific requirements. To obtain a license to act as a broker, the applicant must:

1. Be a citizen or national of the United States or an applicant for citizenship.
2. Not be a minor.
3. File and maintain in effect a $1,000 surety bond with the insurance commissioner. The contingency of the bond is that the broker will account to those dealing with him for insurance moneys and premiums received by him. The annual premium for such bond is generally under $20.
4. Take the qualifying examination for a license to act as an insurance broker after he has:
   a. Successfully completed within three years of the application date a course of instruction previously approved by the insurance commissioner, requiring at least 90 hours of classroom work or the equivalent in correspondence work and covering the principal branches of the insurance business; or
   b. Successfully completed, within three years of the application date, a United States Armed Forces Institute insurance course if it has been previously approved by the insurance commissioner; or
   c. Been regularly employed by an insurance company, insurance broker, or insurance agent, or been licensed as an insurance agent, broker, or solicitor for an aggregate of one year in the three years preceding the date of application. Such employment must have been in responsible insurance duties.
5. Pass an examination given by the insurance commissioner. The examination consists of a number of questions and requires a passing score of 75 percent or better.

Solicitor

A solicitor is employed by a licensed agent or broker to aid in transacting insurance business. A solicitor cannot at the same time be licensed as an agent or a broker. The solicitor is an employee of the agent or broker and is responsible to his employer. On filing with the commissioner a notice of company appointment, he may obtain an agent's license without taking another examination.

Specific requirements. To obtain a license as a solicitor, the applicant must:

1. Be a natural person (individuals only will be issued a solicitor's license) and a citizen or national of the United States or an applicant for citizenship.
2. File a written statement signed by a fire and casualty agent or broker stating that such agent

or broker will employ the applicant if he passes the examination and is licensed.
3. Pass an examination given by the insurance commissioner. This examination is the same as that given for an agent's license, and a score of 70 percent or better is required to pass.

Certificate of convenience

A certificate of convenience is a temporary license issued to a person who wants to transact insurance as an agent or solicitor but has not yet passed the appropriate examination. It allows the holder to gain experience while preparing for the examination, and it is issued for a term not to exceed six months.

General rules governing licensees

Insurance licensees must adhere to certain rules and regulations set by the insurance commissioner and the California Insurance Code in much the same way that real estate licensees are regulated by the real estate commissioner and the Real Estate Law.

HOME WARRANTY INSURANCE PROGRAMS

Brokers have long been aware that a common problem with respect to the sale of homes has to do with the inoperability or malfunction of certain items in the property after the purchaser moves in.

To alleviate this problem, a number of firms have recently been organized which provide insurance for the seller and buyer with respect to repairs which may be necessary to the plumbing, electrical and heating systems, and to common appliances such as a dishwasher, range, oven, garbage disposal, and exhaust fan.

Many brokers claim that the advertising and provision of such protection in connection with the listing is an excellent selling tool. Costs, fees, and the degree of protection vary, but in general, the arrangement for such warranty is made at the time the listing is obtained, and the seller pays for the cost of the policy.

Commonly, such policies provide labor, parts, and materials to repair or replace, as necessary, the following:

Electrical Systems:
Main service panels, all subpanels, all wall receptacles, light switches, and all outside receptacles attached to the main structure.

Built-in Appliances:
Garbage Disposal: Disposal motor, motor shaft bearing, disposal blades, electrical connection, or complete disposal. The repair of disposal is for normal usage. Breakage by foreign object or extreme misuse is not covered under this warranty.
Dishwasher: Gasket leaks, timer, motor and pump, impeller and sprayer unit, dryer element, electrical connections, and safety limit switches. Excluded are door latches and hinges.
Surface Range: (Gas fired) gas controls, burners, orifices, gas valves, gas cocks, flex line, pilot, and pilot lines.
Surface Range: (Electric) burner switches, burner elements, and burner wiring harness.
Oven: (Gas) burners, orifices, thermostat control unit, gas safety valve, pilot, pilot lines, and thermocouplings. Excluded are timers, glass oven doors, latches, and hinges.
Oven: (Electric) elements (bake and broil), wiring, thermostat control unit, and bake and broil selector switches. Excluded are timers, glass oven doors, latches, and hinges.
Bathroom and Kitchen Exhaust Fan: Motor switches, and sockets.

Heating Systems:
Electrical and Gas Fired: Wall furnaces—Electrical Perimeter Heating Systems (excluding baseboard casing). **Floor Furnace—Forced Air Systems** (heat only): Repair and replacement of the following: Gas valves, gas lines, control valves, pilot generators, thermocouplings, pilots, cleaning and regulating of burners, blower limit controls, blower motors, blower belts, variable speed pulleys, vents, vent pipes, thermostat (heat only), and thermostat wiring.
Hot Water and Steam Systems (Gas or Oil Fired): Repair or replacement of circular motors, expansion tanks, boilers, all control valves, pressure guages, pressure switches, burners, thermostat, radiators, convertors, electrical heating units and wiring, fuel pumps, fuel lines, all ignition components necessary for the operation of the heating units. Excluded are all inaccessible radiant and steam lines in floors and interior walls.

Plumbing Systems:
Plumbing: Repair leaks and breaks in water lines on the interior of the house, including riser lines on the interior of the house and riser lines to plumbing fixtures. Excluded are all water lines on the exterior, sewer line waste lines and main service lines.
Toilet Tanks: Repair or replacement of all interior components of the water closet, tank bolts and washers, flushing mechanism and over-flow tube, flapper valve and chain, ball cock, float arm, supply valve and line. Excluded are tank, tank lids, toilet seat, and bowls.
Hot Water Heater: (Gas Fired) Repair and replacement of the following: gas valve, line, thermocouple,

pilot, cleaning and regulating of burners, thermostat heating control, pressure relief valve, vent pipes, and main water tank.

Hot Water Heater (Electrical): Repair and replacement of the following: electrical heating element, heating control, valves, and tanks as necessary.

There are, of course, certain limitations, exclusions, and minimal charges in connection with repair calls, but in general, such policies seem to be excellent protection for the seller and the buyer. They are gaining in popularity in the real estate industry.

QUESTIONS FOR DISCUSSION

1. What is the minimum amount of insurance protection generally required in your locality with respect to various types of buildings?
2. What is meant by the statement that an insurance contract is basically a contract of indemnity?
3. What are some of the advantages to a homeowner who purchases a homeowners policy?
4. Discuss some of the risks a homeowner may want to protect against.
5. Discuss some of the risks an owner of a business may want to protect against.
6. Discuss coinsurance and how it affects the policyholder.
7. What are some of the advantages and disadvantages to being both an insurance and real estate agent?
8. How do the license requirements for an insurance agent differ from those for an insurance broker?
9. In what way does the placing of insurance protection differ between an agent and a broker?
10. With respect to a real estate licensee and an insurance licensee, discuss the similarity of the rules and regulations which govern both licensees.

14

Real estate mathematics

Section 10153 of the California Real Estate Law states that licensees must have an appropriate knowledge of the English language, including reading, writing, and spelling, and must also have a good basic knowledge of elementary mathematics. This knowledge must be sufficient to allow the licensee to correctly calculate and compute mathematical problems common to normal real estate transactions.

This chapter will serve to illustrate how these basic principles of mathematics are used to solve problems such as:

1. Calculation of interest.
2. Prorations, including such items as rent, taxes, and insurance.
3. Percentage problems involving commissions, profit and loss, net listings, capitalization, loan ratio, and discount.
4. Property tax.
5. Depreciation.
6. Amortization and calculation of the present value of a loan.
7. Area measurement.

INTEREST

Interest is an amount of money paid for the use of money. When one leases an apartment, he pays rent to the landlord for use of the apartment. In the same way, when one borrows money he pays for use of the money a rent, or a fee, called interest.

Rate, or rate of interest, is the amount being charged for use of money, expressed as a percentage per annum of the amount being borrowed.

Principal is the amount of money that has been loaned by the lender and borrowed by the borrower.

Time is the number of days, months, or years for which an amount of money has been borrowed and for which interest may be charged.

Simple and compound interest

Simple interest is the type charged by banks, savings and loan associations, insurance companies, and other lenders for the use of money borrowed from them. The principal and the interest of the loan may be repaid in several ways. The most common is for the borrower to make monthly amortized payments over a given period of time. Each payment applies toward paying off both the interest and the principal.

Simple interest is the type the borrower pays to the lender; compound interest is the type the lending institution pays to a depositor for money in a savings account. Compound interest may not be charged by lenders in California to persons who borrow money; it can be paid only to persons who put their money in savings accounts. Compound interest causes interest to be paid on interest. For example, many savings and loan associations pay depositors interest at the end of each quarter, or four times a year. If the depositor does not withdraw any of his funds during the year, not only will he receive a rate of interest on the amount he originally deposited, but also at the end of each quarter, the interest he receives will be added to the amount on deposit. Since the amount of interest paid at the end of each quarter is calculated on the amount on deposit, the depositor is actually receiving interest on interest as well as on the original principal.

Computing time

The two most common methods of measuring time for interest computations are (1) 30-day month time and (2) exact time.

1. Using the 30-day method, the year is divided into 12, 30-day months, and 360 days is one year.

2. Using the exact time method, the year is represented by 365 days or, if a leap year, 366 days.

In computing interest, the time factor is represented by a fraction. The numerator represents the amount of days for which interest is to be charged. In calculating the number of days on which interest is to be charged, the days are counted from the day following creation of the obligation up to and including the last day. The rule is simplified by remembering to skip the first day and include the last day.

Assuming interest is to be calculated for 67 days, the fraction representing time would be 67/360 if the 360-day year is used and 67/365 if an exact time year is used. The 360-day year is the one used in real estate transactions, and it will be used in all subsequent examples.

Where the period of time is expressed in even years, the time factor will not be shown as a fraction but rather as a whole number representing the actual years. Thus, in calculating the interest for a loan in which the time is 11 years, the time factor would be represented by 11. Where the period of time is expressed in even months, the time factor is shown as a fraction with a denominator of 12. Thus, for a loan of 7 months, the time factor fraction will be shown as 7/12. Where the period of time is to be expressed in days, the time factor fraction will show the number of days as the numerator and 360 as the denominator. If the interest is to be calculated for 79 days, the time factor fraction will be shown as 79/360.

Interest formulas

Interest can be calculated by using the formula

$$I = PRT$$
Interest = Principal × Rate × Time.

1. What is the interest on a loan of $7,000 for three years at 9 percent? In calculating interest, the rate is expressed as a decimal. Solution:

Interest = $7,000 × .09 × 3
Interest = $1,890

The $7,000 is first multiplied by .09, giving an answer of $630. This result is then multiplied by three, giving an answer of $1,890.

2. What is the interest on a loan of $6,000 for seven months at 12½ percent? Solution:

Interest = $6,000 × .125 × 7/12
Interest = $437.50

3. What is the interest on a loan of $3,000 at 11 percent for 70 days? Solution:

Interest = $3,000 × .11 × 70/360
Interest = $64.166 = $64.17

Rate of interest may be found by use of formula

$$R = \frac{I}{P \times T}$$

$$\text{Rate} = \frac{\text{Interest}}{\text{Principal} \times \text{Time}}$$

1. If the amount of the loan is $20,000, the time is three years, and the interest charged is $5,400, what is the rate? Solution:

$$\text{Rate} = \frac{\$5,400}{\$20,000 \times 3} = \frac{\$5,400}{\$60,000} = \frac{9}{100}$$

= 9% (9/100 expressed as a percent equals 9%).

2. Amount of loan is $16,000, interest is $1,260, and time is seven months. What is the rate of interest? Solution:

$$\text{Rate} = \frac{\$1,260}{\$16,000 \times 7/12} = \frac{\$1,260}{\$9,333} = .135 = 13½\%$$

Principal can be found by using the formula

$$P = \frac{I}{R \times T}$$

$$\text{Principal} = \frac{\text{Interest}}{\text{Rate} \times \text{Time}}$$

1. What is the principal amount of a loan on which the interest is $5,580, the rate is 15½ percent, and the time is three years? Solution:

$$\text{Principal} = \frac{\$5,580}{.155 \times 3} = \frac{\$5,580}{.465} = \$12,000$$

2. If the interest is $900, the rate is 9 percent, and the time is five months, what is the principal amount of the loan? Solution:

$$\text{Principal} = \frac{\$900}{9/100 \times 5/12} = \$24,000.$$

(Rate is usually stated as a decimal. However, in this problem the 9 percent rate is not expressed as .09 but is shown as the fraction 9/100, because the time, five months, is better expressed as 5/12 than as its decimal equivalent .41⅔.)

3. What is the principal amount of the loan if the interest is $3,200, the rate is 16 percent, and the time is three months? Solution:

$$\text{Principal} = \frac{\$3,200}{.16 \times .25} = \$80,00.$$

(In this problem, the time three months expressed fractionally is ³⁄₁₂, which reduces to ¼. The decimal equivalent of ¼ is .25, so it is more convenient to express both the rate and the time as decimals.)

Time can be found by using the formula

$$T = \frac{I}{P \times R}$$

$$\text{Time} = \frac{\text{Interest}}{\text{Principal} \times \text{Rate}}$$

What is the time on a loan of $8,000 when the rate is 9 percent and the interest is $2,520? Solution:

$$\text{Time} = \frac{\$2,520}{\$8,000 \times .09} = 3½ \text{ years}$$

60-day 6 percent method

Numerous shortcut methods for finding interest are available. One of the more common is the 60-day 6 percent method. The basis of this method is that 6 percent interest for one year equals 1 percent interest for two months, or 60 days. The 1 percent is easily found by merely moving the decimal point in the amount of the principal.

To find interest at 6 percent for 60 days, merely move the decimal point in the principal amount two places to the left.

Example: What is the interest on $2,550 at 6 percent for 60 days?

Solution: Moving the decimal point two places to the left in $2,550, we have $25.50, which is the amount of the interest.

We can check this answer by using the formula previously stated:

$$I = P \times R \times T$$
Interest = $2,550 × .06 × 60/360 = $25.50

With some practice, one can find the interest when the time period varies from 60 days and when the rate differs from 6 percent.

Example: What is the interest on $2,550 at 6 percent for 150 days?
Solution:

$25.50 interest for 60 days
25.50 interest for 60 days more
12.75 interest for 30 days (½ of the 60-day amount)
$63.75 interest at 6% for 150 days

Example: What is the interest on $2,550 at 8 percent for 150 days?

Solution: Calculation of the interest by the 60-day 6 percent method (preceding problem) gives us $63.75 as interest, but this is at 6 percent. To find the interest at 8 percent, we must realize that 8 percent is ⅓ more than 6 percent, so we take ⅓ of $63.75, which equals $21.25, and add it to the $63.75.

Interest on $2,550 at 8% for 150 days equals
$63.75 (at 6%)
 21.25 (additional 2%)
$85.00 interest at 8%

Interest tables

Although each of the preceding methods allows the licensee to accurately calculate interest, anyone who has occasion to regularly make such calculations should obtain a series of interest tables. Such tables supply a numerical multiplier to be used in determining interest on various amounts, for different periods of time, at different interest rates. The principal sum is multiplied by the appropriate multiplier, and the answer is the amount of interest. Table 14–1 is an example of an interest table. It shows the various amounts of interest per $1,000 at different interest rates for from 1 to 30 days.

1. What is the amount of interest on $1 000 at 5 percent for 20 days? Solution: A move to the right from 20 days to the 5 percent column reveals a figure of 2.7778, which rounded off to the nearest cent equals $2.78. Thus the interest on $1,000 at 5 percent for 20 days is $2.78.

2. What is the interest on $18,000 at 7 percent for 26 days? Solution: From the table we can determine that the interest for $1,000 at 7 percent for 26 days is 5.0555, and we must multiply this number by 18 in order to arrive at the interest for $18,000.

$$18 \times 5.0555 = 90.9990 = \$91$$

Finding number of days

One of the many types of tables helpful to the licensee is a table that allows rapid calculation of the exact number of days between two dates. Table 14–2 is an example of a table that shows the number of days from any date in one month to the same date in any other month.

1. How many days from February 12, 1981 to October 12, 1981? Solution: From February in the

TABLE 14–1
Interest figured on $1,000
(360 days to the year)

Days	12 percent	13 percent	14 percent	15 percent	16 percent
1	.333	.361	.389	.417	.444
2	.667	.722	.778	.833	.889
3	1.000	1.083	1.167	1.250	1.333
4	1.333	1.444	1.556	1.667	1.778
5	1.667	1.806	1.944	2.083	2.222
6	2.000	2.167	2.333	2.500	2.667
7	2.336	2.528	2.722	2.917	3.111
8	2.667	2.889	3.111	3.333	3.556
9	3.000	3.250	3.500	3.750	4.000
10	3.333	3.611	3.889	4.167	4.444
11	3.667	3.972	4.278	4.583	4.889
12	4.000	4.333	4.667	5.000	5.333
13	4.333	4.694	5.056	5.417	5.778
14	4.667	5.056	5.444	5.833	6.222
15	5.000	5.417	5.833	6.250	6.667
16	5.333	5.778	6.222	6.667	7.111
17	5.667	6.139	6.611	7.083	7.556
18	6.000	6.500	7.000	7.500	8.000
19	6.333	6.861	7.389	7.917	8.444
20	6.667	7.222	7.778	8.333	8.889
21	7.000	7.583	8.167	8.750	9.333
22	7.333	7.944	8.556	9.167	9.778
23	7.667	8.306	8.944	9.583	10.222
24	8.000	8.667	9.333	10.000	10.667
25	8.338	9.028	9.722	10.417	11.111
26	8.667	9.389	10.111	10.833	11.556
27	9.000	9.750	10.500	11.250	12.000
28	9.336	10.111	10.889	11.667	12.444
29	9.667	10.472	11.278	12.083	12.889
30	10.000	10.833	11.667	12.500	13.333
31 st day	—	—	—	—	—

left column, move to the right and stop under October. The number shown is 242, so from February 12 to October 12 there are 242 days. If 1981 was a leap year, an additional day would have to be added for February, making the total 243.

2. How many days from January 21, 1981 to November 26, 1981? Solution: From January in the left column, moving to the right to November, we find 304. Thus, from January 21 to November 21 there are 304 days. However, the problem asks for the time to November 26, so we must add the 5 days from the 21st to the 26th and arrive at a total of 309 days.

With some additional calculations, this same type of table can be used to determine the exact amount of days from a month and day in one year to a month and day in a subsequent year.

TABLE 14–2
Number of days between dates

From	To Jan.	Feb.	March	April	May	June	July	Aug.	Sept.	Oct.	Nov.	Dec.
January	365	31	59	90	120	151	181	212	243	273	304	334
February	334	365	28	59	89	120	150	181	212	242	273	303
March	306	337	365	31	61	92	122	153	184	214	245	275
April	275	306	334	365	30	61	91	122	153	183	214	244
May	245	276	304	335	365	31	61	92	123	153	184	214
June	214	245	273	304	334	365	30	61	92	122	153	183
July	184	215	243	274	304	335	365	31	62	92	123	153
August	153	184	212	243	273	304	334	365	31	61	92	122
September	122	153	181	212	242	273	303	334	365	30	61	91
October	92	123	151	182	212	243	273	304	335	365	31	61
November	61	92	120	151	181	212	242	273	304	334	365	30
December	31	62	90	121	151	182	212	243	274	304	335	365

PRORATIONS

Proration generally takes place in escrow. Its purpose is to correctly apportion income and expense items between the parties to the sale. The more common items that usually need to be prorated are rents, taxes, insurance, and interest. Table 14-3 shows one of many different types of proration tables employed in such calculations.

1. The sale of a building involves a small store which rents for $500 per month, payable in advance on the first of each month. Escrow is to be closed on the 25th of a 30-day month. How much of the month's rent is due to the seller and how much to the buyer? Solution: To find the value of 25 days of a 30-day month, refer to the left column (years, months, days) of the proration table. To the right of the number 25 we find the factor .8333 for a 30-day month.

$$.8333 \times \$500 = 416.65$$

Thus, the seller gets $416.65 for 25 days, and the buyer receives the remainder, $83.35.

2. Smith purchases a triplex on which the owner Lorvan has already collected the rents amounting to $1,620. Escrow is to be closed on the 18th day of a 31-day month. How is the rent apportioned between Smith and Lorvan? Solution: From the proration table, the factor of .5806 is given for the 18th day of a 31-day month.

$$.5806 \times \$1,620. = \$940.5720 = \$940.57$$
$$\$1,620.00 - \$940.57 = \$679.43.$$

Smith, the buyer, is entitled to $679.43 of the $1,620 which Lorran has already collected.

3. Morgan paid both installments of his property tax amounting to $1,850 and sells his property with escrow to close on May 1. What is the tax proration? Solution: Taxes are paid for the fiscal year July 1 to June 30. The period from July 1 to May 1 is ten months. The factor from the proration table, under the column Taxes and Insurance, is .8333.

$$.8333 \times \$1,850 = \$1,541.6050 = \$1,541.61$$
$$\$1,850.00 - \$1,51.61 = \$308.39$$

TABLE 14-3
Proration for rents, taxes, and insurance

Number of years, months, and days	Rents one month days to month		Taxes and insurance one year		Insurance						Number of years, months, and days
					Three years			Five years			
	30	31	Months	Days	Years	Months	Days	Years	Months	Days	
1	.0333	.0323	.0833	.0028	.3333	.0278	.0009	.2000	.0167	.0006	1
2	.0667	.0645	.1667	.0056	.6667	.0556	.0019	.4000	.0333	.0011	2
3	.1000	.0968	.2500	.0083	1.0000	.0833	.0028	.6000	.0500	.0017	3
4	.1333	.1290	.3333	.0111		.1111	.0037	.8000	.0667	.0022	4
5	.1667	.1613	.4167	.0139		.1389	.0046	1.0000	.0833	.0028	5
6	.2000	.1935	.5000	.0167		.1667	.0056		.1000	.0033	6
7	.2333	.2258	.5833	.0194		.1944	.0065		.1167	.0039	7
8	.2667	.2581	.6667	.0222		.2222	.0074		.1333	.0044	8
9	.3000	.2903	.7500	.0250		.2500	.0083		.1500	.0050	9
10	.3333	.3226	.8333	.0278		.2778	.0093		.1667	.0056	10
11	.3667	.3548	.9167	.0306		.3056	.0102		.1833	.0061	11
12	.4000	.3871	1.0000	.0333		.3333	.0111		.2000	.0067	12
13	.4333	.4194		.0361			.0120			.0072	13
14	.4667	.4516		.0389			.0130			.0078	14
15	.5000	.4839		.0417			.0139			.0083	15
16	.5333	.5161		.0444			.0148			.0089	16
17	.5667	.5484		.0472			.0157			.0094	17
18	.6000	.5806		.0500			.0167			.0100	18
19	.6333	.6129		.0528			.0176			.0106	19
20	.6667	.6452		.0556			.0185			.0111	20
21	.7000	.6774		.0583			.0194			.0117	21
22	.7333	.7097		.0611			.0204			.0122	22
23	.7667	.7419		.0639			.0213			.0128	23
24	.8000	.7742		.0667			.0222			.0133	24
25	.8333	.8065		.0694			.0231			.0139	25
26	.8667	.8387		.0722			.0241			.0144	26
27	.9000	.8710		.0750			.0250			.0150	27
28	.9333	.9032		.0778			.0259			.0156	28
29	.9667	.9355		.0806			.0269			.0161	29
30	1.0000	.9677		.0833			.0278			.0167	30
31		1.0000									31

Morgan, the seller, is credited with $308.39, and the buyer is charged $308.39.

It is interesting to note that the factor used in this problem (.8333) is the same as that used in the preceding Example 1. In that example, .8333 represented the 25th day of a 30-day month. As a fraction, 25 days out of 30 is shown as 25/30 = 5/6. In this problem 10 months out of 12 as a fraction is 10/12 = 5/6. Obviously, .8333 is 5/6 represented decimally.

4. Reagan pays $648 as the premium on a three-year fire insurance policy. He sells his home one year and 17 days later. Assuming that the premium is to be prorated according to this time period, what must the buyer pay to Reagan? Solution: From the proration table,

$$1 \text{ year} = .3333$$
$$17 \text{ days} = \underline{.0157}$$
$$.3490$$

one year and 17 days = .3490 × $648 = $226.152 = $226.15.
$648.00 − $226.15 = $421.85 (amount to be charged the buyer).

5. A five-year policy premium is $1,175. Find the value of three years, five months, and 16 days. Solution: From the proration table,

$$3 \text{ years} = .6000$$
$$5 \text{ months} = .0833$$
$$16 \text{ days} = \underline{.0089}$$
$$.6922$$
$$.6922 \times \$1,175. = \$813,335 = \$813.34$$

The value of three years, five months, and 16 days is $219.43.

The proration of interest enters into a real estate transaction in many ways. One of the most common is in the sale of a house when the buyer arranges for a new loan and the seller must pay off his old loan. When the lender sends his demand to the escrow officer with regard to the loan being paid off, the seller will usually be charged for interest from the time of the last payment to the date of the close of escrow.

If the buyer assumes an existing loan, we may have a different situation. The interest portion of a monthly payment is usually for the month past, thus if escrow closes on the 15th of the month, the seller will be charged for two weeks interest, which will be credited to the buyer since at the end of the month the buyer will make his payment, which will include interest for the entire preceding month.

PERCENTAGE

A great many of the problems encountered in everyday real estate practice are percentage problems. These are generally of three types, since there are three elements in percentage problems, and the problems usually involve finding one of the elements when given the other two. The elements are: (1) base, (2) rate, and (3) part (also referred to as percentage or portion).

The *base* is the principle amount and represents 100 percent.

The *rate* is the relationship between the base and a part of the base and is expressed as a percent.

The *part* of the base will vary in size, depending on the rate used, and may be more or less than the base.

The following formulas are used:

$$\text{Base} = \text{Part divided by rate} = B = \frac{P}{R}$$
$$\text{Rate} = \text{Part divided by base} = R = \frac{P}{B}$$
$$\text{Part} = \text{Base times rate} = P = B \times R$$

The following examples will illustrate the use of the formulas.

1. Pickett receives $3,000, representing an 8 percent return on an investment. What amount has he invested? Solution: Part is $3,000, rate is 8 percent, base is unknown. Using the formula

$$B = \frac{P}{R}$$
$$B = \frac{\$3,000}{.08}$$
$$B = \$37,500$$

2. Stewart sells a building for $280,000 and receives a commission of $19,600. What percent of the selling price is his commission? Solution: Base is $280,000, and part is $19,600. Using the formula

$$R = \frac{P}{B}$$
$$R = \frac{\$19,600}{\$280,000} = .07 = 7\% \text{ rate}$$

3. Szukalski tells Funke that he can expect a 12 percent return on his investment of $385,000. How much will Funke receive? Solution: Base is $385,000, and rate is 9 percent. Using the formula

$$P = B \times R$$
$$P = .09 \times \$385,000 = \$46,200$$

The following are examples of common types of percentage problems found in real estate practice.

Commissions

1. Salesman Thomas gets one half of the commission his firm receives on the sale of a building. If the building sells for $850,000 and the commission rate is 5 percent, Thomas's share is:

Commission = .05 × $850,000 = $42,500
$42,500 ÷ 2 = $21,250

2. Broker Lippitt sells a building for $286,500. He receives a commission of 6 percent of the first $100,000 and 5 percent of the balance of the selling price. How much does he get? Solution:

.06 × $100,000 = $ 6,000
.05 × $186,500 = $\underline{9,325}$
$15,325 Lippitt's total commission

3. Salesman Wagner's contract with broker Samuels states that if Wagner lists and sells a property he is to receive 60 percent of the commission, less 10 percent for advertising expense. On the sale of a house at $128,500, what will Wagner receive? The commission rate is 6 percent of the selling price. Solution:

.06 × $128,500 = $7,710 commission on sale received by office.
.60 × $7,710 = $4,626 Wagner's share before advertising deduction.
.10 × $4,626 = $462.60 deduction for advertising expense.
$4,626 − $462.60 = $4,163.40 Wagner's share of commission.

Profit and loss

1. Irene Anderson purchases a lot for $5,000 and later sells it for $8,000. What is her percent of profit on the original cost? Solution:

$8,000 selling price
− 5,000 cost
$3,000 profit

Rate = Part ($3,000) divided by base ($5,000)
= .60 = 60%

2. Morris Green sells his house for $120,000 and makes a profit of 25 percent based on the original cost. What was the cost? Solution: In this type of problem, the selling price represents the cost plus the profit. The cost is the base, which is always 100 percent, and to this is added 25 percent profit, so that the selling price of $120,000 represents 125 percent.

$$B = \frac{P}{R} = B = \frac{\$120,000}{1.25} = \$96,000 \text{ original cost}$$

3. Louis Shaffer purchases 10 acres of land for $200,000. He wants to sell the land and make a profit of 35 percent. For how much must he sell the property? Solution:

.35 × 200,000 = $70,000 profit of 35%
$200,000 cost plus $70,000 desired profit
= $270,000 selling price

Net listing

1. Joseph Calleja tells broker Batmale that he wants to net $141,000 on the sale of his property. For how much must Batmale sell the property in order to make a 6 percent commission in addition to the $141,000 for Calleja? Solution: Since the selling price must include $141,000 plus a 6 percent commission, the reader should realize that the $141,000 must represent 94 percent. This, when added to the 6 percent commission, equals the selling price or 100 percent.

$$\text{Base (100\%)} = \frac{\$141,000 \text{ (part)}}{.94 \text{ (rate)}}$$
$$= \$150,000 \text{ selling price}$$

The $150,000 selling price minus 6 percent commission of $9,000 equals $141,000 net to the seller. Because net listings may often lead to a misunderstanding between the broker and seller, it is usually better for the broker to calculate the selling price necessary to allow for a normal commission and then list the property in the regular way.

Capitalization

Capitalization of income is treated extensively in Chapter 12, dealing with appraisal and valuation.

1. Luckmann wants to purchase an income property that shows a net yearly income of $120,000. If he wants an 8 percent return on his total investment, how much should he pay for the building? Solution:

$$\frac{\$120,000 \text{ (net income)}}{.08 \text{ (8\% capitalization rate)}}$$
$$= \$1,500,000 \text{ purchase price}$$

TABLE 14-4
Capitalization

Percent rate	Factor	Percent rate	Factor
7½	13.3	13	7.69
8	12.5	13½	7.40
8½	11.7	14	7.14
9	11.1	14½	6.90
9½	10.5	15	6.67
10	10.0	15½	6.45
10½	9.52	16	6.25
11	9.09	16½	6.06
11½	8.69	17	5.88
12	8.33	17½	5.71
12½	8.00	18	5.56

2. Nesbitt purchases a building for $425,000. The building shows a net yearly income of $25,500. What is his rate of return? Solution:

$$R = \frac{\text{Net income}}{\text{Present value}} = \frac{\$25,500}{\$425,000} = .06 = 6\%$$

A capitalization table similar to the one shown in Table 14-4 is often used to simplify such problems. The rate of capitalization desired is selected, and the net income is multiplied by the factor which is shown on the table for the particular rate.

3. What should be the selling price for a building being sold on the basis of its net income of $23,800, capitalized at 8 percent? Solution: From the capitalization table, we find that the factor for 8 percent is 12.5; thus,

$12.5 \times \$23,800 = \$297,500$ selling price

Loan ratio

A broker or salesman often must approximate the amount of first loan available on a property and the down payment that may be necessary by applying the same loan ratio he thinks the lender will use.

1. Broker Barry shows Mr. and Mrs. Katz a house priced at $135,000. He thinks he can get an 80 percent loan from ABC Savings and Loan Company. If the down payment is to be cash over loan, what will be the amount of the loan and the down payment? Solution:

$.80 \times \$135,00 = \$108,000$ loan
$\$135,00 - \$108,000 = \$27,000$ down payment

On conventional home financing, if the first loan is 75 or 80 percent of the selling price, a shortcut method may be employed to determine the amount of first loan and required down payment. For instance, an 80 percent first loan means 4/5 of the selling price with a down payment of 1/5. Dividing the selling price by five gives the down payment (1/5 = 20%), and subtracting this amount from the selling price gives the amount of the first loan (4/5 = 80%).

2. The selling price is $180,000. On the basis of an anticipated 80 percent first loan, what will be the loan and what will be the down payment? Solution:

$\$180,000 \div 5 = \$36,000$ down payment.
$\$180,000 - \$36,000 = \$144,000$ first loan.

Or the calculation may be made as follows:

5) $180,000 selling price
− 36,000 down payment
$144,000 first loan

Thus, five divided into $180,000 equals $36,000, and the $36,000 subtracted from the $180,000 gives $144,000.

3. The selling price is $168,000. On the basis of a 75 percent loan, what is the first loan and what is the required down payment? Here, 75 percent represents ¾, and the down payment is ¼. Solution:

$\$168,000 \div 4 = \$42,000$ down payment
$\$168,000 - \$42,000 = \$126,000$ first loan

or

4) $168,000 selling price
− 42,000 down payment
$126,000 first loan

Discount

1. A second note has been discounted 20 percent, and the amount of the discount is $1,200. What was the original amount of the note? Solution:

$$\frac{\$1,200}{.20} = \$6,000 \text{ original amount}$$

2. Conklin owns an old building in the city which he wants to convert to cash in order to purchase some country acreage. The building is free and clear. Misthos offers Conklin $95,000 on the following terms: Misthos will obtain a first loan of $60,000 form his bank, put down $20,000 in cash, and Conklin is to carry back a second loan of $15,000. Conklin agrees, and after close of escrow, he sells the note to Casey at a 25 percent discount. How much cash does Conklin now have for the

purchase of the country property? Solution: Conklin received $80,000 plus a $15,000 note on the sale of his building. He discounts the note 25 percent:

$$\$15,000 \times .25 = \$3,750 \text{ discount}$$
$$\$15,000 - \$3,750 = \$11,250$$

The $80,000 from the building plus the $11,250 from the note equalt $91,250 Conklin now has to invest.

PROPERTY TAX

1. Murphy owns a 12-unit building with a 1976–77 full cash value of $180,000. If the assessor has allowed for a 2 percent yearly increase compounded on the tax and adds 15 percent for bond payoff, what is Murphy's 1980–81 tax amount? Solution:

$$\begin{aligned}
&.01 \times \$180,000 = \$1,800 \\
(77\text{-}78)\ &1.02 \times \$1,800 = \$1,836 \\
(78\text{-}79)\ &1.02 \times \$1,836 = \$1,872.72 \\
(79\text{-}80)\ &1.02 \times \$1,872.72 = \$1,910.17 \\
(80\text{-}81)\ &1.02 \times \$1,910.17 = \$1,948.37 \\
&1.15 \times \$1,948.37 = \$2,240.62
\end{aligned}$$

2. Smith receives a statement from the assessor showing an assessed valuation of $12,000 on his apartment house. If the assessor uses 24 percent of market value as the basis for his assessment, what value has been set on Smith's property? Solution:

$$\frac{\$12,000}{.24} = \$50,000 \text{ market value}$$

3. If a property was purchased in 1976 for $65,000, what will each installment of taxes for 1980–81 be with a 2 percent yearly increase compounded on the tax and a $70 homeowner's exemption? Solution:

$$\begin{aligned}
&.01 \times \$65,000 = \$650 \\
(77\text{-}78)\ &1.02 \times \$650 = \$663.00 \\
(78\text{-}79)\ &1.02 \times \$663 = \$676.26 \\
(79\text{-}80)\ &1.02 \times \$676.26 = \$689.79 \\
(80\text{-}81)\ &1.02 \times \$689.79 = \$703.59 \\
&\$703.59 - \$70.00 = \$633.59 \\
&\$633.59 \div 2 = \$316.80
\end{aligned}$$

DEPRECIATION

The reader is referred to Chapter 10, Income Tax and Real Estate, for an extensive discussion of depreciation.

1. Scourkes purchases an income property at a price of $85,000. Of the purchase price, 75 percent is to be allotted to the building and the remainder to the land. Scourkes chooses to use the straight-line method of depreciation and a depreciable life of 30 years for the property. What will be the annual amount of depreciation? Solution:

$$.75 \times \$85,000 = \$63,750 \text{ basis for depreciation}$$
$$\$63,750 \div 30 = \$2,125 \text{ yearly depreciation}$$

2. Vincent's property has a depreciable basis of $156,000. He elects to use the 125 percent declining balance method and a depreciable life of 20 years for the property. What will be his first year's depreciation? Solution:

$$\$156,000 \div 20 = \$7,800$$
$$125\% = 1.25$$
$$1.25 \times \$7,800 = \$9,750 \text{ first year's depreciation.}$$

3. In example 2, what will be Vincent's depreciation for the second year? Solution:

$\$156,000 - \$9,750$ (first year's depreciation) $= \$146,250$
$\$146,250 \div 19 = \$7,697.37$
$1.25 \times \$7,697.37 = \$9,621.71$ second year's depreciation.

AMORTIZATION

Real estate loans usually are repaid by an equal monthly payment over the term of the loan. The payment includes principal and interest, and the process is called amortization. All real estate licensees should have in their possession an *Equal Monthly Loan Amortization Payments* booklet. The booklet shows monthly payments necessary to amortize a loan in a given number of years at different rates of interest and for different amounts. The licensee can usually obtain a copy from his local bank or savings and loan association. Anyone may obtain a copy for a nominal fee by writing to the Financial Publishing Company, 82 Brookline Avenue, Boston, Massachusetts.

Table 14–5, reproduced from this booklet, shows the monthly payments necessary to amortize a loan at 15 percent interest per annum in amounts ranging from $100 to $100,000 with terms.

1. What is the monthly payment necessary to amortize a loan of $70,000 at 15 percent interest per annum for a term of 18 years? Solution: The amount shown in the "18 years" column (Table 14–5) for $70,000 is $939.19. This is the fixed monthly payment necessary to completely pay off

TABLE 14-5

15%	MONTHLY PAYMENT NECESSARY TO AMORTIZE A LOAN					
TERM AMOUNT	14 YEARS	15 YEARS	16 YEARS	17 YEARS	18 YEARS	19 YEARS
100	1.43	1.40	1.38	1.36	1.35	1.33
200	2.86	2.80	2.76	2.72	2.69	2.66
250	3.57	3.50	3.45	3.40	3.36	3.33
300	4.29	4.20	4.14	4.08	4.03	3.99
400	5.71	5.60	5.51	5.44	5.37	5.32
500	7.14	7.00	6.89	6.79	6.71	6.65
1000	14.28	14.00	13.77	13.58	13.42	13.29
2000	28.55	28.00	27.54	27.16	26.84	26.57
3000	42.82	41.99	41.31	40.74	40.26	39.85
4000	57.09	55.99	55.08	54.31	53.67	53.13
5000	71.36	69.98	68.84	67.89	67.09	66.41
6000	85.63	83.98	82.61	81.47	80.51	79.70
7000	99.90	97.98	96.38	95.04	93.92	92.98
8000	114.17	111.97	110.15	108.62	107.34	106.26
9000	128.44	125.97	123.91	122.20	120.76	119.54
10000	142.71	139.96	137.68	135.78	134.17	132.82
11000	156.98	153.96	151.45	149.35	147.59	146.11
12000	171.25	167.96	165.22	162.93	161.01	159.39
13000	185.52	181.95	178.99	176.51	174.42	172.67
14000	199.79	195.95	192.75	190.08	187.84	185.95
15000	214.06	209.94	206.52	203.66	201.26	199.23
16000	228.33	223.94	220.29	217.24	214.68	212.52
17000	242.60	237.93	234.06	230.81	228.09	225.80
18000	256.87	251.93	247.82	244.39	241.51	239.08
19000	271.14	265.93	261.59	257.97	254.93	252.36
20000	285.41	279.92	275.36	271.55	268.34	265.64
21000	299.68	293.92	289.13	285.12	281.76	278.93
22000	313.95	307.91	302.89	298.70	295.18	292.21
23000	328.22	321.91	316.66	312.28	308.59	305.49
24000	342.49	335.91	330.43	325.85	322.01	318.77
25000	356.76	349.90	344.20	339.43	335.43	332.05
26000	371.04	363.90	357.97	353.01	348.84	345.34
27000	385.31	377.89	371.73	366.58	362.26	358.62
28000	399.58	391.89	385.50	380.16	375.68	371.90
29000	413.85	405.89	399.27	393.74	389.10	385.18
30000	428.12	419.88	413.04	407.32	402.51	398.46
31000	442.39	433.88	426.80	420.89	415.93	411.75
32000	456.66	447.87	440.57	434.47	429.35	425.03
33000	470.93	461.87	454.34	448.05	442.76	438.31
34000	485.20	475.86	468.11	461.62	456.18	451.59
35000	499.47	489.86	481.87	475.20	469.60	464.87
36000	513.74	503.86	495.64	488.78	483.01	478.16
37000	528.01	517.85	509.41	502.35	496.43	491.44
38000	542.28	531.85	523.18	515.93	509.85	504.72
39000	556.55	545.84	536.95	529.51	523.26	518.00
40000	570.82	559.84	550.71	543.09	536.68	531.28
41000	585.09	573.84	564.48	556.66	550.10	544.57
42000	599.36	587.83	578.25	570.24	563.52	557.85
43000	613.63	601.83	592.02	583.82	576.93	571.13
44000	627.90	615.82	605.78	597.39	590.35	584.41
45000	642.17	629.82	619.55	610.97	603.77	597.69
50000	713.52	699.80	688.39	678.86	670.85	664.10
55000	784.88	769.78	757.23	746.74	737.93	730.51
60000	856.23	839.76	826.07	814.63	805.02	796.92
65000	927.58	909.74	894.91	882.51	872.10	863.33
70000	998.93	979.72	963.74	950.40	939.19	929.74
75000	1070.28	1049.70	1032.58	1018.28	1006.27	996.15
100000	1427.04	1399.59	1376.77	1357.71	1341.70	1328.20

	MONTHLY PAYMENT NECESSARY TO AMORTIZE A LOAN					15%
TERM AMOUNT	20 YEARS	22 YEARS	25 YEARS	30 YEARS	35 YEARS	40 YEARS
100	1.32	1.30	1.29	1.27	1.26	1.26
200	2.64	2.60	2.57	2.53	2.52	2.51
250	3.30	3.25	3.21	3.17	3.15	3.14
300	3.96	3.90	3.85	3.80	3.78	3.76
400	5.27	5.20	5.13	5.06	5.03	5.02
500	6.59	6.50	6.41	6.33	6.29	6.27
1000	13.17	12.99	12.81	12.65	12.57	12.54
2000	26.34	25.98	25.62	25.29	25.14	25.07
3000	39.51	38.97	38.43	37.94	37.71	37.60
4000	52.68	51.96	51.24	50.58	50.28	50.13
5000	65.84	64.95	64.05	63.23	62.85	62.67
6000	79.01	77.94	76.85	75.87	75.41	75.20
7000	92.18	90.93	89.66	88.52	87.98	87.73
8000	105.35	103.92	102.47	101.16	100.55	100.26
9000	118.52	116.91	115.28	113.80	113.12	112.80
10000	131.68	129.89	128.09	126.45	125.69	125.33
11000	144.85	142.88	140.90	139.09	138.25	137.86
12000	158.02	155.87	153.70	151.74	150.82	150.39
13000	171.19	168.86	166.51	164.38	163.39	162.92
14000	184.36	181.85	179.32	177.03	175.96	175.46
15000	197.52	194.84	192.13	189.67	188.53	187.99
16000	210.69	207.83	204.94	202.32	201.10	200.52
17000	223.86	220.82	217.75	214.96	213.65	213.05
18000	237.03	233.81	230.55	227.60	226.23	225.59
19000	250.20	246.80	243.36	240.25	238.80	238.12
20000	263.36	259.78	256.17	252.89	251.37	250.65
21000	276.53	272.77	268.98	265.54	263.94	263.18
22000	289.70	285.76	281.79	278.18	276.50	275.71
23000	302.87	298.75	294.60	290.83	289.07	288.25
24000	316.03	311.74	307.40	303.47	301.64	300.78
25000	329.20	324.73	320.21	316.12	314.21	313.31
26000	342.37	337.72	333.02	328.76	326.78	325.84
27000	355.54	350.71	345.83	341.40	339.34	338.38
28000	368.71	363.70	358.64	354.05	351.91	350.91
29000	381.87	376.69	371.45	366.69	364.48	363.44
30000	395.04	389.67	384.25	379.34	377.05	375.97
31000	408.21	402.66	397.06	391.98	389.62	388.50
32000	421.38	415.65	409.87	404.63	402.19	401.04
33000	434.55	428.64	422.68	417.27	414.75	413.57
34000	447.71	441.63	435.49	429.92	427.32	426.10
35000	460.88	454.62	448.30	442.56	439.89	438.63
36000	474.05	467.61	461.10	455.20	452.46	451.17
37000	487.22	480.60	473.91	467.85	465.03	463.70
38000	500.39	493.59	486.72	480.49	477.59	476.23
39000	513.55	506.58	499.53	493.14	490.16	488.76
40000	526.72	519.56	512.34	505.78	502.73	501.29
41000	539.89	532.55	525.15	518.43	515.30	513.83
42000	553.06	545.54	537.95	531.07	527.87	526.36
43000	566.22	558.53	550.76	543.72	540.43	538.89
44000	579.39	571.52	563.57	556.36	553.00	551.42
45000	592.56	584.51	576.38	569.00	565.57	563.96
50000	658.40	649.45	640.42	632.23	628.41	626.62
55000	724.24	714.40	704.46	695.45	691.25	689.28
60000	790.08	779.34	768.50	758.68	754.09	751.94
65000	855.92	844.29	832.54	821.89	816.93	814.60
70000	921.76	909.23	896.59	885.12	879.77	877.26
75000	987.60	974.18	960.63	948.34	942.61	939.92
100000	1316.79	1298.90	1280.84	1264.45	1256.82	1253.23

the loan, including principal and interest, over a period of 18 years.

2. What is the monthly payment necessary to amortize a loan of $119,500 at 15 percent interest per annum for a term of 25 years? Solution:

$100,000 at 15% for 25 years = $1,280.84
$19,000 at 15% for 25 years = $ 243.36
    500 at 15% for 25 years =   6.41
    Total payment required = $1,530.61

3. What will be the monthly payment necessary to amortize a loan of 275,000 at 15 percent interest per annum for a term of 30 years? Solution:

Payment for $100,000 = $1,264.45
Payment for 100,000 = 1,264.45
Payment for   75,000 =   948.34
Total payment required = $3,477.24

Amortization schedule

For any loan, an amortization schedule can be constructed to show the allocation of each payment into interest and principal, and the balance outstanding after each payment has been made. This is done by (1) computing the interest on the previous balance, (2) deducting the interest from the payment, and (3) crediting the remainder as a repayment of principal. A schedule for any loan can be obtained from the Financial Publishing Company, Boston, Massachusetts.

Present balance of a loan

It is often necessary for the licensee to determine the present balance due on an outstanding loan. He may want to know how much will be necessary to pay off the obligation or what is the present value of the owner's equity.

A call to the bank or savings and loan association usually is all that is needed to find out the balance of the first loan, and many lenders show the balance on the monthly or yearly statement sent to the borrower. Although the licensee may have to calculate the balance due on a first loan, it is usually with respect to second loans that such calculations become necessary.

Tables are available for this purpose. Table 14-6 shows a loan progress chart for the remaining balance per $1,000 on a loan at 12 percent interest per annum. The table assumes that amortized monthly payments have been made.

1. What is the present balance of a $5,000 loan at 6 percent interest per annum with a term of ten years, three years after date of execution of the note? Solution: The age of the loan is three years, and the table shows that the balance per $1,000 on a three-year-old loan originally written for ten years is now $813. Thus, for a $5,000 loan amount, the balance due will be

$$5 \times \$813 = \$4,065$$

The balance due on a second loan for which the monthly payment has not been amortized can be found by using the *Equal Monthly Loan Amortization Payments* information shown in Table 14-7.

1. What is the present balance of a note executed five years ago in the amount of $6,000 at 9¾ percent interest per annum for a term of eight years? Payments have been $60 per month. Solution: From the 9¾ percent table, find the $6,000 amount and the payment closest to $60. This is found as $60.33 in the "17 years" column. Thus, at a monthly payment of $60.33, it will take 15 years to amortize the note. Five years have passed, however, so there are 12 years left. Going to the "12 years" column, we find that the amount closest to $60 to $60.22. A move to the left of $60.22 to the left margin will reveal the sum of $5,100 now due.

Notice that in figuring the balance of the note now due we must take the monthly amount actually being paid ($60) and treat it as though it is an amortized payment. Actually, the loan was for a term of eight years. The monthly payment required to amortize a note of $6,000 at 9¾ percent interest for a term of eight years is $90.26. Since only $60 a month was actually being paid, this note is not amortized, and when the eight-year term is up, a balloon payment will be necessary.

AREA MEASUREMENT

The licensee often must determine the square footage contained in a parcel of land or in a building. Generally, these problems involve finding the area within rectangular or triangular shaped parcels. Certain irregular or circular shaped parcels are best left to a land measurement expert, such as a surveyor.

Example: The area of a rectangular shape is

TABLE 14-6
Loan progress chart
(dollar balance remaining on a 12 percent loan of $1,000)

12% LOAN PROGRESS CHART
Showing dollar balance remaining on a $1,000 loan

AGE OF LOAN	5	8	10	12	15	16	17	18	19	20	21	AGE OF LOAN
1	845	921	945	960	975	978	981	983	985	987	989	1
2	670	831	883	915	946	953	959	964	969	973	976	2
3	473	731	813	865	914	925	935	943	950	956	962	3
4	250	617	734	808	877	894	907	919	929	938	946	4
5		489	645	744	837	858	877	892	906	917	928	5
6		345	545	672	790	818	842	862	879	894	907	6
7		183	432	590	738	773	802	828	849	868	884	7
8			305	499	680	722	758	789	816	838	858	8
9			161	395	614	665	708	745	777	805	829	9
10				279	540	600	652	696	735	767	795	10
11				148	456	528	589	641	686	725	759	11
12					361	446	518	579	632	677	717	12
13					255	353	437	509	571	624	670	13
14					135	249	347	430	501	563	617	14
15						132	245	341	424	495	557	15
16							130	240	336	418	489	16
17								127	237	332	413	17
18									126	234	328	18
19										124	231	19
20											123	20

AGE OF LOAN	22	23	24	25	26	27	28	29	30	35	40	AGE OF LOAN
1	990	991	992	993	994	995	995	996	996	998	999	1
2	979	982	984	986	987	989	990	991	992	996	998	2
3	966	970	974	977	980	982	984	986	988	993	996	3
4	952	958	963	967	971	975	978	980	982	990	995	4
5	936	944	951	957	962	966	970	974	977	987	993	5
6	918	928	937	944	951	957	962	966	970	984	991	6
7	898	910	921	930	939	946	952	958	963	980	989	7
8	875	890	903	915	925	934	941	948	954	975	986	8
9	850	868	884	897	909	920	929	938	945	970	984	9
10	821	842	861	878	892	905	916	926	934	964	980	10
11	788	814	836	855	872	887	900	912	922	958	977	11
12	751	781	807	830	850	868	883	897	909	950	973	12
13	710	745	775	802	825	846	864	880	894	942	968	13
14	663	704	739	770	797	821	842	860	876	933	963	14
15	611	657	698	734	765	793	817	838	857	922	958	15
16	551	605	652	694	730	761	789	814	835	910	951	16
17	485	547	601	648	689	726	758	786	811	897	944	17
18	409	480	542	597	644	686	723	755	783	882	936	18
19	325	406	477	539	593	641	683	720	752	865	926	19
20	229	322	403	473	536	590	638	680	717	846	916	20
21	121	227	319	400	471	533	587	635	677	825	904	21
22		120	225	317	398	468	530	585	633	800	891	22
23			119	224	315	395	466	528	583	773	876	23
24				119	222	314	394	464	526	742	859	24
25					118	221	312	392	462	708	840	25
26						117	220	311	391	669	819	26
27							117	219	310	625	795	27
28								116	219	575	768	28
29									116	519	737	29
30										457	703	30
31										386	664	31
32										306	621	32
33										216	571	33
34										114	516	34
35											453	35

TABLE 14-7
Monthly payments necessary to amortize a 9¾ percent loan (term: 10-17 years)

9¾%	MONTHLY PAYMENT NECESSARY TO AMORTIZE A LOAN								MONTHLY PAYMENT NECESSARY TO AMORTIZE A LOAN							9¾%
TERM AMOUNT	10 YEARS	11 YEARS	12 YEARS	13 YEARS	14 YEARS	15 YEARS	16 YEARS	17 YEARS	TERM AMOUNT	10 YEARS	11 YEARS	12 YEARS	13 YEARS	14 YEARS	15 YEARS	16 YEARS	17 YEARS
$ 100	1.31	1.24	1.19	1.14	1.10	1.06	1.04	1.01	$ 5600	73.24	69.33	66.12	63.46	61.23	59.33	57.71	56.31
200	2.62	2.48	2.37	2.27	2.19	2.12	2.07	2.02	5700	74.54	70.56	67.30	64.60	62.32	60.39	58.74	57.32
300	3.93	3.72	3.55	3.40	3.28	3.18	3.10	3.02	5800	75.85	71.80	68.48	65.73	63.41	61.45	59.77	58.32
400	5.24	4.96	4.73	4.54	4.38	4.24	4.13	4.03	5900	77.16	73.04	69.67	66.86	64.51	62.51	60.80	59.33
500	6.54	6.19	5.91	5.67	5.47	5.30	5.16	5.03	6000	78.47	74.28	70.85	67.99	65.60	63.57	61.83	60.33
600	7.85	7.43	7.09	6.80	6.56	6.36	6.19	6.04	6100	79.77	75.52	72.03	69.13	66.69	64.63	62.86	61.34
700	9.16	8.67	8.27	7.94	7.66	7.42	7.22	7.04	6200	81.08	76.75	73.21	70.26	67.79	65.69	63.89	62.34
800	10.47	9.91	9.45	9.07	8.75	8.48	8.25	8.05	6300	82.39	77.99	74.39	71.39	68.88	66.74	64.92	63.35
900	11.77	11.15	10.63	10.20	9.84	9.54	9.28	9.05	6400	83.70	79.23	75.57	72.53	69.97	67.80	65.95	64.35
1000	13.08	12.38	11.81	11.34	10.94	10.60	10.31	10.06	6500	85.01	80.47	76.75	73.66	71.07	68.86	66.98	65.36
1100	14.39	13.62	12.99	12.47	12.03	11.66	11.34	11.06	6600	86.31	81.71	77.93	74.79	72.16	69.92	68.01	66.36
1200	15.70	14.86	14.17	13.60	13.12	12.72	12.37	12.07	6700	87.62	82.94	79.11	75.93	73.25	70.98	69.04	67.37
1300	17.01	16.10	15.35	14.74	14.22	13.78	13.40	13.08	6800	88.93	84.18	80.29	77.06	74.34	72.04	70.07	68.37
1400	18.31	17.34	16.53	15.87	15.31	14.84	14.43	14.08	6900	90.24	85.42	81.47	78.19	75.44	73.10	71.10	69.38
1500	19.62	18.57	17.72	17.00	16.40	15.90	15.46	15.09	7000	91.54	86.66	82.65	79.33	76.53	74.16	72.13	70.39
1600	20.93	19.81	18.90	18.14	17.50	16.95	16.49	16.09	7100	92.85	87.89	83.83	80.46	77.62	75.22	73.16	71.39
1700	22.24	21.05	20.08	19.27	18.59	18.01	17.52	17.10	7200	94.16	89.13	85.01	81.59	78.72	76.28	74.19	72.40
1800	23.54	22.29	21.26	20.40	19.68	19.07	18.55	18.10	7300	95.47	90.37	86.19	82.73	79.81	77.34	75.22	73.40
1900	24.85	23.52	22.44	21.54	20.78	20.13	19.58	19.11	7400	96.77	91.61	87.38	83.86	80.90	78.40	76.25	74.41
2000	26.16	24.76	23.62	22.67	21.87	21.19	20.61	20.11	7500	98.08	92.85	88.56	84.99	82.00	79.46	77.28	75.41
2100	27.47	26.00	24.80	23.80	22.96	22.25	21.64	21.12	7600	99.39	94.08	89.74	86.13	83.09	80.52	78.31	76.42
2200	28.77	27.24	25.98	24.93	24.06	23.31	22.67	22.12	7700	100.70	95.32	90.92	87.26	84.18	81.58	79.35	77.42
2300	30.08	28.48	27.16	26.07	25.15	24.37	23.70	23.13	7800	102.01	96.56	92.10	88.39	85.28	82.64	80.38	78.43
2400	31.39	29.71	28.34	27.20	26.24	25.43	24.73	24.14	7900	103.31	97.80	93.28	89.52	86.37	83.69	81.41	79.43
2500	32.70	30.95	29.52	28.33	27.34	26.49	25.76	25.14	8000	104.62	99.04	94.46	90.66	87.46	84.75	82.44	80.44
2600	34.01	32.19	30.70	29.47	28.43	27.55	26.80	26.15	8100	105.93	100.27	95.64	91.79	88.56	85.81	83.47	81.45
2700	35.31	33.43	31.88	30.60	29.52	28.61	27.83	27.15	8200	107.24	101.51	96.82	92.92	89.65	86.87	84.50	82.45
2800	36.62	34.67	33.06	31.73	30.62	29.67	28.86	28.16	8300	108.54	102.75	98.00	94.06	90.74	87.93	85.53	83.46
2900	37.93	35.90	34.24	32.87	31.71	30.73	29.89	29.16	8400	109.85	103.99	99.18	95.19	91.84	88.99	86.56	84.46
3000	39.24	37.14	35.43	34.00	32.80	31.79	30.92	30.17	8500	111.16	105.23	100.36	96.32	92.93	90.05	87.59	85.47
3100	40.54	38.38	36.61	35.13	33.90	32.85	31.95	31.17	8600	112.47	106.46	101.54	97.46	94.02	91.11	88.62	86.47
3200	41.85	39.62	37.79	36.27	34.99	33.90	32.98	32.18	8700	113.78	107.70	102.72	98.59	95.12	92.17	89.65	87.48
3300	43.16	40.86	38.97	37.40	36.08	34.96	34.01	33.18	8800	115.08	108.94	103.90	99.72	96.21	93.23	90.68	88.48
3400	44.47	42.09	40.15	38.53	37.17	36.02	35.04	34.19	8900	116.39	110.18	105.09	100.86	97.30	94.29	91.71	89.49
3500	45.77	43.33	41.33	39.67	38.27	37.08	36.07	35.20	9000	117.70	111.41	106.27	101.99	98.40	95.35	92.74	90.49
3600	47.08	44.57	42.51	40.80	39.36	38.14	37.10	36.20	9100	119.01	112.65	107.45	103.12	99.49	96.41	93.77	91.50
3700	48.39	45.81	43.69	41.93	40.45	39.20	38.13	37.21	9200	120.31	113.89	108.63	104.26	100.58	97.47	94.80	92.51
3800	49.70	47.04	44.87	43.07	41.55	40.26	39.16	38.21	9300	121.62	115.13	109.81	105.39	101.68	98.53	95.83	93.51
3900	51.01	48.28	46.05	44.20	42.64	41.32	40.19	39.22	9400	122.93	116.37	110.99	106.52	102.77	99.59	96.86	94.52
4000	52.31	49.52	47.23	45.33	43.73	42.38	41.22	40.22	9500	124.24	117.60	112.17	107.66	103.86	100.64	97.89	95.52
4100	53.62	50.76	48.41	46.46	44.83	43.44	42.25	41.23	9600	125.54	118.84	113.35	108.79	104.96	101.70	98.92	96.53
4200	54.93	52.00	49.59	47.60	45.92	44.50	43.28	42.23	9700	126.85	120.08	114.53	109.92	106.05	102.76	99.95	97.53
4300	56.24	53.23	50.77	48.73	47.01	45.56	44.31	43.24	9800	128.16	121.32	115.71	111.05	107.14	103.82	100.98	98.54
4400	57.54	54.47	51.95	49.86	48.11	46.62	45.34	44.24	9900	129.47	122.56	116.89	112.19	108.24	104.88	102.01	99.54
4500	58.85	55.71	53.14	51.00	49.20	47.68	46.37	45.25	10000	130.78	123.79	118.07	113.32	109.33	105.94	103.04	100.55
4600	60.16	56.95	54.32	52.13	50.29	48.74	47.40	46.26	11000	143.85	136.17	129.88	124.65	120.26	116.53	113.35	110.60
4700	61.47	58.19	55.50	53.26	51.39	49.80	48.43	47.26	12000	156.93	148.55	141.69	135.98	131.19	127.13	123.65	120.66
4800	62.77	59.42	56.68	54.40	52.48	50.85	49.46	48.27	13000	170.01	160.93	153.49	147.32	142.13	137.72	133.96	130.71
4900	64.08	60.66	57.86	55.53	53.57	51.91	50.49	49.27	14000	183.08	173.31	165.30	158.65	153.06	148.32	144.26	140.77
5000	65.39	61.90	59.04	56.66	54.67	52.97	51.52	50.28	15000	196.16	185.69	177.11	169.99	163.99	158.91	154.56	150.82
5100	66.70	63.14	60.22	57.80	55.76	54.03	52.55	51.28	16000	209.24	198.07	188.91	181.31	174.92	169.50	164.87	160.88
5200	68.01	64.37	61.40	58.93	56.85	55.09	53.59	52.29	17000	222.31	210.45	200.72	192.65	185.85	180.10	175.17	170.93
5300	69.31	65.61	62.58	60.06	57.95	56.15	54.62	53.29	18000	235.39	222.82	212.53	203.97	196.79	190.69	185.48	180.98
5400	70.62	66.85	63.76	61.20	59.04	57.21	55.65	54.30	19000	248.47	235.20	224.33	215.31	207.72	201.28	195.78	191.04
5500	71.93	68.09	64.94	62.33	60.13	58.27	56.68	55.30	20000	261.55	247.58	236.14	226.64	218.65	211.88	206.08	201.09

found by multiplying the width times the length. Square feet in lot A:

$50 \times 100 = 5,000$ square feet

Example: The area of a triangular shape, in which two of the sides form a right angle, is found by multiplying the length of these two sides and dividing by two.

Square feet in lot B:

$50 \times 100 = 5,000$
$5,000 \div 2 = 2,500$ square feet

Examples:

1. What is the square footage of lot C? Solution:

$50 \times 100 = 5,000$ square feet

2. What is the square footage of lot D? Solution: Lot D should be solved as though it were two parcels—a rectangle 50 feet by 75 feet and a triangle with the two sides forming the right angle, 50 feet and 25 feet.

$50 \times 75 = 3,750$
$50 \times 25 = 1,250 \div 2 = 625$
$3,750 + 625 = 4,375$ square feet in lot D

3. To find the square footage in lot E, it is necessary to divide the lot into three parts.

$50 \times 50 = 2,500$
$25 \times 50 = 1,250$
$25 \times 50 \div 2 = \underline{625}$
$4,375$ square feet in lot E

4. How many square yards in a room 15 feet by 21 feet? Solution: To find square yards, divide the number of square feet by nine, since there are nine square feet in a square yard.

$15 \times 21 = 315$ square feet $\div 9 = 35$ square yards

TABLE 14-8
Table of monthly payments to amortize a $1,000 loan

Term of years	10%	10½%	11%	11½%	12%	12½%	13%	13½%	14%	14½%	15%	15½%	16%	16½%	17%
1	87.92	88.15	88.38	88.62	88.85	89.08	89.32	89.55	89.79	90.02	90.26	90.49	90.73	90.97	91.20
2	46.14	46.38	46.61	46.84	47.07	47.31	47.54	47.78	48.01	48.25	48.49	48.72	48.96	49.20	49.44
3	32.27	32.50	32.74	32.98	33.21	33.45	33.69	33.94	34.18	34.42	34.67	34.91	35.16	35.40	35.65
4	25.36	25.60	25.85	26.09	26.33	26.58	26.83	27.08	27.33	27.58	27.83	28.08	28.34	28.60	28.86
5	21.25	21.50	21.75	22.00	22.25	22.50	22.76	23.01	23.27	23.53	23.79	24.06	24.32	24.59	24.86
6	18.53	18.78	19.04	19.30	19.56	19.82	20.08	20.34	20.61	20.87	21.15	21.42	21.69	21.97	22.25
7	16.61	16.87	17.13	17.39	17.66	17.93	18.20	18.47	18.75	19.03	19.31	19.58	19.86	20.15	20.44
8	15.18	15.45	15.71	15.98	16.26	16.53	16.81	17.09	17.38	17.66	17.95	18.24	18.53	18.82	19.12
9	14.08	14.36	14.63	14.91	15.19	15.47	15.76	16.05	16.34	16.64	16.93	17.22	17.53	17.83	18.15
10	13.22	13.50	13.78	14.06	14.35	14.64	14.94	15.23	15.53	15.83	16.13	16.44	16.75	17.08	17.38
11	12.52	12.81	13.10	13.39	13.60	13.98	14.28	14.58	14.89	15.20	15.51	15.82	16.14	16.46	16.79
12	11.96	12.25	12.54	12.84	13.14	13.44	13.75	14.06	14.38	14.70	15.02	15.34	15.67	15.99	16.32
13	11.48	11.78	12.08	12.38	12.69	13.00	13.32	13.63	13.96	14.28	14.60	14.93	15.27	15.60	15.94
14	11.09	11.39	11.70	12.01	12.32	12.64	12.96	13.28	13.61	13.94	14.27	14.61	14.95	15.29	15.64
15	10.75	11.06	11.37	11.69	12.01	12.33	12.66	12.99	13.32	13.66	14.00	14.34	14.69	15.04	15.39
16	10.46	10.78	11.10	11.42	11.74	12.07	12.40	12.74	13.08	13.42	13.77	14.12	14.47	14.83	15.19
17	10.22	10.54	10.86	11.19	11.52	11.85	12.19	12.53	12.88	13.22	13.58	13.93	14.29	14.65	15.02
18	10.00	10.33	10.66	10.99	11.32	11.67	12.01	12.36	12.71	13.06	13.42	13.78	14.14	14.51	14.88
19	9.82	10.15	10.48	10.82	11.16	11.50	11.85	12.21	12.56	12.92	13.28	13.65	14.02	14.39	14.76
20	9.66	9.99	10.33	10.67	11.02	11.37	11.72	12.08	12.44	12.80	13.17	13.54	13.91	14.29	14.67
21	9.51	9.85	10.19	10.54	10.89	11.24	11.60	11.96	12.33	12.70	13.07	13.45	13.82	14.20	14.59
22	9.38	9.73	10.07	10.42	10.78	11.14	11.50	11.87	12.24	12.61	12.99	13.37	13.75	14.13	14.52
23	9.27	9.62	9.97	10.33	10.69	11.05	11.42	11.79	12.16	12.54	12.92	13.30	13.69	14.07	14.46
24	9.17	9.52	9.88	10.24	10.60	10.97	11.34	11.72	12.10	12.48	12.86	13.25	13.63	14.02	14.42
25	9.09	9.45	9.81	10.17	10.54	10.91	11.28	11.66	12.04	12.42	12.81	13.20	13.59	13.98	14.38
26	9.01	9.37	9.73	10.10	10.47	10.84	11.22	11.60	11.99	12.38	12.76	13.16	13.55	13.95	14.34
27	8.94	9.30	9.67	10.04	10.41	10.79	11.17	11.56	11.95	12.34	12.73	13.12	13.52	13.92	14.32
28	8.88	9.25	9.61	9.99	10.37	10.75	11.13	11.52	11.91	12.30	12.70	13.09	13.49	13.89	14.29
29	8.82	9.19	9.57	9.94	10.32	10.71	11.09	11.48	11.88	12.27	12.67	13.07	13.47	13.87	14.27
30	8.78	9.15	9.53	9.91	10.29	10.68	11.07	11.46	11.85	12.25	12.64	13.05	13.45	13.85	14.25
35	8.60	8.99	9.37	9.77	10.16	10.56	10.96	11.36	11.76	12.16	12.57	12.98	13.38	13.79	14.21
40	8.49	8.89	9.28	9.68	10.08	10.49	10.90	11.30	11.71	12.12	12.53	12.94	13.36	13.77	14.18

TABLE 14–9
Fraction, decimal, and percentage equivalents

Denominator	*Numerators*														
1.00 or 100%	*1*	*2*	*3*	*4*	*5*	*6*	*7*	*8*	*9*	*10*	*11*	*12*	*13*	*14*	*15*
2	.50 50%														
3	.333 33 1/3%	.666 66 2/3%													
4	.25 25%	.50 50%	.75 75%												
5	.20 20%	.40 40%	.60 60%	.80 80%											
6	.166 16 2/3%	.333 33 1/3%	.50 50%	.666 66 2/3%	.833 83 1/3%										
7	.142 14 2/7%	.285 28 4/7%	.428 42 6/7%	.571 57 1/7%	.714 71 3/7%	.857 85 5/7%									
8	.125 12 1/2%	.25 25%	.375 37 1/2%	.50 50%	.625 62 1/2%	.75 75%	.875 87 1/2%								
9	.111 11 1/9%	.222 22 2/9%	.333 33 1/3%	.444 44 4/9%	.555 55 5/9%	.666 66 2/3%	.777 77 7/9%	.888 88 8/9%							
10	.10 10%	.20 20%	.30 30%	.40 40%	.50 50%	.60 60%	.70 70%	.80 80%	.90 90%						
11	.090 9 1/11%	.181 18 2/11%	.272 27 3/11%	.363 36 4/11%	.454 45 5/11%	.545 54 6/11%	.636 63 7/11%	.727 72 8/11%	.818 81 9/11%	.909 90 10/11%					
12	.083 8 1/3%	.166 16 2/3%	.25 25%	.333 33 1/3%	.416 41 2/3%	.50 50%	.583 58 1/3%	.666 66 2/3%	.75 75%	.813 83 1/3%	.916 91 2/3%				
13	.077 7 9/13%	.153 15 5/13%	.230 23 1/13%	.307 30 10/13%	.385 38 6/13%	.462 46 2/13%	.538 53 11/13%	.615 61 7/13%	.692 69 3/13%	.769 76 12/13%	.846 84 8/13%	.923 92 4/13%			
14	.071 7 1/7%	.142 14 2/7%	.214 21 3/8%	.285 28 4/7%	.357 35 5/7%	.428 42 6/7%	.50 50%	.571 57 1/7%	.642 64 2/7%	.714 71 3/7%	.786 78 4/7%	.857 85 5/7%	.929 92 6/7%		
15	.066 6 2/3%	.133 13 1/3%	.20 20%	.266 26 2/3%	.333 33 1/3%	.40 40%	.466 46 2/3%	.533 53 1/3%	.60 60%	.666 66 2/3%	.733 73 1/3%	.80 80%	.866 86 2/3%	.933 93 1/3%	
16	.062 6 1/4%	.125 12 1/2%	.1875 18 3/4%	.25 25%	.3125 31 1/4%	.375 37 1/2%	.4375 43 3/4%	.50 50%	.5625 56 1/4%	.625 62 1/2%	.6875 68 3/4%	.75 75%	.8125 81 1/4%	.875 87 1/2%	.9375 93 3/4%

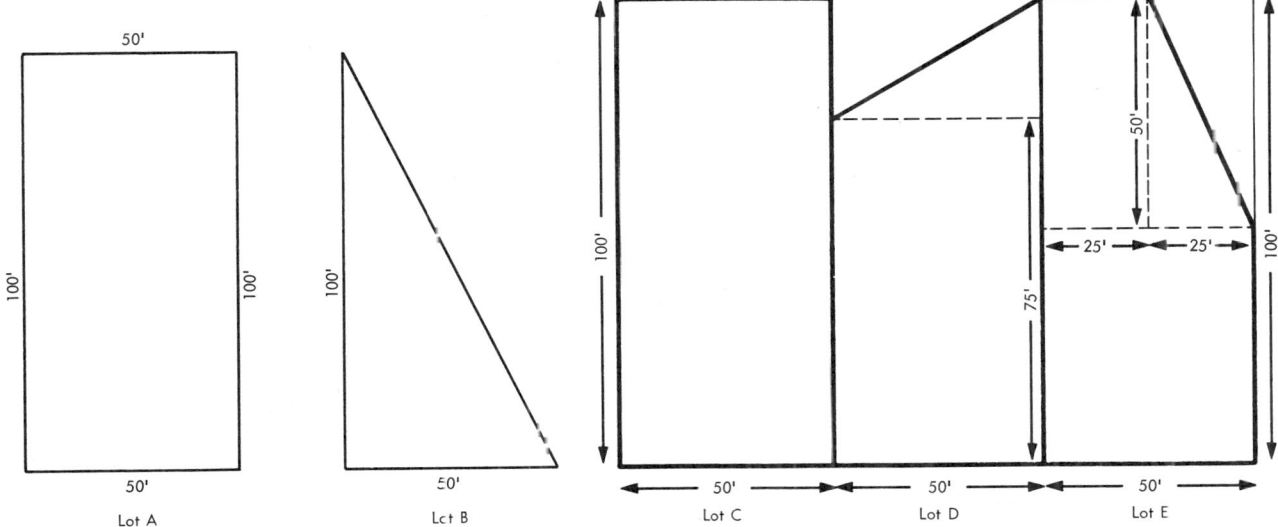

5. At $350 per front foot, what would lots C, D, and E together sell for? Solution: Each of the three lots has a 50-foot frontage. The three together consist of 150 front feet.

$$150 \times \$350 = \$52,500$$

6. Builder Carol owns a 50 by 100-foot lot. The lot zoning is such that he may erect a building on the entire area of the lot, subject only to a ten-foot setback requirement applicable to the front of the lot. If he erects a single-story building, what is the maximum number of square feet it may contain?

A setback requirement prohibits construction between the boundary line of a lot and the setback line. A lot in a higher priced residential district in the suburbs would probably be subject to setback requirements that result in the building being completely detached from those on adjacent lots.

Solution: Carol's lot is 50 by 100, or 5,000 square feet. A ten-foot setback requirement applicable to the front of the lot would mean an area of 50 by 10, or 500 square feet.

5,000 square feet − 500 square feet
= 4,500 square feet,

the maximum square footage a single-story building may contain.

Finding the square footage of a building

The square footage of a building is generally found by using the outside measurements. Thus, everything inside the building—rooms, closets, hallways, and stairways—is included. If the building is more than a single story, one must be careful to note whether the second story has the same outside dimensions as the first story. Such measurements are used in connection with the reproduction cost method in appraising where the building square footage is found and multiplied by the construction cost per square foot.

QUESTIONS FOR DISCUSSION

1. Ten thousand dollars is deposited in a savings and loan association that pays 9½ percent compounded quarterly. How much interest will be credited to the account at the end of the first quarter?
2. What is the interest on a loan of $25,000 at 12 percent interest for 120 days?
3. What rate of interest is being charged if the amount of a loan is $3,000, the time is five years, and the interest paid is $1,200.
4. If the interest is $8,960, the rate is 7 percent, and the time is eight years, what is the principal amount of the loan?
5. Using the 60-day 6 percent method, can you determine the interest on $5,800 at 9 percent for 120 days?
6. Clark purchases an apartment house on which owner Samuels has already collected the rents, amounting to $2,980. Escrow is to be closed on the 16th day of a 30-day month. How is the rent apportioned between them?
7. Barbaix receives $3,565, representing a 15½ percent return on his investment. What amount has he invested?
8. O'Shaughnessy's contract with broker Ohman states that if O'Shaghnessy lists and sells a property, he is to receive 70 percent of the commission, less

10 percent deducted for advertising expense. On the sale of a house at $139,500, what will he receive if the commission rate is 6 percent of the selling price?

9. Everett purchases 20 acres of land at $750 per acre. For how much will he have to sell the land in order to make a 20 percent profit on his investment?

10. Williams purchases a building for $276,000. The building shows a net yearly income of $22,080. What is his rate of return?

11. Buoncristiani wishes to purchase a house offered at $325,000. A 70 percent bank loan can be obtained, and the owner will carry back a second loan in the amount of $35,000. What will be the down payment necessary?

12. What is the original amount of a note which has been discounted 35 percent if the amount of the discount is $9,800.

13. If Brussell's building is assessed for tax purposes at 25 percent of its market value of $532,000 and the tax rate is $4.30 per $100, what will be the amount of his first tax installment payment.

14. At $3.50 per square foot, what must Clift pay for a commercial lot which is 52 feet wide and 223 feet deep?

15. If Moraga purchases a lot for $40,000 and later sells it for $64,000, what is his percent of profit on his original cost?

15

Business opportunities brokerage

In 1943, the California Business Opportunity Act of 1937 was incorporated into the Business and Professions Code and became part of the Real Estate Law. This law required all persons engaged in the sale of a business opportunity to have a business opportunity license. On January 2, 1966, real estate and business opportunity licenses were merged by statute. A real estate license is now required in order to engage in the sale of business opportunities. The special classification of business opportunity license no longer exists, and candidates for a real estate license are now examined to some extent on business opportunity practice. Anyone who holds a real estate license may now legally negotiate the sale of business opportunities.

DEFINITION OF BUSINESS OPPORTUNITY

The Real Estate Law defines "business opportunity" as meaning and including business, business opportunity, and goodwill of an existing business, or any one of a combination thereof. The sale of a business opportunity involves the sale of personal property, and the rules and laws governing transfer of chattels apply. The usual transaction involves such businesses as grocery stores, restaurants, service stations, hardware stores, bakeries, bars, and leases and fixtures of operating rooming houses and hotels. The sale of these general types of businesses almost always includes stock, fixtures, and goodwill. Certain permits, licenses, and the like must be transferred and/or obtained, and other legal requirements not commonly encountered in the sale of houses, multiple units, and other types of nonbusiness opportunity properties must be met.

GOODWILL AS APPLIED TO BUSINESS

The term "goodwill" as applied to a business means the expectation of continued patronage. It includes the value added to the business because of the owner's policies toward his clients and customers with regard to advertising, merchandise, and/or services, as well as the reputation the business had in the particular locale where it operates.

SELLING A BUSINESS OPPORTUNITY

The sale of business opportunities is a specialized field, and brokers who deal in this area are specialists just as are brokers who deal in industrial properties, unimproved acreage, or recreational properties. Even within the broad area of business opportunities, many brokers specialize to the extent of dealing with one type of business opportunity, such as grocery stores or bars.

Most real estate licensees seldom engage in the sale of a business opportunity as such. The closest many have ever come is having sold a building that happened to contain a shop or a few stores on the ground floor. In such cases, the merchant is merely thought of as a tenant as are those persons who occupy the dwelling units in the building. The real estate broker, then, has merely sold a building and not a business opportunity.

Before we turn to a discussion of the various laws and other complexities involved in the sale of business opportunities, let us take a general look at what may be involved in such a sale.

The broker must remember that when he sells a business opportunity, he is dealing with a buyer who may be investing his life savings and therefore expects to be able to earn a livelihood from the business he is purchasing. While real property always retains some value, a bankrupt business is usually worthless. Thus, the business opportunity broker has the tremendous responsibility of correctly representing to the buyer the business for sale and of qualifying the buyer not only on his ability to buy but also, to a certain degree, on his ability to succeed in the business after he purchases it.

Business opportunity listings should be taken by the broker only when he feels that the value of the business is correctly represented by the owner. In the sale of smaller businesses where everything, including the stock, will be sold at a given price, the listing should include a guaranteed inventory to assure the buyer that he is getting a correct dollar value. Prior to completion of the sale, a physical inventory should be taken to assure that the figure previously represented by the seller is correct. Should the inventory fall below or above the figure expected, an adjustment in the purchase price must be made.

The broker should inform the seller that his books and other business records will have to be opened for inspection to the potential purchaser after a deposit has been obtained.

When the broker and the purchaser together prepare the deposit receipt, they should include several important contingencies in the receipt to protect the buyer as well as the broker with regard to representations made to the buyer. The following are examples:

1. Amount of rent being paid.
2. Terms and conditions of the lease, if any.
3. Length of the lease.
4. Seller's ability to transfer the lease to the buyer.
5. Approval and inspection of the business records.
6. Approval and inspection of the inventory.
7. Transfer of various licenses.
8. Securing of necessary permit to operate the business.

Attention to certain legal requirements

Following preparation of the deposit receipt and prior to close of escrow, the broker must be sure that certain legal requirements are met. The Uniform Commercial Code, pertaining to bulk sales of goods, usually requires that certain legal notices be published for the benefit of creditors. If the business being sold requires possession of a sales tax permit, it is necessary to pay sales tax on the furniture and fixtures sold. It is usually necessary to obtain a final clearance form from the California State Board of Equalization before close of escrow. Businesses that require a liquor license pose many special problems.

In addition, the broker must understand and be able to explain the bill of sale for personal property sold, the escrow agreement and instructions, and the prorations of insurance, rents, accounts receivable, licenses, and taxes.

The Federal Small Business Administration provides many pamphlets, books, and programs designed to assist buyers and sellers of small businesses, and real estate brokers dealing in business opportunities should be familiar with these materials.

SPECIFIC RULES AND REGULATIONS

The broker who deals in business opportunities must be familiar with and understand the requirements of (1) the Uniform Commercial Code (UCC), (2) the Bulk Transfer Act of the UCC, (3) California Sales and Tax Provisions, and (4) the Alcoholic Beverage Control Act.

Uniform Commercial Code (UCC)

In 1965, the California Uniform Commercial Code became law and established a unified and comprehensive method for the regulation of security transactions in personal property. It regulates any transaction which is intended to create a security interest in goods, documents, installments, chattel paper, accounts, or contract rights. It excludes consumer goods if they are used or bought for use primarily in personal, family, or household purposes and is not applicable to real property security transactions. The previously used chattel mortgage has now been replaced by the security agreement and the financing statement.

Security agreement. There are three basic methods used when borrowing money and giving personal property as security. The borrower may (*a*) give actual possession of the property to the lender, (*b*) give the lender title to the property but retain possession, and (*c*) retain both title and possession but give the lender a security interest.

It is method (*c*) which is generally used in the sale of a business opportunity. In compliance with the UCC, the borrower executes a note and a security agreement when he obtains the personal property loan. The promissory note evidences the debt, and the security agreement is the instrument whereby the debtor (borrower) gives the secured party (lender) an interest in the personal property.

Financing statement. To protect the lender and give public notice of the security interest, the debtor signs a financing statement which is then filed by the lender with the Secretary of State or in the office of the county recorder. The intent of this law is to protect purchasers and creditors from the rights of prior secured parties who have a security interest in the property. If the financing statement is not filed, subsequent purchasers and secured parties without actual knowledge of the interest take the property free of the prior security interest. Thus, when a lender does properly file, he is protected from the interests of subsequent purchasers and secured parties. Involved here is the same idea as that found with regard to mortgages and deeds of trust. Proper recordation protects the lender from subsequent parties.

It is important that a buyer obtain copies of financing statements that affect the seller. The financing statement is generally filed with the Secretary of State except that with regard to consumer goods or farm equipment and farm products other than crops, it is filed in the office of the county recorder in which the debtor resides. With respect to crops of timber, the filing is in the county in which the crops or timber are located.

A financing statement is effective for five years from date of filing, and the lender must then file a continuation statement if he wishes to extend. A form called a Financing Statement Change is provided whereby the secured party may *(a)* file for continuation, *(b)* release a portion of the secured interest, *(c)* assign his rights to another, or *(d)* terminate the effect of the financing statement by indicating that the obligation has been paid.

The office of the Secretary of State, Sacramento, 95808, publishes a booklet outlining procedures and forms for filing in compliance with Divisions 9 and 10 of the Uniform Commercial Code. Copies of the booklet and forms used may be obtained by request.

Bulk sales and the UCC

Division 6 of the UCC pertains to bulk transfers of goods in California. The purpose of this UCC section is to protect the creditors of a person who sells a business. Recordation and publication are used to warn the transferor's (seller's) creditors of the impending transfer (due to the sale). This allows the creditors to protect their rights before the assets are disposed of or encumbered.

When a retail or wholesale merchant or a manufacturer wants to transfer in bulk (and not in the ordinary course of his business) a substantial part of his material, supplies, merchandise, or other inventory, Division 6 requires that the transferee (buyer) give public notice to the transferor's (seller's) creditors. This requirement is fulfilled by (1) recordation of a notice in the office of the recorder in the county where the property is located at least 12 business days before the bulk transfer is to be made and (2) publication of the notice at least once in a newspaper of general circulation published in the judicial district where the property is located or, if none, then in a newspaper of general circulation in the county where the business is located. Notice must be published at least 12 business days before the bulk transfer is to take place. Figure 15–1 is an illustration of this type of published notice.

Noncompliance may result in fraudulent transfer. When compliance is necessary but the statutory filing and publication requirements are not met, the result is to render the transfer fraudulent and void against those creditors of the transferor who hold claims based on transactions or events occurring before the bulk transfer.

The broker and/or seller often must consult with legal counsel during the sale of a business opportunity because of the specialized and technical legal requirements that may have to be met. The provisions of the UCC Division 6 do not apply to certain transactions, such as a sale made by executors, administrators, receivers, trustees in bankruptcy, or any public officer under judicial process, or to transfers made to create a security interest in durable goods that have a unit retail value of over $500. Also, compliance with Division 6 does not exclude compliance with other applicable statutes as, for instance, the transfer of liquor licenses under the Alcoholic Beverage Control Act.

Assembly Bill 2534, effective January 1979, added to bulk sales legislation. Among the various new law changes is a requirement that any required notice to creditors of an intended bulk transfer must be recorded, published, and delivered to the county tax collector at least 12 business days prior to the transfer and must include the name and address of the person with whom claims may be filed. In any transaction using an escrow agent, the purchaser must deposit with the escrow agent the full amount of purchase price or other consideration, and the agent cannot use any of these funds to pay any commissions or fees prior to actual close of escrow. Manufacturers are now included as a

NOTICE OF INTENDED SALE.

TO THE CREDITORS OF **PHILIP MAUER** and **EVA MAUER**:

Please take notice that you and each of you are, pursuant to §§6105 and 6107 of the Uniform Commercial Code, hereby notified as follows:

1. The transferors, **PHILIP MAUER** and **EVA MAUER**, are about to transfer to the undersigned, **HERBERT B. GREENBAUM**, transferee, in bulk that certain business known as **PHILIP MAUER PHOTO MOUNTS**, located at 894 Folsom Street, San Francisco, California, together with all of the stock, fixtures, inventory, equipment and good will of said business, all as more particularly described in a schedule which, with a list of transferors creditors, is on file and open for inspection and copying by any creditor at all reasonable hours at 894 Folsom Street, San Francisco, California.

2. The names and business addresses at this time of the transferors and the transferee are:

Transferors: **PHILIP MAUER,** 894 Folsom Street, San Francisco, California.

EVA MAUER, 894 Folsom Street, San Francisco, California.

Transferee: **HERBERT B. GREENBAUM**, 96 Fifth Avenue, New York City, New York.

All other business names and addresses used by the transferors within the three years last past, so far as known to the transferee are:

PHILIP MAUER PHOTO MOUNTS, 894 Folsom Street, San Francisco, California.

3. The bulk transfer is to be consummated at the offices of Rhein and Dienstag, Attorneys at Law, 98 Post Street, Suite 300, San Francisco, California 94104, on or after the **1st day** of **August, 1966,** at the hour of 10:00 o'clock a.m.

Dated: June 11, 1966.

HERBERT B. GREENBAUM,
Transferee.

RHEIN & DIENSTAG, Attorneys at Law, 98 Post Street, San Francisco, California.

No. 77538 July 18-1t-R

NOTICE OF BULK TRANSFER.

(Secs. 6101-6107 U.C.C.)

TO WHOM IT MAY CONCERN:

Notice is hereby given to the creditors of JOSE M. ECHAMENDI, transferor, whose business address is 1362 Powell Street, City and County of San Francisco, State of California, that a bulk transfer is about to be made to FELIX BILBAO and BEGONA BILBAO, transferees, whose business address is 691 Hebirdes Way, Sunnyvàle, County of Santa Clara, State of California.

Said property is described in general as: All fixtures, equipment and good will of that hotel and restaurant business known as HOTEL Du MIDI and located at 1362 Powell Street, City and County of San Francisco, State of California.

The bulk transfer will be consummated on or after the 12th day of July, 1967, at the office of Sol A. Abrams, attorney and escrow holder, 400 Montgomery Street, City and County of San Francisco, State of California.

So far as known to the transferees, all business names and addresses used by transferor for the three years last past, if different from the above, are: NONE.

Dated: June 12, 1967.

FELIX BILBAO,
BEGONA BILBAO,
Transferees.
JOSE M. ECHAMENDI,
Transferor.

No. 85967 June 15-1t-Th-R

NOTICE OF INTENTION TO ENGAGE IN THE SALE OF ALCOHOLIC BEVERAGES

TO WHOM IT MAY CONCERN:

Subject to issuance of the license applied for, notice is hereby given that the undersigned propose to sell alcoholic beverages at the premises, described as follows:

1362 POWELL STREET, San Francisco, California.

Pursuant to such intention, the undersigned are applying to the Department of Alcoholic Beverage Control for issuance by transfer of an alcoholic beverage license for these premises as follows:

On-sale beer and wine, bona fide eating place.

Anyone desiring to protest the issuance of such license may file a verified protest with the Department of Alcoholic Beverage Control at Sacramento, California, stating grounds for denial as provided by law. The premises are now licensed for the sale of alcoholic beverages. The form of verification may be obtained from any office of the Department.

FELIX BILBAO.
BEGONA BILBAO.

SOL A. ABRAMS, Attorney, 1029-4th Street, San Rafael, California.

No. 85965 June 15-1t-Th-R

FIGURE 15–1

business required to give prior notice to creditors of any impending bulk transfer.

California sales and use tax provisions

The Sales and Use Tax Law is of interest to brokers engaged in the sale of business opportunities where sales of tangible personal property at retail are made. The following are of particular importance:

1. The necessity of acquiring a seller's permit when engaging in business.
2. The necessity of posting security for the collection of the required sales tax.
3. The obtainment of a clearance receipt in order to protect the purchaser against successor's liability.
4. The obtainment of releases or subordination agreements covering sales tax liens against real or personal property.
5. The matter of tax liability on the sale price of a business in proportion to the fair retail value of the tangible personal property involved.

For the privilege of selling tangible personal property at retail, a tax established as a percentage rate of gross receipts is imposed on all retailers. This includes the state sales tax and the local state administered sales tax. Board of Equalization Ruling 81 states that the tax liability (mentioned in 5, above) applies to the portion of the gross receipts from the sale of an entire business operated by a retailer that represents the fair retail value of the tangible personal property, such as showcases and office or delivery equipment, acquired for use rather than resale by the purchaser of the business. The tax does not apply, however, to tangible personal property, such as stock in trade, sold for the purpose of resale in the regular course of the purchaser's business.

Alcoholic Beverage Control Act

The sale of many businesses involves, as part of the transaction, the sale and transfer of a license or permit to engage in the sale of alcoholic beverages. Thus, the licensee engaged in the sale of business opportunities should be familiar with the legal controls imposed on the sale and distribution of alcoholic beverages and especially with the methods governing the issuance of licenses or permits to those persons engaged in such sale or distribution.

The manufacture, sale, purchase, and possession of alcoholic beverages in California is governed by Article XX, Section 22, California State Constitution, the Alcoholic Beverage Control Act (Division 9 of the Business and Professions Code), Business Regulations of the department (Title 4, Chapter 1, California Administrative Code), and applicable sections of the Health and Safety Code and Penal Codes, as well as certain federal statutes and regulations.

Department of Alcoholic Beverage Control. The Department of Alcoholic Beverage Control is charged with administration of the Alcoholic Beverage Control Act and issues licenses thereunder. Local officials and the department are charged with the duty of enforcing the law.

Alcoholic beverage licenses are issued to qualified adult persons, partnerships, fiduciaries, and corporations for use at particular premises approved by the department.

An on-sale general license and on-sale general license for seasonal business may not be approved for various reasons, including overconcentration of alcoholic beverage licenses in the area, the creation of a police problem, or delinquent tax payments on the part of the transferor.

Transfer of a license. A person who intends to engage in the sale of alcoholic beverages should not make any investment on the assumption that a license authorizing him to engage in such business will be issued or transferred. Before filing a transfer application with the department, the applicant and licensee must file a notice of intended transfer with the county recorder and establish an escrow as required by law. No consideration may be paid out of the escrow before approval of the transfer, and the transfer of title to the licensed business must coincide with the transfer of the license.

Information for brokers and applicants. Brokers who negotiate a business opportunity involving the transfer of a license and persons who seek such a license must be familiar with the statutes and regulations governing such activity. These are available on request through any office of the Department of Alcoholic Beverage Control.

Some of the different types of licenses issued are: retail package off-sale beer and wine license, retail package off-sale general license for distilled spirits, on-sale beer license, on-sale beer and wine license, on-sale general license, on-sale general license for seasonal business. On-sale means that the alcoholic beverage will generally be consumed on the premises as at a restaurant or bar, while off-sale means that the alcoholic beverage will be purchased on the premises but not consumed as in a grocery store or supermarket.

License speculation. The Department of Alcoholic Beverage Control may file a complaint against any broker who participates in speculation on licenses or their transfer. Licenses may not be purchased by a broker at a bankruptcy or trustee's sale, with the exception of transfer to a nominee. The only person who may have an interest in an alcoholic beverage license is the person who is operating or intends to operate the licensed business.

TECHNICAL QUALIFICATIONS LICENSE

Licensees engaged in the sale of business opportunities must be especially careful when selling a business in which the owner must be examined for technical qualifications and licensed by the state. The licensee must be sure that the prospective purchaser is aware of the licensing requirements he must meet. Among the more common businesses with licensing requirements of which a buyer may be unaware are dry-cleaning establishments and beauty shops.

GENERAL CHRONOLOGICAL SALE PROCEDURE

The steps involved in the sale of a business opportunity will vary depending on the size and complexity of the business being sold. The following steps are merely intended to show the general sequence of events as they may occur in an ordinary sale.

1. The broker secures a listing for the sale of a business opportunity or has a client who wants to purchase a certain type of business.
2. When a prospective purchaser evidences interest in a particular business, the broker secures a deposit and prepares a deposit receipt that includes the terms of the sale and any contingencies that may be necessary. The broker obtains the signature of the buyer and gives him a copy of the deposit receipt. A licensee must always remember that a copy

of a listing, deposit receipt, or other important form must always be given to the person who affixes his signature thereto.
3. The broker presents the offer to the seller and, on obtaining his acceptance, has him sign the deposit receipt and gives him a copy.
4. An escrow is opened, and instructions are prepared for the signatures of the buyer and seller. Business escrows are often handled by attorneys but may also be taken care of by a bank, escrow company, or title company.
5. In accordance with Division 6 of the Uniform Commercial Code, provision is made for notice to creditors of the intended sale and transfer of stock in trade by recording and publishing (Figure 15–1) a Notice of Intended Sale in Bulk, thus conforming with the requirements of the Bulk Sales Act.
6. In accordance with Division 9 of the Uniform Commercial Code, the necessary financing statement is filed with the secretary of state and/or the recorder's office, if necessary.
7. The appropriate forms for the transfer of any types of liquor licenses necessary are filed with the Department of Alcoholic Beverage Control.
8. The broker secures the lessor's consent on a lease assignment form so that the lease may be transferred, if necessary.
9. In accordance with the Sales and Use Tax Law, the seller's permit and the clearance receipt are obtained from the board of equalization, thereby protecting the buyer against successor's liability.
10. When the sale of a business involves some employees, adjustments pertaining to prepaid vacation periods or sick leave may have to be worked out, and a clearance may have to be obtained from the Department of Employment with regard to unemployment insurance tax.
11. An inventory of stock-in-trade, fixtures, or other personal property is taken.
12. The seller executes a bill of sale for all personal property involved.
13. Prior to and on close of escrow, the broker delivers to the buyer and seller the closing statements and any other necessary documents pertaining to the sale of the business.

Additional forms, applicable to this chapter, are illustrated in Appendix C as Figures C15–1 and C15–2.

QUESTIONS FOR DISCUSSION

1. How is the broker who sells business opportunities dealing with intangibles?
2. Why is it important that a careful inventory of stock in-trade be taken before close of escrow?
3. If a liquor license is involved in the sale, why should the sale be made contingent on transfer of the license to the purchaser?
4. What should the broker do if the seller refuses to supply adequate information when listing the business opportunity?
5. What kinds of information should the broker request when obtaining a business opportunity listing?
6. What special requirement must a beauty shop purchaser meet that a donut shop purchaser need not?
7. Why might the Department of Alcoholic Beverage Control refuse to issue a new license or transfer an old license to a purchaser?
8. What are some of the more important contingencies that might be included on the deposit receipt for the purchase of a business opportunity?
9. How does Division 9 of the UCC protect a purchaser of certain kinds of personal property?
10. What are some of the kinds of business opportunities in which a broker may specialize exclusively?

16

Public sales, condominiums, and mobilehomes

This chapter will deal with three areas of opportunity available to real estate licensees; public sales of real property, condominium sales, and mobilehome sales.

PUBLIC SALES

A piece of real property is most commonly put on the market for sale by the owner of the property, who either lists it with a real estate broker or attempts to sell it by himself. However, the real estate licensee should also be aware of public sales of real property in which the licensee may effect the sale and earn a standard commission. This section will deal with public sales, which are generally to enforce liens, to carry out court judgments, estate sales, or tax sales of property forfeited to the state or county as the result of nonpayment of taxes.

TRUSTEE'S SALE

When a borrower defaults on his obligations under a note and deed of trust by virtue of his failure to make the necessary payments, the beneficiary notifies the trustee named in the deed of trust, and we have the beginning of what may eventually be a trustee's sale of the real property involved.

Statement of condition

On being notified by the beneficiary of the trustor's default, the trustee obtains from the beneficiary a statement showing the condition of the debt. The statement will show:

1. The amount of the unpaid balance on the obligation.
2. The amounts of periodic payments, if any.
3. The date on which the obligation is due in whole or part.
4. The date to which real estate taxes and special assessments have been paid.
5. The amount of insurance in effect, its terms and premium.
6. The amount in an account, if any, maintained to accumulate funds with which to pay taxes and insurance premiums.

On receipt of the above information, the trustee also obtains the deed of trust and note, together with receipts that may show any advances paid by the beneficiary for the protection of his security. Such advances may be in the form of taxes or insurance paid by the beneficiary because of the trustor's inability to do so.

The notice of default

Section 2924 of the Civil Code states that in order for the power of sale under a deed of trust to be carried out, the trustee must record a notice of default in the county where the property is located. This must be done at least three months before notice of sale is given. Some trust deeds require that the beneficiary execute the notice of default and then deliver it to the trustee with instructions to exercise the power of sale. At any rate, the requirements as set forth in the deed of trust must be fully met.

The notice of default will contain the following:

1. Identification of the deed of trust, usually by means of the legal description of the property involved.
2. The name of the trustor.
3. A statement that a breach of the obligation has occurred.

4. A statement that the trustee has elected to proceed under his power of sale.
5. The names of the trustee and the beneficiary.

Within ten days after the notice of default has been recorded in the county recorder's office, all persons who under Section 2924b of the Civil Code have so requested must be notified by mail that the notice has been filed. If no request for notice is contained in the deed of trust or if no request has been filed, then the notice of default must be published in a newspaper of general circulation once a week for four weeks.

Recent legislation makes it unlawful to take advantage of a property owner in default or foreclosure. The law provides for possible recision of such transactions and provides for strict notice and publication requirements with respect to foreclosure resulting from contracts for the sale of goods or home improvements. Such contracts create what is termed an *Unruh* lien, and conveyance of title within 45 days after notice of default is voidable.

A notice of default is illustrated in Chapter 7.

Trustor's right of reinstatement

At any time during the three-month period following recordation of the notice of default, the trustor may reinstate the obligation by paying to the beneficiary:

1. All sums of money due up to that point.
2. Any additional costs incurred by the beneficiary.
3. A small fee to the trustee, usually consisting of .5 percent of the entire unpaid balance of the loan.

If the above is done during the three-month period, the default is cured, and the proceedings are discontinued. The obligation is restored, and the trustor goes back to making his regular periodic payments.

Payment in full

After the three-month period has passed, the right to reinstate is gone, and the trustor must then pay the entire amount of the obligation. If the entire obligation plus necessary costs and expenses are not paid, the property may then be sold by the trustee.

This is not to say that the beneficiary may not allow the trustor to reinstate, but only that beyond the three-month period, the beneficiary does not have to allow reinstatement if he does not want to do so.

Notice of sale

Assuming that the beneficiary has decided to proceed with the sale of the property, he must now execute a notice of sale, stating:

1. Time of the sale.
2. Place of the sale.
3. Description of the property and occasion for the sale.

The notice of sale must be published in a newspaper of general circulation either in the city in which the property is located or, if there is no newspaper in the city, then in the judicial district or county. The notice must be published once a week for 20 days—that is, three publications not more than seven days apart.

The notice must also be posted in a conspicuous place on the property and in one public place—the reason every city hall has a bulletin board on which such notices are regularly posted. In most areas, when a title insurance company is acting as trustee, a copy of the notice of sale is posted on the premises of the title company.

The sale must be held within the county in which the property is located and may be postponed once or several times if the trustee has good reason to believe that this will best serve the interests of the concerned parties. Often, a sale may be temporarily postponed if it is thought that the trustor may be able to come up with the necessary funds to reinstate the obligation. In most cases, however, the sale is not postponed but is held as scheduled.

The sale

At the time and place specified in the published notice of sale, the trustee or his representative announces the purpose of the sale and identifies the property to be sold. The sale is then officially open to bidding, since the idea is to get the best price possible for the property.

All bids must be on the basis of cash of the equivalent, and only the holder of the debt under foreclosure can offset the amount owing to him without having to put up cash. Thus, the beneficiary can and usually does bid in the amount due him, and if there are no other bidders, the beneficiary obtains the property. If there are other interested purchasers at the sale, the beneficiary begins by bidding in the amount due him, and then bidding by all in attendance continues. Eventually, a high bidding by all in attendance continues. Eventually, a high bid is declared and accepted by the trustee or his representative, and a trustee's deed is issued to the purchaser.

The trustee's deed gives to the buyer the title held by the maker of the deed of trust on the date the deed of trust was executed and also any title that may have been acquired afterward. There is, of course, no right of redemption by the former owner, who has now lost the property, and the purchaser is entitled to immediate possession.

Holder of a second loan

Brokers many times have considerable difficulty in convincing a seller to carry back a small second loan. The property owner usually likes to have all cash, since he thinks that in carrying back a second loan he will face a very difficult and complicated situation should the purchaser fail to make the necessary payments on the note.

Actually, the holder of a junior lien has the same rights as the holder of the first loan. Should a purchaser fail to make payments on a second loan, the holder of the second may record a notice of default, go through all the procedures outlined above, and finally effect a sale of the property.

Practically speaking, when a borrower is unable to make a payment on one loan against his property, he generally cannot make the payment on any other loan, so that he is actually in default with regard to both the first and second loans. To protect his interest, the holder of the second loan must bring action to effect the sale of the property and, in the meantime, must make the payments on the first loan but only for the few months required to effect the trustee's sale.

If the holder of the second note allows the holder of the first note to force the sale, the second loan holder may lose all that he has coming to him. If the beneficiary under the first deed of trust becomes the purchaser or if the sale of the property brings only enough to pay off the first loan, then the holder of the second note cannot sue the trustor, since there cannot be any deficiency judgment on a purchase money loan.

Effect of sale on liens

Although most junior liens are eliminated by a trustee's sale, a few are not. Federal tax liens are eliminated by following the procedures stipulated in the Federal Tax Lien Act of 1966. Mechanic's liens are not eliminated if the work of improvement commenced before the date on which the deed of trust was recorded. Also not affected are taxes and assessments against the property, which may be in the form of state, county, or city taxes.

Additional comments on trustee's sales

Since a trustee's sale is the result of a borrower's failure to make the necessary payments, the beneficiary may want to save the expense and time involved in forcing a sale and may enter into an agreement with the buyer-borrower to take back the property and obtain a deed in lieu of foreclosure.

Since the lender is in a very strong position in this type of situation, the courts are always quite concerned that the lender not take any unfair advantage of the borrower. Generally, however, the debt usually approximates the reasonable value of the property, and no additional consideration may be necessary. The borrower may be very pleased to get out from under and will accept a small amount from the beneficiary and execute a deed in his favor. Many brokers follow the recordation of notices of default and approach the borrower and try to effect a sale of the property before it is sold through a trustee's sale.

Title insurance companies are very careful about insuring this type of transaction and usually require special recitals in a deed in lieu of foreclosure.

Possession after sale

One of the most common problems with regard to properties sold at trustee's sales is that of possession by the purchaser. The former owner, by virtue of having failed to make his payments, has lost his property. He will certainly be in a less than cooperative mood as far as his leaving the premises is concerned. If the purchaser is the former beneficiary under the deed of trust, the best type of arrangement is one wherein the beneficiary and trustor have worked out an agreement that will result in some form of orderly procedure for vacating the premises after the trustee's sale. Many times, the purchaser must pay the former owner a sum of money and/or help him to move from the property.

If the purchaser at the trustee's sale is not the former beneficiary, he may purchase the building and then find that the former owner refuses to leave the premises. Since the new owner has not been able to make any prior arrangements with the former owner, a very difficult situation may result. The new owner may have to go through the complicated and time-consuming procedure of having the sheriff forceably evict the former owner. It is very important that anyone contemplating purchase of a property at a trustee's sale give some thought and prior attention, if possible, to the matter of possession.

Type of property sold

Although there are exceptions to the rule, it may be generally said that most of the properties sold at trustee's sales closely resemble one another in many respects.

1. This type of property was purchased with a very small down payment.
2. The property is usually overfinanced with a first, second, and possibly even a third loan involved.
3. The owner has a small equity in the property.
4. It is generally older property in a less desirable location in the community.
5. It has not been correctly maintained or kept in proper repair.
6. It is sold at trustee's sale within 12 to 18 months after the original date of purchase by the trustor.
7. The property has not appreciated in value much beyond the value at the time of its purchase. For this reason, the beneficiary frequently is able to obtain the property by merely bidding in the amount due him on the note in default.

PROBATE SALES

The subject of probate proceedings is a complex one, and we will not go into any detailed explanation here. We are interested in probate proceedings only as they apply to the sale of real estate therein. The terms "probate sale," "court sale," and "estate sale" are used interchangeably by many persons and may cause some confusion. Thus, in this section, we will be concerned with property that is being offered for sale as the result of the probate of an estate and will hereafter use the term *probate sale*.

In California, the Superior Courts have jurisdiction over the probate and administration of estates. Although called the probate court, the department to which this function is assigned is actually not a separate court at all but merely a department of the Superior Court.

Sale of estate property

A probate sale may be made by either an executor, an administrator, a guardian, or a conservator. An executor is a person specifically named in a will to carry out the wishes of the decedent and administer the estate. An administrator is one appointed by the court to administer an estate when the decedent has not left a will or has not named an executor in the will. An administrator may also be appointed if an executor is unable to perform the function expected of him; then he is called an administrator with the will annexed. A guardian is appointed by the court to administer the estate of a minor or an incompetent. A conservator is one appointed to administer the estates of those who are unable to manage their affairs. Most commonly, the attorney of the decedent or the trust department of a bank acts as the executor of the estate.

Real property usually must be sold in order to pay debts and expenses of administration, including attorney fees and court costs, and for the payment of taxes. The property may be sold either at public auction or by private sale, but since the idea is to get the best price obtainable for the property, it is almost always sold by publishing a Notice of Intended Sale and accepting bids for the property.

Notice of sale

In the following discussion, we will assume a most common situation—an attorney acting as the executor of an estate offers a piece of real property for sale. The attorney begins by publishing a notice of sale for the period and in the manner prescribed by law. The notice resembles the one previously discussed in connection with trustee's sales. Figure 16–1 is an example of a standard notice of sale published by an attorney.

It is important that the notice be read very carefully and that provisions and conditions outlined therein be followed carefully. A bid submitted on conditions other than those stated in the advertised notice of sale may be rejected even though it is the highest price offered.

The notice of sale contains the following:

1. The date, time, and place of the sale—that is, when the bids will be opened.
2. A legal description of the property to be sold. Many times, the street address will also be given for added ease in identifying the property.

> **NOTICE OF SALE OF REAL PROPERTY**
>
> IN THE SUPERIOR COURT OF THE State of California, in and for the City and County of San Francisco.
>
> In the Matter of the Estate of ELLEN M. LYONS, Deceased.—No. 170709.
>
> NOTICE OF SALE OF REAL PROPERTY
>
> Notice is hereby given that on or after July 27th, 1966, the undersigned, James V. Lyons, as administrator of the estate of Ellen M. Lyons, deceased, will sell at private sale to the highest net bidder, subject to confirmation by the above-entitled Superior Court, all the right, title, interest and estate of the decedent at the time of her death and all the right, title and interest the estate has by operation of law or otherwise acquired other than or in addition to that of the decedent at the time of her death, in and to that certain real property located in the City and County of San Francisco, State of California, described as follows:
>
> Commencing at a point on the southerly line of Duncan Street distant thereon 75 feet easterly from the easterly line of Dolores Street, running thence easterly along said southerly line of Duncan Street 25 feet; thence at a right angle southerly 64 feet; thence at a right angle westerly 25 feet; thence at a right angle northerly 64 feet to the southerly line of Duncan Street and the point of commencement.
>
> Being a portion of Horner's Addition Block No. 36.
>
> Bids or offers are invited for the property and must be in writing and may be delivered to the administrator at the office of his attorneys, Tobin & Tobin, No. 1 Jones Street, San Francisco, California, at any time after the first publication of this notice and before the making of the sale.
>
> Terms and conditions of sale: Cash in lawful money of the United States of America; 10% of the amount bid to accompany the offer and the balance to be paid upon confirmation of sale by the Superior Court. Taxes, rents, operating and maintenance expenses and premiums on insurance acceptable to the purchaser shall be prorated as of the date of recording of conveyance. The examination of title, recording of conveyance, and any title insurance policy shall be at the expense of the purchaser or purchasers.
>
> Bids must be sealed and will be opened at the office of Tobin and Tobin at the hour of 2 p. m. on or after July 27th, 1966. The undersigned has the right to reject any and all bids. Information may be obtained by calling the administrator at 474-9947 days, or OV 1-4340 evenings, or Patrick Lyons at 333-1588.
>
> Dated: June 27th, 1966.
>
> JAMES V. LYONS,
> As administrator of estate of Ellen M. Lyons, deceased.
>
> Endorsed: Filed July 12, 1966. MARTIN MONGAN, Clerk. By J. T. MITCHELL, Deputy Clerk.
>
> TOBIN and TOBIN, by JOHN J. FORD, III, Hibernia Bank Building, San Francisco, California.
>
> No. 77236   July 13-26-dly-R

FIGURE 16–1

3. The address at which bids for the property may be delivered prior to the date set for the sale and actual opening of bids.
4. Rules to be observed in preparation of the bid.
5. Terms and conditions of the sale. The two most common conditions are: (1) a certified or cashier's check in the amount of 10 percent of the offered purchase price must be included with the bid; (2) the offer must be all cash, with the property to be purchased in its present as-is condition. Although the bid must be for all cash to the estate, the buyer is given sufficient time to arrange for adequate financing following acceptance of his bid.
6. A statement to the effect that the representative may reject any and all bids. Personal representative is the legal term often applied to an executor or administrator. If the bids opened on the day and time of the sale are considered by the representative to be too low, he may reject all the bids. A new notice of sale then must be published and the procedure repeated. The price offered for probate sale property must be at least 90 percent of the value of the property as set by the inheritance tax appraiser and/or the court. If none of the bids submitted meet this requirement, the sale may have to be repeated.
7. Inspection information. If the notice does not contain information about how the property may be inspected by prospective purchasers before the date of sale, this information can be obtained by calling the representative. Quite often, the representative places a set of keys to the property, if vacant, in the office of a real estate broker in the vicinity of the property.

Listing probate property

A representative of an estate, with court permission, may grant a real estate broker an exclusive right to sell listing for a period of not more than 90 days. Why a listing is given depends on who the representative is and what he wants to do.

When the representative is the trust department of a bank, usually no listing is given to any broker. The bank generally believes that only the notice of sale is needed to bring the sale to the attention of any concerned parties.

An attorney may give a listing to a broker for a variety of reasons. The attorney generally does not have an employee to keep the property open for inspection as does a bank and cannot afford the time to do so himself. He knows that if he gives a listing to a broker in the neighborhood the broker will keep the property open for inspection and may even advertise the property in the local papers. The broker will make an effort to interest a prospective purchaser and will submit the offer for the purchaser, so he has a good chance of earning a standard commission if his client's offer is the highest.

Figure 16–2 and Figure 16–3 illustrate a listing

EXCLUSIVE AUTHORIZATION AND RIGHT TO SELL

(Sale Subject to Probate Court Confirmation)

CALIFORNIA ASSOCIATION OF REALTORS® STANDARD FORM

1. **Right to Sell.** The undersigned, the duly appointed executor or administrator of the estate of _____ _____, deceased, hereby employ and grant _____ herein after called "agent", the exclusive right to sell the real property belonging to the Estate of the decedent, situated in _____, County of _____, California, described as follows: _____
_____
_____

2. **Term.** Agent's right to sell shall be for 90 days, commencing on _____, 19___ and expiring at midnight on _____, 19___.

3. **Terms of Sale**
   (a) The price for the property shall be the sum of $_____, to be paid as follows: _____
   _____
   _____

   (b) The following items of personal property are to be included in the above pre-stated price: _____
   _____
   _____

   (c) Agent is hereby authorized to accept a deposit upon the purchase price of ten per cent (10%) of the purchase price. Said deposit shall be in form of a certified check or cashiers check made payable to the undersigned.

   (d) The bid for the purchase of the property shall be substantially in the form shown on the reverse hereof, which form is incorporated herein by reference.

4. **Compensation to Agent.** I hereby agree to compensate agent as follows: From the proceeds of the sale _____% of the selling price, subject to allowance by the Court, if the property is sold during the term hereof by agent or through any other person, or by me on the terms herein set forth, or any other price and terms I may accept, subject to confirmation of the Court. This agreement is subject to the applicable provisions of the California Probate Code. When said sale is confirmed by the Court, this agreement shall be binding and valid as against the estate for the amount allowed by the Court.

5. I warrant that prior to the execution of this agreement I have obtained the permission of the Court to enter into this agreement. Agent agrees that by the execution of this agreement, no personal liability shall attach to the undersigned, executor or administrator, and no liability of any kind shall be incurred by the estate, unless an actual sale is made and confirmed by the Court.

6. I authorize the agent named herein to cooperate with subagents.

7. I authorize the agent to place a "for sale" sign on the property.

8. This property is offered without regard to race, creed, color, or national origin.

9. Other provisions: _____
_____

10. I acknowledge receipt of a copy hereof.

Dated _____ day of _____, 19___, at _____, California.

_____
Executor/Administrator of the estate of
_____
_____, deceased

11. In consideration of the foregoing, the undersigned agent agrees to be diligent in endeavoring to obtain a purchaser.

_____   _____
Agent   Address/City

By _____   _____
                          Phone

For these forms, address California Association
of Realtors, 505 Shatto Place, Los Angeles 90020.   FORM AP-11   (12-74)

FIGURE 16–2

16 / PUBLIC SALES, CONDOMINIUMS, AND MOBILEHOMES

SUPERIOR COURT OF CALIFORNIA,
COUNTY OF _____

Estate of _____, deceased.

No. _____

BID FOR PURCHASE OF REAL PROPERTY

To _____, _____ of the _____ of the above-named decedent
executor/administrator (etc.)   will/estate

The undersigned hereby offer(s) the sum of $_____

_____

_____
in cash/specify credit terms

for purchase of the real property belonging to the estate of the decedent, commonly known and referred to as _____ (Street Address)
_____, California, and more particularly described as follows: _____
(City)

Subject to current taxes, covenants, conditions, restrictions, reservations, rights, rights-of-way, and easements of record. The following encumbrance is to be assumed by the purchaser: (strike this sentence if it is not applicable) _____

Delivered to you herewith is a certified [ ] cashiers [ ] check in the sum of $_____, being ten per cent (10%) of the purchase price, balance to be paid as follows _____
on confirmation of the sale by the Court/(Other terms)

Rentals, taxes, expenses of operation and maintenance, and premiums on insurance acceptable to the undersigned shall be prorated as of the date of _____ Escrow charges, examination of title, recording of conveyance, transfer
confirmation of sale/recording of conveyance
taxes and any title insurance shall be at the expense of the undersigned.

We have inspected the property and the offer is made as a result of this inspection, and not on any representation based by the seller or any selling agent. We agree that you offer the property without representation, warranty, or covenant of any kind, express or implied.

This sale is conditional upon confirmation of the above-entitled Court, and shall be returned to that Court for confirmation before _____, 19____, and you shall have the same set promptly for hearing. On confirmation of sale by the Court and payment of the balance of the purchase price, you shall deliver to the undersigned possession and a deed conveying all the interest belonging to the estate in the real property.

The undersigned hereby elect(s) _____ to receive title to the property in the following manner:
_____ as _____.
his separate property/joint tenants/husband and wife as their community property/tenants in common

Dated _____   _____

_____
(Purchaser(s))

ACCEPTANCE

Subject to confirmation of the Court, the undersigned, as _____ of the _____, of the above-
Executor/administrator/(Etc.)   will/estate
named decedent, hereby accepts the foregoing bid of _____ as purchaser(s) of all the right, title and interest of the decedent's estate in the real property on the terms therein stated and hereby agrees to pay to _____ real estate broker, form proceeds of the sale whatever sum may be allowed by the above-entitled Court for services in securing the purchaser.

The undersigned also acknowledges receipt of a _____ check for $_____, as deposit.
certified/cashier's

Dated _____

_____ as _____ of the _____ of the above-named decedent.
Executor/administrator (Etc.)   will/estate

ACCEPTANCE BY BROKER

The undersigned real estate broker, duly licensed by the State of California, having secured the purchaser(s) _____
(Name(s))
_____ hereby accepts the foregoing undertaking of _____
as _____ of the _____ of the above-named decedent, to pay to the undersigned from proceeds
Executor/administrator (Etc.)   will/estate
of the sale whatever sum may be allowed by the above-entitled court.

Dated _____   _____
Real Estate Broker

FIGURE 16-3

contract and a purchase contract prepared by CAR in connection with probate properties.

Sale and opening of bids

On the day and at the time set for the sale in the published notice of sale, the bids are opened. The bid accepted at the time of the opening should be the highest net bid to the estate. That is, the representative should actually deduct from the offered price the broker's commission, if one is requested, in order to arrive at the net offer. A bid that does not ask for a commission may possibly be a better net bid than one that is higher in money amount but includes a commission payment. Let us state an example.

Broker A submits a bid of $150,000 and asks for a 5 percent commission. A deduction of 5 percent from $150,000 leaves the amount of $142,500 net to the estate.

Private party B submits a bid of $145,000, which is, of course, net to the estate since a private individual cannot be paid a commission. Thus, we have a situation in which B's offer is better to the estate by $2,500 than broker A's offer, even though broker A's offer was $5,000 higher than private party B's offer.

It is B's offer that the representative should accept as the best offer. A representative's misunderstanding of this procedure often results in some confusion when bids are submitted by brokers as well as by private parties. After a bid has been selected and accepted by the representative, it is subject to confirmation by the court. Within ten days after the date of sale and acceptance of a bid, the representative must file a sale statement and petition the court for confirmation. If the court feels that everything has been done properly and correctly up to this point, the court will set a date for confirmation.

Form of the bid

Bids are usually made on a standard deposit receipt form common to the particular locality in which the sale is taking place or a form similar to that illustrated in Figure 16–3. Often, the representative wants the bid to conform to a certain form and appearance. Anyone who makes a bid should contact the representative before submitting the bid so that no problems in this regard will arise.

Raising the bid in court

On the date set by the court for confirmation of the bid accepted by the representative, the judge of the court, immediately prior to confirmation, asks if anyone in court wants to raise the bid in question. Any interested person or broker may attend the court hearing and, at this point, may step forward and raise the existing high bid. However, this first increased bid must exceed the accepted bid by 10 percent of the first $10,000 and 5 percent of the excess. Any subsequent increase may be in any amount. If the person who submitted the high bid at the time of the sale is present in court or is represented by his broker and, in addition, others present still want to purchase the property, the result is an auction-type affair. No distinction is now made between gross and net bids, and the judge finally accepts the highest amount at this time. If a commission is to be paid, it is fixed by the court at this time.

Issuance of deed

After confirming the sale, the court issues an order to the representative, and he, in turn, executes a deed to the purchaser. The deed refers to the order confirming sale, and both the deed and order should be recorded in the office of the county recorder.

Real estate broker's commission

In this type of sale, it is not necessary that the broker have a written listing in order to obtain a commission. It is standard procedure for the court to pay a commission to a licensed broker if one is asked for in the accepted bid. A broker holding an exclusive right to sell listing will receive half a commission upon sale of the property or a full commission if he is also the selling broker. Although the court usually sets a commission equivalent to those that prevail in the particular locale, it is better practice for a broker not to specify an exact percentage or amount. In the place on the bid where the commission is mentioned, the broker might state:

> Subject to the rate of commission to be set by the Probate Court and payable to _____ Realty Company.

Where there is no increase in court at time of confirmation, the high bid at time of the sale is accepted by the court, and the commission is paid on this accepted bid. Where there is bidding in court at the time of confirmation, the result may vary as far as the commission is concerned. Since court practices may vary, the licensee should consult with the court in any given locality as to its practices.

Additional comments on purchase of probate property

Property sold through probate court sale is sold in its as-is condition, and the estate is not responsible for any termite or dry rot damage or any other condition in need of repair. The purchaser should understand that he must personally inspect the property and use his own judgment on its structural condition.

The notice of sale usually states that responsibility for obtaining a policy of title insurance rests with the purchaser, making it appear that the title to be acquired may be less than acceptable. Actually, the personal representative usually has a preliminary title insurance report, which the prospective purchaser may inspect. In the purchase of such properties, there is usually no problem with regard to title.

MORTGAGE FORECLOSURE

The only form of action that may be brought for the recovery of an obligation secured by a mortgage is foreclosure by court action. The object of the foreclosure is to sell the right, title, and interest held in the property by the mortgagor at the time of execution of the mortgage.

Foreclosure sale

The foreclosure sale is made by a commissioner appointed by the court in accordance with the Code of Civil Procedure. The sale must be made in the same manner as sales by a sheriff on execution and must be made to the highest bidder. A notice of the time and place of sale must be given in writing and must describe the property and be posted in a public place in the city where the property is to be sold. The notice is usually posted at the city hall for the required 20 days. In addition, the notice must be published once a week for 20 days in a newspaper of general circulation, published in the city, judicial district, or county in which the property is located, preferably, the one closest to the location of property.

Method of bidding

Persons who make bids at the foreclosure sale must bid cash, with the exception of the beneficiary, who can bid in the amount due him without the necessity of putting up cash in this amount. The title given to the successful bidder is deemed to relate back to the title of the mortgagor as of the date of execution of the security. Except for certain tax liens, intervening liens are eliminated by the foreclosure purchase.

Redemption rights

The mortgagor, or any one claiming under him, or certain creditors have a statutory right of redemption. This may be undertaken at any time within 12 months after the sale by paying the purchaser:

1. The price paid by the purchaser at the foreclosure sale.
2. In addition, 1 percent per month.
3. Any taxes or assessments paid by the purchaser.
4. Any reasonable sum for fire insurance, maintenance, upkeep, or repair.
5. Interest on these sums.

Right of possession

It should also be noted that after the foreclosure of a mortgage, the mortgagor may remain in possession for the one-year redemption period. The purchaser is entitled to rent and any profits during this period but cannot generally obtain possession. After sale under a deed of trust, however, the purchaser gets the right to possession as soon as he receives the trustee's deed.

TAX SALE OF REAL PROPERTY

Property sold at tax sale is quite simply property on which the taxes have not been paid for a certain period of time and which is finally being sold by the state, county, or city tax collector in order to satisfy the tax delinquency.

First sale

On June 8 of each year, a delinquent tax list is published showing all properties for which one or both installments are delinquent. On June 30, such property is said to be first sold to the state. Although the property is not actually sold at this time, the important point is that at this point, the statutory five-year period of redemption begins. At any time during the five years, the owner of the property may redeem it and save it from ultimately being sold by paying all delinquent taxes and any attendant penalties; this right is granted under the Revenue and Taxation Code, Section 4101.

In certain conditions covered in the code, delinquent taxes may be paid by the property owner under an installment plan. This allows the owner to pay the delinquent taxes in other than a lump-sum payment and makes it easier to redeem a delinquent piece of property.

Second sale

After five years have passed from the date of the so-called first sale, the state of California now actually acquires an absolute title in the tax-delinquent property. The property must be sold for at least the full amount that was due for the year in which the property was first sold to the state, plus the unpaid taxes for each of the five subsequent years. In addition, there must be included in the sale price all statutory penalties, interest, and costs that may have accrued.

Actual sale to public

If the real property to be sold is outside an incorporated area, it is sold under the authority of the state comptroller. If the property is in an incorporated area, the city or county tax collector is in charge of the sale. Because tax may be due to local, state, and federal agencies at the same time, the official in charge of the sale, whoever he may be, and other agencies who may have a tax lien against the property will have reached an agreement on the disposition of the purchase price received for the property.

After publishing the required notice, giving details of the sale, description of the property, and other particulars, the property involved is sold at public auction. A minimum bid is established, and any interested party may bid and purchase the property.

Tax deed

On completion of the sale, the tax collector in charge automatically records and issues to the purchaser a deed commonly referred to as a tax deed.

Title insurance

After the sale, the former owner loses any claim he may have had and cannot redeem the property. During recent years, the California State Legislature has enacted certain legislation to help the stability of tax titles. One such piece of legislation, Section 3711 of the Revenue and Taxation Code, provides that a tax deed is, in fact, conclusive evidence of the regularity of the proceedings that led up to the sale and issuance of the tax deed.

Because of this regulation, most title insurance companies now insure tax titles. The tax deed usually is insured if one year has passed since issuance of the tax deed, if the former owner is not in possession, if current taxes have been paid, and if no serious defects are shown by examination of the events leading up to the sale.

If the title insurance company refuses to insure the tax title after an investigation of the case, the new owner must proceed with a quiet title action against the former owner. This alternative is expensive and usually takes at least a year.

SHERIFF'S SALE

A sheriff's sale of real property is usually the result of a judgment obtained against the owner of the property and the court's subsequent issuance of a writ of execution. This writ directs the sheriff, or other officer whom the court may elect, to enforce the judgment against the property of the one against whom the judgment has been obtained.

Section 577 of the Code of Civil Procedure relates to judgments that may result in a lien against real property. Such judgments are generally of three types:

1. Judgments that foreclose liens on the property and order the sale of such property, the money obtained being used to pay the amount of the judgment.
2. Judgments that award money and impose a lien on property in order to obtain that money—a common practice as a result of divorce proceedings.
3. Judgments for money, awarded against a debtor, that result in a lien against property of the debtor.

Before awarding a judgment, the plaintiff in an action may ask the court to issue a writ of attachment against the defendant's property. The property being so attached cannot be sold or encumbered until the case in court is settled.

Writs of attachment, judgment, and execution

Quite simply, then, a writ of attachment merely holds the property until a judgment is or is not obtained against the property owner. In the event that a judgment is obtained and the property must be sold to satisfy the judgment, the court will issue a writ of execution directing the sheriff to proceed with the sale in order to get such satisfaction.

Sale on writ of execution

Before real property can be sold by the sheriff acting on a writ of execution issued by the court the following must be done:

1. A written notice of sale must be posted, usually at the city hall or in a prescribed public place.
2. The notice must be posted at least 20 days before the sale and must give a description of the property and the time and place of the sale.
3. The notice must be published in a newspaper of general circulation at least once a week during the 20 days, a notice of sale must be mailed to any person who has requested it under Section 692a of the Code of Civil Procedure.

The sale must be held in the county where the property is located, and the property must be sold at public auction to the highest bidder. The sale must be on a business day during normal business hours.

Certificate of sale

At the actual sale, the high bidder becomes the purchaser, and the officer who conducts the sale issues to the purchaser a certificate of sale. A duplicate of the certificate is filed in the office of the county recorder. This certificate of sale is assignable.

Right of redemption

Although the purchaser has a certificate of sale, the property he has just purchased may still be redeemed by the former owner or other creditors. Under Section 700a of the Code of Civil Procedure, real property sold as the result of a writ of execution is subject to redemption at any time within 12 months after the sale.

A redemption may be accomplished by either the judgment debtor or his successor in interest. The redemption is made by paying to the holder of the certificate of sale a sum equal to the sale price plus any interest and any sums advanced by the purchaser for such items as taxes, assessments, insurance, maintenance, and repairs.

On payment of the above sums, the person to whom payment is made must execute, acknowledge, and deliver a certificate of redemption, which is then recorded at the office of the county recorder.

A redemption may be made by a creditor who has a junior lien, but this redemption operates only as an assignment of the certificate of sale, and a redemption may still be made by the debtor or his successor in interest within the 12 months stipulated in the code.

Final issuance of deed

If the 12 months after the date of sale pass and there is no redemption, the officer who originally made the sale executes and delivers a deed to the purchaser. The sale has thus become absolute, and no redemption is possible.

ADDITIONAL SALES OF REAL PROPERTY

This chapter has thus far discussed the more common situations of real property offered for public sale under the jurisdiction of a court and/or as the result of some type of judicial proceeding.

There are other kinds of sales, such as a guardianship sale and a sale by a conservator, referred to as a sale of real property in conservatorship proceedings. A court referee's sale of real property as the result of a partition action takes place when several persons own shares in a piece of property and one owner blocks sale of the property by the others. The owners who want to sell then ask the court to force a sale of the property. This maneuver is known as a partition action.

All the less common types of these sales follow the general procedure, previously discussed, for publishing a notice of sale and making the sale a public one where anyone may attempt to purchase the property.

Role of the real estate broker

The role of the real estate broker in the types of sales discussed varies according to the type of sale involved. When the court will award a commission to a broker if his bid is successful, the broker's role is much the same as in any day-to-day type of transaction. The broker is representing a purchaser, and if he is successful, he will receive a commission from the judicial agency in charge of the sale. When a property is up for public sale but no provision is made for payment of a commission if a licensee represents the successful bidder, he must enter with his client into a prior agreement whereby the client pays the broker a commission if he becomes the purchaser.

The broker may interest his client in the purchase of property at public sale as a business investment, to be resold later, rather than as property for actual use by the purchaser. Here, the broker may receive a commission when the property is purchased and another commission later when he resells the property for his client. Brokers quite often represent speculators and other persons who are looking for properties in need of modernization and repair. These persons hope to buy the property for a price that will allow for the necessary improvements and a satisfactory profit when the property is sold again. Many pieces of real estate available at public sale need repair and modernization. They will not attract offers from the average purchaser, leaving the path open for the speculator.

Finally, many real estate licensees who attend public sales represent only themselves. In addition to representing others, they buy and sell on their own account. A broker who makes such a purchase cannot be paid a commission if he is, in fact, purchasing the property for himself. He must submit his bid in the same way any private purchaser does.

CONDOMINIUM SALES

Prior to 1963, the word "condominium" did not appear anywhere in the California statutes. Condominiums were treated as subdivisions within the Business and Professions Code, but no special legislation had been passed to provide answers to the several legal problems presented to title companies, tax authorities, insurance companies, and others by this variance from conventional development. The 1963 legislature moved to solve the problem and statutes were enacted which defined "condominium" and added provisions to the Civil Code, Business and Professions Code, and Revenue and Taxation Code dealing specifically with this particular type of ownership. Recent estimates predict that during the early 1980s close to 50 percent of all newly built residences will be condominiums.

A condominium in a highrise building, often referred to as a vertical subdivision, consists of a fee simple ownership in a particular unit and the air space it occupies, together with an undivided interest in common with other owners as regards the framework and common areas of the building, land it occupies, and any additional facilities which serve the building.

Planned residential unit developments and townhouses are often referred to as horizontal subdivisions, and the owner generally has a fee ownership in a particular unit and land on which it is built, together with an undivided interest in common with other owners in the common areas and facilities which serve the project.

Condominium features

Increasing land and construction costs in certain areas have made traditional housing extremely expensive. Although studies have shown that most Americans still prefer to purchase traditional homes, economic realities are forcing more and more buyers to consider the concept of condominium homes.

Some of the possible advantages are:

1. Same tax and property appreciation features as traditional property.
2. Relief from yard care and exterior maintenance.
3. Special facilities, such as recreational building, pool, and tennis courts.
4. Certain security and safety features.
5. Location usually convenient to urban facilities.

Some of the possible disadvantages are:

1. Lack of individuality and necessity of having to conform to occupancy rules and regulations.
2. Disturbances and noise by neighbors.
3. Lack of privacy.
4. Minimal parking and storage facilities.
5. Conformance with convenants, conditions, and restrictions and property owners association.

Given the various advantages and disadvantages, the growing number of condominium sales seems to indicate that condominium living provides the housing answer to many individuals.

The licensee and condominium sales

The basic difference with respect to condominium purchase is that the owner of a condominium must be willing to conform to association bylaws and rules and regulations necessary to maximize the benefits to the total population of a condominium complex.

The real estate licensee who engages in the sale of condominium homes performs the same duties and functions as in the sale of any real property, but additionally, the licensee must be sure to prepare the client for the lifestyle and environment usually associated with condominium ownership. Buyers are often attracted to condominiums as the result of advertising which indicates that the condominium owner has little ownership responsibility. The licensee must explain that a condominium owner has very specific ownership responsibilities. The licensee must provide the prospective purchaser with a copy of the Commissioners Subdivision Public Report in connection with the particular condominium development and explain the usual articles of incorporation and bylaws which will regulate the activities of the condominium owner.

California law further requires that a copy of the Real Estate Commissioners Public Report be given to a prospective purchaser of a condominium before any written offer to purchase is made or before any money or other consideration toward purchase of a condominium is accepted by a developer, his agents, or salesmen.

The licensee must be prepared to discuss with his clients such topics as the articles of incorporation and association bylaws, management, maintenance, common areas, recreational facilities, insurance, assessments, and fees.

If an existing building has been converted to condominiums, such conversions may present additional problems. It may be that the conversion is mainly cosmetic, and later problems may arise with respect to plumbing, wiring, heating, roofing and appliances. The quality of construction and general physical condition of the property is always a most important consideration to the purchaser.

MOBILEHOME SALES

California real estate licensees may now sell mobilehomes which have been registered with the Division of Motor Vehicles for 366 days or more and are in place on a lot which is rented or leased within an established mobilehome park, or on a separate site properly zoned for the presence of mobilehomes. These resales are in some ways similar to conventional housing sales, but since mobilehomes are classified as personal property, there are new rules and regulations which the licensee wishing to engage in the sale of mobilehomes must learn.

More than 8 million Americans live in mobilehomes, and approximately 700,000 families will purchase mobilehomes this year. California leads the nation in number of mobilehomes with about 7,000 mobilehome communities and approximately 1 million residents. Mobilehomes must be produced in conformity with standards set by the Secretary of Housing and Urban Development (HUD) in conjunction with the Consumer Product Safety Commission. These standards have to do with safety, body and frame construction, and plumbing, heating, and electrical features. A mobilehome code has also been enacted in California and is administered by the California Department of Housing and Community Development, and the law requires each mobilehome sold in California to have an insignia of approval issued by this agency.

Regulating laws

As of July 1975, A.B. 2194 authorizes real estate brokers to engage in selling or purchasing, offering to sell or purchase, soliciting purchasers of, soliciting the obtaining of, or negotiating purchase, sale, or exchange of certain mobilehomes registered with the Department of Motor Vehicles for 366 days or more.

It provides that real estate brokers engaged in such activities shall not maintain a place of business where two or more of such mobilehomes are displayed and offered for sale by the broker if the broker is not also licensed as a vehicle dealer persuant to the Vehicle Code.

A mobilehome within this section means a vehicle designed and equipped for habitation which is greater than 8 feet in width and 32 feet in length and does not include a motor vehicle. The Real Estate Commissioner has conferred with the Department of Motor Vehicles and prescribed regulations to assure compliance with the Vehicle Code pertaining to mobilehome registration, collection of sales and use taxes, and transaction documentation. Sections 10131.6 and 10131.7 have been added to the Business and Professions Code and Regulations 2860 and 2863 to the Commissioners Rules and Regulations. Some examples of these new provisions are as follows:

1. It is unlawful for a real estate licensee, acting as a mobilehome agent, to advertise or offer for sale in any way a mobilehome unless it is either in place on a lot rented or leased for habitation within an established mobilehome park, or on a separate site properly zoned for the presence of a mobilehome.

2. Since the real estate licensee can only engage in mobilehome activities where the mobilehome has been registered with DMV for 366 days or more, the licensee must ascertain its registration status prior to accepting a listing and should do so by asking the mobilehome owner to furnish his registration certificate.

3. The advertising or offering for sale by a real

estate agent must not be contrary to any terms of an agreement between the seller of the mobilehome and the owner of the mobilehome park.

4. The licensee must withdraw any advertisment of a mobilehome for sale, lease, or exchange within 48 hours after receipt of notice that the mobilehome is no longer available for sale, lease, or exchange, and the law does not specify that any reason be given by the mobilehome owner.

5. The licensee cannot represent or advertise a mobilehome as a new mobilehome and cannot make any representation that a mobilehome is capable of being operated as a vehicle on California highways if it does not meet the necessary requirements. The safest practice for the real estate licensee is to make no representation with respect to operation of the mobilehome on highways. If the licensee has need to know the equipment requirements specifically applicable to the transport of mobilehomes on highways, such information should be obtained from the California Highway Patrol.

Taxing mobiles as real property

It has been argued for a number of years that mobilehomes should no longer be considered as trailers. Today they are mostly 1,000 to 2,000 square foot dwellings with rigid standards in design, construction, and materials. After a mobilehome is purchased, it is generally fixed in place with no intention of being either vehicular or mobile.

This particular trend has been recognized by the California legislature with a new law effective July 1980. All new mobilehomes sold in California and installed on a permanent foundation for occupancy as a residence are now taxed on the same basis as conventional homes. They are assessed and taxed as real property and not subject to Department of Motor Vehicle licensing.

The new tax is 1 percent of market value. The market value (sales price) is reduced by the $7,000 exemption allowed to homeowners. The tax on a $50,000 mobilehome is $430. A purchase price of $50,000 minus $7,000 equals $43,000. Multiplying $43,000 × .01 equals a $430 tax. The tax is limited to a 2 percent increase every succeeding year, and the homeowner may pay the tax in two installments. A small registration fee collected by the Department of Housing and Community Development in 1981 will be charged and not collected again until such time as the mobilehome is sold. Notification to place mobilehomes on the tax rolls is the responsibility of the local building inspection department.

An additional bonus to a purchaser who buys after March 1 of any year will be a tax-free year. The mobilehome will not go on the tax roll until March 1 of the following year.

Mobilehome parks

The real estate licensee who plans to act as an agent in the sale of mobilehomes must be familiar with the local ordinances which apply specifically to the occupancy of mobilehomes. Since a large majority of occupied mobilehomes today are in mobilehome parks rather than on individually owned lots, park rules can have a significant effect on the purchaser's choice of where to buy a particular mobilehome.

In a rental-type mobilehome park, even though the tenant owns his own mobilehome and may have made a significant additional investment in landscaping and other improvements, he is usually renting space on a month-to-month basis. There is no automatic transfer or conveyance of leasehold interest when the mobilehome is sold, and new tenancy must be created between the park operator and the buyer of the mobilehome if he wishes the mobilehome to remain in the park. As in any rental situation, the new tenant must be approved by the owner. While the owner's evaluation of the prospective tenant must not conflict with law regulating discrimination in housing, the park may be geared to certain needs and interests, such as to persons who are in a particular age bracket or are retired.

It is essential that the real estate licensee obtain and be familiar with the written park rules and regulations since most mobilehome parks and communities require a prospective tenant to read and agree to comply with these rules. A copy can be obtained at the time the licensee takes the mobilehome listing.

Financing methods

Mobilehome financing does not differ greatly from traditional real estate financing with respect to sources of funds. Many banks and savings and loan associations are becoming increasingly active in providing funds for mobilehome purchase. FHA and VA loans are available, and certain finance companies and credit unions may provide funds. The amount of the monetary obligation is evidenced by a note and security interest in the mobilehome and any equipment contained in the mobilehome.

In seeking financing for clients, the real estate licensee should find those lenders in the area who specialize in mobilehomes and learn their policies and procedures.

Escrow procedures

Since the sale of mobilehomes involving real estate licensees is relatively new, the licensee should attempt to use an escrow holder who is familiar with the procedures involved in such a transaction. The licensee must be ready with certain information and material.

Principals to the escrow. The DVM requires that names of buyers and sellers be given in full and the social security number of all parties to the transaction must be shown on forms to be filed with the Secretary of State.

Mobilehome description. The description of the mobilehome must include year of manufacture, size, I.D. number, and license plate number. This information can be obtained from the registration certificate. Any additional items to be included in the sale should also be listed and approved by buyers and sellers. A Bill of Sale should be delivered through escrow for the mobilehome and inventory of any personal property in addition to any required by the Department of Motor Vehicles.

Sales price. With respect to consideration or sales price, the buyers may:

1. Pay all cash.
2. Cash to an existing loan on the mobilehome.
3. Cash to an existing loan on the mobilehome and additional personal property, such as patio roof and air conditioning.
4. Cash to a new loan to be obtained by buyer.
5. Cash to a note and security agreement that buyers will sign in favor of sellers.

Registration and ownership certificates. The seller should have a copy of the registration certificate. The seller should also have a copy of the ownership certificate and will sign this certificate releasing the sellers interest as legal owner. If there is an existing loan on the mobilehome, the lender will usually have the ownership certificate. These certificates must be rated and approved by the Department of Motor Vehicles before escrow is closed.

Insurance. Owners of mobilehomes carry fire and liability coverage in the same way as owners of real property, and insurance policies are handled in escrow as with real property. The insurance policy may be transferred and prorated, or the buyer may obtain a new policy.

Search of records. In addition to the promissory note and security agreement, the lender will usually file a financing statement with the Secretary of State of the State of California or with the county recorder. In order to establish any possible liens, the escrow holder should obtain reports which may have been filed with any of these agencies.

When opening escrow, the licensee should be prepared with respect to the following information in order that the escrow proceed properly:

1. Identification of parties, mobilehome and inventory of any personal property included in the sale escrow.
2. Terms of the sale and financing, any liens to be cleared or assumed, and any lease to be assigned or rental agreement.
3. Registration and ownership certificates to be rated and approved by appropriate agencies.
4. Determination of proration and closing dates.
5. Any other items which must be cleared or completed prior to close of escrow.

Listing and purchase contracts

The California Association of Realtors has prepared listing and purchase contracts to be used in connection with mobilehome sales. These are illustrated in Figure 16–4 and Figure 16–5.

Modular construction

With respect to manufactured housing, modular units are assuming increasing importance. Modules are factory-built construction units and typically contain about 400 square feet. Three modules can be put together to produce a 1,200-square-foot residence.

While mobilehomes are built on a permanent steel chassis and later installed on concrete blocks, modular units are brought to a particular site and assembled on poured concrete foundations. Modular homes can be built to conform to any local building codes and, together with mobilehomes, are another alternative to traditional construction methods.

Additional forms, applicable to this chapter, are illustrated in Appendix C as Figures C8–3 and C16–1.

EXCLUSIVE AUTHORIZATION AND RIGHT TO SELL

(MOBILEHOME registered at least one year under Vehicle Code Div. 3)   California Association of Realtors® Standard Form
THIS IS INTENDED TO BE A LEGALLY BINDING AGREEMENT. READ IT CAREFULLY.

1. RIGHT TO SELL. I hereby employ and grant _____ hereafter called "Agent", the exclusive and irrevocable right commencing on _____ 19 ____, and expiring at midnight on _____ 19 ____, to sell or exchange the mobilehome situated at _____,
_____ County, California in _____ Mobilehome Park,
Space # _____ described af follows: Make _____ Model _____ Year _____
Net Length _____ Expando _____ Width _____ Class _____
Type _____ Bedrooms _____ Baths _____ Exterior _____ Roof _____ Skirting _____

Serial #'s: CAL D.O.H. #'s: HUD #'s: 19___ License #'s:
_____ U (A) _____ _____ _____
_____ X (B) _____ _____ _____
_____ XX (C) _____ _____ _____
_____ XXX (D) _____ _____ _____

together with all built in appliances, heating units and water heater and the following equipment:
Refrigerator _____ Range _____ Oven _____ Washer _____ Dryer _____
Disposal _____ Dishwasher _____ Air Conditioner—Serial # — Tonnage _____
Carport Awning _____ Patio Awning _____ Porch _____ Screen Rm. _____
Wheels _____ Tires _____ Other: _____

Park Information

Type _____ Clubhouse _____ Swimming Pool _____ Space Rental _____
Gas _____ Electricity _____ Guests _____ Children _____ Pets _____ Cable TV _____
Name of Manager _____ Phone No. _____ Sign ____ Caravan _____
Has seller obtained written agreement from Park Management permitting overage mobilehome to remain? _____ Yes _____ No

2. TERMS OF SALE. The purchase price shall be $ _____, to be paid on the following terms:
_____
_____

   (a) The following items of personal property are to be included in the above-stated price:
_____
_____

   (b) Agent is hereby authorized to accept and hold on my behalf a deposit upon the purchase price.
   (c) I agree to deliver the above described mobilehome and personal property, if any is included, free of liens, encumbrances, recorded, filed or registered, or known to me.
   (d) Evidence of title shall be in form of a duly endorsed, dated and delivered Certificate of Ownership or mobilehome and delivery of current Registration Certificate, as required by the Vehicle Code.
   (e) I warrant that I am the owner of the mobilehome or have authority to execute this agreement. I warrant that the above described mobilehome complies with equipment requirements of Division 12 (commencing with section 24000) of the Vehicle Code.
   (f) I warrant that the above described mobilehome conforms to the requirements of the Health and Safety Code and the regulations of the Department of Housing and Community Development, HUD Regulations, and any applicable local ordinances and is either 1) located within an established mobilehome park as defined in Section 18214 of the Health and Safety Code and that advertising or offering for its sale is not contrary to any items of any contract between myself and the mobilehome park owner, or 2) located pursuant to a local zoning ordinance or permit, on a lot where its presence has been authorized or its continued presence and such use would be authorized for a total and uninterrupted period of at least one year.
   (g) I agree to deliver as soon as possible to Agent for submission to buyer a copy of my lease or rental agreement and all curent park rules and regulations and inform agent of any changes occuring during the term hereof.

3. COMPENSATION OF AGENT. I hereby agree to compensate Agent as follows:
   (a) _____% of the selling price if the mobilehome is sold during the term hereof, or any extension thereof, by Agent, on the terms herein set forth or any other price and terms I may accept, or through any other person, or by me, or_____% of the price shown in 2), if said mobilehome is withdrawn from sale, transferred, or leased without the consent of Agent, or made unmarketable by my voluntary act during the term hereof or any extension thereof.
   (b) The compensation provided for in subparagraph a) above if the mobilehome is sold or otherwise transferred within _____ days after the termination of this authority or any extension thereof to anyone with whom Agent has had negotiations prior to final termination, provided I have received notice in writing, including the names of the prospective purchasers, before or upon termination of this agreement or any extension thereof.

4. If action be instituted to enforce this agreement, the prevailing party shall receive reasonable attorney's fees and costs.
5. I authorize the Agent named herein to cooperate with sub-agents.
6. The mobilehome is offered in compliance with state and federal Anti-Discrimination Laws.
7. In the event of an exchange, permission is hereby given Agent to represent all parties and collect compensation or commissions from them, provided there is full disclosure to all principals of such agency. Agent is authorized to divide with other agents such compensation or commissions in any manner acceptable to them.
8. I agree to hold Agent harmless from any liability arising from any incorrect information supplied by me, or from any material fact known by me concerning the mobilehome, the park or other location in which it is located, which I fail to disclose.
9. Other provisions: _____
_____

10. I acknowledge that I have read and understand this Agreement, and that I have received a copy hereof.

DATED: _____, 19 ____   _____, California
Owner _____   Owner _____
Address _____   City, State, Phone _____

11. In consideration of the above, Agent agrees to use diligence in procuring a purchaser.
Agent _____   Address, City _____
By _____   Phone, Date _____

NO REPRESENTATION IS MADE AS TO THE LEGAL VALIDITY OF ANY PROVISION OR THE ADEQUACY OF ANY PROVISION IN ANY SPECIFIC TRANSACTION.

FIGURE 16–4

CALIFORNIA ASSOCIATION OF REALTORS® STANDARD FORM

MOBILEHOME PURCHASE CONTRACT AND RECEIPT FOR DEPOSIT

(Mobilehome Registered at Least One Year Under Vehicle Code Div. 3)
THIS IS MORE THAN A RECEIPT FOR MONEY. IT IS INTENDED TO BE A LEGALLY BINDING CONTRACT. READ IT CAREFULLY.

_____ , California _____ , 19 _____
Received from _____
herein called Buyer, the sum of _____ Dollars $ _____
evidenced by cash ☐, cashier's check ☐, or _____ ☐ personal check ☐ payable to _____, to be held uncashed until acceptance of this offer, as deposit on account of purchase price of _____ Dollars $ _____
for the purchase of mobilehome situated at _____ ,
County of _____ , California in _____
Mobilehome Park, Space # _____ , described as follows: Make _____
Model _____ Year _____ Net Length _____ Expando _____ Width _____

Serial #'s:		CAL. D.O.H. #'s:	HUD #'s	19 ___ License #'s:
_____	U (A)	_____	_____	_____
_____	X (B)	_____	_____	_____
_____	XX (C)	_____	_____	_____
_____	XXX (D)	_____	_____	_____

together with all built-in appliances, heating units and water heater and the following additional equipment: _____

1. Buyer will deposit in escrow with _____ the balance of purchase price as follows:

_____

(Set forth above any terms and conditions of this sale, such as financing, repairs and personal property to be included in the sale.)

2. Deposit will ☐ will not ☐ be increased by $ _____ to $ _____ within _____ days of acceptance of this offer.
3. The supplements initialed below are incorporated as part of this agreement.

		Other
___ DMV Form Reg. 347(B)	___ Occupancy Agreement	_____
___ Structural Pest Control Certification Agreement	___ VA Amendment	_____
___ Special Studies Zone Disclosure	___ FHA Amendment	_____

4. Buyer and Seller acknowledge receipt of a copy of this page. Page 1 of _____ Pages

X _____ X _____
BUYER   SELLER

X _____ X _____
BUYER   SELLER

THIS STANDARDIZED DOCUMENT FOR USE IN SIMPLE TRANSACTIONS HAS BEEN APPROVED BY THE CALIFORNIA ASSOCIATION OF REALTORS® IN FORM ONLY. NO REPRESENTATION IS MADE AS TO THE APPROVAL OF THE FORM OF SUPPLEMENTS. THE LEGAL VALIDITY OF ANY PROVISION OR THE ADEQUACY OF ANY PROVISION IN ANY SPECIFIC TRANSACTION. IT SHOULD NOT BE USED IN COMPLEX TRANSACTIONS OR WITH EXTENSIVE RIDERS OR ADDITIONS.

FIGURE 16–5

MOBILEHOME PURCHASE CONTRACT AND RECEIPT FOR DEPOSIT

The following terms and conditions are hereby incorporated in and made a part of Buyer's Offer

5. Title is to be free of liens, encumbrances, recorded, filed or registered, or known to seller except as set forth above.

6. Unless otherwise designated in the escrow instructions of Buyer, title shall vest as follows: _____

(The manner of taking title may have significant consequences. Therefore, give this matter serious consideration.)

7. Evidence of title shall be in form of a duly endorsed, dated and delivered Certificate of Ownership and delivery of current Registration Certificate, as required by the Vehicle Code. If seller fails to deliver title as herein provided, Buyer may terminate this agreement and deposit shall thereupon be returned to Buyer.

8. Buyer acknowledges that present or any future movement of the mobilehome may be limited by law and is subject to the regulations current at that time by the Department of Transportation.

9. Buyer acknowledges that Seller hereby is not assigning or subletting the space the mobilehome occupies in its present location unless such letting is specifically made part of this agreement. If the described mobilehome is located in a mobilehome park in which it is to remain, the buyer by his signature below represents that he has agreed to the terms of a rental agreement for the space involved.

10. Possession shall be delivered to Buyer (a) on close of escrow, or (b) not later than _____ days after closing escrow, or (c) _____.

11. Escrow instructions signed by Buyer and Seller shall be delivered to the escrow holder within _____ days from the Seller's acceptance hereof and shall provide for closing within _____ days from the Seller's acceptance hereof, subject to written extensions signed by Buyer and Seller.

12. If the mobilehome is destroyed or materially damaged prior to close of escrow, then, on demand by Buyer, any deposit made by Buyer shall be returned to Buyer and this contract thereupon shall terminate.

13. If Broker is a participant of a Board multiple listing service ("MLS"), the Broker is authorized to report the sale, its price, terms and financing for the information, publication, dissemination, and use of the authorized Board members.

14. **If Buyer fails to complete said purchase as herein provided by reason of any default of Buyer, Seller shall be released from his obligation to sell the property to Buyer and may proceed against Buyer upon any claim or remedy which he may have in law or equity; provided, however, that by placing their initials here Buyer: ( ) Seller: ( ) agree that Seller shall retain the deposit as his liquidated damages.**

15. If the only controversy or claim between the parties arises out of or relates to the disposition of the Buyer's deposit, such controversy or claim shall, at the election of the parties, be decided by arbitration in accordance with the Rules of the American Arbitration Association, and judgment upon the award rendered by the Arbitrator(s) may be entered in any court having jurisdiction thereof. The provisions of Code of Civil Procedure Section 1283.05 shall be applicable to such arbitration.

16. In any action or proceeding arising out of this agreement, the prevailing party shall be entitled to reasonable attorney's fees and costs.

17. Time is of the essence. All modifications or extensions shall be in writing signed by the parties.

18. This constitutes an offer to purchase the described mobilehome. Unless acceptance is signed by Seller and the signed copy delivered to Buyer, in person or by mail to the address below, within _____ days, this offer shall be deemed revoked and the deposit shall be returned. Buyer acknowledges receipt of a copy hereof.

Real Estate Broker _____ Buyer _____
By _____ _____
Address _____ Address _____
Telephone _____ Telephone _____

ACCEPTANCE

The undersigned Seller accepts and agrees to sell the mobilehome on the above terms and conditions. Seller has employed _____ as Broker(s) and agrees to pay for services the sum of _____ Dollars ($ _____), payable as follows: (a) On close of escrow, or (b) if completion of sale is prevented by default of Seller, upon Seller's default or (c) if completion of sale is prevented by default of Buyer, only if and when Seller collects damages from Buyer, by suit or otherwise and then in an amount of one-half of the damages recovered, but not to exceed the above fee after first deducting escrow expenses and the expenses of collection, if any. In any action between Broker and Seller arising out of this agreement, the prevailing party shall be entitled to reasonable attorney's fees and costs. The undersigned acknowledges receipt of a copy and authorizes' Broker(s) to deliver a signed copy to Buyer. Page 2 of _____ Pages.

Dated: _____ Telephone _____ Seller _____
Address _____ Seller _____
Broker(s) agree to the foregoing. Broker _____ Broker _____
Dated: _____ By _____ Dated: _____ By _____

FIGURE 16-5 *(continued)*

QUESTIONS FOR DISCUSSION

1. What may a trustor do after a notice of default has been recorded and before the actual sale in order to keep his property from being sold?
2. What may a second loan holder do to protect his interests after a notice of default has been recorded for the first loan?
3. What liens are not eliminated by a trustee's sale of real property?
4. Discuss the rights of possession by the purchaser after a trustee's sale of real property.
5. In what ways are most properties sold at a trustee's sale similar?
6. Why is real property often sold as the result of a probate proceeding?
7. What type of listing may a broker obtain for probate property?
8. Who sets the rate of commission to be paid to a broker for a probate property?
9. Discuss the as-is provision in the sale of probate property.
10. What are the redemption rights of a mortgagor?
11. Discuss the rights of possession by the purchaser after a mortgage foreclosure sale of real property.
12. What are the basic differences among a writ of attachment, a judgment, and a writ of execution?
13. What type of buyer may a broker interest in the purchase of public sale property?
14. What general types of judgments may result in a lien against property?
15. What is meant by the first sale and second sale of tax-delinquent property?
16. Discuss condominium sales and special features relevant to your particular locality.
17. Discuss the sale of mobilehomes and special features relevant to your particular locality.

17

Real estate exchanges and trade-in programs

This chapter will deal with two general topics: (1) real estate exchanging and trading and (2) types of trade-in programs the broker can set up for his office in order to increase sales.

EXCHANGES

Real estate exchanging has become one of the specialty areas within the real estate business, and many brokers devote all their time to this field. Groups of licensees interested in exchanges exist on local, state, and national bases. A division of the California Association of Realtors Exchange Committee is the Certified Property Exchangors. Licensees who qualify on the basis of certain education, examination, and experience requirements may qualify for the designation, Certified Property Exchangor (CPE). The National Institute of Real Estate Brokers sponsors the International Traders Club, which provides its members with printed materials and information regarding properties throughout the United States and Canada.

Reasons for an exchange

People enter into a real estate exchange situation for various reasons.

1. By far the most common reason concerns tax advantages. The tax-free exchange and trading up in real estate are tax advantages we shall discuss in detail in this chapter.
2. Many persons who want a change of location or climate seek to exchange their property.
3. An owner who wants no disruption of income may be able to exchange his units for others without losing income during negotiations.
4. An owner who has no cash may want to use his equity in his present property in order to acquire another.
5. During a tight money market, an owner may benefit more by exchanging his property instead of selling outright and having to carry back a large mortgage.
6. A person may want another property but may not want to go through the process of a sale and new purchase, with all the pressures and time factors involved.

The tax-free exchange

Section 1031 of the Internal Revenue Code deals with tax-free exchanges. Such exchanges are generally of most benefit to persons who want to exchange for a property worth substantially more than theirs. This is commonly referred to as trading up. Many persons think that the term "tax-free exchange" means that the Internal Revenue Service will completely forgive a certain amount of gain on the exchange as far as tax payment is concerned. Actually, the tax is merely deferred until a time in the future when the owner disposes of the property in a taxable transaction.

Many owners have exchanged their property a number of times over the years. Each time an exchange was made, the tax was deferred. Also, each exchange was usually for a property of more worth. Years later, if the owner sells the final piece of property in a normal sale, 80 or 90 percent of the sale price will be a taxable gain. If an owner trades up for a number of years and never does sell the property but instead wills it to his heirs, the heirs will discover that a very large amount of tax will be due and payable at the time of inheritance. The recent increased interest in methods of transferring property—for insurance, through a trust—is the result of such situations. How to accomplish such a transfer is best left to a textbook dealing with advanced problems of taxation and/or real estate law. Transfer involves consultation with such persons as an accountant, an attorney, or a trust officer specializing in estate and tax planning.

Section 1031 states that no gain or loss shall be recognized if property held for investment or for productive use in a trade or business is exchanged solely for property of like kind also to be held for investment or for use in a trade or business. In a tax-free exchange, the basis of the property exchanged is transferred to, and becomes the basis of, the new property obtained as a result of the exchange. Taxable gain will result if not only like property is received in the exchange but also other property or money. The extent to which one is relieved of a mortgage indebtedness also constitutes other property. The extent of such other property over and above the value of the property exchanged is subject to tax at the time of the exchange and is generally referred to as boot.

Like kind defined

The Internal Revenue Code states that in order to qualify as a tax-free exchange, the property exchanged must be of like kind. This requirement is met if property held for investment or for use in a trade or business is exchanged for any other business or investment property.

The size or worth of the properties exchanged does not defeat the like kind requirement, so that a four-unit building worth $95,000 may be exchanged for a 12-unit worth $260,000.

Boot defined

Boot is cash or any other property given or received in addition to the property that may be exchanged tax-free. When boot is involved in an exchange, it is important to identify the person "giving" boot and the person "receiving" it.

For the person giving boot, the new basis of the property he receives is the basis of the property he gave in the exchange plus the amount of boot given.

Example: A owns property with a market value of $100,000 and a cost basis of $40,000. A exchanges this building for B's property which has a market value of $60,000. A gives B his building plus $20,000 in cash. The cost basis to A of his newly acquired building is (1) the $40,000 cost basis of the building traded in and (2) the $20,000 cash boot given. Thus, A now has a building with a cost basis of $60,000. This has been a tax-free exchange as far as A is concerned.

For the person receiving boot, the exchange may become partly taxable. The taxable portion, however, is limited to the amount of boot received.

Example: The market value of the building exchanged by B is $120,000, and we will assume that his cost basis is $70,000.

The potential taxable gain to B is $50,000 ($120,000 − $70,000).

Cost basis of building exchanged by B......	$ 70,000
Received by B:	
Fair market value of A's building	100,000
Boot in the form of cash	20,000
Total received	$120,000

Taxable gain when boot is received is limited to the amount of boot received, so B will be taxed on only $20,000 of the $50,000 gain. Thus, for B, who received the boot, the exchange of property between himself and A has resulted in a partially taxable exchange.

Depreciation considered

The necessity for increased depreciation is one of the main tax reasons for entering into an exchange. It is quite common to find many persons who have owned a property for so many years that there is virtually no depreciation left to deduct against the building. In the meantime, the income from the property has greatly increased, and since the owner has very little of an offset, he finds himself paying a considerable amount of tax. Further, many times the mortgage has been paid off, thereby eliminating the interest deduction.

A person in such a position would probably want to acquire another building so that he will have substantial depreciation to offset income. However, in a tax-free exchange, the basis for a newly acquired property is merely what the basis was for the old property. This problem is solved if the owner exchanges his property for one that is worth much more and has a large mortgage against it. The basis for the new property is the basis for the old building plus the difference between the old mortgage, if any, and the new one.

Example: A has a building worth $200,000 with a cost basis of $30,000. He trades his building for another worth $600,000 subject to a mortgage of $400,000. A has no mortgage on his old property; it is clear.

The basis of the new building to A would be

his old basis of $30,000 plus the mortgage of $400,000, which means he now has on the new building a basis of $430,000. Not only is A building up an equity in a building much more valuable than the one he had previously, but also he now has a substantial depreciation and interest deduction to offset the building's income.

Basis for newly acquired property

In any type of real estate exchange involving tax decisions, it obviously is necessary for the broker and his client to have available the services of a professional accountant. Such need is clearly illustrated numerous times with regard to property exchanges and trades. Determination of the basis for property acquired in an exchange is one area that can become quite complex, since so many different factors must be considered. The problem of boot, whether given or received; the exchange of existing mortgages; an exchange involving many pieces of property; an exchange involving more than two parties; an exchange resulting in a partial loss for one party and a gain for the other; and many other possible combinations—each results in a detailed and complex set of calculations.

The following outline shows the basic framework within which calculations are made in order to arrive at the basis for property acquired in an exchange. Old property refers to the property traded off, and new property refers to the property received as a result of the exchange.

Basis of newly acquired property is determined as follows:

1. Start with the basis of the old property.
2. To the basis of the old property, add the following:
   a. Any cash paid.
   b. Any other boot paid.
   c. Any loans on the new property (an existing loan assumed or taken subject to, or a new loan).
   d. <u>Any recognized gain.</u>
      Total (of 1 and 2)
3. From the total above, subtract any of the following:
   a. Any loans on the old property assumed or taken subject to by the other party.
   b. Any cash received.
   c. Any boot received.

Thus, the basis of the newly acquired property will be the total of 1 and 2 minus the total of 3.

Three-way exchange

A three-way exchange, or multiple exchange as it is sometimes called, results when there are more than two parties to an exchange. The three-way exchange is also covered under Section 1031 of the Internal Revenue Code. If certain requirements are met, all parties in a multiple exchange may enjoy the benefits of a tax-free exchange. The Internal Revenue Service is extremely strict in its interpretation of certain rules and regulations regarding exchanges involving three or more persons, and the brokers and clients involved in such an exchange must exercise extreme caution to see that all steps are properly documented and requirements fully met. If not, the Internal Revenue Service may declare that a taxable sale, and not a tax-free exchange, has taken place.

If two owners, each of whom wants to exchange his property, can get together and agree on terms and conditions, it is a fairly simple exchange situation that can take place without any difficulty. Quite often, however, we find a situation in which one party wants to exchange his property, but the other party wants to sell. In such a case, a third party must be brought into the picture.

Example: A wants to exchange his property for property B owns. However, B wants to sell his property rather than exchange it. Thus, a third party, C, who wants to purchase A's property must be found.

A and B can then exchange properties, and C purchases the property B has received in the exchange (A's former property). An alternative method might be for the broker to find someone who will purchase B's property and then enter into an exchange agreement with A.

It is obvious here that a broker involved in such a transaction must be very experienced and knowledgeable in this area. Written agreements must be quite specific in order to insure a tax-free exchange benefit; timing is likewise most important. There are numerous ways of setting up such exchanges, but perhaps the safest method is to provide first for a direct exchange and then for a sale. Thus, in the example above, the broker should first set up a direct exchange between A and B. Following the exchange, the broker then sets up the sale between B and C.

Two escrows are necessary in order to separate the exchange transaction from the sale transaction. A should in no way become involved in negotiations with C; his involvement should be strictly in an exchange with B.

Time-delay exchange—Starker case

California investors who previously avoided an exchange because of the difficulty in locating a necessary property (up-leg) for which to exchange can now take advantage of a recent decision of the Ninth Circuit Court of Appeals.

In *Starker v. Internal Revenue Service*, the court ruled that a time-delay exchange with an "open leg" will qualify for tax deferred treatment if there is a contractual agreement giving the selling party the right to receive like-kind property in exchange at some future time.

If the parties place funds to acquire property in an escrow or impound account, the taxpayer should not have any control over such funds or be able to cancel any agreement and receive the money. Otherwise, the IRS can claim that the taxpayer has constructively received any funds placed into escrow and attempt to refuse allowance of exchange benefits. The exchange party should acquire title to the exchange property and transfer it to the taxpayer.

INVOLUNTARY CONVERSION

In the area of tax-free exchanges, one often hears the term "involuntary conversion." Involuntary conversions and tax-free involuntary exchanges involve many complexities, and again, the services of an expert in such matters is necessary. Thus, we will merely define involuntary conversion and briefly show how it relates to tax-free exchanges.

Involuntary conversion occurs when a person receives money or other property for his property which was destroyed, stolen, or condemned for public use. An example of an involuntary conversion is the destruction or loss of property by hurricane, flood, drought, other casualty, or theft, and the receipt of insurance proceeds for the loss.

Property given up is said to be involuntarily converted if an owner's property or part of it is condemned for public use and he is awarded money or other property in exchange, or if an owner sells his property to the condemning authority or exchanges it with the authority because condemnation was threatened or imminent.

Thus, the person whose property is involuntarily converted may receive a substantial amount of cash by an insurance award or condemnation award. If the money received amounts to more than the adjusted basis of the property destroyed or condemned, the owner will have realized a gain.

However, the Internal Revenue Service, under Section 1033 of the Internal Revenue Code, holds that there is no taxable gain under involuntary conversion if, within a prescribed period of time, the money received as a result of the involuntary conversion is used to purchase property similar to, or similar in use or service to, that property that was involuntarily converted.

Therefore, when an owner reinvests money received in a property that is actually a replacement property, the Internal Revenue Service interpretation is that there has been no cash benefit to the taxpayer and he should not be taxed. If the property owner does not reinvest in a replacement property, he may then be subject to taxation on any gain realized.

Exchange examples

Here are a few further examples of exchanges and their results.

Example 1. Steinberg owns a building free and clear with a present market value of $160,000 and a tax basis of $40,000. He trades it for another building with a market value of $160,000, which is also free and clear. Result: Steinberg's basis of $40,000 is carried over to the new property received. The existing gain of $120,000 is not recognized, and the result is a tax-free exchange.

Example 2. Flynn owns a building free and clear with a present market value of $500,000 and a tax basis (cost basis) of $150,000. Flynn exchanges the building for another building, also free and clear, with a present market value of $450,000. In addition, Flynn receives $50,000 in cash. Result: The $50,000 in cash received by Flynn is boot and is recognized and taxed. The cost basis of the new building is $150,000, reflecting the unrecognized gain of $300,000. Using the outline given previously in this chapter for calculation of the basis of newly acquired property, the calculations are as follows:

	$150,000	basis of old property
plus	50,000	recognized gain
	$200,000	
minus	50,000	cash received
	$150,000	basis of new property

Example 3. Brussell owns a building with a present market value of $750,000 and a tax basis of $400,000. The building has a loan against it, with a present balance due of $150,000. Brussell exchanges his building for another that is free and clear and has a present market value of $600,000. The party who receives Brussell's building will as-

sume the existing loan against it of $150,000. Result: Here is an example of the other party's assuming an existing loan on the building being exchanged. This is known as mortgage relief or debt reduction and is treated as boot received by Brussell. This $150,000 is a recognized gain and subject to tax. The remaining $200,000 of gain is unrecognized at the time of the exchange. The basis for the new property is calculated as follows:

	$400,000	basis of old property
plus	150,000	recognized gain
	$550,000	
minus	150,000	loan assumed by other party
	$400,000	basis of new property

The $400,000 basis for the new property, which has a present value of $600,000, represents the $200,000 of unrecognized gain in this exchange.

Example 4. Calleja exchanges his building with a present market value of $1,000,000 and a cost basis to him of $500,000. His building is encumbered by an existing loan of $200,000 which is assumed by the other party. The building Calleja receives has a present market value of $2,000,000 with an existing loan against it of $1,200,000 which Calleja assumes. Calleja has increased his mortgage debt by $1,000,000 (the difference between the $200,000 loan on the old property and the $1,200,000 loan on the new property). Since Calleja's mortgage debt is increased, no boot is deemed to have been received, and Calleja's gain is unrecognized at the time of this exchange. If Calleja had exchanged a larger debt in return for a smaller one, the difference between the two loans would be a recognized gain to Calleja and, therefore, would have been taxed. The basis of the new property is calculated as follows:

	$ 500,000	basis of old property
plus	1,200,000	loan assumed on new property
	$1,700,000	
minus	200,000	loan on old property assumed by other party
	$1,500,000	basis of new property

Thus, the $1,500,000 basis applied against the $2,000,000 present market value of the new building represents the $500,000 of unrecognized gain to Calleja as the result of this transaction.

Analysis of exchange agreement form

The exchange agreement form is to the exchange as the deposit receipt form is to the usual sale of real property. The exchange agreement must be written in a clear and concise manner and must be complete in all necessary details to the transaction. The agreement form will represent a legal contract when properly executed and signed by the parties involved. For purposes of illustration, we will use the California Association of Realtors Exchange Agreement Form. The parts of the CAR Exchange Form (Figure 17–1) correspond to those of the explanations that follow.

A. The names and addresses of the interested parties are entered. The legal status of the parties should also be noted—for example, John A. Crown and Phyllis Crown, husband and wife.

B. A complete description of the property involved should include the legal description and the post office address of the property.

C. All liens and encumbrances known to exist against the property should be stated in detail. The terms, conditions, and balances of any loans against the property should be shown and, in addition, any tax liens that exist. The property may also be subject to certain covenants, conditions, restrictions, reservations, special rights, rights-of-way, a ground lease, and other matters subject to review by the parties involved prior to the close of escrow.

Terms and conditions of an exchange

The broker must set forth clearly the terms and conditions of the exchange. He must specify in detail what is to be done or accomplished by each party to the exchange, since this will provide a pattern for the steps to be taken during the escrow. This section, which presents the details of the exchange, includes such items as:

a. How the equities of the properties involved in this exchange are to be equalized, which usually is accomplished by stating which party in the exchange must deposit cash in escrow and the amount of such deposit.
b. Any contingencies that are to be made a part of the agreement.
c. Mention of any rental statements that may have to be approved.
d. Provisions for refinancing either of the properties in the exchange.
e. Any trust deeds that may be involved and their terms and conditions.

Page two of the agreement contains various printed clauses.

1. The title company is named and number of days allowed in which to deliver escrow in-

structions is shown together with the number of days allowed for close of escrow. Space is provided for determining how escrow fee is to be paid. In the southern part of the state, escrow instructions are usually delivered within a few days of opening escrow. In other parts of the state, the time limit for both delivery of instructions and for close of escrow are the same.

The amount of time required may vary depending on the particular transaction and the location of the properties involved. Whether the parties involved shall pay for the escrow fee or title policy fee-for the property acquired or conveyed is dependent on the general practice in the particular area.

2. A title clause is provided which refers to liens, encumbrances, easements, restrictions, rights, and conditions of record. Since the status of these matters is not usually known until a preliminary title search is issued, it is general practice to allow the parties to examine the preliminary title reports and then discuss any objections which may result.

The title company issuing the title policy is shown, and provision is made for payment of title policy fees.

3. A clause is provided to show how Richard and Wilma Arthur wish to take title to the property acquired. If there is doubt as to the proper method of acquiring title, the broker should be careful not to give any legal advice and should refer the parties to their attorney and tax advisor.

4. Any prorations which may be necessary are dealt with, and who shall pay for or assume any bond or assessment which may exist is determined.

5. Clauses 5(A) and 5(B) allow separate possession and occupancy provisions relating to each property. Space is provided for mention of a possible rental payment by either party who may wish to remain in possession of all of part of the premises after close of escrow.

6. Numbers 6, 7, and 8, are self-explanatory.

9. The amount of time to be allowed for acceptance of the offer is stated.

10. The broker or brokers representing the parties are shown. The clause allows a broker representing both parties to receive payment from both and allows cooperation between brokers if necessary.

11. An intent to exchange is shown. It is important that the parties clearly state that they are entering into a property exchange to legally defer federal and state taxes as allowed by law.

12. The parties agree to do whatever is necessary to expedite the transaction.

13. Numbers 13 and 14 are self-explanatory.

Page three of the agreement contains the agreement of offerors Richard and Wilma Arthur to pay their broker, Ann Smith, a commission. The exact amount of the commission to be received is shown. Commissions in a three-way or other type of multiple exchange may be quite complicated, and separate detailed instructions relating to the payment of commission may have to be executed by the parties. Richard and Wilma Arthur and their broker, Ann Smith, sign the agreement.

Acceptance

The offerees, Philip and Carol Brown, accept the offer to exchange and agree to pay their broker, ABC Realty Company, a commission. Title is to be vested in Philip Brown and Carol Brown, husband and wife, as community property. The Browns and Realtor Virginia Marsh sign the agreement.

When properly prepared by the broker and signed by all parties to the exchange, the exchange agreement will constitute a valid and binding legal contract. This will allow the escrow officer to begin the escrow procedure. All parties to the exchange must perform as stated in the exchange agreement.

The law of California further requires that the broker, within one month after the closing of the transaction, provide the parties involved with a written statement of the exchange prices of the properties involved.

In the preceding explanation of the exchange agreement, an important point was that the broker must set forth clearly the terms and conditions of the exchange. The following examples are intended to show some common approaches that might be used in differing situations with regard to financial terms and conditions.

Example 1. A owns clear property with a market value of $100,000 and trades for B's clear property with a market value of $200,000. A will have to give his property clear plus $100,000 for B's clear property. The exchange, then, will probably be subject to A's being able to obtain a first loan on B's property in the amount of at least $100,000. If A needed additional money for closing charges and commission, say $20,000, the exchange will have to be subject to A's obtaining a first loan in the amount of $120,000.

CALIFORNIA ASSOCIATION OF REALTORS® STANDARD FORM

EXCHANGE AGREEMENT

THIS IS INTENDED TO BE A LEGALLY BINDING CONTRACT. READ IT CAREFULLY.

(A) Richard Arthur and Wilma Arthur, husband and wife
herein called Arthur, offers to exchange
the following described property, designated as Property No. (A) situated in Los Angeles
County of Los Angeles, State of California

(B) Lot 23, Tract 5998, recorded in Book 21, Page 68 of Maps, commonly known as 178 Harbor Way. Subject to (1) Current taxes, (2) Deed of Trust recorded in book 67,
(C) page 57 O.R., Los Angeles County, with present balance of approximately $ 85,000. payable at $ 714.74 per month including interest at 9 ½ percent per annum, (3) Covenants, conditions, restrictions and easements of record.

for the following described property of Philip Brown and Carol Brown, husband and wife
(A)
herein called Brown, designated as Property No. (B)
situated in Lancaster
County of Los Angeles, State of California

(B) Lot 19, Tract 338, recorded in Book 18, Page 93 of Maps, commonly known as 826 La Habra Avenue. Subject to (1) Current taxes, (d) Deed of Trust recorded in book 78, Page 20 O.R., Los Angeles County, with present balance of approximately $ 78,000 payable at $ 670.15 per month including interest at 9 3/4 percent per annum, (3) Covenants, conditions, restrictions and easements of record.

Terms and Conditions of Exchange:

Value of Arthur property	$ 190,000	Value of Brown property	$ 200,000
Subject to loan balance of	85,000	Subject to loan balance of	78,000
Arthur's Equity is	$ 105,000	Brown's Equity is	$ 122,000

1. Difference in equities of approximately $ 17,000 to be adjusted by Arthur depositing in escrow the sum of $ 17,000. This amount to be paid to Brown on close of escrow.

2. If, at close of escrow, the loans of record are more or less than the approximate amounts shown, differences shall be adjusted in cash to the respective parties.

3. Arthur to take title to Brown property subject to existing loan, and Brown to take title to Arthur property subject to existing loan.

4. Both parties to furnish a termite report for their respective properties and to pay the cost of any corrective work indicated in the report. Funds to pay for said work to be deposited in escrow.

5. Possession and occupancy of both properties to be given within 15 days of close of escrow.

The supplements initialled below are incorporated as part of this agreement.

Other
X Structural Pest Control Certification Agreement
___ Special Studies Zone Disclosure
___ Flood Insurance Disclosure

Both parties acknowledge receipt of a copy of this page. Page 1 of 3 Pages.

X (s) Richard Arthur   X (s) Philip Brown

X (s) Wilma Arthur   X (s) Carol Brown

A REAL ESTATE BROKER IS THE PERSON QUALIFIED TO ADVISE ON REAL ESTATE. IF YOU DESIRE LEGAL OR TAX ADVICE, CONSULT A COMPETENT PROFESSIONAL.

For these forms, address California Association of Realtors®
505 Shatto Place, Los Angeles, California 90020
Copyright 1978, California Association of Realtors®   FORM E-11-1

FIGURE 17–1

EXCHANGE AGREEMENT

The following terms and conditions are hereby incorporated in and made a part of the offer.

1. The parties hereto shall deliver signed escrow instructions to U.S. Title Company
, escrow holder, within 5 days from acceptance, which shall provide for closing within 60 days from acceptance. Escrow fees shall be paid as follows:
Each party agrees to pay escrow fee for property conveyed.

2. Title is to be free of liens, encumbrances, easements, restrictions, rights and conditions of record or known to the conveying party, other than the following: Respective parties to examine preliminary title reports and report any objections within 5 days of receipt.

Each party shall provide the other with (a) a standard California Land Title Association policy, or (b)
, issued by U.S. Title Company
to be paid for as follows: Property (A) Brown, and Property (B) Arthur ,
showing title vested in the acquiring party subject only to the above and to any liens or encumbrances to be recorded in accordance with this agreement. If the conveying party fails to deliver title as above, the acquiring party may terminate this agreement and shall be released from payment of any compensation to broker(s) for services rendered.

3. Unless otherwise designated in escrow instructions, title to the property acquired shall vest as follows:
Richard Arthur and Wilma Arthur, husband and wife, as joint tenants .
(The manner of taking title may have significant legal and tax consequences. Therefore, give this matter serious consideration.)

4. Property taxes, premiums on insurance acceptable to the party acquiring the property insured, rents, interest and
shall be prorated as of (a) the date of recordation of deed, or (b) .
Any bond or assessment which is a lien on a party's property shall be paid or assumed as follows: None

5 (A). Possession of Property No. (A) shall be delivered (a) ~~on close of escrow,~~ or (b) not later than 15 days after close of escrow, or (c)

5 (B). Possession of Property No. (B) shall be delivered (a) ~~on close of escrow,~~ or (b) not later than 15 days after close of escrow, or (c)

6. If, as a part of this exchange, any property is to be sold to a third party, the original transferor shall indemnify and hold harmless the party conveying the property to the third party from all claims, liability, loss, damage and expenses including reasonable attorneys' fees and costs incurred by reason of any warranties or representations made by conveying party to the purchaser provided they conform to the warranties and representations made by the original transferor either by this agreement or in any statement made or document delivered to the conveying party or to the designated escrow holder.

7. Each party warrants that he has no knowledge of the existence of any notices of violations of city, county or state building, zoning, fire and health codes, ordinances, or other governmental regulations filed or issued against his property.

8. Each party represents to the other that no tenant, if any, is entitled to any rebate, concession or other benefit except as set forth in rental agreements and leases, copies of which are to be exchanged or delivered within _____ days of acceptance. If such rental agreements or leases are not disapproved in writing within _____ days of receipt thereof, this condition shall be deemed waived.

9. Unless acceptance of this offer is signed by the other party hereto and the signed copy delivered to the undersigned, in person or by mail to the address below, within 5 days, this offer shall be deemed revoked.

10. Each party agrees that Ann Smith, Realtor, Los Angeles, representing Arthur and ABC broker
address Realty, Lancaster, representing Brown. , California
telephone can act as agent for, and may accept compensation for services from, each party herein. Broker is authorized to cooperate with other brokers and to divide such compensation as agreed by them.

11. It is the intention of the parties to the extent permitted by law, that the mutual conveyances agreed to herein will qualify as an "exchange" within the meaning of Section 1031 of the Internal Revenue Code of 1954 and Section 18081 of the California Revenue and Taxation Code. Failure to so qualify however, shall not affect the validity of this agreement.

12. Each party agrees to execute and deliver to escrow any instrument or to perform any act reasonably necessary to carry out the provisions of this agreement.

13. In any action or proceeding arising out of this agreement, the prevailing party shall be entitled to reasonable attorneys' fees and costs.

14. Time is of the essence of this agreement. All modifications or extensions shall be in writing signed by the parties.

Both parties acknowledge receipt of a copy of this page. Page 2 of 3 Pages.

X (s) Richard Arthur   X (s) Philip Brown
X (s) Wilma Arthur   X (s) Carol Brown

For these forms, address California Association of Realtors®
505 Shatto Place, Los Angeles, California 90020 (Revised 1978)
Copyright ©1978, California Association of Realtors®   FORM E-11-2

FIGURE 17-1 *(continued)*

EXCHANGE AGREEMENT

The following terms and conditions are hereby incorporated in and made a part of the offer.

If the other party hereto accepts the foregoing offer, I agree to pay to <u>Ann Smith, Realtor</u>
as broker for services rendered as follows: <u>Nine Thousand Five Hundred Dollars</u> ($ 9,500.)

payable (a) on recordation of deed or on delivery of a Real Property Contract as defined by Civil Code Section 2985; or (b) upon default if completion of the exchange is prevented by me; or (c)

In any action or proceeding arising out of this agreement, the prevailing party shall be entitled to reasonable attorney's fees and costs.

Receipt of a copy hereof is hereby acknowledged. Page 3 of 3 Pages.

<u>Los Angeles</u>, State <u>California</u>, Dated: <u>July 2</u>, 19 --

Address: <u>178 Harbor Way</u>   x (s) <u>Richard Arthur</u>
<u>Los Angeles</u>   x (s) <u>Wilma Arthur</u>
Telephone: <u>303-1123</u>   x _____

Broker(s) agree to the foregoing.
Dated: <u>July 2</u>, 19 --   Dated: _____, 19 ____
Broker <u>Ann Smith, Realtor</u>   Broker _____
By <u>(s) Ann Smith</u>   By _____

ACCEPTANCE

The foregoing offer and agreement to exchange the properties upon the terms and conditions stated is hereby accepted and I agree to pay <u>ABC Realty Company 620 Center Lane, Lancaster, California</u>

California, telephone <u>350-2329</u> as broker(s) for services rendered as follows: <u>Ten Thousand Five Hundred Dollars</u> ($ 10,500.)

payable as follows: (a) on recordation of Deed or delivery of Real Property Sales Contract as defined by Civil Code Section 2985; (b) upon default if completion is prevented by me; or (c)

Unless otherwise designated in the escrow instructions, title to the property acquired shall vest as follows:
<u>Philip Brown and Carol Brown, husband and wife, as community property</u>
(The manner of taking title may have significant legal and tax consequences. Therefore, give this matter serious consideration.)
In any action or proceeding arising out of this agreement, the prevailing party shall be entitled to reasonable attorneys' fees and costs.

Receipt of a copy hereof is acknowledged and broker is authorized to deliver a signed copy to the other party named above. Page 3 of ____ Pages.

<u>Lancaster</u>, State <u>California</u>, Dated: <u>July 5</u>, 19 --

Address: <u>826 La Habra Avenue</u>   x (s) <u>Philip Brown</u>
<u>Lancaster, California</u>   x (s) <u>Carol Brown</u>
Telephone: <u>350-7389</u>   x _____

Broker(s) agree to the foregoing:
Dated: <u>July 5</u>, 19 --   Dated: _____, 19 ____
Broker <u>ABC Realty Company</u>   Broker _____
By <u>(s) Virginia Marsh</u>   By _____

THIS STANDARDIZED DOCUMENT FOR USE IN SIMPLE TRANSACTIONS HAS BEEN APPROVED BY THE CALIFORNIA ASSOCIATION OF REALTORS® IN FORM ONLY. NO REPRESENTATION IS MADE AS TO THE APPROVAL OF THE FORM OF SUPPLEMENTS. THE LEGAL VALIDITY OF ANY PROVISION OR THE ADEQUACY OF ANY PROVISION IN ANY SPECIFIC TRANSACTION. IT SHOULD NOT BE USED IN COMPLEX TRANSACTIONS OR WITH EXTENSIVE RIDERS OR ADDITIONS.

For these forms, address California Association of Realtors®
505 Shatto Place, Los Angeles, California 90020
Copyright ©1978, California Association of Realtors®   FORM E-11-3

FIGURE 17–1 *(concluded)*

Example 2. A owns property valued at $200,000 subject to a transferable first loan of approximately $146,000. He trades for B's $400,000 property subject to an existing transferable first loan of approximately $328,000.

A's property....	$200,000	B's property....	$400,000
Minus loan.....	146,000	Minus loan.....	328,000
A's equity......	$ 54,000	B's equity......	$ 72,000

Subtracting the smaller equity of $54,000 from the larger equity of $72,000 gives an amount of $18,000 by which B's equity exceeds A's. A must make up the difference to B, by cash or note, as follows.

First party A to give his property subject to a first loan of approximately $146,000, payable at $———— ———— per month, including interest at ———— percent per annum, for Second party B's property subject to a first loan of approximately $328,000, payable at $———— ———— per month, including interest at ———— percent per annum, and in addition, First party A will give Second party B, $18,000 in cash. Adjustments to exact loan balances on existing loans to be made in cash.

In the event that the first party A does not have the necessary cash, the difference in equities may be made up as follows:

First party A will execute a note in the amount of $18,000 secured by a second Deed of Trust on the property he is acquiring, in favor of Second party B, payable at $———— per month, including interest at ———— percent per annum. Adjustments to exact loan balances on existing loans to be made in this second note.

Example 3. A owns property valued at $420,000, subject to two nontransferable loans in the approximate total amount of $280,000. He trades for B's property, valued at $1,050,000, now subject to a transferable first loan of approximately $300,000.

In this example, A must pay off the existing loans on his property so that he will be trading clear property. A must also generate cash by obtaining a new loan on B's property; thus, it can be said that B's property will also be traded clear. Considering that both properties are to be traded clear, the value of A's property at $420,000 must be subtracted from the value of B's property at $1,050,000, arriving at a figure of $630,000. This figure represents the excess of B's equity over A's. A must therefore give B $630,000 in cash or notes to make up this difference. This may be shown as follows:

First party A to give his property clear plus $350,000 in cash for Second party B's property clear, and, in addition, First party will execute a note in the amount of $280,000 secured by a second Deed of Trust on the property he is acquiring in favor of Second party B payable at $———— per month, including interest at ———— percent per annum. This exchange is subject to a new first loan of no less than $690,000 being obtained by A on the property he is acquiring, for a term of ————, with interest not to exceed ———— percent per annum.

The figure $690,000 for loan proceeds is used so that A will be able to pay off the loans on his property and, in addition, the closing costs, commission, and the $350,000 in cash to be paid to B. Second party B will, in turn, use the $350,000 to pay off the existing loan on his property and have cash left over to pay commission and other expenses of the exchange.

The three preceding examples have been brief. Many brokers would probably prepare a more lengthy and detailed wording of some of the items. For instance, a complete reference to the loans would include present balance or new amount, the term, interest rate, possible mention of fees, monthly payment, and mention of a balloon payment and due on sale clause where necessary.

TRADE-IN PROGRAMS

The remainder of this chapter will deal with trade-in programs as they are set up and operate in the real estate business. Such programs are a must for any real estate office that wants to increase sales and revenue. A successful trade-in program is often the major factor in enabling the broker to sell a property to clients who must first solve the problem of disposing of their present property.

Trade-in versus the exchange

There is a sharp and distinct difference between exchanging a property and trading in a property. Exchanging is basically the transferring of one property for another. The broker acts as a negotiator only and is customarily not a principal in the transaction. In a trade-in, however, the broker is active as one who provides time, knowledge, and capital as a principal in the transaction.

Trade-in programs are generally limited to the residential sales field, since the basis of this program as it operates in the real estate industry is to make it easier for a prospective client to purchase a house. Persons who want to exchange larger properties usually tend to favor the benefits inherent in the exchange method discussed previously. In the discussion that follows, we shall refer to the house the purchaser presently owns as the old house and to the property the purchaser wants to buy as the new house.

The basic problem

One of the main problems confronting persons who already own a house but want to purchase another is what to do with the old house. Some common courses of action are the following.

1. Buy a new house and keep the old one. If the old house is in good condition and in a neighborhood where values are stable and will tend to appreciate over the years, it may be argued that to keep the house and rent it out would be a good investment and should be considered. However, the owner must also consider such problems as future maintenance and repair, dealings with tenants, distance between the old house and the new one he wants to buy, and equity he has in the old house. Equity means money, and here is the main reason the average person cannot buy a new house and also keep his old one; it is simply that he needs the money he has invested in the old house in order to buy the new one.
2. Sell the old house first and then buy a new one. While this may seem the logical thing to do, most owners quickly realize that when they enter into an agreement with a prospective purchaser to buy their old house, the buyers will want occupancy on close of escrow. This means that the seller must find a new house within a relatively short period of time and will be under a certain amount of pressure to do so. Very few persons want to be put in such a position, especially if they are going to buy the new house in the same general locality and are not under any particular pressure to sell.
3. Buy a new home first and then sell the old one. Here is another course of action available to the owner, but it too has certain drawbacks. The owner must have enough money to be able to purchase a new house without the funds he has tied up in the old one; he would not be able to immediately move a great distance away; and, most of all, he would generally be making two mortgage payments at the same time—one on the old house and one on the new.
4. Purchase a new house from a real estate firm that offers the owner a trade-in plan. This action will enable him to buy the new house and dispose of the old one at the same time.

Common trade-in programs

The benefits of the various trade-in programs discussed below are available to all types of purchasers and sellers. This includes the average purchaser and real estate licensee and, in addition, speculators, investors, and home builders. Developers of large tracts of new houses have long understood the benefits and increased sales that result from offering to the general public some plan whereby they can trade in their old house and buy a newly constructed one. The FHA also provides special assistance to brokers or builders in financing of property taken in trade on the sale of another.

The conditional trade-in plan. Under this plan, the prospective purchaser agrees to buy a particular house, provided that he can sell his old house within a certain period of time. This is often referred to as a contingent sale—that is, the sale of one house contingent on the sale of another. The prospective purchaser is committed by a written agreement to buy the new house if he sells his old one during the agreed-on time period.

This type of trade-in plan relies to a great extent on the willingness of the seller to wait for the buyer to sell his old house. If a broker or a builder owns the new house, he may be in a better position to wait for the buyer to effect a sale. The broker may, in fact, obtain the listing on the old house and make a commission on its sale as well as on the sale of the new house. Quite often, however, the owner of the property for sale is not willing to wait for a month or two while the buyer attempts to sell his old house. It may be that the prospective purchaser cannot, for any number of reasons, enter into an agreement for the sale of his property, and thus, the seller who has been waiting will have lost a considerable amount of time. Therefore, most sellers may agree to an offer contingent on the sale of another property but will usually reserve the right to accept another offer during the time period agreed on. It is for this reason that the most used trade-in plan is not the conditional trade-in plan but rather the guaranteed trade-in plan.

The guaranteed trade-in plan. Under this plan, the real estate firm guarantees the buyer that it will either sell his old house within a certain period of time or buy it from him for a certain specified price. With such a guarantee, the buyer will be able to negotiate and enter into a contract for the purchase of a new property.

If the broker can sell the client's property within the agreed-on time, generally 90 days, he will usually earn a standard commission on the sale. While many persons feel that they may lose money if they trade in a house, this is not often the case for the following reasons:

1. Since the client is a prospective purchaser and is actively seeking to buy another property, he usually has a fair understanding of the prevailing market conditions and property prices.
2. Thus, the broker must guarantee a price that is fair to the client. In trying to agree with the client on what constitutes a fair price, the broker is also in the position of obtaining a listing on the property. He must very carefully appraise the house and convince the owner of the validity of his final appraisal. In the circumstances, it would be very difficult for the broker to get the owner to agree to a guaranteed price that is very much below market value.
3. In most cases, the guaranteed price is such that it is much more advantageous for the broker to sell the property and earn a commission on the sale than to have to buy the property himself.
4. The responsible broker makes every attempt to sell the trade-in property during the time allowed; he then makes two commissions—one on the old property and one on the new property—and avoids all the detail of actually having to purchase the old property himself and then resell it.

FHA trade-in assistance

The FHA offers a program of assistance to brokers and builders for financing homes taken in trade. This program is sometimes referred to as a straight trade-in plan. Two forms of assistance for financing homes taken in trade are provided: (1) assumption plan and (2) escrow commitment plan. The term "mortgage" as used below refers to either a mortgage or a deed of trust.

Assumption of FHA-insured mortgage. When there is already an FHA-insured mortgage on a house, whoever takes the house in trade can assume the mortgage. The owner can be released from personal liability for the mortgage debt only by obtaining both the mortgagee's and the FHA's consent to the substitution of another mortgagor. The substitute mortgagor may be a builder, broker, or other nonoccupant who assumes the FHA-insured mortgage on a house that he acquires in trade and intends to hold for sale.

When FHA consent to the substitution of a nonoccupant mortgagor is requested, if the unpaid balance of the mortgage is more than 85 percent of the original mortgage amount, the nonoccupant mortgagor must make a cash escrow deposit with the mortgage lender or reduce the outstanding balance by means of a prepayment to the principal. The escrow deposit or prepayment must be the difference between the unpaid balance and 85 percent of the original mortgage principal or whatever higher amount is necessary to comply with statutory and administrative requirements pertaining to the mortgagor's minimum cash investment. The escrow deposit can be returned to the nonoccupant mortgagor when the house is sold to an owner-occupant approved by FHA.

If a person who applies for an FHA insured mortgage to buy a house already has an FHA insured mortgage on another house that he is selling or trading to a nonoccupant and if more than 75 percent of the original amount of that mortgage is outstanding, then his new application will not be approved unless the outstanding mortgage is cancelled or he is released from liability on the mortgage.

FHA escrow commitment procedure. When a house is being exchanged or offered for sale by the owner in order to acquire another house, an FHA mortgage insurance commitment with escrow provisions may be obtained on the traded-in house by a borrower who will not be the occupant, provided the property, location, and borrower are acceptable to FHA. Escrow commitments are issued only on one- or two-family homes.

The maximum mortgage that FHA will insure for a nonoccupant mortgagor is 85 percent of the amount that could be insured for an owner-occupant on the same property. With an escrow commitment, however, a nonoccupant who accepts the house in trade can have an insured mortgage in the same amount and with the same term as that available to a borrower who buys the house to live in it.

The escrow provisions are: (a) the nonoccupant borrower places at least 15 percent of the mortgage proceeds in an escrow fund held by the lender; (b) this fund is released and returned to the borrower, provided he sells the house within 18 months to a buyer who is acceptable to FHA, will assume the insured mortgage, and will live in the

Guaranteed Sales Plan Agreement

THIS AGREEMENT, made this_____day of_____19____ by and between_____and_____
his wife, of_____
California, hereinafter called Seller, First Party, and_____
hereinafter called Buyer, second party. _(Broker)

WITNESSETH

A. Sellers warrant that they are the owners of that certain real property located at_____
_____

B. Sellers have purchased or are in the process of purchasing real property for which they are committed or intend to be committed to pay purchase monies.

C. Sellers are unable to pay said purchase monies unless property now owned by them and hereinabove first described is sold and escrow closed; and

D. Sellers are desirous of establishing a guaranteed sales price; and Buyers for a set fee are willing to guarantee such price;

NOW, THEREFORE, it is understood and agreed by and between the parties hereto as follows;

I. **General Provisions:**

   a. Buyer herein guarantees to seller in consideration of the covenants and conditions herein contained to buy Sellers said property on SELLERS WRITTEN REQUEST on or before the _____day of_____ 19____ for the total purchase price of $_____, subject to the terms and conditions herein contained.

   b. Seller agrees to deliver subject property to Buyer free and clear of bonds, liens, attachments, judgments, or any other items affecting the title or Seller's equity in said property excepting as follows:_____
   _____
   _____

   c. Seller represents that the existing encumbrance(s) on the subject property may be paid in full at any time prior to maturity of said note and trust deed.

   d. Seller represents that he is not in default on any payments for subject property and covenants to make all payments as they fall due until close of escrow. In connection with said purchase agreement Seller agrees to correct any default within twenty-four (24) hours after notification by Buyer.

   e. Seller agrees not to sell, agree to sell, or execute any documents relating to a sale of the subject property without the written consent of Buyer.

   f. Seller represents that (s)he has free and clear title to any and all personal property included in this sale.

   g. Seller agrees to maintain the subject premises in good condition and repair and to deliver the property in the same or better condition than now exists.

   h. Possession of the subject property shall be delivered to Buyer upon close of escrow. In the event Seller fails to surrender possession, Seller agrees to pay as rental two per cent

FIGURE 17-2

(2%) of the sales price per month on a prorata basis and shall be a month to month tenant. Seller agrees to hold Buyer harmless from any and all liabilities for injuries to persons or for property damage as a result of the use and occupation of the property until Seller surrenders possession of the property to Buyer.

i. As Buyer's fee for this guarantee, Seller agrees to pay Buyer $_____.

j. Seller agrees forthwith to list said property with _____
(Broker)
for a period of _____ days, under the terms found in the Standard Exclusive Listing Agreement used by that company.

II. Sale of Seller's Property by Broker

In the event of a sale of said property by _____, Seller
(Broker)
shall pay to Buyer from the proceeds in escrow the amount of Buyer's guarantee fee, and the parties hereto are released from any further obligation under this Agreement.

III. Sale of Seller's Property to Buyer Herein

In the event Buyer is required to purchase hereunder, escrow shall be opened immediately, and sale shall be completed as follows:

A. Buyer will assume the balance due as of the close of escrow upon aforedescribed loans, or at the option of the Buyer, may place new financing on the property.

B. Seller will deliver to Buyer a termite report from a licensed pest control company showing the above property to be free of any visible termites, dry rot and fungus.

C. Seller agrees, at his expense, to furnish Buyer a Standard Policy of Title Insurance.

D. Interest, taxes, insurance and rentals and any and all charges arising out of ownership of the property will be prorated as of the date of closing of escrow.

E. Buyer and Seller agree to pay customary escrow charges.

F. Sellers will execute such deeds and other documents, as may be necessary or desirable to carry out the purpose of this Agreement.

IV. Cancellation

Sellers shall have the right at any time prior to his giving written notice to Buyer to purchase hereunder, to cancel this Agreement upon the payment of guarantee fee to Buyers.

Seller_____   _____
(Broker)

Seller_____ by_____

FIGURE 17–2 *(continued)*

house; (c) if such resale is not made within the 18-month period, the escrow fund is applied to reduction of the mortgage amount.

Beginning a trade-in program

Much has been written about the establishment of a trade-in program for the average real estate firm. The broker interested in beginning a trade-in program for his firm should also have the advice of other brokers in his area who are expert in this type of operation. Most of the common problems of a trade-in program concern (a) correctness of the market value appraisal, (b) availability of necessary capital, (c) ability to successfully market and sell properties, and (d) adequacy of the organization and personnel.

Different real estate offices have different procedures for their trade-in programs. Many firms in the San Francisco Bay area use the following procedure:

1. The house to be traded in is appraised to determine fair market value.
2. An exclusive listing is obtained.
3. The guaranteed price is set at about 85 percent of the appraised price.
4. The firm advances the down payment to the buyer for the new property.
5. If the property is sold, the firm receives a standard commission.
6. If the property is not sold by the end of the listing term, the firm purchases it for the amount agreed on in (3), above.

The availability of necessary working capital is extremely important to the broker. If he must eventually purchase a property, he will have to meet certain expenses connected with the purchase and subsequent resale. In addition, he will have to make loan payments, and he may need to spend some money to improve the property before it can be sold. The trade-in program in some respects is closely akin to speculation. Many times, a client wants to purchase a new property, but the old one is in a run-down condition, which may make it not readily salable. In order to sell the new property, the broker may have to attempt to reach an agreement with the owner to immediately purchase the old property. Many owners realize that for a variety of reasons their old property may be difficult to sell at the moment and are thus willing to accept what they consider to be a fair price from the broker. The broker, in turn, will attempt to purchase at a price that will allow him to make a fair profit.

Guarantee agreement form

Figure 17–2 illustrates a Guaranteed Sales Plan Agreement which states the terms of the agreement between the broker and his client. Should the broker need to advance funds for the down payment on the new property, this can be done by having the client sign a promissory note secured by a deed of trust on his old property.

Additional forms, applicable to this chapter, are illustrated in Appendix C as Figures C17–1 thru C17–3.

QUESTIONS FOR DISCUSSION

1. Discuss why an individual might enter into an exchange of real property for other than tax advantages.
2. What kind of tax picture might eventually result for an individual who has been trading up for a number of years and deferring payment of tax?
3. Discuss the factors that must be considered in determining the basis for property acquired in an exchange.
4. In what type of situation might a three-way exchange occur?
5. What tax benefits are provided for an owner whose property is involuntarily converted?
6. Discuss the items which may be included on the exchange agreement with regard to terms and conditions.
7. What courses of action are available to an individual who has a large equity in an older residence and wishes to purchase something newer in the same general locality?
8. Discuss the differences between a conditional and a guaranteed trade-in plan.
9. How does the FHA help the broker in trade-in programs?
10. With respect to a guaranteed trade-in situation, what are the responsibilities and duties of the broker?

Appendix A

Definitions of real estate and building construction words and phrases

ALTA title policy: A type of title insurance policy issued by title insurance companies that expands the risks normally insured against under the standard type policy to include unrecorded mechanics' liens, unrecorded physical easements, facts a physical survey would show, water and mineral rights, and rights of parties in possession, such as tenants and buyers under unrecorded instruments.

Abatement of nuisance: Extinction or termination of a nuisance.

Abstract of judgment: A condensation of the essential provisions of a court judgment.

Abstract of title: A summary or digest of the conveyances, transfers, and any other facts relied on as evidence of title, together with any other elements of record that may impair the title.

Acceleration clause: A clause in a trust deed or mortgage giving the lender the right to call all sums owing him to be immediately due and payable upon the happening of a certain event.

Acceptance: The act by which the seller or agent's principal agrees to the terms of the agreement of sale and approves the negotiation on the part of the agent and acknowledges receipt of the deposit in subscribing to the agreement of sale.

Access right: The right of an owner to have ingress and egress to and from his property.

Accretion: An addition to land from natural causes, such as from gradual action of ocean or river waters.

Accrued depreciation: The difference between the cost of replacement new as of the date of the appraisal and the present appraised value.

Acknowledgment: A formal declaration before a duly authorized officer by a person who has executed an instrument that such execution is his act and deed.

Acoustical tile: Blocks of fiber, mineral, or metal, with small holes or a rough-textured surface to absorb sound, used as covering for interior walls and ceilings.

Acquisition: The act or process by which a person procures property.

Acre: A measure of land equaling 160 square rods, or 4,850 square yards, or 43,560 square feet, or a square tract 208.71 feet on a side.

Administrator: A person appointed by the probate court to administer the estate of a person deceased.

Ad valorem: According to valuation.

Adverse possession: The open and notorious possession and occupancy under an evident claim or right, in denial or opposition to the title of another claimant.

Affidavit: A statement or declaration reduced to writing sworn to or affirmed before some officer who has authority to administer an oath or affirmation.

Affirm: Confirm, aver, ratify, verify.

Agency: The relationship between principal and agent that arises out of a contract, either expressed or implied, written or oral, wherein the agent is employed by the principal to do certain acts dealing with a third party.

Agent: One who represents another from whom he has derived authority.

Agreement of sale: A written agreement or contract between seller and purchaser in which they reach a meeting of minds on the terms and conditions of the sale.

Alienation: The transferring of property to another; the transfer of property and possession of lands, or other things, from one person to another.

Alluvion (Alluvium): Soil deposited by accretion. Increase of earth on a shore or bank of a river.

Amenities: Satisfaction of enjoyable living to be derived from a home; conditions of agreeable living or a beneficial influence arising from the location or improvements.

Amortization: The liquidation of a financial obligation on an installment basis; also recovery, over a period, of cost or value.

Appraisal: An estimate and opinion of value; a conclusion resulting from the analysis of facts.

Appraiser: One qualified by education, training, and experience who is hired to estimate the value of real and personal property based on experience, judgment, facts, and use of formal appraisal processes.

Appreciation: An increase in value.

Appurtenance: Something annexed to another thing that may be transferred incident to it. That which belongs to another thing, as a barn, dwelling, garage, or orchard is incident to the land to which it is attached.

A.S.A.: American Society of Appraisers.

Assessed value: Value placed on property as a basis for taxation.

Assessment: The valuation of property for the purpose of levying a tax or the amount of the tax levied.

Assessor: The official who has the responsibility of determining assessed values.

Assignment: A transfer or making over to another of the whole of any property, real or personal, in possession or in action, or of any estate or right therein.

Assignor: One who assigns or transfers property.

Assigns; assignees: Those to whom property shall have been transferred.

Assumption agreement: An undertaking or adoption of a debt or obligation primarily resting upon another person.

Assumption of mortgage: The taking of title to property by a grantee, wherein he assumes liability for payment of an existing note secured by a mortgage or deed of trust against the property; becoming a co-guarantor for the payment of a mortgage or deed of trust note.

Attachment: Seizure of property by court order, usually done to have it available in event a judgment is obtained in a pending suit.

Attest: To affirm to be true or genuine; an official act establishing authenticity.

Attorney in fact: One who is authorized to perform certain acts for another under a power of attorney; power of attorney may be limited to a specific act or acts, or be general.

Avulsion: The sudden tearing away or removal of land by action of water flowing over or through it.

Backfill: The replacement of excavated earth into a hole or against a structure.

Balloon payment: The final installment payment on a note that is greater than the preceding installment payments and that pays the note in full.

Base and meridian: Imaginary lines used by surveyors to find and describe the location of private or public lands.

Baseboard: A board placed against the wall around a room next to the floor.

Base molding: Molding used at the top of a baseboard.

Base shoe: Molding used at the junction of baseboard and floor: commonly called a carpet strip.

Batten: Narrow strips of wood or metal used to cover joints, interiorly or exteriorly; also used for decorative effect.

Beam: A structural member transversely supporting a load.

Bearing wall or partition: A wall or partition supporting any vertical load in addition to its own weight.

Bench mark: A location indicated on a durable marker by surveyors.

Beneficiary: (1) One entitled to the benefit of a trust. (2) One who receives profit from an estate, the title of which is vested in a trustee. (3) The lender on the security of a note and deed of trust.

Bequeath: To give or hand down by will; to leave by will.

Bequest: That which is given by the terms of a will.

Betterment: An improvement upon property that increases the property value and is considered as a capital asset, as distinguished from repairs or replacements in which the original character or cost is unchanged.

Bill of sale: A written instrument given to pass title of personal property from vendor to vendee.

Blacktop: Asphalt paving used in streets and driveways.

Blanket mortgage: A single mortgage that covers more than one piece of real estate.

Blighted area: A declining area in which real property values are seriously affected by destructive economic forces, such as encroaching inharmonious property usages and/or rapidly depreciating buildings.

Board foot: A unit of measurement of lumber one foot wide, one foot long, and one inch thick: 144 cubic inches.

Board of Realtors: A local organization of real estate licensees who are additionally members of the National Association of Realtors.

Bona fide: In good faith, without fraud.

Bracing: Framing lumber nailed at an angle in order to provide rigidity.

Breach: The breaking of a law or failure of duty either by omission of commission.

Breezeway: A covered porch or passage, open on two sides, connecting house and garage or two parts of the house.

Bridging: Small wood or metal pieces used to brace floor joists.

BTU: British thermal unit. The quantity of heat required to raise the temperature of one pound of water one Fahrenheit degree.

Building codes: Federal, state, or local laws that set minimum construction standards.

Building line: A line set by law a certain distance from a street line in front of which an owner cannot build on his lot. (A setback line.)

Building paper: A heavy waterproofed paper used as sheathing in wall or roof construction as a protection against air passage and moisture.

Built in: Cabinets or similar features built as part of the house.

Bundle of rights: Beneficial interests or rights.

Capital assets: Assets of a permanent nature being held for investment or used in the production of an income, such as land, buildings, machinery, equipment, and so forth. Under income tax law, it is usually distinguishable from *inventory*, which comprises assets held for sale to customers in the ordinary course of the taxpayer's trade or business.

Capital gain: Gain received from sale of capital assets and given preferential tax treatment.

Capitalization: In appraising, determining value of property by considering net income and percentage of reasonable return on the investment.

Capitalization rate: The rate of interest that is considered a reasonable return on the investment and used in the process of determining value based upon net income.

CAR: California Association of Realtors®.

Casement window: Frames of wood or metal that swing outward.

Caveat emptor: Let the buyer beware. The buyer must examine the goods or property and buy at his own risk.

Chain of title: A history of conveyances and encumbrances affecting the title from the time the original patent was granted or as far back as records are available.

Chattel real: An estate related to real estate, such as a lease on real property.

Chattels: Goods or every species of property movable or immovable that are not real property.

Circuit breaker: An electrical device that automatically interrupts an electric circuit and can be reset.

Clapboard: Boards usually thicker at one edge used for siding.

Cloud on the title: Any conditions revealed by a title search that affect the title to property; usually relatively unimportant items but ones which cannot be removed without a quitclaim deed or court action.

Collar beam: A beam that connects the pairs of opposite roof rafters above the attic floor.

Collateral: Property subject to the security interest. (See definition of security interest.)

Collateral security: A separate obligation attached to a contract to guarantee its performance; the transfer of property or of other contracts or valuables to insure the performance of a principal agreement.

Collusion: An agreement between two or more persons to defraud another of his rights by the forms of law, or to obtain an object forbidden by law.

Color of title: That which appears to be good title but that is not title in fact.

Combed plywood: A grooved building material used primarily for interior finish.

Commercial acre: The remainder of an acre of newly subdivided land after the area devoted to streets, sidewalks, curbs, and so forth, has been deducted from the acre.

Commercial paper: Bills of exchange used in commercial trade.

Commingling: Mixing together the funds of an agent and principal without proper authorization.

Commission: An agent's compensation for performing the duties of his agency; in real estate practice, a percentage of the selling price of property, percentage of rentals, and so forth.

Commitment: A pledge or a promise or firm agreement.

Common law: The body of law that grew from customs and practices developed and used in England "since the memory of man runneth not to the contrary."

Community property: Property accumulated through joint efforts of husband and wife living together.

Compaction: Whenever extra soil is added to a lot to fill in low places or to raise the level of the lot, the added soil is often too loose and soft to sustain the weight of buildings. Therefore, it is necessary to compact the added soil so that it will carry the weight of buildings without the danger of their tilting, settling, or cracking.

Competent: Legally qualified.

Compound interest: Interest paid on original principal and also on the accrued and unpaid interest that has accumulated.

Condemnation: (1) The act of taking private property for public use by a political subdivision; (2) declaration that a structure is unfit for use.

Conditional commitment: A commitment of a definite loan amount for some future unknown purchaser with a satisfactory credit standing.

Conditional sale contract: A contract for the sale of property stating that delivery is to be made to the buyer, title to remain vested in the seller until the conditions of the contract have been fulfilled. (See definition of security interest.)

Condominium: A system of individual fee ownership of units in a multifamily structure, combined with joint ownership of common areas of the structure and the land. (Sometimes referred to as a vertical subdivision.)

Conduit: Usually a metal pipe in which electrical wiring is installed.

Confession of judgment: An entry of judgment upon the debtor's voluntary admission or confession.

Confirmation of sale: A court approval of the sale of property by an executor, administrator, guardian, or conservator.

Consideration: Anything of value given to induce entering into a contract; it may be money, personal services, or even love and affection.

Constructive notice: Notice given by the public records.

Contiguous: Adjacent, touching upon, or adjoining.

Contingency: A condition upon which a valid contract is dependent.

Contract: An agreement, either written or oral, to do or not to do certain things.

Consumer goods: Goods used or bought for use primarily for personal, family, or household purposes.

Conversion: Change from one character or use to another, as in the misappropriation of funds.

Conveyance: The transfer of the title of land from one to another. It denotes an instrument that carries from one person to another an interest in land.

Corporation: A group or body of persons established and treated by law as an individual or unit with rights and liabilities or both distinct and apart from those of the persons composing it. A corporation is a creature of law having certain powers and duties of a natural person. Being created by law, it may continue for any length of time the law prescribes.

Counterflashing: Flashing used on chimneys at roofline to cover shingle flashing and to prevent moisture entry.

Covenant: Agreement written into a deed or other instrument promising performance or nonperformance of certain acts or stipulating certain uses or nonuses of the property.

CPM: Certified Property Manager; a member of the Institute of Real Property Management of the National Association of Realtors.

Crawl space: Exterior or interior opening permitting access underneath a building, as required by building codes.

Curtain schedule: A listing of the amounts by which the principal sum of an obligation is to be reduced by partial payments, and of the dates when each payment will become payable.

Courtesy: The right that a husband has in his wife's estate at her death.

Damages: The indemnity recoverable by a person who has sustained an injury, either in his person, property, or relative rights, through the act or default of another.

Debtor: The party who "owns" the property that is subject to the security interest. Previously he was known as the *mortgagor* or the *pledgor,* and so forth.

Deciduous trees: Trees that lose their leaves in the autumn and winter.

Deck: Usually an open porch on the roof of a ground or lower floor, porch, or wing.

Dedication: An appropriaton of land by its owner for some public use accepted for such use by authorized public officials on behalf of the public.

Deed: A written instrument that, when properly executed and delivered, conveys title.

Default: Failure to fulfill a duty or promise or to discharge an obligation; omission or failure to perform any act.

Defeasance clause: The clause in a mortgage that gives the mortgagor the right to redeem his property upon the payment of his obligations to the mortgagee.

Deferred maintenance: Existing but unfulfilled requirements for repairs and rehabilitation.

Deficiency judgment: A judgment given when the security pledge for a loan does not satisfy the debt upon its default.

Depreciation: Loss of value in real property brought about by age, physical deterioration, or functional or economic obsolescence. Broadly, a loss in value from any cause.

Desist and refrain order: The Real Estate Commissioner is empowered by law to issue an order directing a person to desist and refrain from committing an act in violation of the real estate law.

Deterioration: Impairment of condition. One of the causes of depreciation reflecting the loss in value brought about by wear and tear, disintegration, use in service, and the action of the elements.

Devisee: One who receives a bequest made by will.

Devisor: One who bequeaths by will.

Directional growth: The location or direction toward which the residential sections of a city are destined or determined to grow.

Documentary transfer tax: A method of taxing real property transfers by requiring a tax to be paid prior to deed recordation.

Donee: A person to whom a gift is made.

Donor: A person who makes a gift.

Dower: The right that a wife has in her husband's estate at his death.

Duress: Unlawful constraint exercised upon a person whereby he is forced to do some act against his will.

Easement: The right, privilege, or interest created by grant or agreement for a specific purpose that one party has in the land of another. (Example: right of way.)

Eaves: The lower part of a roof projecting over the wall.

Economic life: The period over which a property will yield a return on the investment, over and above the economic or ground rent due to land.

Eminent domain: The right of the government to acquire property for necessary public or quasi-public use by condemnation; the owner must be fairly compensated.

Encroachment: Trespass; the building of a structure or construction of any improvements partly or wholly on the property of another.

Encumbrance: Anything that affects or limits the fee simple title to property, such as mortgages, easements, or restrictions of any kind. Liens are special encumbrances that make the property security for the payment of a debt or obligation, such as mortgages and taxes.

Endorsement: Signature on reverse side of check or promissory note for purpose of transfering ownership.

Equity: (1) The interest or value that an owner has in real estate over and above the liens against it; (2) branch of remedial justice by and through which relief is afforded to suitors in courts of equity.

Equity of redemption: The right to redeem property during the foreclosure period, such as a mortgagor's right to redeem within a year after a foreclosure sale.

Erosion: The wearing away of land by the action of water, wind, or glacial ice.

Escalator clause: A clause in a contract providing for the upward or downward adjustment of certain items to cover specified contingencies.

Escheat: The reverting of property to the state when heirs capable of inheriting are lacking.

Escrow: The deposit of instruments and funds with instruction to a third neutral party to carry out the provisions of an agreement or contract; when everything is deposited to enable carrying out the instructions, it is called a complete or perfect escrow.

Estate: The degree, quantity, nature, and extent of interest that a person has in real or personal property.

Estate of inheritance: An estate that may descend to heirs. All freehold estates are estates of inheritance, except estates for life.

Estate for life: A freehold estate, not of inheritance, but which is held by the tenant for his own life or the life or lives of one or more other persons, or for an indefinite period that may endure for the life or lives of persons in being and beyond the period of life.

Estate for years: An interest in lands by virtue of a contract for the possession of them for a definite and limited period of time. A lease may be said to be an estate for years.

Estate of will: The occupation of lands and tenements by a tenant for an indefinite period terminable by one or both parties.

Estoppel: A doctrine that bars one from asserting rights that are inconsistent with a previous position or representation.

Ethics: That branch of moral science, idealism, justness, and fairness that treats of the duties that a member of a profession or craft owes to the public, to his clients or patron, and to his professional colleagues or members.

Exclusive agency listing: A written instrument giving one agent the right to sell property for a specified time but reserving the right of the owner to sell the property himself without the payment of a commission.

Exclusive-right-to-sell listing: A written agreement between owner and agent giving the right to collect a commission if the property is sold by anyone during the term of the agreement.

Execute: Complete, make, perform, do, follow out; execute a deed, make a deed, including especially signing, sealing, and delivery; to execute a contract is to perform the contract, to follow out to the end, to complete.

Executor: A person named in a will to carry out its provisions as to the disposition of the estate of a person deceased.

Expansible house: Home designed for further expansion and additions in the future.

Expansion joint: A bituminous fiber strip used to separate units of concrete to prevent cracking due to expansion as a result of temperature changes.

Facade: Front of a building.

Fee: An estate of inheritance in real property.

Fee simple: In modern estates, the terms *fee* and *fee simple* are substantially synonymous. The term *fee* is of Old English derivation. *Fee simple absolute* is an estate in real property by which the owner has the greatest power over the title that it is possible to have, being an absolute estate. In modern use, it expressly establishes the title of real property in the owner, without limitation or end. He may dispose of it by sale, trade, or will, as he chooses.

Fiduciary: A person in a position of trust and confidence, as between principal and broker; a broker as fiduciary owes certain loyalty that cannot be breached under rules of agency.

Financing statement: This is the instrument that is filed in order to give public notice of the security interest and thereby protect the interest of the secured parties in the collateral. (See definitions of security interest and secured party.)

Finish floor: Finish floor strips are applied over wood joists, deadening felt, and diagonal subflooring before finish floor is installed; finish floor is the final covering on the floor: wood, linoleum, cork, tile, or carpet.

Fire stop: A solid, tight closure of a concealed space, placed to prevent the spread of fire and smoke through such a space.

Fixtures: Appurtenances attached to the land or improvements, which usually cannot be removed without agreement since they become real property. Examples: plumbing fixtures, store fixtures built into the property, and so forth.

Flashing: Sheet metal or other material used to protect a building from seepage of water.

Footing: The base or bottom of a foundation wall, pier, or column.

Foreclosure: Procedure whereby property pledged as security for a debt is sold to pay the debt in event of default in payments or terms.

Forfeiture: Loss of money or anything of value due to failure to perform.

Foundation: The supporting portion of a structure below the first floor construction or below grade, including the footings.

Fraud: The intentional and successful employment of any cunning, deception, collusion, or artifice, used to circumvent, cheat, or deceive another person, whereby that person acts upon it to the loss of his property and to his legal injury.

Front foot: Property measurement for sale or valuation purposes; the property measures by the front foot on its street line, each front foot extending the depth of the lot.

Frostline: The depths of frost penetration in the soil. It varies in different parts of the country. Footings should be placed below this depth to prevent movement.

Furring: Strips of wood or metal applied to a wall or other surface to even it, to form an air space, or to give the wall an appearance of greater thickness.

Gable roof: A pitched roof with sloping sides.

Gambrel roof: A curb roof, having a steep lower slope with a flatter upper slope.

Gift deed: A deed for which the consideration is love and affection and where there is no material consideration.

Girder: A large beam used to support beams, joists, and partitions.

Grade: Ground level at the foundation.

Graduated lease: Lease that provides for a varying rental rate, often based upon future determination; sometimes rent is based upon result of periodical appraisals; used largely in long-term leases.

Grant: A technical term made use of in deeds of conveyance of lands to import a transfer.

Grantee: The purchaser; a person to whom a grant is made.

Grantor: Seller of property; one who signs a deed.

Grid: A chart used in rating the borrower risk, property, and the neighborhood.

Gross income: Total income from property before any expenses are deducted.

Gross Multiplier: A method of appraising income property based upon a multiple of the gross annual income of the property.

Ground lease: An agreement for the use of the land only, sometimes secured by improvements placed on the land by the user.

Ground rent: Earnings of improved property credited to earnings of the ground itself after allowance is made for earnings of improvements; often termed *economic rent*.

Header: A beam placed perpendicular to joists and to which joists are nailed in framing for chimney, stairway, or other opening.

Highest and best use: An appraisal phrase meaning that use which at the time of an appraisal is most likely to produce the greatest net return to the land and/or buildings over a given period of time; that use which will produce the greatest amount of amenities or profit. This is the starting point for appraisal.

Hip roof: A pitched roof with sloping sides and ends.

Holder in due course: One who has taken a note, check, or bill of exchange in due course: (1) before it was overdue; (2) in good faith for value; and (3) without knowledge that it has been previously dishonored and without notice of any defect at the time it was negotiated to him.

Homestead: A home upon which the owner or owners have recorded a declaration of homestead as provided by California statutes. The declaration protects the home against judgments up to specified amounts.

Hundred-percent location: A city retail business location that is considered the best available for attracting business.

Hypothecate: To give a thing as security without the necessity of giving up possession of it.

Incompetent: One who is mentally incompetent, incapable; any person who, though not insane, is, by reason of old age, disease, weakness of mind, or any other cause, unable, unassisted, to properly manage and take care of himself or his property and by reason thereof would be likely to be deceived or imposed upon by artful or designing persons.

Increment: An increase. Most frequently used to refer to the increase of value of land that accompanies population growth and increasing wealth in the community. The term unearned increment is used in this connection since values are supposed to have increased without effort on the part of the owner.

Independent contractor: One who exercises independent judgment in doing a job and is responsible to employer only as to the results of the work.

Indirect lighting: The light is reflected from the ceiling or other object external to the fixture.

Indorsement: The act of signing one's name on the back of a check or a note, with or without further qualification.

Injunction: A writ or order issued under the seal of a court to restrain one or more parties to a suit or proceeding from doing an act that is deemed to be inequitable or unjust in regard to the rights of some other party or parties in the suit or proceeding.

Installment note: A note which provides that payments of a certain sum or amount be paid on the dates specified in the instrument.

Instrument: A written legal document created to effect the rights of the parties.

Interest rate: The percentage of a sum of money charged for its use.

Interim financing: A loan used to finance construction and due at its completion.

Intestate: A person who dies having made no will or having made one that is defective in form, in which case his estate descends to his heirs at law or next of kin.

Involuntary lien: A lien imposed against property without consent of an owner, for example taxes, special assessments, federal income tax liens, and so forth.

Irrevocable: Incapable of being recalled or revoked; unchangeable.

Irrigation districts: Quasi-political districts created under special laws to provide for water services to property owners in the district.

Jalousie: A slatted blind or shutter, like a venetian blind but used on the exterior to protect against rain as well as to control sunlight.

Jamb: The side post or lining of a doorway, window, or other opening.

Joint: The space between the adjacent surfaces of two components joined and held together by nails, glue, cement, mortar, and so forth.

Joint note: A note signed by two or more persons who have equal liability for payment.

Joint tenancy: Joint ownership by two or more persons with right of survivorship; all joint tenants own equal interest and have equal rights in the property.

Joist: One of a series of parallel beams to which the boards of a floor and ceiling lath are nailed, and supported in turn by larger beams, girders, or bearing walls.

Judgment: The final determination of a court of competent jurisdiction of a matter presented to it; money judgments provide for the payment of claims presented to the court or are awarded as damages and so forth.

Jurisdiction: The authority by which judicial officers take cognizance of and decide cause; the power to hear and determine a cause; the right and power that a judicial officer has to enter upon the inquiry.

Laches: Delay or negligence in asserting one's legal rights.

Land contract: A contract ordinarily used in connection with the sale of property in cases where the seller does not wish to convey title until all or a certain part of the purchase price is paid by the buyer; often used when property is sold on a small down payment.

Lateral support: The support that the soil of an adjoining owner gives to his neighbors' land.

Lath: A building material of wood, metal, gypsum, or insulating board fastened to the frame of a building to act as a plaster base.

Lease: A contract between owner and tenant, setting forth conditions upon which the tenant may occupy and use the property and the term of the tenant's occupancy.

Lease description: A description recognized by law; a description by which property can be definitely located by reference to government surveys or approved recorded maps.

Lessee: One who contracts to rent property under a lease contract.

Lessor: An owner who enters into a lease with a tenant.

Lien: A form of encumbrance that usually makes property security for the payment of a debt of discharge of an obligation. Example: judgments, taxes, mortgages, deeds of trust, and so forth.

Limited partnership: A partnership composed of some partners whose contribution and liability are limited.

Lintel: A horizontal board that supports the load over an opening such as a door or window.

Liquidated damages: An agreement in a contract providing for a definite sum of money to be paid in the event of a breach of the contract.

Lis pendens: Suit pending, usually recorded so as to give constructive notice of pending litigation.

Listing: An employment contract between principal and agent authorizing the agent to perform services for the principal involving the latter's property; listing contracts are entered into for the purpose of securing persons to buy, lease, or rent property. Employment of an agent by a prospective purchaser or lessee to locate property for purchase or lease may be considered a listing.

Louver: An opening with a series of horizontal slats set at an angle to permit ventilation without admitting rain, sunlight, or vision.

MAI: Designates a person who is a member of the American Institute of Appraisers of the National Association of Realtors®.

Margin of security: The difference between the amount of the mortgage loan(s) and the appraised value of the property.

Marginal land: Land that barely pays the cost of working or using.

Market price: The price paid regardless of pressure, motives, or intelligence.

Market value: (1) The price at which a willing seller would sell and a willing buyer would buy, neither being under abnormal pressure. (2) As defined by the courts, the highest price estimated in terms of money that a property will bring if exposed for sale in the open market allowing a reasonable time to find a purchaser with knowledge of the property's use and capabilities for use.

Marketable title: Merchantable title; title free and clear of objectionable liens or encumbrances.

Material fact: A fact that the agent should realize would be likely to affect the judgment of the principal in giving his consent to the agent to enter into the particular transaction on the specified terms.

Mechanic's lien: May be recorded by any supplier of work, labor, or materials for the construction or improvement of real estate if payment is not received for such work, labor, or materials.

Meridians: Imaginary north-south lines that intersect east-west base lines to form a starting point for the measurement of land.

Metes and bounds: A term used in describing the boundary lines of land, setting forth all the boundary lines together with each of their terminal points and angles.

Minor: All persons under 18 years of age. Any person who is 18 or over is deemed an adult person for the purpose of entering into an engagement or transaction respecting property.

Misrepresentation: False and misleading statements and concealment of material facts.

Molding: Usually patterned strips used to provide ornamental variation of outline or contour, such as cornices, bases, or window and door jambs.

Monument: A fixed object and point established by surveyors to establish land locations.

Moratorium: The temporary suspension, usually by statute, of the enforcement of liability for debt.

Mortgage: An instrument recognized by law by which property is hypothecated to secure the payment of an debt or obligation; procedure for foreclosure in event of default is established by statute.

Mortgage guaranty insurance: Insurance against financial loss available to mortgage lenders from Mortgage Guaranty Insurance Corporation.

Mortgagee: One to whom a mortgagor gives a mortgage to secure a loan or performance of an obligation; a lender. (See definition of secured party.)

Mortgagor: One who gives mortgage on his property to secure a loan or assure performance of an obligation; a borrower. (See definition of debtor.)

Multiple listing: A listing, usually an exclusive right to sell, taken by a member of an organization composed or real estate brokers, with the provisions that all members will have the opportunity to find an interested client; a cooperative listing.

Mutual water company: A water company organized by or for water users in a given district with the object of securing an ample water supply at a reasonable rate; stock is issued to users.

NAR: National Association of Realtors®.

Negotiable: Capable of being negotiated; that is, assignable or transferable in the ordinary course of business.

Net listing: A listing which provides that the agent may retain as compensation for his services all sums received over and above a net price to the owner.

Note: A signed written instrument acknowledging a debt and promising payment.

Notice of nonresponsibility: A notice provided by law designed to relieve a property owner from responsibility for the cost of work done on the property of materials furnished therefor; notice must be verified, recorded, and posted.

Notice to quit: A notice to a tenant to vacate rented property. If a tenant is delinquent in rental payments, a three-day notice to quit is required by law in connection with an unlawful detainer suit.

Obsolescence: Loss in value due to reduced desirability and usefulness of a structure because its design and construction become obsolete; loss because of becoming old-fashioned and not in keeping with modern needs, with consequent loss of income.

Offset statement: Statement by owner of property or owner of lien against property setting forth the present status of liens against said property.

Open-end mortgage: A mortgage containing a clause that permits the mortgagor to borrow additional money after the loan has been reduced, without rewriting the mortgage.

Open listing: An authorization given by a property owner to a real estate agent wherein said agent is given the nonexclusive right to secure a purchaser; open listings may be given to any number of agents without liability to compensate any except the one who first secures a buyer ready, willing, and able to meet the terms of the listing, or secures the acceptance by the seller of a satisfactory offer.

Option: A right given for a consideration to purchase or lease a property upon specified terms within a specified time.

Oral contract: A verbal agreement; one that is not reduced to writing.

Orientation: Placing a house on its lot with regard to its exposure to the rays of the sun, prevailing winds, privacy from the street, and protection from outside noises.

Overhang: The part of the roof extending beyond the walls, to shade buildings and cover walks.

Overimprovement: An improvement that is not the highest and best use for the site on which it is placed by reason of excess size or cost.

Par value: Market value; nominal value.

Partition action: Court proceedings by which co-owners seek to sever their joint ownership.

Partnership: According to the California Supreme Court, "A partnership as between partners themselves may be defined to be a contract of two or more persons to unite their property, labor or skill, or some of them, in prosecution of some joint or lawful business and to share the profits in certain proportions."

Party wall: A wall erected on the line between two adjoining properties, which are under different ownership, for the use of both properties.

Parquet floor: Hardwood flooring laid in squares or patterns.

Patent: Conveyance of title to government land.

Penny: A measure of nail length, represented by the *d* symbol.

Percentage lease: Lease on property, the rental for which is determined by amount of business with provision for a minimum rental.

Perimeter heating: Baseboard heating, or any system in which the heat registers are located along the outside walls of a room, especially under the windows.

Periodic tenancy: Tenancy for successive time periods of the same length.

Personal property: Any property that is not real property.

Pier: A column of masonry, usually rectangular in horizontal cross section, used to support other structural members.

Pitch: The incline or rise of a roof.

Plate: A horizontal board placed on a wall or supported on posts or studs to carry the trusses of a roof or rafters directly; a shoe, or base member as of a partition or other frame; a small flat board placed on or in a wall to support girders, rafters, and so forth.

Pledge: The depositing of personal property by a debtor with a creditor as security for a debt or engagement.

Pledgee: One who is given a pledge or a security. (See definition of secured party.)

Pledgor: One who offers a pledge or gives security. (See definition of debtor.)

Plottage increment: The appreciation in unit value created by joining smaller ownerships into one large single ownership.

Plywood: Laminated wood made up in panels; several thicknesses of wood glued together with grain at different angles for strength.

Points: A fee charged by a lender for making a loan. For example, 1½ points represents a fee of 1½ percent of the loan amount.

Police power: The right of the state to enact laws and enforce them for the order, safety, health, morals, and general welfare of the public.

Power of attorney: An instrument authorizing a person to act as the agent of the person granting it and a general power authorizing the agent to act generally in behalf of the principal. A special power limits the agent to a particular or specific act. For example, a landowner may grant an agent special power of attorney to convey a single and specific parcel of property. Under the provisions of a general power of attorney, the agent having the power may convey any or all property of the principal granting the general power of attorney.

Prefabricated house: A house manufactured, and sometimes partly assembled, before delivery to the building site.

Prepayment penalty: Penalty for the payment of a mortgage or trust deed note before it actually becomes due.

Prescription: The securing of title to property by adverse possession; by occupying it for the period determined by law barring action for recovery.

Prima facie: Presumptive on its face.

Principal: The employer of an agent.

Privity: Mutual relationship to the same rights of property; contractual relationship.

Procuring cause: That cause originating from a series of events that, without break in continuity, results in the prime object of an agent's employment producing a final buyer.

Promissory note: Written instrument used to evidence a basic obligation or debt.

Property: Anything of which there may be ownership rights.

Proration of taxes: To divide or prorate the taxes equally or proportionately to time of use.

Purchase money mortgage or trust deed: A trust deed or mortgage given as part or all of the purchase consideration for property.

Quarter round: A molding that presents a profile of a quarter circle.

Quiet enjoyment: Right of an owner to the use of property without interference of possession.

Quiet title: A court action brought to establish title; to remove a cloud on the title.

Quitclaim deed: A deed to relinquish any interest in property that the grantor may have.

Radiant heating: A method of heating usually consisting of coils or pipes in the floor, wall, or ceiling.

Rafter: One of a series of boards of a roof designed to support roof loads. The rafters of a flat roof are sometimes called *roof joists*.

Range: A strip of land six miles wide determined by a government survey, running in a north-south direction.

Ratification: The adoption or approval of an act performed on behalf of a person without previous authorization.

Real estate trust: A special arrangement under federal and state law whereby investors may pool funds for investments in real estate and mortgages and yet escape corporation taxes.

Real property: Land and anything permanently affixed to it, incidental or appurtenant to it, or immovable by law.

Realtor®: A real estate broker who is a member of the National Association of Realtors®.

Recapture: The rate of interest necessary to provide for the return of an investment. Not to be confused with interest rate, which is a rate of interest on an investment.

Reconveyance: The transfer of the title of land from one person to the immediately preceding owner. This particular instrument of transfer is commonly used in California when the performance or debt is satisfied under the terms of a deed of trust, when the trustee conveys the title he has held on condition back to the owner.

Recordation: To file a document for record in the office of the county recorder. Gives constructive notice of the contents to any party searching the records.

Redemption: Buying back one's property after a judicial sale.

Reformation: An action to correct a mistake in a deed or other document.

Release clause: A stipulation that upon the payment of a specific sum of money to the holder of a trust deed or mortgage, the lien of the instrument as to a specific described lot or area shall be removed from the blanket lien on the whole area involved.

Remainder: An estate that vests after the termination of the prior estate, such as a life estate.

Recision of contract: The abrogation or annulling of contract; the revocation or repealing or contract by mutual consent by parties to the contract, or for cause by either party to the contract.

Reservation: A right retained by a grantor in conveying property.

Restriction: As used relating to real property, it means that the owner of real property is restricted or prohibited from doing certain things relating to the property or using the property for certain purposes—for instance, the requirement in a deed that a lot may be used for the construction of not more than a one-party dwelling, costing not less than ten thousand dollars ($10,000), is termed to be restriction; also, a legislative ordinance affecting all properties in a given area, requiring that improvements on property shall not be constructed any closer than 25 feet to the street curb, is a restriction by operation of law.

Reversion: The right to future possession on enjoyment by the person, or his heirs, creating the preceding estate.

Reversionary interest: The interest that a person has in lands or other property upon the termination of the preceding estate.

Ridge: The horizontal line at the junction of the top edges of two sloping roof surfaces. The rafters at both slopes are nailed at the ridge.

Ridge board: The board placed on edge at the ridge of the roof to support the upper ends of the rafters; also called roof tree, ridge piece, ridge plate, or ridgepole.

Right of survivorship: Right to acquire the interest of a deceased joint owner; distinguishing feature of a joint tenancy.

Right of way: A privilege operating as an easement upon land whereby the owner does by grant or by agreement give to another the right to pass over his land, to construct a roadway or use as a roadway a specific part of his land, or the right to construct through and over his land telephone, telegraph, or electric power lines, or the right to place underground water mains, gas mains, or sewer mains.

Riparian rights: The right of a landowner to water on, under, or adjacent to his land.

Riser: The upright board at the back of each step of a stairway. In heating, a riser is a duct slanted upward to carry hot air from the furnace to the room above.

Roman brick: Thin brick of slimmer proportions than standard building brick.

Sales contract: A contract by which buyer and seller agree to terms of a sale.

Sale-leaseback: A situation where the owner of a piece of property wishes to sell the property and retain occupancy by leasing it from the buyer.

Sandwich lease: A leasehold interest that lies between the primary lease and the operating lease.

Sash: Wood or metal frames containing one or more window panes.

Satisfaction: Discharge of mortgage or trust deed lien from the records upon payment of the evidenced debt.

Scribing: Fitting woodwork to an irregular surface.

Seal: An impression made to attest the execution of an instrument.

Secondary financing: A loan secured by a second mortgage or trust deed on real property.

Section: An area of land established by government survey and containing 640 acres.

Secured party: The party having the security interest. Thus the mortgagee, the conditional seller, the pledgee, and so forth, are all now referred to as the secured party.

Security agreement: An agreement between the secured party and the debtor that creates the security interest.

Security interest: A term designating the interest of the creditor in the property of the debtor in all types of credit transactions. It thus replaces such terms as the following: chattel mortgage, pledge, trust receipt, chattel trust, equipment trust, conditional sale, inventory lien, and so forth.

Separate property: Property owned by a husband or wife that is not community property; acquired by either spouse prior to marriage or by gift or devise after marriage.

Septic tank: An underground tank in which sewage from the house is reduced to liquid by bacterial action and drained off.

Setback ordinance: An ordinance prohibiting the erection of a building or structure between the curb and the set back line.

Severalty ownership: Owned by one person only. Sole ownership.

Shake: A hand-split shingle, usually edge grained.

Sheathing: Structural covering, usually boards, plywood, or wallboards, placed over exterior studding or rafters of a house.

Sheriff's deed: Deed given by court order in connection with sale of property to satisfy a judgment.

Sill: The lowest part of the frame of a house, resting on the foundation and supporting the uprights of the frame. The board or metal forming the lower side of an opening, such as a door sill, window sill, and so forth.

Sinking fund: Fund set aside from the income from property that, with accrued interest, will eventually pay for replacement of the improvements.

Soil pipe: Pipe carrying waste out from the house to the main sewer line.

Sole or sole plate: A member, usually a 2-by-4, on which wall and partition studs rest.

Span: The distance between structural supports such as walls, columns, piers, beams, girders, and trusses.

Special assessment: A public authority created to pay the cost of public improvements, such as street lights, sidewalks, and street improvements.

Specific performance: An action to compel performance of an agreement, as the sale of land.

SRA: Designates a person who is a member of the Society of Residential Appraisers.

Statute of frauds: State law which provides that certain contracts must be in writing in order to be enforceable at law. Examples: real property lease for more than one year; agent's authorization to sell real estate.

Straight-line depreciation: A definite sum set aside annually from income to pay the cost of replacing improvements, without reference to interest it earns.

String, stringer: A timer or other support for cross members. In stairs, the support on which the stair treads rest.

Studs or studding: Vertical supporting timbers in the walls and partitions.

Subject to mortgage: When a grantee takes a title to real property subject to mortgage, he is not responsible to the holder of the promissory note for the payment of any portion of the amount due. The most that he can lose in the event of a foreclosure is his equity in the property. See also *assumption of mortgage* in this section. In neither case is the original maker of the note released from his responsibility.

Sublease: A lease given by a lessee.

Subordinate: To make subject to or junior to.

Subordination clause: Clause in a junior or a second lien permitting retention of priority for prior liens. A subordination clause may also be used in a first deed of trust, permitting it to be subordinate to subsequent liens such as, for example, the liens of construction loans.

Subpoena: A process to cause a witness to appear and give testimony.

Subrogation: The substitution of another person in place of the creditor, to whose rights he succeeds in relation to the debt. The doctrine is used very often when one person agrees to stand surety for the performance of a contract by another person.

Surety: One who guarantees the performance of another; guarantor.

Survey: The process by which a parcel of land is measured and its area ascertained.

Tax-free exchange: A method of deferring capital gains taxes by exchanging real property for other like property.

Tax sale: Sale of property after a period of nonpayment of taxes.

Tenancy in common: Ownership by two or more persons who hold undivided interest, without right of survivorship; interests need not be equal.

Tentative map: The Subdivision Map Act requires subdividers to submit initially a tentative map of their tract to the local planning commission for study. The approval or disapproval of the planning commission is noted on the map. Thereafter a final map of the tract embodying any changes requested by the planning commission is required to be filed with the planning commission.

Tenure in land: The mode or manner by which an estate in lands is held.

Termites: Ant-like insects that feed on wood.

Termite shield: A shield, usually of noncorrodible metal, placed on top of the foundation wall or around pipes to prevent passage of termites.

Testator: One who leaves a will in force at his death.

Threshold: A strip of wood or metal beveled on each edge and used above the finished floor under outside doors.

Time is the essence: One of the essential requirements to forming of a binding contract; contemplates a punctual performance.

Title: Evidence that the owner of land is in lawful possession thereof; an instrument evidencing such ownership.

Title insurance: Insurance written by a title company to protect the property owner against loss if the title is imperfect.

Topography: Nature of the surface of land; topography may be level, rolling, mountainous.

Torrens title: System of title records provided by state law (no longer used in California).

Tort: A wrongful act; wrong, injury; violation of a legal right.

Township: A territorial subdivision 6 miles long, 6 miles wide and containing 36 sections, each 1 mile square.

Trade fixtures: Articles of personal property annexed to real property but which are necessary to the carrying on of a trade and are removable by the owner.

Trade-in: An increasingly popular method of guaranteeing an owner a minimum amount of cash on sale of his present property to permit him to purchase another. If the property is not sold within a specified time at the listed price, the broker agrees to arrange financing to purchase the property at an agreed-upon discount.

Treads: Horizontal boards of a stairway.

Trim: The finish materials in a building, such as moldings, applied around openings (window trim, door trim) or at the floor and ceiling (baseboard, cornice, picture molding).

Trust account: A special account set up by an agent into which monies of principals are deposited with such monies kept separate and not commingled with monies belonging to the agent.

Trust deed: A deed given by the borrower to a trustee to be held pending fulfillment of an obligation, which is ordinarily repayment of a loan to a beneficiary.

Trustee: One who holds property in trust for another to secure the performance of an obligation.

Trustor: One who deeds his property to a trustee to be held as security until he has performed his obligation to a lender under terms of a deed of trust.

Undue influence: Taking any fraudulent or unfair advantage of another's weakness of mind, distress, or necessity.

Unearned increment: An increase in value of real estate due to no effort on the part of the owner, often due to increase in population.

Uniform Commercial Code: Effective January 1, 1965, it establishes a unified and comprehensive scheme for regulation of security transactions in personal property, superseding the existing statutes on chattel mortgages, conditional sales, trust receipts, assignment of accounts receivable, and others in this field.

Urban property: City property; closely settled property.

Usury: On a loan, claiming a rate of interest greater than that permitted by law.

Valid: Having force, or binding force; legally sufficient and authorized by law.

Valley: The internal angle formed by the junction of two sloping sides of a roof.

Valuation: Estimated worth or price. Estimation. The act of valuing by appraisal.

Vendee: A purchaser; buyer.

Vendor: A seller; one who disposes of a thing in consideration of money.

Veneer: Thin sheets of wood.

Vent: A pipe installed to provide a flow of air to or from a drainage system or to provide a circulation of air within such a system to protect trap seals from siphonage and back pressure.

Verification: Sworn statement before a duly qualified officer to the correctness of the contents of an instrument.

Vested: Bestowed upon someone; secured by someone, such as title to property.

Void: To have no force or effect; that which is unenforceable.

Voidable: That which is capable of being adjudged void but is not void unless action is taken to make it so.

Voluntary lien: Any lien placed on property with consent of, or as a result of, the voluntary act of the owner.

Wainscotting: Wood lining of an interior wall; lower section of a wall when finished differently from the upper part.

Waive: To relinquish or abandon; to forego a right to enforce or require anything.

Warranty deed: A deed used to convey real property that contains warranties of title and quiet possession; the grantor thus agrees to defend the premises against the lawful claims of third persons. It is commonly used in other states but not in California, where the grant deed has supplanted it. The modern practice of securing title insurance policies has reduced the importance of express and implied warranty in deeds.

Waste: The destruction, or material alteration of, or injury to, premises by a tenant for life or years.

Water table: Distance from the ground surface to a depth at which natural groundwater is found.

Zone: The area set off by the proper authorities for a specific use subject to certain restrictions or restraints.

Zoning: The act of city or county authorities specifying the type of use to which property may be put in specific areas.

Appendix B

Multiple-choice questions and answers

1. Assignment of a lease generally requires: *(a)* payment of additional rent, *(b)* renegotiation of the lease agreement, *(c)* permission of lessor, *(d)* none of these.
2. A verbal agreement to rent a residence for three months is: *(a)* binding if in writing, *(b)* legally binding, *(c)* not legally binding, *(d)* not enforceable unless the rent is paid by written instrument.
3. An encumbrance which most affects the use of real property is: *(a)* valid easement, *(b)* tax lien, *(c)* trust deed, *(d)* mechanics lien.
4. A term that refers to a borrower is: *(a)* seller, *(b)* trustee, *(c)* trustor, *(d)* purchaser.
5. Broker Stans submits the high bid on behalf of her client for the purchase of a probate property. Her commission is set by: *(a)* seller attorney, *(b)* county clerk, *(c)* the court, *(d)* civil code at 5 percent of sales price.
6. The basic propose in establishing state licensing procedures is to: *(a)* protect the public, *(b)* collect license fees in order to support real estate education, *(c)* conform with federal regulations that require licensing agents, *(d)* comply with Statute of Frauds.
7. An owner who wishes to begin construction or alteration work must obtain: *(a)* a building permit, *(b)* a property appraisal, *(c)* an occupancy certificate, *(d)* a construction loan.
8. What is the number of square yards in an area that measures 75 × 100 feet: *(a)* 11,250, *(b)* 3,750, *(c)* 1,250, *(d)* 225.
9. An offeror is an individual: *(a)* accepting an offer, *(b)* to whom an offer is given, *(c)* making the offer, *(d)* representing a purchaser.
10. Escrow companies must be licensed by: *(a)* real estate commissioner, *(b)* superior court, *(c)* corporation commissioner, *(d)* none of these.
11. The basic purpose of a title insurance policy is to: *(a)* prepare financial statements, *(b)* provide property inspection, *(c)* insure legal title to the property, *(d)* pay taxes and judgments.
12. A California Corporation desiring to obtain a real estate broker license must: *(a)* maintain branch offices, *(b)* offer real property securities to California residents, *(c)* obtain a restricted real estate license or special permit, *(d)* none of these.
13. Which of the following statements is correct as regards two unmarried individuals who hold title to real property as joint tenants: *(a)* they have equal rights of possession and use, *(b)* the joint tenancy automatically terminates upon the marriage of either joint tenant, *(c)* testamentary disposition is allowable, *(d)* none of these.
14. The most common subdivision is a: *(a)* stock cooperative, *(b)* community apartment, *(c)* standard subdivision, *(d)* commercial development.
15. Proper calculation of depreciation helps provide the property owner with: *(a)* better interest rates, *(b)* greater appreciation, *(c)* tax shelter, *(d)* VA financing.
16. A subdivider studies general economic factors by preparing: *(a)* financing statements, *(b)* building plans, *(c)* market analysis, *(d)* public reports.
17. In California, the title insurance policy fee must be paid by: *(a)* seller, *(b)* lender, *(c)* varies according to county, *(d)* buyer.
18. Real property tax assessment rolls are prepared by: *(a)* county supervisors, *(b)* tax collector, *(c)* county assessor, *(d)* none of these.
19. The transfer of property without receipt of monetary consideration is generally by: *(a)* court action, *(b)* gift, *(c)* private grant, *(d)* none of these.
20. Most real property is acquired by: *(a)* gift, *(b)* court order, *(c)* transfer, *(d)* prescriptive easement.
21. The manner in which the rent is to be paid is usually set by: *(a)* real estate law: *(b)* broker, *(c)* owner, *(d)* tenant.
22. Which of the following always adversely affects the value of residential property: *(a)* zoning laws, *(b)* set-back requirements, *(c)* recorded second trust deed, *(d)* none of these.
23. Property acquired by a husband or wife by gift

is: (a) community property, (b) automatically owned by them as tenants in common, (c) separate property, (d) none of these.

24. A broker may escrow a transaction if: (a) broker is acting as agent with respect to the transaction, (b) parties ro the agreement request it and issue a power of attorney to the broker, (c) title company pays the broker a commission, (d) none of these.

25. A deposit receipt: (a) is a contract for the purchase of real property, (b) must include a clause specifying a termite inspection, (c) is legally considered a listing agreement until accepted by seller, (d) must contain a notary stamp.

26. A valid grant deed does not have to state: (a) name of grantor, (b) name of grantee, (c) statement of the amount of consideration, (d) description of the property.

27. Brown purchases an apartment building on which owner Taylor has already collected monthly rents amounting to $3,960. If escrow is to be closed on the 15th day of a 30-day month, the amount of rent Brown will receive is: (a) $2,112, (b) $1,848, (c) $1,980, (d) $3,960.

28. Summary proceedings have to do with: (a) preparation of a lease or rental agreement, (b) periodic rental statements, (c) eviction, (d) appraisal statements in connection with the application for an FHA loan.

29. An example of an attractive nuisance is: (a) loud noises, (b) mechanical equipment, (c) smoke or noxious fumes, (d) none of these.

30. Most real estate offices in California operate as: (a) a partnership, (b) a stock company with branch offices, (c) a corporation, (d) none of these.

31. Which of the following is mostly associated with business opportunities: (a) purchase contract in writing, (b) leases, (c) correct inventory, (d) necessary financing.

32. A broker must be familiar with standard accounting procedures to: (a) properly prepare a purchase contract, (b) appraise residential property, (c) keep adequate trust fund records, (d) prepare listing agreements.

33. An example of an unlawful object is: (a) a listing contract, (b) an assignment clause in a construction contract, (c) an interest rate of 12 percent per annum, (d) a contract of an unlicensed general contractor.

34. Functional obsolescence if generally corrected by: (a) increasing the tax rate, (b) building modernization, (c) rezoning the area, (d) none of these.

35. The best definition of who may appoint an agent is: (a) a property owner, (b) real estate licensee, (c) any individual having the capacity to contract, (d) any individual at least 21 years of age and a citizen of the United States.

36. Which of the following is most likely not classified as real property: (a) producing grape vines, (b) fences, (c) farm tractors, (d) recreational buildings.

37. The Statute of Frauds specifies: (a) time allowed to file a court action, (b) types of fradulent statements, (c) responsibilities of a real estate licensee in preparing contracts, (d) which contracts must be in writing.

38. A homestead most often protects against a: (a) tax lien, (b) zoning restriction, (c) party wall encroachment, (d) judgment.

39. The issuance of a writ of execution may result in: (a) an increase in property tax assessment, (b) the filing of a writ of attachment, (c) a sheriff sale, (d) a mechanics lien.

40. A report prepared by a professional appraiser is most nearly: (a) an FHA checklist sheet, (b) a comprehensive narrative report, (c) a CAR competitive market analysis, (d) a Veterans Administration CRV report.

41. Appreciation generally refers to: (a) increase in interest rates, (b) property value increases, (c) special sales methods to provide tax benefits, (d) none of these.

42. Salvage value is most often considered with respect to: (a) tract sales, (b) cost basis calculation, (c) property acquired by gift, (d) none of these.

43. The rate of commission a broker may charge in the sale of industrial or commercial property is: (a) set by agreement between the principal and agent, (b) 5 percent up to $100,000 and 3 percent of the balance, (c) 10 percent of the sales price, (d) set by the Uniform Commercial Code statutes relating to the sale of business opportunities.

44. The Federal Housing Administration: (a) guarantees loan funds, (b) builds tract developments, (c) provides money to federal banks, (d) acts as insurer.

45. A recital in a deed which excludes a portion of the property being granted is: (a) an acknowledgment, (b) a patent, (c) a restriction, (d) none of these.

46. The payment of various escrow charges between the parties is set by: (a) real estate law, (b) escrow company, (c) agreement by parties and various practices in the area, (d) broker.

47. A real estate licensee must: (a) have the seller approve any advertising in connection with the sale of the property, (b) disclose to the seller any material facts in connection with the transaction, (c) show the property to prospective purchasers when the seller is present, (d) none of these.

48. Real estate licensees in most offices are classified as: (a) special partner, (b) agent by ratification, (c) independent contractor, (d) none of these.

49. The basic requisite to a successful partnership is: (a) financial resources, (b) mutual agreement between the partners, (c) business location and specialization, (d) branch offices.

50. A real estate licensee is said to be practicing law when: (a) preparing a standard purchase contract, (b) listing a property, (c) suggesting various meth-

ods of taking title to prospective purchasers, (d) none of these.
51. Most individuals enter into a property exchange to: (a) receive better property prices, (b) comply with trust account law, (c) gain tax advantages, (d) none of these.
52. A contract is usually enforceable if there is: (a) duress, (b) substantial breach, (c) substantial performance, (d) misrepresentation.
53. A probate sale is administered by: (a) title company, (b) county clerk, (c) assessor, (d) superior court.
54. With respect to a buyer taking possession of purchased property: (a) broker determines date of possession, (b) time of possession is set by law and relates to date of close of escrow, (c) must be given within three days of close of escrow, (d) strictly by agreement between buyer and seller.
55. The real estate commissioner prepares a public report in connection with a subdivision in order to: (a) protect and inform the public, (b) provide financial statements, (c) regulate prices and advertising, (d) set building standards as required by the state housing codes and regulations.
56. The W½ of a section contains: (a) 320 acres, (b) 180 acres, (c) 40 acres, (d) none of these.
57. If shrubs and branches from A's property extend onto B's property: (a) A and B become tenants in common, (b) A must trim the branches at B's request, (c) B has the right to trim the shrubs and branches back to the fence or other boundary line, (d) none of these.
58. The most common type of deed used to transfer title to property in California is: (a) warranty, (b) sheriff, (c) gift, (d) none of these.
59. The most common type of leasehold is: (a) periodic tenancy, (b) rental agreement, (c) tenancy for years, (d) monthly tenancy.
60. Prior to Mexican independence, California belonged to: (a) American settlers, (b) France, (c) King of Spain, (d) Bear Flag Republic.
61. An encumbrance that makes property security with respect to payment of a debt is: (a) a zoning law, (b) an easement, (c) a lien, (d) a homestead.
62. County supervisors can attempt to finance a special street lighting project by establishing: (a) special assessment district, (b) special tax rate scales, (c) eminent domain proceedings, (d) none of these.
63. In order to exchange an apartment building and defer income taxes, an owner must: (a) trade for a smaller building and receive some cash, (b) have owned the building to be traded for at least eight years, (c) trade with an owner having the same or a greater equity in his building, (d) none of these.
64. Smith earned $2,185 which represented a 9½ percent return on his investment. How much does Smith have invested: (a) $20,758, (b) $21,850 (c) $23,000, (d) none of these.
65. Which of the following is not a necessary factor in a valid contract: (a) competent parties, (b) mutual consent, (c) recordation, (d) lawful object.
66. A metes and bounds description generally contains: (a) square feet, (b) block number, (c) measurements and boundaries, (d) street address.
67. A fee which is charged to arrange a loan is called: (a) processing charge, (b) prepayment penalty, (c) origination fee, (d) application and appraisal fee.
68. An irrigation district: (a) provides water stock to county agricultural districts, (b) sets agricultural building requirements, (c) regulates water conservation and production, (d) none of these.
69. An offer to purchase real property must be accepted: (a) within three days of presentation, (b) prior to approval of loan application, (c) exactly as specified in the offer, (d) by seller who must sign acceptance before a notary.
70. Mrs. Brown has an $80,000 investment which earns 8½ percent return per year. Her monthly earnings are approximately: (a) $6,800, (b) $655, (c) $68,000, (d) $567.
71. California counties are required by law to establish: (a) real estate licensing laws, (b) a planning commission, (c) an irrigation district, (d) none of these.
72. Proper interpretation of complex tax laws is best accomplished by: (a) property owner, (b) real estate broker, (c) CPA, (d) tax assessor.
73. A real estate licensees most fundamental right to compensation is based on: (a) advertising the property, (b) showing the property to a prospective client, (c) a written listing contract, (d) presenting an offer to a seller.
74. Cancellation of a lease by mutual agreement is: (a) periodic tenancy, (b) result of court action, (c) recapture, (d) surrender.
75. In order to earn $300 per month on a 10 percent investment, the amount of investment must be: (a) $36,000, (b) $3,000, (c) $30,000, (d) $3,600.
76. An owner wishing to give some real estate to a university could do so by: (a) eminent domain, (b) quiet title action, (c) dedication, (d) tax credit grant.
77. The usual loan amortization table used by a real estate licensee shows: (a) monthly payments which include principal and interest, (b) payment to principal, interest, and taxes, (c) depreciation rates, (d) loan equity buildup.
78. With respect to capital gains, real estate licensees are generally classified as: (a) agent, (b) principal, (c) dealer, (d) investor.
79. Mr. and Mrs. Brown signed a five-year lease on a store and began to operate a coffee shop. Three years later, Mr. Brown expired, and the owner notified Mrs. Brown that the present lease must now be renegotiated: (a) owner is correct, (b) lease

does not have to be renegotiated and is still valid for two years, *(c)* lease is now invalid but owner is automatically required to renew if Mrs. Brown desires, *(d)* when a husband and wife signed a commercial lease, the husband is considered to be the lessee.

80. An individual who meets all the requirements for adverse possession with the exception of payment of taxes is most likely to acquire: *(a)* fee simple title, *(b)* encroachment, *(c)* full estate, *(d)* easement by prescription.

81. The type of interest given to a lessee by an owner is: *(a)* ownership, *(b)* security, *(c)* possessory, *(d)* riparian.

82. Quiet enjoyment of real property relates to: *(a)* method of holding title, *(b)* possession, *(c)* deed restriction, *(d)* encumbrances.

83. When a contract is terminated and the parties are put back in their original position, this is termed: *(a)* recordation, *(b)* abrogation, *(c)* rescission, *(d)* none of these.

84. Which of the following is not a test of whether a piece of property is a fixture: *(a)* method of attachment, *(b)* monetary value, *(c)* intent of annexor, *(d)* none of these.

85. The party most likely to record a request for notice of default is: *(a)* tax assessor, *(b)* trustor, *(c)* holder of second loan, *(d)* tax collector.

86. Broker A wishes to purchase a piece of property he has listed. In order to do so, Broker A must: *(a)* obtain approval of the real estate commissioner, *(b)* wait until the listing terminates, *(c)* make an offer and full disclosure to the owner, *(d)* make an offer through a dummy buyer.

87. The Realtors Code of Ethics is a product of the: *(a)* NAR, *(b)* C.T.A., *(c)* Department of Real Estate, *(d)* HUD.

88. Automatic right of survivorship is associated with: *(a)* tenants in common, *(b)* severalty ownership, *(c)* community property, *(d)* joint tenancy.

89. A deed of reconveyance is generally signed by: *(a)* title officer, *(b)* trustee, *(c)* trustor, *(d)* none of these.

90. Which of the following is not an encumbrance: *(a)* homestead, *(b)* tax lien, *(c)* trust deed, *(d)* none of these.

91. The subsequent deed of an individual judicially judged incompetent is: *(a)* valid, *(b)* voidable, *(c)* void, *(d)* enforceable by the sheriff.

92. A straight note: *(a)* may be used only in connection with an FHA loan, *(b)* provides for payment of interest and principal in equal payments, *(c)* is not negotiable, *(d)* provides for payment of interest only during its term.

93. Which of the following is not regulated by the Subdivision Map Act: *(a)* filing procedures, *(b)* obtaining certificates, *(c)* proper recordation, *(d)* none of these.

94. If the income from a building containing 12 apartments is $5,526 per month, the average monthly rental per apartment is: *(a)* $383.50, *(b)* $525, *(c)* $460.50, *(d)* $425.

95. Title to property purchased with a California Veterans Loan is vested in: *(a)* purchaser, *(b)* title company, *(c)* state of California, *(d)* bank or savings and loan association.

96. The property owner in a lease agreement is *(a)* broker, *(b)* lessor, *(c)* lessee, *(d)* tenant.

97. If seller accepts an offer and buyer refuses to perform: *(a)* deposit must be retained by seller, *(b)* deposit belongs to broker, *(c)* seller may order escrow officer to return deposit to buyer, *(d)* broker and seller automatically split deposit.

98. The basic intent in designating a neighborhood as a conservation area is to: *(a)* require existing buildings to comply with building codes, *(b)* conserve water and basic utilities, *(c)* clear slum areas, *(d)* increase tax assessments.

99. The compensation paid to a broker is generally: *(a)* a percentage of the asking price of the property, *(b)* an hourly rate of pay, *(c)* set by the Real Estate Commissioner, *(d)* a percentage of the selling price of the property.

100. Which of the following statements is most correct as regards a real estate partnership: *(a)* a branch office license is necessary, *(b)* individual partners must hold real estate broker licenses, *(c)* any real estate license allows an individual to be a partner in a real estate firm, *(d)* a special real estate partner license is necessary.

101. Bankruptcy proceedings are regulated by: *(a)* state laws, *(b)* real estate law, *(c)* federal statutes, *(d)* none of these.

102. An example of an encroachment is a: *(a)* local building code, *(b)* portion of a building extending onto the property of an adjoining owner, *(c)* party wall agreement between two property owners, *(d)* restrictive covenant.

103. An appraisal is most commonly used to set: *(a)* utility standards, *(b)* cost estimates, *(c)* market value, *(d)* tax assessment rates.

104. The tax year with respect to collection of real property taxes is: *(a)* calendar year, *(b)* same as federal income tax, *(c)* fiscal year, *(d)* set by county supervisors.

105. Real property taxes must be paid: *(a)* at the time such taxes become a lien, *(b)* in two installments, *(c)* by the individual who resides on the property, *(d)* none of these.

106. $20,000 capitalized at 12½ percent is: *(a)* $2,500, *(b)* $25,000, *(c)* $160,000, *(d)* $250,000.

107. Broker Smith sold some estate property. His commission will be determined by: *(a)* real estate commissioner, *(b)* executor, *(c)* the court, *(d)* the estate administrator.

108. An adverse possessor who satisfies all requirements except payment of real property taxes most often obtains: *(a)* public grant, *(b)* ownership by

court order, (c) easement by prescription, (d) none of these.

109. Property is sold by a trustee as the result of: (a) lien priority, (b) loan that allows future advances, (c) default, (d) deficiency judgment.
110. The cost approach to valuation is most valuable in the appraisal of: (a) city, county, and other public buildings, (b) tract houses, (c) residential complexes, (d) commercial properties.
111. The cooperative method of owning real property is generally found with respect to: (a) community apartments, (b) partnerships, (c) trusts, (d) leaseholds.
112. A term that refers to a lender is: (a) trustor, (b) seller, (c) beneficiary, (d) purchaser.
113. A fee ownership and tenancy in common combination is most often found with respect to: (a) community apartments, (b) condominium ownership, (c) mineral rights, (d) leasehold arrangements.
114. A purchaser takes liability with respect to an existing loan by: (a) purchasing subject to the existing loan, (b) signing a subordination agreement, (c) assuming the existing loan, (d) none of these.
115. Broker Cynthia prepares and presents an offer on a property she has listed. The owner says he will consider it and either accept or reject it within two days. The following day, another client who has been shown the property calls Broker Cynthia and wishes to make an offer. With respect to presentation of the second offer, Broker Cynthia: (a) must present the offer, (b) should wait until the previous offer is rejected by seller, (c) should refuse to prepare another offer for two days, (d) cannot act as agent for both offers.
116. Parol evidence refers to: (a) oral statements, (b) specific conditions in a purchase offer, (c) required signature of a parole officer, (d) none of these.
117. Industrial property is most often sold by the (a) number of acres, (b) front foot, (c) square foot, (d) cubic foot.
118. Stock cooperative projects are generally found in connection with: (a) commercial properties, (b) resort properties, (c) residential apartment buildings, (d) condominiums.
119. Which of the following may properly use the Realtor designation: (a) any individual acting as a real estate agent who expects to receive a commission, (b) real estate licensee who belongs to any professional organization, (c) a real estate broker who belongs to the NAR, (d) any real estate agent licensed by the state of California.
120. All other factors being equal, the greatest determinant of property value is its: (a) tax assessment, (b) utility and age, (c) location, (d) cost of construction.
121. A dealer in real property securities must hold a license as: (a) real estate broker, (b) stockholder, (c) securities analyst, (d) none of these.
122. An instrument which transfers an interest in real property must be: (a) in writing, (b) a contract stating a monetary consideration, (c) approved by the county recorder for recordation, (d) witnessed by an escrow or title officer.
123. A prospective purchaser who receives a copy of the Commissioners Public Report must: (a) sign a deposit receipt, (b) deposit funds in escrow, (c) sign a receipt, (d) none of these.
124. A term which refers to water rights is: (a) township, (b) fixtures, (c) riparian, (d) fluid public utility.
125. A broker listing properties in a large residential tract most often uses: (a) competitive market analysis, (b) tax assessors estimate of value, (c) original square footage costs, (d) opinion of property owner.
126. Broker Allan, in attempting to list a residential complex, is suspicious about the owners statement of income and expenses. The best way to verify the true facts is to ask the owner for a copy of: (a) appraisal report, (b) tax assessors statement of assessed value, (c) schedule submitted by property owner with income tax papers, (d) bank records showing rental deposits.
127. A contract to sell community property: (a) requires court approval, (b) must be signed by both husband and wife, (c) is valid if either spouse signs it, (d) must be prepared by a licensed real estate broker.
128. A sworn statement that the contents of a document are true is: (a) contract, (b) verification, (c) a judicial consideration, (d) an acknowledgment.
129. An owner whose property is acquired by right of eminent domain must by law receive: (a) original cost to owner, (b) fair market value, (c) depreciated value, (d) reproduction cost.
130. The best loan term is generally obtainable with respect to: (a) commercial properties, (b) industrial developments, (c) newer properties, (d) purchasers with a large down payment.
131. The Veterans Administration guarantee provides protection to: (a) veteran, (b) seller, (c) lender, (d) title company.
132. In a typical sale of real property in California, the type of estate transferred is: (a) community property, (b) corporate ownership, (c) a fee, (d) *none of these.*
133. A notice of default is generally recorded by: (a) trustor, (b) trustee, (c) beneficiary, (d) none of these.
134. Which of the following is not controlled by zoning regulations: (a) property uses, (b) building height limits, (c) restrictive convenants in grant deeds, (d) types of buildings.
135. The interest of a joint tenant who expires without a will passes to: (a) state of California, (b) lienholders, (c) surviving joint tenant, (d) those entitled to receive the property through the California law of intestate succession.

136. A township is: (a) 3 miles square, (b) 6 square miles, (c) 6 miles square, (d) 20 square miles.
137. The sale of property by a sheriff is usually the result of: (a) accretion, (b) addition of fixtures, (c) adverse possession, (d) judgment against owner.
138. The individual making a taxable gift: (a) is required to be a trustee, (b) is a donee, (c) is a donor, (d) none of these.
139. Where income property suffers from economic obsolescence, this is generally due to: (a) faulty building plan, (b) poor wiring or plumbing, (c) deferred maintenance, (d) deteriorating neighborhood.
140. The height and construction of fences are often regulated by: (a) local ordinances, (b) state law, (c) individual property owners, (d) real estate law.
141. The cost approach to appraisal is most properly used with respect to which of the following properties: (a) commercial, (b) industrial, (c) newer properties, (d) older properties.
142. Recordation of documents imparts: (a) legal validity, (b) court approval, (c) constructive notice, (d) none of these.
143. Which of the following is a method of removing an easement from the records: (a) obtain a court attachment and deliver it to the easement owner, (b) file a bankruptcy petition, (c) record a quitclaim deed signed by the easement owner, (d) record a note secured by a deed of trust.
144. A property owner owes the least duty of protection to a: (a) tenant, (b) invitee, (c) licensee, (d) trespasser.
145. The owner of a dominant tenement: (a) must hold title as a tenant in common, (b) receives the benefits of an easement, (c) receives a preferential tenement tax rate, (d) acquires an easement by necessity.
146. A type of lease that permits the lessee to purchase the property is: (a) residential, (b) percentage or net, (c) lease option, (d) tenancy agreement.
147. A deed is executed when it is: (a) in writing, (b) given to grantee, (c) signed by a witness, (d) signed by grantor.
148. Arthur receives a real property tax bill of $826.20 based on an assessment ratio of 25 percent of market value and a tax rate of $4.86 per $100. The assessed property value is: (a) $117,000, (b) $118,300, (c) $17,000 (d) $1,880.
149. A conditional sales contract for purchase of real property generally gives buyer: (a) security interest, (b) fee title, (c) right of possession, (d) none of these.
150. Using a straight note, Clark borrows $63,000 with a three-year term and a 9 percent yearly interest rate. How much total interest will Clark have to pay: (a) $5,670, (b) $17,010, (c) 16,670, (d) none of these.
151. A trust account sets aside funds to: (a) pay brokers commission, (b) establish a lien priority, (c) pay insurance and taxes, (d) none of these.
152. A written listing that allows a number of brokers to act as agent is: (a) net, (b) oral, (c) open, (d) none of these.
153. How much must be invested at 12 percent in order to provide the investor with a $550 monthly income payment: (a) $50,000, (b) $6,600, (c) 66,000, (d) none of these.
154. An example of a freehold estate is: (a) a lease for three years, (b) a lease for less than a year, (c) a fee simple, (d) a tenancy at will.
155. Broker A can receive a commission from both buyer and seller in a transaction if: (a) the factor is disclosed to both parties, (b) both parties pay an equal amount of commission, (c) Broker A receives approval of the real estate commissioner, (d) none of these.
156. The best protection a property owner has against possible liability to others is to: (a) post adequate signs, (c) install a burglar alarm on the premises, (c) carry adequate liability insurance, (d) record a notice of nonresponsibility.
157. A married woman can enter into a contract for the purchase of real property when she reaches the age of: (a) 21, (b) 18, (c) at any age so long as she is legally married, (d) only with consent of the husband.
158. A distinctive feature of an agreement of sale or installment sale contract with respect to real property is: (a) title given to a broker who acts as agent for purchaser, (b) buyer pays purchase price in cash, (c) seller retains title, (d) an exchange agreement is made part of the contract.
159. The following property that is subject to taxation is: (a) minicipal court building, (b) apartment building, (c) city and county budgets, (d) state property.
160. A disclosure statement provides buyer with: (a) statement of specific credit charges, (b) property appraisal, (c) amount of money seller owes to existing lender, (d) listing contract.
161. The method by which buyers take title to real property: (a) is set by local ordinance, (b) must be shown on any purchase offer, (c) generally is determined by seller in the listing, (d) none of these.
162. The questionnaire that a subdivider must prepare prior to issuance of a public report is obtained from: (a) county recorder, (b) state engineer, (c) real estate commissioner, (d) planning commission.
163. The best protection to the parties in a rental situation is: (a) agreement in writing, (b) large rental deposit, (c) dealing directly with the owner, (d) real estate commissioner.
164. A suit by a co-owner against other co-owners requesting a severance of respective interests is: (a) private grant, (b) sale by sheriff, (c) partition action, (d) none of these.
165. An acceptance that slightly modifies an offer: (a) results in a legal contract, (b) is valid with respect

to real property, *(c)* constitutes a ratification, *(d)* none of these.

166. A riparian owner: *(a)* is responsible for repair and maintenance of fences on boundary lines, *(b)* must provide special lateral support for adjacent buildings, *(c)* has certain water rights in common with other owners, *(d)* none of these.
167. The holding of property by an individual for the benefit of another individual is a: *(a)* leasehold, *(b)* joint venture, *(c)* condominium, *(d)* trust.
168. If an offer is rejected by a seller, the broker will usually try to obtain: *(a)* ratification, *(b)* option agreement, *(c)* counteroffer, *(d)* listing extension.
169. A charge in excess of the interest rate allowed by law is: *(a)* trust account, *(b)* usury, *(c)* subordination, *(d)* acceleration.
170. Broker Smith has a listing which does not make any mention of acceptance of a deposit. If Broker Smith accepts a deposit check for $2,000 in connection with an offer, it is legally held as agent for: *(a)* title company, *(b)* seller, *(c)* buyer, *(d)* bank or savings and loan association.
171. A social guest is generally considered to be: *(a)* licensee, *(b)* an invitee, *(c)* an agent, *(d)* a tenant.
172. The cost basis of property is its: *(a)* purchase cost, *(b)* appraisal set by tax collector, *(c)* net proceeds to seller, *(d)* none of these.
173. Smith makes and signs an offer to purchase, giving seller five days to accept. The offer may be withdrawn: *(a)* if broker agrees, *(b)* if seller agrees, *(c)* prior to expiration of the listing, *(d)* prior to acceptance by seller and notification to buyer.
174. The individual who employs an agent is: *(a)* a trustee, *(b)* a broker, *(c)* a principal, *(d)* an attorney.
175. A handwritten will is: *(a)* holographic, *(b)* signed by witnesses, *(c)* nuncupative, *(d)* none of these.
176. The income approach to appraisal uses application of a capitalization rate to: *(a)* purchase price, *(b)* gross income, *(c)* net income, *(d)* none of these.
177. A real property appraiser may determine value by applying a gross multiplier to: *(a)* purchase price, *(b)* gross income which property produces, *(c)* functional design pattern, *(d)* real property taxes.
178. An acknowledgment is made by a: *(a)* notary public, *(b)* judge or clerk of a municipal court, *(c)* grantor, *(d)* title officer during an escrow.
179. The funds to support real estate education and research are mostly provided by: *(a)* state grants, *(b)* real estate license fees, *(c)* community colleges, *(d)* bond issues.
180. A real estate license is necessary in order to act as: *(a)* a rental agent, *(b)* an escrow agent, *(c)* a bookkeeper in a real estate office, *(d)* a secretary in a real estate office.
181. Joan Thomas owns a building containing a small store. She rents the store to a tenant who begins extensive modernization work on the interior. Joan Thomas can best protect herself against possible mechanics liens by: *(a)* notifying the tenant, *(b)* preparing a lease, *(c)* properly affixing to the store entrance a notice of nonresponsibility, *(d)* taking out the proper building permits.
182. A real estate appraisal license may be obtained by applying to: *(a)* real estate commissioner *(b)* state building inspection department, *(c)* state of California department of housing and appraisal, *(d)* none of these.
183. The escrow holder: *(a)* arranges financing, *(b)* must request a termite inspection, *(c)* generally pays a referral fee to broker, *(d)* none of these.
184. The greatest amount of loan funds in the California real estate market is provided by: *(a)* FHA, *(b)* commercial banks, *(c)* savings and loan associations, *(d)* VA.
185. A standard section contains: *(a)* 640 acres, *(b)* 180 acres, *(c)* 640 acres and is six miles square, *(d)* 20 square miles.
186. Which of the following is not a test used to determine fixtures: *(a)* method of attachment, *(b)* intention of the parties, *(c)* adaptation to the property, *(d)* none of these.
187. The type of note that calls for periodic payments is: *(a)* straight, *(b)* trust, *(c)* installment, *(d)* none of these.
188. California law presumes that real property purchased by a husband and wife is: *(a)* tenancy in common, *(b)* community property, *(c)* tenancy in partnership, *(d)* joint tenancy.
189. The basic restrictive feature of zoning laws has to do with: *(a)* financing, *(b)* property maps, *(c)* property uses, *(d)* building codes.
190. The filing of a financial statement in accordance with the UCC has to do with: *(a)* sale of recreational property, *(b)* apartment buildings, *(c)* industrial properties, *(d)* none of these.
191. The Real Estate Law authorizes which of the following to suspend real estate licenses: *(a)* state licensing commission, *(b)* real estate commissioner, *(c)* state legislature, *(d)* state real estate commission.
192. Charges to the parties in connection with the escrow are best shown in: *(a)* purchase contract prepared by a real estate licensee, *(b)* title search, *(c)* escrow or settlement statements, *(d)* tax statements.
193. Which of the following statements best describes the escrow holder: *(a)* is paid by the listing broker, *(b)* neutral party, *(c)* gives legal advice to the parties in the escrow, *(d)* guarantees validity of purchase contract.
194. Broker Laura prepares an $160,000 offer on a deposit. The seller accepts and signs the offer. Two weeks later both buyer and seller agree to terminate the contract, and seller tells Broker Laura to return the deposit. She should: *(a)* return $6,400 and retain $9,600 as commission, *(b)* return the $16,000, *(c)* keep half the deposit and

return the other half, (d) keep the entire deposit as liquidated damages.
195. Which of the following is not required of a real estate license applicant: (a) state examination, (b) 18 years of age or older, (c) U.S. citizenship, (d) submit set of fingerprints.
196. A seller will generally elect to use an installment sale in order to: (a) provide FHA or VA financing, (b) meet capital gain requirements, (c) spread tax payments, (d) none of these.
197. Bank appraisal policies are generally: (a) very liberal with respect to residential properties, (b) set by FHA (c) conservative, (d) very favorable to speculative purchasers.
198. State law requires a residential building with a market value of $200,000 to be assessed at: (a) $200,000, (b) $75,000, (c) varies according to tax rate, (d) none of these.
199. The right given a utility company to string wires across a number of private properties is an: (a) easement appurtenant, (b) easement in gross, (c) encroachment, (d) appurtenant reservation.
200. A possible tax advantage to investors in real property as against common stock investors is: (a) tax provision allowing capital gains, (b) appreciation, (c) depreciation, (d) none of these.
201. The duties and authority of an agent are found in the: (a) California housing codes, (b) California Civil Code, (c) local ordinances, (d) none of these.
202. The various uses to which real property may be put is regulated by: (a) rules and regulations of the real estate commissioner, (b) state housing and construction laws, (c) local zoning ordinances, (d) intent of owners.
203. The listing that affords a broker the greatest amount of protection is: (a) exclusive agency, (b) exclusive right to sell, (c) open listing, (d) none of these.
204. Property distributed by the court according to the statutes of succession is most often: (a) community property, (b) tenancy in common, (c) separate property, (d) joint tenancy property.
205. Laws with respect to racial discrimination in connection with the sale or purchase of real property: (a) vary between counties, (b) affect only certain types of real property, (c) permit discrimination only if the owner acts as a principal, (d) none of these.
206. Factory housing construction is regulated by the: (a) State Housing Act, (b) City Planning Commission, (c) State Department of Housing and Community Development, (d) none of these.
207. The amount at which a recently purchased property is assessed for tax purposes is best reflected by: (a) utility laws, (b) zoning regulations, (c) current market values, (d) city and county budgets.
208. Smith purchases a property for $260,000. If assessed valuation for tax purposes is 25 percent of market value and the current tax rate is $4.20 per $100 of assessed value, what is the amount of tax Smith will have to pay: (a) $1,092, (b) $10,920, (c) $27,300, (d) $2,730.
209. Most builders obtain their construction financing directly from: (a) Veterans Administration, (b) bank or savings and loan association, (c) Small Business Administration, (d) private lenders.
210. A second trust deed is most readily obtainable from: (a) private party, (b) FHA, (c) state chartered savings and loan association, (d) savings bank.
211. The number of square feet in an acre is: (a) 180, (b) 43,560, (c) 5,280, (d) 320.
212. The record law was introduced into California by: (a) U.S. Government, (b) Mexican Government, (c) California legislature, (d) King of Spain.
213. The establishment of title insurance policy rates are within the jurisdiction of the: (a) real estate commissioner, (b) title insurance companies, (c) insurance commissioner, (d) none of these.
214. An executory contract: (a) is generally prepared by court order, (b) must contain a monetary consideration, (c) has yet to be completed by the parties, (d) generally contains alienation clauses.
215. Real property is generally taxed according to its: (a) location, (b) size, (c) value, (d) zoning status.
216. The instrument used to remove the lien of a trust deed from record is called a: (a) satisfaction, (b) release, (c) deed of reconveyance, (d) certificate of redemption.
217. Community property is property owned by: (a) the municipality, (b) husband and wife, (c) city and county, (d) any township incorporated in California as a charter city.
218. The stock and fixtures that are to be transferred with the sale of a business are generally listed in: (a) sales tax statement, (b) an inventory, (c) a contract of sale, (d) a settlement statement.
219. A valid bill of sale must contain: (a) a verification, (b) an acknowledgment, (c) seller's signature, (d) none of these.
220. A security agreement is usually given in connection with: (a) real property, (b) agricultural property, (c) rentals, (d) none of these.
221. The rate of commission to be charged for selling a business is determined by: (a) real estate commissioner, (b) buyer and seller, (c) agreement between seller and broker, (d) UCC.
222. When the purchaser is ready, willing, and able to buy, the broker binds the transaction by: (a) obtaining a deposit, (b) preparing a rental agreement, (c) ordering a title search, (d) none of these.
223. The Bulk Sales Act is part of the: (a) Real Estate Law, (b) Industrial Sales Act, (c) Real Estate Commissioners Regulations, (d) Uniform Commercial Codes.
224. The maximum term for which urban property in California may be leased is: (a) 99 years, (b) 20 years, (c) 51 years, (d) none of these.
225. Which of the following methods of calculating de-

preciation for income tax purposes is not an accelerated method: (a) sum-of-the-years-digits, (b) 125 percent declining balance, (c) straight-line, (d) 200 percent declining balance.

226. Chin sold a building for $92,250 which represented a 23 percent increase on original purchase price. What did Chin originally pay: (a) $71,032, (b) $75,000, (c) $21,217, (d) $79,500.

227. The Veterans Administration guarantees a loan in order to protect the: (a) broker, (b) borrower, (c) lender, (d) U.S. Treasury.

228. A real property securities dealer must: (a) be a real estate broker, (b) obtain a stockbroker permit, (c) make a monthly report to the real estate commissioner, (d) file a $20,000 bond.

229. Which of the following cannot receive the protection of a homestead: (a) condominium, (b) triplex, (c) residence encumbered by an FHA or VA loan, (d) none of these.

230. A real estate listing providing a ten percent commission to the broker is: (a) valid, (b) against the rules of the real estate commissioner, (c) against the civil code, (d) void.

231. Which of the following most closely defines an installment sale contract: (a) transfer of ownership, (b) a lease option, (c) security device, (d) none of these.

232. A voidable contract can generally be rescinded by: (a) either party to the contract, (b) the innocent party, (c) by both parties only if they do so in escrow, (d) none of these.

233. An industrial building was listed at $275,000 with an agreed commission of 10 percent. The owner later agreed to accept an offer of 12 percent less than the listed price, and the broker agreed to an 8 percent commission. What was the amount of commission paid to the broker: (a) $19,360, (b) $24,360, (c) $24,200, (d) $27,500.

234. The type of interest that lenders most generally charge for home loans is: (a) bank, (b) discount, (c) simple, (d) compound.

235. The maximum market value of a residence on which a homestead may be filed cannot be more than: (a) $20,000, (b) $35,000, (c) $50,000, (d) none of these.

236. A title to California real property is considered marketable if the purchaser can obtain: (a) financing, (b) warranty certificate, (c) policy of title insurance, (d) recordation.

237. An individual must hold a real estate license in order to: (a) collect rents and charge a fee, (b) act on order of a superior court, (c) act as a trustee or administer, (d) none of these.

238. Smith pruchases a restaurant business from Brown. The instrument Brown uses to transfer his possessory interest in real property is: (a) security agreement, (b) purchase contract, (c) assignment of lease, (d) business license permit.

239. In order to sell a piece of property containing an oil lease, a real estate broker must: (a) obtain a special permit from the real estate commissioner, (b) obtain a license as a mineral, oil, and gas broker, (c) be a real property securities broker, (d) none of these.

240. An individual who wishes to purchase property using substantial leverage should: (a) pay cash, (b) obtain conventional financing, (c) purchase with a very small down payment, (d) use a 29 percent down payment.

241. In order to be valid, a deed must: (a) be acceptable to the county recorder, (b) have a granting clause, (c) contain an acknowledgment, (d) be given to purchaser by escrow officer.

242. A building 75 × 100 is constructed at a cost of $47.50 per square foot. The cost of construction is: (a) $83,125, (b) $39,567.50, (c) $356,250, (d) none of these.

243. The California Real Estate Law prohibits real estate licensees from: (a) signing an option listing, (b) participating in a real estate trade as a principal, (c) negotiating a loan secured by a deed of trust, (d) none of these.

244. A building is purchased for $196,000 subject to a savings and loan association loan of $97,000 and a second loan provided by seller in the amount of $14,400. The purchaser's equity is: (a) $82,600, (b) $111,400, (c) $84,600, (d) $59,000.

245. The brokers commission rate in the sale of a business opportunity is set by: (a) real estate commissioner, (b) Uniform Commerical Code, (c) agreement between principal and agent (d) state of California.

246. Broker Smith obtained an exclusive agency listing on an apartment building. When the owner sold the property himself, Broker Smith requested a 6 percent commission. Broker Smith is entitled to receive: (a) 3 percent commission, (b) advertising expenses, (c) full commission, (d) none of these.

247. A deposit check given to a broker by a prospective purchaser is properly classified as a: (a) straight note, (b) promissory note, (c) negotiable instrument, (d) none of these.

248. Which of the following is an income tax benefit to the owner of a residence who resides in it (a) principal payment, (b) interest payment, (c) plumbing repair expenses, (d) none of these.

249. A real estate broker may conduct an escrow: (a) with respect to a transaction in which the broker acts as the agent, (b) in any real estate transaction if buyer and seller request it, (c) if licensed as an escrow agent, (d) if broker is the listor.

250. Broker Brown has a property listed at $135,000. Smith wishes to offer $122,000. (a) broker should contact owner about the price and prepare the offer if seller agrees, (b) broker should wait until Smith increases offer, (c) Brown must prepare the offer and present it, (d) Smith must obtain property appraisal.

ANSWERS TO MULTIPLE CHOICE QUESTIONS

1. c	26. c	51. c	76. c	101. c	126. c	151. c	176. c	201. b	226. b
2. b	27. c	52. c	77. a	102. b	127. b	152. c	177. b	202. c	227. c
3. a	28. c	53. d	78. c	103. c	128. b	153. d	178. c	203. b	228. a
4. c	29. b	54. d	79. b	104. c	129. b	154. c	179. b	204. c	229. d
5. c	30. d	55. a	80. d	105. d	130. c	155. a	180. a	205. d	230. a
6. a	31. c	56. a	81. c	106. c	131. c	156. c	181. c	206. c	231. c
7. a	32. c	57. c	82. b	107. c	132. c	157. b	182. d	207. c	232. b
8. c	33. d	58. d	83. c	108. c	133. b	158. c	183. d	208. d	233. a
9. c	34. b	59. c	84. b	109. c	134. c	159. b	184. c	209. b	234. c
10. c	35. c	60. c	85. c	110. a	135. c	160. a	185. a	210. a	235. d
11. c	36. c	61. c	86. c	111. a	136. c	161. d	186. d	211. b	236. c
12. d	37. d	62. a	87. a	112. c	137. d	162. c	187. c	212. c	237. a
13. a	38. d	63. c	88. d	113. b	138. c	163. a	188. b	213. c	238. c
14. c	39. c	64. c	89. b	114. c	139. d	164. c	189. c	214. c	239. d
15. c	40. b	65. c	90. d	115. a	140. a	165. c	190. d	215. c	240. c
16. c	41. b	66. c	91. c	116. a	141. c	166. c	191. b	216. c	241. b
17. c	42. d	67. c	92. d	117. c	142. c	167. d	192. c	217. b	242. c
18. c	43. a	68. c	93. d	118. c	143. c	168. c	193. b	218. b	243. d
19. b	44. d	69. c	94. c	119. c	144. d	169. b	194. b	219. c	244. c
20. c	45. d	70. d	95. c	120. c	145. b	170. c	195. c	220. d	245. c
21. c	46. c	71. b	96. b	121. a	146. c	171. a	196. c	221. c	246. d
22. d	47. b	72. c	97. c	122. a	147. d	172. a	197. c	222. a	247. c
23. c	48. c	73. c	98. a	123. c	148. c	173. d	198. d	223. d	248. b
24. a	49. b	74. d	99. d	124. c	149. c	174. c	199. b	224. a	249. a
25. a	50. c	75. a	100. c	125. a	150. b	175. a	200. c	225. c	250. c

Appendix C

FIGURE C2-1

INDEPENDENT CONTRACTOR APPLICATION

GENERAL INFORMATION

Name _____ Date _____

Address _____ Own ☐ Rent ☐ Phone _____

Birth Date _____ Social Security Number _____

If applicable:

Spouse's Name _____ Number of Dependents _____

Spouse Employed? _____ Position _____ How Long? _____

Do you belong to local Community and Civic organizations, etc., if so please list:
_____
_____

Vehicle: ☐ own ☐ lease Make _____ Type _____ Year _____

Do you carry auto liability insurance? _____ Amount? _____

Name of Carrier _____

If you do not carry any of the above insurance, would you be willing to secure it? _____

In Case of Accident Notify: _____ Telephone(s) _____

    Address _____

    My Doctor is: _____ Telephone(s) _____

EDUCATIONAL HISTORY

High School graduate? _____ College or University? _____

Major? _____ Years _____ Degree? _____

Advanced Real Estate courses? _____ How many units? _____ R. E. Certificate? _____

GRI courses? _____ How many units? _____ Graduate? _____

Other Real Estate designations? _____

State what special qualifications or training you have which you think will assist you in the Real Estate profession:
_____
_____

FIGURE C2–1 *(continued)*

REAL ESTATE HISTORY

First entered Real Estate _____ Where? _____

Type of license now held: Broker _____ Salesman _____ License # _____

Do you intend to engage in the Real Estate profession full time _____ Part-time _____

If part-time, when do you plan to become full-time? _____

Are you presently associated with a Broker? _____ How long? _____

Broker's name and address _____

Have you given notice that you intend to leave? _____ Why do you desire a change? _____

_____

Are you a member of a Real Estate Board? _____ Name _____

Membership Classification _____

Were you referred to this Company? _____ By Whom? _____

Why do you wish to associate with this Company? _____

_____

Do you know Associates in this Company? _____ If so, please list their names: _____

_____

PERSONAL REFERENCES

Please list three references:

NAME	ADDRESS	Years Known	POSITION	PHONE

When do you wish to start? _____

I hereby declare that my answers to the foregoing questions are true and correct, and that I have not knowingly withheld any fact or circumstance that would, if disclosed, effect my application unfavorably.

I authorize you to communicate with references, former employers or associates, and any others you desire to contact, including a credit information agency and agree to hold you and such persons harmless with respect to any information furnished.

Applicant _____

DATE OF INTERVIEW _____ NAME OF INTERVIEWER _____

FIGURE C3–1

EXCLUSIVE EMPLOYMENT OF BROKER TO EXCHANGE, SELL, LEASE OR OPTION
CALIFORNIA ASSOCIATION OF REALTORS® STANDARD FORM

THIS IS INTENDED TO BE A LEGALLY BINDING AGREEMENT – READ IT CAREFULLY

1. The undersigned _____
(PRINCIPAL), hereby grants to _____
a licensed real estate broker, hereinafter called "agent," the EXCLUSIVE AND IRREVOCABLE RIGHT commencing on _____, 19____ and terminating at midnight on _____, 19____ to advise, offer, solicit and negotiate for the disposition of the Principal's right, title, and interest, through exchange, sale, lease or option on terms acceptable to Principal of the real and personal property described as follows: _____

SUBJECT TO: _____

TERMS: _____

2. Agent is hereby authorized to accept and hold on my behalf a deposit from any offer or pending my acceptance. No offer shall be submitted to me unless signed by the offeror or his authorized agent.

3. I warrant that I am the owner of or have the right to obtain and deliver marketable title to the property described above. Evidence of title of the real property shall be in the form of a California Land Title Association Standard Coverage Policy of Title Insurance to be paid for by _____

4. Agent may ☐ may not ☐ place a for sale or exchange sign on the property.

5. Compensation to Agent: (a) I hereby agree to pay Agent a fee of $ _____ upon exchange, sale, lease or exercise of an option which has been executed during the term hereof or any extension thereof by Agent, or through any other person, or by me, or if said property is withdrawn from exchange, sale, lease or option without the consent of Agent, or made unmarketable by my voluntary act during the term hereof or any extension thereof; or

(b) If within _____ days after expiration hereof, or any extension thereof, I enter into an agreement with anyone with whom Agent has had negotiations prior to final expiration, provided I have received notice in writing thereof before or upon expiration of this agreement or any extension thereof.

6. If any action or proceeding be instituted to enforce this agreement, the prevailing party shall receive reasonable attorney's fees and costs.

7. In the event of an exchange agent may represent all parties and collect compensation or commission from them provided there is full disclosure to all principals of such Agency. Agent may cooperate with sub-agents and other agents and divide such compensation or commission in any manner acceptable to them.

8. Other Provisions: _____

NOTICE: The amount or rate of compensation is not fixed by law. They are set by each broker individually and may be negotiable between the seller and broker.

9. I acknowledge that I have read and understand this Agreement, and that I have received a copy hereof.

DATED: _____, 19____ _____, California

PRINCIPAL _____ PRINCIPAL _____

ADDRESS CITY STATE PHONE

10. In consideration of the above, Agent agrees to use diligence in the performance of his obligations.

AGENT ADDRESS CITY STATE

NO REPRESENTATION IS MADE AS TO THE LEGAL VALIDITY OF ANY PROVISION OR THE ADEQUACY OF ANY PROVISION IN ANY SPECIFIC TRANSACTION. A REAL ESTATE BROKER IS THE PERSON QUALIFIED TO ADVISE ON REAL ESTATE. IF YOU DESIRE LEGAL ADVICE CONSULT YOUR ATTORNEY.

FIGURE C3–2

SELLING YOUR HOME

Here's what a REALTOR® does for YOU!

1. A REALTOR® knows real estate values, can intelligently determine the fair market price of a home at the time of sale—helping to assure top dollar for your property.
2. A REALTOR® has a list of pre-screened prospects: people seriously interested in buying a home.
3. A REALTOR® is familiar with zoning codes, neighborhoods, schools, churches, transportation and shopping centers.
4. A REALTOR® does not have personal ties or fond memories concerning the property. Therefore, he or she is better able to answer all questions objectively and unemotionally.
5. Because of his or her many years of experience, a REALTOR® can offer many valuable suggestions on how to make your home more salable.
6. A REALTOR® knows how to advertise a property to gain maximum results, and has referrals from others.
7. A REALTOR® pre-screens all prospects, sets up appointments and personally shows the property. You are not bothered with lookers, curious and undesirable traffic.
8. A REALTOR® knows how to "sell" the property and obtain a firm offer without pressuring the buyer.
9. A REALTOR® knows how to assist the buyer in obtaining a mortgage, the amount of down payment required, points, escrow, property taxes, closing costs and utility bills.
10. At closing time, a REALTOR® will assist in guiding you through the paperwork to help assure that title evidence and all other documents are properly and legally executed.
11. A REALTOR® operates under a strict Code of Ethics enforced by the NATIONAL ASSOCIATION OF REALTORS®, assuring you the most competent, professional and ethical performance available.

REALTOR®

BUYING A HOME

Here's how a REALTOR® is of service to YOU!

1. A REALTOR® has a list of available properties in various neighborhoods and in different price ranges, and works closely with other REALTORS® in sharing information about what properties are available.
2. A REALTOR® is familiar with each house he or she offers for sale and, in most cases, has personally inspected the property.
3. Because a REALTOR® knows your financial position, your basic needs and desires, he or she will only show you homes that "fit the bill." He or she will not waste your time on properties you can't afford or would not be interested in.
4. A REALTOR® knows real estate values, can recommend homes that will fit your budget, and will answer all questions concerning zoning, the neighborhood, schools, churches, shopping centers and transportation.
5. A REALTOR® knows the tax structure of the communities he or she services and can intelligently answer questions such as cost of maintenance and utilities.
6. A REALTOR® does not have personal ties or fond memories concerning the property. He or she will answer all questions objectively, pointing out any defects or advantages in a particular home.
7. A REALTOR® is familiar with local lending institutions, knows how much down payment will be required, what the approximate monthly payments and closing costs will be.
8. A REALTOR® will work closely with you, showing you every available property that meets your specifications. He or she will never "high pressure" you into buying something that you're not completely satisfied with.
9. Once you select the home you want, a REALTOR® will help to guide you through the complex maze of title evidence and other legal documents to help protect your interest and investment.
10. A REALTOR® operates under a strict Code of Ethics enforced by the NATIONAL ASSOCIATION OF REALTORS®, assuring you the most competent, professional and ethical performance available.

APPENDIX C

FIGURE C3-3

MULTIPLE DWELLING UNITS—APARTMENTS
CALIFORNIA ASSOCIATION OF REALTORS® STANDARD FORM

This is an attachment to a listing contract (A-11/L-11/EX-11) — read it carefully.

LISTING NO. _____

HAVE _____ CITY _____ NUMBER OF UNITS _____
ADDRESS _____ CO. _____ STATE _____ LIST PRICE (LP) $_____
MOTIVATION _____ DP _____ RPT. PRESENT LOANS $_____
WANT _____ CAN ADD $ _____ RPT. GROSS EQUITY $_____

FINANCIAL ANALYSIS (Annual)

RPT. GROSS SCH. INCOME (GS)	$_____
RPT. VACANCY ALLOW. ____%	$_____
RPT. GROSS OPER. INC. (GOI)	$_____
RPT. OPERATING EXP. ____%	$_____
RPT. NET OPER. INC. (NOI)	$_____
LOAN PAYMENT (P & I)	$_____
RPT. GROSS SPEND. INC. (SI)	$_____
RESERVES (CAP. IMPROV.)	$_____
CAP. RATE (NOI ÷ LP)	____%
GROSS MULTI. (LP ÷ GSI) = _____ X GROSS	

ASS'D VAL. CODE AREA _____ Yr ___ / ___
LAND $_____ ____
IMPR. $_____ ____
PERS. PROP. $_____ ____
TOTAL $_____
LEGAL DES. LOT _____ B_K ____
SUBDIVISION _____ MAP NO. _____

(LEAVE BLANK)

Reserved for photograph—printing or writing in this space will not be reproduced. Material for this section should be identified and clipped to the back. This material should be no larger than this blank space. If the material is a map, sketch, or list it should be drawn or typed in black ink (blue will not reproduce). You may use this space for other remarks if no map or picture.

INSTRUCTIONS FOR LISTING
Complete all information requested. Listing may be withheld for clarification if incomplete.
This is an attachment to a listing contract. Read it carefully. If Sale attach A-11, if Exchange attach EX-11 and if Lease attach L-11.

ABBREVIATIONS, DEFINITIONS

DP = Down Payment P&I = Principal and Interest
GOI = Gross Operating Income RPT = Reported
GSI = Gross Scheduled Income SCH = Reported or Projected by Seller
LP = Listing Price SI = Gross Spendable Income
NOI = Net Operating Income

No.	BRS.	BA.	Rms.	RENT PER UNIT	MONTH	RPT. OPER. EXP. ANN.	
				$	$	TAXES EST. NEW	$
				$	$	INS. — F & L	$
				$	$	WK. COMP.	$
				$	$	GAS & ELEC.	$
				$	$	WATER/SEWER	$
				$	$	TRASH	$
				$	$	SUPPLIES	$
				$	$	ELEVATOR	$
				$	$	CABLE T.V.	$
				$	$	MAINT. ____%	$
				$	$	PEST CONT.	$
				$	$	LICENSES	$
				$	$	GARDENER	$
			TOTAL	$		POOL	$

LOAN INFORMATION as of _____ 19 ___
1st TD $_____ @ $_____ Mo. P & I @___%
Due _____ Lender _____ Loan No. _____
Assumable _____ V/R/FIXED FEE _____
2nd TD $_____ @ $_____ Mo. P & I @___%
Due _____ Lender _____ Loan No. _____
Assumable _____ V/R/FIXED FEE _____

Other Terms—Remarks: _____

NO. APTS. LEASED: ____ MO. MO. ____ FURN. ____ MANAGER $____
OTHER INCOME $____ PROF. MGMT. $____
GARAGES NO. ____ @ $____ $____ FURN. REPL. $____
LAUNDRY EQUIP. OWNED $____ ____ $____
RPT. MONTHLY GROSS SCH. INC. $____ TOTAL $____

ADDITIONS, ALTERATIONS, REPAIRS YES ____ NO ____
RPT. BLDG. PERMITS AND INSP. YES ____ NO ____
PARKING _____ GARAGES NO. _____ SPACES NO. _____
CARPORTS NO. _____ PATIO _____ RECR. ROOM _____
TYPE PLUMBING _____

ZONING ____ LOT SIZE ____ X ____ NO. BLDGS. ____ AGE ____ TENANTS PAY: GAS ____ ELEC. ____ WATER ____ REFUSE ____
CONST. ____ STORIES ____ SEWER ____ HEAT ____ A/COND. ____ ELEV. ____ FLOORS ____ CARPETS NO. ____ DRAPES NO. ____ RANGES NO. ____ REFRIGS. NO. ____
DISPOSALS ____ CIRC. H/WTR. ____ D/WASH ____ TILE: ____ KITCHEN ____ BATH ____ POOL ____ HEATED ____ SAUNA ____ ALLEY ____ PAVED ____

TO SHOW CONTACT: LISTING OFFICE _____ OWNER _____ OTHER _____ PHONE (___) _____
PROP. ZIP CODE _____ COMMISSION TO COOP. OFFICE % _____ /$_____

BROKER _____ ADD. _____ CITY _____ STATE _____
OFFICE PHONE (___) _____ SALESMAN _____ HOME PHONE (___) _____

All information is from sources believed reliable but is not guaranteed.
Owner certifies that the above information as to income and expenses is accurate and complete to the best of his knowledge.

OWNER _____ OWNER _____
This listing expires _____ DATE _____

FIGURE C3–4

COMMERCIAL-INDUSTRIAL BUILDINGS
CALIFORNIA ASSOCIATION OF REALTORS® STANDARD FORM

This is an attachment to a listing contract (A-11/L-11/EX-11) — read it carefully.

LISTING NO. _____

HAVE _____ CITY _____ NO. TENANTS _____
ADDRESS _____ CO: _____ STATE _____ LIST PRICE (LP) $ _____
MOTIVATION _____ DP _____ RPT. PRESENT LOANS $ _____
WANT _____ CAN ADD $ _____ RPT. GROSS EQUITY $ _____

FINANCIAL ANALYSIS (Annual)

RPT. GROSS SCH. INCOME (GS) $ _____
RPT. VACANCY ALLOW. _____ % $ _____
RPT. GROSS OPER. INC. (GOI) $ _____
RPT. OPERATING EXP. _____ % $ _____
RPT. NET OPER. INCOME. (NOI) $ _____
LOAN PAYMENT (P & I) $ _____
RPT. GROSS SPEND. INC. (SI) $ _____
RESERVES (CAP. IMPROV.) $ _____
CAP. RATE (NOI ÷ LP) _____ %
GROSS MULTI. (LP ÷ GSI) = _____ X GROSS

ASS'D VAL. CODE AREA _____ Yr ____ / ____
LAND $ _____ _____ %
IMPR. $ _____ _____ %
PERS. PROP. $ _____ _____ %
TOTAL $ _____
LEGAL DES. LOT _____ BLK. _____
SUBDIVISION _____ MAP NO. _____

(LEAVE BLANK)

Reserved for photograph — printing or writing in this space will not be reproduced. Material for this section should be identified and clipped to the back. This material should be no larger than this blank space. If the material is a map, sketch, or list it should be drawn or typed in black ink (blue will not reproduce). You may use this space for other remarks if no map or picture.

INSTRUCTIONS FOR LISTING

Complete all information requested. Listing may be withheld for clarification if incomplete.
This is an attachment to a listing contract. Read it carefully. If Sale attach A-11, if Exchange attach EX-11 and if Lease attach L-11.

ABBREVIATIONS, DEFINITIONS

DP = Down Payment
GOI = Gross Operating Income
GSI = Gross Scheduled Income
LP = Listing Price
NOI = Net Operating Income
P&I = Principal and Interest
RPT = Reported
SCH = Reported or Projected by Seller
SI = Gross Spendable Income

Unit No.	TENANT	SIZE	LEASE Length	LEASE Expires	Base Rent-Mo
					$
					$
					$
					$
					$
					$
					$
					$
					$
					$

RPT. GROSS SCHEDULED INCOME $ _____ Mo.
RPT. OVERAGE PAID $ _____ Yr.
RPT. TOTAL ANNUAL INCOME (GSI) $ _____ Yr.

LOAN INFORMATION as of _____ 19 ____
1st TD $ _____ @ $ _____ Mo. P & I @ ____ %
Due _____ Lender _____ Loan No. _____
Assumable _____ VIR/FIXED ____ FEE _____
2nd TD $ _____ @ $ _____ Mo. P & I @ ____ %
Due _____ Lender _____ Loan No. _____
Assumable _____ VIR/FIXED ____ FEE _____
Other Terms — Remarks: _____

LOT SIZE _____ X _____ ZONING _____
NO. BLDGS. _____ AGE _____
STORIES _____ ELEVATORS _____

RPT. OPERATING EXPENSES (Annual)

TAXES YR. ____ $ _____   MANAGEMENT $ _____
____ / ____ $ _____   ELEVATOR $ _____
FIRE INSURANCE $ _____   GARDENER $ _____
LIABILITY INSUR. $ _____   PARKING LOTS $ _____
GAS & ELECTRIC $ _____   TRASH JANITOR $ _____
WATER $ _____   _____ $ _____
MAINTENANCE ____ %   _____ $ _____
                                   TOTAL $ _____

CONSTRUCTION _____
PARKING SPACES _____ RAIL _____ DOCK _____
ROOF _____ AGE _____ SPAN _____
CEILING HEIGHT _____ GAS _____
HEAT _____ TYPE _____
SEWER _____ H/WTR. _____ CAP. _____
ELEC: ____ VOLT ____ AMP. ____ PHASE _____
AIR COND. _____ TYPE _____ BASEMENT _____

TO SHOW CONTACT: LISTING OFFICE _____ OWNER _____ OTHER _____ PHONE (____) _____
PROP. ZIP CODE _____ COMMISSION TO COOP. OFFICE % _____ /$ _____

BROKER _____ ADD. _____ CITY _____ STATE _____
OFFICE PHONE (____) _____ SALESMAN _____ HOME PHONE (____) _____

All information is from sources believed reliable but is not guaranteed.
Owner certifies that the above information as to income and expenses is accurate and complete to the best of his knowledge.

OWNER _____ OWNER _____
This listing expires _____ DATE _____

APPENDIX C

FIGURE C4–1

RESIDENTIAL ANALYSIS

PURCHASE PRICE	: 180,000
AMOUNT OF LOAN #1	: 144,000
INTEREST RATE LOAN #1	: 12.5
TERM IN YEARS LOAN #1	: 30
IF ASUMP – CURRENT YEAR #	:
AMOUNT OF LOAN #2	:
ANNUAL REAL ESTATE TAXES	: 2,160
TAX GROWTH RATE	: 2
ANNUAL APPRECIATION RATE	: 15
EST. ANNUAL HAZARD INS.	: 600
MONTHLY ASSOCIATION FEE	:
BUYERS EST. TAX BRACKET	: 40
CURRENT MONTHLY RENT	:

	YEAR 1	YEAR 2	YEAR 3	YEAR 5	YEAR 10
MONTHLY					
PAYMENT (PITI)	1,766.85	1,777.95	1,790.25	1,819.14	1,927.86
− TAX SAVINGS	671.13	670.50	669.63	667.00	652.97
− PAID ON LOAN(S)	39.04	44.21	50.06	64.20	119.55
ACTUAL COST	1,056.69	1,063.25	1,070.56	1,087.95	1,155.35
− APPRECIATION	2,250.00	2,587.50	2,975.63	3,935.26	7,915.23
EFFECTIVE COST	−1,193.31	−1,524.25	−1,905.06	−2,847.32	−6,759.88
YEARLY					
+ PAID ON LOAN(S)	468.47	530.48	600.72	770.34	1,434.58
+ INTEREST	17,973.75	17,911.74	17,841.50	17,671.88	17,007.64
+ PROPERTY TAXES	2,160.00	2,203.20	2,247.26	2,338.05	2,581.40
+ HAZARD INS.	600.00	690.00	793.50	1,049.40	2,110.73
TOTAL CASH OUTLAY	21,202.22	21,335.42	21,482.98	21,829.68	23,134.35
TAX SAVINGS	8,053.50	8,045.97	8,035.51	8,003.97	7,335.62
TOTAL					
PAID ON LOAN(S)	468.47	998.95	1,599.67	3,050.30	8,730.63
INTEREST PAID	17,973.75	35,885.49	53,726.99	89,160.80	175,691.58
PROPERTY VALUE	207,000.00	238,050.00	273,757.50	362,044.28	728,200.44
− LOAN BALANCE(S)	143,531.53	143,001.05	142,400.33	140,949.70	135,269.38
EQUITY	63,468.47	95,048.95	131,357.17	221,094.58	592,931.06
EFFECTIVE COST	−14,319.75	−32,610.79	−55,471.54	−117,757.95	−416,412.47

FIGURE C5-1

RECEIPT FOR INCREASED DEPOSIT AND SUPPLEMENT TO REAL ESTATE PURCHASE CONTRACT

CALIFORNIA ASSOCIATION OF REALTORS® STANDARD FORM

THIS IS INTENDED TO BE A LEGALLY BINDING CONTRACT. READ IT CAREFULLY.

Received from _____ herein called Buyer, the sum of _____

Dollars ($_____) evidenced by cash ☐, personal check ☐, cashier's check ☐ as additional deposit payable to _____ for the purchase of the property described in the Real Estate Purchase Contract and Receipt for Deposit dated _____, executed by _____ as Buyer and accepted by Seller on _____, 19_____.

DATE _____

Real Estate Broker _____ By _____

The following is hereby incorporated in and made a part of said Real Estate Purchase Contract and Receipt for Deposit, which remains in full force and effect:

Buyer hereby increases the total deposit to $_____ and Buyer and Seller agree that should Buyer fail to complete the purchase by reason of any default of Buyer, Seller shall retain the total deposit as liquidated damages. If the described property is a dwelling with no more than four units, one of which the Buyer intends to occupy as his residence, Seller shall retain as liquidated damages the deposit actually paid, or an amount therefrom, not more than 3% of the purchase price, and promptly return any excess to Buyer.

The undersigned agree to the above and acknowledge receipt of a copy hereof.

Date _____ Date _____

Buyer _____ Seller _____

FIGURE C5–2

RELEASE OF REAL ESTATE PURCHASE CONTRACT AND RECEIPT FOR DEPOSIT

CALIFORNIA ASSOCIATION OF REALTORS® STANDARD FORM
THIS IS INTENDED TO BE A LEGALLY BINDING CONTRACT. READ IT CAREFULLY.

The undersigned Buyer and Seller who were parties to that certain Real Estate Purchase Contract and Receipt for Deposit dated, _____, 19____, covering the following described property:

_____
_____
_____
_____
_____
_____
_____
_____

hereby mutually release each other from any and all claims, actions or demands which each may have up to the date of this Agreement against the other by reason of said Real Estate Purchase Contract and Receipt for Deposit.

It is the intent of this Agreement that all rights and obligations arising out of said Real Estate Purchase Contract and Receipt for Deposit are declared null and void.

_____ holding
(Name of Broker or Escrow Holder)

the deposit under the terms of said Real Estate Purchase Contract and Receipt for Deposit is hereby directed and instructed to disburse said deposit in the following manner:

$_____ TO _____
$_____ TO _____
$_____ TO _____
$_____ TO _____

Dated _____   Dated _____

Buyer _____   Seller _____

Dated _____   Dated _____

Broker _____   Broker _____

By _____   By _____

FIGURE C5–3

INTERIM OCCUPANCY AGREEMENT
(Buyer in Possession)

THIS IS INTENDED TO BE A LEGALLY BINDING AGREEMENT — READ IT CAREFULLY

CALIFORNIA ASSOCIATION OF REALTORS® STANDARD FORM

_____, California _____, 19____.
_____, "LESSOR" and
_____, "LESSEE" agree:

1. On _____, 19____, LESSOR as SELLER and LESSEE as BUYER entered into an agreement for the sale and purchase of the real property commonly known as _____, _____, California ("Premises") and the escrow thereof is scheduled to close on or before _____, _____, 19____.

2. Pending completion of sale and close of escrow, LESSEE is to be given immediate occupancy of the premises in accordance with the terms of this agreement.

3. LESSEE acknowledges an inspection of, and has found the premises in satisfactory condition and ready for occupancy, except as follows: _____
_____.

4. LESSEE shall pay to LESSOR for the occupancy of said premises the sum of $ _____ per _____
                                                                                              day/week/month
commencing _____, 19____, to and including _____
                                                           specific date/other
_____. Said sum shall be paid _____ in advance.
                                                       weekly/monthly
Prorations, if any, shall be predicated upon a 30 day month. As additional consideration, LESSEE shall pay for all utilities and services based upon occupancy of the premises and the following charges: _____
except _____ which shall be paid by LESSOR.

5. If the purchase and sale agreement between LESSOR and LESSEE is not completed within its designated term, or any written extension thereof through no fault of LESSOR, LESSEE agrees to vacate the premises upon service of a written notice in the form and manner provided by law. Any holding over thereafter shall create a day-to-day tenancy with a fair rental value of $ _____ per day. Except as to daily rent and tenancy, all other covenants and conditions herein contained shall remain in full force and effect.

6. Except as provided by law LESSEE shall keep the premises and yards clean, sanitary, and in good order and repair during the term hereof and shall surrender the same in like condition if the said sale is not completed, reasonable wear and tear excepted. Additionally, LESSEE shall save and hold LESSOR harmless from any and all claims, demands, damages or liabilities arising out of LESSEE'S occupancy of the premises caused or permitted by LESSEE, LESSEE'S family, agents, servants, employees, guests and invitees.

7. As additional consideration passing from LESSEE to LESSOR, LESSEE shall obtain and maintain during the term of this agreement public liability insurance naming both LESSOR and LESSEE as co-insureds in the amount of not less than $ _____ for injury to one person; $ _____ for injury to a group; and $ _____ for property damage. If permitted, LESSOR agrees to retain his fire insurance on the premises until close of escrow. Otherwise, LESSEE shall obtain fire insurance on the premises in a sum of not less than that designated as the sales price of the subject property.

8. The premises are to be used as a residence only by LESSEE and his immediate family and no animal, bird or pet except _____
_____ shall be kept on or about the premises without LESSOR'S prior written consent. LESSEE shall not violate any law or ordinance in the use of the premises, nor permit waste or nuisance upon or about the premises and, except as provided by law, LESSEE shall not make any additions, alterations, or repairs to the premises without the prior written consent of LESSOR.

9. $ _____ as security has been deposited. LESSOR may use therefrom such amounts as are reasonably necessary to remedy LESSEE defaults in the payment of rent, to repair damages caused by LESSEE, or to clean the premises if necessary upon the termination of tenancy. If used toward rent or damages during the term of this agreement, LESSEE agrees to reinstate said total security deposit upon 5 days written notice delivered to LESSEE in person or by mail. The balance of the security deposit, if any, shall be mailed to LESSEE'S last known address within 14 days of surrender of premises. Alternatively, and upon completion of sale, said security deposit shall be mailed to LESSEE at the subject premises within 10 days of close of escrow.

10. In the event of any action or proceeding between LESSOR and LESSEE under this agreement, the prevailing party shall be entitled to recover reasonable attorney's fees and costs.

11. The right to occupy the premises as granted LESSEE herein is personal to LESSEE and any attempt to assign, transfer, or hypotecate the same shall be null and void.

12. The undersigned LESSEE acknowledges having read the foregoing and receipt of a copy.

LESSOR and LESSEE have executed this agreement on the day and year above written.

_____ _____
LESSOR   LESSEE

_____ _____
LESSOR   LESSEE

NO REPRESENTATION IS MADE AS TO THE LEGAL VALIDITY OF ANY PROVISION OR THE ADEQUACY OF ANY PROVISION IN ANY SPECIFIC TRANSACTION. A REAL ESTATE BROKER IS THE PERSON QUALIFIED TO ADVISE ON REAL ESTATE. IF YOU DESIRE LEGAL ADVICE CONSULT YOUR ATTORNEY.

SPECIAL STUDIES ZONE DISCLOSURE

CALIFORNIA ASSOCIATION OF REALTORS® STANDARD FORM

This Addendum is attached as Page_____ of _____ Pages to the Real Estate Purchase Contract and Receipt for Deposit dated _____, 19_____ in which _____
_____
is referred to as Buyer and _____
_____ is referred to as Seller.

The property which is the subject of the contract is situated in a Special Study Zone as designated under Sections 2621-2625, inclusive, of the California Public Resources Code; and, as such, the construction or development on this property of any structure for human occupancy may be subject to the findings of a geologic report prepared by a geologist registered in the State of California, unless such report is waived by the city or county under the terms of that act. No representations on the subject are made by Seller or Agent, and the Buyer should make his own inquiry or investigation.

Note: California Public Resources Code #2621.5 excludes structures in existence prior to May 4, 1975;
California Public Resources Code #2621.6 excludes wood frame dwellings not exceeding two (2) stories in height and mobile homes over eight (8) feet in width;
California Public Resources Code #2621.7 excludes conversion of existing apartment houses into condominiums;
California Public Resources Code #2621.8 excludes alterations and additions under 50% of value of structure from the Special Studies Zone Act.

Buyer is allowed_____days from date of Seller's acceptance to make further inquiries at appropriate governmental agencies concerning the use of the subject property under the terms of the Special Study Zone Act and local building, zoning, fire, health and safety codes. When such inquiries disclose conditions or information unsatisfactory to the Buyer, Buyer may cancel this agreement. If notice in writing has not been delivered within such time, this condition shall be deemed waived.

Receipt of a copy is hereby acknowledged.

DATED:_____, 19_____   BUYER_____

_____

Receipt of a copy is hereby acknowledged.

DATED:_____, 19_____   SELLER:_____

_____

FIGURE C7-1

DO NOT DESTROY THIS ORIGINAL NOTE: When paid, said original note, together with the Deed of Trust securing same, must be surrendered to Trustee for cancellation and retention before reconveyance will be made.

ALL INCLUSIVE PURCHASE MONEY PROMISSORY NOTE SECURED BY LONG FORM ALL-INCLUSIVE PURCHASE MONEY DEED OF TRUST
(Installment Note, Interest Included)

$ _____   _____, California, _____, 19___

In installments as herein stated, for value received, I/We ("Maker") promise to pay to _____
_____
_____
("Payee") or order, at _____
the principal sum of _____ DOLLARS,
with interest from _____ on unpaid principal at the rate of
_____ per cent per annum; principal and interest payable in installments of _____
_____
or more on the _____ day of each _____ month, beginning
on the _____ day of _____ 19_____, and continuing until said principal and interest have been paid.

Each installment shall be applied first on the interest then due and the remainder on principal; and interest shall thereupon cease upon the principal so credited.

The total principal amount of this Note includes the unpaid principal balance of the promissory note(s) ("Underlying Note(s)") secured by Deed(s) of Trust, more particularly described as follows:

1. (A) PROMISSORY NOTE:
   Maker: _____
   Payee: _____
   Original Amount: _____
   Date: _____

   (B) DEED OF TRUST:
   Beneficiary: _____
   Original Amount: _____
   Recordation Date: _____
   Document No. _____ Book _____ Page _____
   Place of Recordation: _____, County, California

2. (A) PROMISSORY NOTE:
   Maker: _____
   Payee: _____
   Original Amount: _____
   Date: _____

   (B) DEED OF TRUST:
   Beneficiary: _____
   Original Amount: _____
   Recordation Date: _____
   Document No. _____ Book _____ Page _____
   Place of Recordation: _____, County, California

By Payee's acceptance of this Note, Payee covenants and agrees that, provided Maker is not delinquent or in default under the terms of this Note, Payee shall pay all installments of principal and interest which shall hereafter become due pursuant to the provisions of the Underlying Note(s) as and when the same become due and payable. In the event Maker shall be delinquent or in default under the terms of this Note, Payee shall not be obligated to make any payments required by the terms of the Underlying Note(s) until such delinquency or default is cured. In the event Payee fails to timely pay any installment of principal or interest on the Underlying Note(s) at the time when Maker is not delinquent or in default hereunder, Maker may, at Maker's option, make such payments directly to the holder of such Underlying Note(s), in which event Maker shall be entitled to a credit against the next installment(s) of principal and interest due under the terms of this Note equal to the amount so paid and including, without limitation, any penalty, charges and expenses paid by Maker to the holder of the Underlying Note(s) on account of Payee failing to make such payment. The obligations of Payee hereunder shall terminate upon the earliest of (i) foreclosure of the lien of the All-Inclusive Purchase Money Deed of Trust securing this Note, or (ii) cancellation of this Note and reconveyance of the All-Inclusive Purchase Money Deed of Trust securing same.

Should Maker be delinquent or in default under the terms of this Note, and Payee consequently incurs any penalties, charges or other expenses on account of the Underlying Note(s) during the period of such delinquency or default, the amount of such penalties, charges and expenses shall be immediately added to the principal amount of this Note and shall be immediately payable by Maker to Payee.

OFC 1017

FIGURE C7-1 *(continued)*

Notwithstanding anything to the contrary herein contained, the right of Maker to prepay all or any portion of the principal of this Note is limited to the same extent as any limitation exists in the right to prepay the principal of the Underlying Note(s). If any prepayments of principal of this Note shall, by reason of the application of any portion thereof by Payee to the prepayment of principal of the Underlying Note(s), constitute such prepayment for which the holders of the Underlying Note(s) are entitled to receive a prepayment penalty or consideration, the amount of such prepayment penalty or consideration shall be paid by Maker to Payee upon demand, and any such amount shall not reduce the unpaid balance of principal or interest hereunder.

At any time when the total of the unpaid principal balance of this Note, accrued interest thereon, all other sums due pursuant to the terms hereof, and all sums advanced by Payee pursuant to the terms of the All-Inclusive Purchase Money Deed of Trust securing this Note, is equal to or less than the unpaid balance of principal and interest then due under the terms of the Underlying Note(s), Payee, at his option, shall cancel this Note and deliver same to Maker and execute a request for full reconveyance of the Deed of Trust securing this Note.

Should default be made by Maker in payment of any installments of principal, interest, or any other sums due hereunder, the whole sum of principal, interest and all other sums due from Maker hereunder, after first deducting therefrom all sums then due under the terms of the Underlying Note(s), shall become immediately due at the option of the holder of this Note. Principal, interest and all other sums due hereunder payable in lawful money of the United States. If action be instituted of this Note, I/we promise to pay such sums as the Court may fix as attorney's fees. This Note is secured by a **LONG FORM ALL-INCLUSIVE PURCHASE MONEY DEED OF TRUST** to **FOUNDERS TITLE COMPANY**, a California corporation, as Trustee.

_____   _____

_____   _____

_____   _____

(Maker)   (Maker)

The undersigned hereby accept(s) the foregoing All-Inclusive Purchase Money Promissory Note and agree(s) to perform each and all of the terms thereof on the part of Payee to be performed.

Executed as of the date and place first above written.

_____   _____

_____   _____

_____   _____

(Payee)   (Payee)

(THIS NOTE IS FOR USE ONLY IN PURCHASE MONEY TRANSACTIONS. IT IS RECOMMENDED THAT PRIOR TO THE EXECUTION OF THIS NOTE, THE PARTIES CONSULT WITH THEIR ATTORNEYS WITH RESPECT THERETO.)

FIGURE C7-2

```
                RECORDING REQUESTED BY


                AND WHEN RECORDED MAIL TO

    Name   ┌                         ┐
   Street
   Address
    City &
    State  └                         ┘
                                              SPACE ABOVE THIS LINE FOR RECORDER'S USE
```

LONG FORM ALL-INCLUSIVE PURCHASE MONEY DEED OF TRUST AND ASSIGNMENT OF RENTS

This All-Inclusive Purchase Money Deed of Trust, made this _____ day of, _____
between _____,
herein called TRUSTOR, whose address is _____
                            (number and street)   (city)   (state)   (zip)
                FOUNDERS TITLE COMPANY, A California corporation, herein called TRUSTEE, and
_____, herein called BENEFICIARY,
Witnesseth: That Trustor IRREVOCABLY GRANTS, TRANSFERS AND ASSIGNS to TRUSTEE IN TRUST, WITH POWER OF SALE, that property in _____ County, California described as:

TOGETHER WITH the rents, issues and profits thereof, SUBJECT, HOWEVER, to the right, power and authority hereinafter given to and conferred upon Beneficiary to collect and apply such rents, issues and profits.
For the Purpose of Securing:
    1. Performance of each agreement of Trustor herein contained. 2. Payment of the indebtedness evidenced by one all-inclusive purchase money promissory note of even date herewith, and any extension or renewal thereof, in the principal sum of $_____ executed by Trustor in favor of Beneficiary or order.
Underlying Obligations:
    This is an all-inclusive purchase money deed of trust, securing an all-inclusive purchase money promissory note in the original principal amount of _____ Dollars ($ _____)
(the "Note") which includes within such amount the unpaid balance of the following:
    (a) A promissory note in the original principal sum of _____ Dollars ($ _____)
in favor of _____
as Payee, secured by a deed of trust recorded _____, 19 ____, as Document No. _____, in Book _____,
Page _____, Official Records of _____ County, California, and
    (b) A promissory note in the original principal sum of _____ Dollars ($ _____)
in favor of _____
as Payee, secured by a deed of trust recorded _____, 19 ____, as Document No. _____, in Book _____,
Page _____, Official Records of _____ County, California.
(The Promissory Notes secured by such deeds of trust are hereinafter called the "Underlying Notes").
To Protect the Security of This Deed of Trust, Trustor Agrees:
    (1) To keep said property in good condition and repair; not to remove or demolish any building thereon; to complete or restore promptly and in good and workmanlike manner any building which may be constructed, damaged or destroyed thereon and to pay when due all claims for labor performed and materials furnished therefor; to comply with all laws affecting said property or requiring any alterations or improvements to be made thereon; not to commit or permit waste thereof; not to commit, suffer or permit any act upon said property in violation of law; to cultivate, irrigate, fertilize, fumigate, prune and do all other acts which from the character or use of said property may be reasonably necessary, the specific enumerations herein not excluding the general.
    (2) To provide, maintain and deliver to Beneficiary fire, vandalism and malicious mischief insurance satisfactory to and with loss payable to Beneficiary. The amount collected under any fire or other insurance policy may be applied by Beneficiary upon any indebtedness secured hereby and in such order as Beneficiary may determine, or at option of Beneficiary the entire amount so collected or any part thereof may be released to Trustor.
    Such application or release shall not cure or waive any default or notice of default hereunder or invalidate any act done pursuant to such notice. The provisions hereof are subject to the mutual agreements of the parties as below set forth.
    (3) To appear in and defend any action or proceeding purporting to affect the security hereof or the rights or powers of Beneficiary or Trustee; and to pay all costs and expenses, including cost of evidence of title and attorney's fees in a reasonable sum, in any such action or proceeding in which Beneficiary or Trustee may appear, and in any suit brought by Beneficiary to foreclose this Deed.
    (4) To pay: at least ten days before delinquency all taxes and assessments affecting said property, including assessments on appurtenant water stock; subject to the mutual agreements of the parties as below set forth, to pay when due, all incumbrances, charges and liens, with interest, on said property or any part thereof, which appear to be prior or superior hereto; all costs, fees and expenses of this Trust.
    Should Trustor fail to make any payment or to do any act as herein provided, then Beneficiary or Trustee, but without obligation so to do and without notice to or demand upon Trustor and without releasing Trustor from any obligation hereof, may: make or do the same in such manner and to such extent as either may deem necessary to protect the security hereof, Beneficiary or Trustee being authorized to enter upon said property for such purposes; appear in

OFC 1016

FIGURE C7-2 (continued)

and defend any action or proceeding purporting to affect the security hereof or the rights or powers of Beneficiary or Trustee; pay, purchase, contest or compromise any incumbrance, charge or lien which in the judgment of either appears to be prior or superior hereto; and, in exercising any such powers, pay necessary expenses, employ counsel and pay his reasonable fees.

(5) To pay immediately and without demand all sums so expended by Beneficiary or Trustee, with interest from date of expenditure at the amount allowed by law in effect at the date hereof, and to pay for any statement provided for by law in effect at the date hereof regarding the obligation secured hereby any amount demanded by the Beneficiary not to exceed the maximum allowed by law at the time when said statement is demanded.

(6) That any award of damages in connection with any condemnation for public use of or injury to said property or any part thereof is hereby assigned and shall be paid to Beneficiary who may apply or release such moneys received by him in the same manner and with the same effect as above provided for disposition of proceeds of fire or other insurance. The provisions hereof are subject to the mutual agreements of the parties as below set forth.

(7) That by accepting payment of any sum secured hereby after its due date, Beneficiary does not waive his right either to require prompt payment when due of all other sums so secured or to declare default for failure so to pay.

(8) That at any time or from time to time, without liability therefor and without notice, upon written request of Beneficiary and presentation of this Deed and said note for endorsement, and without affecting the personal liability of any person for payment of the indebtedness secured hereby, Trustee may: reconvey any part of said property; consent to the making of any map or plat thereof; join in granting any easement thereon; or join in any extension agreement or any agreement subordinating the lien or charge hereof.

(9) That upon written request of Beneficiary stating that all sums secured hereby have been paid, and upon surrender of this Deed and said note to Trustee for cancellation and retention and upon payment of its fees, Trustee shall reconvey, without warranty, the property then held hereunder. The recitals in such reconveyance of any matters or facts shall be conclusive proof of the truthfulness thereof. The grantee in such reconveyance may be described as "the person or persons legally entitled thereto." Five years after issuance of such full reconveyance, Trustee may destroy said note and this Deed (unless directed in such request to retain them).

(10) That as additional security, Trustor hereby gives to and confers upon Beneficiary the right, power and authority, during the continuance of these Trusts, to collect the rents, issues and profits of said property, reserving unto Trustor the right, prior to any default by Trustor in payment of any indebtedness secured hereby or in performance of any agreement hereunder, to collect and retain such rents, issues and profits as they become due and payable. Upon any such default, Beneficiary may at any time without notice, either in person, by agent, or by a receiver to be appointed by a court, and without regard to the adequacy of any security for the indebtedness hereby secured, enter upon and take possession of said property or any part thereof, in his own name sue for or otherwise collect such rents, issues and profits, including those past due and unpaid, and apply the same, less costs and expenses of operation and collection, including reasonable attorney's fees, upon any indebtedness secured hereby, and in such order as Beneficiary may determine. The entering upon and taking possession of said property, the collection of such rents, issues and profits and the application thereof as aforesaid, shall not cure or waive any default or notice of default hereunder or invalidate any act done pursuant to such notice.

(11) That upon default by Trustor in payment of any indebtedness secured hereby or in performance of any agreement hereunder, Beneficiary may declare all sums secured hereby immediately due and payable by delivery to Trustee of written declaration of default and demand for sale and of written notice of default and of election to cause to be sold said property, which notice Trustee shall cause to be filed for record. Beneficiary also shall deposit with Trustee this Deed, said note and all documents evidencing expenditures secured hereby.

After the lapse of such time as may then be required by law following the recordation of said notice of default, and notice of sale having been given as then required by law, Trustee, without demand on Trustor, shall sell said property at the time and place fixed by it in said notice of sale, either as a whole or in separate parcels, and in such order as it may determine, at public auction to the highest bidder for cash in lawful money of the United States, payable at time of sale. Trustee may postpone sale of all or any portion of said property by public announcement at such time and place of sale, and from time to time thereafter may postpone such sale by public announcement at the time fixed by the preceding postponement. Trustee shall deliver to such purchaser its deed conveying the property so sold, but without any covenant or warranty, express or implied. The recitals in such deed of any matters or facts shall be conclusive proof of the truthfulness thereof. Any person, including Trustor, Trustee, or Beneficiary as hereinafter defined, may purchase at such sale.

After deducting all costs, fees and expenses of Trustee and of this Trust, including cost of evidence of title in connection with sale, Trustee shall apply the proceeds of sale to payment of: all sums expended under the terms hereof, not then repaid, with accrued interest at the amount allowed by law in effect at the date hereof; all other sums then secured hereby; and the remainder, if any, to the person or persons legally entitled thereto.

(12) Beneficiary, or any successor in ownership of any indebtedness secured hereby, may from time to time, by instrument in writing, substitute a successor or successors to any Trustee named herein or acting hereunder, which instrument, executed by the Beneficiary and duly acknowledged and recorded in the office of the recorder of the county or counties where said property is situated, shall be conclusive proof of proper substitution of such successor Trustee or Trustees, who shall, without conveyance from the Trustee predecessor, succeed to all its title, estate, rights, powers and duties. Said instrument must contain the name of the original Trustor, Trustee and Beneficiary hereunder, the book and page where this Deed is recorded and the name and address of the new Trustee.

(13) That this Deed applies to, inures to the benefit of, and binds all parties hereto, their heirs, legatees, devisees, administrators, executors, successors and assigns. The term Beneficiary shall mean the owner and holder, including pledgees, of the note secured hereby, whether or not named as Beneficiary herein. In this Deed, whenever the context so requires, the masculine gender includes the feminine and/or neuter, and the singular number includes the plural.

(14) That Trustee accepts this Trust when this Deed, duly executed and acknowledged, is made a public record as provided by law. Trustee is not obligated to notify any party hereto of pending sale under any other Deed of Trust or of any action or proceeding in which Trustor, Beneficiary or Trustee shall be a party unless brought by Trustee.

The Undersigned Trustor requests that a copy of any Notice of Default and of any Notice of Sale hereunder be mailed to him at his address hereinbefore set forth.

Trustor and Beneficiary Mutually Agree:

(A) By Beneficiary's acceptance of this All-Inclusive Purchase Money Deed of Trust, Beneficiary covenants and agrees that provided Trustor is not delinquent or in default under the terms of the Note secured hereby, Beneficiary shall pay all installments of principal and interest which shall hereafter become due pursuant to the provisions of the Underlying Note(s) as and when the same become due and payable. In the event Trustor shall be delinquent or in default under the terms of the Note secured hereby, Beneficiary shall not be obligated to make any payments required by the terms of the Underlying Note(s) until such delinquency or default is cured. In the event Beneficiary fails to timely pay any installment of principal or interest on the Underlying Note(s) at the time when Trustor is not delinquent or in default under the terms of the Note secured hereby, Trustor may, at Trustor's option make such payments directly to the holder of such Underlying Note(s), in which event Trustor shall be entitled to a credit against the next installment(s) of principal and interest due under the terms of the Note secured hereby equal to the amount so paid and including, without limitation, any penalty, charges and expenses paid by Trustor to the holder of the Underlying Note(s) on account of Beneficiary's failing to make such payment. The obligations of Beneficiary hereunder shall terminate upon the earlier of (i) foreclosure of the lien of this All-Inclusive Purchase Money Deed of Trust, or (ii) cancellation of the Note secured hereby and reconveyance of this All-Inclusive Purchase Money Deed of Trust.

Should Trustor be delinquent or in default under the terms of the Note secured hereby, Beneficiary consequently incurs any penalties, charges, or other expenses on account of the Underlying Note(s) during the period of such delinquency or default, the amount of such penalties, charges and expenses shall be immediately added to the principal amount of the Note secured hereby and shall be immediately payable by Trustor to Beneficiary.

If at any time the unpaid balance of the Note secured hereby, accrued interest thereon, and all other sums due pursuant to the terms thereof and all sums advanced by beneficiary pursuant to the terms of this Deed of Trust, is equal to or less than the unpaid principal balance of the Underlying Note(s) and accrued interest thereon, the Note secured hereby, at the option of Beneficiary, shall be cancelled and said property shall be reconveyed from the lien of this Deed of Trust.

(B) Trustor and Beneficiary agree that in the event the proceeds of any condemnation award or settlement in lieu thereof, or the proceeds of any casualty insurance covering destructible improvements located upon said property, are applied by the holder of the Underlying Note(s) in reduction of the unpaid principal amount thereof, the unpaid principal balance of the Note secured hereby shall be reduced by an equivalent amount and be deemed applied to the last sums due under the Note.

(C) At such times as the Note secured hereby becomes all due and payable, the amount of principal and interest then payable to Beneficiary thereunder shall be reduced by the then unpaid balance of principal and interest due on the Underlying Note(s).

(D) Any demand hereunder delivered by Beneficiary to Trustee for the foreclosure of the lien of this Deed of Trust may be not more than the sum of the following amounts:

(i) The difference between the then unpaid balance of principal and interest on the Note secured hereby and the then unpaid balance of principal and interest on the Underlying Note(s); plus

FIGURE C7-2 *(concluded)*

(ii) The aggregate of all amounts theretofore paid by Beneficiary pursuant to the terms of this Deed of Trust prior to the date of such foreclosure sale, for taxes and assessments, insurance premiums, delinquency charges, foreclosure costs, and any other sums advanced by Beneficiary pursuant to the terms of this Deed of Trust, to the extent the same were not previously repaid by Trustor to Beneficiary; plus

(iii) The costs of foreclosure hereunder; plus attorneys fees and costs incurred by Beneficiary in enforcing this Deed of Trust or the Note secured hereby as permitted by law.

(E) Notwithstanding any provision to the contrary herein contained, in the event of a Trustee's sale in furtherance of the foreclosure of this Deed of Trust, the balance then due on the Note secured hereby, for the purpose of Beneficiary's demand, shall be reduced, as aforesaid, by the unpaid balance, if any, of principal and interest then due on the Underlying Note(s), satisfactory evidence of which unpaid balances must be submitted to Trustee prior to such sale. The Trustee may rely on any statements received from Beneficiary in this regard and such statements shall be deemed binding and conclusive as between Beneficiary and Trustor, on the one hand, and the Trustee, on the other hand, to the extent of such reliance.

Signature of Trustor

_____   _____

_____   _____

Signature of Beneficiary

_____   _____

_____   _____

STAPLE APPROPRIATE ACKNOWLEDGMENTS HERE

(THIS DEED OF TRUST FOR USE ONLY IN PURCHASE MONEY TRANSACTIONS. IT IS RECOMMENDED THAT, PRIOR TO THE EXECUTION OF THIS DEED OF TRUST, THE PARTIES CONSULT WITH THEIR ATTORNEYS WITH RESPECT TO SAME).

Title Order No._____   Escrow or Loan No._____

— DO NOT RECORD —

REQUEST FOR FULL RECONVEYANCE
To be used only when note has been paid.

To **FOUNDERS TITLE COMPANY**, Trustee: Dated _____

The undersigned is the legal owner and holder of all indebtedness secured by the within Deed of Trust. All sums secured by said Deed of Trust have been fully paid and satisfied; and you are hereby requested and directed, on payment to you of any sums owing to you under the terms of said Deed of Trust, to cancel all evidences of indebtedness, secured by said Deed of Trust, delivered to you herewith together with said Deed of Trust, and to reconvey, without warranty, to the parties designated by the terms of said Deed of Trust, the estate now held by you under the same.

MAIL RECONVEYANCE TO:

_____   _____

_____   By_____

_____   By_____

Do not lose or destroy this Deed of Trust OR THE NOTE which it secures. Both must be delivered to the Trustee for cancellation before reconveyance will be made.

OFC 1016-A

VA AND FHA AMENDMENTS
CALIFORNIA ASSOCIATION OF REALTORS® STANDARD FORM

This addendum is attached as Page _____ of _____ Pages to the Real Estate Purchase Contract and Receipt for Deposit dated _____, 19 _____ in which _____
_____
is referred to as Buyer and _____
_____ is referred to as Seller.

VA LOAN

It is expressly agreed that, notwithstanding any other provisions of this contract, the purchaser shall not incur any penalty by forfeiture of earnest money or otherwise or be obligated to complete the purchase of the property described herein, if the contract purchase price or cost exceeds the reasonable value of the property established by the Veterans Administration. The purchaser shall, however, have the privilege and option of proceeding with the consummation of this contract without regard to the amount of the reasonable value established by the Veterans Administration.

Receipt of a copy is hereby acknowledged.

DATED: _____, 19 _____   BUYER: _____

Receipt of a copy is hereby acknowledged.

DATED: _____, 19 _____   SELLER: _____

FHA LOAN

It is expressly agreed that notwithstanding any other provisions of this contract, the buyer shall not be obligated to complete the purchase of the premises and shall not incur any penalty or loss of his deposit money or otherwise unless the seller has delivered to the buyer a written statement issued by the Federal Housing Commissioner setting forth the appraised value of the property for mortgage insurance purposes of not less than $_____, which statement the seller shall deliver to the buyer promptly after such appraised value statement is made available to the seller.

The buyer shall, however, have the privilege and option of proceeding with the consummation of this contract without regard to the amount of the appraised valuation made by the Federal Housing Commissioner.

The appraised valuation is arrived at to determine the maximum mortgage the Department of Housing and Urban Development will insure. HUD does not warrant the value or the condition of the property. The purchaser should satisfy himself/herself that the price and condition of the property are acceptable.

Receipt of a copy is hereby acknowledged.

DATED: _____, 19 _____   BUYER: _____

Receipt of a copy is hereby acknowledged.

DATED: _____, 19 _____   SELLER: _____

NO REPRESENTATION IS MADE AS TO THE LEGAL VALIDITY OF ANY PROVISION OR THE ADEQUACY OF ANY PROVISION IN ANY SPECIFIC TRANSACTION. A REAL ESTATE BROKER IS THE PERSON QUALIFIED TO ADVISE ON REAL ESTATE. IF YOU DESIRE LEGAL ADVICE CONSULT YOUR ATTORNEY.

FIGURE C8-1

RECORDING REQUESTED BY

ORDER #

APN

WHEN RECORDED MAIL TO

Name
Street Address
City & State

———— SPACE ABOVE THIS LINE FOR RECORDER'S USE ————

Joint Tenancy Grant Deed

ALL PTN.

The undersigned grantor(s) declare(s):
Documentary transfer tax is $........................
( ) computed on full value of property conveyed, or
( ) computed on full value less value of liens and encumbrances remaining at time of sale.
( ) Unincorporated area: ( ) City of.., and
( ) Realty not sold.

FOR A VALUABLE CONSIDERATION, receipt of which is hereby acknowledged,

hereby GRANT(S) to

, AS JOINT TENANTS,

the following described real property in the
County of .... , State of California:

Mail tax statements to _____

Dated _____

STATE OF CALIFORNIA
COUNTY OF _____ } SS.
On _____ before me, the undersigned, a Notary Public in and for said State, personally appeared
_____
_____
_____, known to me
to be the person____ whose name____ subscribed to the within instrument and acknowledged that____ executed the same.
WITNESS my hand and official seal.

Signature _____
Name (Typed or Printed)

(This area for official notorial seal)

1003-OFC-74   MAIL TAX STATEMENTS AS DIRECTED ABOVE

APPENDIX C

FIGURE C8-2

RECORDING REQUESTED BY

ORDER #

APN

WHEN RECORDED MAIL TO

Name
Street Address
City & State

―――― SPACE ABOVE THIS LINE FOR RECORDER'S USE ――――

Grant Deed

ALL PTN.

The undersigned grantor(s) declare(s):
Documentary transfer tax is $..........................
( ) computed on full value of property conveyed, or
( ) computed on full value less value of liens and encumbrances remaining at time of sale.
( ) Unincorporated area: ( ) City of..., and
( ) Realty not sold.
FOR A VALUABLE CONSIDERATION, receipt of which is hereby acknowledged,

hereby GRANT(S) to

the following described real property in the
County of   , State of California:

Mail tax statements to _____

Dated _____

STATE OF CALIFORNIA
COUNTY OF _____ } SS.
On _____ before me, the undersigned, a Notary Public in and for said State, personally appeared
_____
_____
_____ known to me
to be the person_____ whose name_____ subscribed to the within
instrument and acknowledged that _____ executed the same.
WITNESS my hand and official seal.

Signature _____
_____
Name (Typed or Printed)

(This area for official notorial seal)

1005-OFC-74   MAIL TAX STATEMENTS AS DIRECTED ABOVE

FIGURE C8–3

RECORDING REQUESTED BY

ORDER #

APN

AND WHEN RECORDED MAIL TO

Name
Address
City & State

———— SPACE ABOVE THIS LINE FOR RECORDER'S USE ————

CONDOMINIUM GRANT DEED

– I –

The undersigned grantor(s) declare(s):
Documentary transfer tax is $_____$.
(   ) computed on full value of property conveyed, or
(   ) computed on full value less value of liens and encumbrances remaining at time of sale.
(   ) Unincorporated area: (   ) City of _____, and
(   ) Realty not sold.
FOR A VALUABLE CONSIDERATION, receipt of which is hereby acknowledged,

hereby GRANT(S) to

the following described real property in the City and County of San Francisco, State of California: — (See EXHIBIT A) —

– II –

EACH of the foregoing Grants is subject to the lien of real property taxes and assessments not delinquent, the Restrictions referred to in III-C, below, and all covenants, easements, restrictions and liens of record. The property herein granted is a Condominium, as defined in Section 783 of the California Civil Code, and the Project as hereinafter defined is subject to the provisions of Sections 1350 through 1370, inclusive, of said Code.

– III –

A. "UNIT" means a numbered Parcel, as shown on the Map, and includes the elements of a Condominium which are not owned in common with the Owners of other Condominiums in the project. The boundary lines of a Unit are the interior unfinished surfaces (exclusive of paint, paper, wax, tile, enamel or other finishings) of its perimeter walls, bearing walls, floors, ceilings, windows and window frames, doors and door frames and trim, and the Unit includes both the portions of the building so described and the air space so encompassed.
B. "COMMON AREA" means that portion of the project not located within any Unit, including, but not by way of limitation, all land, staircases and light wells, lobby areas, common patio areas, corridors, garages, walkways, roofs, roof deck, driveways, foundations, pipes, ducts for the mutual use of adjoining Units, flues, chutes, conduits, wires, elevators and elevator equipment, and other utility installations to the outlets, bearing walls, columns and girders, to the unfinished surfaces thereof, all regardless of location.
C. "RESTRICTIONS" means that certain Declaration of Covenants, Conditions and Restrictions executed by
_____ on the _____ day of _____, 19____,
and recorded in the office of the Recorder of the City and County of San Francisco, State of California, in Book _____,
Page _____, Official Records, and following.
D. "PROJECT" means the entire parcel of real property, as shown on the Map, divided or to be divided into Condominiums, including all structures thereon.

– IV –

THIS DEED is made and accepted subject to all the provisions contained in that certain Document defined herein as "RESTRICTIONS", all of which are incorporated herein by reference with the same effect as though fully set forth herein, and by this conveyance said Restrictions are imposed on said land.

– – –

Mail tax statements to _____

Dated _____

_____ (Grantor)

STATE OF CALIFORNIA } SS.
COUNTY OF _____

_____ (Grantor)

On _____ before me, the undersigned, a Notary Public in and for said State, personally appeared
_____
_____

ACCEPTED:

_____ (Grantee)

_____ , known to me
to be the person___ whose name_____ subscribed to the within
instrument and acknowledged that _____ executed the same.
WITNESS my hand and official seal.

_____ (Grantee)

Signature _____

Name (Typed or Printed)

(This area for official notorial seal)

OFC-2052 SF   MAIL TAX STATEMENTS AS DIRECTED ABOVE

APPENDIX C

FIGURE C8-4

STATEMENT OF IDENTITY

For confidential use in connection with   Order No._____

This Statement is to be SIGNED PERSONALLY by each party to the transaction and by BOTH HUSBAND AND WIFE, before a policy of title insurance can be written. This information is necessary because we have been asked to insure a title to real property in which you are interested. In searching your title we may encounter judgements, bankruptcies, divorces, and income tax liens against persons with names similar to yours. We can quickly eliminate any such matters which otherwise cloud the title to this property if you will help us by COMPLETELY filling in the following statement.

_____ _____ _____
(First Name)   (Full Middle Name)   (Last Name)

_____ _____ _____
(Birthplace)   (Date of Birth)   (Social Security No.)

(if married complete the following:)

Full name of Wife / Husband

_____ _____ _____
(First Name)   (Full Middle Name)   (Last Name)

_____ _____ _____
(Birthplace)   (Date of Birth)   (Social Security No.)

We were married on_____at_____

Wife's maiden name_____

RESIDENCES

	Number and Street	City	From (Date)	To (Date)

RESIDENCE AND OCCUPATIONS DURING PAST 10 YEARS

OCCUPATIONS

	Firm Name	Location	From (Date)	To (Date)
Husband				
Husband				
Husband				
Wife				
Wife				

(if no former marriage or marriages, write "none" otherwise complete the

Name of former wife_____
Deceased_____ Divorced_____ When_____ Where_____
Name of former husband_____
Deceased_____ Divorced_____ When_____ Where_____

I have never been adjudged bankrupt, nor are there any unsatisfied judgements or other matters pending against me which might affect my title to this property EXCEPT as follows:
_____
_____

The street address of the property in this transaction is:_____

Home Phone_____   Signature_____

Business Phone_____   Signature_____

Date_____

FIGURE C10-1

INDIVIDUAL TAX ANALYSIS

NAME: ADDRESS: DATE:

WIFE'S NAME: CHILDREN NO: AGES: PREPARED BY:

LINE		(1) (2) PRESENT INCOME POSITION	(3) (4) PROPERTY	(5) (6) PROPERTY	LINE
1	GAINFUL OCCUPATION INCOME				1
2	Dividends				2
3	Interest				3
4	Annuities				4
5	Capital Gains Reportable				5
6	Other Income				6
7	TOTAL SECURITY INCOME				7
8	REAL ESTATE NET TAXABLE				8
9	TOTAL ORDINARY INCOME				9
10	Less: Personal Deductions & Exemptions				10
11	TOTAL TAXABLE INCOME				11
12	**TOTAL TAX LIABILITY**				12
13	Gainful Occupation Income (L1)				13
14	Less: Personal Deductions & Exemptions (L10)				14
15	Taxable Income, Gainful Occupation				15
16	**TAX LIABILITY GAINFUL OCCUPATION**				16
17	Gainful Occupation Income (L1)				17
18	Security Income (L7)				18
19	Total Gainful Occupation & Security Income				19
20	Less: Personal Deductions & Exemptions (L10)				20
21	Tax, Gainful Occupation & Security Income				21
22	**TAX LIABILITY, GAINFUL OCCUPATION & SECURITY INCOME**				22
23	Total Tax Liability (L12)				23
24	Less: Tax Liability, Gainful (L22) Occupation & Security Income				24
25	**TAX LIABILITY REAL ESTATE**				25
26	Tax Liability, Gainful Occupation & Security Income (L22)				26
27	Less: Tax Liability, Gainful Occupation (L16)				27
28	**TAX LIABILITY SECURITY INCOME**				28
29	Dividends (L2 ÷ L7)	% X L28	% X L28	% X L28	29
30	Interest (L3 ÷ L7)	% X L28	% X L28	% X L28	30
31	Annuities (L4 ÷ L7)	% X L28	% X L28	% X L28	31
32	Capital Gain (L5 ÷ L7)	% X L28	% X L28	% X L28	32
33	Other Income (L6 ÷ L7)	% X L28	% X L28	% X L28	33
34	Gainful Occupation Income (L1)				34
35	Security Income (L7)				35
36	Capital Gains not included in Line 5 above				36
37	Real Estate Gross Spendable				37
38	TOTAL INCOME				38
39	Less: Total Tax Liability (L12)				39
40	**NET AFTER TAX**				40
41	Overall Rate (L39 ÷ L38)	%	%	%	41

(Column 29-33 left margin label: TAX ALLOCATION)

FIGURE C11-1

EXCLUSIVE AUTHORIZATION TO LEASE OR RENT

THIS IS INTENDED TO BE A LEGALLY BINDING AGREEMENT — READ IT CAREFULLY

CALIFORNIA ASSOCIATION OF REALTORS® STANDARD FORM

In consideration of the services to be rendered by _____
hereinafter called agent, I hereby grant said agent the exclusive and irrevocable right to lease or rent for a period of _____
days from date hereof, and ending at midnight _____, 19 ___, the property situated in the _____
County of _____ State of California, described as follows, to wit:

_____

within said time for _____
DOLLARS ($ _____) per _____ payable in advance on the _____
and I hereby authorize said agent to accept and hold a deposit thereon.

Terms of Lease:

_____

I hereby agree to compensate agent as follows: _____

_____

whether property is leased or rented through the efforts of agent, or by me, or by another agent, or through any other source. Said compensation shall be paid to agent in the event the property is transferred or conveyed or withdrawn from agent's authority during the time set forth herein.

In the event lease is extended or renewed, I agree to pay an additional compensation of _____

I hereby agree to pay agent the compensation stated above if property is leased or rented within _____ days after the termination of this authority or any extension thereof to anyone with whom agent has had negotiations prior to final termination, provided I have received notice in writing, including the names of prospective lessees before or upon termination of this agreement or any extension thereof. If action be instituted on this agreement to collect compensation or commissions, the prevailing party shall be entitled to recover reasonable attorneys fees and costs.

This property shall be offered in compliance with state and federal anti-discrimination laws.

I hereby acknowledge receipt of a copy of this exclusive authorization to lease or rent.

In consideration of the foregoing employment, the undersigned agent agrees to use diligence in procuring a lessee for said property.

DATED: _____

OWNER: _____

_____

Listing Agent _____

ADDRESS: _____

By _____

PHONE: _____

NO REPRESENTATION IS MADE AS TO THE LEGAL VALIDITY OF ANY PROVISION OR THE ADEQUACY OF ANY PROVISION IN ANY SPECIFIC TRANSACTION. A REAL ESTATE BROKER IS THE PERSON QUALIFIED TO ADVISE ON REAL ESTATE IF YOU DESIRE LEGAL ADVICE CONSULT YOUR ATTORNEY.

FIGURE C11-2

RESIDENTIAL LEASE AGREEMENT AFTER SALE

(Possession Retained by Seller)

THIS IS INTENDED TO BE A LEGALLY BINDING AGREEMENT — READ IT CAREFULLY

CALIFORNIA ASSOCIATION OF REALTORS® STANDARD FORM

_____, California, _____, 19 _____.
_____, "LESSOR" and
_____, "LESSEE"
agree:

    1. On _____, 19 ____, LESSOR as Buyer and LESSEE as Seller entered into an agreement for the sale and purchase of the real property commonly known as _____, _____, California ("Premises"), wherein escrow is designated to close on or about _____, 19 _____.

    2. LESSOR leases to LESSEE the premises as LESSEE'S personal residence in accordance with the terms of this lease.

    3. Occupancy shall commence on the day following close of escrow and terminate _____ thereafter
                                                                                                     days/weeks/months
at which time the premises shall be vacated and possession surrendered to LESSOR.

    4. LESSEE shall pay to LESSOR as rent for the said premises the sum of $ _____ per _____
commencing _____, 19 ___ to and including _____. Said
                                                                                                                 specific date/other
sum shall be paid _____ in advance. Prorations, if any, shall be predicated upon a 30 day month. Additionally,
                       weekly/monthly
LESSEE shall pay for all utilities and services based upon occupancy of the premises and the following charges: _____
except, _____ which shall be paid by LESSOR. Any holding over without the express written consent of LESSOR shall create a day-to-day tenancy with a fair rental value of $ _____ per day. Except as to daily rent and tenancy, all other covenants and conditions herein contained shall remain in full force and effect.

    5. As part of the consideration passing from LESSEE to LESSOR, but for which LESSOR would not have entered into this agreement, except as provided by law, LESSEE shall maintain the premises and yards and all real and personal property as conveyed by LESSEE to LESSOR in clean, sanitary, operable condition and repair, reasonable wear and tear excluded, at LESSEE'S sole cost and expense. LESSEE further agrees upon surrendering possession that said premises shall otherwise be in the same condition as required of LESSEE to have delivered them to LESSOR at close of escrow.

    6. $ _____ as security has been deposited. LESSOR may use therefrom such amounts as are reasonably necessary to remedy LESSEE'S defaults in the payment of rent, to repair damages caused by LESSEE, or clean the premises if necessary upon the termination of tenancy. If used toward rent or damages during the term of this agreement, LESSEE agrees to reinstate said total security deposit upon 5 days written notice delivered to LESSEE in person or by mail. The balance of the security deposit, if any, shall be mailed to LESSEE's last known address within 14 days of surrender of the premises.

    7. As additional consideration passing from LESSEE to LESSOR, LESSEE shall obtain and maintain during the term of this lease, public liability insurance naming both LESSOR and LESSEE as co-insureds in the amount of not less than $ _____ for injury to one person; $ _____ for any injury to a group; and $ _____ for property damage. If permitted, LESSEE agrees to retain his fire insurance on the premises in a sum of not less than designated as the sales price of the subject property.

    8. In the event of any action or proceeding between LESSOR and LESSEE under this agreement, the prevailing party shall be entitled to recover reasonable attorney's fees and costs.

    9. The undersigned LESSEE acknowledges having read the foregoing and receipt of a copy.

LESSOR and LESSEE have executed this lease on the day and year above written.

_____ _____
                     LESSOR   LESSEE

_____ _____
                     LESSOR   LESSEE

NO REPRESENTATION IS MADE AS TO THE LEGAL VALIDITY OF ANY PROVISION OR THE ADEQUACY OF ANY PROVISION IN ANY SPECIFIC TRANSACTION. A REAL ESTATE BROKER IS THE PERSON QUALIFIED TO ADVISE ON REAL ESTATE. IF YOU DESIRE LEGAL ADVICE CONSULT YOUR ATTORNEY.

FIGURE C11-3

EXCLUSIVE AUTHORIZATION TO LEASE OR RENT A SINGLE FAMILY DWELLING

THIS IS INTENDED TO BE A LEGALLY BINDING AGREEMENT — READ IT CAREFULLY

CALIFORNIA ASSOCIATION OF REALTORS® STANDARD FORM

In consideration of the services to be rendered by _____ hereinafter called agent, I hereby grant said agent the exclusive and irrevocable right to lease or rent for a period of _____ days from date hereof, and ending at midnight _____, 19___, the property situated in the _____ County of _____ State of California, described as follows, to wit:

_____
_____
_____
_____
_____
_____
_____
_____
_____
_____

within said time for _____
DOLLARS ($ _____) per _____ payable in advance on the _____
and I hereby authorize said agent to accept and hold a deposit thereon.

Terms of Lease:

_____
_____
_____
_____
_____
_____

I hereby agree to compensate agent as follows: _____
_____
_____
_____

whether property is leased or rented through the efforts of agent, or by me, or by another agent, or through any other source. Said compensation shall be paid to agent in the event the property is transferred or conveyed or withdrawn from agent's authority during the time set forth herein.

In the event lease is extended or renewed, I agree to pay an additional compensation of _____

I hereby agree to pay agent the compensation stated above if property is leased or rented within _____ days after the termination of this authority or any extension thereof to anyone with whom agent has had negotiations prior to final termination, provided I have received notice in writing, including the names of prospective lessees before or upon termination of this agreement or any extension thereof. If action be instituted on this agreement to collect compensation or commissions, the prevailing party shall be entitled to recover reasonable attorneys fees and costs.

I hereby acknowledge receipt of a copy of this exclusive authorization to lease or rent.

In consideration of the foregoing employment, the undersigned agent agrees to use diligence in procuring a lessee for said property.

DATED: _____

OWNER: _____

_____

Listing Agent _____

ADDRESS: _____

By _____

PHONE: _____

NO REPRESENTATION IS MADE AS TO THE LEGAL VALIDITY OF ANY PROVISION OR THE ADEQUACY OF ANY PROVISION IN ANY SPECIFIC TRANSACTION. A REAL ESTATE BROKER IS THE PERSON QUALIFIED TO ADVISE ON REAL ESTATE. IF YOU DESIRE LEGAL ADVICE CONSULT YOUR ATTORNEY.

FIGURE C11-4

STATEMENT OF CONDITION
CALIFORNIA ASSOCIATION OF REALTORS® STANDARD FORM

PROPERTY _____ UNIT _____

Type of Unit _____ Occupant _____ Move in Date _____

This move-in, move-out form is for your protection. When completing this form, be specific and check carefully. Among things you should look for are dust, dirt, grease, stains, burns, damages and wear. Use additional paper if necessary. California Civil Code 1950.5 stipulates that your security deposit is refundable to the extent not used for unpaid rent, damage and reasonable cleaning charges, normal wear and tear excepted.

ITEMS	CONDITION	
	MOVE-IN	MOVE-OUT
Living Room & Dining Room		
Doors and Locks		
Carpeting		
Floors and Baseboards		
Walls and Ceiling		
Draperies		
Electrical Fixtures		
Electrical Switches, Outlets		
Windows, Screens		
Misc. _____		
Kitchen		
Floors and Baseboards		
Walls and Ceiling		
Electrical Fixtures		
Electrical Switches, Outlets		
Range, Fan, Hood		
Oven		
Refrigerator		
Plumbing		
Sink & Disposer		
Cabinets, Counter Surfaces		
Windows, Screens		
Draperies/Curtains		
Misc. _____		

FIGURE C11-4 *(continued)*

	CONDITION			
	MOVE-IN		MOVE-OUT	
Bedrooms	#1	#2	#1	#2
Doors and Locks				
Carpeting				
Floors & Baseboards				
Walls and Ceiling				
Windows and Screens				
Draperies				
Electrical Fixtures				
Electrical Switches, Outlets				
Closets, Doors, Tracks				
Misc._____				
Bedrooms	#3	#4 or ____	#3	#4 or ____
Doors and Locks				
Carpeting				
Floors & Baseboards				
Walls and Ceiling				
Windows and Screens				
Draperies				
Electrical Fixtures				
Electrical Switches, Outlets				
Closets, Doors, Tracks				
Misc._____				
Bathrooms	#1	#2	#1	#2
Doors and Locks				
Floors & Baseboards				
Walls and Ceiling				
Windows and Screens				
Window Covering				
Shower, Tub				
Shower Door, Curtain				
Toilet				
Sink, Medicine Cabinet				
Plumbing Fixtures				
Electrical Fixtures, Fan				
Electrical Switches, Outlets				
Towel Racks				
Misc._____				
Other Items				
Heating				
Air Conditioning				
Patio, Balcony				
Yard Areas				
Fencing				
Garage or Carport				
Misc._____				

UNIT INSPECTED AND ACCEPTED AS NOTED

Date _____

Signature of Tenant _____

Signature of Landlord/Agent _____

UNIT INSPECTED AND VACATED AS NOTED

Date _____

Signature of Tenant _____

Signature of Landlord/Agent _____

FIGURE C11-5

NOTICE TO PAY RENT OR QUIT

CALIFORNIA ASSOCIATION OF REALTORS® STANDARD FORM

To _____
      All tenants and subtenants in possession (full name)
      and all others in possession

WITHIN THREE DAYS after the service on you of this notice, you are hereby required to pay to the undersigned or _____, his authorized agent, the rent of the premises hereinafter described, of which you now hold possession amounting to the sum of _____ dollars ($_____) enumerated as follows:

$ _____ Due From _____ 19_____ To _____ 19_____

$ _____ Due From _____ 19_____ To _____ 19_____

$ _____ Due From _____ 19_____ To _____ 19_____

OR QUIT AND DELIVER UP THE POSSESSION OF THE PREMISES.

The premises herein referred to are situated in the city of _____, County of _____, State of California, designated by the number and street as _____, apt._____.

YOU ARE FURTHER NOTIFIED THAT, the undersigned does hereby elect to declare the forfeiture of your lease or rental agreement under which you hold possession of the above-described premises and lessor will institute legal proceedings to recover rent and possession of said premises which could result in a judgment against you including costs and necessary disbursements together with treble damages as allowed by law for such unlawful detention.

Dated this _____ day of _____, 19_____.

_____   _____
             AGENT   LESSOR

FIGURE C11-6

THIRTY (30) DAY NOTICE
OF TERMINATION OF TENANCY

CALIFORNIA ASSOCIATION OF REALTORS® STANDARD FORM

To _____
    All tenants and subtenants in possession (full name)
    and all others in possession

PLEASE TAKE NOTICE that your tenancy of the below-described premises is terminated, effective at the end of a thirty (30) day period after service on you of this notice.

The purpose of this notice is to terminate your tenancy of the below-described premises.

If you fail to quit and deliver possession, legal proceedings will be instituted against you to obtain possession and such proceedings could result in a judgment against you which could include costs and necessary disbursements.

The premises herein referred to are situated in the city of _____

County of _____, State of California, designated by

the number and street as _____

Apartment _____

Dated this _____ day of _____, 19 _____

_____   _____
                 AGENT   LESSOR

FIGURE C11-7

INDUSTRIAL AND COMMERCIAL LEASES
BUILDING SPACE

CALIFORNIA ASSOCIATION OF REALTORS® STANDARD FORM
This is an attachment to a listing contract — read it carefully.

Information Sheet

LISTING NO. _____

Property _____ Available Area _____ Est. Square Ft. _____
Address _____ City-State _____ Map Code _____

STORIES _____
CONSTRUCTION _____
TYPE _____
PARKING RESERVED _____
PARKING PUBLIC _____
FLOOR COVERING _____
WALLS _____
ELEVATOR _____
CEILING HEIGHT _____
TYPE CEILING _____
LIGHTING _____
WINDOW COVERING _____
ELECTRICAL _____
GENERAL CONDITION _____
MISC _____
_____
_____
_____
SIGN RESTRICTIONS _____
_____
HEAT TYPE _____
A/C TYPE _____

(LEAVE BLANK)

Reserved for photograph—printing or writing in this space will not be reproduced. Material for this section should be identified and clipped to the back. This material should be no larger than this blank space. If the material is a map, sketch, or list it should be drawn or typed in black ink (blue will not reproduce). You may use this space for other remarks if no map or picture.

INSTRUCTIONS FOR LISTING

Complete all information requested. Listing may be withheld for clarification if incomplete.
This is an attachment to a listing contract. Read it carefully, attach L-11.

ABBREVIATIONS, DEFINITIONS

DP = Down Payment   P&I = Principal and Interest
GOI = Gross Operating Income   RPT = Reported
GSI = Gross Scheduled Income   SCH = Reported or Projected by Seller
LP = Listing Price   SI = Gross Spendable Income
NOI = Net Operating Income

ADDRESS OR OFFICE NO.	DIMENSIONS	SQ. FT.	RENT	SEC. DEPOSIT	TERM	POSS.	UTIL. FURN.

SPECIAL BUILDING FEATURES _____
_____ ZONING _____
OWNER WILL DIVIDE _____ REMODEL _____ PARTITION _____
LEASE TO BE NEGOTIATED: _____ MIN _____ YEARS C.P.I. CLAUSE _____
REQUIRED LEASE TERMS _____
_____
_____
_____
_____

TO SHOW CONTACT: LISTING OFFICE _____ OWNER _____ OTHER _____ PHONE (___) _____
PROP. ZIP CODE _____ COMMISSION TO COOP. OFFICE % _____ /$ _____

BROKER _____ ADD. _____ CITY _____ STATE _____
OFFICE PHONE (___) _____ SALESMAN _____ HOME PHONE (___) _____

All information is from sources believed reliable but is not guaranteed.
Owner certifies that the above information as to income and expenses is accurate and complete to the best of his knowledge.

OWNER _____ OWNER _____
This listing expires _____ DATE _____

APPENDIX C

FIGURE C12-1

PROPERTY ANALYSIS

Purpose: _____ Date: __/__/__ | List Price $ _____ Market Value $ _____
Name: _____ | Loans $ _____ Loans $ _____
Location: _____ | List Price Equity $ _____ Market Value Equity $ _____
Type of Property: _____ | Existing Financing: Annual Payment   Interest

Assessed Value:
- Land $ _____ ____%   1st $ _____ _____ ____%
- Improvement $ _____ ____%   2nd $ _____ _____ ____%
- Personal Property $ _____ ____%   3rd $ _____ _____ ____%
- TOTAL $ _____ 100%   Potential 1st $ _____ _____ ____%

Adjusted Cost Basis as of _____ $ _____   2nd $ _____ _____ ____%

#		%	2	3	Comments	
1	SCHEDULED GROSS INCOME					1
2	Less: Vacancy and Credit Losses					2
3	GROSS OPERATING INCOME					3
4	Less: Operating Expenses					4
5	Taxes					5
6	Insurance					6
7	Utilities					7
8	Licenses, Permits, Advertising					8
9	Management					9
10	Payroll, Including Payroll Taxes					10
11	Supplies					11
12	Services					12
13	Maintenance					13
14	Other					14
15						15
16						16
17	TOTAL EXPENSES					17
18	NET OPERATING INCOME Cap Rate List Price ____% Cap Rate Market Value ____%					18

ESTIMATE OF MARKET VALUE

#					4	5	
19	INCOME APPROACH: Estimated Value Capitalized at Rate of ____%						19
20	Cost Approach:						20
21	Sq. Ft. @ Per Sq. Ft.						21
22	Sq. Ft. @ Per Sq. Ft.						22
23	Sq. Ft. @ Per Sq. Ft.						23
24	Less: Estimate of Accumulated Depreciation ____%						24
25	Depreciated Value of Improvements						25
26	Plus: Site Improvements						26
27	Plus: Land Sq. Ft. @ Per Sq. Ft.						27
28	ESTIMATE OF MARKET VALUE BY COST APPROACH						28
29	MARKET DATA APPROACH: @						29
30	FINAL ESTIMATE OF MARKET VALUE (CORRELATED)						30

INCOME ADJUSTED TO FINANCING

#		1	2	3	4	5	
31	NET OPERATING INCOME (Line 18)						31
32	Less: Loan Payments	3rd Loan	2nd Loan	1st Loan	Total		32
33	Interest						33
34	Principal						34
35	Total Loan Payment						35
36	GROSS SPENDABLE INCOME	Rate: ____% (Line 36 ÷ MV Equity)					36
37	Plus: Principal Payment						37
38	GROSS EQUITY INCOME	Rate: ____% (Line 38 ÷ MV Equity)					38
39	Less: Depreciation	Personal Property		Improvements			39
40	REAL ESTATE TAXABLE INCOME						40

The statements and figures presented herein, while not guaranteed, are secured from sources we believe authoritative.

FIGURE C12-2

COMPARATIVE INVESTMENT ANALYSIS

NAME: _____ DATE ____/____/____

PURPOSE: _____

LINE No.		(1) PRESENT POSITION	(2) PROPERTY	(3) PROPERTY	(4) PROPERTY	(5) PROPERTY	(6) PROPERTY	
1	List Price							1
2	Market Value							2
3	Less: Total Loans							3
4	Equity							4
5	Plus: Available Cash							5
6	Total Effective Equity							6
7	Less: Transaction Costs							7
8	NET EFFECTIVE EQUITY							8
	CASH POTENTIAL							
9	Cash From Owner							9
10	Plus: Cash from Potential Loan							10
11	Total Cash Available							11
12	Less: Transaction Costs							12
13	NET CASH AVAILABLE							13
	PROPERTY INCOME ANALYSIS							
14	Gross Scheduled Income							14
15	Less: Vacancy & Credit Losses							15
16	Gross Operating Income							16
17	Less: Operating Expenses							17
18	NET OPERATING INCOME							18
19	Capitalization Rate							19
OWNERSHIP ANALYSIS OF PROPERTY INCOME:			**TAXABLE INCOME**					
20	Net Operating Income							20
21	Less: Interest Payments							21
22	Less: Depreciation							22
23	TAXABLE INCOME							23
	SPENDABLE INCOME							
24	Net Operating Income							24
25	Less: Principle & Interest Payments							25
26	GROSS SPENDABLE							26
27	Less: Income Tax							27
28	Less: Capital Improvements							28
29	NET SPENDABLE ANNUALLY							29
30	Per Month							30
	EQUITY INCOME							
31	Net Operating Income							31
32	Less: Interest on Loans							32
33	Less: Income Tax							33
34	NET EQUITY INCOME							34
35	Net Equity Income Rate	%	%	%	%	%	%	35
36	Plus: Equity Growth Rate %	%	%	%	%	%	%	36
37	TOTAL EQUITY RATE	%	%	%	%	%	%	37

FIGURE C12–3

Standard Residential Appraisal Data Sheet
CALIFORNIA ASSOCIATION OF REALTORS

1. Location _____ City _____ Parcel _____
2. Legal _____
3. Owner _____ Address _____ Phone _____
4. Tenant _____ Rent Paid $ _____ Mo. to Mo. _____ ☐ Leased to _____ Fair Mo. Rental $ _____

LAND DESCRIPTION

5. Location	On		side of			St.		Feet from				St.
6. Lot	x	ft.		sf	Typical ☐	Alley ☐	Level ☐	Hilly ☐	Filled ☐			
	At Grade ☐	Above	ft.	Below	ft.	Drainage			Retaining Wall			
7. Street	Paved ☐	Oiled ☐	Dirt ☐	Walks ☐	Curbs ☐	Gutters ☐	St. Lights ☐					
8. Utilities	Water ☐	Gas ☐	Light ☐	Phone ☐	Sewer ☐	Cesspool ☐	Sep. Tank ☐					
9. Zoning												
10. Deed Restrictns.	Use			Area	Cost $	Race ☐	Liquor ☐	Expire	Yr.			
11. Taxes	County Taxes:	Land $	Imprs. $	City:	Land $	Imprs. $	Total $					

DESCRIPTION OF IMPROVEMENTS

12. Building	Age yrs.	Useful Life yrs.	No. Rooms	No. B. Rms.	No. Baths	No. Porches	No. Stories			
13. Style	Spanish ☐	Colonial ☐	English ☐	Monterey ☐	Farm House ☐	Plain ☐	Calif. ☐			
14. Livability	Plan	Housework	Socially	Homey	Built-ins	Closets	Yard			
15. Garage— x	Attached ☐ Detached ☐	Floor	Roof	Walls	Type Door		Work Bench ☐			
16. Special										

YARD DESCRIPTION

17. Lawn	Front ☐	Side ☐	Rear ☐	Flowers ☐	Vines ☐	Hedge ☐	
18. Sprinkling Sys.	Front ☐	Side ☐	Rear ☐	Fountain ☐	Fish Pond ☐	No. Faucets ☐	
19. Shrubs—Trees	Front	Side	Rear	Shade	Fruit	Ornamental ☐	
20. Wall—Fence	Height ft.	Lineal ft.	Concrete Tile ☐	Wood ☐	Stucco ☐	Brick ☐	
21. Special	Rock Garden ☐	Barbecue ☐	Plunge ☐	Dressing Rooms ☐	Sun Deck Sun Patio ☐	Tennis Badminton ☐	
22. Driveway	Width ft	Area sf	Cement ☐	Asphalt ☐	Ribbon ☐	Dirt ☐	
23. Walks	Front ☐	Area sf	Side ☐	Area sf	Back ☐	Area sf	Total

DESCRIPTION OF DISTRICT

24. District	Years old	Built up %	Growing ☐	Static ☐	Receding ☐	
25. Property Adj.	To left	To right	Opposite			
26. Setting	Typical ☐	Fits District ☐	Over-Improved	Under-Improved		
27. Distances to	Gr. School blks	Hi. School blks	Bus/Car blks	Stores blks	Park blks	Theatre blks
28. Nuisances	Noises ☐	Odors ☐	Smoke ☐	Dust ☐	Encroachments	
29. Owner occupied	Pride in ☐					

PLAT OF BUILDING / STREET LOCATION

COMPARABLE SALES IN DISTRICT

Location	No. Rooms	Price	Date Sold
1.		$	
2.		$	
3.		$	

FIGURE C12-3 *(continued)*

BUILDING DESCRIPTION

REMARKS

30.	Building type	Single	☐	Double	☐	Duplex	☐	Flat	☐	Court	☐	Apt. ☐
31.	Class of Bldg.	1 story	☐	1½ story	☐	2 story	☐	Frame	☐	Stucco	☐	Brick ☐
32.	Exterior	Siding	☐	B.B.	☐	Stucco	☐	Tile	☐	Brick	☐	Adobe ☐
33.	Foundation	Concrete	☐	Stone	☐	Brick	☐	Mudsill	☐	Piers	☐	Posts ☐
34.	Under-pinning	Joists x in.		Set in. o.c.		Clearance in.		Vents		Bracing		
35.	Floors	Hdw.	☐	Pine	☐	Cement	☐	Sub-floor	☐	Diagonal	☐	Horizontal ☐
36.	Basement	x ft.		Height ft.		Conc. floor		Conc. wall		Dirt		Furnace ☐
37.	Roof	Shingle	☐	Tile	☐	Slate	☐	Comp.	☐	Flat	☐	Pitch
38.	Porches	Front	☐	Side	☐	Back	☐	Conc. floor	☐	Wood floor	☐	Tile Floor ☐
39.	Heating	Unit heat	☐	Floor heater	☐	Wall heater	☐	Gas jets	☐	Fireplace	☐	Elect. ☐
40.	Elec. wiring	Conduits	☐	B.X.	☐	Tube	☐	Ceiling	☐	Wall	☐	Floor Plugs ☐

ROOM DESCRIPTION

					CONDITION		
					Poor	Fair	Good
41. Living Room	Floor	Walls	Ceiling	Trim			
42. Dining Room	Floor	Walls	Ceiling	Trim			
	Built-Ins						
43. Breakfast Room	Floor	Walls	Ceiling	Trim			
44. Bed Rooms. No.	Floor	Walls	Ceiling	Sleeping Porch ☐			
45. Bath Rooms. No.	Floor	Walls	Ceiling	Gas Heat ☐ / Electric ☐			
	Toilet ☐	Basin ☐	Tub (shower) ☐	Stall shower ☐			
46. Kitchen	Floor	Walls	Ceiling	Trim			
	Sink	Built-Ins					
47. Service Porch	Floor	Walls	Ceiling	Laundry tray ☐			
	Basin ☐	Toilet ☐	Water heater ☐	Ironing Board ☐			
48. Servants Quarters	Maids room	Chauffeur ☐	Bath ☐	Area sf			
Guests House	No. rooms	Built on Separate Bldg. ☐	Bath ☐	Area sf			
49. Other	Den ☐	Powder Room ☐	Sun Room ☐	Wash room ☐			

CONSTRUCTION AND CONDITION

50.	Construction	Poor ☐	Fair ☐	Good ☐	Best ☐			
51.	Sq. Ft. Area	House sf	Porches sf	Basement sf	Garage sf			
52.	General	Termites	Dampness	Dry Rot	Settling			
53.	Repairs Needed							

REPLACEMENT COST

54. House (Porches ½)   sf @ $. $
55. Basement   sf @ $. $
56. Other   sf @ $. $
    Garage   sf @ $. $
57. Walks–Drive   sf @ $. $
58. Fence–Walls–Special $
59. Landscaping–Sprinkling $
60. Replacement Cost New $
61. Less Depreciation   Yrs. $
62. Less Needed Repairs $ $
63. Depreciated Cost Improvements $
64. Value Land as Improved $
65. Replacement Cost Depreciated $
66. Value Indicated by Comparable Sales $
67. Estimated Fair Market Value $

SUMMARY ITEMS

Taxes $
Insurance $
Street Bonds $
Yearly Rental $
Present Loan $
Loan Recommended $
Mortgagee?

Lessee?

Remarks

Date   Signed   Address   Phone

Moore Business Forms, Inc. f

APPENDIX C

FIGURE C15-1

This **FINANCING STATEMENT** is presented for filing pursuant to the California Uniform Commercial Code

1. DEBTOR (LAST NAME FIRST)			1A. SOCIAL SECURITY OR FEDERAL TAX NO.
1B. MAILING ADDRESS	1C. CITY, STATE		1D. ZIP CODE
1E. RESIDENCE ADDRESS (IF AN INDIVIDUAL AND DIFFERENT THAN 1B)	1F. CITY, STATE		1G. ZIP CODE
2. ADDITIONAL DEBTOR (IF ANY) (LAST NAME FIRST)			2A. SOCIAL SECURITY OR FEDERAL TAX NO.
2B. MAILING ADDRESS	2C. CITY, STATE		2D. ZIP CODE
2E. RESIDENCE ADDRESS (IF AN INDIVIDUAL AND DIFFERENT THAN 2B)	2F. CITY, STATE		2G. ZIP CODE
3. DEBTOR(S) TRADE NAME OR STYLE (IF ANY)			3A. FEDERAL TAX NO.
4. ADDRESS OF DEBTOR(S) CHIEF PLACE OF BUSINESS (IF ANY)	4A. CITY, STATE		4B. ZIP CODE

5. SECURED PARTY
   NAME
   MAILING ADDRESS
   CITY   STATE   ZIP CODE

5A. SOCIAL SECURITY NO., FEDERAL TAX NO. OR BANK TRANSIT AND A.B.A. NO.

6. ASSIGNEE OF SECURED PARTY (IF ANY)
   NAME
   MAILING ADDRESS
   CITY   STATE   ZIP CODE

6A. SOCIAL SECURITY NO., FEDERAL TAX NO. OR BANK TRANSIT AND A.B.A. NO.

7. This FINANCING STATEMENT covers the following types or items of property (if crops or timber, include description of real property on which growing or to be grown)

8. Check ☒ If Applicable
   A ☐ Proceeds of collateral are also covered
   B ☐ Products of collateral are also covered
   C ☐ Proceeds of above described original collateral in which a security interest was perfected
   D ☐ Collateral was brought into this State subject to security interest in another jurisdiction

9. _____ (Date) _____ 19____

By: _____
    SIGNATURE(S) OF DEBTOR(S)   (TITLE)

By: _____
    SIGNATURE(S) OF SECURED PARTY(IES)   (TITLE)

CODE: 1 2 3 4 5 6 7 8 9

10. This Space for Use of Filing Officer (Date, Time, File Number and Filing Officer)

11. **Return Copy to**
    NAME
    ADDRESS
    CITY, STATE
    AND ZIP

FIGURE C15–2
UCC financing statement

BUSINESS OPPORTUNITY
CALIFORNIA ASSOCIATION OF REALTORS® STANDARD FORM

This is an attachment to a listing contract (A-11/L-11/EX-11) — read it carefully.

LISTING NO. _____

HAVE _____ CITY _____ LIST PRICE (LP) $ _____
ADDRESS _____ COUNTY _____ RPT. PRESENT LOANS $ _____
MOTIVATION _____ STATE _____ RPT. GROSS EQUITY $ _____
WANT _____   DOWN PAYMENT (DP) $ _____
BUSINESS NAME _____ KIND _____ CAN ADD $ _____

OWNER _____
_____ BUS. PH. _____
ADDRESS _____
CITY _____ ZIP ____
LANDLORD _____
_____ PH. _____
ADDRESS _____
CITY _____ ZIP ____
LEASE TERMS _____
EXPIR. DATE _____ MO. RENT $ ___
LEASE SECURITY _____ ANY LEASE % ___
YRS. LEFT ON LEASE _____ RENEWAL OPT? ___
EQUIP. ON LEASE _____
BALANCE $ _____ PER MO. $ ___
OUTSTANDING OBLIGATIONS ___

BALANCE $ _____ PER MO. $ ___
HOW LONG ESTAB. _____ AV. CUST. COUNT ___
LOCATION CLASS: 1 2 3 PARKING NO. ___
NO. EMPLOYEES ___ TOT. WAGES & SAL. $ ___
OWNER WORKS ___ DAYS & HOURS OPEN ___

(LEAVE BLANK)

Reserved for photograph—printing or writing in this space will not be reproduced. Material for this section should be identified and clipped to the back. This material should be no larger than this blank space. If the material is a map, sketch, or list it should be drawn or typed in black ink (blue will not reproduce). You may use this space for other remarks if no map or picture.

INSTRUCTIONS FOR LISTING
Complete all information requested. Listing may be withheld for clarification if incomplete.
This is an attachment to a listing contract. Read it carefully. If Sale attach A-11, if Exchange attach EX-11 and if Lease attach L-11.

ABBREVIATIONS, DEFINITIONS
DP = Down Payment   P&I = Principal and Interest
GOI = Gross Operating Income   RPT = Reported
GSI = Gross Scheduled Income   SCH = Reported or Projected by Seller
LP = Listing Price   SI = Gross Spendable Income
NOI = Net Operating Income

TERMS OF SALE: _____
STORAGE FACIL.: _____ AVE. MARK UP ___

RPT. TOTAL ANN. SALES $ _____ RPT. TOTAL ANN. PURCH. $ _____ RPT. MARGIN $ _____
INVENTORY INCLUDES: _____ RPT. VALUE $ _____
EQUIPMENT INCLUDES: _____ RPT. VALUE $ _____
REAL ESTATE INCLUDED: _____ RPT. VALUE $ _____ DESCRIBE _____ ZONING _____

RPT. GROSS MONTHLY SALES		RPT. ANNUAL EXPENSES		RPT. ANNUAL	
YEAR ___	YEAR ___	RENT	$ ___	TOTAL SALES	$ ___
JAN. ___	JAN. ___	UTILITIES	$ ___	TOTAL PURCHASES	$ ___
FEB. ___	FEB. ___	INSURANCE	$ ___	GROSS NET INCOME	$ ___
MAR. ___	MAR. ___	ADVERTISING	$ ___	EXPENSES	$ ___
APR. ___	APR. ___	ACCOUNTING	$ ___	NET INCOME	$ ___
MAY ___	MAY ___	SUPPLIES	$ ___	PRICE INCLUDES:	
JUN. ___	JUN. ___	TELEPHONE	$ ___	GOODWILL	$ ___
JUL. ___	JUL. ___	TAXES	$ ___	EQUIPMENT	$ ___
AUG. ___	AUG. ___	LICENSES	$ ___	INVENTORY	$ ___
SEP. ___	SEP. ___	EQUIP. RENTAL	$ ___	LEASE VALUE	$ ___
OCT. ___	OCT. ___	REPAIRS	$ ___	REAL ESTATE	$ ___
NOV. ___	NOV. ___	PAYROLL	$ ___	LICENSE	$ ___
DEC. ___	DEC. ___	PAYROLL TAX	$ ___	OTHER	$ ___
TOTAL $ ___	TOTAL $ ___	REPL. RESERVE	$ ___	OTHER	$ ___
LIVING QUARTERS		OTHER	$ ___	TOTAL	$ ___
___		OTHER	$ ___	REMARKS: ___	
___		TOTAL	$ ___		

TO SHOW CONTACT: LISTING OFFICE ___ OWNER ___ OTHER ___ PHONE (___) ___
PROP. ZIP CODE ___ COMMISSION TO COOP. OFFICE % ___ /$ ___

BROKER ___ ADD. ___ CITY ___ STATE ___
OFFICE PHONE (___) ___ SALESMAN ___ HOME PHONE (___) ___

All information is from sources believed reliable but is not guaranteed.
Owner certifies that the above information as to income and expenses is accurate and complete to the best of his knowledge.

OWNER _____ OWNER _____
This listing expires _____ DATE _____

FIGURE C16-1
Condominium DRE public report

DEPARTMENT OF REAL ESTATE
OF THE
STATE OF CALIFORNIA

In the matter of the application of

CADILLAC FAIRVIEW HOMES WEST -
CALIFORNIA, a Partnership

for a Final Subdivision Public Report on

CROWN COLONY

SAN MATEO COUNTY, CALIFORNIA

CONDOMINIUM
FINAL SUBDIVISION
PUBLIC REPORT

FILE NO. 17,706 SF

ISSUED: APRIL 25, 1980

EXPIRES: APRIL 24, 1985

This Report Is Not a Recommendation or Endorsement of the Subdivision
But Is Informative Only.

Buyer or Lessee Must Sign That He Has Received and Read This Report.

This Report Expires on Date Shown Above. If There Has Been a Material Change in the Offering, an Amended Public Report Must Be Obtained and Used in Lieu of This Report.

Section 35700 of the California Health and Safety Code provides that the practice of discrimination because of race, color, religion, sex, marital status, national origin or ancestry in housing accommodations is against public policy.

Under Section 125.6 of the California Business and Professions Code, California real estate licensees are subject to disciplinary action by the Real Estate Commissioner if they make any discrimination, distinction or restriction in negotiating a sale or lease of real property because of the race, color, sex, religion, ancestry or national origin of the prospective buyer. If any prospective buyer or lessee believes that a licensee is guilty of such conduct, he or she should contact the Department of Real Estate.

Information Regarding Schools can be found on Page 6.

READ THE ENTIRE REPORT on the following pages before contracting to purchase a lot in this SUBDIVISION.

R/E Form 618
10/76

Page 1 of 6 Pages

FIGURE C16-1 *(continued)*

COMMON INTEREST SUBDIVISION GENERAL INFORMATION

The project described in the attached Subdivision Public Report is known as a common-interest subdivision. **Read the Public Report carefully** for more information about the type of subdivision. The subdivision includes common areas and facilities which will be owned and/or operated by an owners' association. **Purchase of a lot or unit automatically entitles and obligates you as a member of the association and, in most cases, includes a beneficial interest in the areas and facilities.** Since membership in the association is mandatory, **you should be aware of the following information** before you purchase:

Your ownership in this development and your rights **and remedies as a member of its association will be controlled by governing instruments** which generally include a Declaration of Restrictions (also known as CC&R's), Articles of Incorporation (or association) and Bylaws. The provisions of these documents are intended to be, and in most cases are, enforceable in a court of law. **Study these documents** carefully before entering into a contract to purchase a subdivision interest.

In order to provide funds for operation and maintenance of the common facilities, **the association will levy assessments against your lot/unit. If you are delinquent in the payment of assessments, the association may enforce payment through court proceedings or your lot/unit may be liened and sold through the exercise of a power of sale.** The anticipated income and expenses of the association, including the amount that you may expect to pay through assessments, are outlined in the proposed budget. **Ask to see a copy of the budget** if the subdivider has not already made it available for your examination.

A homeowner association provides a vehicle for the ownership and use of recreational and other common facilities which were designed to attract you to buy in this subdivision. The association also provides a means to accomplish architectural control and to provide a base for homeowner interaction on a variety of issues. **The purchaser of an interest in a common-interest subdivision should contemplate active participation in the affairs of the association.** He or she should be willing to serve on the board of directors or on committees created by the board. In short, "they" in a common-interest subdivision is "you". Unless you serve as a member of the governing board or on a committee appointed by the board, your control of the operation of the common areas and facilities is limited to your vote as a member of the association. **There are actions that can be taken by the governing body without a vote of the members of the association which can have a significant impact upon the quality of life for association members.**

Until there is a sufficient number of purchasers of lots or units in a common-interest subdivision to elect a majority of the governing body, it is likely that the subdivider will effectively control the affairs of the association. It is frequently necessary and equitable that the subdivider do so during the early stages of development. **It is vitally important to the owners of individual subdivision interests that the transition from subdivider to resident-owner control be accomplished in an orderly manner and in a spirit of cooperation.**

When contemplating the purchase of a dwelling in a common-interest subdivision, you should consider factors beyond the attractiveness of the dwelling units themselves. **Study the governing instruments and give careful thought to whether you will be able to exist happily in an atmosphere of cooperative living where the interests of the group must be taken into account as well as the interests of the individual.** Remember that managing a common-interest subdivision is very much like governing a small community . . . the management can serve you well, but **you will have to work for its success.**

DRE

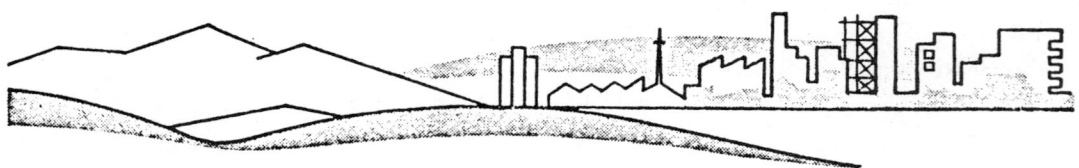

File No. 17,706 SF   Page 2 of 6 Pages

FIGURE C16-1 *(continued)*

SPECIAL NOTES

THIS PROJECT IS A COMMON-INTEREST SUBDIVISION OF THE TYPE REFERRED TO AS A CONDOMINIUM. IT WILL BE OPERATED BY AN INCORPORATED OWNERS ASSOCIATION.

SINCE THE COMMON PROPERTY AND FACILITIES WILL BE MAINTAINED BY AN ASSOCIATION OF HOMEOWNERS, AND IT'S ESSENTIAL THAT THIS ASSOCIATION BE FORMED EARLY AND PROPERLY, THE DEVELOPER MUST:

1. PAY ALL THE MONTHLY ASSESSMENTS WHICH HE OWES TO THE HOMEOWNERS ASSOCIATION FOR UNSOLD UNITS -- THE PAYMENTS MUST COMMENCE IMMEDIATELY AFTER SUBDIVIDER CLOSES FIRST SALE (Regulations 2792.9 and 2792.16).

THE HOMEOWNER ASSOCIATION MUST:

2. CAUSE THE FIRST ELECTION OF THE ASSOCIATION'S GOVERNING BODY TO BE HELD WITHIN 45 DAYS AFTER 51% SELL-OUT, OR IN ANY EVENT, NO LATER THAN SIX MONTHS AFTER CLOSING THE FIRST SALE. (Regulations 2792.17 and 2792.19); AND

3. PREPARE AND DISTRIBUTE TO ALL HOMEOWNERS A BALANCE SHEET AND INCOME STATEMENT. (Regulation 2792.22).

THE SUBDIVIDER STATED THAT HE WILL PROVIDE YOU WITH A COPY OF THE ARTICLES OF INCORPORATION, RESTRICTIONS AND BYLAWS, BY POSTING THEM IN A PROMINENT LOCATION IN THE SALES OFFICE AND/OR FURNISHING YOU COPIES PRIOR TO CLOSE OF ESCROW. THESE DOCUMENTS CONTAIN NUMEROUS MATERIAL PROVISIONS THAT SUBSTANTIALLY AFFECT AND CONTROL YOUR RIGHTS, PRIVILEGES, USE OBLIGATIONS, AND COSTS OF MAINTENANCE AND OPERATION. YOU SHOULD READ AND UNDERSTAND THESE DOCUMENTS BEFORE YOU OBLIGATE YOURSELF TO PURCHASE A UNIT.

THE SUBDIVIDER STATED HE WILL FURNISH THE CURRENT BOARD OF OFFICERS OF THE HOMEOWNERS ASSOCIATION THE BUILDING PLANS TO INCLUDE DIAGRAMS OF LOCATION OF MAJOR COMPONENTS, UTILITIES AND RELATED DATA.

THESE ITEMS WILL BE IMPORTANT TO THE BOARD OF OFFICERS OR THOSE WHO WILL MANAGE OR REPAIR COMMON FACILITIES IN THIS SUBDIVISION.

File No. 17,706 SF   Page 3 of 6 Pages

FIGURE C16–1 *(continued)*

IF YOU PURCHASE TWO OR MORE UNITS YOU MAY BE REQUIRED TO OBTAIN AMENDED PUBLIC REPORT BEFORE OFFERING TWO OR MORE OF THE UNITS FOR SALE TO OTHERS. IF YOU INTEND TO SELL TWO OR MORE UNITS OR LEASE THEM FOR MORE THAN ONE YEAR, YOU ARE REQUIRED TO OBTAIN AN AMENDED SUBDIVISION PUBLIC REPORT BEFORE YOU CAN OFFER THE UNITS FOR SALE OR LEASE.

WARNING: WHEN YOU SELL YOUR CONDOMINIUM UNIT TO SOMEONE ELSE, YOU MUST GIVE THAT PERSON A COPY OF THE DECLARATION OF RESTRICTIONS, THE ARTICLES OF INCORPORATION, AND OF THE BYLAWS. IF YOU FORGET TO DO THIS, IT MAY COST YOU A PENALTY OF $500.00 -- PLUS ATTORNEY'S FEES PLUS DAMAGES. (SEE CIVIL CODE SECTION 1360).

INTERESTS TO BE CONVEYED: You will receive title to a specified unit, together with undivided fractional interest as tenant in common in the common area together with a membership in the Crown Colony Homeowners Association and rights to use the common area.

LOCATION AND SIZE: This subdivision is located at Junipero Sierra Blvd. and Hickey Blvd. within the city limits of Daly City and is serviced by the usual city amenities.

This is a condominium which consists of approximately 23.685 acres on which twenty seven buildings containing 920 units and 1362 parking spaces have been constructed, together with common facilities consisting of private streets, a recreation center, 2 swimming pools, tennis courts, landscaping which have been constructed.

The subdivider has posted a bond into escrow to assure completion of renovation work.

MANAGEMENT AND OPERATION: The Crown Colony Homeowners Association, which you must join, will manage and operate the common area(s) in accordance with the Restrictions, Articles of Incorporation, and the Bylaws.

MAINTENANCE AND OPERATIONAL EXPENSES: The subdivider has submitted a budget for the maintenance and operation of the common areas and for long-term reserves. This proposed budget was reviewed by the Department of Real Estate, in March, 1980, but you should obtain a copy of this proposed budget from the subdivider. Under this proposed budget, the average monthly assessment against each subdivision unit is estimated at $88.05 of which $9.53 is to be a monthly contribution to long-term reserves and is not to be used to pay for current operating expenses. Actual expenses vary from $76.62 to $147.47 per unit per month.

File No. 17,706 SF   Page 4 of 6 Pages

FIGURE C16–1 (continued)

IF THE FINAL, APPROVED BUDGET FURNISHED TO YOU BY THE DEVELOPER SHOWS A MONTHLY ASSESSMENT FIGURE WHICH VARIES 10% OR MORE FROM THE ASSESSMENT AMOUNT SHOWN IN THIS PUBLIC REPORT, YOU SHOULD CONTACT THE DEPARTMENT OF REAL ESTATE BEFORE ENTERING INTO AN AGREEMENT TO PURCHASE.

The association may increase or decrease assessments at any time in accordance with the procedure prescribed in the proposed CC&R's or Bylaws. In considering the advisability of a decrease (or a smaller increase) in assessments, care should be taken not to eliminate amounts attributable to reserves for replacement or major maintenance.

THE BUDGET INFORMATION INCLUDED IN THIS PUBLIC REPORT IS APPLICABLE AS OF THE DATE OF BUDGET REVIEW AS SHOWN ABOVE. EXPENSES OF OPERATION ARE DIFFICULT TO PREDICT ACCURATELY AND EVEN IF ACCURATELY ESTIMATED INITIALLY, MOST EXPENSES INCREASE WITH THE AGE OF FACILITIES AND WITH INCREASES IN COST OF LIVING.

Monthly assessments will commence on all units during the month following the closing of the first sale of a unit. From that time, the subdivider is required to pay the association a monthly assessment for each unit which he owns.

The remedies available to the association against owners who are delinquent in the payment of assessments are set forth in the CC&R's. These remedies are available against the subdivider as well as against other owners.

The subdivider has posted a bond as partial security for his obligation to pay these assessments. The governing body of the association should assure itself that the subdivider has satisfied his obligations to the association with respect to the payment of assessments before agreeing to a release or exoneration of the security.

This development is a conversion of an existing apartment to condominium use. The structure is 6 years old.

EASEMENTS: Easements for utilities and other purposes are shown on the title report and subdivision map recorded in the Office of the San Mateo County Recorder, in Book 83 of Maps, Pages 21-24.

RESTRICTIONS: This subdivision is subject to restrictions to be recorded in the Office of the San Mateo County Recorder, in Reel 7952 at Image 1582, Official Records, and is subject to Condominium Plan recorded in Reel 7952, at Image 1675, Official Records.

File No. 17,706 SF

FIGURE C16–1 *(concluded)*

FOR INFORMATION AS TO YOUR OBLIGATIONS AND RIGHTS, YOU SHOULD READ THE RESTRICTIONS. THE SUBDIVIDER SHOULD MAKE THEM AVAILABLE TO YOU.

TAXES: The maximum amount of any tax on real property that can be collected annually by counties is 1% of the full cash value of the property. With the addition of interest and redemption charges on any indebtedness, approved by voters prior to July 1, 1978, the total property tax rate in most counties is approximately 1.25% of the full cash value.

For the purchaser of a lot or unit in this subdivision, the "full cash value" of the lot or unit will be the valuation, as reflected on the tax roll, determined by the county assessor as of the date of purchase of the lot or unit or as of the date of completion of an improvement on the lot if that occurs after the date of purchase.

PURCHASE MONEY HANDLING: The subdivider must impound all funds received from you in escrow depository until legal title is delivered to you. (Ref. Section 11013.2(a) of the Business and Professions Code). If the escrow has not closed on your lot within six (6) months of the date of your deposit receipt, you may request return of your deposit.

GEOLOGIC CONDITIONS: THE UNIFORM BUILDING CODE, CHAPTER 70, PROVIDES FOR LOCAL BUILDING OFFICIALS TO EXERCISE PREVENTIVE MEASURES DURING GRADING TO ELIMINATE OR MINIMIZE DAMAGE FROM GEOLOGIC HAZARDS SUCH AS LANDSLIDES, FAULT MOVEMENTS, EARTHQUAKE SHAKING, RAPID EROSION OR SUBSIDENCE. THIS SUBDIVISION IS LOCATED IN AN AREA WHERE SOME OF THESE HAZARDS MAY EXIST. SOME CALIFORNIA COUNTIES AND CITIES HAVE ADOPTED ORDINANCES THAT MAY OR MAY NOT BE AS EFFECTIVE IN THE CONTROL OF GRADING AND SITE PREPARATION.

PURCHASERS MAY DISCUSS WITH THE DEVELOPER, THE DEVELOPER'S ENGINEER, THE ENGINEERING GEOLOGIST, AND THE LOCAL BUILDING OFFICIALS TO DETER-MINE IF THE ABOVE-MENTIONED HAZARDS HAVE BEEN CONSIDERED AND IF THERE HAS BEEN ADEQUATE COMPLIANCE WITH CHAPTER 70 OR AN EQUIVALENT OR MORE STRINGENT GRADING ORDINANCE DURING THE CONSTRUCTION OF THIS SUBDIVISION.

PUBLIC TRANSPORTATION: There is a Sam Trans Bus stop at Gellert and Hickey, approximately 1/4 mile from the subdivision.

For further information in regard to this subdivision, you may call (415) 557-0486, or examine the documents at the Department of Real Estate 185 Berry Street, Room 5816, San Francisco, CA 94107.

CWK:vld

File No. 17,706 SF

APPENDIX C

FIGURE C17-1

EXCHANGE ESCROW INSTRUCTIONS

Parcel I: *in*   Parcel II:
Property known as   *Exchange for*   Property known as
_____   _____

Escrow No. _____   Escrow No. _____

I hand you herewith:
( ) Deed to _____   ( ) Addendum to Escrow Instructions
( ) Deed to _____   ( ) _____
( ) Rental Statement on Parcel # _____   ( ) _____
( ) Note ( ) Trust Deed for $ _____ payable to _____ on Parcel # _____
( ) Note ( ) Trust Deed for $ _____ payable to _____ on Parcel # _____

( ) Note and ( ) first ( ) second Trust Deed for $ _____ on Parcel # _____ payable to _____
_____ at $ _____ or more per month ( ) plus ( ) including interest at _____ %
per annum. First payment due _____. Due in full: _____.
YOU MAY COMPLETE SAID NOTE UPON CLOSE OF ESCROW.
( ) Note and ( ) first ( ) second Trust Deed for $ _____ on Parcel # _____ payable to _____
_____ at $ _____ or more per month ( ) plus ( ) including interest at _____ %
per annum. First payment due _____. Due in full: _____.
YOU MAY COMPLETE SAID NOTE UPON CLOSE OF ESCROW.

You are authorized to deliver or record all of said documents and disburse all funds deposited in this escrow for my account, in accordance with the instructions herein, and the statement attached hereto when you can cause to be issued a CLTA form policy of title insurance in the amount of $ _____
and an ALTA Loan policy (if required by lender) showing record title of real property described in the Preliminary Report No. _____ dated _____
vested in _____
_____

Subject to the printed provisions, exceptions and stipulations in said Policy, and subject to:
1. Taxes for the fiscal year 19 ____ -19 ____ , _____.
2. Assessments not delinquent, and Covenants, Conditions, Restrictions, Rights of Way, Easements and Reservations shown in your title report.
3. Exceptions No. _____ of Preliminary Report No. _____ dated _____ ; and
    ( ) Trust Deed for $ _____ in favor of _____.
    ( ) Trust Deed for $ _____ in favor of _____.
    ( ) _____
    ( ) _____ ;

and when you can cause to be issued a CLTA form policy of title insurance in the amount of $ _____ and an ALTA Loan policy (if required by lender) showing record title of real property described in Preliminary Report No. _____ dated _____ vested in
_____

Subject to the printed provisions, exceptions and stipulations in said Policy, and subject to:
1. Taxes for the fiscal year 19 ____ -19 ____ , _____.
2. Assessments not delinquent, and Covenants, Conditions, Restrictions, Rights of Way, Easements and Reservations shown in your title report.
3. Exceptions No. _____ of Preliminary Report No. _____ dated _____ ; and
    ( ) Trust Deed for $ _____ in favor of _____.
    ( ) Trust Deed for $ _____ in favor of _____.
    ( ) _____
    ( ) _____

PRORATE AS OF: _____ ( ) Taxes (based on latest available tax bill) on each parcel.
(on basis of 30-day month)   ( ) Assessments on Parcel # _____.
                                      ( ) Prepaid fire insurance premium on Parcel # _____.
                                      ( ) Interest on existing loan on Parcel # _____.
                                      ( ) Rents on Parcel # _____.

Additional Instructions: _____
_____
_____

These instructions shall remain in full force and effect until rescinded in writing.

_____   _____
_____   _____
_____   _____
_____   _____

DATE RECEIVED: _____   MAILING ADDRESS: _____
FOUNDERS TITLE COMPANY   _____

BY: _____   Phone: _____

FIGURE C17-2
EXCHANGE ESCROW STATEMENT

EXCHANGE STATEMENT

PROPERTY: _____ ESCROW # _____
VALUATION $ _____ DATE _____
ENCUMBERANCES $ _____ ESCROW OFFICER _____
EQUITY $ _____ Page _____ of _____ pages.

	( ) ESTIMATED STATEMENT ( ) FINAL STATEMENT	DEBITS	CREDITS
PROPERTY BEING ACQUIRED	VALUATION - PROPERTY:		
	DEPOSIT PAID BY UNDERSIGNED TO:		
	DEPOSIT PAID BY UNDERSIGNED TO:		
	1st TRUST DEED ( ) EXISTING ( ) NEW		
	2nd TRUST DEED ( ) EXISTING ( ) NEW		
	LOAN TRUST FUND		
	TAX PRO RATA		
	FIRE INSURANCE ( ) PRO RATA ( ) NEW		
	INTEREST ( ) PRO RATA ( ) NEW		
	INTEREST ( ) PRO RATA ( ) NEW		
	RENT PRO RATA		
	RENT DEPOSIT		
	TITLE INSURANCE PREMIUM — CLTA $		
	TITLE INSURANCE PREMIUM — ALTA $		
	TITLE BINDER FEE		
	ESCROW FEE		
	RECORDING		
	DOCUMENT PREPARATION $ NOTARY FEE $		
	OF: LOAN #		
	NEW TAX RESERVE $ INS. RESERVE $		
	LOAN CREDIT REPORT $ TAX SERVICE $		
	CHARGES LOAN FEE $ APPRAISAL FEE $		
	TOTAL OF LINES 21 THRU 23		
	TERMITE ( ) WORK ( ) REPORT		
PROPERTY BEING CONVEYED	VALUATION - PROPERTY:		
	DEPOSIT RECEIVED OUTSIDE OF ESCROW BY UNDERSIGNED		
	1st TRUST DEED — EXISTING		
	2nd TRUST DEED — EXISTING		
	LOAN TRUST FUND		
	TAX PRO RATA		
	FIRE INSURANCE PRO RATA		
	INTEREST PRO RATA		
	INTEREST PRO RATA		
	RENT PRO RATA		
	RENT DEPOSIT		
	RECONVEYANCE FEE		
	RECORDING		
	TRANSFER TAX ( ) CITY $ ( ) COUNTY $		
	DOCUMENT PREPARATION $ NOTARY FEE $		
	PAY TAXES		
	OF: LOAN #		
	PAY PRE-PAYMENT CHARGE $		
	CHARGES RECON/FORWARDING FEE $		
	TOTAL OF LINES 45 THRU 47		
	COMMISSION:		
	COMMISSION:		
	ESCROW FEE:		
	TERMITE ( ) WORK ( ) REPORT		
	BALANCE DUE ( ) THIS ESCROW ( ) THIS EXCHANGOR		
	TOTALS		

APPENDIX C

FIGURE C17-3

EXCHANGE BASIS ADJUSTMENT

NAME _____ DATE ___/___/___

PROPERTY CONVEYED _____

		PROPERTY BASIS	
		CAPITALIZED TRANSACTION COSTS	
		ADJUSTED COST BASIS	

	Item No.		(1) PROPERTY	(2) PROPERTY	(3) PROPERTY	(4) PROPERTY	(5) PROPERTY	(6) PROPERTY	
INDICATED GAIN	1	Market Value of Property Conveyed							1
	2	Less: Adjusted Cost Basis							2
	3	INDICATED GAIN							3
BALANCE EQUITIES	4	Equity Conveyed							4
	5	Equity Acquired							5
	6	Difference							6
	7	Cash or Boot Received							7
	8	Cash or Boot Paid							8
DETERMINE RECOGNIZED GAIN	9	Old Loans							9
	10	Less: New Loans							10
	11	NET LOAN RELIEF							11
	12	Less: Cash or Boot Paid (L8)							12
	13	Recognized Net Loan Relief							13
	14	Plus: Cash or Boot Received (L7)							14
	15	TOTAL UNLIKE PROPERTY RECEIVED							15
	16	RECOGNIZED GAIN (LESSER OF L3 OR L15)							16

TRANSFER OF BASIS

TRANSFER OF BASIS	17	Adjusted Cost Basis (L2)							17
	18	Plus: New Loans (L10)							18
	19	Plus: Cash or Boot Paid (L8)							19
	20	Plus: Recognized Gain (L16)							20
	21	Total Additions							21
	22	Less: Old Loans (L9)							22
	23	Less: Cash or Boot Received (L7)							23
	24	NEW ADJUSTED COST BASIS							24

NEW ALLOCATION AND DEPRECIATION

			(1)	(2)	(3)	(4)	(5)	(6)	
ALLOCATION	25	Land Allocation							25
	26	Improvement Allocation							26
	27	Personal Property Allocation							27
	28	NEW ADJUSTED COST BASIS (L24)							28

			PP	IMP	PP	IMP	PP	IMP	PP	IMP	PP	IMP	PP	IMP	
DEPRECIATION	29	Estimated Life Term													29
	30	Depreciation Method													30
	31	ANNUAL DEPRECIATION IMPROVEMENTS													31
	32	ANNUAL DEPRECIATION PERSONAL PROPERTY													32

The statements and figures presented herein, while not guaranteed, are secured from sources we believe authoritative.

Index

A

Acceleration clause, 94
Acceptance of offer, 73
Adjusted basis, 159
Advertising, 78
  A-I-D-A approach, 78
  answering ad calls, 83
  classified, 81
  general versus specific, 78
  office, 79
  switch sheet and call register, 85
  writing the ad, 81
Agency, 14
  agent's authority, 15
  creation of agency, 14
  divided, 11
  fiduciary relationship, 15
  statements made by licensees, 15
Agent, insurance, 205
Agreement of sale, 99
Alcoholic beverage control act, 230
All-inclusive trust deed, 100, 300, 302
Amortization, 219
Amortized note, 87
Appraisal and valuation of real property, 189
  appraisal report, 198
  building construction details, 194
  capitalization rate, 193
  comparative investment analysis form, 320
  competitive market analysis form, 191
  cost approach, 190, 198
  definition of, 190
  depreciation, 197
  factors influencing value, 189
  income capitalization approach, 193, 198
  income property statement, 201
  market comparison approach, 190, 198
  market value, 190
  property analysis form, 319
  property tax reassessment, 148
  residential appraisal data sheet, 321
  residential appraisal report, 200
Area measurement, 221
Assessment of real property; see Taxation
Assignment of debt, 92
Assumption of loan, 94

B

Banks, commercial, 113
Board of equalization, 147
Boards, real estate, 1
Boot, 161, 253
Broker
  acting as loan agent, 121
  insurance, 208
  public sales, 243
  real estate, 7, 19
  salesman contract, 21, 22, 26
Broker's commission, 46
Broker's loan statement, 121
Building construction details, 194
Bulk sales, 229
Business opportunities brokerage, 227
  alcoholic beverage control act, 230
  bulk sales and the UCC, 229
  definition of business opportunity, 227
  notice of
    bulk transfer, 230
    intended sale, 230
    intention to sell alcoholic beverages, 230
  sales and use tax, 230
  selling a business opportunity, 227
  steps in, 231
  uniform commercial code, 228

C

California Association of Realtors, 5
California-Veterans loans, 119
Capital assets, 157
Capital gains and losses, 157, 159, 161
Capitalization
  rate, 193
  table, 217
CAR purchase contract and receipt form, 64
Certificate of sale, 243
Certified Property Manager, 173
Chattel mortgage, 99
Closing costs, 71, 128
Code of ethics, 3, 12
Coinsurance, 204
Commingling, 11
Commission, 45, 46
Commissioners code of ethics, 12
Comparative Investment Analysis form, 320
Competitive Market Analysis form, 191
Condominium grant deed, 308
Condominium sales, 244
Construction details, residential, 194
Continuing education requirement, 10
Contract to purchase real estate; see Offer and deposit receipt
Cost basis, 153, 159
Counteroffer, 74, 80

D

Deeds
    condominium, 308
    grant, 307
    joint tenancy, 306
    tax, 242
    trust, 88, 90
Deferred payment sale, 167
Deficiency judgment, 92
Department of Real Estate, 5
Deposit receipt; see Offer and deposit receipt
Depreciation
    accelerated, 164
    appraisal, 197
    declining balance, 164
    exchanges, 253
    income tax, 162
    mathematics, 219
    recapture, 166
    straight-line, 163
    traditional, 197
Disclosure statement, 103, 104
Documentary transfer tax, 150

E

Escrow, 126
    checklist for closing, 129
    complete, 127
    duties and responsibilities of escrow holder, 127
    escrow agent defined, 127
    escrow charges, 128
    escrow procedure chart, 131
    essentials of a valid escrow, 126
    northern California escrow practices, 128, 132
    sample escrow illustrated, 132
    southern California practices, 128, 130
    statements and settlement sheets, 134, 135
    statement of identity, 309
    termination of escrow, 128
    termite report, 127
    title insurance policy, 136, 137
Estate and Gift Tax Act of 1980, 151
Estate sales, 236
Estate tax, federal, 154
Estates, leasehold, 178
Estimating sellers proceeds, 50
Exchanges and trade-in programs, 252
    exchanges
        basis for newly acquired property, 254
        boot defined, 253
        depreciation, 253
        escrow instructions, 331
        escrow statement, 332
        examples, 255
        exchange agreement form, 258
            analysis of, 256
        exchange basis adjustment, 333
        involuntary conversion, 255
        like kind defined, 253
        reasons to exchange, 252
        Starker case, 255
        tax-free, 252
        three-way, 254
    trade-in versus exchange, 261
    trade-ins
        conditional, 262
        FHA assistance, 263
        guaranteed, 262
        guaranteed trade-in form, 264

F

Finance, 86
    acceleration clause, 94
    agreement of sale, 99
    all-inclusive promissory note, 300
    all-inclusive trust deed, 100, 302
    assignment of debt, 92
    assumption of a loan, 94
    beneficiary, 89
    broker acting as loan agent, 121
    broker's loan statement, 121
    California-Veterans loans, 119
    chattel mortgage, 99
    commercial banks, 113
    deed of trust, 88, 90
    deficiency judgment, 92
    disclosure, Regulation Z, 101
    Federal Housing Administration (FHA), 115
    FNMA, 120
    fully amortized note, 86
    GI loan, 118
    GNMA, 120
    government loan table, 116
    graduated payment loan, 100
    holder in due course, 87
    hypothecation, 92
    impound account, 95
    insurance companies, 114
    interest, 88
    investment trusts, 115
    land contract, 99
    lock-in provision, 95
    mortgage, 88
    mortgage companies, 115
    mortgagee, 88
    mortgagor, 88
    note secured by deed of trust, 87
    notice of default, 98
    offset statement, 94
    open-end loan, 95
    partial release clause, 94
    points, 96
    portable loan, 101
    prepayment penalty, 95
    promissory note, 86, 87
    purchase money, 92
    real property securities dealer, 124
    reconveyance, 92
    redlining, 121
    request for notice, 96, 97
    reverse loan, 101
    rollover loan, 100
    savings and loan associations, 110
    second trust deeds and mortgages, 96
    Settlement Procedures Act, 109
    subject to a loan, 94
    subordination clause, 94
    swing loan, 101
    trust account, 95
    trust deed, 88, 90
    trustee, 89
    trustor, 89
    Truth-in-Lending Law, 101
    Tucker v. *Lassen*, 99
    usury, 88
    various methods of finance, 66
    variable rate loan, 100
    Veterans Administration (VA), 118
    Wellenkamp v. *Bank of America*, 95
Fixtures, 67
Franchising, 30

G

GI loan, 118
Gift tax
  California, 151
  federal, 154
Graduated payment loan, 100
Grant deed, 307
Grant deed, condominium, 308
Grant deed, joint tenancy, 306
Gross lease, 185
Ground lease, 185
Guaranteed Sales Plan Agreement, 264

H

Holder in due course, 87
Home warranty insurance, 209
Homeowners insurance policy, 205
Homeowners' tax exemption, 148
Hypothecation, 92

I

Income Property Statement, 201
Income tax and real estate, 157; see also Taxation
  accelerated depreciation, 163
  adjusted basis, 159
  boot, 161
  capital assets, 157
  capital gains and losses, 157
  cost basis, 153, 159
  dealer or investor, 158
  declining balance depreciation, 164
  deferred payment sale, 167
  depreciation, 162, 197
  determination of gain or loss, 161
  installment sale, 167
  individual tax analysis, 310
  long-term capital gain or loss, 159
  principal residence, 160
  recapture of depreciation, 166
  residence, sale of, 160
  Revenue Act of 1978, 166
  salvage value, 163
  Schedule E, 169
  Section 1231 property, 157
  short-term capital gain or loss, 159
  straight-line depreciation, 163
  Tax Reform Act of 1976, 166
Independent contractor status, 21
Inheritance tax, California, 151
Installment sales, 167
Insurance; see Property insurance
Insurance companies, 114
Interest, 211
Investment trusts, 115
Involuntary conversion, 255

J–L

Joint tenancy
  grant deed, 306
  property, 151
Judgments, 242
Land contract, 99
Law, real estate, 10, 12
  agency, 14
  commissioners code of ethics, 12
  continuing education, 10
  fiduciary, 15
  statements, 15
  violations, 10
Leases and leasing, 175
  analysis of lease form, 179

Leases and leasing—Cont.
  assignment of lease, 182
  clauses for leases, 183
  exclusive authorization to lease, 311, 313
  gross lease, 185
  ground lease, 185
  industrial and commercial, 318
  lease-option, 187
  leasehold estates, 178
  lessee, 179
  lessor, 179
  maintenance, repairs, and injury, 182
  monthly tenancy agreement, 186, 187
  net lease, 185
  notice to pay rent or quit, 316
  oil, gas, and mineral leases, 185
  origin of leases, 175
  percentage lease, 185
  remedies of the lessor, 184
  rental determination, 185
  requirements for creation of a lease, 178
  residential rental agreement, 186, 187
  retaliatory eviction, 184
  rights and obligations of parties, 178
  sale-and-leaseback, 185
  security, 179
  standard lease, 180, 312
  statement of premises condition, 314
  subletting, 182
  tenancy, periodic, 178
    at sufferance, 178
    at will, 178
    for years, 178
  termination of the lease, 183
  30 day notice, 317
Licensees, real estate, 8
Lien priorities, 92
Listing and prospecting, 41
  estimating sellers proceeds, 50
  exclusive authorization to lease, 311, 313
  listing forms, 41, 291, 292
  obtaining the listing, 49
  proper procedures, 49
  prospecting, 46
  types of listings
    exclusive agency, 42
    exclusive right to sell, 42, 44
    mobilehome, 248
    multiple, 42
    net, 42
    open, 41
    option, 43
    oral, 41
    probate property, 237
Management; see Property management
Management contract, 175
Marital deduction, 155
Market value, 190
Marketing; see Selling and marketing techniques
Mathematics; see Real estate mathematics
Misrepresentation, 11
Mobilehome sales, 245
  escrow procedures, 247
  financing methods, 246
  listing contract, 248
  mobilehome parks, 246
  modular construction, 247
  purchase contract, 249
  regulating laws, 245
  taxing mobilehomes, 246
Monthly rental agreement, 186, 187
Mortgage, 88, 89

Mortgage companies, 115
Mortgage foreclosure; see Public sales of real property

N

National Association of Realtors, 2
Net lease, 185
Nonperformance of contract, 76
Note secured by trust deed, 87
Notice of
  bulk transfer, 230
  default, 98, 233
  intended sale, 230
  intention to sell alcoholic beverages, 230
  right-to-cancel, 106
  sale, 234, 236
Notice to pay rent or quit, 316
Notice to quit, 30 day, 317

O

Offer and deposit receipt, 61
  agreement of sale, 99
  closing costs, 71
  counteroffer, 73, 74
  deposit funds, 63
  deposit receipt
    as a contract, 61
    form, 64
  fixtures, 67
  forfeit of deposit, 72
  interim occupancy agreement, 298
  legal status of parties, 63
  marketable title, 72
  nonperformance, 76
  note as deposit, 63
  option to purchase, 76
  possession after sale, 72
  preparing the deposit receipt, 62
  purchase contract and receipt form, 64
  receipt for increased deposit, 296
  release of contract, 75, 297
  special studies zone disclosure, 299
  termite report, 66, 68, 69
  terms and conditions of sale, 63
Office; see Real estate office
Offset statement, 94
Option, 43, 76

P

Partial release clause, 94
Percentage lease, 185
Periodic tenancy, 178
points, 96
Policy and procedure manual, 30, 32
Portable loan, 101
Possession, 72
Preliminary title report, 133
Preparation of deposit receipt, 62
Probate property, 237
Promissory note, 86, 87
Property analysis form, 319
Property insurance, 203
  agent, 205
  broker, 208
  business risk coverages, 206
  certificate of convenience, 209
  coinsurance, 204
  commercial coverages, 206
  home warranty insurance, 209
  homeowners policy, 205
  insurance concept of property, 203
  licenses, 205
  personal risk coverages, 207

Property insurance—*Cont.*
  solicitor, 208
  workmen's compensation, 205
Property management, 187; see also Leases and leasing
  Certified Property Manager, 173
  functions and duties of manager, 174
  management contract, 175
  types of managers, 174
Prorations, 215
Prospecting; see Listing and prospecting
Public sales of real property, 233
  mortgage foreclosure, 241
  probate sale, 236
  sheriff's sale, 242
  tax sale, 241
  trustee's sale, 233
Purchase contract, real estate, 64
Purchase money deed of trust, 92
Purchase money mortgages, 92

R

Real Estate Advisory Commission, 6
Real Estate Commissioner, 6
Real estate law violations, 10
Real estate licenses, 8
Real estate mathematics, 211
  amortization, 219
  area measurement, 221
  capitalization, 217
  commissions, 217
  depreciation, 219
  interest, 211
  loan ratio, 218
  net listing, 217
  percentage, 216
  present loan balance, 220
  profit and loss, 217
  property tax, 219
  prorations, 215
    tables, 215
Real estate office, 17
  broker-salesman contract, 21, 22, 26
  corporation, 18
  desk cost, 26
  employee status, 21
  franchising, 30
  independent contractor application, 290
  independent contractor status, 21
  individual proprietorship, 17
  operating costs, 26
  partnership, 17
  physical features and location, 28
  policy and procedure manual, 30, 32
  sales manager, 18
  salespersons, 19
  training of personnel, 19
  trust fund records, 28
Real Estate Settlement Procedures Act, 109
Real property securities dealer, 124
Realtist, 5
Realtor, 5
Reconveyance, full, 92
Redemption rights, 89, 241, 243
Redlining practices, 121
Regulation Z, 101
Request for notice, 97
Residential Appraisal Data Sheet, 321
Residential Rental Agreement, 186, 187
Retaliatory eviction, 184
Reverse loan, 101
Rollover loan, 100

S

Sale-and-leaseback, 185
Sales and Use Tax Law, 230
Salesman, real estate, 7, 9, 19
Salvage value, 163
Savings and Loan associations, 110
Second trust deeds, 96
Secret profit, 11
Section 1231 property, 157
Securities dealer, real property, 124
Security and Leases, 179
Selling and marketing techniques, 52
  buyers analysis, 56
  estimated buyers cost, 57
  points of emphasis for buyer, 58, 292
  presale preparation, 53
  qualifying the buyer, 54
  real estate sales kit, 59
  reasons for sale or purchase, 53
  showing a property, 55
Senior citizens property tax assistance, 148
Settlement sheet, 134, 135
Sheriff's sale, 242
Solicitor, insurance, 208
Solar tax credits, 149
Starker Case, 255
Statement of condition, 233
Statement of identity, 309
Stepped-up tax basis, 153
Subject to loan, 94
Subordination clause, 94
Swing loan, 101

T

Tax deed, 242
Tax-free exchange, 252
Tax Reform Act of 1976, 154, 166
Tax sale of real estate, 150, 241
Taxation, 145; *see also* Income tax and real estate
  assessment of real property, 146, 148
  assessments, special, 149
  board of equalization, 147
  cost basis, 153
  documentary transfer tax, 150
  estate tax, federal, 154
  exempt properties, 150
  gift tax
    California, 151
    exemptions, 152
    federal, 154
  inheritance tax
    California, 151
    exemptions, 152
    Federal estate tax, 154
    homeowners' tax exemptions, 148

Taxation—*Cont.*
  joint tenancy property, 151
  marital deduction, 155
  ownership changes, 147
  personal property tax, 148
  proceedings in probate, 153
  proposition 13—Jarvis-Gann, 145
  renter's tax credit, 148
  senior citizens property tax assistance, 148
  senior citizens property tax postponement, 149
  solar tax credits, 149
  stepped-up tax basis, 153
  tax collection calendar, 146
  tax rate, 146, 155
  tax sale, 150, 241
  tax statement, 147
  transfers of property, 156
  veteran's tax exemption, 149
Tenancies, leasing, 178
Termite
  disclosure, 12, 127
  inspection, 66
  reports, 66, 68, 69
Title insurance, 136
  policy, 137
  rates, 143
Trade-in forms, 264
Trade-in programs; *see* Exchanges and trade-in programs
Trust deed, 88, 90
Trustee's sale, 233
Truth-in-Lending Law, 101
  disclosure, 101
  disclosure statement, 103, 104
  enforcement, 108
  notice of right to cancel, 106
  Regulation Z, 101
  right to rescind, 105
  secondary financing, 108
Tucker v. *Lassen,* 99

U–V

Uniform Commercial Code, 228
Unruh lien and notice of default, 254
Usury, 88
Valuation; *see* Appraisal and valuation of real property
Value, 189
Variable rate loan, 100
Veterans Administration, 118
Veteran's tax exemption, 149
Violations of real estate law, 10

W

Wellenkamp v. *Bank of America,* 95
Workmen's compensation insurance, 205
Writ of attachment, 242
Writ of execution, 242

This book has been set CAP in 10 and 9 point Baskerville, leaded 2 points. Chapter numbers are in 24 Spectra, and chapter titles are in 16 point Spectra bold. The size of the type page is 40 by 56 picas.